Social and Cultural Mobility

Social and Cultural
MOBILITY

By PITIRIM A. SOROKIN

Containing complete reprints of *Social Mobility* and Chapter V from Volume IV of *Social and Cultural Dynamics*

The Free Press of Glencoe, Illinois

PRINTED IN THE UNITED STATES OF AMERICA

Library of Congress Catalog Card No. 59-13122

LITHOGRAPHED FOR THE PUBLISHERS BY
NOBLE OFFSET PRINTERS, INC., NEW YORK

Foreword

THIS VOLUME is a reprint of the original edition of my *Social Mobility*, supplemented by a reprint of Chapter Five, "Genesis, Multiplication, Mobility, and Diffusion of Sociocultural Phenomena in Space," from Volume Four of my *Social and Cultural Dynamics*. While *Social Mobility* deals with a change in social position of *persons and groups in social space*, Chapter Five is concerned with mobility of *cultural phenomena in cultural space*. Combined, these works give an essential knowledge of both forms of mobility—social and cultural—that are different from, but supplementary to, one another.

Though both works are available in foreign translations, their American edition has been out of print for a number of years. As a pioneer work that opened the vast domain of social mobility for subsequent explorations, *Social Mobility* (published in 1927), is still, according to Dr. Glass, editor of *Social Mobility in Great Britain* (London, 1953, p.v.), "the only comprehensive work" in this field. I am naturally gratified that *Social Mobility* has initiated numerous and ever increasing studies in this realm, that my main concepts and terminology have become commonly accepted by other investigators (even by those who use them without any reference to my volume), and that practically all my main generalized conclusions have been confirmed by the subsequent important studies of these phenomena.

Pitirim A. Sorokin
Winchester, Massachusetts

CONTENTS

Social Mobility

INTRODUCTION

PART ONE
THE FLUCTUATION OF SOCIAL STRATIFICATION

PART TWO
SOCIAL MOBILITY

PART THREE
POPULATION OF DIFFERENT SOCIAL STRATA

SOCIAL MOBILITY

INTRODUCTION

CHAPTER I

SOCIAL SPACE, SOCIAL DISTANCE, AND SOCIAL POSITION

I. GEOMETRICAL AND SOCIAL SPACE

EXPRESSIONS like "upper and lower classes," "social promotion," "N. N. is a climber," "his social position is very high," "they are very near socially," "right and left party," "there is a great social distance," and so on, are quite commonly used in conversation, as well as in economic, political, and sociological works. All these expressions indicate that there is something which could be styled "social space." And yet there are very few attempts to define social space and to deal with corresponding conceptions systematically. As far as I know, after Descartes, Thomas Hobbes, Leibnitz, E. Weigel and other great thinkers of the seventeenth century only F. Ratzel, G. Simmel, and recently E. Durkheim, Robert E. Park, Emory S. Bogardus, Leopold von Wiese, and the writer have tried to give greater attention to the problem of social space and to some others connected with it.[1]

As the subject of this book is social mobility—that is, the phenomenon of the shifting of individuals within social space—it is necessary to outline very concisely what I mean by social space and its derivatives. In the first place, *social space is something quite different from geometrical space*. Persons near each other in geometrical space—*e.g.*, a king and his servant, a master and his slave—are often separated by the greatest distance in social space. And, *vice versa*, persons who are very far from each other in geometrical space—*e.g.*, two brothers, or bishops of the same religion, or generals of the same rank in the same army, some staying in America, others being in China—may be very near each other in social space. Their social position is often identical, in spite of the great geometrical distance which separates them from each other. A man may cross thousands of miles of geometrical space without changing his position in social space; and, *vice versa,* a man may stay at the same geometrical place, and yet, his social position may change enormously. President Harding's position in geometrical space was changed greatly when he went from Washington to Alaska; and yet, his social position remained the same as it was in Washington. Louis XVI and the Czar Nicholas II remained in the same geometrical space, in Versailles and in Czarskoie Selo, when their social positions were changed enormously.

These considerations show that social and geometrical space are quite different things. The same may be said of the derivatives from these conceptions, such as "geometrical and social distance," and "climbing in geometrical and in social space," "shifting from position to position in geometrical and in social space," and so on.[2]

In order to define social space positively, let us remind ourselves that geometrical space is usually thought of as a kind of "universe," in which physical phenomena are located. The location in this universe is obtained through definition of the position of a thing in relation to other things chosen as "the points of reference." As soon as such points are established (be it the sun, the moon, Greenwich, the axes of abscissas and ordinates) we can locate the spatial position of all physical phenomena with relation to them, and then through that, with relation to each other.

In a similar way we may say that *social space is a kind of universe composed of the human population of the earth.* As far as there are no human beings, or there is only one human creature, there is no human social space or universe. One man in the world cannot have any relation to other men; he may be only in geometrical but not in social space. Accordingly, *to find the position of a man or a social phenomenon in social space means to define his or its relations to other men or other social phenomena chosen as the "points of reference."* What are taken as the "points of reference" depends upon us. It is possible to take a man, or a group of men, or several groups. When we say that "Mr. N., Jr. is a son of Mr. N., Sr.," we take a step toward the location of Mr. N. in the human universe. It is clear, however, that such location is very indefinite and imperfect; it gives us only one of the coordinates of location (the family relation) in a complex social universe. It is as imperfect as a geometrical location which says: "The tree is two miles from the hill." If such a location is to be satisfactory, we must know whether the hill is in Europe or in some other continent of the earth, and in what part of the continent, and under what degree, and if the tree is two miles to the north or south, east or west, from the hill. In brief, more or less sufficient geometrical location demands an indication of the located thing to the whole system of spatial coordinates of the geometrical universe. The same is true in regard to the "social location" of an individual.

An indication of a man's relation to another man gives something, but very little. An indication of his relation to ten or to one hundred men gives somewhat more but cannot locate the man's position in the whole social universe. It is similar to the location of a thing in geometrical space through a detailed indication of the different things around it, without indication of the latitude and longitude of the things. On this planet there are more than one and a half billion of human beings. To indicate a man's relations to several dozens of men, especially when they are not prominent, may mean nothing. Besides, the method is very complex and wasteful. In place of it, social practice has already invented another method, which is more satisfactory and simple, and which reminds one somewhat of the system of coordinates used for the location of a thing in geometrical space. This method consists in: (1) *the indication of a man's relations to specific groups,* (2) *the relation of these groups to each other within a population, and* (3) *the relation of this population to other populations included in the human universe.*

In order to know a man's social position, his family status, the state of which he is a citizen, his nationality, his religious group, his occupational group, his political party, his economic status, his race, and so on must be known. Only when a man is located in all these respects is his social position definitely located. But even this is not all. As within the same group there are quite different positions, *e.g.,* that of the king and a common citizen within a State group, the man's position within each of the fundamental groups of a population must also be known. When, finally, the position of the population itself, *e.g.*, the population of North America, is defined in the whole human universe (mankind), then the social position of an individual may be thought to be quite sufficiently defined. Paraphrasing the old proverb, one may say: "Tell me to what social groups you belong and what function you perform within each of those groups, and I will tell you what is your social position in the human universe, and who you are as a socius." When two people are introduced this method is usually applied: "Mr. A. (family group) is a German professor (occupational group), a staunch Democrat, a prominent Protestant, formerly he was an ambassador to," and so on. This and similar introductions are complete or incomplete indications of the groups with which a man has been affiliated. The biography of a man in its essence is largely a description of the groups to which the man has had a relation, and the man's place within each of them. Such a method may not always inform us whether the man is tall or not, whether blond or dark, "introvert or extrovert"; but all this, though it may have a great significance for a biologist or a psychologist, is of relatively small value for a sociologist. Such information does not have any direct importance in the defining of a man's social position.

To sum up: (1) *social space is the universe of the human population;* (2) *man's social position is the totality of his relations toward all groups of a population and, within each of them, toward its members;* (3) *location of a man's position in this social universe is obtained by ascertaining these relations;* (4) *the totality of such groups and the totality of the positions within each of them compose a system of social coordinates which permits us to define the social position of any man.*

From this it follows that human beings, who are members of the same social groups and who within each of these groups have the same function, are in an identical social position. Men who differ in these respects from each other have different social positions. The greater the resemblance of the positions of the different men, the nearer they are toward each other in social space. The greater and the more numerous are their differences in these respects, the greater is the social distance between them.[3]

2. THE HORIZONTAL AND THE VERTICAL DIMENSIONS OF SOCIAL SPACE

Euclid's geometrical space is space of the three dimensions. The social space is space of many dimensions because there are more than three different social groupings which do not coincide with each other (the groupings of the population into state groups, into those of religion, nationality, occupation, economic status, political party, race, sex and age groups, and so on). The lines of differentiation of a population among each of these groups are specific or *sui generis* and do not coincide with each other. Since relations of all these kinds are substantial components of the system of social coordinates, it is evident that the social space is a universe of many dimensions; and the more differentiated is the population, the more numerous are the dimensions. In order to locate an individual in the universe of the population of the United States, which is more differentiated than that of the natives of Australia, a more complex system of social coordinates must be used to indicate the more numerous groups with which one is connected.

For the sake of a simplification of the task it is possible, however, to reduce the plurality of the dimensions into two principal classes, provided that each is to be subdivided into several subclasses. *These two principal classes may be styled the vertical and the horizontal dimensions of the social universe.* The reasons for this are as follows: several individuals who belong to the same social groups are easily found, *e.g.*, all may be Roman Catholics; Republicans; engaged in the automobile industry; Italians, according to native language; American citizens, according to citizenship; and so on. And yet, their social position may be quite different from the vertical standpoint. One of them may be a bishop, within the Roman Catholic group, while others may be only common parishioners; one of them may be a boss, within the Republican party, while others are only common voters; one may be the president of an automobile corporation, while others are only the common laborers; and so on. While their social position from the horizontal standpoint seems to be identical, from a vertical standpoint it is quite different. The horizontal dimension and its coordinates are not sufficient for a description of these differences. The same may be said about the positions of a commander-in-chief and a soldier in an army; and of those of a president and a clerk in a university. One cannot help thinking of their interrelations in terms of vertical dimensions. Our common representations of social position are very closely associated with it. Such expressions as: "he is a social climber," "he goes socially down," "the upper and the lower classes," "he is at the top of a social pyramid," "the bottom of a society," "social ranks and hierarchies," "social stratification," "horizontal and the vertical differentiation," "the superposition of social groups," and so on are commonly used. The interrelations of individuals, as well as those of groups, are thought of either as situated on the same horizontal level, or as hierarchically superimposed upon each other. Shifting from group to group sometimes does not involve any social rise or descent; at other times it is thought of as inseparable from the vertical dimensions. A social promotion is thought of as a social ascent; a degradation, as a social sinking. This common manner of thinking may be conveniently used for scientific description. On account of its familiarity, it helps to obtain a proper orientation in the complex social universe. The discrimination between the vertical and the horizontal dimensions expresses something which really exists in the social universe: the phenomena of hierarchy, ranks, domination and subordination, authority and obedience, promotion and degradation. All these phenomena and corresponding interrelations are thought of in the form of stratification and superposition. For a description of such relations the vertical dimension is very helpful and convenient. On the other hand, interrelations free from such elements may be conveniently described in terms of the horizontal dimension. In brief, from the technical standpoint, as well as from that of the nature of the social universe, there is no reason to avoid the above rather common discrimination of the two principal dimensions of the social universe.

This book deals with social phenomena in their vertical dimension. It studies the height and the profile of the "social structures"; their differentiation into social strata; the people who live within each stratum; the shifting of the population along the lines of the vertical dimension. In short, it deals with social stratification and the vertical social mobility. Horizontal structure of the social bodies is omitted[4] and is touched only by the way, incidentally. Such being the object of the book, it is necessary to make a constant use of such terms as "the upper and the lower social strata," "people socially inferior and superior," and so on. In order to avoid any misunderstanding, I must emphatically stress, that such terminology does not signify any evaluation on my part, and means only some formal location of the people within the different social strata. Maybe the inhabitants of the upper strata are really better than those of the lower ones; may be they are worse. It is up to the reader to make such judgments. For me these terms are no more than convenient tools for analysis and description of the corresponding phenomena and their factual interrelations. The task of any scientific study is to define the interrelations of the studied phenomena as they exist. The task of the evaluation is entirely out of the field of such a study. This should be constantly kept in mind in order to avoid misunderstanding.

So much for the general conceptions of social space and its dimensions. The details and development will be given in the course of the book.

[1] *Vide* Spektorsky, E., *The Problem of Social Physics in the Seventeenth Century,* Vol. I, Warsaw, 1910; Vol. II, Kiev, 1917, (in Russian); Ratzel, F., *Politische Geographie,* Chaps. XII to XV, 1903; Simmel, G., *Soziologie,* Chap. ix, 1908; Park, Robert E., "The Concept of Social Distance," *Journal of Applied Sociology,* Vol. VIII, No. 6; Bogardus, Emory S., several papers on Social Distance in the *Journal of Applied Sociology,* 1925-1926; Sorokin, P., *Systema Soziologii,* Vol. II, 1920, Chap. I, and *passim;* von Wiese, Leopold, *Allgemeine Soziologie,* pp. 104, 154, 178 ff., 1924; Durkheim, E., *Les formes élémentaires de la vie religieuse,* introduction and conclusion.

[2] From this it follows that the so-called "ecological approach" to the study of social phenomena may have only a limited value and is not suitable for a study of the greater part of social changes. The ecological approach may grasp the phenomena and changes as far as they are located and reflected on the geometrical territory, *e.g.,* different territorial zones on the city (loop, residential zone, and so on) and shifting of the population from one geometrical place to another. But it cannot grasp all "zones" of social groups dispersed and not located at a definite geometrical territory (*e.g.,* a Masonic society); it cannot grasp all non-territorial shiftings in social space; it is helpless in regard to vertical circulation within a society and so on. The greater part of social phenomena belong to this type and are not reflected properly on the geometrical territory. Hence, the limited possibilities of the ecological approach

in the study of social phenomena. Within its appropriate limits it is useful and may be welcomed. The approach is not new. Without the term "ecological" it has been excellently used by many statisticians for a long time. See VON MAYR, G., *Statistik und Gesellschaftslehre,* Vol. II, pp. 45-65, 109-126, 329 ff., 1897. Similar good "ecological" chapters may be found in many other statistical works dealing with the problem of migration and demography. The same approach styled "ecological" is given by the works of MCKENZIE, R. D., *The Neighborhood,* 1923; PARK, ROBERT E., and BURGESS, ERNEST W., *The City,* 1925; GALPIN, CHARLES T., *Rural Life,* Chap. IV, 1918; KOLB, J. H., *Rural Primary Groups,* Mad., 1921; E. WAXWEILER'S (*Esquisse d'une Sociologie,* p. 39 ff., 1906,) "ecology" is quite different from the ecology of the abovementioned authors.

[3] This conception of social distance is quite different from that offered by R. Park and E. Bogardus. Their conception is purely psychological and not sociological. From their standpoint persons who psychologically like each other are socially near; the persons who dislike each other are socially far from each other. There is no doubt that the study of such psychology of sympathy and antipathy is very valuable. But it seems to me it is not a study of social distance in the sociological sense of the word. A master and a slave, a king and a beggar, may like each other very much. But to conclude from this that their social positions are similar, or that there is no great social distance between them, would be utterly fallacious. The Orsini and the Colonna in Italy of the fifteenth century hated each other. Their social positions, however, were very similar. This clearly shows that my conception of social space and social distance is objective (because the groups exist objectively) and sociological, while Dr. Park's and Dr. Bogardus's conception is purely psychological and subjective (as far as it measures the social distance by the subjective feelings of liking and disliking). Even in regard to the *psychology of solidarity,* the above sociological conception may be very helpful. Similarity of social position of individuals results usually in a "likemindedness" because it means the similarity of habits, interests, customs, mores, traditions, inculcated in the individuals by similar social groups to which they belong. Being "likeminded" they are likely to be more solidary than the people who belong to the different social groups. See the details in SOROKIN, P., *Systema Soziologii,* Vol. II, *passim.* See the quoted works of Robert E. Park and Emory S. Bogardus. As a concrete example of the use of a sociological system of social coordinates for the definition of leadership see the paper of CHAPIN, F. STUART, "Leadership and Group Activity," *Journal of Applied Sociology,* Vol. VIII, No. 3. In essence his method is identical with that above outlined and quite different from the psychological approach of Robert E. Park and Emory S. Bogardus. Another example is given by the study of HOAG, E., *The National Influence of a Single Farm Community,* 1921.

[4] Two volumes of my *Systema Soziologii* are devoted to an analysis of the horizontal differentiation of human population. There is also given a classification of social groups into (*a*) simple and (*b*) cumulative and it analyzes the structure of a population from the standpoint of this classification.

CHAPTER II

SOCIAL STRATIFICATION

I. CONCEPTIONS AND DEFINITIONS

SOCIAL stratification means the differentiation of a given population into hierarchically superposed classes. It is manifested in the existence of upper and lower social layers. Its basis and very essence consist in an unequal distribution of rights and privileges, duties and responsibilities, social values and privations, social power and influences among the members of a society. Concrete forms of social stratification are different and numerous. If the economic status of the members of a society is unequal, if among them there are both wealthy and poor, the society is *economically stratified,* regardless of whether its organization is communistic or capitalistic, whether in its constitution it is styled "the society of equal individuals" or not. Labels, signboards and "speech reactions" cannot change nor obliterate the real fact of the economic inequality manifested in the differences of incomes, economic standards, and in the existence of the rich and the poor strata.[1] If the social ranks within a group are hierarchically superposed with respect to their authority and prestige, their honors and titles; if there are the rulers and the ruled, then whatever are their names (monarchs, executives, masters, bosses), these things mean that the group is *politically stratified,* regardless of what is written in its constitution or proclaimed in its declarations. If the members of a society are differentiated into various occupational groups, and some of the occupations are regarded as more honorable than others, if the members of an occupational group are divided into bosses of different authority and into members who are subordinated to the bosses, the group is *occupationally stratified,* independently of the fact whether the bosses are elected or appointed, whether their position is acquired by social inheritance or personal achievement.

2. PRINCIPAL FORMS OF SOCIAL STRATIFICATION AND THEIR INTERRELATIONS

Concrete forms of social stratification are numerous. The majority of them may, however, be reduced to three principal classes: the economic, the political, and the occupational stratification. As a general rule, these forms are closely intercorrelated with each other. Usually, those who occupy the upper strata in one respect happen to be in the upper strata also in other respects, and *vice versa.* The men who dwell in the upper economic layers happen also to be in the upper political and occupational strata. The poor, as a rule, are politically disfranchised and dwell in the lowest strata of the occupational hierarchy. Such is the general rule, though there are, however, many exceptions to it. Not always are the wealthiest men at the apex of the political or occupational pyramid; and not always are the poor men the lowest in the political or the occupational gradations. This means that the intercorrelation among the three forms of stratification is far from being perfect; the strata of each form do not coincide completely with one another. There is always a certain degree of overlapping among them. This fact does not permit us to analyze in a summary way all three fundamental forms of social stratification. For the sake of a greater accuracy each form has to be studied separately.[2] A real picture of social stratification in any society is very complex. In order to make its analysis easier, only the most fundamental traits must be taken. Many details must be omitted, and the situation simplified, without, however, disfiguring it. This is done in any science and has to be done especially here where the problem is so complex and so little studied. In such cases the Roman *minima non curat prætor* is completely justified.

3. SOCIAL STRATIFICATION IS A PERMANENT CHARACTERISTIC OF ANY ORGANIZED SOCIAL GROUP

Any organized social group is always a stratified social body. There has not been and does not exist any permanent social group which is "flat," and in which all members are equal. Unstratified society, with a real equality of its members, is a myth which has never been realized in the history of mankind. This statement may sound somewhat paradoxical and yet it is accurate. The forms and proportions of stratification vary, but its essence is permanent, as far as any more or less permanent and organized social group is concerned. This is true not only in human society, but even in plant and animal communities. Let us consider the principal corroborations.

Plant and Animal Communities.—As far as it is possible to apply the conceptions of human sociology to plant and animal communities, social stratification may be said to exist here also. In the plant communities there are different "social" classes, the phenomena of parasitism and exploitation, suppression and domination, different "economic" standards of living (the amount of air, sunlight, moisture, and soil ingredients consumed) and so on. Of course, these phenomena are but roughly analogous to those of social stratification in human society; and yet they signify clearly that the plant community is in no way a community of "equal units," whose positions are equal and whose interrelations are identical within the community.[3]

With still greater reason the same may be said of animal societies. Within them social stratification is manifested in: (*a*) the existence of different and sharply divided classes in the communities of bees, ants, and other insects; (*b*) the existence of leaders among gregarious mammals; (*c*) the general facts of parasitism, exploitation, domination, subordination, and so on. In brief, one cannot find here any society which may be styled an unstratified group.[4]

Pre-literate Human Tribes.—Except, perhaps, the few cases where the members of a population are leading an isolated life, where no permanent social life and interaction exist, where, therefore, we do not have a social organization in the proper sense of the word, as soon as organization begins primitive social groups exhibit the trait of stratification. It is manifested in various forms. First, in the existence of the sex and age groups with quite different privileges and duties. Second, in the existence of a privileged and influential group of the tribe's leaders. Third, in the existence of the most influential chieftain or headman. Fourth, in the existence of outcasts and outlawed men. Fifth, in the existence of inter- and intratribal division of labor. Sixth, in the existence of different economic standards, and in that of economic inequality generally. Traditional opinion about primitive groups as communistic societies which do not have any commerce or private property, or economic inequality, or inheritance of fortune, are far from being correct. "The primitive economy (*Urwirtschaft*) is neither an economy of isolated individuals searching for food (as K. Bücher thinks), nor the economy of communism or collective production. What we really have is the economic group composed of mutually dependent and economically active individuals and of the smaller parts of the group which have a system of commerce and barter with each other." [5] If in many tribes economic differentiation is very slight, and customs of mutual aid approach communism, this is due only to the general poverty of the group. These facts support the contention that primitive groups also are stratified bodies.[6]

More Advanced Societies and Groups.—If we cannot find a non-stratified society among the most primitive groups, it is useless to try to find it among more advanced, larger and compound societies. Here, without any single exception, the fact of stratification is universal. Its forms and proportions vary; its essence has existed everywhere and at all times. Among all agricultural and, especially, industrial societies social stratification has been conspicuous and clear. The modern democracies also do not present any exception to the rule. Though in their constitutions it is said that "all men are equal," only a quite naïve person may infer from this a non-existence of social stratification within these societies. It is enough to mention the gradations: from Henry Ford to a beggar; from the President of the United States to a policeman; from a foreman to the most subordinate worker; from the president of a university to a janitor; from an "LL.D." or "Ph.D." to a "B.A."; from a "leading authority" to an average man; from a commander-in-chief of an army to a soldier; from a president of a board of directors of a corporation to its common laborer; from an editor-in-chief of a newspaper to a simple reporter; it is enough to mention these various ranks and social gradations to see that the best democracies have social stratification scarcely less than the non-democratic societies.

It is needless to insist on these obvious facts. What should be stressed here is, that not only large social bodies, but any organized social group whatever, once it is organized, is inevitably stratified to some degree.

Gradations, hierarchies, shining leaders, cumulative aspirations—all these appear spontaneously whenever men get together, whether for play, for mutual help, for voluntary association, or for the great compulsory association of the State. Every Englishman is said to love a lord; every American is said to love a title.[7]

Family, church, sect, political party, faction, business organization, gang of brigands, labor union, scientific society—in brief, any organized social group is stratified at the price of its permanency and organization. The organization even of groups of ardent levelers, and the permanent failure of all attempts to build a non-stratified group, testify to the imminency and unavoidability of stratification in an organized social group. This remark may appear somewhat strange to many people who, under the influence of high-sounding phraseology, may believe that, at least, the societies of the levelers themselves are non-stratified. This belief, as many another one, is utterly wrong. Different attempts to exterminate social feudalism have been successful, in the best cases, only in ameliorating some of the inequalities, and in changing the concrete forms of stratification. They have never succeeded in annihilating stratification itself. And the regularity with which all these efforts have failed once more witnesses the "natural" character of stratification. Christianity started its history with an attempt to create an equal society; very soon, especially after 313 A. D., it already had a complicated hierarchy, and soon finished by the creation of a tremendous pyramid, with numerous ranks and titles, beginning with the omnipotent pope and ending with that of a lawless heretic. The institution of Fratres Minorum was organized by St. Francis of Assisi on the principle of perfect equality. Seven years later equality disappeared. Without any exceptions, all attempts of the most ardent levelers in the history of all countries have had the same fate. They could not avoid it even when the faction of the levelers has been victorious. The failure of the Russian

Communism is only an additional example in a long series of similar experiments performed on small and large scale, sometimes peacefully, as in many religious sects, sometimes violently, as in social revolutions of the past and present. If many forms of stratification were destroyed for a moment, they regularly reappeared again in the old or in a modified form, often being built by the hands of the levelers themselves.[8]

Present democracies and Socialist, Communist, Syndicalist, and other organizations, with their slogan of "equality" do not present any exception to the rule. In regard to democracies this has been shown above. The inner organization of different socialist and similar groups pleading "equality" shows that perhaps in no other organization does such an enormous hierarchy and "bossism" exist as in these groups of levelers. "The Socialist leaders regard the masses only as the passive tools in their hands, as a series of zeros destined only to increase the significance of the figure on the left" (the importance of the leaders themselves), says E. Fournière, himself one of these socialists.[9] If in the statement there is an exaggeration, it is hardly considerable. At least, the best and the most competent investigators of the situation are unanimous in their conclusions of an enormous development of oligarchy and stratification within all these groups.[10] The enormous potential taste for inequality of numerous "levelers" becomes at once conspicuous, as soon, indeed, as they happen to be victorious. In such cases they often exhibit a greater cruelty and contempt toward the masses than former kings and rulers. This has been repeated regularly in victorious revolutions where the levelers become dictators.[11] Classical descriptions of the situation given by Plato and Aristotle, on the basis of the ancient Greek social revolutions, may be literally applied to all such cases, including the Bolshevist experiment.[12]

To sum up: social stratification is a permanent characteristic of any organized society. "Varying in form, social stratification has existed in all societies which proclaimed the equality of men." [13] Feudalism and oligarchy continue to exist in science and arts, in politics and administration, in a gang of bandits, in democracies, among the levelers, everywhere.

This, however, does not mean that the stratification quantitatively or qualitatively is identical in all societies and at all times. In its concrete forms, defects or virtues, it certainly varies. The problem to be discussed now is these quantitative and qualitative variations. Begin with the quantitative aspect of social stratification in its three forms: economic, political and occupational. This is what is meant by the height and the profile of social stratification, and, correspondingly, the height and the profile of a "social building." How high is it? How long is the distance from the bottom to the top of a social cone? Of how many stories is it composed? Is its profile steep, or does it slope gradually? These are the problems of the quantitative analysis of social stratification. It deals, so to speak, exclusively with the exterior architecture of a social building. Its inner structure, in its entirety, is the object of the qualitative analysis. The study should begin with the height and the profile of the social pyramid. After that the pyramid should be entered and an investigation of its inner organization made from the standpoint of stratification.

[1] *Methodological Note.*—If a picture is drawn of a tree whose title is nevertheless, "A Fish," only one insane may say, "This is a picture of a fish." Unfortunately, in social sciences such insane statements are still very numerous. Authors still do not understand that the labels and the real situation, the speech reactions of a man and his real behavior may be quite different. If in a constitution is written "all men are equal," they often conclude that in such a society the equality is realized. If a man abundantly produces sonorous phrases, then for this reason he is judged as "open-minded," "progressive," "protector of the laboring classes" and so on, regardless of his real behavior. For the same reason, the periods of Revolution are styled as periods of progress and so forth. Such "thinkers" do not see what was clear for Bayle several centuries ago. "Opinions (speech reactions and labels) are not the rules for actions, and men do not follow them in their conduct," says Bayle. "The Turks believe in Fatalism and Predestination; and yet, they flee from a danger just as the French who do not have such a belief." According to speech reactions, the Christians are those who, being smitten on the right cheek, turn to the offender their left one. I wish I could see such Christians. These examples show that between the labels and the real situation may be the greatest discrepancy. This is one reason for not relying on labels and speech reactions in the description of social phenomena. The second reason is that this discrepancy is rather common. The third reason is that in many cases speech reactions are only "the minor, but not the major reactions." For these reasons it is unscientific to give to them such an exclusive importance, as many authors do. The above explains why I disregard the labels in all cases where the real situation shows "a tree" but not a "fish." See the reasons for this in the works: Bayle, P., *Pensées diverses . . . à l'occasion de la comète,* etc., pp. 266, 272-273, 361-362, Paris, 1704; Weiss, A. P., "Relation Between Functional and Behavior Psychology," *The Psychological Review,* pp. 353-568, 1917; Bechtereff, W., *Obschija osnovy reflexologii,* p. 15 ff., Petrograd, 1918; Sorokin,

P., *Sociology of Revolution,* Chap. IV, and *passim,* Philadelphia, 1925; and especially PARETO, V., *Traité de sociologie générale,* Vol. I, Chap. III, and *passim,* Paris, 1917-1919.

[2] This is the reason why I do not use the term "social classes" in a general sense, and prefer to talk separately of the economic, the occupational, and the political strata or classes. The best possible definition of social class is the totality of the people who have a similar position in regard to occupational, economic, and political status. Although convenient for some summary use, in a special study of social stratification, it becomes unsatisfactory in view of the indicated fact of overlapping and exceptions. Other definitions of social class are nothing but inconsequential indication of one of the three forms of the social stratification under the name of "social class." Plato, M. Agrippa, Sallustius, Voltaire, D'Aeth, Raynal, Guizot, Enfantine, Considérant, Godwin, E. Bernstein, and many others have understood by social classes the strata of the poor and the rich. This means they took the economic stratification, wrongly generalized it, and wrongly exhibited it as the only form of social stratification. Helvetius, S. Simon, A. Bauer, Blondel, and many others have discriminated the dominating, or aristocratic, or exploiting, or privileged classes, and the subjugated, subordinated, exploited or disfranchised classes. This means that by social class they understood what I style political stratification. The third group of authors such as Turgot, A. Bauer partly, K. Bücher partly, G. Schmoller, F. W. Taussig, and many others have taken the occupational status as the principal basis of social classes. Finally, there is a group of authors like K. Marx, A. Smith, W. Sombart, K. Kautsky, and others, who have taken as a basis and a characteristic of social class a combination of these three principles: occupational, political, and economic status. The weak point of the three first "monistic" conceptions of social classes is that they take one of the forms of social stratification, make it exclusive and disregard other forms which are different from the form taken. Such one-sidedness leads these authors to an undue simplification of social reality, to its disfiguring and to many logical and factual fallacies. The fourth mixed group of the class definitions are purely local and temporary, and, on this account, could not be applied to different societies and to different times. Besides, they show also a great many logical inconsistencies and factual mistakes. These reasons are enough to explain why I prefer to study each of the mentioned forms of stratification separately. See a detailed analysis and criticism of the social class theories in SOROKIN, P., *Systema Soziologii,* Vol. II, pp. 283-306. See also SOLNTZEV, S., *Obschestvennyje klassy,* Tomsk, 1917; BAUER, A., *Les classes sociales,* Paris, 1902; SCHMOLLER, G., *Grundriss der Allgemeinen Volkswirtschaftslehre,* Vol. I, pp. 428-456; Vol. II, pp. 562-647, 1923.

[3] See the facts and analysis in the works: MOROSOFF, *Wood as a Plant-community* (Russian), pp. 1-23, *et passim,* St. Petersburg, 1913; SOUKACHEFF, W., *Introduction to the Study of Plant Communities* (Russian), *passim,* St. Petersburg, 1919; WARMING, E., *Oecology of Plants,* Oxford University Press, pp. 12-15, 91-95, 1909; CLEMENTS, F. E., *Plant Succession,* 1916.

[4] See the facts in the works: PETRUCCI, *Origine Polyphiletique . . . des societés animales,* Bruxelles, 1906; WHEELER, W. M., *Ants, Their Structure, Development, and Behavior,* Columbia University Press, 1916; WAGNER, W., *Biological Foundations of Comparative Psychology* (Russian), Vols. I and II, Wolf Company, St. Petersburg; WHEELER, W. M., *Social Life Among the Insects,* New York, 1923; ESPINAS, A., *Des Societés Animales,* Paris, 1878; BREHM, *Tierleben,* in different volumes; MUMFORD, E., "The Origins of Leadership," *American Journal of Sociology,* Vol. XII, p. 224 ff.; MORGAN, L., *Animal Behavior,* p. 191 ff., 1908; many facts are given also in principal works of CHARLES DARWIN, in KROPOTKIN, P., *Mutual Aid;* HOUZEAU, *Étude*

sur les facultés mentales des animaux, Vol. II; PERRIER, *Les colonies animales et les formations des organisms,* 1898; FABRE, J. H., *Souvenirs entomologiques,* 1 er Série, p. 177 and *passim.*

[5] SOMLÓ, F., *Der Güterverkehr in der Urgesellschaft, Inst. of Solvay,* pp. 65-67, 155, 177 ff., 1909. See also PANSKOW, H., "Betrachtungen über das Wirtschaftsleben der Natürvölker," *Zeitschrift der Gesellschaft für Erdkunde zu Berlin,* Vol. XXXI, 1896; MAUNIER, R., "Vie Religieuse et vie économique," *Revue International de Sociologie,* December, 1907, January and February, 1908; LOWIE, R. H., *Primitive Society,* Chap. IX, New York, 1920; THURNWALD, R., *Die Gestaltung d. Wirtschaftsentwicklung aus ihren Aufangen heraus,* 1923; MALINOWSKI, B., "The Argonauts in the West Pacific," *Economics Journal,* March, 1921.

[6] See SPENCER, H., *Principles of Sociology,* Vol. II, Pt. V, *passim,* New York, 1909; MUMFORD, E., *op. cit., passim;* DESCAMPS, P., "Le pouvoir publique chez les sauvages," *Revue International de Sociologie,* pp. 225-261, 1924; VIERKANDT, A., "Führende Individuen bei den Natürvölkern," *Zeitschrift für Sozialwis.,* Vol. XI, pp. 542-553, 623-639, 1908; KOVALEVSKY, M., "Political Organization" (Russian), *Sociology,* Vol. II, 1910; POST, A. H., *Evolution of Law,* Boston, 1915 (incorrect in many respects); SCHURZ, H., *Alterklassen und Männerbunde,* Berlin, 1902; RIVERS, W. H., *Social Organization,* New York, 1924; LOWIE, R. H., *Primitive Society,* Chaps. XII and XIII; GOLDENWEISER, A., *Early Civilization,* p. 271 ff., 1922; CHAPIN, F. S., "Primitive Social Ascendancy," *Publications of American Society of Sociology,* Vol. XII, pp. 61-74; HOBHOUSE, L., WHEELER, G., GINSBERG, M., *The Material Culture and Social Institutions of the Simpler Peoples,* Chaps. II and IV, 1915.

[7] TAUSSIG, F. W., *Inventors and Money Makers,* p. 126, New York, 1915

[8] See SOROKIN, P., *Sociology of Revolution,* Chap. XII, and *passim;* LEOPOLD, L., *Prestige,* pp. 13 ff., London, 1913.

[9] FOURNIÈRE, E., *La Sociocratie,* p. 117, 1910.

[10] See OSTROGORSKI, M., *La democratie et les parties politiques, passim,* 1912; MICHELS, R., *Political Parties,* New York, 1915; MOSCA, G., *Elemente di scienza politica,* 1896; BRYCE, J., *Modern Democracies,* Vols. I and II, New York, 1921; BORGATA, "Democrazia e oligarchia nelle organizz. democr.," *Rivista Ital. di sociologia,* p. 664 ff., 1912; NOVGORODZEFF, P., *Social Ideal* (Russian), 1923; NAVILLE, A., *Liberté, Egalité, Solidarité,* Geneva, 1924. See further the works of the ideologists of syndicalism and their criticism of all these traits in the socialist organization: *e.g.,* LAGARDELLE, "Le socialisme ouvrier," *Movem. Soc., June,* 1904; POUGET, *La Confederation générale du travail,* 2nd ed., Paris; SOREL, *Reflections on Violence,* 1912; FOURNIÈRE, E., *La Crise Socialiste,* Paris, 1908. See further the criticism of all these organizations and their exposure by the ideologists of Anarchism, *e.g.,* in the works of P. Kropotkin, M. Bakunin, Malatesta, and others. See also a very substantial analysis of the real situation in V. Pareto's quoted work, *passim.* In spite of the most different political affiliations of these and many other authors, they are unanimous in this respect. See SOROKIN, P., *Systema Soziologii,* Vol. II, p. 173 ff.

[11] See the facts in my *Sociology of Revolution, passim.*

[12] See PLATO, *The Republic,* translated by JOWETT, B., Bks. VIII and IX, 1894; ARISTOTLE, *Politics,* Bk. V, Chap. V, and *passim.* Rereading recently these works, I have been struck by the identity of the picture of ancient tyranny drawn by Plato and Aristotle with that of the Russian Revolution and the Bolshevist picture. Even the details in almost all cases appear to be identical.

[13] PARETO, V., *op. cit.,* Vol. I, p. 613.

Part One

THE FLUCTUATION OF SOCIAL STRATIFICATION

CHAPTER III

ECONOMIC STRATIFICATION

I. TWO FUNDAMENTAL TYPES OF FLUCTUATION

THERE are two principal kinds of fluctuations which must be discriminated in the economic status of a group. The first is an economic rise or decline of the group as a whole; the second is an increase or a decrease of economic stratification within the group. The first phenomenon is an increase of economic prosperity or impoverishment of the social group as a whole; the second may be expressed as a change in the economic profile of the group or an increase or decrease of the height and steepness of the economic pyramid. Correspondingly, there are the following two kinds of fluctuation of the economic status of a society: I. Fluctuation of the economic status of a group as a whole: (*a*) increase of economic prosperity; (*b*) its decrease. 2. Fluctuation of the height and the profile of economic stratification within the society: (*a*) heightening of the economic pyramid, (*b*) its flattening. A beginning is made with the study of the fluctuations of the economic status of a group as a whole.

2. FLUCTUATION OF THE ECONOMIC STATUS OF A GROUP AS A WHOLE

Whether a group, as a whole, is rising economically to a higher level or is falling, is a question which can be judged approximately on the basis of the fluctuation of its per capita wealth and income measured in money units. On the same basis, it is possible to measure the comparative economic status of different groups.

This criterion permits us to make the following statements:

I. *The Wealth (and Income) of Different Societies Varies Considerably from Country to Country, from Group to Group.*— The following figures illustrate the statement. Taking the average wealth of Wisconsin, as 100, in 1900, the corresponding indices of the average wealth are: for the United Kingdom (1909) 106, for France (1909) 59, for Prussia (1908) 42.[1] In such societies as China, or India, or many primitive groups, the difference will be still greater. The same may be said about the income.[2] Taking, not whole nations, but less extensive territorial groups (provinces, districts, counties, different sections of a city or of a village, finally, even different families of a neighborhood), the result will be similar: their average wealth and income vary.

2. *The Average Wealth and Income of the Same Society Are Not Constant, but Vary in Time.*—Whether it is a family group or a corporation, or a county population, or a whole nation, their average wealth and income fluctuate upward and downward in the course of time. There has scarcely been any family whose wealth or income has been identical throughout many years or several generations. The economic "ups" and "downs," sometimes sharp and great, sometimes slight and gradual, are normal phenomena in the economic history of any family. The same may be said about all the larger social groups. As a corroboration the following figures may be given:

THE ESTIMATED INCOME OF THE PEOPLE OF THE UNITED STATES PER CAPITA MEASURED IN DOLLARS

Census Year	Income per Capita	Census Year	Income per Capita
1850	95	1912	340
1860	116	1913	344
1870	174	1914	*330*
1880	*147*	1915	357
1890	192	1916	449
1900	236	1917	525
1910	332 or 338	1918	595
1911	332	1919	637 [3]

These figures translated into dollars' purchasing power would be somewhat different, but would show a similar fluctuation. In spite of a general upward tendency, the figures exhibit a considerable fluctuation from census to census, from year to year. Another example of the opposite fluctuation is given by the average income of the Russian population during the last few years.

Years	Income per capita of the population (in gold rubles).
1913	101.35
1916-17	85.60
1921	38.60
1922-1923	40.
1924	47.3[4]

In the United Kingdom, according to A. L. Bowley's computation, "average incomes were quite one-third greater in 1913 than in 1880; the increase was gained principally before 1900, since when it barely kept pace with the diminishing value of money."[5] There is no necessity to add to these data. Statistics of income of different European countries, without any exception, show the same phenomena of the average incomes' fluctuations. Its concrete forms are different in various countries, but the phenomenon of fluctuation is general among all nations.

3. *In the History of a Family, or a Nation or Other Group There Seems to Exist no Perpetual Trend either toward Prosperity or Impoverishment.—All known trends seem to have continued only for a limited period of time. In a long period of time they may swing to the opposite direction. History does not give a certain basis for belief in either a paradise of prosperity or a hell of misery toward which societies drift perpetually. History shows only goalless fluctuations.*[6]

The next problem is whether in these fluctuations of the average income and wealth of the same society there exists a perpetual secular trend. There seems to be no quite certain basis for a definite answer to the question. All that is possible to do is to give a mere hypothesis which may, and may not, be true. With this reservation, consider these hypothetical propositions.

In the first place, the statistics of incomes of the United States, United Kingdom, Germany, France, Denmark, Russia, and several other countries show that since the second half of the nineteenth century there has been a trend of increase in the average income and wealth of these countries.[7] Granting that the computations of the statisticians have been correct, is the trend a real secular trend, or is it only a part of a "parabola" which may be superseded by a stagnation or by the opposite downward movement? The second possibility appears more probable. In a schematic way economic change in the course of time is neither a straight line (*A*), nor a spiral line (*B*) rising up or perpetually

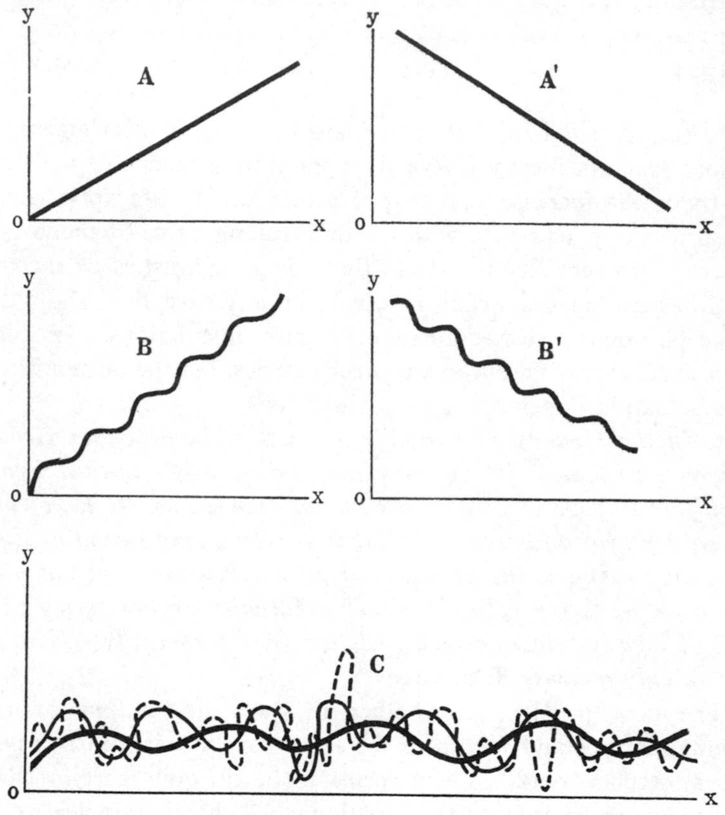

going down, but is nearer to the figure (*C*) fluctuating without any perpetual trend. The principal arguments in favor of this opinion are as follows:

In the first place, the economic history of a family, or a corporation, or any economic organization shows that there scarcely has been one among such groups which has been permanently rising economically. After a short or long period, within one or several generations, the rising trend has been superseded by the sinking one. In this way many wealthy families, firms, corporations, cities, districts, of ancient, medieval and modern times have become poor and have disappeared from the top of the financial pyramid. Among the present magnates of wealth in Europe and America there are not many (if there are any, except perhaps some of the royal families) which were wealthy two or three centuries ago, whose wealth has since that time been steadily increasing. The great majority, if not all, of the present wealthiest families sprang up during the last two centuries, or even the last two decades. All the rich families of previous times have disappeared and sunk into poverty again. This means that after a period of rising they have undergone one of impoverishment. Similar, it seems, has been the fate of many financial corporations, firms, and houses. If such is the fate of these social groups, why must the fate of whole nations be quite different?[8]

In the second place, the history of many nations of the past shows that they, on a broader scale, have repeated the fate of the smaller social groups. However imperfectly the economic history of Ancient Egypt, or Babylon, or Persia, or Greece, or Rome, or Venice, or other Italian Republics of the Middle Ages, or China is known, it seems certain that all these nations have had many "ups" and "downs" in their economic prosperity until finally some of them became enormously impoverished. And have not any of the present countries had the same "ups" and "downs" during their history? Has it not been common for all of them in the Middle Ages to have years of the acutest starvation superseded by those of comparative prosperity, the decades of economic welfare superseded by decades of calamity, the periods of accumulation of wealth followed by its destruction?[9]

Concerning the economic status of the large masses of the population of the most unlike countries, this may be said with a reasonable degree of certainty. It is known that the economic situation of the masses in Ancient Egypt about the time of the thirteenth and nineteenth dynasties after Seti II, and in the later period of the Ptolemaic dynasty became much worse than it was before these periods.[10] Similar periods of decline have occurred in the history of China. Such, *e.g.*, were the periods at the end of the Shang dynasty, in 1115 to 1079 and 781 to 771; 202-3; 140; 33; B. C. 9 to 23 A. D.; 107; in the eighth (755 to 763), in the ninth (875 to 907) and the eleventh century, during the twentieth and twenty-first dynasties, not to mention many other periods of great famines and impoverishment which continue to recur up to this time.[11] Similar waves we have in the economic history of Ancient Greece and Rome. As examples of a great economic decline in many Greek states may be cited the seventh century, B. C., and the time at the end of the Peloponnesian war; and finally the third century B. C. Athens became rich after the Median wars and poor after the disaster of Sicily.[12] Sparta became rich in the period of its supremacy and poor after the battle at Leuctra. In Rome, we may cite possibly the second and first centuries B. C. and the fourth and fifth centuries A. D.[13] Similar "ups" and "downs" took place several times in the history of the economic situation of the masses in England, in France, in Germany, in Russia, and in many other countries. They are well enough known not to be mentioned in detail.[14] And what is especially important is the fact that in many of the past societies, as well as in some of the still existing ones, (China), the final or later stages of their history have not been better in regard to the economic situation of the masses, but rather worse, than many preceding periods. If such is the case, these facts of history do not give any basis for an admission of a perpetual trend in either direction.

In the third place, the following computation seems to testify also against the hypothesis of a perpetual increase of wealth in the course of time. One centime, put at 4 per cent, compound interest, at the time of Jesus Christ, would have given in 1900 an enormous capital expressed by the figure: 2,308,500,000,000,000,000,000,000,000,000 francs. Supposing that the earth is composed of gold, it would require 31 gold earths to represent this enormous sum of money. The real situation, as we know, is far from being such. In the time of Christ there was an enormous capital, and yet it did not yield an amount of wealth remotely approaching the above sum. The sums of 100,000 francs, put at 3 per cent interest at the time of Christ, would, in the first 495 years, increase to 226 billion francs, a fortune near to the present national wealth of France. As the real amount of wealth at the present time is incomparably less than it would have to be according to these computations, it follows that the rate of its increase has been much less than the supposed rate of interest, and that the periods of wealth accumulation have been superseded by those of its destruction and spoliation.[15]

In the fourth place, the cyclical hypothesis is confirmed by the fact of business cycles. The existence of "small business cycles" (whether in the forms of periods of 3 to 5 years or 7 to 8 years, or 10 to 12 years) at the present moment is not questioned. There is difference of opinion only as to the time span of the cycles.[16] "Change takes place by a succession of jumps or spurts, periods of rapid increase being followed by periods of stagnation or even of decline." [17] But has not the whole progress of the second half of the nineteenth century been, in its turn, a part of a larger cycle? A study by Prof. N. Kondratieff answers this question in the affirmative. Besides the above small cycles, he has found that there have been larger cycles with periods of about 40 to 60 years.[18] This is a direct confirmation of the hypothesis that the above progressive economic trend of the second half of the nineteenth century has been only a part of a long-time cycle. But why stop at the cycles of this type and not go to still larger economic waves? If their periodicity is difficult to prove,[19] the existence of long-time economic "ups" and "downs" seems to be beyond doubt; the history of any country, taken in a sufficiently long period of time, shows it with a reasonable degree of certainty.

In the fifth place, the slowing down and stagnation in the growth of the average real income in England and France and Germany, and in some other European countries, since approximately the beginning of the twentieth century,[20] and a decided impoverishment during and after the war, are doubtless symptoms of at least a temporary and considerable downward movement.

In the sixth place, "the law of diminishing returns is inexorable. As more and more people crowd our soil, each one must have less and less from Nature in making a living. After a certain density is reached, therefore, more population means more poverty for someone. Inventions and discoveries may postpone, but they cannot avert, the day of reckoning." [21] It is true that the birth rate of European and American countries has been going down; but not so much as to lead to a cessation in the growth of the population, and it is still very high in the Slav countries, not to mention the Asiatic peoples. It is true also that inventions are increasing more and more; but, in spite of their increase, they still are not so great as to guarantee a high standard of living for everybody in the world, nor even in Europe. These reasons explain why, in my opinion, the hypothesis of a permanent trend of an increase of the average income (or its permanent decrease) is improbable, and why the hypothesis of small and large economic cycles appears to me nearer the reality. When we are told that the present standard of living of a Paris middle-class man is almost as high as that of Charles IV of France,[22] when we see the enormous and wonderful technical machinery of production, it is difficult to admit that all this may go to the wall and be ruined. And yet, the years of the World War and especially those of the Revolution, have shown how easily wealth and a tiny veneer of civilization might be destroyed in a period of some 14 years.

On the other hand, our time is especially fortunate in the discovery of many past civilizations. The more we study them the more fallacious appears the opinion that, up to the nineteenth century, there has been nothing but primitive culture and primitive economic organization. Even the civilizations which existed several thousands of years ago, were in many respects splendid. And yet, their splendor perished, their prosperity succumbed, their wealth disappeared. This does not mean that, since they were destroyed, our wealth must meet the same fate. But, on the other hand, it does not give any basis for thinking that the present European and American countries are to be an exception.

But, it may be asked, how about the spiral line of progress? If by progress is meant a spiral line of permanent improvement of economic conditions of a country, such a hypothesis has not yet been proved by anybody or by anything. The only possible evidence in its favor is the economic progress of some of the European countries for the second half of the nineteenth century. But the above reasons show why this fact cannot prove the contention. In addition to the above argument, it is possible to say that the same trend, during the same time, did not take place among many Asiatic, African, and other aggregates of population. More than that, a part of European prosperity was bought at the cost of the exploited population of primitive and less advanced countries. The native population of New Zealand was 104,000 in 1841; 55,467 in 1858; and no more than 47,000 in 1864. At the beginning of the nineteenth century the native population of Van Diemen's Land was about 6,000; in 1864 only 4,000. At the time of Cook's visit the native population of Tahiti was between 150,000 and 200,000. In the 'sixties of the nineteenth century, it was only about 15,000. In the Sandwich Islands in 1778, according to Cook's opinion, the natives numbered about 400,000; in 1823, according to Hopkins' computation they had decreased to 123,000; in 1849 to 80,000, in 1860 to 67,000.[23] In the Fiji Islands, from 1875 to 1912, the native population decreased from 150,000 to 75,000.[24] These are only a very few of many similar facts. What do they mean, and why have they been mentioned? Because such facts show that, instead of improvement, the level of economic and social welfare in the nineteenth century went down and led to the extinction of these peoples; and that European economic improvement in the nineteenth century was due in part to their exploitation and plundering. What was good for one group, was disastrous for others. To ignore these other groups—hundreds of millions of people of India, Mongolia, Africa, China, the natives of all non-European continents and islands, at least some of whom the European progress cost a great deal and who scarcely have improved their standard of living for the last century—to ignore them and to advance "the permanent spiral progress" theory only on the basis of some European countries is to be utterly subjective, and partial, and fantastic. The very multitude of primitive and civilized societies of the past which have finished their economic history by misery and impoverishment decidedly does not permit us to talk about any "spiral or non-spiral" law of progress for all societies.[25] In the best cases, such progress has been a local and temporary phenomenon.

To sum up:

1. The average wealth and average income fluctuate from group to group, from society to society.

2. The average wealth and income fluctuate within the same society or group at different times.

3. There scarcely is any perpetual trend in these fluctuations. All "trends"—upward or downward—may be the "trends" only in a very relative sense: in the sense of typical tendency for a definite period of time. Taken from the standpoint of a longer time period, they are likely to be a part of a longer time cycle.

4. From this viewpoint there are different time cycles: besides the known small business cycles there seem to exist larger cycles, in social phenomena and in economic processes also.

5. The trend of an increase of the average income and wealth for the second half of the nineteenth century in European and American countries is likely to be part of a large economic cycle.

6. The theory of an endless economic progress seems not to be true.

[1] KING, W. I., *The Wealth and Income of the People of the United States*, p. 96, New York, 1922.

[2] See *ibid.*, pp. 235 *ff.*

[3] KING, W. I., *op. cit.*, p. 129; *Income in the United States*, National Bureau of Economic Research, Vol. II, p. 338, 1922.

[4] PROKOPOVICZ, C., *Ocherki khosaistva Sovetskoi Rossii*, p. 119, Berlin, 1923; *Ekonomicheskaja Jisn*, Mar. 29, 1925; PERVOUCHIN, S., *Narodnoje i Gosudarst. Khosaistvo*, S.S.S.R., v. 1922-1923 g., p. 10, Moscow, 1924; PROKOPOVICZ, C., *Narodny dokhod*, C.C.C.R., Dni, No. 757, May 6, 1925.

[5] BOWLEY, A. L., *The Change in the Distribution of the National Income, 1880-1913*, p. 26, Oxford University Press, 1920.

[6] *Methodological Note.*—Since the second half of the nineteenth century, under the influence of the theory of evolution, social sciences and sociology have given a great deal of attention to the so-called "tendencies of evolution," "historical trends," and "laws of historical development," or to "the secular trends." Since August Comte's "law of the three stages," and Herbert Spencer's "formula of progress," the greater part of sociologists, anthropologists, historians, and social philosophers have been busy with "the discovery" of hundreds of "historical tendencies" and "laws of progress" and "evolution." Unfortunately, following the fate of Comte's "laws," these trends and tendencies have turned out to be nothing but fiction. Meanwhile, this hunting for the laws of historical development and "progress" has diverted the attention of the investigators from a study of the phenomena of repetitions, fluctuations, oscillations, and cycles in social life, phenomena which attracted a great deal of attention on the part of social thinkers in the past (Ecclesiastes, Confucius, Plato, Polybius, Florus, Seneca, Campanella, Machiavelli, Vico, etc.). Fortunately, however, this current of thought seems to have been renewed since the end of the nineteenth century, and is growing more and more. In spite of my

desire to view the historical process as a kind of college curriculum where the societies pass through the same stages of the Freshman, the Sophomore, and so on, to be graduated in a paradise granted by a corresponding "progress-law-maker," I failed to find a corroboration for such a delightful conception of history. For this reason, I must satisfy myself with a less charming but, probably, a more correct conception of the goallessness of historical fluctuations. Maybe there is some transcendental goal and some unseen drift toward it, but, unfortunately, it is not manifested. This goalless conception seems to be true also in regard to the discussed economic fluctuations.

See about this in detail in SOROKIN, P., "A Survey of the Cyclical Conceptions of Social and Historical Process," to be published in *Social Forces* in 1927. See here also literature and references.

[7] See the data for Prussia in the study of WAGNER, A., "Zur Methodik der Statistik des Volkseinkommen, etc.," published in the *Zeitschrift des Königlich Preussischen Statistik Bureau,* Vol. XLIV, pp. 41-122, 229-267, Berlin, 1904; for other countries: KIAER, "Répartition sociale des revenues," *Bull. de l'Inst. Int. de Stat.,* Vol. XVIII; for Italy: MORTARA, I., "Numeri indici delle condizioni econ. d'Italia," *Bulletin de L'Institut International de Stat.,* Vol. XX, pp. 663-675; for Japan: TAKANO, "Étude sur le développement et la répartition du revenu national au Japon," *Bull. de l'Inst. Int. Stat.,* Vol. XVIII. See the works of A. L. Bowley, E. Woods, Giffen, E. Levasseur, and others mentioned further.

[8] According to an appropriate remark of Pareto, the difference is only in the time span of cycles; it is very long for the whole of mankind; it is shorter, but still long, for nations; it is very short for a family or small social group. PARETO, V., *op. cit.,* p. 1530 *ff.*

[9] See the facts in the work of CURSCHMAN, F., *Hungersnöte in Mittelalter,* pp. 39-91 and *passim,* Leipzig, 1900.

[10] TURAEFF, *The Ancient Egypt* (Russian), p. 70, Petrograd, 1922; BREASTED, *History of the Ancient Egyptians,* pp. 155, 161, 174, 332, 1911; ROSTOVTZEFF, M. I., *A Large Estate in Egypt,* Madison, 1922; ROSTOVTZEFF, M. I., "Gosudarstvo i lichnoct v khos. jizni Ptol. Egipta," *Sovr. Zapiski,* No. 10; PETRIE, W. M. F., *Revolution of Civilization,* 1922.

[11] See LEE, MABEL P. H., *The Economic History of China,* pp. 40-121, New York, 1921; HIRTH, *The Ancient History of China,* pp. 105-106, 173, 1908; IVANOFF, *Van-an-Shi,* pp. 12, 27-28, 38-39, Petrograd, 1909; BOULGER, *History of China,* Vol. I, pp. 398-401, 1881; PARKER, E., *China Past and Present,* pp. 23 *ff.,* 1903; SMITH, A., *Village Life in China,* pp. 49, 161, 310, 1906. See also *The Shû-King, The Sacred Books of the East,* Vol. III; CHEN HUAN CHANG, *The Economic Principles of Confucius,* Vol. II, pp. 507 *ff.,* Columbia University Press, 1911; GROUSSET, R., *Histoire de l'Asie,* Vol. II, pp. 179 *ff.,* 249 *ff.,* 331 *ff.,* Paris, 1922.

[12] ARISTOTLE, *On the Athenian Constitution,* Chaps. XXVIII and XXIX, London, 1907.

[13] About Rome and Greece, see any of the fundamental works in their history, and especially their economic history, such as the books of Beloch, Pöhlman, Bury, Guiraud, Marquardt, Salvioli, Mommsen, Rostovtzeff, Waltzing, and Duruy, cited and quoted further.

[14] See further the quoted works of T. Rogers, D'Avenel, and some other authors.

[15] PARETO, V., *op. cit.,* Vol. II, p. 1528 *ff.* On the history of the treasuries of Delphi and the Church, Pareto conspicuously shows the existence of a perpetual rhythm of accumulation and spoliation of wealth. While, thanks to the savings of the population, these treasuries have been permanently receiving money and

accumulating wealth, other social forces and agencies in the form of war, invasion, revolution, spoliation, and so on, have steadily plundered and destroyed the accumulated capital. In this way they have checked successfully the perpetual process of accumulation. The same may be said of the wealth of other social groups and societies. See PARETO, V., *Ibid.*, p. 1515 *ff.* To this it may be added that, in spite of several thousands of years of the existence of China, in its history there has not been manifested anything like the imagined trend of a perpetual increase of average wealth and income.

[16] See TUGAN-BARANOVSKY, *Les Crises industrielles en Angleterre, passim;* AFTALION, *Les Crises périodiques de surproduction,* Paris, 1913; ROBERTSON, *A Study of Industrial Fluctuation;* MITCHELL, W., *Business Cycles,* 1913; MOORE, H. L., *Economic Cycles,* 1914.

[17] PIGOU, A. C., *The Economics of Welfare,* p. 799, 1920.

[18] KONDRATIEFF, N., "Bolshie tzykly konjunktury," *Voprosy Konijunktury,* No. 1, Moscow, 1925. The existence of such long-time cycles has been admitted by several other authors, such as V. Pareto, A. Spiethoff, H. L. Moore, and others. See PARETO, V., *op. cit.*, p. 1490 *ff.;* MOORE, H. L., *Generating Economic Cycles,* 1923; SPIETHOFF, A., "Krisen," 4th ed., *Handwörterbuch der Staatswiss.*

[19] The number of works intended to prove the existence of the periodical long-time cycles in various fields of social life has been growing rapidly for the last few decades. Many authors, like O. Lorenz and G. Ferrari, insist on the existence of cycles of 100 and 125 years. Some others, like K. Joël and W. Scherer, tried to show the existence of cycles of 300 years. Some others, like Millard, indicate cycles of 500 years. Men like John Brownlee found a cycle of 200 years. Besides the periodic cycles, a great many investigators indicated the existence of non-periodic long-time cycles in various fields of social processes (V. Pareto, Sensini, Kolabinska, Guignebert, Veber, G. Schmoller, G. Hansen, O. Ammon, O. Spengler, H. Spencer, F. Stuart Chapin, W. F. Ogburn, and many others). If the periodicity of the long-time cycles may often be questioned, the fact of long-time fluctuations is beyond doubt. See SOROKIN, P., *A Survey of the Cyclical Conceptions of Social and Historical Process.*

[20] Concerning the future of income-growth in England, Dr. Bowley says, "The wealth of the country, however divided, was insufficient before the war for a general high standard; there is nothing as yet to show it will be greater in the future." BOWLEY, A. L., *The Division of the Product of Industry,* p. 58, Oxford University Press, 1919. For America, see MENDELSOHN, S., *Saturated Civilization,* Chaps. IX to XII, New York, 1926.

[21] KING, W. I., *op. cit.*, p. 176; see also EAST, E. M., *Mankind at the Crossroads,* pp. 69-70 and Chap. IV, 1923.

[22] D'AVENEL, *Le Méchanisme de la vie moderne,* 1 er série, pp. 158-159, Paris, 1908.

[23] ARNOLDI-LAVROFF, *Czivilisatzia i dikie plemena,* pp. 141-148, St. Petersburg, 1904. See series of similar facts in the above work of Arnoldi-Lavroff, and especially in ENGELGARD, *Progress as an Evolution of Cruelty, Progress kak evolutzia jestokosti,* Pavlenkoff Company, St. Petersburg.

[24] TRIGGS, "The Decay of Aboriginal Races," *Open Court,* October, 1912.

[25] I am inclined to think that the same is true in many other respects. The following quotation from a prominent Russian thinker Leontieff appears to me correct. Criticizing the popular theories of progress he says: "Is it not horrible and fallacious to think that Moses climbed Sinai, that the Greeks built their acropolises, that the Romans carried out the Punic wars, that the wonderful and beautiful Alexander the Great crossed Granicus and fought at

Arbil, that the apostles preached, the martyrs suffered, the poets sang, the great painters painted, and the knights shone in tournaments only in order that a contemporary French or German or Russian bourgeois, in his ugly and comical cloth, could have his saving account and could satisfactorily exist on the ruins of all this past grandeur? It would be shame for mankind if this were true." LEONTIEFF, K., *Visantism i Slavianstvo*.

CHAPTER IV

FLUCTUATION OF THE HEIGHT AND THE PROFILE OF ECONOMIC STRATIFICATION

Having discussed the fluctuation of the economic status of a society as a whole, let us now turn to the fluctuations of the height and the profile of economic stratification. The principal points to be discussed are as follows: first, are the height and profile of the economic pyramid of a society permanent things, or do they fluctuate from group to group, and, within the same group, from time to time? Second, if they fluctuate, is there in the fluctuation any regularity and periodicity? Third, is there any perpetual trend in these fluctuations, and if there is, what is it?

PRINCIPAL HYPOTHESES

Among many answers to these questions in current economic science, the most important probably are: the hypothesis of V. Pareto, that of Karl Marx, and some others mentioned later.

A. Pareto's Hypothesis.—Its essential point consists in a contention that the profile of an economic stratification or frequency distribution of income in any society (earlier contention) or, at least, in many societies (later restriction of Pareto) represents something permanent and uniform and may be expressed through a definite mathematical formula. This is approximately as follows: Let x represent a given income and y the number of persons with income above x. If a curve be plotted of which the ordinates are logarithms of x and the abscissæ logarithms of y, the curve for all countries, studied by Pareto, is approximately a straight line. Furthermore, in all countries studied, the slope of the straight line to the axis of x has approximately the same angle, about 56 degrees. Deviations do not exceed 3 or 4 degrees. As tan 56 degrees = 1.5, hence, if the number of incomes exceeding x is equal to y, the number greater than mx is $\frac{1}{m^{15}} \cdot y$ whatever the value of m may be. This means that the shape of the income frequency distribution curve on a double logarithmic scale is the same for all countries and at all times.

We have something reminding us of a great number of crystals of the same chemical composition. There may be very large crystals, middle-sized crystals and small ones, but all have the same form.[1]

Later on he restricted this law, saying that it is "an empirical law" and that "empirical laws have little or no value outside the limits for which they were found experimentally to be true."[2] It is not the intention to lay down here all the arguments which may be brought against this law. It is enough to say that many competent critics have shown that Pareto's figures disclose considerable deviations from his curve; that Pareto, in order to prove the rigidity of his law, has made some logical changes in the terms used by him; that the frequency distribution of income of the United States or other countries and at different times shows, in fact, a considerable deviation from the law; that, as Pareto admits himself, under a radical change of social conditions, for instance, when the institution of private property is superseded by collectivism, or the institution of inheritance is changed, or education of the people is radically modified, the form of his curve is changed.[3] The conclusions of a very careful mathematical analysis of Pareto's law by F. R. Macaulay with the assistance of E. G. Benjamin, are as follows:

1. Pareto's Law is quite inadequate as a mathematical generalization, for the following reasons:

(*a*) The tails of the distribution on a double logarithmic scale are not, in a significant degree, linear; (*b*) they could be much more nearly linear than they are without that condition being especially significant, as so many distributions of various kinds have tails roughly approaching linearity; (*c*) the straight lines fitted to the tails do not show even approximately constant slopes from year to year or between country and country; (*d*) the tails are not only not straight lines of constant slope but are not of the same shape from year to year or between country and country.

2. It seems unlikely that any useful mathematical law describing the entire distribution can ever be formulated.[4] This is enough to show that the height and the profile of eco-

nomic stratification (the curve of income distribution) *fluctuates from country to country, from time to time. The economic stratification may become higher or lower, steeper or less steep.* Such is the conclusion from the foregoing discussion.

If it fluctuates, does this mean that the fluctuation may be unlimited and the economic cone may become extraordinarily steep or, on the contrary, quite flat? The analysis of these problems leads us to the hypothesis of Karl Marx, on the one hand; on the other, to many current Socialist and Communist theories of economic equality. Let us turn to Karl Marx's hypothesis.

B. Karl Marx's Hypothesis.—Its essential point is the contention that among European societies there is going on a process of greater and greater economic differentiation. The middle economic strata become thinner and poorer; the economic situation of the proletariat tends to be more and more pitiful; at the same time, wealth is concentrating in fewer and fewer hands. A narrow stratum of the middle classes, a big stratum of the impoverished proletariat at the bottom, and a small group of the magnates of capital at the top—such must be the profile of economic stratification, according to this theory of society. The rich are getting ever richer and the poor are to be more poverty stricken. Should such a state come, Marx adds, it would be enough to nationalize the wealth of the few magnates to have socialism established. Such is the essence of Marx's theory of a catastrophic advent of socialism. In the words of Marx it runs as follows:

> The small tradespeople, shopkeepers, and retired tradesmen generally, the handicraftsmen and peasants—all these sink gradually into the proletariat. . . . Entire sections of the ruling classes are by the advance of industry precipitated into proletariat. . . . At the same time the centralization of industry goes on. One capitalist always kills many. The modern laborer . . . instead of rising with the progress of industry, sinks deeper and deeper below the conditions of existence of his own class. He becomes a pauper and pauperism develops more rapidly than population and wealth.[5]

Thus, this theory, announced at the middle of the nineteenth century, contended that fluctuation in the height and the profile of economic stratification may be practically unlimited and may disfigure completely not only Pareto's curve but any shape of economic stratification. At the same time, Marx contended that the above trend is only temporary and must be superseded by the opposite trend toward the annihilation of economic stratification through expropriation of the exploiters and the realization of socialism. This means that Marx admitted the possibility, even the necessity, of an unlimited fluctuation in the economic shape of a social body, from the extreme pointed profile, to the "flat" form of a society with economic equality. At the present moment there is no need to insist upon the fallacy of Marx's theory and prediction. The 75 years which have elapsed since the *Communist Manifesto* did not corroborate Marx's expectation and prophecy.

In the first place in all European countries and in the United States since the second half of the nineteenth century up to the time of the World War, the economic conditions of the laboring class have been improving and not becoming worse, as Marx predicted. In England, from 1850 to the beginning of the twentieth century the index number of the real wages of the laboring class increased from 100 to approximately 170; from 1790 to 1900, from 37 to 102; from 1880 to 1910, from 100 to 134.[6] In the United States the average wage per employee in purchasing power has increased between 1850 and 1910 from 147 to 401; from 1820 to 1923 the real wages increased from 41 to 129.[7] Similar was the situation in France, Belgium, Germany, Austria, Denmark, Italy, Japan, and in some other countries.[8] On the other hand the proportion of the poor according to the poor relief statistics of Sweden, Prussia, England, Holland, and some other countries, did not increase during the second half of the nineteenth century, but decreased.[9] In brief, this part of the theory was disproved by history.

No more fortunate has been that part of the theory which predicted the impoverishment and disappearance of the middle economic classes and the concentration of wealth into fewer and fewer hands. Of many data which disprove these predictions only a few representative instances shall be cited.

In Germany, from 1853 to 1902 the number of middle-class

incomes and the number of rich men and millionaires increased absolutely and relatively (in regard to the increase of the population), while the relative numbers in the lower economic strata (with an income less than 900 marks) decreased. For instance, in the population of Prussia the per cent of the people with an income lower than 900 marks was in 1896, 70.7; in 1906, 61.7; in 1910, 42.8.[10] The following table[11] gives an idea of the change:

Years	Population in thousands	Number of Incomes of Specified Size in Thousands					
		900 to 3,000 Marks	3,000 to 6,000 Marks	6,000 to 9,500 Marks	9,500 to 30,500 Marks	30,500 to 100,000 Marks	100,000 Marks and Over
1853	16,870	825	32.0	7.2	4.4	0.6	0.06
1902	35,551	3,310	291.3	77.6	64.7	13.2	2.76

This means that instead of a decrease in numbers in the middle-class economic strata there was an increase, in general at the cost of the lower economic classes with an income of 900 marks and below. While population increased approximately two times in 50 years, the groups with incomes of from 900 to 3,000 marks increased approximately four times, those with incomes of from 3,000 to 6,000 marks, nine times, and remaining groups correspondingly: 11, 15, 22, and 46 times. Finally the number of multimillionaires with an income of 2,000,000 marks and over increased from 4 to 16 in the period from 1875 to 1902. All this shows how fallacious are Marx's predictions.

A similar picture is presented by England. This may be seen from the following data: First, "the average of all incomes was about £76 in 1880 and £104 in 1913, an increase of 37 per cent"; the income per head of the population was about £33 in 1880, and £47 in 1913, an increase of 42 per cent (the population increased less rapidly than the incomes owing mainly to the diminishing proportion of young children). Second, the number of taxpayers, with an income of above £160 increased from 618,000 in 1881 to 1882 to 1,240,000 in 1914 to 1915. As the index of wholesale prices (Sauerbeck) was 88 in 1880 and 80 to 85 in 1911 to 1913, and as the gainfully engaged population increased during this period only by 39 per cent, the above increase of the number of the taxpayers means that the middle income classes did not decrease but, on the contrary, increased. Third, "the average wage per earner has increased in the 33 years at almost exactly the same rate as the average of all incomes." This is seen from the following figures:

Year	Average of Incomes Other Than Wages	Average of Wage Income
1880	100	100
1891 to 1895	105	110
1901 to 1905	119	121
1911	134	128
1912	135	132
1913	139	134

In other words, the lower economic classes received their share from the increase of national income, divided "with remarkable equality among the various economic classes." Taking many other data into consideration, Dr. Bowley says: "I can find no statistical evidence that the rich as a class were getting rapidly richer in real income in the years preceding the war." The same conclusion is reached by him on the basis of the data about the assessed annual values of private dwelling houses in Great Britain. Fourth, a considerable part of the wage earners, during this period, rose from a lower economic class to a higher one.[12] All this represents a decided refutation of Marx's statements.

Still stronger refutation is given by the data of the United States income statistics, not to mention other sources. This is seen from the following figures:[13]

The table shows that the share of labor in the national income has been fluctuating and does not show any perpetual tendency.

The Estimated Percentages of the Total National Income Received Respectively by Labor, Capital, Land, and the Entrepreneur

Census Year	Shares of Product				
	Wages and Salaries	Interest	Rent	Profit	Total
1850	35.8	12.5	7.7	44.0	100.0
1860	37.2	14.7	8.8	39.3	100.0
1870	48.6	12.9	6.9	31.6	100.0
1880	51.5	18.6	8.7	21.3	100.0
1890	53.5	14.4	7.6	24.6	100.0
1900	47.3	15.0	7.8	30.0	100.0
1910	46.9	16.8	8.8	27.5	100.0

The share of profit has been rather decreasing; the share of interest, increasing; but, the shares of interest and profit, taken together, are rather constant. At any rate, the figures do not indicate the existence of any marked tendency of concentration of capital in fewer and fewer hands, nor, as we have seen, for the theory of systematic impoverishment of the lower classes. The comparison of wages and profits for 60 years shows further that "the general trend of wages and profits has been upward, and at about the same rate." This is seen from the following figures: [14]

Year	Average Wage per Employee in Purchasing Power	Average Profits per Entrepreneur in Purchasing Power
1850	147	318
1860	188	231
1870	179	224
1880	244	212
1890	350	368
1900	410	607
1910	401	711

An analysis of the income distribution among families gives practically similar results. It shows a possible slight increase of concentration of wealth in the hands of a few of the very rich for the last 20 years, but "the marked stability shown by the distribution of wealth during the preceding 70 years makes us doubt that the shift in the relative shares of income held by the different fractions of the population has been so great as to be at all startling." [15]

To the above must be added a comparatively new phenomenon which has already attracted the attention of American economists: namely, the "diffusion of ownership" in the United States and European countries which seems to have taken on extraordinary proportions during the last few decades. Here are a few data which illustrate the situation: According to the data of Robert S. Binkerd, from 1918 to 1925 the number of stockholders of certain industries (railroads, street railways, gas, light, electric, telegraph, telephone companies, packers, ten oil companies, five iron and steel companies, and ten miscellaneous manufacturing companies) has increased from 2,537,105 to 5,051,499, an increase of 2,514,394 stockholders. About one-half of them have been recruited from the employees and wage earners and the consumers of the companies, another half from the general public.[16] The number of farmers financially interested in cooperative buying and selling increased from 650,000 in 1916 to 2,490,000 in 1925. The number of savings-account depositors and the aggregate amount of their savings increased correspondingly from 10,631,586 and $11,115,790,000 in 1918, to 38,867,994 and $20,873,552,000 in 1925. Besides the increase in the number of stockholders, the number of the bondholders has increased on the most conservative basis by at least 2,500,000.[17] These figures indicate but a part of the enormous process of diffusion of ownership which has been going on in the United States since the time of the war.[18] Perhaps, it is too much to say that this process is a great revolution, but it is not an exaggeration to say that it is enough to disprove completely the theory of Marx. Concentration of industry does not mean at all a concentration of wealth in fewer and fewer hands, as Marx thought.[19]

Similar data are available from some other countries. Here

are examples taken from the work of Kiaer. According to his method, he computed a general increase in the national income of the indicated countries, and, besides, the rate of increase of each of the five principal economic strata, beginning with the richest and ending with the poorest.[20] The results are as follows:

PER CENT OF INCREASE OF INCOME FOR EACH ECONOMIC GROUP[21]

Economic Groups	Saxony, 1888 to 1906	Prussia, 1892 to 1906	Denmark, 1870 to 1903
First (richest)	40.3	40.8	52.5
Second	28.7	24.7	32.7
Third	34.6	45.2	54.4
Fourth	40.9	18.0[a]	86.0[a]
Fifth	36.0		
Average	35.4	24.7	61.4

[a] Fourth and fifth groups together.

These data again do not all support the prophecy of Marx. The same may be said about Japan and some other countries.[22]

Finally, how far the profile of economic stratification of European societies at the beginning of the twentieth century—50 years after Marx's prediction—varied from Marx's anticipated shape, may be seen from the following figures which show the average income of each of the five income classes in francs and the number of incomes in each class per 100,000 individual incomes:

[Income Classes	Great Britain		France		Prussia	
	Number of Incomes	Average Income	Number of Incomes	Average Income	Number of Incomes	Average Income
First (richest)	260–270	160,000	1,477	27,300	978	29,383
Second	2,895	15,195	8,000	3,888	7,603	3,781
Third	13,060	3,369	?	?	16,922	1,699
Fourth	27,425	1,604	?	?	26,558	1,082
Fifth	56,356	780	?	?	47,939	600

Income Classes	Denmark		Sweden		Norway	
	Number of Incomes	Average Income	Number of Incomes	Average Income	Number of Incomes	Average Income
First (the richest)	1,971	13,204	1,170	16,189	2,192	7,930
Second..........	8,669	3,001	8,029	2,359	8,582	2,024
Third...........	16,792	1,550	16,906	1,120	15,772	1,102
Fourth..........	26,493	982	25,589	740	24,901	698
Fifth...........	46,075	564	48,306	392	48,553	458[23]

So much for the theories of Marx. The above data are enough to show that practically all his predictions have failed. This means that Marx's predicted trends have not taken place. But, is the right hypothesis then the opposite one of an existence of a trend in the direction of a steady equalization of distribution of income? Perhaps the economic stratification of a society tends to become flatter? We know that many levelers, and socialists, and communists believe that such a transformation is possible and must take place in the future. This leads us to a discussion of this hypothesis.

C. Hypothesis of Flattening of Economic Stratification.—The discussion of this hypothesis will be brief. The above figures show that, if Marx's opposite theory is fallacious, at the same time there is no basis for the belief that during the second half of the nineteenth century and at the beginning of the twentieth century a marked and consistent tendency of economic equalization has been taking place. It is true that all classes of European and American society have become wealthier; and that the middle economic strata have not been decreasing; it is true, also, that the number of millionaires and multimillionaires has been increasing; but in many countries the income of the richest has been increasing more rapidly than that of the poorer economic classes; and the relative economic contrasts among the poor and the rich have not been decreasing; and in some countries, as we have seen, for instance, in America, since 1890, there has appeared a slight tendency toward a concentration of wealth;[24] and in other societies, *e.g.,* in England, in Germany, in France, if the economic stratification has not increased, at any rate, it has not decreased either. These facts, followed by other similar data, make certain that, as far as the European and American countries are concerned, their economic evolution for the last 60 or 70 years does not give any basis for the contention that economic stratification has tended to decrease. So much for the fantasy of many disheartened and dissatisfied social dreamers.[25] Farther on it will be pointed out under what conditions their dream may be realized and what this realization would mean.

Thus, if neither the hypothesis of a constant shape of economic stratification, nor that of its perpetual increase or decrease is true, it seems, there is left only one possible conclusion, namely, the theory of trendless fluctuation and cycles regardless of whether the fluctuations are periodic or not. This hypothesis seems the most probable. Keeping in mind that the necessary data are not complete, the further outlines have to be taken as only tentative. They need to be tested before they can pretend to certain validity.

2. HYPOTHESIS OF FLUCTUATION OF THE HEIGHT AND PROFILE OF ECONOMIC STRATIFICATION

In order to make the hypothesis clearer an analogy may be used. In natural phenomena a "natural" direction of some processes is often seen. The water of a river moves from the higher level to the lower one, unless it meets an obstacle or artificial arrangement which forces it to move upward. Material things heavier than air tend to fall downward, unless there is a force coercing them to fly up. In a similar way, within a social group numerous and as yet unknown forces in a "natural" way tend to increase economic stratification, unless there is an intervention of opposite forces acting as a check. Of course, such forces and interventions are also natural; but, in contrast with the forces which seem to work permanently and smoothly in the way of an increase of the stratification, the forces and interventions which tend to check it seem to work convulsively and spasmodically, and manifest themselves clearly only from time to time. Being always marked by a special effort to stop the natural process of stratification, they remind us of the artificiality of the cutting of permanently growing hair. In this sense they are artificial, though from a broad standpoint they are quite "natural."

If such is the case, then small and large fluctuations of economic stratification are inevitable. Postponing the discussion of whether these fluctuations are unlimited—from the steepest profile to a flat economic square—or not, and whether there are regularities and periodicity, it is easy to show that the fluctuations have existed in all societies at different times. Their scheme is as follows:

Economic stratification among the most primitive tribes is relatively very slight. Parallel to their growth and complication, the institution of private property emerges in its clear forms. The stratification becomes more conspicuous. It grows until it reaches a point of saturation, which is different for different societies. In growing, it calls forth the opposite leveling forces. Earthquake, inundation, fire, revolution, war, plundering the belongings of the rich, reforms, and laws of redistribution of land and capital, progressive taxes, cancellation of debts, expropriation of large profits—such are the forms of the leveling forces. They manifest themselves in cutting off the higher strata of the pyramid. The operation of cutting performed, the natural forces of stratification set off again in their work; and, in the course of time, they cause a renewed stratification; but when its new saturation point is reached, a new "surgical operation" takes place. In this way the monotonous repetition of the same story has been going on hundreds of times in various societies at various periods. The concrete forms of this play have been many and diverse. The play has been staged at not quite regular intervals and with not the same actors and not quite identical speeches in different societies; but its essence has been the same everywhere from the earliest records of history up to this moment. Here are a few corroborations selected from the many known.

Ancient Rome.—It is reasonable to think that in Ancient Rome, at its earliest period, economic differentiation was very slight. With the continuation of its history such stratification began to grow. At the time of Servius Tullius it was already clear, though moderate. The difference between the richest and the poorest classes, according to his reform, was that of 2 to 5 jugera and 20 jugera of land. As the land at that moment represented the principal kind of wealth, and as out of 193 "centurions" 98 were composed of people of the richest class, it seems that the economic profile of Roman society was still a gradual slope. The forces of stratification continued to work, and, at the time of the "XII tables," seem to have produced the necessity of the first attempts to stop it in the form of an alleviation of the obligations of debts, prohibition of interest above 8⅓ per cent per annum, facilitation of the use of the *ager publicus* by the poor, and so on. After this period, a legislative cancellation and diminution of debts (*tabulae novae*) and of similar "checks," often occurred. Although temporarily successful, yet they could not stop the process for a long time, hence new and newer attempts at "leveling." Among the principal of these were the laws of Licinius and Sextius, which cancelled debts and stipulated the maximum amount (500 jugera) of land (*ager occupatorius*) which might be possessed by one man. After this economic inequality again began to grow. From the fact that the equites up to 180 B. C. had to have property of above £4,000 (400,000 sesterces) [26] we must conclude that it grew notably. Hence, the necessity of new checks. And we see them in the attempts of the Gracchi to decrease the economic stratification, by extra taxation of luxury, by their land-debt-frumentaria and other laws. The next leveling was made during the period of the civil wars and revolutions, at the end of the Republic (in the forms of confiscation, plundering, different "nationalizations," expropriations, redistributions of land and what not). And yet, the "natural" forces continued their work. Concentration of wealth at the end of the Republic and during the first three centuries A. D. seems to have reached an enormously high degree. Rome became "the Republic of millionaires and beggars." Such estates as $70,000,000 brought by Gaius Julius Caesar from Gallia; Crassus' fortune worth about $7,000,000; and Seneca's amounting to $15,000,000; the enormous fortunes, at that time, of Sixtus Roscius, Demetrius, Augus, Cnaeus Lentulus, Narcissus, and others; these facts testify to the continuation of economic stratification. The advance in size of fortunes was not less at that time than in the United States of the nineteenth century. Naturally, many efforts at "flattening" the economic pyramid, in the form of revolutions, redistribution and an establishment of a state socialism in the fourth and fifth centuries A. D., were not lacking. And yet, economic stratification never disappeared. The end of this story is well known. As the result of great economic disorganization there came general poverty, disorder, invasions of the barbarians, and the so-called end of the Western Roman Empire. Thus, regarded as a whole, Roman history reminds us of a large curve which is very gentle at its beginning; then slowly, and with many sudden and sharp fluctuations, it tends to go up, reaches its climax at the end of the Republic and during the first centuries of Imperial Rome, and thereafter fluctuates without a definite trend to the end of the Empire.[27]

Greece.—The fluctuation of economic stratification in the Greek states seems to have been similar. Its beginning is a slight economic differentiation. Further on it increases. Already in the time of Hesiod, as may be seen from his complaints in *Works and Days,* it grew considerably. The same is shown by Theognis' works. In the eighth and seventh centuries B. C. it reached its point of relative saturation (for the conditions of that time) [28] and in the form of revolution and reform it called forth the first strong attempt, as far as is known, to check it. By this is meant the reforms of Solon,[29] in Athens, and similar "checks" in other Greek states. Temporarily these reforms decreased economic differentiation,[30] but could not undo it. Things resumed their "natural course." Hence, there were renewed attempts to check it: the measures of Pisistratus, those of Cleisthenes and Pericles who in various ways tried to help the poor at the cost of the rich, and at the cost of other states exploited by Athens.

The situation is well characterized by P. Guiraud:

> All ambitions of the politicians and statesmen consisted in the transference of wealth from the rich to the poor. Innumerable attempts which were made in the course of centuries, had their only purpose in a redistribution of wealth. It goes without saying that this purpose was never achieved. In the first place they did not try to make the partition strictly equal. In the second place, they did not take precautions to prevent inequality in the future. In brief,

it was a permanent new starting. They put their hand on everything economically valuable. Sometimes they give an appearance of legality to these spoliations. The most common was the method of violence. A riot broke out against the rich. If it was successful the conquerors murdered or banished their victims and confiscated their fortunes. The history of Greece is saturated with revolutions of this kind. They began with the first conflicts between the aristocratic and democratic parties and continued to the Roman conquest.[31]

Add to this numerous taxes and levies on capital (the eisphora, proeisphora, liturgiae, etc.) which took in some periods up to 20 per cent of the income of the rich. And yet, in spite of all these measures, from the time of Solon to the fourth century B. C. economic differentiation seems to have been increasing. The four economic classes created by Solon's constitution were those differentiated as having a probable capital of 500, 300, 150, and less than 150 medimnes of grain or its substitutes. While later on, according to Böckh, the probable capital of the four economic classes in its maximum and minimum was as follows: 500 to 12 talents for the first, the richest class; 11 to 6 talents for the second; 5 to 2 talents for the third; and 1.5 and less talents for the fourth class.[32] If this computation is valid, it shows a considerable increase of the economic stratification. The course of the curve of the economic stratification in other Greek states was similar. In Sparta, in spite of the severest measures taken to check an increase of economic inequality, including even the military communism of Sparta, it was impossible to stop its upward trend. And to the end of the Peloponnesian War, or later to the times of Cleomenes III and Agis IV it became very considerable and great in comparison with the earlier stages of Spartan history. (Division of the Spartans into "The Peers" and "The Inferiors.")[33] The last centuries of the Greek states, beginning approximately with the third century, represent their economic decline which in some states seems to have been followed by a decrease of economic stratification due to many causes, among which oppressive taxes, expropriations, and social revolutions played important rôles.[34]

Still more conspicuous are these waves in the long history of China. Though its history is known very little, especially in its earliest periods, nevertheless, the big cycles of increase and decrease in economic stratification, during the last two thousand years, seem to be evident.

This is shown by the cycles of concentration and diffusion of land ownership which seem to have been repeated several times in the last two thousand years. We are told that thanks to the Tsing Tien System (a kind of state ownership of land) before the fourth century B. C. there was not a great concentration of land in the hands of the rich few. After approximately 350 B. C. this system was followed by that of private property. This led to a rapid concentration of land in the hands of the few, and, as a result, to several attempts to check it (in 120, and in 7 B. C.). The Chinese, however, could not check it for a long time. In 280 A. D. such an attempt was carried out again; the land was equally redistributed and the Tsing Tien System reestablished. As the growth of inequality resumed, several new redistributions, in the way of reform and revolution, followed and have been carried on at the beginning of the dynasties Tsin, Wei, Tang, Sung, and others. With interruptions the system existed up to 713 A. D. when it gave way to private property again, and to new concentration. Later on, in different ways, several attempts at equalization have been made again in the form of different nationalizations, state socialism measures, governmental control of industry and so on (the reforms of Liu An, 755 to 762; Wang An-Shih, 1069 to 1086, and others).[35] Such is the course of the history of China to this time.

If a great non-territorial group, such as the Christian Church, especially the Roman Catholic Church, is taken, similar cycles may be seen. At the beginning is the Christian Community economically not differentiated and near to the state of *communis omnium possessio*. Further on, with the increase of the Christians and the legalization of Christianity, a rapid increase of church wealth followed with rapid growth of economic stratification. In the seventh and eighth centuries the wealth of the church became enormous; paralleling this, the social and economic standards, the wealth and incomes of its different strata, beginning with the Pope and ending with a common parishioner or the lowest clergyman, became also quite incomparable. Previous equality disappeared. The Church organization represented now a very high pyramid divided into numerous economic strata. After this many measures were employed to cut off the wealth and stratification of the Church. Confiscations and taxation of the Church wealth by the Carolingians, and later on, by the secular powers in England, in France and in other places; the appearance of the numerous sects, inimical to the Church authorities, which tried to "return the Church to the Gospel poverty"; (the Cathari, Bogomili, Waldenses, Beggards, Lollards, Humiliati, Arnoldists, and so on); the Renaissance and the Reformation—these and many similar factors worked for a decrease of the wealth of the Church and its economic stratification. Of a similar sort was "the economic history" of the Christian churches in the separate countries, such as England, Italy, France, Germany, and Russia. To be brief, if the wealth and incomes of the highest representatives of the National Christian Churches in these countries are compared approximately with those of their average priests, on the one hand; and then if the same comparison for the highest and the lowest church authorities in the Middle Ages, on the other are made, the inference, with considerable probability, is that the present economic cone of the Christian Religious group is considerably more flat than that of the Middle Ages. The upward trend of the first fourteen centuries of the Christian Church in the field of its economic stratification seems, since that time, and especially after the eighteenth century, to have been superseded by a trend toward flattening. This fundamental curve has been in reality much more complicated; many series of smaller cycles have been fluctuating around this fundamental curve. Taken together they signify the existence of cycles but not of a perpetual trend. If we take the whole story of many religious orders, a similar result is obtained.

The history of the European nations (still relatively short) shows similar waves in economic stratification. Its beginning is known. Among the Teutons in the time of Cæsar "each man sees that his own wealth is equal to that of the most powerful." [36]

In the time of Tacitus' *Germania* economic stratification among them had made already considerable progress; later on, not without fluctuations, parallel to the expansion and complication of the social bodies, it continued to grow, and resulted in the complex system of feudalism which, in the first place, was a system of very complex economic stratification. At the end of the Middle Ages stratification was already enormous. According to Luther the annual income of a peasant was at his time about 40 guldens, that of a noble (Ritter) 400 guldens, that of a count, a prince and a king, 4,000, 40,000, and 400,000 respectively. About A. D. 1500 the rich man's income was between 100,000 and 130,000 ducats; an average annual income of a German artisan fluctuated between 8 and 20 guldens; the income of Charles V is supposed to have been no less than 4,500,000 ducats.[37] Thus, the highest income of the economic cone exceeded, at least, 500,000 times an average income of an artisan—a difference which is scarcely exceeded by any of the present societies, even by England and the United States. In a similar way, in France of the thirteenth and fourteenth centuries, was found great economic stratification. Besides the king and nobility, there were five economic classes of the artisans (*gens de métiers*) paying taxes from 5 sous to 10 livres and above; and a class of the *bourgeoisie* superposed on the class of the *gens de métier,* and stratified in its own terms, according to their incomes. Such *bourgeois* as Ganduffle de Lombart had 458,000 livres of yearly income—an amount several tens of thousands times the income of an average artisan.[38] The fortune of Lorenzo Medici (1440) was about 235,137 gold guldens; that of the banker Chigi (1520) about 800,000 ducats; that of the pope Julius II, about 700,000 ducats. In Spain, in the sixteenth century, the greater part of the land was owned by 105 persons.[39] According to G. King's historical document, in England, in the seventeenth century, the gradation of annual income began with £5—the income of the ill-paid pursuits; further on gradually rose to £15 for the agricultural laborers and country folks; to £38, for the artisans and craftsmen; to £42, 10 shillings for the farmers; to £45, for the shopkeepers and tradesmen; to £60, for those engaged in the arts and sciences; to £60-80, for the naval and military officers; to £55 to £90, for the freeholders; to £50, for the inferior clergy; to £72, for the dignified clergy; to £154, for the lawyers; to £200 to £400, for the merchants; to £280, for the country gentleman; to £450, for an esquire; to

£650, for a knight; to £880, for a baronet; to £1,300, for a bishop; to £3,200, for a nobleman; and finally, at the top of a cone we have the king and the richest men with incomes much greater still.[40] It is enough to compare these data with those of F. A. Woods, concerning the present difference between the highest and an average income in the United States to see that the previous centuries knew economic contrasts scarcely less than those of the present society with its multimillionaires and enormous financial corporations.[41]

This process of the growth of economic inequality has been many times checked in various ways; through revolutions, wars, reforms, confiscations, expropriations, taxes, levies; through the free gifts of rich men; and so on. That these "checks" have been relatively efficient, is proved by the fact that the present inequality, measured from the average modal income to the highest one in a society, is no greater than it was before in some periods. If the trend in increase of economic stratification were permanent, the present inequality should have been much greater than that in England or in Germany in the past. If this seems not to be the case, it must be concluded that the checks have not been quite impotent.

The existence of cycles may be seen even from these few figures concerning the share of the different income strata in the whole national income in the nineteenth and twentieth centuries in European countries. The figures show that the shares fluctuate from month to month, from year to year, from one period of several years to another period (see the above figures for the United States from 1850 to 1890, and from 1890 to 1910; for the United Kingdom, from 1880 to 1900, and from 1900 to 1913). The Russian Revolution in the period 1917 to 1921 is a contemporary example of a sudden and radical flattening of the economic stratification of Russian society; since 1922 it has shown the opposite trend again, which has manifested itself in a rebuilding of many strata destroyed in the first period of the Revolution.[42]

Finally the existence of a rhythm in economic stratification is manifested also by many "ups" and "downs" in the economic status of the largest economic strata. Some of the "ups" and "downs" were parallel to an increase and decrease of the national income; some of them have happened independent of this general cause. In England, for instance, the economic status of the laboring classes was bad in the fourteenth century, and was excellent in the fifteenth and at the beginning of the sixteenth century; in the second half of the sixteenth and in the seventeenth century it became much worse; in the first half of the eighteenth century it improved again, to be aggravated later on, especially at the end of the eighteenth and at the beginning of the nineteenth century; these periods, in their turn, gave way to a new improvement in the second half of the nineteenth century, to be aggravated again during the last 10 years.[43] Similar waves have existed in the history of France. The thirteenth and the beginning of the fourteenth centuries were periods of a good economic situation, for the laboring classes. The second half of the fourteenth and the first half of the fifteenth centuries were the periods of its great aggravation; in the second half of the fifteenth and in the first part of the sixteenth centuries it became again better, to be aggravated once more in the second part of the sixteenth and at the beginning of the seventeenth centuries; the next period was again a period of a relative improvement which after the second half of the eighteenth century was superseded by an aggravation which continued throughout the first part of the nineteenth century to give way to an improvement of the second half of the nineteenth century which, in its turn, was interrupted by the World War and the post-war conditions.[44]

Similar waves have existed in the history of Russia, Germany, and practically all countries. In regard to China, Ancient Egypt, Greece, and Rome, some indications are given above.

The preceding seems to give a basis for the conclusion *that the existence of fluctuations in the economic stratification of a society is reasonably certain.*

3. ARE THE FLUCTUATIONS PERIODIC?

The next problem to be discussed briefly is whether these fluctuations are periodic or not. The problem unfortunately cannot be answered with certainty, owing to the lack of data, and to the impossibility of deciding definitely at what time an increase or decrease of stratification has begun. The fluctuations go on so gradually that it is almost impossible to indicate a definite year as the beginning or the end of a cycle. Any such attempt is somewhat subjective. Yet in a purely tentative way it is possible to admit the existence of several kinds of approximate periodicity. The above data concerning the economic status of the laboring classes in France and England may suggest the probability that there have been periods of about 50, 100, and 150 years. The indexes of purchasing power of money and prices given by D'Avenel for France may show something on this point. Taking the purchasing power of money at the end of the nineteenth century as 1, D'Avenel [45] gives the following indices for the previous centuries:

Periods	Purchasing Power of Money	
1201 to 1225	4.5	150 years (1201 to 1350), decreasing trend.
1226 to 1300	4	
1301 to 1350	3.5	
1376 to 1400	4	150 years (1351 to 1500), increasing trend.
1401 to 1450		
1451 to 1500	5	
1501 to 1525	5	150 years (1501 to 1650), decreasing trend.
1526 to 1550	4	
1551 to 1575	3	
1576 to 1600	2.5	
1601 to 1650		
1651 to 1700		
1701 to 1725	2.75	150 years, no trend.
1726 to 1750	3	
1751 to 1775	2.33	
1776 to 1790	2	

If it is true that "rising prices amount to a redistribution of the national income in favor of the entrepreneur class," [46] then the above figures show a periodicity of 150 years in the fluctuation of stratification, which, however, is not shown by the last 150 years. Similar periodicity is suggested also by the mentioned fluctuation of the economic status of the laboring classes in England. Studying from this standpoint many long-time series of indices of price, cost of living, nominal and real wages, and so on, it is possible, sometimes, to notice a periodicity of about 30, 15, 20, 10, 40, 50 years. Any certain negative or positive inference from these data is impossible, however, in view of their fragmentary, incidental, and inadequate character. As the problem of the periodicity is not very important, it is dropped here, with the suggestion that the existence of a not quite rigid periodicity may be probable, but is not yet proved.

4. IS THERE, IN THE FLUCTUATION OF ECONOMIC STRATIFICATION, A LIMIT?

The most probable tentative answer to this question seems to be as follows: *Under normal conditions, free from any social catastrophe, for a society which has passed beyond the primitive stage and is compound in its structure, and maintains the institution of private property, the fluctuations in the height and the profile of its economic stratification are limited.* This means that the shape of the stratification is likely not to become too "pointed" or too "flat." It is relatively constant, and permanently varies only within definite limits. This is shown by Pareto, Schmoller, and by some others who have shown that the shape of the economic cone of different societies and of the same society at different times is somewhat similar. This is illustrated by the following selected figures:

The figures show that the shape of the economic cone of different societies and of the same society at different times fluctuates, but the variations are limited and the profiles are substantially similar.

Does this mean that a more radical change in the shape of the stratification is impossible? Not at all. Not to go far into the past it is enough to look at the Russian experiment to see that under extraordinary circumstances, the shape and the height of the stratification may be almost flat. The Bolshevist annihilation of private property and expropriation of all money, valuable and precious objects; their nationalization of all banks, factories, workshops, houses, and land; their equalization of all wages and salaries (the difference between the highest wage and the lowest one, according to the decree of 1918 had to be not greater than

PER CENT OF THE CORRESPONDING FOUR INCOME CLASSES [47]

Social Groups and Periods	Richest Class	Second Income Class	Third Income Class	Poorest Class	Total, Per Cent of All Classes
Population of Basel:					
In 1453–1454	4.3	17.0	27.8	50.9	100.0
In 1881	4.6	17.2	18.2	60.0	100.0
Population of Augsburg:					
In 1471	0.29	2.7	31.6	65.4	100.0 [a]
In 1554	2.29	3.98	40.5	53.2	100.0 [a]
Population of Oldenburg:					
In 1892	2.8	5.8	33.4	57.6	100.0 [a]
Population of Prussia:					
In 1893–1894	1.4	2.5	26.1	70.0	100.0
Population of England:					
In 1688	0.6	2.9	34.1	62.4	100.0
In 1867	0.5	1.5	30.2	67.7	100.0 [a]
Population of Saxony:					
In 1892	0.7	2.7	30.5	66.9	100.0 [a]

a Approximately.

the relation of 175 to 100; the same may be said of the differences in the salaries) [48] in brief, the Communist "measures" in 1917 to 1921 cut off all the well-to-do strata of the Russian economic cone, greatly diminished the economic differences among the peasants and the industrial wage earners, and in this way made the economic shape of the Russian society almost entirely flat. Instead of a cone, at that period the shape resembled a kind of trapezium. This fact—far from being unique in the history of different countries—means that *the most radical transformation of the height and the shape of the economic stratification happens. But, it always has the character of a great catastrophe, takes place under extraordinary, unfavorable circumstances, and if the society does not perish, its "flatness" is regularly replaced by recreation of the cone and its inevitable economic layers.*

During these years this has been seen in Russia, in Hungary, and in Bavaria, where such "flattenings" have taken place. In the past, a similar course of events has been exhibited by many

Communist Revolutions in Greece, in Persia (Mazdac's Communist experiment), in many Mohammedan countries, in China (the experiments of Wang Mang, and Wang An-Shih), in the Middle Ages in Bohemia (the Taborits' Communist State), in Germany (the Communist Societies of Th. Münzer and John of Leiden), in France during the Great French Revolution, and so on. In other words, as far as more or less advanced and large social aggregates are concerned, the radical flattening of economic stratification always has been catastrophic; always has been accompanied by a great economic disorganization, famine, starvation and poverty; never has been successful; always has been short lived; and as soon as the society has begun to recover economically, always has been replaced by a new stratification. These statements are not speculations but the result of an inductive study of the corresponding experiments.[49] No exception to this rule is known. Those "State Socialist" or "Military Communist" societies which, like Lipara, Sparta, or the Roman Empire of the fourth and fifth centuries A.D., or the Kingdom of the Incas, or that of Ancient Mexico, or Egypt under the Ptolemei, or the state of the Jesuits, which existed comparatively for a long time, are not exceptions to the rule simply because they were really highly stratified societies, with a great social and economic inequality of different layers within each of them.[50]

Therefore, we must agree, with the extreme levelers, that the radical "flattening" of the shape of the stratification is possible, and has sometimes happened. But we must add that this has been accompanied by a catastrophic destruction of the economic life of the society; by a still greater increase of the misery of the majority of its population, and by anarchy and death. He who wants such "flattening" should be ready to meet these accompaniments. Either a flat economic society, and then poverty is to be expected; or a relatively prosperous society, and then a certain degree of inequality is unavoidable.[51]

The above, with corresponding variation, may be said about an unlimited heightening and steepening of the profile of economic stratification. *There seems also to be a point of "saturation" beyond which the society cannot go without risk of great catastrophe. When such a point is transgressed, the social building is doomed to crumble, and its higher economic layers to fall. . . .* in what way the operation is made, through revolution or reform, invasion or inner disorganization, taxation or robbery, does not matter; what matters is that in some way it has always been done. As a physical building has its point of excessive strain, in an analogous way there exists also a point of excessive strain for a "social building." Depending on many conditions, the point of "overloading" is different for different physical structures. In a similar way, the danger point of overstrain of economic stratification is different for different societies, according to their size, the environment, the human material, the character of the distribution of wealth, and so on. As soon as a society begins to approach its point of overstrain, the revolutionary, leveling, Socialist, and Communist "fever" starts to go up; it begins to infect larger and larger masses; calls forth greater and greater public indignation, and either in a reform or else in a revolutionary way "the operation" takes place. Such seems to have been this ever-revolving cycle of history. So much about the limits of the fluctuation of the height and profile of economic stratification. Let us now turn to the last problem.

5. IS THERE ANY PERPETUAL TREND IN THE FLUCTUATIONS OF THE HEIGHT AND THE PROFILE OF ECONOMIC STRATIFICATION?

I do not see it. That there is no permanent trend toward economic equality is evident to everybody who is acquainted with this field, and who does not substitute for thousands of years of factual historical processes the fiery "speech reactions" and "noisy verbosity" of disheartened levelers. Beyond doubt, the economic pyramid of all primitive societies, and that of the earliest stages of the European, American, Asiatic, and African societies, has been very low, and near to a "flatness." Further evolution of each of these has consisted not in an increase of economic equality but in that of inequality. The earliest economic "flatness" in the later stages has never been achieved by any of these societies, just as no man can return to his childhood when he has passed it. This is certain beyond any doubt. And since, in the course of thousands of years, such "return" has not happened, except in the short-lived catastrophic cases, there is no basis for any claim for such a trend in economic equality. Although complete liberty is given to everybody, even to an insane person, to believe what he pleases, nevertheless, as for science, there is only one answer: *any society, as it proceeds from its earliest primitive stages to more advanced ones, shows not a decrease but an increase of economic inequality.* And neither the speeches of levelers, nor those of the Christian liberal preachers, in spite of their everyday repetition, can change this process.[52]

Does this mean that there is the opposite permanent trend toward an increase of economic inequality? I do not think so. In the way of an analogy it may be said: it is true that a newborn baby shows a growth of his body and mind during several years; but it is false to infer from this that his physical and mental growth continues indefinitely. After a definite number of years the growth stops and somewhat opposite processes take place. This means that from the mere fact of an increase of economic stratification during the first stages of the evolution of a society it is impossible to infer that this tendency is to be permanent and must go on indefinitely. The analogy is surely not an argument. But the facts of history are the arguments. What do they show in this respect? In the first place, they show that in many societies of the past, at their earlier stages, economic stratification grew; having reached its point of culmination it began to fluctuate and, from time to time, to crumble; the last stages of their economic evolution were often (not always) marked by a decrease of economic contrasts, though it was not a return to the primitive "flatness." Such is the schematic curve of their history in this respect. The second series of relevant historical facts is given in the history of some long-lived societies, such as China. In spite of the 6,000 years of its history, and many fluctuations, it is scarcely possible to say that there has been a permanent trend of increase in economic stratification in Chinese society during the last millenniums. At the present moment it is scarcely greater than in many previous periods. All that we see here during the last 2,000 or 3,000 years are fluctuations in the stratification. The third series of facts is supplied by the history of present European societies. The data given above indicate that in their past they have shown economic contrasts no less than those of the present. During the last few centuries their stratification has been fluctuating up and down; that is all. No perpetual trend in the direction of either a growth of the economic inequality or its decrease has been definitely shown.

Finally, the history of the better-known and statistically studied nineteenth and twentieth centuries, as we have seen, also does not show any definite trend in this respect. The division of the national income in these countries, being pretty stable, shows only fluctuations in either direction. Therefore, in spite of our inclination to see a definite trend in anything; in spite of our desire that the unknown forces which shape the history of mankind lead it toward a definite goal; in spite of the common opinion, which depicts the process of historical development as a passing through a college where all students (societies) enter the freshman class, pass consecutively through the sophomore, junior, and senior classes and, finally, are graduated to become happy members of a final "socialist," "communist," "anarchist," "equal," "unequal," or what-not social paradise prescribed to history by the sense or the nonsense of a "theoretician of progress"—in spite of all that, we have to conclude that for such "finalism" and "eschatology," whatever it may be, there is no serious basis. And the historical process in this, as well as in many other respects, reminds me rather of a man circling in various directions without any definite goal or point of arrival.

To the above the following brief remarks should be added: First, as Schmoller and Pareto properly noticed, there may be a correlation between the period of an intensive economic development and an increase of economic stratification,[53] and contrariwise; second, other conditions being equal, an enlargement of the size of a society, in the form of an increase of its members, is likely to facilitate an increase of inequality, and *vice versa*. These, however, are not very close, and are often broken by an interference of heterogeneous and unexpected factors. So much about the fluctuation of the height and the profile of economic stratification.

6. SUMMARY

1. Neither the hypothesis of a constant height and profile of the economic stratification, nor that of its growth in the nineteenth century, is warranted.

2. The most probable is the hypothesis of their fluctuations from group to group, and, within the same group, from time to time. In other words, there are cycles in which increase in economic inequality is superseded by decrease.

3. In these fluctuations there may be a kind of periodicity, but, for various reasons, its existence is not yet proved.

4. Except in the first stages of the economic evolution of a group, which are marked by an increase of economic stratification, there seems to be no perpetual trend in the fluctuations of the height and the shape of economic stratification.

5. There surely has not been manifested any perpetual trend toward decrease of economic inequality. On the other hand, there is no serious basis for an admission of the existence of the opposite trend.

6. Under normal conditions, the economic cone of an advanced society fluctuates within definite limits. Its shape is relatively constant. Under extraordinary circumstances, however, these limits may be surpassed, and the profile of economic stratification may become either extraordinarily flat or extraordinarily steep and high. In both cases, however, such a situation is very short lived; if an "economically flat" society does not perish, the "flatness" very rapidly is followed by an increase of economic stratification. If the economic inequality becomes too great and reaches the point of overstrain the top of the society is doomed to crumble and fall.

7. Thus, in any society at any time there is going on a struggle between the forces of stratification and those of equalization. The former work permanently and steadily; the latter, convulsively, violently, and from time to time.

[1] PARETO, V., *Cours d'économie politique,* Vol. II, pp. 306-308.

[2] PARETO, V., *Manuale di economia politica,* pp. 371-372. In his later *Traité de sociologie générale,* he made still greater reservations.

[3] See the analysis and criticism of Pareto's law: MACAULAY, F. R., and BENJAMIN, E. G., "The Personal Distribution of Income in the United States,"

Income in the United States, Its Amount and Distribution, Vol. II, pp. 341-394, National Bureau of Economic Research, New York, 1922; PIGOU, A. C., *The Economics of Welfare,* pp. 693-700, 1920.

[4] MACAULAY, F. R., and BENJAMIN, E. G., *op. cit.,* pp. 393-394.

[5] MARX, KARL, *Communist Manifesto* (Kerr ed.), pp. 21-31; *Capital,* Vol. I, pp. 788-789, London, 1891.

[6] WOOD, G. H., "Real Wages and the Standard of Comfort Since 1850," *Journal of the Royal Statistical Society,* pp. 102-103, 1909; BOWLEY, A. L., *Wages in the United Kingdom in the Nineteenth Century, passim,* 1900; BOWLEY, A. L., *The Change in the Distribution of the National Income,* pp. 15, 18; GIFFEN, "The Progress of the Working Classes," in his *Essay in Finances,* 2nd series, London, 1890. BEVERIDGE, SIR WILLIAM, paper in *Economics Journal,* p. 462, September, 1923.

[7] KING, W. I., *op. cit.,* p. 168; HANSEN, A., "Factors Affecting the Trend of Real Wages," *American Economics Review,* Vol. XV, No. 1, p. 32. See also "Income per Family" in BERRIDGE, WINSLOW, & FLINN, *Purchasing Power of the Consumer,* Bk. II, Straw Company, 1925.

[8] See, for France, LEVASSEUR, E., *Histoire des classes ouvrières,* Vol. II, pp. 795-904; and *passim,* 1904; CAUDERLIÈR, *L'évolution économique du XIX siècle,* pp. 73 *ff.,* Stuttgard, 1903; for Belgium, ENGEL, "Die Lebenskosten Belgischer Arbeiter-Familien früher und jetzt," *Bull. de l'Inst. Int. Stat.,* Vol. IX, pp. 123-124; for Denmark, Prussia, and some other European countries, see WAGNER, A., *op. cit., passim;* ASCHLEY, W. J., *The Progress of the German Working Classes in the Last Quarter of a Century,* 1904; KIAER, *op. cit., passim;* for the United States, see KING, W. I., *op. cit.,* Chap. VII; for Japan, see TAKANO, *op. cit., passim;* for Italy, MORTARA, G., *op. cit.;* general data and survey of the situation is given in SOMBART, W., *Der Proletarische Sozialismus* (new and greatly changed edition of his *Sozialismus und soziale Bewegung*) Bds. I and II, Jena, 1924; SIMKHOVITCH, W. G., *Marxism versus Socialism,* Chaps. VI and VII, New York, 1913; SOLNTZEFF, S. *Zarabotnaia plata kak predmet raspredelenia* (Russian), *passim;* MOORE, H. L., *Laws of Wages,* New York, 1911; SCHMOLLER, G., *Grundriss der Allgemeinen Volkswirtschaftslehre,* Vol. II, 523 *ff.,* 1919; TUGAN-BARANOVSKY, M., *Osnovy polit. economii,* pp. 682 *ff.*

[9] See the figures in SCHMOLLER, G., *op. cit.,* Vol. II, pp. 378 *ff.*

[10] TUGAN-BARANOVSKY, M., *Osnovy polit. economii,* pp. 682-683; *Die Zeitschrift d. königlich Preussischen Statistik Landesamts,* Vols. XLVI and XLVII, pp. 4, 8-10, 1911.

[11] The data are taken from WAGNER, A., *Zur Methodik der Statistiks des Volkseinkommens,* etc. See other similar data for Saxony, for Prussia (from 1893 to 1913) in SCHMOLLER, G., *op. cit.,* Vol. II, pp. 526-529.

[12] BOWLEY, A. L., *The Change in the Distribution of the National Income,* pp. 10, 12, 21-22, 26, *passim.* See also STAMP, SIR JOSIAH, *British Incomes and Property,* Chaps. XII to XIV, 1920; STAMP, SIR JOSIAH, *Studies in Current Problems,* pp. 126 *ff.,* 1924; GOSHEN, VISCOUNT, *Essays and Addresses on Economic Questions,* London, pp. 230 *ff.,* 1905.

[13] KING, W. I., *op. cit.,* p. 160; see many valuable details for the period from 1910 to 1920 in *Income in the United States, Its Amount and Distribution,* National Bureau of Economic Research, Vols. I and II, *passim.*

[14] KING, W. I., *op. cit.,* p. 168.

[15] *Ibid.,* p. 219.

[16] BINKERD, ROBERT S., "The Increase in Popular Ownership Since the World War," *Proceedings of the Academy of Political Science,* Vol. XI, No. 3, pp. 33, April, 1925. CARVER, THOMAS N., *The Present Economic Revolution in the United States,* Boston, 1925.

[17] *Ibid.*, pp. 36-37. See other detailed data in other papers of this volume, *passim.*

[18] The same process has been proceeding in other countries. See the figures in SCHMOLLER, G., *op. cit.*, Vol. II, pp. 520-522.

[19] See some other facts and proper remarks in SIMKHOVITCH, *Marxism versus Socialism*, Chaps. IV and V.

[20] See the method of computation and the details in KIAER, "Répartition sociale des revenus," *Bull. de l'Inst. Int. de Stat.*, Vol. XVIII, and KIAER, "La répartition des revenus et fortunes privés," *Bull. de l'Inst. Int. de Stat.*, Vol. XX, pp. 619-648.

[21] KIAER, *op. cit.*, p. 130.

[22] For Japan, see the quoted paper of Takano; for Italy, that of G. Mortara.

[23] KIAER, *op. cit.*, pp. 121-125.

[24] From this standpoint the computation of F. A. Woods concerning the contrast between the fortunes of the richest and the relatively poor groups in this country at different times, may have some interest. According to his data, in the seventeenth century "the richest men were not more than fifty times as rich as the average; at the middle of the eighteenth century they were three hundred times as rich as the average; for the middle of the nineteenth century the figure is about six hundred; at the present time the richest men are ten thousand and even one hundred thousand times as rich as the average." The accuracy of these data may be questioned, but Dr. Woods may be right in the contention that the economic distance between the top of the social cone and its average economic strata has increased. See WOODS, F. A., "The Conification of Social Groups," *Eugenics, Genetics, and the Family*, Vol. I, pp. 312-328, Baltimore, 1923.

[25] With a reason, Dr. Schmoller styles such theories as "childish and contradictory to all historical knowledge." *Op. cit.*, Vol. II, p. 516.

[26] LIVY, 39, 19, 4.

[27] See the details in the works: WEBER, M., *Römische Agrargeschichte*, 1891; PÖHLMANN, *Geschichte d. Antiker Socialismus und Kommunismus;* SALVIOLI, *Capitalism in the Antique World;* ROSTOVTZEFF, M. I., *Studien zur Geschichte des Römischen Kolonats*, 1910; WALTZING, *Étude Historique sur les corporations professionnelles chez les Romaines*, Bruxelles, 1896; further the works of J. Ferrero, Mommsen, Duruy, Friedländer, Druhmann, O. Seek; GUIRAUT, P., *Études économiques sur l'antiquité*, Chap. V, Paris, 1905. See especially M. Rostovtzeff, *Social and Economic History of the Roman Empire*, Oxford, 1926, *passim.*

[28] "Land was in the hands of few," and "many were in slavery to the few"; therefore, "the people rose against the upper class." ARISTOTLE, *On the Athenian Constitution*, Chaps. IV to VI, London, 1907.

[29] "Solon liberated the people once and for all, by prohibiting all loans on the security of the debtor's person; and at the same time he made laws by which he cancelled all debts, public and private," and so on. *Ibid.*, Chaps. IV to VII.

[30] Though any leveling, on the other hand, creates a new source of economic inequality. Such was the course of events, according to Aristotle, which happened here also. "It so happened that, when Solon was about to enact the Seisachteia (that means removal of burden), he announced his intention to some members of the upper classes . . . and these persons borrowed money and bought up a large amount of land, and so, when a short time afterwards, all debts were cancelled, they became wealthy; and this was the origin of the families which were afterwards looked upon as possessing wealth from primeval

times." *Ibid.*, Chap. VI. This shows that any reform and revolution has its own profiteers and machinators.

[31] GUIRAUD, P., *Études économiques sur l'antiquité*, pp. 68-69, Paris, 1905.

[32] A talent is about 6,000 French francs.

[33] XENOPHON, *Hellenica*, 3.3, 5, and 6.

[34] See GUIRAUD, P., *op. cit.*, *passim;* BÖCKH, *Staatshaushaltung der Athener*, Bk. IV, and *passim;* PÖHLMANN, *op. cit.*, *passim;* BUSOLT, *Griechische Geschichte*, all volumes: NIESE, B., *Geschichte d. Griechischen und Maked. Staaten*, all volumes; BEER, M., *Social Struggles in Antiquity;* ZIMMERN, *The Greek Commonwealth*, 1915; BURY, *History of Greece*, 1906.

[35] See LEE, MABEL P. H., *op. cit.*, pp. 58-123, 162, 214 and Chap. VII; CHEN HUAN CHANG, *The Economic Principles of Confucius and His School*, Vol. II, Bk. VIII, and *passim;* IVANOFF, *Wang An-Shih* (Russian), *passim.*

[36] CÆSAR, GAIUS JULIUS, *Gallic Wars*, Bk. VI, Chap. 22, and Bk. LV, Chap. I.

[37] SCHMOLLER, G., "Die Einkommensverteilung in alter und neuer Zeit," *Bull. de l'Inst. Int. de Stat.*, Vol. IX, Pt. I, No. 17, pp. 2-3; *Grundriss der Allgemeinen Volkswirtschaftslehre*, Vol. II, p. 517.

[38] See SAINT-LEON, É. MARTIN, *Histoire de Corporations de Métiers*, pp. 177*ff.*, Paris, 1922. The annual income of Louis XIV was about 21,000,000 francs; of Richelieu, 14,000,000; Mazarini left a fortune amounting to 195,000,000 francs; J. Coeur, 27,000,000. See other figures in D'AVENEL, G., *Découvertes d'histoire sociale*, pp. 220 *ff.*, Paris, 1910.

[39] SCHMOLLER, G., *Grundriss der Allgemeinen Volkswirtschaftslehre*, Vol. II, p. 517.

[40] ROGERS, J. E. T., *Six Centuries of Work and Wages*, pp. 463-465, New York, 1884. Annual revenue of Edward II fluctuated from £60,111 to £128,-248; that of Edward III, from £67,603 to £253,126. See RAMSAY, SIR JAMES H., *A History of the Revenues of the Kings of England*, Vol. II, pp. 292, 422, and *passim*, Oxford, 1925.

[41] G. Schmoller says that the economic contrasts of the present time are rather less than that of some past periods. *Ibid.*, p. 519. Opposite is the opinion of D'Avenel, *Découvertes*, pp. 229 *ff.*

[42] See SOROKIN, P., *Sociology of Revolution*, Pts. III and IV.

[43] ROGERS, *op. cit.*, pp. 327 and 480, Chaps. XII and XVI, and *passim;* BOWLEY, A. L., *Wages in the United Kingdom in the Nineteenth Century*, pp. 32-34, 40; WELBY, LORD, "The Progress of the United Kingdom from the War of the French Revolution to 1913," *Journal of the Royal Statistical Society*, pp. 2-15, 1915; CUNNINGHAM, W., *The Growth of English Industry and Commerce*, 1892.

[44] See D'AVENEL, *Paysans et Ouvriers*, pp. 11-18, 28, 152-157, 290, and *passim*, Paris, 1899; D'AVENEL, *La fortune privée*, pp. 7, 17, 37, and *passim*, Paris, 1895; SCHMITZ, O., *Die Bewegung der Warenprise in Deutschland*, Berlin, 1913; TOOKE and NEWMARCH, *Die Geschichte und Bestimmung der Preise*, *passim*, 1858; LEVASSEUR, E., *Histoire des classes ouvrières*, Vols. I and II, *passim;* LEVASSEUR, E., "Le prix du blé dans divers pays au XIX siècle," *Bull. l'Inst. Int. Stat.*, Vol. XVIII.

Besides general historical characteristics these works give the indices of the wages, purchasing power of money and the prices of principal necessities, which allow us to define the economic status of the labor classes more or less clearly.

[45] D'AVENEL, *La fortune privée*, pp. 7, 17, 37.

[46] HANSEN, A., *op. cit.*, p. 40.

[47] SCHMOLLER, G., *Die Einkommensverteilung in alter und neuer Zeit*, pp.

13-22. See here the bases and methods of the comparison. See other figures in PARETO, V., *Cours d'économie politique*. See also KING, W. I., *op. cit.*, Chaps. IV to VIII.

[48] See the details in my *Sociology of Revolution*, Chaps. V, XII, and XIV.

[49] Something in this respect may be found in my *Sociology of Revolution;* the detailed study of the problem has been made by me in my *Inanition as a Factor*, destroyed by the Bolshevist Government.

[50] See PARETO, V., *Les systèmes socialistes, passim*, Paris, 1902-1903; SPENCER, HERBERT, *Principles of Sociology*, Pt. V, Chap. XVII; WIPPER, T., *History of Communist Societies* (Russian), Riga, 1925; PÖHLMANN, R., *op. cit., passim.*

[51] In a small face-to-face group, like the Communist sects and communities, the chances of keeping economic equality are incomparably greater. They are like a family group or a small primitive tribe. But, as is well known, even such groups, composed of highly selected individuals, have always failed, and ended either by a dispersion of the group or by its transformation into a stratified—capitalistic—body. Apparently, the chances for an existence of a large complicated society without economic stratification, and without misery, are almost *nil*. All arguments against it, set forth by Aristotle and Herbert Spencer, not to mention other names, are still quite valid and true. See ARISTOTLE, *Politics*, Bk. II, and *passim;* SPENCER, HERBERT, *Principles of Sociology*, Vol. III, Chaps. XXII and XXIII. See also PARETO, V., *Les systèmes socialistes, passim.* A greater part of the books about socialism and equality are scientifically quite valueless. They deal not with the facts but almost exclusively with speech reactions in form of description and speculative reasoning in favor of or against different socialist Utopias and speculative theories.

[52] The patent medicine for an establishment of such equality in the form of annihilation of private property and universal nationalization—the medicine many times tried in China, Ancient Egypt, Sparta, Athens, Rome, Peru, Mexico, Persia, and Arabia never has given a real equality and has not prevented the appearance and growth of an excessive economic stratification. The contemporary Communist experiments in Hungary, and especially in Russia, where the Communists themselves are rebuilding a highly stratified society, after its destruction—these experiments are only an additional confirmation of the inefficiency of this prescription for an achievement of economic equality.

[53] See SCHMOLLER, G., *Die Einkommensverteilung in alter und neuer Zeit*, pp. 14-22. See also proper remarks of HANSEN, A., *op. cit.*, pp. 39-40.

CHAPTER V

POLITICAL STRATIFICATION

As has already been said, the universality and permanency of a political stratification does not mean that it is everywhere and always identical. The problems to be discussed now are: first, do the profile and height of political stratification fluctuate from group to group, and from time to time; second, are there any ascertainable limits to these fluctuations; third, are the fluctuations periodical; fourth, is there in the fluctuations any perpetual secular trend. In this field we must be especially careful not to be bewitched with sonorous speech reactions. The problem is very complex. We must approach it gradually, step by step.

I. FLUCTUATION OF THE UPPER PART OF POLITICAL STRATIFICATION

In order to simplify the situation let us take, in the first place, only the upper part of the political pyramid composed of its free members. All strata which are below this, such as the slaves and the serfs, for a moment we put out of the field of our attention. Similarly, we do not now consider by whom, in what way, how long, and for what reasons the different layers of the political pyramid are occupied. Our present concern is with the height and the shape of the political building inhabited by the free members of a society. The problem to be discussed is whether in its fluctuations there is a perpetual trend in the direction of "flattening"—that is, reducing the height and the steepness of the pyramid, or in that of "heightening" it.

The common opinion is, of course, in favor of its flattening. It is thought, as something quite certain, that in history there is a definite trend toward political equality and annihilation of political feudalism and hierarchy. Such an opinion is natural at the present moment because, as Graham Wallas rightly says, "Most of the political opinions of most men are the result, not of reasoning tested by experience, but of unconscious or half-conscious inference fixed by habits." "Things that are nearer sense, nearer to our past, produce a readier inference as well as a more compelling impulse."[1] As far as the height of the indicated part of a political pyramid is concerned, I am not sure that this common opinion is warranted by the facts. My arguments are as follows:

In primitive tribes and at the earliest stages of present societies, the political stratification of their members was very insignificant and inconspicuous. Few leaders and a layer of the elderly influential men—these constitute all that has been superposed on the layer of the general free population. The political shape of a social body has been something only remotely resembling a gently sloping and very low pyramid. It has approximated rather a rectangular parallelopiped with a low elevation upon it.[2] As societies have advanced and grown, whether through unification of some previously independent tribes or through the natural increase of a tribe's population, political stratification has increased and the number of different ranks among the citizens has multiplied rather than diminished.[3] The political cone has begun to heighten but not to flatten. Four principal ranks of the semicivilized societies among the Sandwich Islanders, and six grades among the New Zealanders or the Ashantees, may illustrate this growth of stratification.[4] The same may be said of the earliest stages of the present European peoples, as well as of the Ancient Greek and Roman societies. Regardless of the further political evolution of all these societies, it is certain that in no later stage has their political hierarchy been as flat as it was in these earliest stages. If such be the case, it would seem impossible to contend that in the history of the political stratification there is a secular trend toward a political "flatness."

The second point is that, whether we take the political history of Ancient Egypt, of Greece, or Rome, or China, or of present European societies, it does not show that in the course of time the pyramid of political hierarchy becomes lower and the political cone more flat. In the history of Rome of the Republican period we see, instead of the few ranks of the preceding time, the highest pyramid of different ranks and dignities, superimposed on the layer of the general stratum of the Roman citizens. At the top of the cone is the *Senatorial Cursus honorum* with its numerous ranks beginning with the different minor offices, as *vigintiviri* and *triumviri capitalis*. Above these are higher ranks, like *tribuni militum laticlavius;* still higher is the position of *questorship;* next is the rank of *ædilship* or *tribunate* of the *plebs,* followed by that of *prætorship;* finally comes the rank of *consulship,* not to mention the *dictatorship*. Next below comes the *Equestrian Cursus honorum* with its numerous ranks, beginning with lowest military or civil positions and climbing through many steps to *procuratorship* and to the different *præfecturæ*. Below this were the officials of the *Third Class,* who did not belong either to the Senatorial or to the Equestrian Classes and who filled the numerous lowest positions, which also present definite stratification. And at last, below it there was the stratum of the general citizens.[5] It is enough to compare this complicated hierarchy of the ranks with that of the preceding stages to see that there has been no flattening of the political stratification with the political evolution of Rome. Nor is any trait of flattening to be noted in the period of the monarchy. In brief, the political evolution of Rome belies the popular notion concerning the increasing lessening of stratification.

The same may be said of stratification in the Greek states. In fact, whether Greek, Teutonic, Slavic, or any other European society is taken, it is seen that from its earliest stages through the more advanced stages, up to the Middle Ages, its political stratification became higher and more complex than previously. Consider, finally, the present democratic societies. Have they a flat political structure? Do they have no political ranks and dignities and hierarchy? Such questions seem almost puerile. As an example consider England—surely one of the most democratic societies. Above its general population there yet are sixty-five principal ranks of dignities, with the King at the top, and the fundamental ranks of the Dukes, Marquises, Earls, Viscounts, Barons, Knights, Baronets, Companions, Esquires, and Gentlemen. For these there are definite and strict rules of social precedence. For India, the number of the stratified ranks is seventy-eight, above the general stratum of the British citizen and also above the Indian population. Taking the hierarchy of the officials, civil and military, one finds the same stratified ladder. Beginning with the Admiral of the Fleet or the Field Marshal, and ending with a common soldier or sailor, the Army and the Navy consist of at least thirty-six hierarchical ranks. And the same condition exists everywhere, in any field of social and political organization of Great Britain. Among intellectuals, for example, one finds Doctor of Philosophy, Master of Arts, Bachelor of Arts; the President of the University, Deans, Full-, Associate-, Assistant-Professors, Instructors, Fellows, etc. In a business corporation there is a hierarchy from the president to the lowest wage earner. In a church one finds a hierarchy from the Pope or Archbishop to the parish priest and parishioner. In labor and party unions one finds a hierarchy of the long series of different bosses and leaders.[6] And this stratification is not a "speech reaction" only, and not an "out of date" survival of the past, but it still actually exists, and functions, and determines the psychology, the attitudes, the privileges and social position of the individuals.[7]

Similar conditions are also found in the United States. Here, to be sure, the rankings of Duke, Marquis, Count, and Baron are absent. But does this mean that in the United States the political stratification is absent or flat? Such is by no means the case. Under the names of the President of the United States, the Vice-president, Senators, Representatives, Secretaries, Under-secretaries, Assistant Secretary to Assistant Secretary, Directors of Divisions, Chiefs or Chairmen of Divisions, Commissioners of different ranks, Chief Clerks, Executive Clerks, Senior and Junior members, Clerks, Stenographers, Agents, and so on, we have a high and complex and stratified pyramid of the governmental ranks and positions, whether in the executive, the legislative, or the judicial branches, with different rights, privileges, and responsibilities, with the right to command some and the duty to obey others.[8] A similar pyramid exists also in the state governments, in the Army and Navy, and, in fact, in every other organization.[9] The names are different than in England, but the height of the political cone and the number of its hierarchical strata are scarcely less than in any European country. And this is true not only as regards the height of the pyramid and the number of the ranks subordinated to and superimposed upon one another, but even as regards the degree of privileges and entitlements given to the higher ranks, in contradistinction to the lower ones or to the population. The specialists in Constitutional Law point out, properly enough, that the rights of the President of the United States are somewhat greater than those of any constitutional monarch. The orders given by United States higher officials to subordinates, or by the general to those of subordinate military rank, are as obligatory as in any non-democratic country. Obedience to the orders of a superior officer in the United States Army is quite as compulsory as in any army. There are differences in the methods of recruiting, etc., which will be discussed further, but they by no means signify that the political building of the present democracies is flat or less stratified than that of many non-democratic countries. Thus, as far as the height of the political hierarchy among the citizens is concerned, *I do not see any perpetual trend in political evolution toward the lowering or flattening of the cone.* In spite of different methods of recruiting the members of the higher strata in modern democracies, the cone is now as high and as stratified as at any other time in the past, and it is surely higher than in many less advanced societies. Although stressing this point, I do not wish to be understood as saying that there is in history a permanent trend to the heightening of the political hierarchy. Such is by no means clearly demonstrable. What we seem to have is "disorderly," trendless, "blind fluctuation," not leading to any permanent increase or decrease of stratification.

2. FLUCTUATION OF POLITICAL STRATIFICATION WITHIN THE WHOLE BODY POLITIC

The above discussion is concerned with only the upper part of bodies politic. It seems obvious enough that in all societies there are strata below those of the full citizens. And even among the citizens themselves, either juridically or factually, there are different layers of varying degrees of privilege and responsibility. Hence we now have to turn to an analysis of the vertical distance and profile of the *whole* political body from the very bottom to its apex.

The Hypothesis of Disappearance of Political Inequalities and Political Stratification.—The predominating opinion seems to be that there is a perpetual trend toward the disappearance of political inequalities. According to this notion, in the course of time the political cone tends to be flattened, with the number of strata decreasing. Since the opposite hypothesis is upheld seriously by no one to-day, we may, therefore, leave it without analysis and concentrate our attention upon this other opinion, common to the eighteenth, the nineteenth, and the twentieth centuries. On the first approach this hypothesis seems to be unquestionable. Indeed, slavery and serfdom, the hierarchy of castes and numerous feudal social ranks, all seem to be quite annihilated in the present civilized society. The dominant motto is: "Men are born and continue equal in respect of their rights" (The French Declaration of the Rights of Man and Citizen, 1791); or "We hold these truths to be self-evident, that all men are created equal, that they are endowed by their creator with certain inalienable rights, that among these are Life, Liberty, and the pursuit of Happiness" (American Declaration of Independence, 1776).

During these centuries we see a great wave of democracy sweeping over an increasing number of countries. Equality before the law is introduced, suffrage is eventually made universal, monarchies are overthrown, juridical class barriers and distinctions are exterminated. Inordinate privileges of men, as well as disinheritance of women, are abolished. Government by "the will of God" is replaced by government by "the will of the people." This wave of equality is going further and trying to put an end to all distinctions of race, nationality, occupation, economic privilege, or what not. Briefly, the trend toward political equality, during the last two centuries at least, has been so noticeable and so conspicuous and so sweeping that there seems to be no room for any doubt or contradiction of this common belief.[10]

A closer study of the problem, however, especially one based not so much on speech reactions as on the real facts and real behavior, makes the situation more doubtful. In the first place, granting that this wave of "equalization" in the nineteenth and twentieth centuries has been really such as it is usually depicted, may it not be merely a temporary phenomenon, a part of a cycle which may be superseded by the opposite wave? Viscount Bryce, properly enough, makes the following statement in this connection:

> Free government had been tried (in the past), and had to all appearances failed. Despotic monarchies everywhere held the field. . . . Peoples that had known and prized freedom resigned it, did not much regret it, and forgot it. . . . The thing did happen; and whatever has happened may happen again.[11]

At the present moment for an attentive observer of events there are several symptoms which are a menace to democracy and parliamentarism, to political equality, to political freedom, and to other essential features of democracy and political equality. Among these may be mentioned Bolshevism, Fascism, Communism, exaggerated Socialism, Class Struggle, Ku Klux Klanism, dictatorship of various kinds, etc. Those who know these phenomena may not have any doubt concerning the nature of these social movements and their results. It is hoped that, in the near future, at present, they will become relatively innocuous. But the success which they have had in various social strata and the numerous responses of *"Ave, Cæsar"* with which they have been welcomed by the masses and "intellectuals" signify that the roots of a real democracy are still very weak, and that the desire of human beings to be ruled (not knowing about their enslavement at the beginning) as has happened in Russia, is by no means moribund, but is yet quite potent. There unfortunately is no guarantee, therefore, that the trend toward political equality may not be superseded by the opposite one. One or two centuries is too short a period in the course of history to give us any absolute basis for the prediction of a perpetual trend. So much for this point.

In the second place, there are other more serious reasons for questioning the above opinion. That these reasons may be perfectly clear, all "high-sounding phraseology" which too often disfigures reality, is to be put aside.[12] In fact, these phraseologies with their corresponding ideologies of equality, the people's government, socialism, communism, democracy, universal suffrage, political and economic equality, are not new but were known a very long time ago, at least several centuries before Christ.[13]

What is important is the real situation and real behavior. Let us consider the matter from this standpoint.

Slavery.—If the common opinion is true and the indicated trend is universal, then in the history of all bodies politic we must find that slavery appeared during the earliest stages, gradually dying out at the later stages of their evolution. Is that statement true as a universal rule? It seems not, because in the first place at the earliest stages, slavery practically did not exist.[14] Furthermore, in the long history of China, during its earliest stages, slavery was unknown, except for a few enslaved criminals. It appeared as an institution at the time of the Ch'in dynasty (fourth century B.C.). Later on it was abolished several times, but reappeared when famine hit the land. This disappearance and reappearance has happened several times.[15] In the long history of China, the real changes in this field do not show anything like the above trend. The same must be said about the evolution of slavery in Ancient Rome and Greece. During the earlier stages there were very few slaves. These were treated as well as the members of the family and their dignity and social status did not have anything like the horrors of slavery later.[16] With the political evolution of these bodies politic, slavery grew quantitatively and qualitatively. In Rome it reached its climax at the end of the Republic, in Greece in the fifth and fourth centuries. If in the last centuries of the history of Rome or Greece there was some quantitative diminution of the slaves and some qualitative mitigation of slavery (the edict of Claudius, *lex Petronia, lex* of Antonius Pius, and so on), this was compensated by the forcing of many free citizens into serfdom and by other laws which restricted the liberation of the slaves *(lex Ælia Sentia, lex Fufia Caninia,* etc.).[17] Taken as a whole, the histories of these political bodies do not seem to follow the expected course. These bodies politic, not to mention others in which the evolution of this institution has been similar, testify that the above trend cannot pretend to be the universal rule typical for the political evolution of any large body politic.[18] It may be objected, however, that "the history of mankind, taken as a whole, shows that slavery is disappearing: it existed and does not exist any more." To this may be replied that only a little more than half a century has passed since it was abolished in the most democratic country, the United States; that serfdom, which surely was no better than slavery in many countries, was abolished in Russia only in 1861. History, it thus appears, waited a long time, many thousands of years, before it decided to show "the trend to an equality in this field." On the basis of such a short time it is impossible to say surely that this "action of history" is final and irrevocable. Furthermore, slavery, if not juridically, at least factually, still exists and is propagated by nobody else so much as by members of civilized nations in their colonies, among the "savage and barbarian natives." The treatment and the conditions of the natives, due to the presence of the "civilizers," are often such that the slaves of the past scarcely would envy them. This is well known. And just now Prof. E. A. Ross, in his official report to the League of Nations, indicated the existence of a real slavery in some colonies of Africa. Similar "discovery" is made by the two governments of Colombia and Venezuela.[19] And these phenomena which concern millions of peoples are usually forgotten because those who are enslaved are not "the white people" and do not belong to "the cultural nations."[20] Twenty or thirty thousand Athenians boasted of their liberty and democracy, forgetting that they were exploiting tens of thousands of slaves. In similar way we boast of our democracy and equality, forgetting that under thirty or forty millions of the citizens of Great Britain there are 300,000,000 people in the British Empire who do not enjoy at all the benefits of a democracy, and who are often treated in the same way in which slaves were treated in the past. We often reproach Aristotle and Plato for their "narrow-mindedness" in regard to slavery. But we likewise boast of the equality of only a small fraction of mankind, forgetting the condition of those outside of this fraction. This means that the social distance between the most advanced democracies of Great Britain, France (African and Indo-Chinese colonies), Belgium (the Congo), Netherlands (Java), not to mention other European countries, and their colonial native population is scarcely less than that which existed between the Athenians or the Spartans and their slaves, Helots, and semi-free classes.

Perhaps one of the most outstanding examples is India. In

her 400,000,000 population we see that slavery, in the form of the lowest castes, still exists, in spite of the fact that history has had plenty of time to manifest a "liberating tendency." Furthermore, the social distance from this lowest stratum of the population of the British Empire to the stratum of full citizens of Great Britain is surely not shorter than from the slaves to the *Civis Romanus* in Rome. The social distance from the stratum of the native population of the Congo to that of the working class of Belgium, from the natives of the colonies of the Netherlands, France, or Portugal, to the status of the population of these countries, is scarcely less than the social distance from a serf to his master, in the past. Slavery means a complete dependence of the behavior of one individual upon another individual, who has the right of life and death over the slave. Slavery in this sense continues to exist in many countries. One of the sources of slavery has been the commitment of crimes. This category of slaves still exists in the form of criminals whose behavior is completely controlled by other men, and who in some cases are executed—who, in fact, are treated just as was the slave in the past, being subjected to hard labor and having practically no control over their own conduct. Incarcerated prisoners we may not call slaves, but the essence of the phenomenon is practically identical with that of nominal slavery.

Another principal source of slavery in the past was war. Do the experiences of the World War lead us to believe that times have changed? To the contrary, it was seen that the treatment of war prisoners was often as bad as the treatment of slaves in the past. Furthermore, before our very eyes, a group of adventurers enslaved and completely deprived of their property millions of people in Russia during 1918 to 1921. These adventurers killed hundreds of thousands, tortured many others, and imposed upon tens of millions of individuals compulsory hard labor no better than that of the Egyptian slaves during the erection of the pyramids. In brief, they deprived the Russian population of all liberty and rights, and created for four years a real slavery in its worst form. This condition, in mitigated form, still exists, and is even welcomed by many "free thinkers."

Whether the indicated categories are styled as slavery or not, matters little. What does matter is that within the present European countries and their colonies there still exist millions of people who are virtually slaves. Many of the natives were free before their colonization, only to lose their rights after it. This lower stratum in some countries is very large. All of these facts seem sufficient to show that neither the slave conditions, nor slave-master interrelations, nor slave-master psychology, nor slave depravity and master's privileges, nor the social distance from a slave to a master, are factually and entirely abolished. Being charmed with our speech reactions, we beautify excessively the present while exaggerating the horrors of the past.[21] In brief, I think that even in respect to slavery the situation is not so brilliant as is usually depicted.

Upper Classes.—Turn now to the opposite, or upper strata of bodies politic. Like children many boast that despotism and autocratic monarchs are destroyed; that the government of the minority is substituted for the "people's government of the majority"; that suffrage is made universal; that aristocracy exists no more; that the social distance from the lower social strata to the higher ones is enormously reduced. Correspondingly, some "social thinkers" have already formulated many laws of "historical trends," such as: (1) the law of historical transition from monarchy to republic; (2) from autocracy to democracy; (3) from government of the minority to that of the majority; (4) from political inequality to equality, etc. Is all this true? Is it warranted by the facts? I wish that it were true, but unfortunately my wish seems not to be confirmed by the facts. Let me briefly point out the principal categories of the stubborn facts which seem not to want to follow the course which we desire.

1. In the first place, *there is no perpetual trend from monarchy to republic.* Whether we take Ancient Rome, or Greece, or the Medieval Italian and German and French city-states, or England, or France, or Spain, or Italy, not to mention "the hopeless" (in this respect) Asiatic countries, we see that throughout the history of these countries monarchy and republic have been in turn superseding each other without any definite trend in favor of either. Rome and Greece began as monarchies, later on became republics, and finished their histories as monarchies again. Theories of

the cyclical writers of the past like Confucius, Plato, Thucydides, Aristotle, Polybius, Florus, Cicero, Seneca, Machiavelli, and Vico, were much more scientific and grasped the reality much better than many speculative theories of the contemporary "tendency lawmakers." Similar "turns" we find in the history of all enumerated and many other countries. Many of the Medieval Italian Republics are now a part of a monarchy. France, at the end of the eighteenth century and throughout the nineteenth century, had several "turns" of this kind. Many European republics founded by revolution disappeared. In England, the Republic of the seventeenth century was short-lived. In Spain the Republic established in 1873 existed a still shorter time. In Greece during the last few years we have seen these turns several times. It is of no use to continue citing these facts.[22] Only a person who knows little of history or who prefers to deal with fiction, instead of reality, may believe in the above trend.[23]

2. *There is no historical trend from the government of the minority to that of the majority.*—Here again the theories of past thinkers are much more valid than many popular theories of present political writers. In the first place, it is naïve to think that the so-called absolute despots can do anything that they please, independently from the desire and pressures of their subjects. To hold that there is such an "omnipotence" of the despots and their absolute freedom from social pressures, is nonsense. Already Herbert Spencer has shown that in the most despotic societies "political power is the feeling of the community, acting through an agency which it has either informally or formally established. . . . As the evidence shows, the despot's individual will is but a small factor; and the authority he wields is proportionate to the degree in which he expresses the wills of the rest. . . ." And the despot himself, "nominally all-powerful, is really less free than a subject" amidst the *mores* and customs of a group.[24] On the other hand, Renan has elucidated the idea that every day of the existence of any given social order is in reality a constant plebiscite of the members of society and, if it continues to exist, it betokens that the stronger part of society answers the question with a silent "yes." Since that time these statements have been tested many times and at the present mo-

ment become a kind of platitude. By this is not meant that in despotic societies the government is an instrument of the majority. This may or may not be the case. But it is true that the despots are not the omnipotent gods who may rule as they please, in spite of the wishes of the stronger part of the society, and independently from all social pressures of their subjects. And the same is true about any régime, whatever its name. If the despotism may be sometimes the government of majority, though more often it is the government of the stronger minority, the democracy, too, is sometimes the government of majority, but more often it is the government of the stronger minority. This statement scarcely needs to be proved after the most careful studies of the problem by James Bryce and M. Ostrogorsky, by G. Mosca and R. Michels, by Kropotkin and Lagardell, by G. Sorel and Berth, by V. Pareto and Borgata, by Sir James Stephen and Sir Henry S. Maine, by Graham Wallas and Charles E. Merriam, and by many other competent investigators.[25] In spite of their different political affiliations, they are unanimous in the conclusion that "the proportion of citizens who take a lively and constant interest in politics is so small, and likely to remain so small that the direction of affairs inevitably passes to a few," and that "the free government cannot but be, and has in reality always been, an oligarchy within a democracy." [26] And this is true not only in regard to a democracy, but in regard to any Socialist, Communist, Syndicalist, or what not, organization.[27] The formal criteria of universal suffrage, as has been proved by M. Ostrogorsky and recently by Charles E. Merriam and H. F. Gosnell, do not guarantee at all the rule of majority. "A citizen, declared free and sovereign in democracies, in fact plays in politics a rôle of a zero, rather than that of a sovereign. He does not have any influence on the election of the men who rule in his name and in his authority." Such is the real situation.[28] In the United States the study made by Professor Merriam has shown that the minority parties formulate most of the legislation in the United States.[29] The same is practically true in regard to all democracies. The real situation may be seen from the following figures: [30]

Country and the Date of Election	Population of Age Twenty years and Over	Number of Electors Enrolled	Number of Electors Who Voted	Per Cent of Those Who Voted to the Electorate	Per Cent of Those Who Voted to the Population Over Twenty Years of Age
Switzerland:					
1920	2,410,125	985,651	500,751	50.6	20.7
Denmark:					
1921	1,900,000[a]	1,586,259	1,217,080	76.7	64.0
Netherlands:					
1921	3,376,965[b]	....	....	97.7	....
1910	1,352,508[b]	....	....	63.2	....
1880	935,665[c]	....	....	13.1	....
London:					
Parliamentary election, 1922	4,488,120[a]	2,129,790	1,228,838	60.3	28.0[a]
Election of County Councillors, 1922	4,488,120[a]	....	....	36.8	17.0[a]
Election of Guardians, 1922	4,488,120[a]	....	....	22.8	10.0[a]
Bavaria:					
1919	....	4,024,479	3,319,329	82.5	....
France:					
1906	22,000,000[a]	11,231,025	8,818,000	79.0	40.0[a]
The Commonwealth of Australia:					
1922	3,140,137[a]	2,771,274	1,646,863	57.95	52.0[a]
The U. S. of America (1920) (President's election)	63,000,000[ad]	....	26,674,171	52.36[e]	42.0[d]

[a] Approximately.

[b] The population at the age of above 25 years.

[c] The women did not vote.

[d] The population at the age of above 21 years in 1921.

[e] For 1924. LIPPMANN, W., *The Phantom Public*, p. 16.

To this it may be added that in the French Colonies the per cent of the non-voting Frenchmen who had the right to vote, fluctuated from 72.74 to 40.09 per cent; that in Egypt this per cent was about 98.0. These figures, especially those of the last columns, are instructive in many respects. They show that even in the most advanced democracies, excluding completely their white citizens and the whole native population of their colonies, the per cent of the full-right citizens who participate in the fundamental parliamentary elections is, on the average, not above 50 per cent of the total full-right citizens of twenty years of age and above. If to this is added the information that out of the voting citizens a part has to vote as it is ordered by its "masters" or by those who buy their votes; that the government and the laws enacted are not a result of the unanimous desire of all representatives elected by the electors, but usually, and especially in Europe, are a result of only an insignificant fraction of the whole body of the representatives which has a relative majority among many parliamentary factions and parties, and which therefore represents only an insignificant part of the population; that, further, owing to skilful machinations and heterogeneous influences of different bosses, committees and subcommittees, the possibility of getting the upper hand for an insignificant minority is still greater; when these and many similar conditions, well known to the politicians and underhand dealers, are taken into consideration, it becomes clear why neither universal suffrage, nor any democratic device, could be taken as an equivalent of the rule of the majority.[81]

But this is not all. A greater part of the present European bodies politic have their colonies, which formally are a part of the corresponding democratic republics, empires, and kingdoms. The former are ruled by the latter. What about the population of these colonies? Does it participate in the election of the government that rules it? Does it have a participation in the enactment of the laws which they must obey? Not at all. They are ruled in the most autocratic way. The following quotation from Bryce may be applied to all of them. In British India, "taking together the Central Government and the Government of the Provinces, the persons 'who count,' that is, those from whom all important decisions on policy proceed, do not exceed thirty or forty. Within a large oligarchy of some hundreds of the British officials, this inner oligarchy rules." [32] It seems these appointed, not elected, rulers of British India, where the population is about 300,000,000, could not be regarded as a government of the majority of India.[33] The same condition is found in almost all colonies. Therefore the government of the majority of the present democracies is, as a rule, only that of a small minority, if the population of colonies is taken into consideration. In the total population of the British Empire of 21 years of age and above, the number of those who have the privilege of suffrage and who really vote, is probably no more than 8 or 10 per cent of this population.

On the basis of the above data it seems proper to conclude that the alleged historical trend from a government of minority to that of majority may be seriously questioned. Bryce has been right in saying: "How extremely small is the number of persons by whom the world is governed! *Quantula regitur mundum sapientia!*" [34]

3. *The political stratification of the present bodies politic is scarcely less than that of the past societies.* The above deviation from the main topic is made in order to dissipate many preconceptions which hinder one's seeing the real situation in the field of the political stratification. The question is: Was the social distance, measured by income, standard of living, psychological and cultural level, like-mindedness, by manner of life, by juridical and factual privileges, by factual political influence, and what not—was this distance between the highest and the lowest ranks of primitive, or of Roman society greater than the social distance between the highest and the lowest strata of the British Empire? The answer may be only tentative. And it seems that the negative answer to the question has at least as much support as has the positive one. In all indicated respects an English peer or the Viceroy of India is no nearer to a sudra or an African negro, than a Roman patrician to a Roman slave. This means that the political cone of the present British Empire is scarcely less high and less stratified than that of many ancient and medieval bodies politic. A flattening of British society which seems to have taken place during the last few centuries has been

compensated by a heightening due to the acquisition of colonies and establishment of the new colonial lower political strata. The same may be said of France, the Netherlands, and other European countries which have colonies. If this be the case, then the theory of the alleged trend becomes doubtful. If to this is added the statement that the primitive groups have been less stratified politically than the present large European bodies politic, the trend is still more questioned. Furthermore, taking into consideration that in other parts of the earth, in India and non-colonial Africa, in China and among the natives of Mongolia, Manchuria, Tibet, and among the natives of Australia and many islands, political stratification still exists as it was several centuries ago; that in comparison with these stagnant aggregates of the population European population is in the minority; that among the European population, for example, in Russia, political stratification rather increased during the last few years; taking all this into consideration one has a sufficient basis to question the existence of the alleged perpetual trend toward a flattening of political stratification.[35]

3. FLUCTUATION OF POLITICAL STRATIFICATION

On the basis of the above it must be concluded that political stratification seems to fluctuate in space and time without any perpetual trend. Whether within a separate body politic or within a series of bodies politic, there are cycles of an increase and decrease of the political stratification. The Christian Church, as a religious organization, had a very slight stratification at the beginning of its history; later on, the stratification increased enormously, reached its climax, and during the last two centuries has shown a trend toward flattening out.[36] The Roman or the Medieval Guilds give another example of the same kind. R. H. Gretton has shown a similar cycle in the evolution of the English middle class. The large bodies politic, like China or Ancient Egypt, France or Russia, exhibit a series of waves of this kind throughout their history. Within any body politic, forms of stratification "originate, grow, spread, elaborate, reach a point of maximum, fluctuate, gradually decline, disintegrate, or metamorphose into some other organization" or form.[37] In this way fluctuation of the political stratification may go on without any perpetual trend in either direction. This course would be comprehensible if we take into consideration some of the factors which are responsible for the fluctuation of the political (and also other forms) of stratification.

4. CORRELATION OF POLITICAL STRATIFICATION'S FLUCTUATION WITH THE FLUCTUATION OF THE SIZE AND HOMOGENEITY OF BODY POLITIC[38]

Not attempting here to elucidate the problem of the factors which determine the fluctuation of stratification in all its complexity, two factors among many others which seem noticeably to influence the fluctuation of political stratification are indicated. They are: *the size of body politic; and the biological (race, sex, health, age), psychological (intellectual, volitional, and emotional), and social (economic, cultural, moral, etc.) homogeneity or heterogeneity of its population.*

1. Other conditions being equal, *when the size of a body politic enlarges, that is, when its membership increases, the political stratification tends to increase also. When the size decreases it tends to decrease also.*

2. *When the heterogeneity of its members increases the stratification tends to increase also;* and *vice versa.*

3. *When both of these factors increase, the stratification tends to increase still more;* and *vice versa.*

4. *When one or both of these factors increase suddenly, as in the case of a military conquest or other compulsory expansion of the size of a body politic, or, though rarely, in the case of a free union of some previously independent bodies politic, the political stratification increases quite strikingly.*

5. *When one of the factors increases while another decreases they may check each other's effects.*

Such are the principal statements concerning the factors of the fluctuations of a political stratification. Let us explain briefly why the factors lead to the fluctuation of the stratification.

An enlargement of the size of a body politic tends to increase the stratification, in the first place, because a *more numerous population makes necessary a more developed and larger ma-*

chinery. An increase of the governing personnel calls forth its hierarchization and stratification because, contrariwise, ten thousand equal officials, say, without subordination, would disintegrate any society and make the functioning of a body politic impossible. Enlargement and stratification of the governmental machinery facilitate separation of the governing personnel from the population, the possibility of its exploitation, abuses and misuses, and so on, and in this way has been, is, and probably will be a factor in stratification. In the second place, an enlargement of the size of a body politic leads to an increase of the political stratification because *the larger membership is likely to be accompanied by greater differences among its members* in their inner capacities, as well as in acquired talents. Such differences, as we shall see, are likely to facilitate political stratification.

For the same reason, *an increase of heterogeneity of the population of a body politic facilitates an increase of the political inequality.* It is physically impossible for a man and a child to be equal; for an idiot and a genius; for a weak and a strong person; for an honest and a dishonest person; and so on. When in the same body politic you have a savage and an English peer; a native of the Congo and a Belgian professor; a "barbarian" Riff and a French literary man, you may preach equality as much as you like, but it will not exist. There will appear a stratification, whether you like it or not. If we add to this many "prejudices" and emotional sympathies and antipathies; frictions and wars and all inimical emotions, aroused by them, it is clear that heterogeneity must work in favor of stratification. If we add to this human cupidity, avarice, lust for power, struggle for existence, and many similar human "virtues," then weakness of one part and strength of another part of a heterogeneous population must lead to the disfranchisement of the former and increase of privilege for the latter. All of these and many similar satellites of a heterogeneity occur when, in the way of war and coercion, one body politic swallows another one. Let the conquerors consist of sinless angels (in fact they more often resemble devils); even they are unable to avoid the stratification. When such a completely heterogeneous body politic as India is incorporated into the British Empire, be all the British the most sincere levelers, they cannot establish a real political equality. On paper and in speech reactions it may be established; but not in reality.

The above reasons explain also why a decrease in the size of a political body, or a decrease in the heterogeneity of its population, facilitates a decrease of political stratification. As a specific form of a decrease of heterogeneity must be mentioned the fact of *a long temporal and spatial coexistence of a given population within the limits of the same political body.* Such coexistence means long social contact and interaction, which are followed by an increase of homogeneity in habits, manners, social traits, standards, ideas, beliefs, and in "like-mindedness." This, according to the above, must lead to a decrease of social stratification.[39]

Corroborations of the Hypothesis.—The above hypothesis is corroborated by, and is in accordance with, the following fundamental facts:

1. When the size and the heterogeneity of the primitive groups is small, their political stratification is also of necessity relatively inconspicuous. The factual situation completely confirms this expectation.

2. The size and heterogeneity of such European bodies politic as Switzerland, Norway, Sweden, Finland, Denmark, the Netherlands, Serbia, Bulgaria, and several other bodies is small, and their political stratification, as a matter of fact, is considerably less than that of the large bodies politic, such as the British Empire (with colonies), Germany, France (with colonies), Russia, or Turkey (before the separation from it of Serbia, Bulgaria, Rumania and other parts of it). The economic, political, and other contrasts within the above small bodies politic in general are less conspicuous than within the indicated large bodies, in spite of the disturbing influences of different factors which often mask or weaken the effects of the discussed factor.

3. Since the size of the present bodies politic, on the average, is much larger than that of the primitive groups,[40] it is natural that the political stratification of the present bodies should be greater than that of the primitive tribes.

4. Since up to this time the sudden and great enlargement in the size and an increase in the heterogeneity of the population of

the bodies politic have taken place principally through war, it must be expected that the factor of war calls forth an increase of political stratification. The studies of Herbert Spencer, Gumplowicz, Ratzenhofer, M. Vaccaro, F. Oppenheimer, J. Novicov, not to mention other names, seem to substantiate this expectation.[41] In this way in the ancient Jewish body politic appeared the disfranchised strata of subjugated population; in Greece, the Helots and Metöken; the *peregrini* in Rome; the disfranchised strata among the ancient Celtic and Teuton population; lower castes in India and so on.

5. Independent of the military enlargement of the size of the bodies politic, any considerable increase of the body politic is likely to produce a growth in the stratification unless it is checked by influence of levelling factors. A rough historical verification of this statement seems to confirm it. Parallel to an expansion of the size of the ancient Roman body politic during the period of the Republic, the simple political machinery and the stratification of the population became increasingly complicated. The governmental ranks began to multiply and the population began to differentiate into more and more numerous political strata: besides the *cives* and *clientes* and small number of the well-treated slaves, there appeared many and various ranks of the population: *latini,* the members of the *civitates cum suffragio* and without *suffragio,* that of the *civitates federatæ* and *liberæ* subdivided into *"æqum"* and *"iniquum"*; members of the *"provinciæ"* with the different ranks of the *peregrini, peregrini dediticii,* and so on. As a result of an immense expansion of the Roman Empire toward the end of the Republic, the whole governmental machinery of Rome, and the whole political stratification beginning with the citizens of the lowest political ranks of the most depraved *"provinciæ"* and ending with the highest strata of the central government, and the population of Rome grew enormously in the vertical and horizontal directions.[42] And contrariwise, when after the beginning of the Principatus, the enlargement of the size of the Roman Empire practically stopped, and thanks to a permanent contact the heterogeneity of the populations seemed to diminish, we see all these gradations begin to disappear, until in 212 A.D., Roman citizenship was granted

to all subjects of the Roman Empire except *peregrini dediticii.* Similar parallelism, though not so conspicuous nor on such a large scale, we see in the history of Ancient Greece, especially of the Athenian, Spartan, Achæan Leagues, and Confederations. An establishment of the League of Delos, under the Athenian hegemony, or that of the Achæan League, or an expansion of the Spartan hegemony in Peloponnesus, called forth the existence of new strata in the governmental machinery, as well as new strata among the free population of the confederations.[43] And a decrease in the size of these bodies politic in the third and fourth centuries B.C., called forth the opposite phenomenon. Still more conspicuous was this process in the creation of the World Empire by Alexander the Great, or in the unification of many tribes by the first Merovingians and by Charles the Great, or in the attempts to establish the Holy Roman Empire, or in the expansion of Great Britain, Medieval Spanish Empire, Russia, or finally, in the establishment of the German Empire (1871). The common trait of all these processes, however different they are from other viewpoints, is that the periods of expansion of these bodies politic were followed by the creation of additional political or governmental layers—Imperial, Federative, Confederative—the strata of the conquerors being above those of the conquered, and above those which had existed before. As a result, in the period of such political enlargement or a little later, the whole political cone of the corresponding societies became higher and more complicated. A decrease of the political stratification which has been gained among the population of Russia, England, Belgium, or France has been smashed or weakened by the acquisition of the new colonies, such as India, or the Congo, or the Philippine Islands, or Morocco, or the Asiatic and Finnish and Polish provinces of Russia, with their quite heterogeneous population. These general facts (which are but a few of many similar ones), seem to corroborate the above hypothesis.[44]

6. In the period of reduction of the size of a body politic and heterogeneity of its population, the opposite process, of a "flattening" in political stratification, of necessity takes place. Again, in spite of many disturbing factors, such a parallelism seems to have been manifested many times. A series of "feudalizations"

of Ancient Egypt or China, that of disintegration of a large body politic into the independent parts, led to an annihilation of the higher strata of the central governments and the most privileged part of the population, superposed on that of the provinces. A similar process happened as a result of the dismemberment of the Ancient Roman Empire, or of the Empire of Alexander the Great, or the Greek Leagues, or the Holy Roman Empire, or the Empire of Charles the Great, or, in our day, of the Austrian body politic, or of the decrease of the size of Russia. The dismemberment of Austria abolished the political inequalities of the Czechs, Slavs, Hungarians and Austrians, which existed before in the Austrian Empire. The separation of Finland, Poland, Latvia, etc., from Russia abolished these strata of the disfranchised citizens in the political cone of Russia. If there happens a separation of India, or the Congo, or Morocco, from the corresponding European bodies, the result will be the same: a flattening of the stratification of these European bodies politic. The independence of the previous parts of a large body politic means a putting away of the political superstructure of the previous large bodies and a step toward a flattening of the political cone.

7. Since, in the changes of size and correspondingly, in the heterogeneity of the population of the bodies politic, there has not been manifested any definite trend; since, in other words, they fluctuate in the course of time, it is to be expected that political stratification as a "function" of these "independent variables" necessarily fluctuates also without any definite trend. This is to be the explanation of the above stressed "trendless" fluctuation of political stratification. Everybody who has studied somewhat the history of the bodies politic knows that their size fluctuates most irregularly. It sometimes grows, and sometimes decreases.[45] Many past societies, such as Ancient Egypt, Persia, Rome, Greece, Carthage, Assyro-Babylon, the Empire of Alexander the Great, Charles the Great, the Holy Roman Empire, the Empire of Tamerlan, Jenghiz Khan, Arabian Califates, not to mention other bodies, appeared, grew with fluctuations, reached the climax of their size, and with fluctuations declined and finally disappeared. The existing bodies politic, whether we take China or any European or American bodies, throughout their history show the

same changes in size. Some of them have already experienced the most opposite fluctuations (*e.g.*, China, Turkey, and Spain), the large cycle of an enlargement and the large cycle of a decrease of their size; some others seem to be still in the period of an enlargement (*e.g.*, the British Empire and the United States) but even they have known many fluctuations of size throughout their history. Such changes of size, in the history of some bodies politic, are very rapid and great; in the history of other bodies they are gradual and relatively slow. Side by side with the large fluctuations which for their realization demand a time-span of several centuries, there are the smaller fluctuations which happen within a very few years or within a few decades. The decrease of the size of Russia from 178,000,000 of its subjects in 1914 to 133,000,000 in 1923; or the fluctuation of the size of European Turkey from 9,500,000 subjects in 1800, to 15,500,000 in 1860, to 5,900,000 in 1900; the decrease of the size of Austria and partially of Germany during the last few years, is an example of these fluctuations. G. De Greef has shown that such fluctuations are a normal phenomenon in the history of any body politic; he has shown also that for any body politic there is a point of saturation in its expansion after which there comes a period of "shrinking" which sometimes leads to the end of the body, or which at other times is followed by a period of expansion again; and so on.[46] If such is the situation, and if there is no definite perpetual trend in the fluctuation of the size of the bodies politic; and if the political stratification is a function of the size of the body and of heterogeneity of its population, then it is natural not to find any long-time trend in the fluctuation of political stratification. Since our "independent variables" fluctuate trendlessly, their "function," the political stratification, must also fluctuate trendlessly. In this way the result found above is satisfactorily corroborated.

The fact that in the field of political stratification we did not find any trend is in complete accordance with the similar result obtained above in the field of economic stratification. This identity of results in both fields is an additional confirmation of our hypothesis of a "trendless cycle of history." Furthermore, the fact that the partisans of the existence of a trend have not succeeded in proving it, but rather have failed in their task, is a further testimony of our contention. All this gives a basis for this hypothesis to pretend to be at least as scientific as the opposite fashionable theories of different trends, and "historical tendencies." Correlative with the forces of political leveling there are the forces which work in the way of the stratification. Their mutual fight has been, is, and will probably be continued. Sometimes, in one place the leveling forces may take the upper hand; sometimes the stratifying forces may be victorious. Any increase of the leveling influences, according to the basic law of physics, calls forth an increase of the counteraction of the opposite forces. In this way history has been going on and is likely so to continue.

5. IS THERE A LIMIT IN THE FLUCTUATION OF THE SHAPE AND THE HEIGHT OF POLITICAL STRATIFICATION?

On the basis of the above it is possible to say that under more or less normal conditions the profile of political stratification fluctuates within limits larger than those of economic stratification. In contradistinction to the economic profile the fluctuations of the shape of political stratification seem to be less smooth and more convulsive. A serious political reform, like liberation of the negroes or a change of electoral laws, or a new constitution, which may only very slightly alter economic stratification, often leads to a very serious alteration of political stratification. Through change of duties and privileges, in the form of legislation, the whole political strata may be annihilated, transposed within the political pyramid or removed. As a result its whole shape is altered. This may explain the greater variability of the political profile as compared with that of economic stratification.

Moreover, under conditions of catastrophe or great upheaval, very radical and extraordinary alterations of the profile have occurred. A society in the first period of a great revolution often suggests a kind of flat trapezium, without upper strata, without any recognized authorities and their hierarchy. Everybody tries to command and nobody to obey. However, such a situation is quite transitory. In a short time an authority appears; the old or a new hierarchy of ranks is soon established; and the destroyed political pyramid is recreated again. In this way, a too flat profile is only a transitional state. On the other hand, if the stratification becomes too high and too steep, its upper layers or apex are likely to be cut off in some way: through revolution and war, through murder, through banishment of the king or oligarchy, or through peaceful new laws. The ways are different and numerous. Their result is similar: flattening of a too high and too unstable political body. In the above way, the shape of a body politic is returned to its form of equilibrium every time that it alters too much either in the way of flattening or of heightening.

6. IS THERE A PERIODICITY IN FLUCTUATION OF POLITICAL STRATIFICATION?

Several attempts have been made to prove the existence of a periodicity in the modifications of political régimes. O. Lorenz, K. Joël, G. Ferrari, and some others have tried to show that there are periods of from 30 to 33 years, which mark a serious change in the political régime of a country.[47] Justin Dromel tried to show the existence of periods of 15 or 16 years.[48] The same authors have endeavored to prove the existence of periods of from 100 to 125 years, 300, 600, and 1,200 years. Colonel Millard has contended the existence of periods of 500 years.[49] However interesting are these theories, corroborations given by the authors are, nevertheless, not sufficient. There is no reason to announce in advance that all such attempts are nothing but "numerical mysticism" as do some writers. Contrariwise, the problem deserves to be studied very attentively. But at the same time the periods have not yet been proved, and the theories need to be tested by new studies. Whether the periodicity exists or not, the fact of the fluctuation of political stratification and its trendless character seems to stand as the most probable hypothesis.

SUMMARY

1. The height of the profile of political stratification fluctuates from country to country and from time to time.

2. In these fluctuations there seems to be no perpetual trend toward either flattening or heightening of the stratification.

3. There is no perpetual trend from monarchy to republic, from autocracy to democracy, from government of the minority to that

of the majority, from an absence of governmental interference to universal governmental control; or *vice versa*.

4. Among many forces which facilitate political stratification, an enlargement of the size of a body politic and of the heterogeneity of its population plays an important part.

5. The profile of political stratification is more flexible, varies within larger limits, and more often and more suddenly than the profile of economic stratification.

6. In any society at any moment a permanent struggle is going on between the forces of stratification and political leveling. Sometimes the first kind of forces, sometimes the opposite ones, get the upper hand. When the swing of the profile in either direction becomes too great, the opposite forces, in various ways, increase their power and cause the return of the profile of the stratification toward its point of equilibrium.

[1] Wallas, Graham, *Human Nature in Politics,* pp. 203-206, 1919.

[2] See the above quoted works of Herbert Spencer, R. Maunier, P. Descamps, E. Mumford, A. Vierkandt, R. H. Lowie, Goldenweiser, M. Kovalevsky, Post, Kohler, Henry S. Maine, and others.

[3] According to Hobhouse, Wheeler, and Ginsberg (*op. cit.,* pp. 236-237) as we pass from more primitive to the more advanced simple peoples the per cent of the peoples of each specified stage who have social ranks of nobility to the total number of the peoples of this stage is as follows:

	Per cent.
Lower hunters	0
Higher hunters	11
Lower agricultural peoples	3
Lower pastoral peoples	20
Higher agricultural peoples	15
Higher pastoral peoples	24
Still higher agricultural peoples	23

[4] Spencer, Herbert, *op. cit.,* Vol II, pp. 302-303.

[5] *Cursus honorum* in *Harper's Dictionary of Classical Literature and Antiquities,* p. 842, edited by H. T. Peck, American Book Company.

[6] See Burke, A. P., *A Genealogical and Heraldic History of the Peerage and Baronetage,* pp. xv *ff.,* 2433-2438, 2444-2452, and *passim,* 1910; Debrett, *Baronetage, Knightage, Companionage, passim,* 1923.

[7] See the series of facts in Pareto, V., *op. cit.,* Vol. I, pp. 613-616; Vol. II, 1050 *ff.* The psychology of superiority and inferiority in different forms is perhaps more conspicuous in democratic than in other societies. Our psychologists have even coined a special term to designate it: "Inferiority Complex."

[8] See *Official Register of the United States,* pp. 5 *ff.,* Washington, D. C., 1922.

[9] See the ranks in the *Register of the Army of the United States,* 1924.

[10] As an example of such optimistic views, see Hall, G. Stanley, "Can the Masses Rule the World," *Scientific Monthly,* Vol. XVIII, pp. 456-466, 1924.

[11] BRYCE, J., *Modern Democracies,* Vol. II, p. 599, New York, 1921. See the whole of Chap. LXXX. See also MAINE, HENRY S., *Popular Government,* pp. 13 *ff.*, 70 *et seq.*, 131 *et seq.*, 131 *et seq.*, London, 1886.

[12] *E.g.*, according to the phraseology and "the Declaration of Independence" one must think that, since the end of the eighteenth century in the United States, slavery did not exist because it was said that all men are created equal; and are endowed with certain inalienable rights, as life, liberty and the pursuit of happiness. And yet, the reality was far different from these labels.

[13] For Ancient Rome and Greece, see PÖHLMAN, R., *Geschichte d. Antik. Communismus und Sozialismus, passim;* for the Middle Ages, CARLYLE, R. W., and A. J., *History of Medieval Political Theory,* Vols. I to IV, Edinburgh, 1903-1922; KAUTSKY, K., *Vorläufer des neuen Sozialismus;* BEER, M., *Social Struggles in Antiquity,* London, 1921, and *Social Struggles in the Middle Ages,* London, 1924; JARRET, B., *Medieval Socialism,* E. C. Jack Company, London.

[14] Passing from the lowest hunters to the more advanced peoples of the high agriculture, we have the following per cent of the peoples of each stage who have slavery to the total number of the peoples of this stage:

	Per cent.
Lower hunters	2
Higher hunters	32
Lower agricultural peoples	33
Lower pastoral peoples	37
Higher agricultural peoples	46
Still higher agricultural peoples	78

This shows that with the advance of civilization, up to a definite stage, slavery has been growing. HOBHOUSE, WHEELER, and GINSBERG, *op. cit.*, Vol. II, p. 236.

[15] See *Chen Huan Chang, op. cit.*, Vol. II, pp. 374-379.

[16] See Schmoller's fitting remarks concerning the common mistake of portraying ancient slavery in too dark colors. In its earlier stages it did not have anything in common with these terrible characteristics of slavery in its later stages. The condition of the slave among the preliterate peoples often has been almost identical with that of the members of his master's family. SCHMOLLER, G., *Die Tatsachen der Arbeitsenteilung,* pp. 1010 *ff.*

[17] MEYER, ED., *Die Sklaverei im Altertum,* 1898; CICOTTI, *Der Untergang der Sklaverei im Altertum,* 1909; GUIRAUD, P., *Etudes,* Chap. II, "La main-d'oeuvre industrielle dans l'ancienne Grèce," 1900.

[18] See SPENCER, HERBERT, *Principles of Sociology,* Vol. III, Chap. XV.

[19] A United Press dispatch from Bogota, Colombia, appearing in the *Minneapolis Journal,* Nov. 11, 1925, reads as follows: "The alleged existence of an Indian slave trade along the borders of Colombia and Venezuela, marked by the enforced labor of natives on rubber plantations and the sale of young Indian girls to white traders, is being investigated by the two governments. This slave trade, long rumored to exist and said to include many of the same cruel features which characterized the notorious Belgian rubber industry in the African Congo a few years ago, was made the object of public and official attention by a recent sensational address in the Colombian chamber of representatives by Representatives Lanao Loayza and Duran Duran. Loayza, a member of the liberal party, declared a slave trade 'of shameful proportions' did exist in the regions of Vichada and of the Peninsula of Goajira, territories isolated from the rest of Colombia and difficult to administer. . . . .The whites who buy either male or female Indians have the right of life and death over them. Traders, lacking all humanitarian feelings, plunder the poor Indians in the

most shameful manner. The Indians grow zarrapia, a natural product of that region, and the traders take from them many kilos of the product in exchange for a few grains of salt or for a few boxes of matches. Many times the traders will despoil the natives of the fruits of their labor by force. . . . . But the most flagrant outrages against the Indians are committed on the rubber plantations. The Indians are forced to work for the plantation owners, and if they refuse they are miserably slain. . . .The life of the Indian, in those regions, is worth nothing to those who call themselves civilized. The Minister of the Interior informed the press after the debate in the chamber that a diplomatic complaint regarding the slave trade had again been addressed to the government of Venezuela and that he had summoned to Bogota the special commissioner of Goajira, Señor Pantaleon Escobar, to inform the government in detail on conditions among the Indians in those regions."

[20] If during the last few decades their situation has become somewhat better, the improvement is still less than the corresponding improvement of the situation of the European population. The difference between them, therefore, has scarcely diminished in comparison with the difference in the past.

[21] Herbert Spencer rightly says: "The current assumption is that of necessity a slave is a downtrodden being, subject to unlimited labor and great hardship, whereas in many cases he is well cared for, not overworked, and leniently treated. Their subjection is sometimes so little onerous that they jeer at those of their race who have no masters. . . . We regard them as necessarily unhappy; whereas they are often more light-hearted than their superiors. Again, when we contrast the slave with the free man we think of the latter as his own master; whereas, very generally, surrounding conditions (and especially social conditions) exercise over him a mastery more severe and unpitying than that exercised over the slave by his owner." "The liberty (of the present working man) amounts in practice to little more than the ability to exchange one slavery for another." *Principles of Sociology,* Vol. III, pp. 464-465, 525, New York, 1912.

[22] See an interesting survey, MAINE, HENRY S., *Popular Government,* pp. 13-20, 70-71.

[23] For a judgment concerning the degree of governmental despotism and that of the freedom of the subjects, the size and the character of governmental control and interference is a much more important criterion than the republican or monarchic régime. The curve of governmental control and interference is also not constant; it fluctuates from country to country, and, within the same society, from time to time. (See the facts and corroborations in SOROKIN, P., *System of Sociology,* Vol. II, pp. 125-145.) Neither the anarchists who promise to us the disappearance of government and its interference in the future society; nor the Communists and Socialists who prophesy unlimited governmental control in the future in the form of all-regulating and everything-controlling government (industry, agriculture, education, family life, and so on) with the system of "nationalization" of everything—neither is right. History has been balancing to and fro in this respect, and there is no reason to think that from now on it will change its trendless course to please the Anarchist or the Communist "lawgivers." And this is likely to be true in spite of the present expansion of governmental control manifested in the form of Communism, Socialism, Fascism, many dictatorships, and other basic facts of the present moment. It is to be expected that such a trend is to be temporary, to be superseded by the opposite one.

[24] SPENCER, HERBERT, *Principles of Sociology,* Vol. II, pp. 253, 321; FRAZER, J. G., *op. cit., passim;* see also right statement of Dr. Breasted concerning the Pharaoh's power, *History of the Ancient Egyptians,* p. 76, 1911.

[25] See the indicated above works of these authors: in addition see MERRIAM,

CHARLES E., *The American Party System,* Chaps. VIII, XIV, and *passim,* New York, 1922; WALLAS, GRAHAM, *Human Nature in Politics,* Chapter on "Representative Government."

[26] BRYCE, J., *op. cit.,* Vol. II, pp. 549-550. Even "The Constitution of the United States was ratified by a vote of probably not more than one-sixth of the adult males." BEARD, CHARLES A., *An Economic Interpretation of the Constitution of the United States,* p. 324, New York, 1913.

[27] See about the oligarchy in these organizations in MICHELS, R., *Political Parties,* pp. 93 *ff.,* 239 *ff.* and *passim,* New York, 1915; see also his "La crisi psicologica del socialismo," *Rivista Ital. di sociologia,* pp. 365-376, 1910; FOURNIÈRE, E., *La crise socialiste,* pp. 365, 371, and *passim,* Paris, 1908, and *La Sociocratie,* pp. 117 and *passim,* Paris, 1910. In the Russian experiment we have the ruling of 130,000,000 of the population by about 600,000 Communists. Such is here the "government of majority"!

[28] "Il n'exerce que le simulacre de la souveraineté dont on lui fait homage aussi pompeusement qu'hypocritement; il n'a, en realité, aucun pouvoir sur le choix des hommes qui gouvernent en son nom et par son autorité; le gouvernment est un monopole." OSTROGORSKY, M., *La democratie et les parties politiques,* 1912, pp. 614-615 and *passim;* NAVILLE, A., *op. cit., passim.*

[29] MERRIAM, CHARLES E., *op. cit.,* Chap. VIII; also MERRIAM, CHARLES E., and GOSNELL, H. F., *Non-voting: Causes and Methods of Control,* Chicago, 1924. See also LIPPMANN, W., *The Phantom Public,* Chaps. I to IV, New York, 1925.

[30] The figures are taken and computed from the following sources: *Statistisches, Jahrbuch der Schweiz,* 1923, pp. 40, 355-356; *Statistik Aarbog* (of Denmark), pp. 154-161, 1923; *Jaarcijeers voor Nederland,* 1923-1924, pp. 285-286; *London City Council, London Statistics,* 1921-1923, Vol. XXVIII; pp. 14, 16, 1924; *Statistisches Jahrbuch für den Freistaat Bayern,* pp. 578-588 *ff.,* 1919; LE CHARTIER, E., *La France et son Parlement,* pp. 1013-1014, Paris, 1911; *Official Year Book of the Commonwealth of Australia,* No. 17, pp. 89, 894, 1924; *Statistical Abstract of the United States,* pp. 2, 13, 775, 1923.

[31] See appropriate analysis in NAVILLE, A., *op. cit.,* chapters on "Liberty" and "Equality."

[32] BRYCE, J., *op. cit.,* Vol. II, p. 543.

[33] By this I do not mean either to blame or to praise such a situation. I only state the facts as it seems they are.

[34] BRYCE, J., *op. cit.,* Vol. II, Chap. LXXX.

[35] See also an attempt of F. A. Woods to show that in the United States social stratification has been increasing during the last century. He tries to measure it through the per cent of intermarriage among yeomanry, officer's yeomen, and gentry. According to his data, the intermarriages among these strata have been systematically decreasing as we pass from the eighteenth to the twentieth century. Such a criterion is surely significant, if the data of the author are typical and representative. See WOODS, F. A., *The Conification of Social Group,* p. 318.

[36] See SPENCER, HERBERT, *op. cit.,* Vol. III, Chap. VIII, Secs. 616 *et seq.*

[37] CHAPIN, F. STUART, "A Theory of Synchronous Culture Cycles," *Journal of Social Forces,* p. 598, May, 1925.

[38] With some modification the statements may be applied also to economic and occupational stratification.

[39] *Cf.* ELLWOOD, C. A., *The Psychology of Human Society,* pp. 208 *ff.,* 1925; BOGARDUS, EMORY S., *Fundamentals of Social Psychology,* chapter on "Isolation," 1924; PARK, ROBERT E., and BURGESS, ERNEST W., *Introduction to the*

Science of Sociology, Chap. IV; Ross, E. A., *Principles of Sociology*, Chaps. XI to XVII.

My thesis is almost opposite to that of C. Bouglé and partially to that of E. Durkheim, in so far as they think that occupational heterogeneity always leads to an establishment of "organic solidarity." The criticism of many authors, among them especially that of M. Kovalevsky, has shown that the theory of Bouglé, and partially that of Durkheim, is not warranted by the facts. See Bouglé, C., *Les Idées Egalitaires, passim;* Durkheim, E., *La division du travail social, passim.* See criticism in Kovalevsky, M., "Contemporary Sociologists" (*Sovremennyie Soziologi*), Chaps. III and IV, St. Petersburg, 1905.

[40] According to A. Sutherland, the average size of the savage societies fluctuates between 40 and 360 members; that of the barbarian groups, between 6,500 and 442,000; that of the civilized peoples between 4,200,000 and 24,000,000; that of the cultured peoples between 30,000,000 and more than 100,000,000. Sutherland, A., *The Origin and Growth of the Moral Instinct*, London, 1898.

[41] See Spencer, Herbert, *op. cit.*, chapters about militant types of society; Gumplowicz, *Die Rassenkampf* and *Outlines of Sociology;* Ratzenhofer, *Soziologische Erkenntniss;* Oppenheimer, F., "Der Staat," 1908, and "Soziologie des Staates," *Jahrbuch für Soziologie*, Vol. I, pp. 64-87, 1925; Vaccaro, M., *Les bases sociologiques du droit et de l'État*, 1898; Novicov, J., *Les Luttes entre sociétés humaines*, Paris, 1896.

[42] See Girard, *Manuel éléméntaire de droit roman*, 1911; Mommsen, *Abriss des römishen Staatsrechts*, 1893; Willems, *Le droit publique romain*, 1910; Pokrovsky, I., *Istoria Rimskago Prava*, 1924.

[43] See Hammond, B. E., *Bodies Politic and Their Government*, Chaps. IX, X, XXV, and *passim*, Cambridge, 1915.

[44] Spencer, Herbert, *Principles of Sociology*, Vol. II, Pt. V, *passim*, and Sec. 461.

[45] This roughly may be seen from different historical atlases, showing, for example, the territory of the different states and the names of the kingdoms at different centuries.

[46] See De Greef, G., *La structure générale des sociétés*, Vols. I, II and III, *passim*, Paris, 1908.

[47] See Lorenz, O., *Die Geschichtswissenschaft in Hauptrichtungen und Aufgaben*, pp. 271-311, Berlin, 1886; *Leopold von Ranke*, pp. 143-276, and *passim*, Berlin, 1891; Joël, K., "Der Seculare Rythmus der Geschichte," *Jahrbuch für Soziologie*, Vol. I, 1925; *Wandlungen der Weltanschauung*, 1925; Ferrari, G., *Teoria dei periodici politici*, Milano, 1874.

[48] Dromel, Justin, *La loi de revolutions.*

[49] Millard, "Essai de physique social et de construction historique," *Revue Internationale de sociologie*, February, 1917. See Sorokin, P., *A Survey of the Cyclical Conceptions.*

CHAPTER VI

OCCUPATIONAL STRATIFICATION

1. INTEROCCUPATIONAL AND INTRAOCCUPATIONAL STRATIFICATION

THE existence of occupational stratification may be seen from two fundamental series of facts. In the first place, from the fact that certain classes of occupation have almost always composed the upper social layers while other occupational groups have almost always been at the bottom of the social cone. The principal occupational classes are not situated horizontally on the same social level but they are, so to speak, superimposed upon each other. In the second place, the phenomenon of occupational stratification manifests itself also within each occupational pursuit. Whether we take the field of agriculture, or industry, or commerce, or governing, or the professions, it is seen that the people engaged in each of these pursuits are stratified into many ranks and layers, from the upper ranks, which control, to the lower ranks, which are controlled and hierarchically subordinated to their "bosses," "directors," "authorities," "superintendents," "managers," "chiefs," and what not. *Occupational stratification, then, manifests itself in these two fundamental forms:* namely, in the form of a hierarchy among the principal occupational groups (interoccupational stratification), and in the form of a stratification within each occupational class (intraoccupational stratification). Let us turn to an analysis of the interoccupational stratification.

2. INTEROCCUPATIONAL STRATIFICATION, ITS FORMS AND BASES

The existence of the interoccupational stratification is manifest in various ways in the past, as well as in the present. In the caste-society it is manifest in the existence of the lower and higher castes. As is known, one of the most important characteristics of a caste is its specific occupation. From the classic theory of the caste-hierarchy we see that caste-occupational groups are superimposed rather than situated side by side on the same level.

There are four castes—Brâhmanas, Kshatriyas, Vaisyas, and Sûdras. Among these each preceding caste is superior by birth to the one following. The lawful occupations of a Brâhmana are studying, teaching, sacrificing, officiating as priest, giving alms, inheriting, and gleaning corn in the fields. The lawful occupations of a Kshatriya are the same, with the exception of teaching, officiating as a priest, and receiving alms. But governing and fighting must be added. The lawful occupations of a Vaisya are the same as those of a Kshatriya, with the exception of governing and fighting. But in his case agriculture, the tending of cattle, and trade must be added. To serve the other three castes is ordained for the Sûdra. The higher the caste which he serves, the greater the merit.[1]

Though the real number of the castes in India is much more numerous, nevertheless, their occupational hierarchy still exists.[2] In Ancient Rome, among the eight guilds established by Numa or Servius Tullius, three of them "which played a considerable political rôle and were important from the social standpoint," were higher than the others; their members were put into the first or the second social classes established by the reform of S. Tullius.[3] This stratification of the occupational corporations, in a modified form, existed throughout their history in Rome. Consider the Medieval Guilds. Their members were stratified not only within a guild, but among the guilds very early there appeared the more and the less privileged guilds. In France they were represented after 1431, by the so-called "Six Corps"; in England by Guilda Mercatoria, not to mention other guilds.[4] As is seen among present occupational groups also, there is, if not a juridical, at least a factual stratification. The problem is now to find whether there is a general principle which forms the basis of this interoccupational stratification.

General Basis of Interoccupational Stratification.—Whatever be the different temporary bases of interoccupational stratification at different times and in different societies, side by side with these partially changing bases there seem to exist some bases which are *permanent and universal.*

At least two conditions seem to have been fundamental: *first, the importance of an occupation for the survival and existence of a group as a whole; second, the degree of intelligence necessary for a successful performance of an occupation.*[5] The socially important occupations are those which are connected with the *functions of organization and control of a group.* Their members suggest the analogy of the locomotive engineer, on whom depends the fate of all the passengers in the train. The occupational groups dealing with the functions of social organization and control are placed at the center of "the engine of society." Bad behavior of a soldier may not have a great influence on the whole army, or the failure of a manual worker may have little effect on others, but every action of a commander-in-chief of an army or of an executive of a group influences the whole army or the whole group over which he has power of control. Furthermore, being at the controlling point of a "social engine," by virtue of holding such an objectively influential place, the corresponding occupational groups can secure for themselves the maximum of privileges and power. This explains the correlation between the social importance of an occupation and its rank in the hierarchy of the occupational groups. Then, too, a successful performance of the occupational functions of social organization and control demands a degree of intelligence considerably greater than is essential for successful manual work of a routine character. Consequently, the two conditions are closely correlated with one another—a successful performance of the functions of organization and control demands a high degree of intelligence, while a high degree of intelligence usually is manifest in the achievements directly or indirectly connected with the organization and control of a group (in the broad sense of these terms). Hence, we may say that *in any given society, the more occupational work consists in the performance of the functions of social organization and control, and the higher the degree of intelligence necessary for its successful performance, the more privileged is that group and the higher rank does it occupy in the interoccupational hierarchy, and vice versa.*

To this general rule it is necessary to add at least four corollaries. First, the general rule does not exclude the possibility of overlapping of the higher layers of a lower occupational class with the lowest layers of the next higher occupational class. Second, the general rule is not valid for the periods of a decay of a society. In such periods, the above correlation may be broken down. But such periods usually lead to an upheaval, after which, if the group does not perish, the correlation is reestablished. Third, the rule does not deny the possibility of individual exceptions. As exceptions, however, they do not invalidate the rule. Fourth, since the concrete character of the societies is different and their conditions vary, and since the same is true for the same societies at different periods, therefore, it is natural that the concrete character of occupational work corresponding to the above general proposition may vary in its detailed forms. In time of war the functions of social organization and control consist in the organization of victory and military leadership; in time of peace these functions are considerably different. Such is the general principle of stratification of occupational groups. Following are some series of facts which corroborate the general proposition.

The first confirmation of the principle is the almost universal and permanent fact that the occupational groups of unskilled manual workers have always been at the bottom of the occupational cone. They were the slaves and the serfs in the past societies. They are the most poorly paid, enjoy the least prestige, maintain the lowest standard of living, and have the least participation in controlling power in a society.

The second confirmation is that the manual occupational groups as a whole have been always less privileged, less paid, less influential, and less esteemed than the intellectual occupational groups. This fact is manifest in a general gravitation of the mass of manual workers toward the intellectual occupations, while the opposite current is rarely a matter of free will and is almost always a result of unpleasant necessity. This universal hierarchy of the intellectual and manual occupations is expressed well in the classification of Professor Taussig, which is quite generally accepted. It runs as follows: At the top of the occupational classes we find the group of the "professions," including the high officials and big business men; then we have the class of "semiprofessional" including small business men and higher clerks; below these, the class of "skilled labor," "semiskilled labor," and finally "common labor." It is easy to see that the classification is based on the principle of a decreasing intellectuality and controlling power of the occupations, which at the same time is parallel to a decreasing payment and hierarchical place in the occupational stratification.[6] This statement is confirmed by F. E. Barr's "Scale Ratings of Occupational Status" from the standpoint of the degree of intelligence necessary for satisfactory performance of an occupation. In an abbreviated form it gives the following intelligence indices necessary for a satisfactory performance of the corresponding occupational functions (the number of units of intelligence runs from 0 to 100):

Indices of the Units of Intelligence	Occupations
From 0 to 4.29	Hobo, odd jobs, garbage collection, hostler, day laborer, farm laborer, laundry worker, etc.
From 5.41 to 6.93 ...	Teamster, dairy hand, delivery man, cobbler, barber, etc.
From 7.05 to 10.83 ...	General repair man, cook, farm tenant, policeman, bricklayer, letter carrier, stone mason, plumber, carpenter, potter, tailor, telegraph operator, dairy owner, linotype operator, etc.
From 10.86 to 16.28 ...	Detective, clerk, traveling salesman, foreman, stenographer, librarian, nurse, chief, editor, primary and grammar school teacher, pharmacist, master mechanic, high school teacher, preacher, chemist, mechanical engineer, artist, mining engineer, architect, etc.
From 16.58 to 17.50 ...	Great wholesale merchant, consulting engineer, education administrator, physician, journalist, publisher, etc.
From 17.81 to 20.71 ...	University professor, great merchant, great musician, high national official, prominent writer, research leader, great inventive genius.

The table shows that *the three characteristics: manual nature of an occupational work, the low intelligence necessary for its performance, and a remote relation to the functions of social organi-*

zation and control, all run parallel and are correlated. On the other hand, we see *the same parallelism and correlation among: the "intellectual nature" of an occupational work, the high intelligence necessary for it, and its connection with the functions of social organization and control.* To this it is possible to add that as we proceed from the less "intelligent" to the more "intelligent" occupations, the average amount of their incomes shows an increasing trend, in spite of some partial fluctuations.

The third confirmation of the statement is given by the nature of occupation of those individuals and groups which have composed the highest strata in different societies, which have had the highest prestige, the highest income, and which have composed their aristocracy. As a general rule, the occupations of such strata have consisted in the functions of social organization and control, and demanded a high degree of intelligence. Such individuals and groups have been as follows:

(*a*) The leaders, the chieftain, the medicine men, the priests, the clever old men, have been the most influential and privileged group in preliterate society. As a general rule, they have represented the most intelligent and experienced men within the group. Their occupations have been higher than those of the general run of the group, being connected with the business of social organization and control. This is seen from the fact that all legendary leaders of the primitive peoples, such as Oknirabata among the tribes of Central Australia, Manco Ccapac and Mama Occllo among the Incas, To Kabinana among the natives of the New Britain, Fu Hi among the Chinese, Moses among the Jews, and many similar heroes among other peoples, are all depicted as the great teachers, lawgivers, great inventors, judges—in brief, as the great social organizers.[7] This is corroborated completely by the factual material which has been collected about leadership among primitive groups.[8]

(*b*) Subsequently, among many groups, the most privileged occupations have been those of priesthood, military leadership, governing, economic organization and social control. There is no need to say that these occupations, under the conditions at that time, have all the characteristics indicated in my proposition. "A king and a Brâhmana deeply versed in the Vedas—

these two uphold the moral order in the World. On them depends the existence of the fourfold human race," says the ancient wisdom.[9]

Upon successful war has depended the very existence of all other phases of association; hence the high esteem in which the efficient leaders in this kind of activity have been held. War makes an urgent demand for leaders with great courage, persistence, and endurance, and with ability to organize and control others, and to form decisions rapidly, yet carefully, and to act promptly, forcefully, and efficiently.[10]

The occupation of the priesthood was no less important and vital for the whole group. The early priesthood was an embodiment of the earliest and highest knowledge, experience, and invention. It has been the bearer of the medical and natural sciences, of moral, religious, and educational control, the inventor of the applied sciences and arts; in brief, it has been the economic, mental, physical, social, and moral organizer of societies.[11] As to the high position of the rulers in the occupational cones of the earlier societies, it goes without saying that their "job" was directly connected with social organization and control, demanded the highest degree of intelligence, and was vitally important for the existence of a group. Among many investigators, Doctor Frazer especially has made it clear that the early kingship was an embodiment of these traits and capacities. The early kings were not only the rulers, but they were the priests, the magicians, the reformers, "the men of the keenest intelligence and superior sagacity." [12]

(*c*) At the later stages of evolution, the performance of the same kinds of work in diversified forms were the occupations of the corresponding aristocracies and intelligentsia, whatever their names. The king or the president of a republic; the nobility in a monarchy or the ranking in a republic; the Holy See and the medieval clergy or the present scholars, scientists, politicians, inventors, teachers, preachers, educators, and leaders; the ancient or the present organizers of agriculture, industry, commerce, and economic enterprises—these occupational groups have been and are at the top of the interoccupational stratification of both past and present societies. Their titles may vary, but their social functions are in substance the same. The functions of a monarch and the functions of a republican president, the functions of the medieval clergy and those of present scientists, scholars and intelligentsia; the functions of the ancient landlords and merchants, and those of the present captains of industry and finance are similar. Identical in substance also is the high position of those occupational groups in the hierarchy of occupations. Doubtless a high degree of intelligence is necessary for a successful performance of these occupations, considering the purely intellectual character of the work. Doubtless also a successful performance of these functions is of the highest importance for the whole society. And, except for the periods of decay, the great social service performed by these leaders and the great abilities of many of them are indubitable. Studies of royalty by Dr. F. A. Woods,[13] studies of money makers, inventors, and captains of finance and industry, by Professors Taussig and Sombart,[14] and by the writer; studies of the great service of the Brahmanic caste, the medieval clergy, the *real* scientists, scholars, and other *real* intellectuals who have enriched the amount of real knowledge and experience;[15] studies of the great services of prominent statesmen, educators, writers, and other prominent professionals—these studies show the very high degree of intelligence displayed by such groups and the great services performed by them for the corresponding societies. The personal unscrupulousness of some of them has been far outweighed by objective results of their organizing and controlling activity. In this respect Doctor Frazer is quite right in saying:

> If we could balance the harm they do by their knavery against the benefits they confer by their superior sagacity, it might well be found that the good greatly outweighed the evil. For more mischief has probably been wrought in the world by honest fools in high places than by intelligent rascals.[16]

This simple truth seems not to have been understood by many sociologists up to the present time.

On the other hand, the manual workingmen, and a considerable strata of the lowest clerical occupations in all societies, have been considered either as "not decent" and "shameful" (especially in past societies), or, at any rate, have composed the less-esteemed, less-privileged, less-paid, and less-influential occupations. Whether it is just or unjust it matters not here.[17] What matters is that such has been the real situation. And its explanation, perhaps, is given by the following words of Professor Giddings, which sound not very "popular" but which seem to be near the truth:

> We are told incessantly that unskilled labor creates the wealth of the world. It would be nearer the truth to say that large classes of unskilled labor hardly create their own subsistence. The laborers that have no adaptiveness, that bring no new ideas to their work, that have no suspicion of the next best thing to turn to in an emergency, might much better be identified with the dependent classes than with the wealth creators.[18]

Whether it be so or not, the facts remain as they have been outlined in the above statement. The large number of facts mentioned above seems to corroborate, in the first place, the very existence of the interoccupational stratification, and in the second place, the above fundamental principle of the interoccupational hierarchy.

3. INTRAOCCUPATIONAL STRATIFICATION: ITS FORMS

The second form of occupational stratification is the intraoccupational hierarchy. The members of almost any occupational group are divided into at least three principal strata. First, *the entrepreneurs,* or masters, who are economically independent in their occupational activity, who are their own "bosses" and whose activity consists either exclusively, or at least partially, in an organization and control of their "business" and their employees. Second, *the higher employees,* such as directors, managers, high engineers, members of the board of directors of the corporation, and so on; they are not the owners of the "business"; they have above them a boss; they sell their services and receive salary; they play a very important part in the organization of the "pursuit"; and their occupational functions consist in intellectual and not manual work. Third, *the wage earners,* who, like the higher employees, sell their services for a salary; but, in contradistinction to them, they receive lower remuneration, are subordinate in function, being mainly manual workers. In turn, each of these classes is stratified into many ranks. In spite of the various names of these intraoccupational strata, they have been existing in all more or less advanced societies. In ancient and caste-society, we find it within the same occupational group, *e.g.*, in the same Brahmin caste in the form of the ranks of the pupil, the householder, the teacher, the hermit and different categories strongly subordinated to each other.[19] In Roman occupational corporations we find it in the form of the apprentices, ordinary members (*populus, plebs*) and *magistri* of the different ranks; in the medieval guilds, in the form of the maîtres, valets, and apprentices; in modern time, in the form of entrepreneurs, high employees, and wage earners. The names are different; the essence is very similar. At the present moment in this form of intraoccupational stratification, we have a new form of occupational feudalism, which is real and manifest in the most sensible ways: in difference of salary and control; in difference of domination and subordination; in a dependence of one's behavior, success, and often happiness on the self-will and attitude of the "boss," and what not. Take a payroll of any "business corporation" or a register of any public and governmental institution and you will find a complicated hierarchy of the ranks and positions within the same enterprise or institution. This is sufficient to indicate that any democratic society is highly stratified and, in a new form, is a feudal society.

4. FLUCTUATION OF THE OCCUPATIONAL COMPOSITION OF THE POPULATION

That occupational composition of a population permanently fluctuates in its horizontal direction is clear and beyond doubt. The studies of K. Bücher, G. Schmoller, O. Petrenz, C. Bouglé, E. Durkheim, L. Deschesne, not to mention others, have shown this clearly.[20] In the course of time, the technical division of labor in all its principal forms (*Berufsbildung, Berufsspaltung, Productionsverteilung, Arbeitszerlegung, Arbeitsverschiebung*) changes; some new occupations appear and some old occupations disappear. For instance, in Leipzig, in the period from 1751 to

1890, the number of occupations increased from 118 to 557; during the same period 115 occupations, which had previously existed, disappeared.[21] In a similar way the occupational composition of a population permanently changes. As an example of this social regrouping may be given the following figures which show the number of workers engaged in a specified occupation in the United States per million of population:[22]

Occupation	Number of Workers per Million of Population of the United States							
	1850	1860	1870	1880	1890	1900	1910	1920
Farmers	103,097	79,809	77,320	84,318	83,904	74,606	64,231	57,550
Wheelwrights	1,323	1,040	543	311	204	178	41	35
Brick and stone masons and plasterers	2,733	.....	.....	.....	.....	.....	.....	1,676
Physicians and Surgeons	1,757	1,751	1,618	1,708	1,665	1,737	1,643	1,372
Clergymen	1,157	1,194	1,138	1,290	1,401	1,469	1,283	1,204
Plumbers	81	.....	.....	.....	.....	.....	.....	1,956
Clerical	4,369	.....	.....	.....	.....	.....	.....	41,246
Chauffeurs	.....	.....	.....	.....	.....	.....	498	2,697

The figures show that in the course of time some occupations, such as farmer, wheelwright, and mason, are "shrinking"; whereas others, such as physician and clergyman, are fluctuating but slightly; still others, such as the clerical, plumber, and chauffeur groups, are "swelling." As a result of such fluctuation of the size of different occupational groups, the occupational composition of the whole population of the United States or other countries, undergoes a permanent change and may be modified considerably in the course of time. In spite of the great interest and importance of these "horizontal" or technical changes in the occupational composition of a population, we are not here directly concerned with them. These will be touched upon here only in so far as they bear upon the changes in occupational stratification. The problem to be discussed now is as follows: does the occupational stratification fluctuate from group to group, and from time to time? If so, is there in the fluctuation any perpetual trend?

5. HEIGHT, GRADATION, AND PROFILE OF OCCUPATIONAL STRATIFICATION

In order to avoid vagueness it is necessary to indicate how to measure an increase or decrease of occupational stratification. In the first place, the *height* of the occupational stratification must be studied. It may be approximately measured: (*a*) by the difference in the control of the occupational institution between the head and the lowest occupational subgroup of it; (*b*) by the amount of dependence of the lower strata on the head; (*c*) by the difference in remuneration of the highest and the lowest members engaged in the occupation. If all members of an occupation are independent in their occupational activity and do not have any boss above them, for example, when all are independent farmers, then the height of the occupational stratification is almost nil. If, on the contrary, only the highest apex of the members of an occupational institution completely controls it and may close, change or do whatever it pleases, then the phenomenon of an *occupational monarchy or oligarchy* with an unlimited "despotism" of the rulers and complete dependence of the employees exists. The height of the stratification in this case would be the greatest. Therefore, when in the occupational stratification a trend toward such a situation is seen, it is said that the height of the occupational stratification is increasing, and *vice versa.*

In the second place the *gradation* of the occupational stratification *measured by the number of the ranks in the hierarchy of the bosses* must be studied. In the third place, the *"profile"* or the *"shape"* of occupational stratification measured by the relative proportion of the people in each occupational substratum to the total population of this occupational group and to that of other occupational strata should be studied. For the sake of simplicity, take only three principal strata: heads or entrepreneurs, higher employees, and manual wage earners. From this standpoint the profile may be quite flat when all people engaged in an occupation are independent producers and do not have any boss controlling their activity. If an enterprise consists of wage earners, higher employees and heads, then a profile is shown which varies in its steepness or slope according to the proportion of each of these classes of the occupational population to the whole number of people engaged in the occupation.

Though these three traits—height, gradation, and profile—of occupational stratification do not describe all its traits, nevertheless they give an approximate characterization of its most important properties. They may therefore be considered satisfactory for purposes of studying the fluctuation of occupational stratification.

6. FLUCTUATION OF THE HEIGHT OF OCCUPATIONAL STRATIFICATION

Viewing existing institutions from the occupational standpoint, great differences are seen among them. Consider, for example, the head of a public institution, such as a university, compared with the head of a private business. The amount of the control of the president of the university and that of the owner of the business is far from identical. The president cannot close the university, cannot radically change its constitution, or discharge the members of the faculty and other employees, as he pleases. The owner can do this. His power and liberty are much greater. This comparison shows that *the height of the occupational stratification varies from institution to institution.* It may fluctuate in the same institution in the course of time. Political scientists distinguish between an absolute and a constitutional régime. In similar fashion it is possible to distinguish an absolute and a constitutional régime in occupational stratification. Any step toward limiting the rights and self-will of the heads of an occupational institution may be regarded as a diminution of the height of the occupational stratification (increase of occupational democracy).

Is there any trend in the fluctuation of this height? Some theorizers contend that it tends to decrease; some others assert that it tends to increase. Which of these two hypotheses is true? I think neither. Consider briefly the arguments of the first hypothesis. Its partisans base their belief on the alleged tendency of the substitution of socialistic or communistic organization for private property. Under socialist organization, they say, the occupational distance between the managers and working people will disappear, and the height of the occupational stratification will be reduced greatly or completely annulled. In spite of the popularity of this hypothesis at the present moment, I think that it is very doubtful. In the first place, the future abolition forever of private property and the establishment of the "eternal" socialist or communist paradise is not certain. Temporarily it may be established, as has happened several times in the history of different countries: in Ancient Egypt and China, in Sparta, Lipara and some other Greek states, in Ancient Persia and in the state of the Taborites, in Mulhgausen and in New Jerusalem, in contemporary Hungary and Russia, not to mention other cases.[23] But in all such cases the "paradise" was established and disappeared, in some cases in a very short period, in some others, in a longer one. If such has been the case there is no reason to think that the same "story" would not happen in the future. In brief, history does not show any factual manifestation of an existence of such a trend, as a perpetual one. On this point the argument of the occupational levelers is not valid.

My second reason is that, even though socialist organization were come to stay, there is no guarantee that such an organization leads to a decrease of the height of occupational stratification. In the above historical experiments of state or military socialism such a decrease has not taken place. The last experiments in Russia and in Hungary have shown the same results. Under communist régime the workingman was transformed into a slave of the governmental commissaries; he did not dare object to them, lest he be executed; he had to go where and when he was ordered. He could not even leave his job or strike because strikes were prohibited; he could not have the protection of the government against his employer, because his employer was the government; he could not appeal to public opinion because, due to absence of all but the government publications and due to the prohibition of all meetings, public opinion did not exist. He could not appeal to the court because the judges were the agents of the same government. Under these conditions the wage earner was helpless. The distance between him and the commissary was far greater than that between Henry Ford and his wage earner. And those who have studied similar experiments in history should know that the Russian picture just described is typical of all of them. I do not see any scientific reason to hold that in any future socialist or communist experiment the situation will be different. I know that the intentions of many socialists are of the best. But with good intentions hell is paved: what is important is not the intentions but the objective results of their realization. The lessons of history do not give any basis of belief in future socialist miracles.

My third reason is that in any occupational institution which has several dozen workers—be it a private industrial corporation or a public organization—a certain height of the occupational stratification is unavoidable. A successful functioning of the institution demands the existence of managers and subordinate workers. Contrariwise, if all people are commanders and nobody is to obey, everybody will do what he pleases. Neither the elaboration of one systematic plan of activity nor its realization is possible under such conditions. Failure of the institution is inevitable. This consideration is the more valid, the greater the complexity of the technics of production. At the present moment it is already so complex that an average worker can scarcely competently organize and manage a large corporation. The more incompetent he be in the future the more important will be the rôle of the specialists and managers. Furthermore, as the present big factories show, the work of an average wage earner tends to be more and more monotonous and automatic. Under such conditions, neither socialization nor nationalization can annihilate the height of the stratification. Nationalization of the Ford factories cannot abolish the great controlling power of their "public managers," if the factories are going to work efficiently. Lack of efficient functioning of the complex machinery of organization would break down the organization and lead to failure of production. Such failure, for similar reasons, taking place in other industries, would ruin the whole economic life of society. This would lead to want, poverty and suffering. These results coming, society would be imperatively urged to increase its production. This means the reestablishment of occupational stratification.

Such is the circle which has occurred many times in history, and has been going on, before our eyes, in Russia.[24] There is only one possibility of avoiding a considerable height of the occupational stratification: to return to the primitive economic organization of "savage" hunters, fishers, and primitive agriculturists. As this is impossible, the conclusion is reached that, as long as there are occupational institutions with their contemporary complex machinery of production, any organization of labor is doomed to be stratified.

The opposite trend—toward an increase of the height—is not proved either. There are also objective conditions of production which do not permit an unlimited increase in the height of stratification. Among these conditions the most important are two: first, the limited capacity of any individual; second, the proclivity of human beings to fight any extraordinary form of inequality. The present technics of organization and control of a large industrial institution are so complex that even such extraordinary managers as Henry Ford cannot go on without the cooperation of specialists and collaborators. Any head of such an enterprise, whether he wants it or not, has to heed and obey the advice of his many experts. On the contrary, managers may make many mistakes which lead to disorganization of the enterprise. Such factual restriction of the control of the heads of institutions is nothing but a limitation of the height of the occupational stratification. In the second place, it is but a platitude to say that the success of an institution depends not only upon its high specialists but upon many subordinate agents and upon all workers. Their dissatisfaction leads to a sluggish performance of their functions, to strikes, and to similar disastrous results which greatly handicap the success of an institution. To avoid them the heads must adapt their behavior to the demands of the employees, to seek their cooperation, to limit their own self-will and absolutism. This means that objective conditions imperatively limit the height of occupational stratification. When it becomes too high the institution cannot function successfully and is doomed to fail. This is the more important since at the present moment the currents toward equality in different forms are especially strong.

Since there are limits to the height of occupational stratification in both directions, it follows *in the history of either an occupational institution, or in that of the occupational population of a whole country, there appear only temporary fluctuations of the height,* i.e., *not perpetual trends.* Thanks to many concrete conditions, in some periods the height of occupational stratification may grow; in others it may decrease. Whether we take the Medieval Guilds and the history of the relationship among the occupational strata of the maîtres, the valets, and the apprentices; or the amount of the factual control of the Roman Catholic Church by the popes and the cardinals; or the distance between the power of a head of a state and his subordinate agents in the control of state affairs; or that of the owner of an industrial enterprise and his employees; or the varying controlling influence of different presidents of the same university; or that of commanders-in-chief of the same army; we see that in all these occupational fields the controlling power of the heads of the same institution is not something equal at all periods but something which fluctuates considerably in the course of time. The controlling power of Gregory VII or of Innocent III was far greater than that of many of the popes. The same may be said about any occupational institution, either public or private.

Fluctuating in time, the height fluctuates also in space, from institution to institution, from one occupational field to another. We are told that the management of the Ford factories is more autocratic than that of many other factories. The personal influence of the presidents of different universities is again different. In the field of military occupation the height of the occupational stratification between the commander-in-chief and a soldier is far greater than between the head of a scientific research institution and a research worker. The occupational behavior of a soldier, especially in the time of war, is completely dependent on his "boss," and the soldier's part in the control of the army is almost nil. Meanwhile a research worker is more independent of his boss. The method of a study, the procedures and the results are determined by a competent worker himself, not by the orders of his boss. This illustrates the fluctuation of the height of occupational stratification in space.

To sum up: though accurately to measure the height of the

occupational stratification is almost impossible, nevertheless an approximate attempt to do it does not give any valid reason to think that there is a perpetual trend in its fluctuation.

7. FLUCTUATION OF THE GRADATION OF OCCUPATIONAL STRATIFICATION

In this respect we find a great variety of grades in different occupational groups beginning with two (farmer and laborer, artisan and his laborer) and ending with the twenty, forty or sixty grades of employees in great occupational institutions. Among numerous factors of this gradation the most important seem to be two: *the nature of the occupation, and within the same occupation the size of the occupational body.* Other conditions being equal, those occupational bodies whose functions are principally *executive* and whose work consists in action rather than in deliberation tend to be more clearly graded and their gradation tends to be more centralized than that of the bodies whose principal function is research, deliberation, and meditation. Army, government and industrial business are examples of executive bodies. Hence their definite, clear-cut and numerous gradations which are centralized and have the form of a pyramid. On the other hand, the occupational group of teachers, scholars, scientists, as well as many groups of professionals (physicians, artists, actors, musicians, writers, and so on), present typical examples of the deliberative body. Within these occupations the gradation is neither into so numerous subgroups, nor so clear cut, nor so centralized as in purely executive bodies. This is due to the nature of the occupation. In an army a commander-in-chief is absolutely necessary for the greatest efficiency; in a scientific work such a commander-in-chief would be only a nuisance and an obstacle to scientific progress.

The second factor of gradation is the size of the occupational institution. The larger occupational institutions tend to be more graded than the smaller ones. It is evident that the greater the number of the employees the more grades of bosses are necessary to coordinate their actions. When in an organization there are five employees they may be controlled by one boss. When the number of the employees amounts to 50,000, it is obvious that they could not be controlled by one or ten bosses of the same rank.

Without entering the discussion as to whether in this field there is or is not any perpetual trend I will state quite dogmatically here that the existence of such a trend has not been proved as yet.

8. FLUCTUATION IN THE PROFILE OF OCCUPATIONAL STRATIFICATION

It is quite certain that the profile of occupational stratification varies from institution to institution, from group to group, from the city to the country (fluctuation in space). The following data illustrate this: [25]

GERMANY, 1895

THE PER CENT OF EACH STRATUM IN THE TOTAL POPULATION GAINFULLY ENGAGED IN A SPECIFIED OCCUPATION

Occupational Strata	Agriculture	Industry	Commerce and Transport	Professions and Officials
Employers and independent	31.1	24.9	36.1	54.4
Higher employees........	1.2	3.2	11.2	24.7
Wage earners............	67.7	71.9	52.7	20.9
Total.................	100.0	100.0	100.0	100.0

The figures show that the proportion of each of the principal occupational strata in the different fields has been different, and consequently the profiles have been dissimilar. If instead of the total occupational population of a country we take a series of occupational institutions—such and such factories, such and such universities, or hospitals—we may see the same variety of profiles in occupational stratification.

The Profile Varies Also in Time.—This is true in regard to a single occupational institution or group, as well as in regard to the whole occupational population of a country. The following figures may give an illustration of the fluctuation of the profile within an occupational group of officials in Germany: [26]

Occupational Classes of the Officials	The Per Cent of Each Class in the Total Population of the Officials	
	In 1914	In 1923
The highest officials	2.5	2.3
The middle ranks	34.8	30.4
The lower ranks	62.7	67.3
Total	100.0	100.0

In 1923 the proportion in the lower strata of officials considerably increased in comparison with that in 1914. Another example is given by the following figures which show the proportion of the different strata in the occupational population of the United States engaged in agriculture: [27]

Occupational Strata	The Per Cent of Each Specified Stratum in the Total Population of the United States Actively Engaged in Agriculture in:				
	1880	1890	1900	1910	1920
Farmers-owners	38.9	38.7	36.2	32.4	37.5
Tenants	13.4	15.3	19.8	19.0	23.1
Wage-laborers	47.7	46.0	44.0	48.6	39.4
Total	100.0	100.0	100.0	100.0	100.0

Still another example is furnished by Ziegelindustrie in Germany.[28] (See the table on p. 119).

In a similar way the fluctuation of the profile takes place within any occupational institution, as well as within the whole occupational population of a country.

The problem to be discussed now is whether or not in this fluctuation of the profile there is a perpetual trend. Of many hypotheses about this problem, that of Karl Marx and that of many levelers may introduce us into the heart of it. As we have seen, Karl Marx has prophesied that the class of independent

Occupational Strata	The Per Cent of Each Stratum in the Total Population Actively Engaged in this Industry in:	
	1895	1907
Owners and managers	4.2	3.4
Employees	1.4	4.0
Common laborers	94.4	92.6
Total	100.0	100.0

entrepreneurs had to decrease more and more, and that the middle classes had to fall down into the class of the proletariat. In this respect he predicted the same transformation in the shape of the occupational stratification toward a "pointed" cone which has been discussed previously.[29] The prediction has failed. This may be seen from the following data, which at the same time give a picture of the fluctuation in the profile of occupational stratification of present societies:[30]

Occupational Classes in the United States	Per Cent of the Specified Occupational Classes in the Total Gainfully Engaged Population in:			
	1870	1900	1910	1920
Farmers	24.0	19.8	16.3	15.5
Proprietors and officials	4.6	6.2	7.5	7.6
Professional	3.3	5.4	5.4	6.6
Salaried lower	2.5	4.6	6.3	9.6
Total independent and middle occupational strata	34.4	36.0	35.5	39.3
Farm laborers	23.1	15.2	16.1	10.0
Servants	7.8	5.0	4.1	3.1
Industrial wage earners	26.6	35.3	38.2	42.4
Total lower wage-earner class	57.5	55.5	58.4	55.5
Unclassified	8.1	8.5	6.0	5.1

In another form the relative change in the capital and labor groups is as follows:[31]

	1870	1900	1910
Capital	7.1	10.8	13.8
Labor	26.6	35.3	38.2
Public[a]	58.2	45.4	41.9
Unclassified	8.1	8.5	6.0

[a] Those who are not directly involved in the industrial conflict.

These figures do not corroborate at all Marx's expectation. They show that the total independent and middle occupational strata do not decrease but only fluctuate within relatively narrow limits. They show also that the occupational class of capitalists has been even more rapidly increasing than that of industrial labor. Similar is the picture given by other countries. Here are some data:

SWITZERLAND[32]

Occupational Strata	Per Cent of the Specified Occupational Classes per 1,000 Gainfully Engaged Population in:		
	1900	1910	1920
Independent	289.4	272.1	247.3
Higher employees	91.3	120.7	148.8
Wage earners	583.4	572.8	562.2
Apprentices	35.9	34.4	41.7
Total	1,000.0	1,000.0	1,000.0

The independent class somewhat decreased, but the middle occupational class has increased very markedly, partly at the cost of the independent, partly at that of the wage-earner stratum. As a result the class of wage earners and apprentices has decreased rather than increased.

GERMANY[33]

Occupational Strata	1882	1895	1907
Independent and entrepreneurs	32.0	29.0	23.1
Higher employees	1.9	3.3	6.1
Wage earners	66.1	67.7	70.8
Total	100.0	100.0	100.0

The proportion of the independent class from 1882 to 1907 has decreased partly in favor of the stratum of wage earners, but principally in favor of the higher employees. This middle stratum, contrary to the prediction of Marx, has been most intensively increasing instead of decreasing. And the tempo of its increase has been far greater than that of the wage earners.

FRANCE[34]

	1886	1901
Independent	51.3	50.0
Employees and wage earners	48.7	50.0

Here the change was very slight, and there is reason to think that it was principally in favor of the high employees rather than of the wage earners. The studies of F. Chessa and R. Michels, concerning the middle class, showed that this class made up partly of small independent entrepreneurs but especially of the high employees, has shown instead of a decrease, an increase. "Middle strata, according to the specific conditions, may sometimes decrease, sometimes increase; but one thing is certain, they cannot be absorbed completely by other classes"; such are the conclusions of both of the investigators.[35] These data are enough to show the fallacy of Marx's theory. The middle strata have been growing so rapidly that Max Weber has ventured to prophesy that "the future will belong to the bureaucrats," *i.e.*, to the class of the high employees.

On the other hand, there is no serious reason to think that there is a perpetual trend toward a flattening of the occupational profile. Neither the above data, nor the indicated enormous occupational gradation within most modern large corporations, nor anything else, show such a tendency. Within each occupation, according to its nature, there are some objective limits for alteration in the profile of stratification. These limits are between "too much" and "too little" control. When in an institution there is too large a stratum of the managers and controlling people, we have "too much control" which works to the disadvantage of the whole institution compared with another one free from this defect. As a result, such a badly "shaped" group is either eliminated in favor of the better one; or, progressing in its way, is doomed to disintegrate under the burden of its upper strata. The same may be said about "too little" control or too large a proportion in its lower strata and too small a proportion in the controlling layers.[36] These "too much" and "too little" are limits different for different occupational institutions and for the same institution at different times. But one thing is certain: within present societies a disappearance of either the stratum of wage earners or that of the managers is highly improbable. Hence the oscillations in the profile of the occupational stratification. Sometimes one of the strata may relatively increase, sometimes one may decrease, but if the occupational institution normally functions, these oscillations go on within limits. "Too much control" calls forth the trend toward its decrease; "too little control" produces the opposite reaction. There are, however, those cases in which a group does not make the necessary changes in its profile in time and continues to progress in its "onesidedness." As a result, we have a catastrophe of this occupational institution or a catastrophe of the whole economic life of a country, if the defect concerns the largest occupational groups of the country. Such a situation is often seen in the time of revolution. An example is given by the Russian Revolution. Here, at its beginning, almost the whole stratum of entrepreneurs and high employees was put down. The profile of occupational stratification became almost flat in 1918. This "ill-proportioned profile" was one of the causes which ruined the economic life of Russia in 1918 to 1919. Then to check the calamity, in Moscow and in many cities, was introduced the opposite extreme: a very large stratum of controlling and managing agents of the government, so large that in many industries in Moscow, according to the census of 1920, there were one or two controlling agents for every workingman.[37] Naturally, this only aggravated the situation more. Therefore, since 1922, when the period of the restoration of the economic life of Russia began, a systematic process of reduction of the enormous layer of the controlling personnel and an approach toward a more normal "occupational profile" of stratification is seen. On a smaller scale similar processes take place within many occupational institutions.[38] One of the most important tasks of a good organization of any enterprise is to find out the best profile for the distribution of its employees among different strata.

In addition to the foregoing data a few other quantitative data from the past are added. If they are valid they seem to show the same trendless fluctuation in the field of the occupational profile. In Ancient Attica the class of slaves, as a general rule, may be thought of as comprising the lowest occupational stratum, while the class of full-privileged citizens, in the majority, belonged to the administrative personnel or to the high occupational stratum. The classes of other citizens and the Metoeken represented something similar to the present middle and the lower-middle occupational strata. According to Beloch, there was the following fluctuation of these layers, and correspondingly, the following oscillation in the occupational profile of the population of Attica and Peloponnesus:[39]

Periods	Attica			
	Number of Bürgers (Full Citizens)	Number of Bürger. Bevölk. (Free Population)	Number of Metoeken	Number of Slaves
Before the Persian wars	25,000 to 30,000 [a]	75,000 to 90,000 [a]	few	few
Before the Peloponnesian war..........	35,000 [a]	135,000 [a]	10,000 [a]	100,000
To the end of the Peloponnesian war.....	20,000 [a]	75,000 [a]	5,000 [a]	30,000
In 327 B.C.	20,000	70,000 [a]	10,000 [a]	100,000

[a] Approximately

Periods	Peloponnesus		
	Free Population	Helots	Slaves
Fifth Century B. C.	530,000	175,000	150,000
Second Century B. C.	700,000	....	250,000

The profile fluctuated considerably, but there was no definite trend in the fluctuation. The per cent of the slaves in the total population of Attica (1) was very small at the earliest period, (2) about 40 per cent before the Peloponnesian war; (3) about 23 per cent at the end of these wars; (4) about 50 per cent in 327 B.C. The data concerning the principal classes in Italy and Rome also show a similar trendless fluctuation.[40] If the proportion of the principal occupational strata of medieval guilds (maîtres, valets, and apprentices) is considered, some fragmentary data show also that their mutual proportion, for example in Paris, fluctuated too. But up to the end of the guilds all strata existed. With the disappearance of the guilds, after the French Revolution, other names for these strata were substituted for the old, but the strata themselves, in modified forms, have continued to exist. As is seen from these figures their proportion has been fluctuating but no definite trend has been shown in the oscillation of the profile of the occupational stratification.

The conclusion is that here also the trendless theory is, it seems, nearer to reality than many pessimistic and optimistic theories of "the regress and progress lawmakers."

9. FLUCTUATION OF THE STRATA OF THE INTELLECTUAL AND THE MANUAL WORKERS

As a general rule, the intellectual occupations, taken as a whole, have always been regarded more highly than the manual occupations, taken as a whole. For this reason, fluctuation in the proportion and in the relative value or rank of these two fundamental occupational classes may be regarded as the fluctuation of the profile of the occupational stratification. Is the fluctuation in their proportion and their value? I think such fluctuations exist, and they also do not show any trend.

In some societies, like the United States, manual work is appreciated somewhat more highly than in many European societies. The difference in appreciation is manifest in the fact that in America manual work is paid, not only absolutely but relatively, in comparison with the remuneration of an intellectual work, somewhat higher than in Europe; in the fact that the difference between the two classes of occupations is not so much emphasized as in Europe; in the fact that the shifting from one class of work to another is somewhat more frequent than in Europe. This shows the fluctuation in the ranks of these two classes *in space,* from society to society. Their ranks fluctuate also within the same society at different periods. An example of this kind of fluctuation may be seen in several societies. In India, though the ladder of ranks of the principal castes is fixed, nevertheless within the secondary caste subdivisions a fluctuation of their relative ranks has been going on.[41] At the earlier stages of Greek history manual labor was not at all regarded as something degrading or indecent.

> At the beginning, nobody held in contempt manual labor, and even the king's sons could be seen busy with the work of an artisan. Later on, first of all aristocracy, further, bourgeoisie, finally, all free citizens, more and more gave up manual work.[42]

It began to be considered contemptuously as something degrading. Later on, in Athens, approximately in the time of Pisistratus, this contempt seems to have decreased and the contrast between intellectual and manual work became somewhat less conspicuous again. But, at the later stages, owing to many causes, the contrast increased again and led to a strong contempt of manual work by all free citizens. Similar fluctuation may be seen in the history of Rome and in the history of medieval and modern Europe. One of the waves of this kind we have experienced during the last few years throughout Russia, Europe, and America. These years have been the years of an increase in the appreciation of manual labor—the trend which has manifested itself in an increase of its social influence, political power, relative remuneration, and higher estimation. In Russia in the period of 1918 to 1921, it led to the "dictatorship of the proletariat." Since 1922 this trend seems to have been slowly superseded by the opposite one. These examples show that the relative estimation of both the classes of occupation fluctuates.

The same may be said of the proportion of people in these occupations in the total occupational population of a country. The following data give a corroboration and an illustration of the statement:

Country and Period	Per Cent of Those Who Are Engaged in Intellectual Occupation in the Total Population Gainfully Engaged	Per Cent of Those Who Are Engaged in Manual Occupation in the Total Population Gainfully Engaged	Unclassified or Intermediary Occupations
United States of America:[43]			
1870	7.9[a]	81.5[b]	10.6[c]
1920	14.2[a]	71.0[b]	14.7[c]
Switzerland:[44]			
1900	6.7[e]	78.3[f]	15.0[n]
1920	8.3[e]	71.2[f]	20.5[n]

[a] Classes: "Proprietors, officials, and professionals."

[b] Classes: farm laborers, farmers, servants, and industrial wage earners.

[c] Unclassified; lower salaried.

[e] Classes: professions, officials, and rentiers.

[f] Classes: engaged in agriculture, industrial wage earners, engaged in mining and forestry.

[n] Unclassified, commerce, transport.

The data approximately show that during the last few decades in both countries and practically in the greater part of European societies a process of increase in intellectual occupations at the cost of manual ones has been going on—similar tendency of a relative "swelling" of intellectual professions has taken place in almost all European countries. In the period from 1895 to 1907, or from 1900 to 1910, or from 1901 to 1911, according to the country, the groups of professions and officials have increased: in Germany from 3.6 to 3.9 per cent of all gainfully engaged in an occupation; the corresponding figures are: for Austria, 2.9 and 3.5; for Italy, 4.0 and 4.2; for France, 5.0 and 5.9; for Netherlands, 5.4 and 7.2; for Denmark, 3.8 and 4.4; for Sweden, 2.9 and 3.5; only in England and Finland we do not see this increase.[45] Similar fluctuation may be observed within any more detailed and specific occupational group.

As to a perpetual trend in this field it seems that no trend exists. In the first place, the above increase in the proportion of the intellectual occupations during the last few years has not taken place in England and Finland. In the second place, there are some symptoms which show that during the last two or three years this trend either has been stopped or, in some countries, like Russia, superseded by the opposite one. In the third place, the very fact of a decreasing remuneration of many kinds of professional work—the fact which seems to be true of several countries recently and an increasing difficulty to find a corresponding position in the professions—these facts show that the point of saturation is almost reached in this direction and, whether wanted or not, the law of supply and demand will of necessity call forth the opposite trend. In the fourth place, it is evident that the development of industry and technics does not lead to an elimination of manual work. It only diminishes the necessity of physical strain and reduces the physical suffering of a manual worker. But it does not and cannot eliminate manual labor completely. Hundreds of thousands of wage earners in the largest and the most technically perfect factories continue to do nothing but a monotonous, and automatic, manual work. The above figures concerning the proportion of the classes of entrepreneurs, high employees and laborers do not show any sign of a decrease in the class of the laborers. On the other hand, as already indicated, are the reasons and the facts which show that an elimination of the class of intellectual workers cannot be expected. Thus, the conclusion which results from the above is that in this field occur trendless oscillations and nothing more.

The preceding discussion of the fluctuation of the economic, political and occupational stratification has not shown the existence of any perpetual trend in all these fields.[46] Now it is time to finish the analysis of the changes in the height and profile of social stratification. The exterior architecture of social buildings is now somewhat known. The student should now enter the buildings and try to study their inner construction: the character and the disposition of the floors, the elevators and staircases leading from one story to another; the ladders and accommodations for climbing up and going down from story to story. In brief, study the inner structure of these many-storied social buildings. This done, turn to the study of the dwellers in the different social strata.

[1] *Apastamba,* Prashna I, Patala I, Khanda 11, Prashna II, Patala V, Khanda 10, *The Sacred Books of the East,* Vol. II, Oxford, 1879. For similar statements see in *The Laws of Manu,* I, 87-91; *Gautama, Narâda, Brihaspati* and other sacred books of India in the same series: *The Sacred Books of the East.*

[2] See *The Imperial Gazetteer of India,* Vol. I, p. 323 *et seq.,* Oxford, 1907.

[3] See SAINT-LEON, É. MARTIN, *Histoire de Corporation de Mètiers,* pp. 5-6, Paris, 1922; WALTZING, J. P., *Étude historique sur les corporations professionnelles chez les Romains,* Vol. I, p. 62 *et seq.,* Louvain, 1895.

[4] See SAINT-LEON, É. MARTIN, *op. cit.,* p. 260 *et seq.,* 289 *et seq.;* LAMBERT, J. M., *Two Thousand Years of Guild Life,* p. 59 *et seq.,* Hull, 1891.

[5] *Cf.* Ross, E. A., *op. cit.,* Chap. XXVIII.

[6] Even in the United States where manual work seems to be more highly paid than in other countries, the average income of the groups of the unskilled, semiskilled, and even skilled labor, taken as a whole, is apparently lower than the groups of the professions and semiprofessional occupations.

[7] See MUMFORD, E., *The Origin of Leadership,* p. 43 *et seq.,* Chicago, 1909.

[8] See the analysis and facts in the works of E. Mumford and in the quoted works of P. Descamps, A. Vierkandt, Herbert Spencer, M. Kovalevsky, Goldenweiser; see also MAUNIER, R., "Vie Réligieuse et économique," *Revue Internationale de Sociologie,* p. 23 *et seq.,* 1908.

[9] GAUTAMA, *The Sacred Book of the East,* Vol. II, Chap. VIII.

[10] MUMFORD, E., *ibid.,* p. 28.

[11] See especially MAUNIER, R., *op. cit.,* p. 23-31.

[12] See FRAZER, J. G., *Lectures on the Early History of the Kingship,* Chaps. II and III, especially p. 83 *et seq.* and *passim,* London, 1905.

[13] See WOODS, F. A., *Mental and Moral Heredity in Royalty,* 1906; *The Influence of the Monarchs,* New York, 1913; SOROKIN, "The Monarchs and the Rulers," *Journal of Social Forces,* September, 1925, and March, 1926.

[14] TAUSSIG, F. W., *Inventors and Moneymakers;* SOMBART, W., *Der Bourgeois;* SOROKIN, P., "The American Millionaires and Multimillionaires," *Journal of Social Forces,* May, 1925.

[15] Under the real scientists and scholars I mean only those who really have

enriched the amount of human experience and knowledge. See LITTLE, A. D., *The Fifth Estate*, published by The Chemical Foundation.

[16] FRAZER, J. G., *op. cit.* p. 83.

[17] According to my personal taste, I wish they would be paid higher than many intellectuals. But this, my subjective opinion, is not obligatory upon anybody and does not have any relation to science.

[18] GIDDINGS, FRANKLIN H., *Democracy and Empire*, p. 83, New York, 1900; compare LITTLE, A. D., *The Fifth Estate*, pp. 6-7.

[19] See *Apastamba*, I, 1-6.

[20] See BÜCHER, K., *Die Enstehung der Volkswirtschaft*, 1921 ed.; SCHMOLLER, G., *Grundriss der Allgemeinen Volkswirtschaftslehre*, Vol. I, pp. 346-456; PETRENZ, O., *Die Entwickelung der Arbeitsteilung in Leipziger Gewerbe*, Leipzig, 1901; DURKHEIM, E., *De la division du travail social*, 1902; BOUGLÉ, C., "Revue général des théories récentes sur la division du travail," *L'Année sociologique*, Vol. VI; DESCHESNE, L., *La specialisation et ses consequences*, Paris, 1901; JONES, M. Z., *"Trend of Occupation in the Population," Monthly Labor Review*, May, 1925; UHL, AUGUST, *Arbeitsgliederung und Arbeitsverschiehung*, Chaps. I and II, Jena, 1924.

[21] PETRENZ, O., *op. cit.*, p. 89.

[22] JONES, M. Z., *op. cit.*, pp. 14-22. See here the data concerning all occupations. See BROWN, R. M., "Occupations in the United States," *Scientific Monthly*, Vol. XVIII, pp. 196-204, 1924.

[23] All these experiments have consisted in a substitution of state socialism or governmental unlimited control for private property and private management of economic affairs. In this way they have realized the fundamental demand of different varieties of socialism, collectivism and communism. For this reason these experiments have the right to be styled as socialistic or communistic. The principal difference between the past and the contemporary experiments of this kind is the difference in the "speech reactions" which accompany and "justify" them. But, as I indicated above, we must not give any important significance to verbosity and sonorous phraseology. What are important are the objective results of a social experiment but not "the desires, motives and speech reactions."

[24] See about Russia in my *Sociology of Revolution*, Chap. XIV.

[25] *Statistisches Jahrbuch für das Deutsche Reich*, p. 13, 1921-1922.

[26] *Allgem. Statistisches Archiv*, Bd. XIV, Heft 1 and 3, pp. 246-248.

[27] The United States Department of Agriculture, *Agriculture Yearbook*, p. 511, 1923.

[28] UHL, AUGUST, *op. cit.*, p. 71.

[29] See *Communist Manifesto*, Secs. 18, 25 and 31.

[30] HANSEN, A. H., "Industrial Classes in the United States in 1920," *Journal of the American Statistical Association*, Vol. XVIII, pp. 503-506.

[31] HANSEN, A. H., "Industrial Class Alignment," *Quarterly Publications of the American Statistical Association*, Vol. XVII, pp. 417-425. See also BROWN, R. M., "Occupations in the United States," *The Scientific Movement*, Vol. XVIII, pp. 109-204.

[32] *Statist. Jahrbuch der Schweiz*, p. 56, 1923.

[33] Computed from *Statistisches Jahrbuch für das Deutsche Reich*, p. 13, 1921-1922; see also VON-MAYR, G., *Statistik und Gesellschaftslehre*, Vol. II, p. 140, 1897.

[34] LEVASSEUR, E., "La démographie Française comparée," *Bull. de l' Inst. Int. Stat.*, Vol. III, p. 46; see other data in GUYOT, YVES, "La répartition des industries," *Bull. de l'Inst. Int. Stat.*, Vol. XVII, pp. 92-118.

[35] CHESSA, F., *La classe médie, Rivista Ital. di sociologia*, pp. 62-83, 1911; MICHELS, R., "Sulla decadenza della classe media industriale antica e sul sorgere

di una classe media moderna," *Giornale dei Economisti*, January, 1909; see also SCHMOLLER, G., *Grundriss der Allgemeinen Volkswirtschaftslehre*, Vol. II, pp. 527-528.

[36] This is a specific form of a general system of the social "checks and balance" so brilliantly indicated already by Polybius. See also some suggestive considerations in CHAPIN, F. STUART, "A Theory of Synchronous Culture Cycles," *Journal of Social Forces*, May, 1925.

[37] See *Red Moscow*, Moscow, 1921; see also SOROKIN, P., *Sociology of Revolution*, Pt. III.

[38] In America an interesting example is given in the field of the municipal government and in the attempts of its reorganization. See the quoted paper of F. Stuart Chapin.

[39] BELOCH, J., *Die Bevölkerung der Griechisch-Römischen Welt*, pp. 99-100, 149-150, 1886.

[40] *Ibid.*, pp. 149 *ff.*, 435 *ff.*

[41] *The Imperial Gazetteer of India*, Vol. I, pp. 311-331.

[42] GUIRAUD, P., *op. cit.*, pp. 41 *ff.*, 51, and 63 *ff.*, 128 *ff.*

[43] Computed from the data given by HANSEN, A. H., "Industrial Classes in the United States in 1920."

[44] *Statist. Jahrbuch der Schweiz*, p. 51, 1923.

[45] *Statistisches Jahrbuch für das Deutsche Reich*, 1921-1922, p. 29.

[46] When this book was already written I came across P. E. FAHLBECK'S book: *Die Klassen und die Gesellschaft*, Jena, 1923, in which this prominent sociologist, starting from quite a different point, comes to conclusions somewhat similar to my own, laid down in my *Systema Soziologii* (in Russian), 1920, Vol. II, and in this book.

Part Two
SOCIAL MOBILITY

CHAPTER VII

SOCIAL MOBILITY, ITS FORMS AND FLUCTUATION

1. CONCEPTION OF SOCIAL MOBILITY AND ITS FORMS

BY SOCIAL mobility is understood any transition of an individual or social object or value—anything that has been created or modified by human activity—from one social position to another. There are two principal types of social mobility, *horizontal* and *vertical.* By horizontal social mobility or shifting, is meant the transition of an individual or social object from one social group to another situated on the same level. Transitions of individuals, as from the Baptist to the Methodist religious group, from one citizenship to another, from one family (as a husband or wife) to another by divorce and remarriage, from one factory to another in the same occupational status, are all instances of social mobility. So too are transitions of social objects, the radio, automobile, fashion, Communism, Darwin's theory, within the same social stratum, as from Iowa to California, or from any one place to another. In all these cases, "shifting" may take place without any noticeable change of the social position of an individual or social object in the vertical direction. By *vertical* social mobility is meant the relations involved in a transition of an individual (or a social object) from one social stratum to another. According to the direction of the transition there are two types of vertical social mobility: *ascending* and *descending*, or *social climbing* and *social sinking.* According to the nature of the stratification, there are ascending and descending currents of economic, political, and occupational mobility, not to mention other less important types. The ascending currents exist in two principal forms: as an *infiltration* of the individuals of a lower stratum into an existing higher one; and as a *creation of a new group by such individuals, and the insertion of such a group into a higher stratum instead of, or side by side with, the existing groups of this stratum.* Correspondingly, the descending current has also two principal forms: the first consists in a dropping of individuals from a higher social position into an existing lower one, without a degradation or disintegration of the higher group to which they belonged; the second is manifested in *a degradation of a social group as a whole, in an abasement of its rank among other groups, or in its disintegration as a social unit.* The first case of "sinking" reminds one of an individual falling from a ship; the second of the sinking of the ship itself with all on board, or of the ship as a wreck breaking itself to pieces.

The cases of individual infiltration into an existing higher stratum or of individuals dropping from a higher social layer into a lower one are relatively common and comprehensible. They need no explanation. The second form of social ascending and descending, the rise and fall of groups, must be considered more carefully.

The following historical examples may serve to illustrate. The historians of India's caste-society tell us that the caste of the Brahmins did not always hold the position of indisputable superiority which it has held during the last two thousand years. In the remote past, the caste of the warriors and rulers, or the caste of the Kshatriyas, seems to have been not inferior to the caste of the Brahmins; and it appears that only after a long struggle did the latter become the highest caste.[1] If this hypothesis be true, then this elevation of the rank of the Brahmin caste as a whole through the ranks of other castes is an example of the second type of social ascent. The group as a whole being elevated, all its members, *in corpore,* through this very fact, are elevated also. Before the recognition of the Christian religion by Constantine the Great, the position of a Christian Bishop, or the Christian clergy, was not a high one among other social ranks of Roman society. In the next few centuries the Christian Church, as a whole, experienced an enormous elevation of social position and rank. Through this wholesale elevation of the Christian Church, the members of the clergy, and especially the high Church dignitaries, were elevated to the highest ranks of medieval society. And, contrariwise, a decrease in the authority of the Christian Church during the last two centuries has led to a relative abasement of the social ranks of the high Church dignitaries within the ranks of the present society. The position of the Pope or a cardinal is still high, but undoubtedly it is lower than it was in the Middle Ages.[2] The group of the legists in France is another example. In the twelfth century, this group appeared in France, as a group, and began to grow rapidly in significance and rank. Very soon, in the form of the judicial aristocracy, it inserted itself into the place of the previously existing nobility. In this way, its members were raised to a much higher social position. During the seventeenth, and especially the eighteenth centuries, the group, as a whole, began to "sink," and finally disappeared in the conflagration of the Revolution. A similar process took place in the elevation of the Communal *Bourgeoisie* in the Middle Ages, in the privileged Six Corps or the *Guilda Mercatoria*, and in the aristocracy of many royal courts. To have a high position at the court of the Romanoffs, Hapsburgs, or Hohenzollerns before the revolutions meant to have one of the highest social ranks in the corresponding countries. The "sinking" of the dynasties led to a "social sinking" of all ranks connected with them. The group of the Communists in Russia, before the Revolution, did not have any high rank socially recognized. During the Revolution the group climbed an enormous social distance and occupied the highest strata in Russian society. As a result, all its members have been elevated *en masse* to the place occupied by the Czarist aristocracy. Similar cases are given in a purely economic stratification. Before the "oil" and "automobile" era, to be a prominent manufacturer in this field did not mean to be a captain of industry and finance. A great expansion of these industries has transformed them into some of the most important kinds of industry. Correspondingly, to be a leading manufacturer in these fields now means to be one of the most important leaders of industry and finance. These examples illustrate the second collective form of ascending and descending currents of social mobility.

The situation is summed up in the following scheme:

- SOCIAL MOBILITY
  - (*a*) of individuals
  - (*b*) of social objects [3]
    - Horizontal
      - Territorial, religious, political party, family, occupational, and other horizontal shiftings without any noticeable change in vertical position
    - Vertical
      - Ascending
        - Individual infiltration
        - Creation and elevation of a whole group
          - Economic, occupational, political, etc.
      - Descending
        - Individual sinking
        - Sinking or disintegration of a whole group
          - Economic, occupational, political, etc.

2. INTENSIVENESS OR VELOCITY AND GENERALITY OF VERTICAL SOCIAL MOBILITY

From the quantitative point of view, a further distinction must be made between the intensiveness and the generality of the vertical mobility. By its *intensiveness* is meant the vertical social distance, or the number of strata—economic or occupational or political—crossed by an individual in his upward or downward movement in a definite period of time. If, for instance, one individual in one year climbed from the position of a man with a yearly income of $500 to a position with an income of $50,000, while another man in the same period succeeded in increasing his income only from $500 to $1,000, in the first case the intensiveness of the economic climbing would be fifty times greater than in the second case. For a corresponding change, the intensiveness of the vertical mobility may be measured in the same way in the field of the political and occupational stratifications. By *the generality of the vertical mobility,* is meant the number of individuals who have changed their social position in the vertical direction in a definite period of time. The absolute number of such individuals gives the *absolute generality* of the vertical mobility in a given population; the proportion of such individuals to the total number of a given population gives *the relative generality of the vertical mobility.*

Finally, combining the data of intensiveness and relative generality of the vertical mobility in a definite field (*e.g.*, in the economic), *the aggregate index of the vertical economic mobility of a given society* may be obtained. In this way a comparison of one society with another, or of the same society at different periods may be made, to find in which of them, or at what period, the aggregate mobility is greater. The same may be said about the aggregate index of the political and occupational vertical mobility.

3. IMMOBILE AND MOBILE TYPES OF STRATIFIED SOCIETIES

On the basis of the above, it is easy to see that a social stratification of the same height and profile may have a different inner structure caused by the difference in the intensiveness and generality of the (horizontal and) vertical social mobility. Theoretically, there may be a stratified society in which the vertical social mobility is nil. This means that within it there is no ascending or descending, no circulation of its members; that every individual is forever attached to the social stratum in which he was born; that the membranes or hymens which separate one stratum from another are absolutely impenetrable, and do not have any "holes" through which, nor any stairs and elevators with which, the dwellers of the different strata may pass from one floor to another. *Such a type of stratification may be styled as absolutely closed, rigid, impenetrable, or immobile.* The opposite theoretical type of the inner structure of the stratification of the same height and profile is that in which the vertical mobility is very intensive and general; here the membranes between the strata are very thin and have the largest holes to pass from one floor to another. Therefore, though the social building is as stratified as the immobile one, nevertheless, the dwellers of its different strata are continually changing; they do not stay a very long time in the same "social story," and with the help of the largest staircases and elevators are *en masse* moving "up and down." *Such a type of social stratification may be styled open, plastic, penetrable, or mobile.* Between these two extreme types there may be many middle or intermediary types of stratification.

Having indicated these types and the types of the vertical mobility, turn now to an analysis of the different kinds of societies and the same society at different times, from the standpoint of the vertical mobility and penetrability of their strata.

4. DEMOCRACY AND VERTICAL SOCIAL MOBILITY

One of the most conspicuous characteristics of the so-called "democratic societies" is a more intensive vertical mobility compared with that of the non-democratic groups. In democratic societies the social position of an individual, at least theoretically, is not determined by his birth; all positions are open to everybody who can get them; there are no judicial or religious obstacles to climbing or going down. All this facilitates a "greater vertical mobility" (capillarity, according to the expression of Dumont) in such societies. This greater mobility is probably one of the causes of the belief that the social building of democratic societies is not stratified, or is less stratified, than that of autocratic societies. We have seen that this opinion is not warranted by the facts. Such a belief is a kind of mental aberration, due to many causes, and among them to the fact that the strata in democratic groups are more open, have more holes and "elevators" to go up and down. This produces the illusion that there are no strata, even though they exist.

In pointing out this considerable mobility of the democratic societies, a reservation must be made at the same time, for not always, and not in all "democratic" societies, is the vertical mobility greater than in the "autocratic" ones.[4] In some of the non-democratic groups mobility has been greater than in the democracies. This is not often seen because the "channels" and the methods of climbing and sinking in such societies are not "the elections," as in democracies, but other and somewhat different ones. While "elections" are conspicuous indications of mobility, its other outlets and channels are often overlooked.

Hence the impression of the stagnant and immobile character of all "non-electoral" societies. That this impression is far from being always true will be shown.

5. GENERAL PRINCIPLES OF VERTICAL MOBILITY

1. *First Proposition.—There has scarcely been any society whose strata were absolutely closed, or in which vertical mobility in its three forms—economic, political and occupational—was not present.* That the strata of primitive tribes have been penetrable follows from the fact that within many of them there is no hereditary high position; their leaders often have been elected, their structures have been far from being quite rigid, and the personal qualities of an individual have played a decisive rôle in social ascent or descent. The nearest approach to an absolutely rigid society, without any vertical mobility, is the so-called caste-society. Its most conspicuous type exists in India. Here, indeed, vertical social mobility is very weak. But even here it has not been absolutely absent. Historical records show that in the past, when the caste-system had already been developed, it did happen that members of the highest Brahmin caste, or the king and his family, were overthrown or cast out for crimes. "Through a want of modesty many kings have perished, together with their belongings; through modesty even hermits in the forest have gained kingdoms. Through a want of humility Vena perished, likewise king Nahusha, Sudâs, Sumukha and Nevi," etc.[5] On the other hand, the outcasts, after a suitable repentance, might be reinstated, or individuals born in a lower social stratum might succeed in entering the Brahmin caste, the top of the social cone of India. "By humility Prithu and Manu gained sovereignty, Kubera the position of the Lord of wealth and the son of Gâdhi, the rank of a Brâhmana."[6] Because of the mixed intercaste marriages, it was possible slowly to climb or sink from caste to caste in several generations. Here are the juridical texts corroborating these statements. In *Gautama* we read: "From a marriage of Brâhmana and Kshatriya springs a Savarna, from a Brâhmana and Vaisya a Nishada, from a Brâhmana and Sûdra a Parasava." In this way intercaste subdivision was appearing. But "In the seventh generation men obtain a change of caste either being

raised to a higher or being degraded to a lower one." [7] "By the power of austerities and of the seed from which they sprang the mixed races obtain here among men more exalted or lower rank in successive birth." [8] Articles concerning the degradation and casting-out for the transgression of the caste rule are scattered throughout all the Sacred Books of India. [9] The existence of the process of social climbing is certainly vouched for, too. At least, in the period of Early Buddhism, we find "many cases of Brahmans and Princes doing manual work and manual occupations. Among the middle classes we find not a few instances revealing anything but castebound heredity and groove, to wit, parents discussing the best profession for their son—no reference being made to the father's trade." "Social divisions and economic occupations were very far from being coinciding." "Labor was largely hereditary, yet there was, withal, a mobility and initiative anything but rigid revealed in the exercise of it." Moreover, at different periods, "slave-born kings are known in history but tabooed in Law." "The spectacle of the low-born man in power was never a rarity in India." The case of Chandragupta, a low-born son of Mura who became the founder of the great dynasty of the Maurya and the creator of the great and powerful Maurya Empire (321 to 297 B. C.) is only one conspicuous example among many.[10]

For the last few decades we see a similar picture. The weak current of the vertical mobility has been active in different ways: "through enrolling in one of the more distinguished castes" by those who became wealthy and could obtain a sanction from the Brahmins; through creation of a new caste; through change of occupation; through intercaste marriages; through migration; and so on.[11] Quite recently a considerable rôle began to be played by education, and by political and religious factors.[12] It is evident, therefore, that, in spite of the fact that the caste-society of India is apparently the most conspicuous example of the most impenetrable and rigidly stratified body, nevertheless, even within it, the weak and slow currents of vertical mobility have been constantly present. If such is the case with the India caste-society, it is clear that in all other social bodies vertical mobility, to this or that degree, must obviously be present. This statement is warranted by the facts. The histories of Greece, Rome, Egypt,[13] China, Medieval Europe, and so on show the existence of a vertical mobility much more intensive than that of the Indian caste-society. The absolutely rigid society is a myth which has never been realized in history.

2. *The Second Proposition.—There has never existed a society in which vertical social mobility has been absolutely free and the transition from one social stratum to another has had no resistance.* This proposition is a mere corollary to the premises established above, that every organized society is a stratified body. If vertical mobility were absolutely free, in the resultant society there would be no strata. It would remind us of a building having no floors separating one story from another. But all societies have been stratified. This means that within them there has been a kind of "sieve" which has sifted the individuals, allowing some to go up, keeping others in the lower strata, and contrariwise.

Only in periods of anarchy and great disorder, when the entire social structure is broken and where the social strata are considerably demolished, do we have anything reminding us of a chaotic and disorganized vertical mobility *en masse*.[14] But even in such periods, there are some hindrances to unlimited social mobility, partly in the form of the remnants of the "sieve" of the old régime, partly in the form of a rapidly growing "new sieve." After a short period, if such an anarchic society does not perish in anarchy, a modified "sieve" rapidly takes the place of the old one and, incidentally, becomes as tight as its predecessor. What is to be understood by the "sieve" will be explained further on. Here it is enough to say that it exists and functions in this or that form in any society. The proposition is so evident and in the future we shall indicate so many facts which warrant it, that there is no need to dwell on it longer here.

3. *The Third Proposition.—The intensiveness, as well as the generality of the vertical social mobility, varies from society to society (fluctuation of mobility in space).* This statement is quite evident also. It is enough to compare the Indian caste-society with the American society to see that. If the highest ranks in the political, or economic, or occupational cone of both

societies are taken, it is seen that in India almost all these ranks are determined by birth, and there are very few "upstarts" who climbed to these positions from the lowest strata. Meanwhile, in the United States, among its captains of industry and finance, 38.8 per cent in the past and 19.6 per cent in the present generation started poor; 31.5 per cent among the deceased and 27.7 per cent among the living multimillionaires started their careers neither rich nor poor;[15] among the twenty-nine presidents of the United States 14, or 48.3 per cent, came from poor and humble families.[16] The differences in the generality of the vertical mobility of both countries are similar. In India a great majority of the occupational population inherit and keep throughout their lives the occupational status of their fathers; in the United States the majority of the population change their occupations at least once in a lifetime. The study of occupational shifting by Dr. Dublin has shown that among the policyholders of the Metropolitan Life Insurance Company 58.5 per cent have changed their occupation between the moment of issuance of the policy and death.[17] My own study of the transmission of occupation from father to son among different groups of the American population has shown that among the present generation the shifting from occupation to occupation is high. The same may be said about the generality of the vertical economic mobility.

Furthermore, the differences in the intensity and generality of the vertical political mobility in different societies may be seen from the following figures which show what per cent among the monarchs and executives of the different countries were "newcomers" who climbed to this highest position from the lower social strata. (See following table.)

These figures may be taken as an approximate indication of the intensiveness and generality of the vertical political mobility from the bottom of the political structure to its top. The great variation of the figures is an indication of the great fluctuation of the political mobility from country to country.

4. *The Fourth Proposition.—The intensiveness and the generality of the vertical mobility—the economic, the political and the occupational—fluctuate in the same society at different times.* In the course of the history of a whole country, as well as of any

Country	Per Cent of "Upstarts" Among the Monarchs and Presidents
Western Roman Empire	45.6
Eastern Roman Empire	27.7
Russia	5.5
France	3.9
England	5.0
United States of America	48.3
Presidents of France and Germany	23.1

social group, there are periods when the vertical mobility increases from the quantitative as well as from the qualitative viewpoint, and there are the periods when it decreases.

Though accurate statistical material to prove this proposition is very scarce and fragmentary, nevertheless, it seems to me that these data, together with different forms of historical testimony, are enough to make the proposition safe.

A. The first series of corroborations is given by the great social upheavals and revolutions which have occurred at least once in the history of every society. It is certain that in the periods of such upheavals vertical social mobility in its intensiveness and generality is far greater than in periods of order and peace. Since, in the history of all countries, periods of upheaval have taken place, this means that the intensiveness and generality of the vertical mobility in every country has oscillated also.[18] Here are a few examples:

In one or two years of the Russian Revolution, almost all people in the richest strata were ruined; almost the whole political aristocracy was deposed and degraded; the greater part of the masters, entrepreneurs, and the highest occupational ranks were put down. On the other hand, within five or six years, a great many people who before the revolution were "nothing," became "everything" and climbed to the top of the political, economic and occupational aristocracy. The revolution reminds one of a great earthquake which throws topsy-turvy all layers in the area of the geological cataclysm. Never in normal periods has Russian society known such a great vertical mobility.

The picture given by the French Revolution, or by the English Revolution of the seventeenth century, or by the great medieval mutations, or by the social revolutions of Ancient Greece, Rome, Egypt, or any other country, is similar to that of the Russian Revolution.[19]

What has been said of the revolutions may be said also of upheavals in the form of foreign invasion, great wars, and conquests.

The Norman Conquest appears to have almost completely supplanted the aristocracy of the Anglo-Saxon race, and to have put the adventurers who accompanied William into the place of those nobles who had ruled the peasantry . . . Anglo-Saxon lords were degraded . . . The dignitaries of the old monarchy were constrained to retire.[20]

This is quoted to show that almost any military upheaval practically calls forth—directly or indirectly—similar results. The conquest by the Aryans of the native population of Ancient India; by the Dorians, of the earlier population of Greece; by the Spartans, of Messenia; by the Romans of their "predia"; by the Spaniards of the native population of America and so on, have involved similar great depressions of the previous highest strata and the creation of a new nobility out of the people who had often been before very low. Even when a war is concluded without conquest or subjugation, it nevertheless calls forth similar results because of a great loss of the higher strata—especially political and military aristocracy—and because of the financial bankruptcy of some of the rich people and the enrichment of skilful swindlers from the new people. The "vacuum" in the nobility caused by the losses has to be filled, and this leads to a more intensive promotion of the new people to the higher positions.

For the same reason in such periods there is a greater occupational shifting, and, hence, a greater occupational mobility, than in a more normal time. The above considerations show the existence of a rhythm of static and dynamic periods in the vertical mobility within the same society at different periods.

B. The second corroboration of the proposition is given by the factual history of many nations.

India.—The historians of India indicate that the rigid caste-system was not known in India at the earlier stages of its history. The Rigveda says nothing of caste. This period appears as a period of great migrations and invasions and struggle and mobility.[21] Later on, the caste-system grew and reached its climax. Correspondingly, vertical social mobility became almost nil. Birth, almost exclusively, began to determine the social position of an individual and this position grew to be "eternal" for all generations born from the same family. At that period, "there is no instance recorded in the Vedic texts of a Vaisya rising to the rank of priest or a prince." [22] Still later, about the time of the appearance of Buddhism (fifth and sixth centuries B. C.) a weakening of the caste-system and an increase of mobility seems to have occurred. Buddhism itself was an expression of the reaction against the rigid caste-régime and an attempt to break it.[23] After approximately the third century B. C. a new wave of social immobility, an increase of the caste-isolation and the triumph of the Brahmins, superseded the preceding period of social mobility.[24]

Later on such waves occurred, it seems, several times,[25] and in this way the alternation of periods of a comparative mobility with those of a comparative stability or decrease of the circulation from stratum to stratum has been going on up to this time, when India seems to have entered again a period of an increase of vertical social mobility and of a slackening of the rigidity of its caste-system.[26] It is certain that the real process of these fluctuations has been much more complex than its above outlines; and yet, there seems to be no doubt that such waves have really been present.

China.—That in the long history of China similar waves have existed is indicated, in the first place, by several alternations of periods of a social order with great upheavals in the form of inner social revolutions and foreign invasions. They have repeated many times. The greater part of them have manifested themselves usually at the end of the existing dynasty and the establishment of a new one.[27] The existence of such fluctuations is witnessed and generalized in the "law of the three stages" ascribed to Confucius and given in the Chinese canonical books. These stages are: "The Disorderly Stage, the Small Tranquillity, and The Great Similarity or Equilibrium." They are repeated, according to the text.[28] The characteristic of the stages suggests that the mobility has been different in each stage; therefore, their repetition has meant also a repetition of the static and dynamic cycles of vertical social mobility. In the third place, the existence of these fluctuations is witnessed indirectly, at least, in regard to political mobility by many pages of the Chinese Sacred Books. They say that during the reign of the good emperors, social positions, especially the highest (even the position of the emperor) were given to the men who deserved them through their personal talent and virtue. In such periods, "every three years there was an examination of merits, and after three examinations the undeserving were degraded, and the deserving advanced. By this arrangement the duties of all the departments were fully discharged."[29] Correspondingly, the Book of Historical Events (*The Shû-King*) records many cases where the highest officials, even the emperors, were taken from the lowest social strata: "Shun rose to Empire from among the channeled fields; Foo Yueh was called to office from the midst of his building-frames; Kaou Kih from his fish and salt; E. Yin was a farmer"; Ti Yao "set forth his successor from among the poor and mean"; and so on.[30] These records say that in "normal and prosperous" periods in Chinese society the circulation was intensive. (By the way, the records show that climbing from a farmer to a king or a president is as old as human history.) In the periods of decay, however, the mobility seems to have been less. This is seen from regular reproach of the overthrown emperors that in the periods of decay "superior men are kept (by the Emperor) in obscurity, and mean men fill all his offices"; such is also the accusation of a great lord Miao by the king Yoi: "He has put men into offices on the hereditary principle"; such is also the crime of the last Shang in the words of Wu, the founder of the Chou dynasty.[31] At the present moment China seems to have entered again a period of increased mobility. However uncertain and indefinite are these indications, none the less, they witness the existence of cycles of comparative mobility and immobility.[32]

Greece.—Something similar may be traced also in the history of the Ancient Greek states. Here we must distinguish the transition from the strata of non-full citizens to that of the full citizens, on the one hand; on the other, from the lowest ranks of the full citizens to the highest positions. In both fields we see a fluctuation of the mobility. As to infiltration from the non-citizen rank to that of the citizen in Sparta, since the time of the enslaving of the Helots, there seems to have been no chance for a Helot to become a free citizen. If such cases happened, they were very few. Later on, after 421 B. C. and especially after the Peloponnesian War, we see that the Helots began to be liberated *en masse,* and to become the Neodâmôdeis, the free men.[33] Such rising to a higher position *en masse* is certainly proof of increased vertical mobility. On the other hand, if in the days of the war against Xerxes the Spartiatæ were equal to one another, then, after the end of the Peloponnesian War, some of them climbed up and became the Homoioi, the Peers, while the majority sank lower and became the Hypomeiones, the Inferiors.[34] The periods of social revolutions led by Agis IV (242 B. C.) and Cleomenes III (227 B. C.) caused great havoc in the circulation of full citizens and were periods of marked mobility. From these facts, it seems to be possible to conclude that in the history of Sparta there was a rhythm of relatively mobile and immobile periods.

That similar cycles took place in the history of Athens is corroborated by the establishment of the eleven different constitutions of Athens within two hundred years. The new constitutions, especially such as those of Solon, Pisistratus, Cleisthenes, of the Four Hundred, of the Thirty and the Ten Tyrants, signified not only a simple change in the form of the government, but a new and fundamental redistribution of citizens within the social cone of Athenian society. For instance, as a result of an introduction of the Solon constitution, a great many people were liberated from slavery, and climbed up, while many previous masters lost their power and went down. The substitution of aristocracy of birth by the aristocracy of wealth had the same result. The effects of some of the other constitutions indicated by Aristotle were similar.[35] Among them, the tyranny of the Thirty and the Ten Tyrants was nothing but a great social earthquake. Therefore, the periods of abolition of an old constitution and introduction of a new one—the periods which in some cases were followed by a civil war and a great upheaval—may probably be regarded as the periods of especially intensive vertical mobility within Athenian society. The *Politics* and *On the Athenian Constitution* of Aristotle, at any rate, conspicuously stress such a conclusion.[36]

Ancient Rome.—For the non-citizens, the infiltration into the stratum of the Roman citizens was very difficult at the earlier stages. It became easier and more intensive after the end of the Republic (*lex Julia,* 90 B. C. and *lex Plautia Papiria,* 39 B. C.). With a decrease of obstacles, however, the privileges of the Roman citizenship decreased also. In 212 A.D. (*lex Caracalla*), all the population of the Roman Empire, except the *latini Juniani,* became Roman citizens. But at that time citizenship practically lost all specific privileges. Such is the curve of circulation from the strata of the non-citizens to that of the *civus Romanus.*

The circulation from the lower strata of citizens or the non-full citizens shows conspicuous fluctuation in generality and intensiveness. The centuries before the fifth and sixth centuries B. C. seem to have been the period of a weak mobility from the layer of the plebeians to that of the patricians. The period after 449 B. C. (*leges Valeriae* and *Horatiae*) to the middle of the fourth century B. C. (*leges Liciniae Sextiae,* 367 B. C.) could be regarded as the period of an intensive circulation because during this period the plebeians obtained almost a complete equality with the patricians, and in this way passed from a lower to a higher stratum. These differences being obliterated, new ones took their place. In spite of their complex character and many unknown details, it is possible to say, with a reasonable degree of certainty, that the period from the last century of the Republic to that of the third century A. D. was in general a period of intensive mobility. The vertical currents were going on from the very bottom of Roman society (the slaves) to its apex (the highest positions, including that of the emperor). Through the avenues of money making, plunder, violence, fraud, swindling, love affairs, and in a less degree through military courage and social service, men with short or with no ancestry rose to great offices, commands, and finally to the purple.[37] As a contrast to this period, the time from the third century A. D. to the end of the Western Roman Empire was marked by a great decrease of the mobility. Inheritance of social position and attachment "forever" to the position of the parents grew to be the rule. Society drifted toward a rigid caste-system.

Every avenue of escape from an inherited position was closed. A man was bound to his calling not only by his father's but by his mother's condition.[38]

Whatever may have been the details of this fluctuation of the mobility throughout Roman history, the existence of cycles of relative immobility and mobility is beyond doubt.

The Middle Ages and the Modern Period.—The fluctuation of the mobility in the Middle Ages may be shown by the history of the highest strata of the privileged social classes. For the sake of brevity, France only is taken. What is said about it, with the corresponding modification, may be said of other European countries.

The Political Mobility.—The beginning of the Middle Ages in Europe may be generally regarded as a period of the most intensive vertical mobility. Among the Teutons, Franks, and Celtic peoples at that moment the stratum of the chiefs and leaders was still open to almost anybody who displayed the necessary talent and ability. Systematic invasion by the Goths, Huns, Lombards, Vandals, and so on, disintegrated social stratification; kept it in a disorderly state; ruined one aristocracy after another; and raised new and newer upstarts and adventurers. In this way the old Roman aristocracy and senatorial families were ruined and disappeared. The bold new adventurers became, and continued to be, the founders of the new dynasties and the new nobility. In this way appeared and grew the Merovingians and, later, the Carolingians, with their nobilities. From what social strata were recruited the nobility of that period, the *noblesse du palais* which superseded the senatorial nobility of Rome? The answer is as follows:

In the sixth century it was possible to see yet the few senatorial families noble by the virtue of their ancestors and rich through their inherited wealth. But in the seventh century this nobility disappeared completely and was replaced by the new nobility of the king's officials or *noblesse du palais*. . . . The law of the Franks gave a value not so much to the ancient noble families as much as to those who were in the king's service. Not a long list of prominent ancestors, but the governmental service, was what ennobled men. In the practice of the Merovingian society even the highest ranks of the government nobility were so open as to permit a slave rather easily to climb to the highest position. The genealogy of the nobility of that time can indicate only the father of a noble, no further.[39]

Correspondingly we have here many counts and nobles, such as Ebrion, *maître des Palais,* Leudastes, and others, who came of slaves, of brigands, and of able people of a humble origin. The situation continued to be similar under the Carolingians. Here also a considerable number of the dukes and counts and the high nobility came of slaves or the lower classes generally (Rahon, Count of Orléans, Bertmund, Sturminius, etc.).[40]

Generally, until the thirteenth century, there were no juridical obstacles for social climbing. The last of the villains, if he was a brave and capable man, might become a noble—a *chevalier;* a man who could buy a fief might become a noble also. And no sanction of the king was necessary for the validity of this ennoblement. After the thirteenth century there appeared the first definite symptoms of a social seclusion of the nobility and one avenue after another began to be closed (the ordinances of Philip III, 1275, and others).[41] Mobility did not disappear completely, but it became somewhat diminished throughout the thirteenth and the first half of the fourteenth centuries.

Owing to the Hundred Years' War, to the Peasant and Paris revolutions, to the struggle of the Cabochiens and Armagniacs, and anarchy, vertical mobility, from the second half of the fourteenth century in the form of an infiltration of newcomers into the high strata of nobility, and in the form of the disappearance and sinking of many previous nobles, seemed to become somewhat more intensive again. Side by side with the previous channels for social climbing, some new ones also appeared: through the profession of the royal *legists;* through the municipalities and the city communes; and through the guilds and money making. With fluctuations the process went on up to the beginning of the eighteenth century (from 1715 to 1789) when the mobility was strongly checked again.[42] The great French Revolution and the period of the Napoleonic Empire, when those "who had been nothing became everything," and contrariwise, were again the periods of most intensive vertical social mobility. Such, in brief, were the principal cycles of vertical social mobility in this field.

A consideration of other countries in regard to vertical mobility within political stratification brings out some periods in their history especially conspicuous for an intensive vertical shifting. In the history of Russia such are the second half of the sixteenth and the beginning of the seventeenth centuries (the time of Ivan the Terrible and the anarchy); the time of Peter the Great; and finally, the time of the last Russian Revolution. In these periods almost all the previous political and governmental nobility has been exterminated or put down and quite new "upstarts" filled the highest ranks of political and governmental aristocracy.[43] It is well known that in the history of the Italian states a similar period was the fifteenth and the sixteenth centuries. "The fifteenth century was rightly styled the age of adventurers and bastards. Borso d'Este at Ferrara, Sigismondo Malatesta at Rimini, Francesco Sforza at Milan, Ferdinand of Aragon at Naples, and a great many other lords and princes were bastards. No one was longer bound by any conventions or traditions; everything depended on personal qualities."[44] Such is in brief the character of the period.

In the history of England such periods were the period of the conquest of England by William the Conqueror, and the second half of the seventeenth century, not to mention other periods.

In the history of the United States such periods were the end of the eighteenth century, and the period of the Civil War.

In most European countries, the age of the Renaissance and

Reformation represented the period of an extraordinarily intensive social mobility.

Finally, the present time, since the beginning of the twentieth century, seems to belong to a very "mobile" age in regard to political and economic circulation. It is also the age of bastards, adventurers, and climbers. Lenin and other dictators in Russia; Mussolini and the Fascist leaders in Italy; Masaryk and the Czech political leaders; Stambuljisky, and even the Tzankoff government in Bulgaria; Mustapha Kemal-pasha, in Turkey; Radich and other "newcomers" in Serbia; Risa-Chan, in Persia; the quite new men at the top of the political cone in Esthonia, Poland, Latvia, Lithuania; the Labor government in England and the Social-Democratic government in Germany; the new leaders in France and so on, on the one hand—on the other, almost a complete extermination or putting down of many royal families (Hohenzollerns, Hapsburgs, Romanoffs, Ottomans, Koburgs, and so on) and the political aristocracies of the end of the nineteenth century—these facts witness very decisively the mobile character of our epoch, at least in the field of political mobility.

And what has been said of the fluctuation of vertical mobility in the sphere of political stratification may be repeated in the sphere of economic and occupational vertical mobility.

For the sake of brevity, a corresponding historical survey for the confirmation of this statement will be omitted, but the materials which will be given further on may, to some extent, show it.

On the basis of the above and what will be given further, it seems safe to say that the fourth proposition is warranted by the facts.

5. *The Fifth Proposition.—As far as the corresponding historical and other materials permit seeing, in the field of vertical mobility, in its three fundamental forms, there seems to be no definite perpetual trend toward either an increase or a decrease of the intensiveness and generality of mobility. This is proposed as valid for the history of a country, for that of a large social body, and, finally, for the history of mankind.* Thus, in the field of vertical mobility, the same conclusion of "trendless" change is reached which was met with in the field of social stratification.

In these dynamic times, with the triumph of the electoral

system, with the industrial revolution, and especially a revolution in transportation, this proposition may appear strange and improbable. The dynamism of our epoch stimulates the belief that history has tended and will tend in the future toward a perpetual and "eternal" increase of vertical mobility. There is no need to say that many social thinkers have such an opinion.[45] And yet, if its bases and reasons are investigated it may be seen that they are far from convincing.

A. In the first place, the partisans of the acceleration and increase of mobility used to point out that in modern societies there are no juridical and religious obstacles to circulation, which existed in a caste—or in a feudal society. Granting for a moment that this statement is true, the answer is: first of all, it is impossible to infer an "eternal historical tendency" on the basis of an experience only of some 130 years; this is too short a period, beside the course of thousands of years of human history, to be a solid basis for the assertion of the existence of a perpetual trend. In the second place, even within this period of 130 years, the trend has not been manifested clearly throughout the greater part of mankind. Within the large social aggregates of Asia and Africa, the situation is still indefinite; the caste-system is still alive in India; in Tibet and Mongolia, in Manchuria and China, among the natives of many other countries, there has been either no alteration of the situation or only such as had happened many times before. In the light of these considerations reference to feudalism compared with the "free" modern times loses a great deal of its significance.

B. Grant that the removal of the juridical and religious obstacles tended to increase mobility. Even this may be questioned. It would have been valid if, in place of the removed obstacles, there were not introduced some other ones. In fact, such new obstacles were introduced. If in a caste-society it is rarely possible to be noble unless born from a noble family, it is possible nevertheless to be noble and privileged without being wealthy; in the present society it is possible to be noble without being born in a prominent family; but, as a general rule, it is necessary to be wealthy.[46] One obstacle gone, another has taken its place. In theory, in the United States of America, every citizen may become the President of the United States. In fact, 99.9 per cent of the citizens have as little chance of doing it as 99.9 per cent of the subjects of a monarchy have of becoming a monarch. One kind of obstacle removed, others have been established. By this is meant that the abolition of obstacles to an intensive vertical circulation, common in caste-society and feudal society, did not mean an absolute decrease of the obstacles, but only a substitution of one sort of impediment for another. And it is not yet known what kind of obstacles—the old or the new—is more efficient in restraining social circulation. A more detailed discussion of this problem will be given later. Meanwhile, this consideration is enough to show that the removal of juridical and religious obstacles cannot necessarily signify an increase of the mobility.

C. The third argument against a perpetual trend is the factual movement of mobility in the history of different nations and large social bodies. It is certain that the least hereditary, and therefore the most mobile, have been primitive societies, with their non-hereditary and temporary leaders, with social influence easily shifted from man to man, according to circumstances and abilities. If in later history there arose a trend toward an increase of mobility it would seem that it could not be a perpetual tendency, because at the beginning of the social life, the social circulation was more intensive than at some advanced stages. Further, the above outlines of the movement of mobility in the history of India and China, in Ancient Greece and Rome, in France and other countries mentioned, have not shown anything like a steady trend of increase in vertical mobility. What has been happening is only an alternation—the waves of a greater mobility superseded by the cycles of a greater immobility—and that is all. If such is the case, the "trend theory," it seems, cannot be based on the data of history. True, from the fact that something has not yet happened, it is impossible to infer that it will not happen in the future; but it is still less possible to infer from the fact that something has not happened in the past that it will happen in the future.

D. Furthermore, it is assumed often, as something quite obvious, that vertical social mobility at the present time is much greater than in the past. But such an assumption is a mere belief which has not been tested as yet. And it seems to me that such competent investigators as E. Levasseur have been not quite wrong in questioning this assumption and contending that social circulation in the seventeenth century was not less than that of the nineteenth century.[47] From a distance everything is gray and formless, and we are prone to think that in the remote past everything was flat and gray and static. But such is not the real situation. And it is really difficult to decide whether the vertical mobility of the present democratic societies is greater than that of the previous centuries in the history of Europe or elsewhere. If it cannot be said that it is less intensive, still it cannot be said that it is greater. And this means that the trend is uncertain.

E. As a proof of the upward trend, its partisans indicate often a decrease in the inheritance of high social positions and their substitution by elective ones. The elected presidents instead of the hereditary monarchs; the elected or appointed high officials instead of the hereditary nobility; talented climbers instead of the hereditary office holders, and so on—so runs this argument. I regret that I must indicate some elementary historical facts which seem to be forgotten by the proponents of this argument. In the first place, the principle of elective leaders and kings and other high social officials was known to the past not less than to the present. The chiefs and the kings of the greater part of the primitive societies have been elected.[48] The consuls, tribunes, and other political positions in ancient Rome and Greece were elected. The Roman emperors were elected or became emperors through violence and struggle. The kings and the emperors of the Holy Roman Empire of the Middle Ages, as a rule, were elected or made themselves kings through violence and desperate struggle. The Roman Catholic Popes and the highest dignitaries of the medieval Church were elected. The authorities of the medieval republics were elected.[49] This is evident to everybody who has studied a little history. But, it may be objected, in the past these authorities were elected by a narrow circle of the privileged few, while we have now a universal suffrage. This, also, is not true. In the past in many bodies politic, the vote was also universal. On the other hand, it is shown that the three hundred millions of the population of India or other colonies of Great Britain; the native population of the colonies of France, of Belgium, and some other countries, do not have any vote in the election of the authorities nor in the enactment of the laws which rule them. Some other facts about the universality of suffrage at the present time have been indicated above. Therefore, the whole argument of the trend from inherited to elected authorities is fallacious.

The non-existence of the trend from monarchy to republic is also indicated. Moreover, it is also not true that the highest social positions: *e.g.* that of a monarch, remain within the same dynasty a much shorter time now than in the past.

The answer is given by the following figures: While the existing dynasties of England, Denmark, Netherlands, Spain, Savoy, and Italy, have already been reigning more than 200 years, and while contemporary dynasties of the Hapsburgs, Romanoffs, Ottomans, Hohenzollerns, not to mention others, reigned more than 200, 300 and 400 years (we must not forget that they were abolished only yesterday), in the past the duration of dynasties was no longer but rather shorter. In Ancient Egypt the Third Dynasty reigned 80 years; the Fourth, 150 years; the Fifth, 125; the Sixth, 150; the Seventh and the Eighth together, 30; the Ninth and the Tenth together, 285; the Eleventh, 160; the Twelfth, 213; the Thirteenth, the Fourteenth, the Fifteenth, the Sixteenth and the Seventeenth dynasties together, 208; the Eighteenth, 230; the Nineteenth, 145; the Syrian dynasty, 5; the Twentieth, 110; the Twenty-first, 145; the Twenty-second, 200; the Twenty-third, 27; the Twenty-fourth, 6; the Twenty-fifth, 50; the Twenty-sixth, 138; some other "upstart" dynasties reigned from 3 days up to 1 or 2 years.[50] The duration of the dynasties in China in chronological sequence of time was as follows: the Yao dynasty reigned 96 years; the Shun, 50; the Hsia, 439; the Shang or Yin, 644; the Chow, 862; the Chin, 44; the Han, 422; the Tsin, 154; the Sui, 28; the Tang, 287; the Five dynasties of the period of anarchy, 57; the Sung, 316; the South Sung, 149; the Yuan, 90; the Ming, 275; the Tsing, (the last dynasty) 267.[51] In ancient Rome, no dynasty reigned more than 100 years, and the greater part of "the dynasties" reigned only a few years or few months, or even few days. There was a similar situation in the Eastern Roman Empire. The Merovingians reigned about 269 years; the Carolingians about 235 years; the Capets, 341; the Valois, 261; the Bourbons, 204; the Saxon dynasty in ancient Germany, 113 years; the Franconia house, about 101; the Hohenstaufens, about 119. These figures are enough to show that there is no "acceleration" or shortening of the "hereditary holding of the position of a monarch" in modern times compared with the past. If anyone would say that this occurs in the case of a republic substituted for a monarchy, I point out again that there is no perpetual trend from a monarchy to a republic. The newly established republics may easily give way to monarchies in the future, as has happened many times in the past. The present republic must be compared with the ancient republic. Such a comparison results in the conclusion that in the ancient republics the holding of the position of a state executive within the same family was as short as at the present moment.

What is true of monarchs is still more valid of other high positions in the past and in modern societies. If one thinks that in the past these positions were held in a long hereditary line, he is mistaken; on the other hand, it is possible with some facts of this kind to confront "the Morgans," "the Rothschilds," "the Astors," "the Vanderbilts," and so on, who also have held their prominent positions several generations.

F. As to the newcomers and climbers in the past and in the present, the list of the upstarts among the monarchs and executives of several countries is given above. This list shows that the per cent of newcomers among the emperors of the Western and the Eastern Roman Empire was higher than among the presidents of France and Germany; it was very near to the percentage of the Presidents of the United States who came from the poor classes; it was much higher than the percentage of upstarts among the monarchs and rulers of European countries for the last few centuries. Even in these countries, with the exception of Russia, the percentage of climbers from the lower strata to the position of monarch in the past, was higher than during the last two centuries. To these data may be added that the percentage of Roman Catholic popes who came of the poor classes has been 19.4; from the middle classes, 18.8; and from the noble and wealthy classes, 61.8; and the popes from the lower social strata were more common in the past than in the last two centuries.[52] The tendency to nepotism, or the hereditary holding of the position of the Pope within the same family, was conspicuous not at the beginning of Church history, as we have to expect according to the trend hypothesis, but much later, in the thirteenth, the fourteenth, the fifteenth and the sixteenth centuries. The same is true of the high church dignitaries. Finally, it may be remarked that the same condition obtained among the nobility and the high social positions in European society at the beginning and during the first half of the Middle Ages.

These factual indications which may be multiplied *ad libitum*, are enough to make very questionable, at least, the above alleged "tendencies" from an inherited to an elected or freely obtained "position."

G. If I were to believe in any perpetual trend in this field, I would rather have tried to prove that, like an organism, a social body, as it grows older, tends to become more and more rigid and the circulation of its individuals tends to become less and less intensive. Though I do not think that there is such a trend, there are many facts which exhibit it. In Egypt a strictly hereditary holding of offices became conspicuous rather lately, in the time of the Sixth dynasty.[53] In Sparta at the earliest period, foreigners were admitted into the rank of the full-right citizens.[54] Later on, the group of Spartan aristocracy became closed and only in extraordinary conditions admitted the newcomers. In Athens, in spite of many convulsive waves of mobility in the time of upheavals, the same trend toward rigidity appeared in the later periods. The Athenian citizens were not very numerous. In order better to enjoy money extorted from the Allies, in 451 B.C., Pericles introduced a bill, according to which "no one should be admitted to the franchise (of full citizenship) who was not of citizen birth by both parents."[55] Though later on, among the citizens we find few men who had been slaves or freemen, "nevertheless, the rarity of the corresponding texts proves that the right of the citizenship was granted rarely and under difficulty to the Metiokes and freemen."[56] In Venice, up to 1296, the ranks of the aristocracy were open. Since that time up to 1775, when the aristocracy lost its significance, its ranks were closed, only from time to time being broken by an infiltration of a few newcomers.[57] The Roman senatorial nobility, to 151 B. C., became more and more restricted. This also was the tendency of the Nobiles and the Equestrians. Being at the beginning an open class, later on (approximately after the time of Augustus) they began to close the doors to newcomers.[58] At the end of the Roman Empire all social strata and groups became quite closed.[59] The highest strata of the Christian Church, being quite open during the first centuries of its existence, even for the slaves, later on, began to be closed also to upstarts from the lower social strata. The nobility of the royal court, accessible for everybody under the Merovingians and Carolingians, later on began to become more exclusive and impenetrable for newcomers. This also was the trend in the Guilds. Even their highest stratum, of the masters, during the first centuries of the history of the Guilds, was accessible for the infiltration of the valets and apprentices and for other people. But after the beginning of the sixteenth century there appeared a trend to the same seclusion and caste-tendency. The Communal *Bourgeoisie,* or the Middle Class in England, an open group at the beginning of its history, later exhibited the same caste-tendency; also in France, after the twelfth, and in England, after the fifteenth century. The same may be said of the financial and industrial and juridical (the legists) aristocracy in France and in other European countries.[60] Even in the United States of America, in spite of the short and rather humble ancestry of the families of "The Social Register," these families already compose a kind of secluded aristocracy, with a special "Social Register," with rules which decide whether a man deserves to be admitted in the Social Register or not; in brief, they show all pretensions of an aristocratic caste.

There is no use in multiplying the facts. It is evident that the tendency to social seclusion and rigidity in the later stages of development of many social bodies has been rather common. While not trying to claim for this tendency a permanent trend, it is mentioned only to oppose the alleged tendency of an increase of social mobility in the course of time.

What has been said seems to be enough to challenge the alleged trend theories.

SUMMARY

1. The principal forms of social mobility of individuals and social objects are: horizontal and vertical. Vertical mobility exists in the form of ascending and descending currents. Both have two varieties: individual infiltration and collective ascent or descent of the whole group within the system of other groups.

2. According to the degree of the circulation, it is possible to discriminate between immobile and mobile types of society.

3. There scarcely has existed a society whose strata were absolutely closed.

4. There scarcely has existed a society where vertical mobility was absolutely free from obstacles.

5. The intensiveness and the generality of vertical mobility vary from group to group, from time to time (fluctuation in space and in time). In the history of a social body there is a rhythm of comparatively immobile and mobile periods.

6. In these fluctuations there seems to be no perpetual trend toward either an increase or decrease of vertical mobility.

7. Though the so-called democratic societies are often more mobile than autocratic ones, nevertheless, the rule is not general and has many exceptions.

Before proceeding to a detailed analysis of vertical mobility within present Western societies, an analysis of the general characteristics of mobility and its mechanism should be made. When this is done, the study of mobility within contemporary societies should be resumed.

[1] See BOUGLÉ, C., "Remarques sur le régime des castes," pp. 53 *et seq.; The Cambridge History of India,* pp. 92 *et seq.*

[2] See GUIZOT, F., *The History of Civilization,* Vol. I, pp. 50-54, New York, 1874.

[3] The mobility of social objects and values and the horizontal mobility, in spite of the great importance of the problem, is not an object of this study.

[4] This is natural because under the signboard "democracy" are usually put societies of the most different types. The same is true of "autocracy." Both terms are very vague and scientifically defective.

[5] *Laws of Manu,* VII, 40-42; see also XI, 183-199.

[6] *Laws of Manu,* VII, 42; XI, 187-199.

[7] GAUTAMA, Chap. IV, pp. 8-21.

[8] *Laws of Manu,* X, 42; see also 5-56.

[9] See also LILLY, W. S., *India and Its Problems,* pp. 200 *et seq.,* London, 1922.

[10] *The Cambridge History of India,* Vol. I, pp. 208 *ff.,* 223, 268-269, 288, 480, New York, 1922.

[11] See *The Imperial Gazetteer of India,* Vol. I, pp. 311-331.

[12] See WOODBURNE, A. S., *Decline of Caste in India,* in CASE, C., *Outlines of Introductory Sociology.*

[13] See BREASTED, J. H., *op. cit.,* pp. 120, 173, 289, 333, 360.

[14] See SOROKIN, P., *Sociology of Revolution,* Pt. III.

[15] SOROKIN, P., "American Millionaires and Multimillionaires," *Journal of Social Forces,* p. 638, May, 1925.

[16] SOROKIN, P., "The Monarchs and the Rulers," *Journal of Social Forces,* March, 1926.

[17] DUBLIN, L. J., "Shifting of Occupations Among Wage Earners," *Monthly Labor Review,* April, 1924.

[18] *Cf.* ROSS, E. A., *Principles of Sociology,* pp. 338-339.

[19] See SOROKIN, P., *Sociology of Revolution,* Pt. III.

[20] ROGERS, J. E. T., *Six Centuries of Work and Wages,* p. 19, New York, 1884.

[21] See *The Cambridge History of India,* Vol. I, pp. 38, 54, 92; ZIMMER, *Altindische Leben,* p. 185; BOUGLÉ, C., "Remarques sur le régime des castes," *L'Année sociologique,* pp. 28-44, 1900; *The Imperial Gazetteer of India,* Vol. I, pp. 345-347.

[22] *The Cambridge History of India,* Chap. V, p. 127.

[23] *Ibid.,* Chap. VII, pp. 208-210, 260. Here the hereditary transmission of an occupation seems to decrease; "the freedom of initiative and mobility in trade and labour" existed; "the merchants and farmers and the mass of working people were endowed with a new influence, which superseded for a short time the influence of priests and nobles."

[24] *Ibid.,* Chaps. IX and X. Here we have "the beginning of that formal theory of defilement which results in a pure man of the upper castes being defiled by the shadow of an impure man, and in the taboo of all contact with the impure." *Ibid.,* p. 234. In the Maurya Empire "there is no transference from one class to another." *Ibid.,* p. 477.

[25] See GROUSSET, RENÉ, *Histoire de l'Asie,* "L'Inde et la Chine," Paris, 1922.

[26] See WOODBURNE, A. S., *Decline of Caste in India.* However, see the opposite statement of J. T. Marten, director of the census of India, who says that the caste-system now is as strong as it was before. MARTEN, J. T., "Population Problems from the Indian Census," *Journal of the Royal Society of Arts,* Mar. 20, 1925.

[27] See, *e.g.,* HIRTH, *The Ancient History of China,* New York, 1908; GROUSSET, RENÉ, *op. cit.,* Vol. II, *"La Chine." The Shû-King, The Sacred Books of the East,* Vol. III, pp. 101 *ff.,* 125 *ff.,* and *passim.*

[28] See *Lî Kî,* Bk. VII, pp. 2 *ff.*

[29] *The Shû-King,* pp. 45, 55, 143, and *passim.*

[30] LEGGE, J., *Life and Works of Mencius,* Bk. VI, Pt. II, Chap. XV, p. 1; Bk. V, Pt. I, pp. 2, 3; *Lî-Kî, The Sacred Books of the East,* Vol XXVII, pp. 223, 312 *ff.; The Shû-King,* pp. 45, 51, 55, 85 *ff.,* 101, 104, 143, and *passim.*

[31] See *The Shû-King, The Sacred Books of the East,* Vol. III, Pt. I, pp. 32 *et seq.;* Pt. II, pp. 51-55, 125, 143, and *passim; Lî-Kî,* Bk. XXVIII; LEE, MABEL P. H., *op. cit.,* 39 *ff.,* 50 *ff.*

[32] Similar waves seem to have existed in the history of Ancient Egypt, too. Here several of the pharaohs, like Neferhotep, were upstarts; some periods, like that of the end of the thirteenth dynasty, were periods of an extraordinary mobility. "King followed a king with unprecedented rapidity, the length of reign being usually but a year or two, while in two cases we find after a king's name but three days." BREASTED, J. H., *op. cit.*, pp. 173-174. See also GARDINER, A., *Admonition of an Egyptian Sage, passim*, Leipzig, 1909.

[33] THUCYDIDES, *History of the Peloponnesian War*, 4.80; 5.34 and 67; 7.19 and 58; 8.5.

[34] XENOPHON, *Hellenica*, 3.3.5 and 6.

[35] Here are a few illustrations: "Cleisthenes attracted the people to his side by giving the franchise to the masses." His redistribution of the population into ten new tribes resulted in breaking down the old families and the creation of a "large number of new citizens by the enfranchisement of emancipated slaves and resident aliens." During the leadership of Miltiades, "five years after the death of Ephialtes, it was decided that the candidates (for the archonship) might be selected from the Zeugitae as well as from the higher classes. The first Archon from that class was Mnesitheides. Up to this time all the Archons had been taken only from the Pentacosiomedimni and Knights, two highest classes, while the Zeugitæ were confined to the ordinary magistracies." ARISTOTLE, *On the Athenian Constitution*, Chaps. XX, XXI, and XXVII.

[36] See ARISTOTLE, *On the Athenian Constitution*, Chaps. I, II, III, IV, VI, XLI, and *passim*.

[37] Within one or two generations a slave became an equestrian, or a member of the *nobilitas*. Cicero speaks even about a six-year period during which a slave may become free. *"Etenim, patres conscripti, cum in spem libertatis, sexenio post simus ingressi, diutiusque servitutem perpessi, quam captivi frugi et diligentes solent."* CICERO, *Phil.* VIII, 11. In his *Pro Cornelio Balbo*, he speaks about social promotion from the bottom to the top of society—"through virtue, intelligence and knowledge"—as of a quite common occurrence. Among the richest people and the highest magistracies of that time we meet many names of freemen and slaves (Trimalchio, Pallas, Demetrius, and others). About other avenues of promotion we have a good description of Dionysii Halicarnassensis. "In the past they obtained liberty through their courage and honesty and through buying it for money earned by an honest work. Now the morals became so vile that some people to buy their liberty and citizenship get money through theft, fraud, prostitution, and through other bad actions. Some others are granted their liberty by their masters and distinction by their patrons for help in their crimes of homicide, poisoning and other felonies against the Gods and the Republic." *Roma Ant.*, IV, 24. There is no doubt that after the time of Augustus there appeared some obstacles to promotion into the highest strata; nevertheless, on the whole the time was one of intensive social shifting. See also Rostovtzeff, *Social and Economic History of the Roman Empire*, pp. 19, 22, 42-3, 47-8, 55, 58, 81, 99, 117-19.

[38] DILL, *Roman Society in the Last Days of the Western Empire*, Bk. III, Chap. I. See also WALTZING, J. P., *op. cit.*, Vol. II, pp. 268 *ff.*, 466-484. Rostovtzeff, *op. cit.*, pp. 472 *ff.*

[39] DE COULANGES, F., *Les Transformations de la royauté pendant l'époque Carolingienne*, pp. 47, 66, 96, 424; VIOLLET, *Histoire du droit civil franc*, p. 251, Paris, 1893; KOLABINSKA, M., *La Circulation des élites en France*, Lausanne, 1912, pp. 11-15.

[40] See also LUCHAIRE, A., *Manuel des instituts françaises*, pp. 257 *et seq.* FLACH, *Les origines de l'ancienne France, X et XI Siécles*, Vol. 1, p. 721; GUIZOT, F., *The History of Civilization*, Vol. I, pp. 67 *ff.*, 203-205, N. Y.

[41] See Kolabinska, M., *op. cit.*, pp. 19-32; Esmein, *Cours d'histoire du droit français*, pp. 231 *et seq.*, 680 *et seq.*

[42] Kolabinska, M., *op. cit.*, Chaps. II to IV.

[43] See Kluchevsky, *Cours Russkov Istorii*, Vol. III, pp. 88-89; Vol. IV, *passim;* Sorokin, P., *Sociology of Revolution*, Pt. III.

[44] Villari, P., *The Life and Times of N. Machiavelli*, Vol. I, p. 8, T. Fisher Unwin, London.

[45] See, *e.g.*, Fahlbeck, "Les classes sociales"; "La noblesse de Suede"; "La décadence et la chute des peuples," in *Bull. de l'Inst. Int. de Stat.*, Vols. XII, XV, and XVIII; D'Aeth, F. G., "Present Tendencies of Class Differentiation," *The Sociological Review*, pp. 269-272 et seq., 1910.

[46] Such is the condition necessary for a man to be included in the American "Social Register."

[47] See the statement of E. Levasseur in *Bulletin de l'Institut International de Statistiques*, Vol. XVIII, pp. 123-124.

[48] Passing from the lower to the higher simple peoples not a decrease but rather an increase is seen in "hereditary government." See the data of Hobhouse, L., Wheeler, G., and Ginsberg, M., *op. cit.*, pp. 50 *ff.*

[49] See the corresponding theories in Carlyle, R. W., and A. J., *A History of Medieval Political Theory*, Vol. I, Chap. IV, 1903; Vol. II, pp. 75, 253-254, 1909; Vol. III, pp. 30, 31, 51, 94-95, 168-169, 1916; De Wulf, M., *Philosophy and Civilization in the Middle Ages*, Chap. XI, 1922; De Labriolle, P., *History and Literature of Christianity*, Bks. I, III, and IV, New York, 1925.

[50] Breasted, J. H. A., *Ancient Records of Egypt*, Vol. I, pp. 40-47; Chicago, 1906. The data are interesting also in that they do not show any trend in the history of Egypt.

[51] Lee, Mabel P. H., *op. cit.*, pp. 38 *ff.* Here also no trend is shown.

[52] Sorokin, P., "The Monarchs and the Rulers."

[53] Breasted, J. H. A., *A History of the Ancient Egyptians*, pp. 117, 146. The same is partly true in regard to China.

[54] Strabo, VIII, 5, 4; Aristotle, *Politics*, II, 6, 12; Schoeman, G. F., *Antiquités grecques*, Vol. I, p. 244, Paris, 1884.

[55] Aristotle, *On the Athenian Constitution*, Chap. XXVI.

[56] Beauchet, *Histoire du droit privé de la republique athénienne*, Vol. I, p. 488, Paris, 1897.

[57] Sandi, Vetton, *Principj di Storia Civile della Rep. di Venezia*, Vol. I, Bk. V, pp. 1-10, 1769.

[58] "The old system, when all official positions were open to all citizens, was abolished; the magistracies and sacerdotal positions were closed to all except to the nobilitas and the equestrians. Nobilitas became a hereditary peerage." Mommsen, *Le droit pub. romaine*, VI, 2, p. 48; Waltzing, J. P., *op. cit.*, Vol. II, p. 7.

[59] Waltzing, J. P., *ibid.*, Vol. II, pp. 480-484.

[60] See the quoted works of F. de Coulanges, M. Kolabinska, A. Luchaire, Viollet, Esmein, R. Gretton, E. Martin Saint-Leon. See also Luchaire, A., *La commune française*, pp. 153, 213; De La Tour, Imbart, *Les élections épiscopales dans l'église de France du XI au XII siècle.*

CHAPTER VIII

THE CHANNELS OF VERTICAL CIRCULATION

SINCE vertical mobility actually functions to some degree in any society, there must be in the "membranes" between the strata "holes," "staircases," "elevators," or "channels" which permit individuals to move up and down, from stratum to stratum. The problem to be discussed now is: What are these channels of social circulation?

Various Social Institutions Perform This Function.—Among them there are few especially important from our standpoint. Of these few, which may be in different societies or in the same society, at different periods, one or two are particularly characteristic for a given type of society. The most important institutions of this kind have been: army, church, school, political, economic, and professional organizations.

1. THE ARMY AS A CHANNEL OF SOCIAL CIRCULATION

This institution plays an especially important part in periods of militarism, or international or civil war. There is no need to say how greatly the fate of a society depends on success in time of war. Whether intentionally or not, any service of a talented strategist, or a brave soldier, regardless of his social status, is highly appreciated at such periods. Besides, the war is apt to test the talent of the low-born soldier or inability of a privileged noble. The great danger to the army and to the country imperatively urges the army and the country to put the soldier in the rank corresponding to his real ability. The services of the low-born soldiers force rewards by promotion. The great losses among the commanding officers make it necessary to fill their places by people taken from the lower ranks. The war continuing, a leadership once obtained by a low-born soldier is likely to grow, if he is a talented commander. A power once obtained may be used by him for the sake of his own promotion. The opportunity to rob; to plunder; to degrade his victims; to revenge his enemies; to surround himself by pomp, ceremonies, titles and what not may in this way increase and give to such a leader all the splendor of luxury, all the power of a hereditary noble, all the fame of a good or a bad hero.

These considerations explain why the army has always played the rôle of "social stairway" through which many low-born people became generals, dukes, princes, monarchs, dictators, and rulers of the world; and many "born aristocrats," princes, dukes, kings, and rulers, have lost their ranks, titles, fortunes, social positions, and even their lives. Facts of this kind are so numerous and so abundantly fill the annals of history that a few examples are enough to illustrate the statement.

In the first place, the majority of the chieftains of the militant tribes have become chieftains and rulers through war and the army.

In the second place, of 92 Roman Emperors, at least 36 climbed to this position from the lowest social strata up the army ladder.

Of 65 Emperors of Byzantium, at least 12 were really upstarts who obtained this position through the same "army ladder."

In the Middle Ages, the founders of the Merovingians and Carolingians, and their highest nobility, rose to the top of the social cone through the same channel. A great many medieval slaves, brigands, serfs, and men of humble origin, in this way became nobles, masters, princes, dukes, high officials. Mercadier, the friend and general-in-chief of Richard the Lion-Hearted; Cadoc, the ally of Philip Augustus; Fulc de Breauté, the agent of John Lackland;[1] Ebrion, *maître des Palais;* Leudastes; Beranger de Nattes; Jeane Boyleane; Crocquard; Bacon; Convers; and so on are the examples of this kind of upstarts.[2] In the seventeenth century in France, such men as Villars, Catinat, Fabert, Chevert, Vauban, Châteaurenaud, and many other "aristocrats" came out of the lower strata up the ladder of the army. In the eighteenth century, in 1787, in the privileged military colleges of France, there were 603 *élèves du roi;* 989 offspring of nobility; and 799 sons of laborers who had to be the future members of nobility. Napoleon and his aristocracy, the marshals, generals, and kings placed by him in Europe, climbed from a humble origin to the top by the same ladder. Cromwell, Grant, Washington, and thousands of other military men and *condottieri* climbed to the highest positions through the army. The heroes of the last war, the contemporary Kemal Pashas, Frunzes, the military leaders in international and civil wars;[3] world rulers like Jenghiz Khan, Tamerlane, and so on, give further illustrations of the upward movement through the channels of the army. On the other hand, thousands of unsuccessful military commanders, who, having been defeated, were turned into slaves, were degraded, ostracized, expelled, banished, in brief, went down rapidly, give an illustration of the downward movement through the same channel of the army.

In time of peace, the army continues to play the rôle of channel for vertical circulation, but at such periods this rôle is far less extensive than in time of war.

2. THE CHURCH AS A CHANNEL OF VERTICAL CIRCULATION

The second principal channel of vertical circulation has been the Church. The Church plays this rôle only when it is growing in social importance. In periods of its decay, or at its very beginning, the rôle of the Church, as a channel for social circulation, is small and insignificant. In periods of its greatest expansion, the rôle tends also to be diminished, thanks to the tendency of social seclusion of the highest Church strata and to an intensive influx of nobility into these strata, as an easy way to further elevation. The history of the Christian Church may give a corroboration and illustration of these statements.

After the legalization of the Christian religion, the Christian Church began to play the rôle of ladder up which a great many slaves and serfs began to climb, sometimes to the highest and most influential social positions. The followers of the Christian religion, at its beginning, were recruited principally out of the lowest social strata. After the legalization of Christianity, the doors of the Christian Church and of its high ranks, were still open to humble people. The slaves and serfs and men of humble origin, who became Church officials, obtained through the Church their liberty and high positions.

Under the Merovingians and Carolingians, we see many of the

most influential bishops and statesmen who came of the strata of slaves, serfs, peasants, artisans, and so on. This process continued later. Taking into consideration the fact that a bishop in the Middle Ages was not only head of a diocese, but at the same time "a great lord, holding a high position in the hierarchy of the nobility, a feudal prince, and often a very rich man,"[4] it is easy to understand the great rôle of the Church as a ladder for social promotion, or social degradation. Persons who became Popes, Cardinals, the nuncios, patriarchs or highest dignitaries of other Christian denominations, thereby obtained either the highest, or one of the few highest, social positions in medieval society. The Church, as a channel, transposed a great many people from the bottom of society to its apex. Hebbon, archbishop of Rheims, previously a slave; the greatest Pope, Gregory VII, a son of a carpenter; the powerful Archbishop of Paris, Maurice of Sully, a son of a peasant; Bishops Fulbert, Suger; Archbishops Pierre, Robert, Jean Peraud—are a very few examples of a great many climbers of the Church ladder. My study of the Roman Catholic Popes has shown that of 144 Popes, for whom the data are available, 28 were of humble origin, and 27 came from the middle classes.[5] In England, Gretton says:

> In the old days (of a rigid stratification) the only ladder of advancement from the lower grades of society to the higher had been the Church. The poor men who became great ecclesiastical dignitaries and thereby great political forces had for the most part risen from the peasantry, the yeomen farmers, and the skilled laborers.[6]

In this way some humbly born became world rulers, who were able to put down and raise up kings (Gregory VII and Henry IV), to elevate thousands of people of a low and noble origin. The institution of celibacy of the Roman Catholic Church still more facilitated the intensiveness of its shifting rôle. Its dignitaries, at least, juridically, did not have a posterity; after their death their positions were filled by new people, partly, at least, from the lower ranks. This called forth an incessant upward current in medieval society. As mentioned, at the climax of the power of the Roman Catholic Church, especially in the twelfth, thirteenth, fourteenth, and fifteenth centuries, a great influx of nobles into its high ranks (as Popes and Cardinals), the influx of such families as Visconti, Orsini, Segni, Gaetani, Borgia, Guidoni, Colonna, Medici, Savelli, and the influx into the less high ranks of the less prominent noble families, somewhat weakened the intensiveness and generality of the circulation througn this channel. None the less, the mobility continued in a fair degree.

Being a channel for an upward current, the Church was also a channel for a downward current. It is enough to point out the hundreds of thousands of heretics, pagans, Church enemies, criminals, who were put down by Church agencies, tried, tortured, degraded, ruined, executed, banished. We know well that among these degraded people there were a considerable number of kings and dukes, princes and lords, aristocrats and nobles of high rank and position.

During the last few centuries, when the social power of the Church began to decline, its function as a channel began to decrease also. Moving up and down within the Church ranks still goes on, but it does not have the same importance among the totality of social ranks as it had before. The vertical currents within the Church stratification do not agitate other social currents to such an extent as they did before. This is a natural result of a decreasing social power of the Christian Church during the last two centuries.

What has been said of the Christian Church may be said also of other religious organizations. Buddhism and Mohammedanism, Tao-ism and Confucianism, even Hinduism and Judaism, in spite of the caste-character of these religious organizations, have played the rôle of channels of vertical circulation in the corresponding societies. In the periods of their growth and expansion they elevated their partisans, not only within their own organizations, but within the ranks of the whole society. The greater part of such organizations, having been open at the earlier stages of their history, and having recruited their followers from all social strata and especially from the lower ones, gave people of such origin the possibility of climbing to high social strata generally, through their ladder. The personal example of Mohammed himself, and his first successors, is a conspicuous illustration of this. The history of Buddhism, and of

Confucianism in China, gives many further corroborations of the statement. And while elevating some people, these religious organizations, at the same time, degraded others. As in the Christian Church, their importance has been relatively great in the period of their growth and triumph; greatly decreased in the period of their decay or weakening.

3. THE SCHOOL AS A CHANNEL OF VERTICAL CIRCULATION

The institutions for training and education, whatever their concrete forms may be, have always been channels of vertical social circulation. In societies where "the schools" are accessible to all members, the school system represents a "social elevator" moving from the very bottom of a society to its top. In societies where the schools generally, or the privileged kind of schools, are accessible only to its higher strata, the school system represents an elevator moving only within the upper floors of a social building and transporting up and down only the dwellers of these upper stories. Even in such societies, however, some individuals from the lower layers always have succeeded in slipping into the school elevator and, through it, in climbing. As an example of a society in which the school system represents "an elevator" going up and down from the very bottom of a social cone to its top, may be taken Chinese society, on the one hand; on the other, the greater part of the present European countries.

In China recruiting of the people for the highest social and political ranks has been going on principally through school machinery. This fact, not known to many people, gives a reason for styling the Chinese political régime "a system of educational election" or a system of educational selection. The schools are open to all classes. The best pupils, regardless of their family status, are selected and promoted to the higher schools, then to the university; from the university they are placed in high governmental positions; and the most talented, in the highest social ranks. In this way the Chinese school has been permanently elevating the humble born to the upper ranks, and barring or putting down those born in the highest strata, who have not been able to meet its demands. Dr. Chen Huan Chang properly says:

According to Confucius, the school is not only a system of education, but also a system of elections; hence, it combines politics with education. His political doctrine is democratic, and no aristocracy is allowed. . . . Since the students elected from the common people become high officials, the different institutions are really the places where the representatives of the people are elected. The educational test takes the place of universal suffrage. . . . Under the influence of Confucius the Chinese government has been that of Imperial democracy, and everyone has the chance to be prime minister.[7]

The Chinese Mandarin government has been, perhaps more than any other one, the government of the Chinese intellectuals recruited and elevated through the school machinery. Something similar existed in Turkey in some periods, especially at the time of Suleiman the Magnificent. The aristocracy of the Sultans, their guard and higher officials, were recruited from the corps of the Janizaries. This corps was recruited from all social strata. For this purpose the special officials traveled through the Turkish Empire and selected the best children from all, especially from the lowest social classes. After selection, the children were put into special schools and were given a special training. In this way they climbed higher and higher, sometimes to the highest positions in the Empire.[8]

In present Western societies, the schools represent one of the most important channels of vertical circulation. This is manifested in hundreds of forms. Without university or college graduation, an individual cannot factually (in some European countries even juridically) be appointed or obtain any prominent place among the high ranks of government or of many other fields; and, contrariwise, a graduate with a brilliant university record is easily promoted and given a responsible position, regardless of his origin and family. Many fields of social activity (especially professions) are practically closed to a man who does not have a corresponding diploma;[9] a graduate is often paid better than a non-graduate at the same position. Social promotion of a great many prominent men in present democracies has been made essentially through the channels of the school machinery: in spite of their humble origin, they made a good record in the schools and in this way climbed to a relatively high stratum from which a further promotion was much easier than from the low stratum in which they were born. The comparative easiness of social climbing through the school channel is understood now by a great many people. Hence at the present moment is seen an inundation of our universities and colleges by hundreds of thousands of students. This is a brilliant confirmation of the above statements. This "channel rôle" of the present schools has now become much greater than before because the present schools have taken many functions previously performed by the Church and family and some other organizations. From this increase in the social importance of the schools follows the possibility of doing either a great social service, if the schools are properly organized, or a great harm, if their organization is defective (see below).

As a type of society in which the school functions as a channel of circulation in the upper strata only, may be mentioned the Indian caste-society as it is depicted in religious and juridical sources. Perhaps in no other society has learning and knowledge been so highly appreciated as in the Indian caste-society. In *The Sacred Books of India,* beginning with *The Upanishads* and ending with the codes like *The Instituts of Vishnu, The Laws of Manu, Gautama, Brichaspati, Narâda, Apastamba,* etc., knowledge is declared to be a power which holds the World in order and rules the Universe. Initiation and learning are declared here as the second birth which is more important than the physical birth. Because "the father and mother produce the body only," while "the teacher causes the pupil to be born a second time by imparting to him sacred learning, therefore, this second birth is the best." [10] "It is real, exempt from age and death." [11]

Correspondingly, through education and training an individual passes from one order to another: the orders of student, householder, ascetic, and hermit; passes from one social position to a higher one. In this sense the school here, as everywhere, performs the same function of "social elevator." But—and this is the difference from the previous type of society—in a caste-society education and instruction have been forbidden for the lower caste. This is seen in the codes, for the caste of Sûdra.[12] Similar situations we find in some periods of the European societies also. In England under Richard II, was issued the following decree: "No bondman or bondwoman shall place their children at school, as has been done, so as to advance their children in the world." The decree manifests clearly the rôle of the school as a channel of circulation and makes an attempt to close it for the members of the lower strata. Since entering "the elevator" has been forbidden to them, naturally this way of social elevation, as a rule, has not been accessible for the members of the lower castes and classes. They have had to have other channels for their upward movement.

4. GOVERNMENTAL GROUPS, POLITICAL ORGANIZATIONS, AND POLITICAL PARTIES AS CHANNELS OF VERTICAL CIRCULATION

Political organizations, beginning with the government and ending with the political party, have played the rôle of "the elevator" also. A man who sometimes enters the lower ranks of the officials or the personal service of an influential ruler is automatically carried up by "the elevator" because in a great many countries there has existed a rule of automatic promotion of officials in the course of time. Besides, an official, or a personal servant of a ruler has always had a chance of rapid elevation, if his service has been especially valuable. As a result, a great many persons, born in the strata of slaves or serfs or peasants or artisans, have climbed to prominent and conspicuous positions. This is true of the past, as well as of the present. In Rome, especially after the time of Augustus, the elevation of slaves, serfs, or freemen through this "ladder" was proceeding on a large scale. We meet a similar picture in the Merovingian and the Carolingian periods, and throughout the Middle Ages. Personal serfs of different rulers, being engaged in governmental functions, became rulers themselves. Such was the origin of many medieval dukes and counts, barons and nobles.

In a somewhat different form, this condition continues to exist now. The careers of a considerable number of prominent statesmen were begun either at the post of private secretary of an influential politician, or as an official of a low rank. By grasping any opportunity, they have succeeded in promoting themselves sometimes into higher ranks; sometimes to the highest positions. Their children, born in a higher stratum than their parents, continue the upward movement; as a result, within two or three generations, the family has risen considerably.

In democratic countries, where the institution of election plays a decisive rôle in the recruiting of rulers and leaders, political organizations continue to play their rôle as channel, though in a somewhat different form. In order to be elected, a man must manifest in some way his personality, aspirations, and ability to perform successfully the functions of a governor, or a representative, or a senator, or a mayor, or a minister, or a president. The easiest way is in political activity and participation in a political organization. Without this, there is small chance of coming to the attention of the electorate and of being elected. Besides, almost all candidates now are nominated by political organizations, and there is little possibility of being elected without political affiliation. Hence, as a channel of social circulation, political organizations play now an especially important part. Many functions which previously belonged to the Church, to the government, and to other social bodies, are now taken over by political parties. There is no need to say that a great majority of political leaders, rulers, statesmen, senators, representatives and officials of present democratic countries have climbed to their positions through the channel of political parties. This is especially true of those of them who were born in a low social stratum. R. Michels rightly says:

> Without party organization many socially useful elements would be lost, in the sense that they would never change their social class, and remain all their life long in the proletariat. . . . All gifted elements (among the proletariat) consider party organization with its places and its careers as a very anchor of salvation.[13]

Lloyd George, R. Macdonald, J. Jaures, Guesde, Vandervelde, Turati, Bebel, Adler, Troelstra, Labriola, Herriot, Viviani, O. Braun, Liebnecht, Ebert, Th. Masaryk, E. Benesh, Snowden, Coolidge—these are only a few names out of thousands. But for this channel, many of the most prominent politicians and statesmen never could climb to high position.

What is true of large political parties is also true of the local and small political organizations, whatever their names may be. Every town and village has its political bosses and leaders. One of the channels for their local promotion has been the local political organization or party.

5. THE PROFESSIONAL ORGANIZATIONS AS CHANNELS OF VERTICAL CIRCULATION

Some of these organizations have also played a prominent part in the vertical transposition of individuals. Such are scientific, literary, and art institutions and organizations. As the entrance to these organizations has been relatively free to all who displayed a corresponding ability, regardless of the status of families, and as an ascent within these institutions has been followed by a general elevation in the social position of a corresponding individual, therefore, many scientists and scholars, lawyers and literary men, artists and musicians, painters and architects, sculptors, physicians, and players, dancers, and singers, born in humble families, have climbed up through this channel. The same is true of many people born in the middle strata and elevated to still higher social layers. Among 829 British men of genius, studied by Havelock Ellis, there were 71 who were the sons of unskilled laborers and climbed to very high positions principally through this channel. About 16.8 per cent of the most prominent men of Germany were born in the laboring class and climbed up through the professional ladder. In France, among the most prominent literary men, we find about 10 or 13 per cent who came from the laboring class and obtained prominence and high social position in the same way. In the United States, out of 1,000 men of letters, at least 187 rose to prominence through this channel. Four per cent of the most prominent Russian scientists (academicians) who came of peasantry, rose through the same channel. If such is the situation with the most prominent men of genius, it is comprehensible that a great many less prominent professionals have somewhat improved their social position by the same "elevator." Illustrations may be given of many motion-picture players (Gloria Swanson, Douglas Fairbanks, etc), many singers (Chaliapin), many actors, painters, artists, composers, and writers who, being born in a humble family, through this channel have promoted themselves to a very high economic, occupational, and social position, and have obtained wealth, fame, titles, degrees, and so on. Such is the situation now; such in essence has it been in the past.[14]

The press, especially newspapers, must be mentioned as a specific kind of professional institution, important as a channel of vertical circulation. At the present moment the press plays a considerable rôle in this respect. It may efficiently create, at least for a certain time, a brilliant career for a nullity, and ruin the career of a man of great capacity. Directly and indirectly it plays an enormous rôle as a "social elevator." "Publicity" is now something without which any rapid promotion is extremely difficult. It creates fame, often out of nothing; it discovers and ruins talent; it may transform average ability into a genius; it may suffocate a real genius and make of him a social stupidity. Hence, those social groups which control the press and publications play a great part in social circulation. They represent one of the most noisy, efficient, and rapidly moving elevators of social circulation.

6. WEALTH-MAKING ORGANIZATIONS AS A CHANNEL OF SOCIAL CIRCULATION

Whatever may be the concrete forms of wealth-making organizations—land owning or commerce, automobile- or oil-producing and manufacturing, mining or fishing, speculation or brigandage, profiteering or military plundering—the corresponding groups, institutions, and gangs have always played the rôle of channel for rise or fall in vertical social circulation. Already, in a great many primitive tribes the leaders have been those who have been wealthy. Accumulation of wealth led to the social elevation of such persons. Such has been the situation among the Janklits, the Takuli, the Chinks, the Kirghizes, the Kurijaks, the Ovaherere, and among many other preliterate groups.[15] Since the earliest time throughout history is seen a close correlation of wealth and aristocracy. As a general rule, which is broken only in some exceptional periods, those who have been noble have been rich, and *vice versa.* When a discrepancy between nobility and wealth appears (the nobles are poor; the wealthy are disfranchised), such discrepancy has usually been very short-lived: either the poor nobles, through violence and plundering, appropriated the wealth and became rich; or the rich bought and obtained privileges and nobility. The ways of history have been various; its balance has always been the same: a cumulation of wealth and high social position. In this way the discrepancy is abolished and the equilibrium reestablished. René Worms, Pareto and Bouglé are right, saying, "If it is easy to maintain a prestige being idle, it is difficult to keep it being poor." [16] The Patricians, the *nobiles,* the equestrians, and the senatorial class in Rome; the upper classes in Greece, after the reforms of Solon and others; the ancient highest strata among Russians, among Germans, French, and Celts, and so on, were at the same time the wealthiest classes, as long as they kept their power and privileges. Even in a society with a nobility of birth, the nobility sprang often from non-noble but prosperous ancestors; only in later generations has it become "noble by birth." Even in such a society, the promotion of a successful wealth maker, regardless of his origin, has always been possible. To perceive this, it is enough to remember the great social influence of the rich slaves, like Trimalchio, Pallas, Narcissus, and others, in Roman society; it is enough to remember the great social influence of the Jewish money lenders in Europe and in Turkey in the Middle Ages: in spite of the relatively disinherited status of the poor Jews, their richest strata have always been among the upper social strata of medieval and modern society. As money began to play a more important part in medieval Europe, money makers from the lower classes began to climb up; the rôle of the money-making class as a whole began to increase with their privileges and social status. Doctor Gretton, in regard to the rise of the English money-making class (middle class in his terminology) properly says:

> While in the fifteenth century the aristocracy and landed gentry were cutting one another's throats, the Middle class went on making money . . . And, as a result, the nation awoke suddenly to the fact that new masters had arisen in the land. The Middle class, and especially its most successful money-makers rapidly promoted themselves and superseded, in considerable part, the aristocracy of birth, or that of the Church, or that of an intellectual ability. With their

money they bought all wanted titles and privileges from the Crown. In the time of James I, already, "mercers, grocers, customs comptrollers, goldsmiths, merchants and mayors of provincial towns appear as country gentlemen with their coats of arms." The men of this class rose to the most prominent positions. Illustration is given by the Princes of the East India Company. "The path by which they rose to eminence was open to any man in the kingdom."[17]

The process was similar in France. The elevation of the French bourgeoisie and of its most successful money makers was due to the same "channel" of successful money making. Especially since the fifteenth century "money began to rule France; everything now could be bought: power and honors, civil and military positions, and even nobility itself."[18] "The money makers were those who rose to eminence. They constituted a new feudalism and a new aristocracy." The prominent aristocratic families of these centuries such as Ponchet, de Briconnet, de Beanne, les du Peirat, les Princes, les Bonald, les Vigouroux, les Roquette and so on, all are families from a lower social stratum which climbed to the top of the society through successful money making. "Since Louis XIII up to the Revolution every rich man became a noble, as at the beginning of the Middle Ages every brave man became a cavalier. . . . In this period money meant everything and was everything." The humble money makers bought any title and any position that they wanted. The letters of ennoblement began to be sold by the crown *en masse*.[19] The father of Mme. Pompadour, Poisson, exclaimed at one aristocratic party: "A foreigner probably would accept us for the princes. In fact, you, Mr. Montmartel, are a son of a saloon-keeper; you, Salvalette, are a son of a gardener; you, Bouret, are a son of a lackey; and I myself?" This picture is representative.

The later stages of the history of Greece and Rome were in the same state. The aristocracy of these periods was recruited principally from the class of the successful money makers, regardless of their origin.[20]

Even in a caste-society, money making is a "social elevator," regardless of the caste. With an increase of wealth a man's social status rises. "Last year I was a jolaha (weaver); now I am a sheikh (because I am more wealthy); next year if prices rise, I shall be a saiyid"—such is the typical promotion through the channel of wealth.[21]

There is no need to say that at the present time money making is one of the most common and omnipotent ways of social promotion. A successful money maker is the greatest aristocrat of modern democratic society. If a man is rich, he is at the top of the social cone, no matter whence he has come, nor how he got his money. Governments and universities, princes and churchmen, poets and writers, societies and organizations, abundantly pour upon him all honors and titles, scientific and other degrees, positions and what not. All doors are open to him, beginning with that of king of a great empire to the door of a "very radical anticapitalist revolutionary." As a rule, almost all may be bought and almost all may be sold. A new Jugurtha may say of the present society: *urbem venalem et mature perituram, si emptorem invenerit.*

The following data may show to some extent what kind of activities in the nineteenth and twentieth centuries in the United States have been leading to money making and, through it, to rise in the economic and social strata:[22]

American Millionaires According to Their Occupations	Number	Per Cent
Manufacturers	193	29.2
Bankers, brokers	138	20.9
Merchants	78	11.8
Transport organizers	63	9.5
Lawyers	40	6.0
Inventors	29	4·4
Editors, publishers	22	3·3
Mining	18	
Real estate	17	
Lumbermen	17	
Artists, actors, theatre managers	17	
Telegraph, telephone, gas, light	12	
Statesmen	8	14.9
Land owners	4	
Physicians, psychiatrists	4	
Clergymen	2	
Total	662	100.0

The groups which, like the editors, publishers, statesmen, clergymen, succeeded in climbing by the ladder of the profession and at the same time by the ladder of money making, could be regarded as people climbing up through a combined system of the money making and other "elevators."

7. FAMILY AND OTHER CHANNELS OF SOCIAL CIRCULATION

Of other channels of vertical circulation may be mentioned the family and marriage with a person of another social stratum. Such a marriage usually leads one of the parties either to social promotion or degradation. In this way some people have made their careers; some others have ruined them. In the past, a marriage to a slave or a member of the lower caste led to the degradation of a higher party and his offspring.

According to the Roman law, a free woman married to a slave became a slave and lost her *status libertatis;* a child born of a slave woman, though by a free citizen, became a slave also. Similar degradation fell on a man or a woman of a high caste who married a woman or a man of lower caste.

At the present moment in our democratic societies, we see a mutual "gravitation" of rich brides by the poor but titled bridegrooms. In this way both parties try: one to get a financial basis for keeping his titled position on a necessary level, the other to get a social promotion through money.

Besides these channels there undoubtedly are many others, but they seem to be not so important as the preceding ones. These have always been the most common and convenient elevators which have carried up and down the streams of people "traveling" in the vertical plane. Those who, like farmers and manual workers, have not tried to enter one of these elevators, have been doomed to stay in the lower strata, having very little chance either to go up or down. Playing in all periods to this or that degree the rôle of channels, each of the above institutions has played an especially important part in a definite society in a certain period. The army plays a great rôle in a period of war and social disturbances; a moderate one in a period of peace. The Church had a great importance in the Middle Ages, and has a less one at the present time. Money making and political activity have great significance now and had less a few centuries ago.

Varying in their concrete forms and in their size, the channels of vertical circulation exist in any stratified society, and are as necessary as channels for blood circulation in the body. So much for this point. Let us now pass to another problem closely connected with that of channels.

[1] LUCHAIRE, A., *Social France at the Time of Philip Augustus*, pp. 10, 147, 271, New York, 1922.

[2] See COULANGES, DE, F., *op. cit.*, pp. 96 *et seq.*, 424, and *passim;* VIOLLET, *op. cit.*, p. 251; FLACH, *Les origines de l'ancienne France*, Vol. I, pp. 111 *et seq.;* KOLABINSKA, M., *op. cit., passim.*

[3] Charles B. Davenport rightly says of the American military officers: "In time of actual battling, selection for advancement is made on the ground of performance—the inferior officers fall; the successful ones are given the higher commands. Our Civil War showed this clearly." *Naval Officers, Their Heredity and Development*, p. 1, Washington, D. C., 1919.

It is enough to look through such publications as BURKE's *Peerage and Landed Gentry*, to see what a great percentage of the English aristocracy originated through the military service and climbed up by the army ladder.

[4] See DE LA TOUR, IMBART, *Les élections épiscopales dans l'église de France du XI au XII siècles*, pp. 219 *et seq., passim;* GUIZOT, F., *The History of Civilization*, Vol. I, pp. 115 *et seq.;* KOLABINSKA, M., *op. cit.*, pp. 16-17, 22-23, 57-61; LUCHAIRE, A., *Social France at the Time of Philip Augustus*, Chaps. II to VII.

[5] SOROKIN, P., "The Monarchs and the Rulers."

[6] GRETTON, R., *The English Middle Class*, p. 151.

[7] CHEN HUAN CHANG, *The Economic Principles of Confucius*, Vol. 1, pp. 87-94. See also *Lî-Kî*, Bk. IX, Sec. III, p. 5.

[8] See LYBYER, *The Ottoman Empire in the Time of Suleiman the Magnificent.*

[9] As an illustration of the above, the following figures concerning occupation and education of 24,442 employed boys in New York are representative:

Last Grade Completed	Boys' Present Occupation			
	Professions, Per Cent	Clerical, Per Cent	Business, Per Cent	Labor, Per Cent
Fifth	1.1	13.4	3.0	22.4
Sixth	1.4	13.3	4.7	19.0
Seventh	1.6	18.5	4.8	13.0
Eighth	2.4	35.2	6.9	8.5
1 year high school	3.2	46.0	6.6	6.9
2 years	4.9	49.2	9.5	4.5
3 years	6.1	51.6	11.1	3.6
4 years	9.2	59.4	10.0	2.4

"The more education a boy has the more likely he is to get into the professional, clerical, and retail business occupations. The less education a boy has the greater his chances are of becoming a laborer." BURDGE, H. G., *Our Boys,* p. 339, New York, 1921.

It is possible to give hundreds of tables which show the same correlation between social status and education.

[10] See, *e.g., Apastamba,* I.I, 14-17; I.I, 5-6.

[11] *Laws of Manu,* II, 148.

[12] *Laws of Manu,* II, 148.

[13] MICHELS, R., "Eugenics in Party Organization," *Problems in Eugenics,* pp. 232-237, 1912.

[14] It is interesting to note that the "elevator" of arts seems to have been more accessible to the humble born than that of science and other professions. F. Maas's study of the German men of genius has shown that out of all such men who came from the strata of the peasants, and proletariat (635 men were studied) 32 per cent were in arts, 27.8 in science, 4.3 in medicine, 4.6 in law, 5.0 in education. Dr. Philiptschenko's study of the contemporary Russian scientists, scholars, and representatives of arts, has shown that among the scientists only 2.9 per cent came out of the class of proletariat and artisans, while this per cent among the representatives of arts is 9.6. See MAAS, F., "Uber die Herkunftsbedingungen der Geistigen Führer," *Archiv für Sozialwiss.,* Vol. XLI, pp. 161-167; PHILIPTSCHENKO, T., "Stat. resultaty ankety, etc." *Bulletin of the Bureau of Eugenics,* No. 1, p. 12, Petrograd, 1922; No. 2, p. 12, 1924.

[15] *Cf.,* DESCAMPS, P., *op. cit., passim;* KOVALEVSKY, M., *Soziologija,* Vol. II, pp. 188 *ff.*

[16] BOUGLÉ, CHARLES, *La démocratie devant la science,* p. 92; WORMS, RENÉ *Philosophie des sciences sociales,* Vol. III, pp. 66 *ff.,* 1907; PARETO, V., *Systèmes socialistes,* Vol. I, p. 8.

[17] GRETTON, R., *op. cit.,* pp. 91 *et seq.,* 105 *et seq.,* 146 and *passim.*

[18] D'AVENEL, *Les riches depuis sept cents ans,* pp. 9, 10; LUCHAIRE, A., *Social France at the Time of Philip Augustus,* pp. 325 *et seq.,* 421 *et seq.,* and Chap. XIII.

[19] KOLABINSKA, M., *op. cit.,* Chaps. II to IV.

[20] See, besides the works of Plato, Aristotle, Thucydides, Polybius and Xenophon, HALLIDAY, W. R., *The Growth of the City State,* pp. 111 *et seq.* and *passim,* Small & Maynard Company; DAVIS, W., *The Influence of Wealth in Imperial Rome,* pp. 62, *et seq.,* 1910.

[21] *The Imperial Gazetteer of India,* Vol. I, p. 329.

[22] SOROKIN, P., "American Millionaires and Multimillionaires," p. 639.

CHAPTER IX

MECHANISM OF SOCIAL TESTING, SELECTION, AND DISTRIBUTION OF INDIVIDUALS WITHIN DIFFERENT SOCIAL STRATA

I. DEFINITION

IN ANY society there are a great many people who want to climb up into its upper strata. Since only a few succeed in doing this, and since, under normal conditions, the vertical circulation does not have an anarchical character, it seems that in any society there is a mechanism which controls the process of vertical circulation. This control seems to consist in the first place, in testing individuals with respect to their suitableness for the performance of a definite social function; in the second place, in the selection of individuals for a definite social position;[1] in the third place, in a corresponding distribution of the members of a society among different social strata, in their promotion, or in their degradation. In other words, within a stratified society, there seem to exist not only channels of vertical circulation, but also a kind of a "sieve" within these channels which sifts the individuals and places them within the society. The essential purpose of this control is to distribute the individuals so that each is placed according to his talents and able to perform successfully his social function. Wrongly placed, individuals do their social work poorly; and, as a result, all society suffers and disintegrates. Though there scarcely has existed any society in which the distribution of individuals has been quite perfect, in complete accordance with the rule, "Everybody must be placed according to his ability,"[2] nevertheless, many societies have existed for a long time and this very fact means that their mechanism of social testing, selecting, and distributing their members has not been wholly bad and has performed its function in a more or less satisfactory way. The problems to be discussed now are: What represents this mechanism of selection and distribution of individuals? How and on what bases does it test, select and distribute them?

The first question may be answered in the following way: in any given society this mechanism is composed of all the social institutions and organizations which perform these functions.

As a general rule these institutions are the same as those which function as channels of vertical circulation. These institutions, such as the family, army, church, school, political, professional, and occupational organizations are not only a channel of social circulation, but are at the same time, the "sieves" which test and sift, select and distribute the individuals within different social strata or positions.

Some of them, as the school and family, are the machinery which tests principally the *general qualities* of individuals necessary for a successful performance of a great many functions; such as their general intelligence, health, and social character. Some other institutions, such as many occupational organizations, are the machinery which tests the *specific quality* of individuals necessary for a successful performance of a specific function in a given occupation; the voice of a prospective singer, the oratorical talent of a prospective politician, the physical strength of a future heavyweight champion, and so forth. Turn now to the problem of how these institutions perform these functions and what principal types of testing, selection, and distribution exist in different societies. This will give us a somewhat deeper insight into many institutions, and will show that many of them, quite absurd at first sight, have been, indeed, quite understandable under existing circumstances.

2. FAMILY STATUS AS AN INDIRECT TEST OF ABILITIES AND AS A BASIS FOR SOCIAL SELECTION AND DISTRIBUTION OF INDIVIDUALS

It is easy to say that in a perfect society all its members should be placed in such positions as correspond to their abilities. But it is difficult to decide whether one has a definite ability or not, whether he has it in a greater degree than another man, and what kind of talent there is in every individual. Even now with psychological testing devices these problems cannot be solved successfully in a great many cases. Still more difficult was the solution in the past. Under such circumstances society had to invent an indirect criterion for discovering and ascertaining the abilities of its members. By way of trial and error, one of the most important criteria for this purpose was found in the character and the social status of a family in which an individual was born. Parents who were clever and of high standing were accepted as a proof of an offspring's superior intelligence and suitableness for a high social position; an origin in a humble family was taken as evidence of a man's inferiority which made him suitable only for a humble position. Thus arises the institution of inheritance of the social position of the parents by the children; one born in a family of high standing deserves to be placed also in high strata; one born in a humble family should be placed in a humble position. Such has been the situation in many past societies, and such, to some extent, it is still.

In this way the family has been made a first criterion for the judgment of a man's general and specific abilities, and correspondingly, a first basis for a prospective social placement of individuals. In this sense, the family has played an enormous rôle as a first basis for social selection of individuals for a definite social position. It has also been a piece of machinery which has controlled the social distribution of members of a society. Though using the family as a social test, and as an instrument of social distribution of individuals has, probably, been established by way of a "trial and error," nevertheless, the fundamental reasons for such a use were well known long ago, many centuries before Christ. These reasons are two: heredity and education. Origin from a prominent and good family makes probable a good heredity and good education; origin from a poor family often means a poor heredity socially, mentally, and physically, and poor training. These two reasons, which the present eugenists, criminologists, and pyschiatrists stress, were well known in the past; more than this, many devices of the present eugenists were already in use long ago.[3]

The above explains why this method of testing individuals came about, and why the family became one of the earliest bases for the social distribution of the members of a society within its layers. This rôle the family has played throughout history.

The importance of the family in this respect, however, has varied from country to country, from period to period. Among the many conditions which have influenced this important function of the family, it is possible to mention here only two: the first, the stability of the family; the second, the number and the character of other educational and testing agencies in a society. As an empirical, and for this reason, an approximate, generalization may be formulated the following proposition:

Other conditions being equal, *in a society where the family is stable, marriage is sacred and durable; intermarriages between different social strata are few; the training and education of the children go on principally within the family; the number of other testing and selective agencies is small; and they receive the young generation for training only at a relatively late age; in such a society, the family, as a testing, selecting, and distributing agency plays an exclusively important rôle. In such a society, an inheritance of the father's position by the son is usual and natural. And contrariwise, in a society where the family is unstable, the marriage is easily dissolved; intermarriages between different strata are common; the education of the children after their early period, goes on outside of the family, in other institutions; and their number is relatively numerous; in such a society the family as a testing and selecting agency plays a rôle far less important than in the first type of society.* In such a society an inheritance of the social position of a father by his children is less necessary and becomes less common. The reasons for this generalization are at hand. Since the family is unstable and intermarriage is common, and the marriage is easily dissolved (divorces), there cannot be either purity of blood, as a hereditary basis for a superiority and inferiority; or a sacredness of the family, or family pride, or a high social evaluation of the family institution. Since the family is easily disintegrated, such a family could not be a good and efficient educational agency. Since the children, at an early age, pass into the hands of the kindergarten, public or private schools, and other similar agencies, the family cannot play an exclusive rôle as an educational and testing institution; it cannot shape the children so strongly as in a society where all mental and moral equipment of the children is furnished in and by the family. In brief, in such a society the family loses its hereditary as well as its exclusive educational value; hence, naturally, it loses its exclusive importance as the basis for an evaluation and social placing of an individual. These functions then are performed by other agencies. Finally, in such a society a hereditary caste or hereditary transmission of social position becomes impossible, as well as much less reasonable than it is in a society where the family determines—biologically and socially—the innate and acquired properties of the individual. Such in brief are the reasons for the above generalization. As an example of a society of the first type it is possible to point out: the India caste-society, the early Roman and Greek societies, the society of the Middle Ages in the period from about the tenth to the fourteenth centuries, and many other groups having the so-called patriarchal family. In them, the family was stable; the marriage bond, sacred and indissoluble. Intercaste, or interplebeian and patrician, or interstrata marriages were prohibited. The education and vocational training of the children went on principally within the family. There were very few schools outside of it. If there were, the teachers, as in the caste-society, had a purely private character, and the relation of a pupil and the teacher was the relation of a father and son. Occupations were learned principally within the family. The family was a school, a vocational training center, and an industrial institution at the same time. The hereditary transmission of the parents' social status to children was a natural outcome of such a situation; hence, an exclusive importance of the family status as a decisive basis for a social placement of individuals. This shows that the correlation of all these traits was almost inevitable and under such conditions very reasonable. Now take the same Roman and Greek society at a later period of its history; or European society in the nineteenth century and especially at the present moment; or during such periods as that of the Renaissance in Italy, or the Reformation in Europe, not to mention other periods of social upheaval.

The family is disintegrated. It no longer has a sacred character. Marriage is easily dissolved and divorce is an everyday occurrence. Interstrata marriages are common and are no longer prohibited by either law, religion or morals. The purity of blood of the noble and the humble no longer exists. Children are kept within the family bosom for only a few years. Even during this period the parents, especially the father, see them only in the morning and at night. They grow up outside of the family. At an early age they are taken by neighborhood gangs, by kindergartens, by schools, and after that time they are almost beyond the influence of the parents. The education, the test, the occupational training, the equipment for their life in society is going on outside of the family. Under such conditions the function of testing is then performed factually by other institutions. Under such conditions the family test naturally loses its exclusive importance. The family status ceases to be an exclusive basis for social placement of the individuals; hereditary transmission of occupation or social status becomes factually much less possible and less necessary. With the disappearance of the closed hereditary castes and orders in such a society, and, an intensive vertical circulation, the habit develops of judging the individuals not so much according to their family status as according to their personal qualities as they are discovered by the school, by their occupations, and other testing and selecting institutions. Such is the correlation of all these traits and their mutual adhesion. Such is "the style" of the two types of societies in this respect. The above shows what is meant by the fluctuation in the importance of the family as a testing and selecting agency. At the present moment, in democratic countries, its rôle is much less important in this respect than in societies of other types. However, even now the family continues to perform this function.

3. THE SCHOOL AS A TESTING AND SELECTIVE AND DISTRIBUTIVE AGENCY

The second fundamental kind of machinery for testing the abilities of the individuals and determining their social position has been the school. The family is the agency which gives the first test; earlier than any other group, it determines the life career and the prospective social position of the children. But even in the caste-society the family test and influences, to some degree, are retested and reconsidered by other agencies, the educator and the teacher among them; still more true is this of societies of another type, especially of those in which we live.

If at the present time the family status and education outline roughly the life career of its children, the school is the next agency which retests the "decisions" of a family, and very often and very decisively changes them. Up to the last few years, the school was regarded primarily as an educational institution. Its social function was seen in "pouring" into a student a definite amount of knowledge, and, to some extent, in shaping his behavior. The testing, the selective, and the distributive functions of the school were almost completely overlooked, although these functions of the school are scarcely less important than that of "enlightenment" and "education." During the last few years many specialists in different fields have begun to see these functions. At the present moment it is certain that the school, while being a "training and educational" institution, is at the same time, a piece of social machinery, which tests the abilities of the individuals, which sifts them, selects them, and decides their prospective social position. In other words, *the essential social function of the school is not only to find out whether a pupil has learned a definite part of a textbook or not;* but through all its examinations and moral supervision to discover, in the first place, which of the pupils are talented and which are not; what ability every pupil has and in what degree; and which of them are socially and morally fit; in the second place, to eliminate those who do not have the desirable mental and moral qualities; in the third place, through an elimination of the failures to close the doors for their social promotion, at least, within certain definite social fields, and to promote those who happen to be the bright students in the direction of those social positions which correspond to their general and specific abilities. Whether successful or not, these purposes are some of the most important functions of the school. From this standpoint *the school is primarily a testing, selecting, and distributing agency.*[4] In its total the whole school system, with its handicaps, quizzes, examinations, supervision of the students, and their grading, ranking, evaluating, eliminating, and promoting, is a very complicated "sieve," which sifts "the good" from "the bad" future citizens, "the able" from "the dull," "those fitted for the high positions" from those "unfitted." This explains what is meant by the testing, selective, and distributive functions of school machinery.

The intensiveness of this function of the school naturally fluctuates from society to society, from time to time. Among other conditions, it *strongly depends on the extent to which the testing and the sifting of individuals is carried out by other institutions, and especially by the family.* If the family performs this rôle efficiently, in such a way that only an already selected group of children reaches the doors of the schools and enters them, then the testing and the selecting and sifting rôle of the school is not so necessary as in the case when the doors of the school are open for all children, when there is no selection and elimination preceding school entrance. Under such conditions, naturally, there are a great many children incapable of progressing further than the first few grades of school; the number of failures is greater than where there is pre-school selection. Therefore, the elimination work of the school becomes much greater and more pitiless. It increases as it proceeds, going from the lower grades to the higher, from the elementary to the secondary school, from the secondary school to the college. As a result, out of the many pupils who enter the door of the elementary school only an insignificant minority reach the stage of university graduation. The great majority (see below for figures) are eliminated, not only from school, but automatically thereby from climbing up this ladder to high social positions. Part of those eliminated succeed in climbing through another ladder (money making, etc.), but only a small part.[5] The majority of those eliminated from the school through "the school sieve" are doomed to be placed at a relatively lower social position. In this way, in certain societies the school does the work of selection, and bars the social promotion of individuals who have not been barred and selected by the family. This explains the fact that, contrary to the common opinion, universal education and instruction leads not so much to an obliteration of mental and social differences as to their increase. The school, even the most democratic school, open to everybody, if it performs its task properly, is a machinery of the "aristocratization" and stratification of society, not of "leveling" and "democratization." The following representative data show clearly the testing, selective, and eliminating rôle of the school in the United States of America. According to Doctor Ayres,[6] for every 1,000 children who enter the first grade, we have in the higher grades:

723 in the second grade
692 in the third grade
640 in the fourth grade
552 in the fifth grade
462 in the sixth grade
368 in the seventh grade
263 in the eighth grade
189 in the first grade of the high school
123 in the second grade of the high school
81 in the third grade of the high school
56 in the fourth grade of the high school

Admitting that out of 1,000 children who enter the first grade, there must be, owing to the death and increase of population, in the eighth grade, 871, we see that, in fact, we have instead of this figure only 263. The remaining 608 pupils are eliminated and dropped out of school. A similar conclusion is given by Doctor Thorndike.[7] According to his data, 25 per cent of the white children in the United States at the beginning of the twentieth century could reach only the fifth grade. According to Doctor Strayer and Doctor Terman, out of 100 children entering elementary school only about 40 remain to enter the high school and only 10 are graduated from high school.[8] The eliminating rôle of the high school is still greater. According to the data of the Bureau of Education for 1917 and 1918 the students in the first year of high school constituted:

39.8 per cent of the total high-school enrollment, in the second year,
26.9 per cent of the total high-school enrollment, in the third year,

18.8 per cent of the total high-school enrollment, in the fourth year,
14.5 per cent of the total high-school enrollment.[9]

According to data of Francis P. O'Brien, out of 6,141 students who entered high school, only 1,936 were graduated.[10] In this way only an insignificant and highly selected group reaches the college or university. Here the elimination again is continued, and only a part of those who enter the freshman class achieve college graduation.

Later on, the causes of this enormous elimination will be seen; now it is enough to state the fact that the school which is accessible to all, nevertheless, debars eventually the greater part of the entering pupils, and in this way performs the work of social selection of the prospective "dwellers on the higher social strata." With the development of the mental test, this tendency of sifting is likely to become more severe. It is already manifest in such facts as the present testing of prospective students before their college enrollment, and debarring those who do not show a necessary I.Q. and other requisite qualities.[11] In different forms, the school has always performed in the past the same function of physical, moral, and mental selection and elimination of the unfit. For the sake of brevity only one or two illustrations will be given here.

In Indian caste-society, in order to become a member of the high orders of the high caste, a successful student had to overcome such enormous obstacles and to display such physical and especially mental and moral qualities that only few men could meet such a test without failure. According to *Apastamba,* the course of the study of the Vedas continued from 12 to 40 years. During this period the student "shall obey his teacher; except crimes"; he must not contradict him; must care for him, feed him, take food only after the teacher has finished his eating; "every day he shall put his teacher to bed after having washed his teacher's feet and after having rubbed him"; he must go to bed only after having received the teacher's permission; talk to the teacher only standing or sitting and never lying; "and if the teacher stands he shall answer him after having risen also; he shall walk after him, if he walks, run after him, if he runs." Furthermore, "he shall not look at the sun; he shall avoid honey, meat, perfumes, garlands, sleep in the daytime, ointments, collyrium, a carriage, shoes, a parasol, love, anger, covetousness, perplexity, garrulity, playing musical instruments, bathing (for pleasure), cleaning the teeth, elation, dancing, singing, calumny and terror; he shall avoid the gaze and touch of women; gambling, low service; taking things not offered; injuring animate beings; making bitter speeches; he shall speak the truth"; and so on. Contrariwise: "If these rules are transgressed, study drives out the knowledge of the Veda acquired already, from the offender and from his children, besides he will go to hell and his life will be shortened" (not to mention that he loses all chances to become a man of high order).[12]

To suppose that many of the novitiates must have failed in fulfilling these and many other prescriptions would be not far from the truth. Therefore this type of school seems to have performed in the severest form the same function of social testing and selection of the prospective leaders of the Indian society.[13]

Thus in India the aristocracy and the aristocracy of the aristocracy has been sifted, at least, through the two severest social sieves; that of the family and that of the school. In this way, it has been tested biologically, mentally, and morally. As a result we have the most powerful aristocracy of biological and social selection.

Turning to China we see a somewhat different Chinese school which in its own way performs, again, the same sifting of the prospective leaders of the country. In China, unlike India, the schools have been open for all people of all classes. In this respect, the system is similar to that of democratic countries. But, perhaps, more than in the present democracies, education has determined man's social position. If we are to believe the Chinese sources and scholars, there, at least, in some periods, the sifting rôle of the school has been decisive:

Even among the sons of the emperor, the princes, and great officials, if they were not qualified to rites and justice, they should be put down to the class of common people; even among the sons of common people, if they have good education and character and are qualified to rites and justice, they should be elevated to the class of ministers and nobles. . . . Education is the only determining force in social standing.[14]

Only a few individuals could slip through the most complicated scholastic system of the Chinese education and examinations, and reach university graduation. A great majority of those who entered the "school race" have been dropping out of the school, and thus were eliminated as prospective candidates for the highest social positions.

The same may be said of many another school and educational system. So much for the school as a testing and selective agency which controls the social distribution of individuals.

4. THE CHURCH AS A TESTING, SELECTIVE, AND DISTRIBUTIVE AGENCY

What has been said of the school may be said of the Church. In many countries the Church has been the school; and the school, the Church. In such countries their functions have been practically the same. Where these two institutions are strongly separated, as, for instance, in many present societies, the principal difference between the two institutions in regard to social testing and selecting seems to have been that the school has tested principally the intellectual qualities of individuals, the Church, principally, their moral and social characteristics. Where, as in medieval society, the Church was also the school, it performed the universal, intellectual, moral and social-testing function and the selection of individuals. In such societies the selective rôle of the Church has been enormous. In the first place, all "pagans and heretics" have been eliminated from those who could obtain responsible positions. In the second place, they were persecuted and placed at the bottom of the social world, imprisoned, disfranchised, executed. In the third place, the persons who, in the opinion of the Church, have been virtuous, *eo ipso,* have been promoted upward. In this way, the Church has played an enormous rôle in social selection and distribution of individuals among different social strata. At the present moment, in societies like the United States of America the "selective" rôle of the Church, in comparison with that of the school, is considerably less. Nevertheless, it still exists. The opinion of the Church community, the Church affiliation of a man, the man's characterization by the Church authorities and leaders, still play a considerable part in the career of a great many people, beginning with men in a parish and ending with teachers and professors (the Tennessee trial is only a conspicuous example of a great many similar cases), officials, senators, governors and even the presidents of the United States. After what has been said of the school there is no need to dwell longer on the functions of the Church in this respect.

5. FAMILY, SCHOOL, AND CHURCH AS THE AGENCIES OF THE TESTING OF THE GENERAL QUALITIES OF THE INDIVIDUALS. THEIR DECISIVE RÔLE IN DETERMINING THE PROPERTIES OF THE DIFFERENT SOCIAL CLASSES

Before turning to the social agencies which test the specific qualities of individuals, and selecting them for a specific social or occupational group, it is proper to say a few words about the enormous rôle which family, school, and Church play in determining the typical qualities of the higher and lower social strata. As mentioned, these agencies test principally the general biological, mental, and moral qualities of individuals which are relevant for a successful performance of a great many social functions. The point which is to be stressed now is that the character of these selective agencies, or their standards of what is desirable and undesirable, what is good and bad, greatly determines what kind of people will fill the upper and the lower strata of a society. The agencies are the social "sieves" and on the nature of the sieves depends what "human particles" will remain in the upper and what will slip into the lower strata. A few examples are enough to make this clear.

As we have seen, in order to pass successfully the test of the Brahmin school a student had to display not only an ability to learn Vedas, but extraordinary moral and social qualities; a wonderful patience, and self-control, a supernormal power to control all biological impulses, to conquer all temptations, to stand all physical privations, to despise worldly goods and comforts, to seek for the truth, not to fear any earthly authority, and any physical suffering, and so forth. Only men with an extraordinary will power and spirit could meet such a test. As a result, the high Brahminic orders were composed of highly selected men, far above the general intellectual and moral level. Now take the Chinese school. Here also some attention is given to the moral and social qualities of the pupils. But the principal test, nevertheless, has consisted in the knowledge of the classics, in the excellence of the style and literary composition, and in similar matters which have small practical value, do not give any real knowledge of the nature or of causal relations.[15] Hence, the purely literary character of the Chinese governing class recruited from those who successfully have passed this "literary test," its impracticability, and its inability to handle many practical affairs. The "literary character of the school" has determined "the literary and impractical" character of the Mandarin government which is the government of the literary intelligentsia *par excellence*. "What the sieve is, the flour will be." Take, further, the medieval church and school. The people with strong bodily proclivities, especially such as the sex impulse, the people with an independence of opinion, with an anti-dogmatic mind, and so on, as a rule, could not pass through this "ascetic, dogmatic, intolerant" sieve; such people were left either at the bottom of society or were put down, or had to find other social channels for their elevation.

Finally, take the present school in Western countries. Recently its test has been almost exclusively intellectual, plus physical athletics. The present school does not demand any extraordinary moral quality, or anything remotely similar to the demand of the Brahmin school. If a student is not below a general moral standard, he may brilliantly pass the test, providing he is bright from the intellectual standpoint. As far as the upper strata are recruited from such people, they display a pretty intellectual ability and pretty conspicuous moral slackness; cupidity, corruption, demagogy, sexual licentiousness, unstable families, profiteering, hunting for worldly goods often at the cost of social and moral values, dishonesty, cynicism, and "plutocracy." Such are the conspicuous qualities which in abundance are displayed by the governmental, intellectual, and financial aristocracy of our modern time. On the other hand, a natural result of the indicated organization of the present school is its complete inefficiency to improve the moral standard of the population generally. For the last few decades in all European countries and in the United States the number of schools and of those graduated from the elementary and the secondary schools and colleges has increased enormously, far more than the increase of population; and yet, the number of crimes did not decrease but rather increased, and the proportion of the "literate criminals" is relatively increasing while that of the illiterate is relatively decreasing.[16]

These facts are the *"testimonium pauperitatis"* of the moral inefficiency of the present school generally. The relatively low moral standard of the contemporary upper strata in Western countries is partly due to the indicated school organization. These examples show how greatly the qualities of the different "aristocracies" depend on the school organization as a testing and selecting agency. The same may be said of all other similar agencies. On the character of the "sieve" greatly depends the character of the upper as well as the lower social layers. Any social reformer must give careful attention, therefore, to all such agencies not only as institutions of education and training, but, especially, as testing and selective machinery. Many traits which are not important from the "educational standpoint" may have great importance from the testing and selective viewpoints, and contrariwise. However important the traits inculcated by Church, school, and family, not less important are the kind of people who are barred and promoted by them. The selective rôle of social institutions, as Lapouge has brilliantly shown, is, perhaps, even more important for the future of a country, than their "transforming and educational" rôle.[17] Such is the *qualitative* side of the organization of the testing and selective and distributive agencies, in determining the kind of people placed in the upper and lower social strata. Besides the qualitative aspect of the problem, there is also a *quantitative* side

The quantitative problem consists in the number of people passed by the above agencies into the upper strata. The point which I want to stress is that the proportion of the *élite* within the total population is not a small matter. We know that the upper stories of a building must be proportionate to its lower stories; they cannot be too heavy nor too large; if they are, the building crumbles (see above, Part I). After Malthus, we are accustomed to talk about overpopulation or underpopulation in relation to the necessities. I wonder, however, why we do not talk over an overproduction or underproduction of the candidates for the upper strata. It is apparent that no society can exist prosperously if its upper strata compose, say, 50 per cent of the whole population. It is also apparent that the whole government of a country with one hundred millions of population cannot consist of 50 men; they would be omnipotent gods to be able by themselves to perform all governmental functions. This means that for any prosperous society there is an optimal proportion of the upper strata in relation to its population. A great deviation from the point of optimum is likely to be disastrous for a society. Hence, the possibility of an overproduction or underproduction of candidates for the upper strata.

According to the type of society, an overproduction of the upper strata may result either from a disproportionately great procreation of the upper layers in an immobile society or from a too easy testing of the social agencies which permits too many people to slip into the upper classes. An underproduction may follow from a too weak differential procreation of the upper strata or from a too severe sifting of the candidates for the upper strata. The results are that only a very few individuals can pass the sieve. An overproduction of the *élite* through a too great, or underproduction through a too low, procreation may be inferred from the following computation. Let us imagine that we have a small society which consists of five subjects and one ruler. Let us imagine further, that in each generation each of the ruled families leaves five surviving children, while the ruling family leaves seven or four surviving children. Somewhat simplifying the situation, thus, we would have the following picture within a few generations:

Generation	Number of Sub-jects	Their Percentage in the Total Population in Case of Seven and Four Children in Ruling Families		Number of Rulers Who Leave Seven and Four Offspring		Per Cent of the Ruling Class in the Total Population Leaving Seven and Four Children	
1...........	5	83.3	83.3	1	1	16.7	16.7
2...........	25	....	....	7	4	....	....
3...........	125	....	....	49	16	....	....
4...........	625	....	....	343	64	....	....
5...........	3,125	....	....	2,401	256	....	....
6...........	15,630	48.2	94.4	16,807	1,024	51.8	5.6

This hypothetical computation shows what a great difference may come out of a small differential fecundity of the upper and lower classes, and how easy in this way may happen either an overproduction (51.8) or an underproduction of the upper strata.

Still more easily may both cases occur through a too severe or a too loose sifting of the candidates by the testing and selecting agencies for the social distribution of individuals.

Let us glance now at what may be the results of an overproduction, either through the high fertility of the higher classes which in countries of polygamy, as in Turkey, may easily happen; or through a too lenient sifting. All the overproduced prospective *élite* cannot find room in the upper strata. A sharp struggle and competition is inevitable for the high positions among them. In the immobile societies it leads to a pitiless fight among the many candidates for the same high positions of a monarch or other prominent places. We read in history how the sons of the same father in the dynasties of the Osmans, Merovingians, Constantine the Great, Carolingians, and many other noble families systematically assassinated, poisoned, killed, and overthrew each other, not to mention the feuds and warfare among the sons of other different families. From this standpoint these are nothing but a repressive means to reduce the overproduction and to re-establish the necessary equilibrium. Descriptions of such processes fill all the chronicles of the Eastern and Western countries in the past. If an overpopulation generally leads to a war, why not admit that an overproduction of the population of the upper strata may lead to similar results. And the facts just indicated seem to corroborate this hypothesis. A great many palace plots, overthrows and disorders seem to have arisen not without this cause. Somewhat different in form, but similar in substance, are the results of an overproduction of the *élite* in the mobile society. In this case the process runs approximately as follows: The overproduced prospective *élite* cannot find the corresponding high positions. For this reason, the unlucky fellows are dissatisfied and try to start their own "elevating" organizations. As this organization cannot find a privileged place under the existing régime, it has to be critical, undermining, oppositional, radical, revolutionary. The "petty ambitions" of these *élite,* being unsatisfied under existing conditions, seek outlet in social reconstruction or revolution. An additional justification for this is that those who succeed in obtaining the high places under the existing régime cannot have either the necessary prestige or a real ability to "silence" the oppositional forces, because, having slipped through the loosened sieve, they may be simply "lucky fellows" not at all more capable than those who have had "hard luck" and had to remain in the lower strata. In this way, an overproduction of the *élite* due to a too easy test and selection of the testing and selecting agencies leads to social instability, disorders, revolutions.[18]

The same result may be reached in a different way by an underproduction of the *élite* due to a low fertility of the upper strata in an immobile society or to a too severe system of sifting (not to mention its defectiveness from the qualitative standpoint) in a mobile society. In this case the number of the *élite* may be much less than is necessary for filling all high social positions. A part of these positions, therefore, have to be given to unselected men. Such a distribution may spoil *all* benefits of severe selection. Besides, non-admission of the newcomers into the upper aristocracy of birth or too severe a system of sifting may bar from climbing a great many people who deserve to be placed in the upper strata. In this way it may lead to an accumulation of these dissatisfied capable *élite* in the lower strata and create explosive material which may supply the leaders for a dissatisfied mass.

This means that such a system may lead again to social instability and disorders. If, on the contrary, in spite of the severe sifting among the lower strata, there are no real *élite,* the system may lead to an unquestionable supremacy of the severely selected *élite,* and in this way to a social stagnation—the situation which is found in part in the history of India. The same results take place when "the social sieves" are qualitatively bad, when the hereditary aristocracy is degenerated and uncapable, or the system of testing is quite incidental, and the criteria of the selection are defective. If, for instance, such a criterion is only the color of eyes or a gracious literary style, or a hereditary status of the father, without any further inquiry as to what the son's talent may be and what quality of heredity he has, it is evident that the population of the upper governmental strata, recruited on these bases, would scarcely be fitted for a successful performance of governmental functions. As a result, the government developed in this way will be incapable. Below, in the lower strata, there will be many "inborn rulers" who will necessarily try to reach the position corresponding to their talents. Hence, social stability will be undermined from the top, through the government's inability, and from the bottom, through the subversive activity of the badly placed "inborn rulers." The result is again social disorder and instability.

These statements here are almost dogmatic. But it might be possible to lay down a considerable number of historical facts which may corroborate them. Part of them will be given later. Only one contemporary fact is indicated here, for the sake of illustration, and as a practical suggestion.

The statistics of college graduates in the United States give the following ratio of male college graduates per 100,000 males over 20 years of age in the population.

Year	One College Male Graduate Per 100,000 Males Over 20 Years of Age	Year	One College Male Graduate Per 100,000 Males Over 20 Years of Age
1880	687	1910	875
1890	710	1920	1,137
1900	745		

Since 1815, 496,618 degrees have been granted, but more than half of these 496,618 have been conferred since 1900, and of the 358,026 male graduates living June 1, 1920, over half received their degrees after 1905.[19]

This shows a very rapid increase of college graduates in the United States. This means an increase of competition among them and difficulty in finding a position proper to the degree. A greater and greater number of these people must satisfy themselves with a comparatively modest position, poorly paid, and not very attractive. Being convinced that their degree entitles them to a better place, and seeing around them the luxury and the prosperity of other people often without any degree, they cannot help thinking that this country is a bad country, that it treats them with injustice, and that this is the result of capitalist exploitation. To summarize: by increasing the rapidity of production of university graduates; by making graduation comparatively easy; by singing hymns to the great significance of university graduation; by paying little attention to moral education; and by failure to place graduates in proper positions; our universities are preparing dissatisfied elements out of these graduates (the people cursing the existing régime, directly and indirectly helping its undermining), under emergency conditions capable of supplying leaders for any radical and revolutionary movement. Even now, the proportion of sympathizers in a radical "reconstruction" of a "reactionary and plutocratic United States" in this group seems to be much higher than in any other group. "The saloon-socialists" and "pink" and "radical" elements are recruited principally from this and similar groups. To check this result of a relative "overproduction" of *élite* or the pseudo *élite,* it is necessary either to find for them a corresponding place or to increase the severity of the demands necessary for passing through college or any other social "sieve." Contrariwise, instead of a social benefit, a further increase of graduates, B.A.'s., masters, Ph.D's., and so on, may lead to social harm. This may sound like a paradox, to a great many thinkers, and yet, it seems to be true.

This example illustrates the statement about the importance of the proper organization of the qualitative and quantitative sides of the social "sieves." Other testing and selective and distributive agencies will now be taken up.

6. OCCUPATIONAL INSTITUTIONS AS TESTING, SELECTING, AND DISTRIBUTING AGENCIES

The family, the Church and the school are the institutions which principally test the general qualities of men and determine only in general and tentatively in which of the fundamental strata an individual is to be placed, and what kind of activity he is to follow. Their decisions even for those who have successfully passed these "sieves" is, however, not final. It is further retested and reconsidered by those occupational organizations in which the individuals engage. With still greater reason this may be said of those who have not passed through all stages of these general agencies, or have failed in passing. This group is tested principally by the occupational machinery of social testing. The decisions of the general agencies are somewhat final, in the sense that a series of the privileged occupations are closed for a great majority of the "failures" in the family, Church, and school test; and the great majority of the men successfully passing this test is directed principally toward these privileged occupational groups. Even in these fields, however, there are the exceptional revisions and alterations of the decisions of the general agencies by an occupational group. These organizations are especially important as the agencies testing the specific abilities of individuals necessary for successful performance of a given form of occupational work. From all these viewpoints the testing and selecting rôle of an occupational organization is enormous.

Occupational testing and selection is manifested, in the first place, in that the very existence of a specific occupation calls forth a definite selection of the kind of people who may enter and stay in the occupation and who can pursue it. Only individuals who have good voices may enter the occupation of professional singer. Individuals who do not have this quality cannot engage in this occupation, or, if some, by any chance, slip into it, they very soon must leave it, or be discharged. Only a man who has extraordinary physical force may enter and stay in the occupation of a professional heavyweight prizefighter. An absent-minded man cannot be a cashier or a bookkeeper; an absolutely frank and truthful individual, a diplomatist; a feeble-minded, a university professor; a deaf-mute, an orator, preacher or politician; a man who fears blood, a successful surgeon or soldier; a cripple, a professional dancer; and so on. Add to this, the fact that, in order to enter many qualified occupations it is necessary to have good references, different kinds of diplomas, a good school record, a good family status and so on. The man who does not have a corresponding diploma cannot enter the occupations of a teacher or physician, or pharmacist, or engineer, or pastor, or architect, or hundreds of other occupations.

These examples show that the very existence of the occupational division of labor is a powerful selective agency. As a result of such a selection, before and quite independently from the modifying influence of occupational work, the population of a greater part of the occupational groups is biologically, mentally, and morally selected; the members of each occupation must often have some specific common traits different from the members of other occupations. Such is the first form of testing, selection, and social distribution of individuals performed by the occupational groups.[20]

The second fundamental form of social testing, selection, and distribution of individuals by occupational groups is manifested in upward promotion or barring from it, or in a degradation of individuals within the ranks of an occupation, as well as within the interoccupational strata. It is well known that the social careers of those who are admitted to an occupation, whatever it may be, are not equal; some are rapidly climbing up, from an office boy to the president of the corporation, from a soldier to a general, from an instructor to a full professor, from an insignificant official to a governor, from a minister to an archbishop, from a third-class author to a famous writer, from an insignificant actor to a star and so on. Some others throughout their life remain in the same position at which they started; some others are going down: a magnate of capital becomes a poor man; a high officer sinks to a subordinate position; a monarch becomes an overthrown nullity; a pope, a simple priest; a professor, a clerk; a prince, a manual laborer, and so on. Such phenomena of social transposition or social redistribution of individuals are of everyday occurrence. The agencies which do this work are almost exclusively the occupational groups.

After an individual enters an occupation, every day and every hour of his work is a permanent test of his general, as well as his specific ability. Those who, under the existing conditions, happen to be quite fitted for a successful performance of their functions are rapidly rising; the opposite type of men are either static in their career, or are discharged or degraded. In this way, the occupation organization tests and retests individuals, confirms or alters the decisions of the family, the Church, and school testing; distributes its members either according or contrary to the decisions of the agencies of general testing. In many cases there is a complete accordance, the greater and more adequate is the system of testing by the family, Church, and school. The more defective is this testing, the more often it is rejected and altered. In the majority of cases, as the occupational test is quite factual and pragmatic, free from speculation and theorizing, it naturally has a great value, and as a general rule it is final.

The third form of occupational testing, selection, and distribution of individuals is expressed in the fact of shifting an individual from an occupation unsuitable for him to another which better corresponds to his ability and vocation. One of the most important things in the life of everyone is to know exactly to what kind of occupation he is best fitted. Unfortunately a great many people do not know, hence their permanent mistake in choosing a wrong occupation for which they do not have the necessary ability. In such cases occupational testing is an agency which corrects such mistakes. A permanent failure of an individual in performance of his occupational work is an objective and often a pitiless proof that he has entered a wrong occupation. Failure causes his own dissatisfaction, degradation, or discharge. This urges him to try another occupation. Failure here forces him to go to a new occupation, from that to another one, until he is lucky enough to find the job corresponding to his vocation or to be tested objectively as "good for nothing." In the first case, having found "his line," he stays and will do his best in "his occupation." In the second case, he may have to give up his ambitions and satisfy himself with a modest position and simple manual or clerical work. In this way the occupational group permanently controls the vertical circulation of individuals, and corrects their ignorance of an adequate knowledge of themselves, shifts them from a wrong line to a proper one, dissipates many false pretensions and baseless ambitions, distributes and redistributes the individuals among different social strata and different groups of the same stratum.

Such in essence are the functions performed by occupational groups in the way of controlling the social circulation and distribution of individuals. This work is done by them permanently and incessantly. Its social importance is enormous. Its results are decisive. A few facts and figures will make these statements clear. A Chicago industrial firm advertised to fill vacant positions. As a result, it received 11,988 replies. Of these replies 54 per cent were rejected for various reasons. This means that 54 per cent of those who wanted to enter the occupation, were not admitted. This is an illustration of the first form of the occupational selection (elimination). Of the remaining 46 per cent of the applicants who were given an appointment, only 33 per cent were able to keep it. Of them, after an examination, only 4.4 per cent were hired. This means that practically 95.6 per cent of the applicants were excluded from the occupation. And finally, only .7 per cent (84 men out of 11,988 applicants) were making good and had the chance to be promoted.[21] This ordinary case shows all the significance and rough efficiency of occupational testing, selection, and distribution of men. Take another example. In 1924, of 415,593 competitive positions, 222,915 persons were examined by the Civil Service of the United States. Of them only 133,506 persons passed the examination, or 59.9 per cent. Of those who passed the examination only 68,287 persons, or 30.6 per cent of the examined were appointed; 69.4 per cent were eliminated before appointment to the position.[22]

Besides this preventive elimination there is an elimination of the unsuitable persons after entering an occupation. In 1915, in a leading metal industry corporation, 30.7 per cent of the employees were discharged owing to failure to perform their work successfully; in printing and binding this per cent was 40.0; in the shoe industry, 7.2; in stores, 46.4; and so on.[23] According to the data of Dr. V. A. C. Henmon, among those who want to enter the occupation of flying from 50 to 60 per cent of the applicants are at once eliminated; 15 per cent are eliminated by the Ground School, as a result of their testing, and only 6 per cent reach the flying field and remain in the occupation. P. F. Brissenden and E. Frankel's study of the causes of the labor turnover has shown that 16 per cent of the shifting laborers are due to discharge, 11 per cent, to layoff, and 73 per cent, to voluntary separations.[24] This illustrates the above second and third forms of the occupational control of social circulation. The study of economic moral failures among the skilled and qualified occupations by D. C. Jones has shown that discharges owing to failure take place within all occupations, in spite of a careful selection by the employers.[25]

A study made by the American Bankers Association has shown that in the United States of 100 average men, healthy and vigorous in mind and body, who engage in business, and who at the age of twenty-five years are getting their living through their work, about 14 men, after 10, 20, or 30 years, become wealthy, about 10 men are in good circumstances, about 45 are still very moderate, and about 30 men are poor.[26] This is a financial manifestation of differing success of the people engaged in a gainful occupation.

Similar incessant test and selection is going on within every occupation—in the Army and in government, in the professions and the Church, in scientific, literary, art, and other activities. A great many "fitted" to certain occupations are rapidly climbing from a soldier to a general, from a slave to a monarch, from a serf to a Pope, from a beggar to a millionaire, from an office boy to the president of a corporation. A great many others, owing to the same occupational test and selection, are sinking; finally, the majority are rather stationary or move up and down very slowly and within narrow limits. Such in essence is the testing, selecting, and distributing function of the occupational groups.

SUMMARY

1. Except in periods of anarchy and social disorders,[27] in any society the social circulation of individuals and their social distribution is not a matter of chance, but is something which has the character of necessity, which is firmly controlled by many and various institutions by the mere virtue of their existence.

2. These institutions in their totality compose an enormously complex and inevitable machinery which controls the whole process of social testing, selection and distribution of individuals within the social body.

3. The Church, school, family, and occupational institutions are not only the agencies for education and transformation of human beings; but besides these functions, they perform the functions of social selection and distribution of the members of a society. These functions have an enormous social importance, scarcely less than that of education and training.

4. The concrete forms of the institutions of selection and distribution may vary from society to society, from time to time; but in this or that form they exist in any society. They are as inevitable a part of a social body as the organs of control of blood circulation in a complex biological body.

5. In its entirety the whole mechanism of social selection and distribution of individuals is responsible for the kind of people that inhabit the upper and the lower strata—the kind of people who are climbing and falling, and the characteristics of the aristocracy as well as those of the "lower classes" of a society.

6. These things are determined by the qualities, nature, and character of the organization of the selecting institutions, and partially by the character of the impediments which they set up to a successful passing through their sieve. If they are qualitatively poor and wrong, the social distribution of the individuals will be wrong also. As a result, society will suffer as a whole. If they are proper, then social distribution of individuals, being proper also, results in a strong and prosperous development of the whole society.

7. The same may be said of the quantitative side of the work of these institutions; over- or underproduction of the various

kinds of *élite* seriously influences the whole social life and both, as far as possible, must be avoided.

8. This means that any social reformer must pay the most serious attention to the problem of a proper reorganization of these institutions, not so much as educative agencies, but as testing, selecting, and distributing machinery. If they are defective from this standpoint, no social improvement can have a deep and durable effect. History finally is built by men. Men located in places for which they are not fitted can successfully destroy society but they cannot create anything valuable, and contrariwise.

Having studied the height and the profile of the social building and its inner structure turn now to the population of different social strata. This will be the object of study in Part III of this book.

[1] From the text it is clear that the selection here means not a biological selection in the sense of a differential survival but a social sorting of individuals among the different strata or groups: non-admission or rejection of the unsuitable and placement or taking in of suitable individuals.

[2] This social placement to everybody according to his talent was known long ago; it is the motto of the Indian, of the Chinese, and of the Greek and the Roman writers. It composes the central idea of Plato's *Justice* in his *Republic;* it is the dominant idea of Confucius, Aristotle, and of the *Sacred Books of India.*

[3] As is known, Plato's ideal Republic had to be built on the basis of an eugenic selection and breeding of Guardians as the best, according to their innate qualities. Plato's treatise shows that in his time, all the basic principles of the present theory of heredity and all the suggestions of present eugenics were well known. In Sparta, in Rome, in Assyria, in Egypt, and in some other countries the principles of heredity were put in practice. One finds still greater knowledge of applied eugenics and the principles of heredity in *The Sacred Books of India and China.* The principle of inheritance of the qualities of the parents lay at the basis of an absolute prohibition of intercaste marriage. The same principle, it seems, called forth a detailed physical and mental examination of a prospective bridegroom and bride before marriage, the dissolution of a marriage with an impotent husband or unhealthy wife, the cruelest sterilization (in the form of cutting the sexual organ) of some kinds of criminals, the murdering of weak and defectively born children, and so on. *The Sacred Books of India* are full of eugenic statements. These are a few out of a great many. "In the blameless marriages, blameless children are born to men; in blamable marriages, blamable offspring; one should avoid blamable marriages." Further, there goes on the enumeration of the blamable families from which a bride must not be taken, "be they great or rich." Such are the families "where no male children are born, which are subject to hemorrhoids, phthisis, weakness of digestion, epilepsy, or leprosy, which neglect the sacred rights" and so on. *Laws of Manu,* III, 42, 7; see Chapters II, III, IV, and V, *passim.* "The man must undergo an examination with regard to his virility; when the fact of his virility has been placed beyond doubt, he shall obtain the maiden (but not otherwise) . . . If a man is impotent (after a

year and a half after waiting) another husband must be procured (for his wife). Women have been created for the sake of propagation, the wife being the field, and the husband the giver of the seeds. The field must be given to him who has (good) seeds. He who has no seeds is unworthy to possess the field." These are but few examples out of many very detailed prescriptions for the practical eugenics of Ancient India scattered in abundance throughout the Sacred Books of India. Similar statements are found in the Canonical and Ancient sources of China, in the *Laws of Hammurabi,* not to mention other sources. See Plato, *The Republic,* translated by JOWETT, B., pp. 191-192, 197, Bks. II and III, *passim,* New York, 1874; *Narada,* XII, 1-27; XXV, 9; *Brihaspati,* XXIII and XXIV; *Gautama,* IV to VI; *Apastamba,* I, 9 to 25, II; and other sacred books of India, in *The Sacred Books of the East,* edited by MÜLLER, M. *Generally speaking, we must abandon our habit of thinking that past peoples had no knowledge save superstitions,* and that experience and knowledge have been obtained only in Europe, in the nineteenth and twentieth centuries. Though such an opinion is very pleasant, nevertheless, especially in the field of social, moral, and psychological sciences, it is quite wrong. In the way of trial and error, the past knew in this field almost as much as we know now. The deepest analysis and appreciation of the family as the most powerful, most important, and most efficient educational agency, belongs again to the past and was given by Confucius in his theory of "Filial Piety." This analysis and its practical applications by Confucianism are unsurpassed up to this time. Even the school of Le Play, which more than any other, stressed the tremendous social rôle of the family and, deeper than any other school, grasped the essential functions of family, practically only repeated and systematized what had been said in the Sacred Books of China upon that topic. See *The Hsiâo King* or *Classic of Filial Piety, passim;* The *Lî-Kî,* Bk. XVI, *Hiso-Kî,* or *Record on the Subject of Education, The Sacred Books of the East,* Vol. XXVII. *Cf.* LE PLAY, *Constitution Essentielle de l'Humanité, passim;* PINO, R., *La Classification des éspeces de la famille établie par Le Play est-elle exacte;* DEMOLIN, E., "Comment on analyse et comment on classe les types sociaux," both papers in *Science Sociale,* 19 Année, 1er fasc.; DE TOURVILLE, H., *The Growth of Modern Nation,* New York, 1907; VIGNES, M., *La Science Sociale d'après les principes de Le Play,* Paris, 1897, Vol. I, Chap. I, and *passim;* DEMOLIN, E., *Anglo-Saxon Superiority, passim. Cf.* COOLEY, CHARLES H., *Social Organization,* Chap. III; SOROKIN, P., *Sistema Soziologii,* Vol. II, pp. 115-125; SOROKIN, P., *Ocherki Sozialnoy politiki,* chapter on "Family," Prague, 1923.

[4] See DE LAPOUGE, V., *Les sélections sociales,* Chap. IV, Paris, 1896; AMMON, O., *Die Gesellschaftsordnung und ihre natürlichen Grundlagen,* pp. 52, *et seq.,* Jena, 1895; PILLSBURY, W. B., "Selection—an Unnoticed Function of Education," *Scientific Monthly,* pp. 62-75, January, 1921. See the sources indicated further.

[5] Even in the field of money making the majority of the successful money makers have been those who successfully met the school test. Part of those who have not had such a test in no way could be regarded as the school failures. They do not have the degrees simply because they did not have the chance to enter the school. Out of 631 richest men of America, 54 per cent hold a college degree; 18.5 per cent went to high school; 24.1 went to elementary school, only 3.4 per cent had no education except self-education. SOROKIN, P., "American Millionaires and Multimillionaires," p. 637.

[6] AYRES, LEONARD P., *Laggards in Our Schools,* p. 13, New York Survey Association, 1913.

[7] THORNDIKE, E., *The Elimination of Pupils from School,* p. 9.

[8] STRAYER, G. D., "Age and Grade Census of Schools and Colleges," *United*

States Bureau of Education, Bull. No. 451, p. 6; TERMAN, L., *"The Intelligence of School Children,"* pp. 87-89.

[9] COUNTS, SYLVESTER G., "The Selective Character of American Secondary Education," *University of Chicago, Supplementary Education Monographs,* No. 19, pp. 36, and *passim,* May, 1922.

[10] O'BRIEN, FRANCIS P., *The High School Failures,* Teachers College, pp. 13 *et seq.*, New York, 1919; KELLEY, T. L., "A Study of High School and University Graduates with the Causes of Elimination," *Journal of Educational Psychology,* 6: 365; VAN DENBOURG, J. K., *The Elimination of Pupils from Public Secondary Schools.* See especially Wooley, Helen Thompson, *An Experimental Study of Children at Work and in School between the Ages of Fourteen and Eighteen Years,* N. Y., 1926.

[11] At the present moment in the universities and the colleges of the United States preliminary testing of the prospective students has become a common rule. It results in a preliminary elimination from entering a university of all whose intelligence is found below the level necessary for a successful passing of college work. As a series of corresponding tests and studies show, the per cent of mistakes in predicting who of the prospective students is to be a failure is very small. This system is likely to grow, and it manifests clearly the selective rôle of school. See about this the studies of Dean J. B. Johnston and other authors in *Journal of Educational Research,* February, 1926; *Journal of Educational Psychology,* May, 1926; *School and Society,* Vol. XIX, Nos. 496 and 497, 1924. See also Kelly, Frederick, J., *The American Arts College,* Ch. III, N. Y., 1925.

[12] *Apastamba,* Prashna I, Patala I, Khanda I, 11-19; Khanda II, 19-41; Patala II, 5.2-3, *et seq. Laws of Manu,* III, *passim; Gautama,* Chaps. I, II, III.

[13] At first thought all this may appear as something childish and superstitious. And yet, the historical reality shows that in this way the Brahmin school succeeded in selecting and training leaders of an efficiency which scarcely has been rivaled anywhere at any time. Whether we like it or not, "for more than 2,000 years the Brahmins have maintained, unchallenged, their position at the apex of Hindu civilization, and this, not merely in virtue of the supernatural endowment attributed to them, but by force of intellectual superiority. They have been the priests, the philosophers, the physicists, the poets, the legislators of their race. Yes: and we may say the rulers, too." This is the more miraculous in that the Brahmins, as rightly remarks C. Bouglé, do not have any physical force at their disposal nor do they have wealth and money, nor represent a Church organization, with a definite system of hierarchy, nor do they have any dogmas of religion. They are "the priests without church, a religion without dogmas; a power without any wealth or army or force." To a thoughtful thinker the power of the Brahmins must appear a riddle. I wish I could see any intelligentsia as powerful as the Brahmins, under the same absence of the force and wealth and organization. One of the causes seems to be the indicated high biological and social selection of this caste and exclusively efficient training which any candidate must undergo for a high order within this caste. See LILLY, W. S., *India and Its Problems,* pp. 200-204, London, 1922; BOUGLÉ, C., "Rémarques sur le régime des castes," *L'Année sociologique,* pp. 54-60, 1900; KETKAR, *The History of Caste in India, passim,* 1909; MAZZARELLA, "Le Forme di aggregazione Soziale nell', India," *Rivista Italiana di sociologia,* pp. 216-219, 1911.

[14] CHEN HUAN CHANG, *op. cit.,* pp. 88-92; *Lî-Kî,* Bk. IX, 3-5.

[15] See CHEN HUAN CHANG, *op. cit.,* Vol. II, pp. 718-725.

[16] See PARMELEE, M., *Criminology,* Chap. VIII; SUTHERLAND, E., *Crimin-*

ology, pp. 171-174; DE LAPOUGE, V., *op. cit.*, Chap. IV; VON MAYR, G., *Statistik und Gesellschaftslehre*, Vol. III, pp. 677, *et seq.*, Tübingen, 1917.

[17] See DE LAPOUGE, V., *Les Sélections Sociales*, the work which is unsurpassed up to this time in a brilliant analysis of the enormous rôle of social selections.

[18] PEARSON, K., *The Function of Science in the Modern State*, 2d ed., pp. 9-12, Cambridge, 1919; AMMON, O., *Die Gesellschaftsordnung*, Secs. 13-14, Jena, 1900.

[19] SHAW, J. P., "Statistics of College Graduates," *Quarterly Publication of the American Statistical Association*, Vol. XVII, p. 337.

[20] For this, see SOROKIN, P., "The Influence of Occupation on Human Behavior and Reflexology of Occupational Groups" (Russian), *Psychologia, Neorologia i Experimental Psyciologia*, No. 2, Petrograd, 1922.

[21] LAIRD, D. A., *The Psychology of Selecting Men*, p. 31, 1925.

[22] *Statistical Abstract of the United States*, p. 140, 1924.

[23] LAIRD, D. A., *ibid.*, p. 30.

[24] BRISSENDEN, P. F., and FRANKEL, E., *Labor Turnover in Industry*, p. 80, New York, 1922. See also LESCOHIER, DON D., *The Labor Market*, Chap. IV, New York, 1919.

[25] JONES, D. C., "An Account of an Inquiry into the Extent of Economic Moral Failures Among Certain Types of Regular Workers," *Journal of the Royal Statistical Society*, pp. 520-533, 1913.

[26] LESCOHIER, DON D., *op. cit.*, p. 259.

[27] See about the social circulation in such periods in my *Sociology of Revolution*.

Part Three

POPULATION OF DIFFERENT SOCIAL STRATA

CHAPTER X

BODILY DIFFERENCES OF THE POPULATION OF DIFFERENT STRATA

1. THE PROBLEM OF DISTRIBUTION OF INDIVIDUALS WITHIN A SOCIETY

THE distribution of *wealth* or economic values became long ago an object of investigation on the part of economists and social thinkers. But the distribution of the *individuals within a society* has not arrested the attention of investigators up to this time. If something has been done in this line it has been fragmentary, far from being systematic or exhaustive. Yet the problem of distribution of individuals within a society is in no way less important or less interesting than that of the distribution of wealth. Why are some individuals at the top of a social pyramid while others are at the bottom? Why are some dwelling in the privileged and wealthy social strata while others are dwellers in the economic and social "slum"? What are the causes of these phenomena?

One of the fundamental conditions which determine man's social position has been explicitly indicated above: this is environment, and particularly social environment. Among its many constituents from this viewpoint especially important are: (1) *the degree of mobility;* (2) *the character of the channels;* and (3) *the mechanism of social testing, selection and distribution of individuals.* These chiefly are responsible for the kind of people that dwell within each stratum. With their alteration, the kind of dwellers within different layers must alter also. But is this factor sufficient to explain the whole phenomenon of social distribution of individuals? The answer depends on whether the individuals "sifted" by the social sieve have equal ability or not. If they are identical then all have an equal chance to slip through the sieve and the whole social distribution of individuals becomes a mere matter of chance. If they have not identical ability, then some of them may have characteristics which facilitate slipping through a definite system of "sieves" while some others may have the traits which hinder such slipping. We know certainly that human beings are physically and mentally dissimilar. There are not even two cells quite identical in Nature. With still greater reason the same may be said of human beings.[1] Therefore, *we must conclude that another fundamental factor of social distribution of individuals is the human material itself, the physical and mental qualities of individuals, regardless of whether they are inherited or acquired. The dissimilarity of the inherited and acquired traits is the second independent variable which, together with the mechanism of social distribution, is responsible for a kind of social distribution of men within any given society.* This statement is quite certain. But it is not certain which traits in fact facilitate social climbing and which traits hinder it. Are there some traits which, under *all conditions,* favor a social ascent, or are such *permanent* "favorable" characteristics non-existent? If they do exist, what are they? If they do not exist, what individual characteristics and what kind of mechanism of social distribution favor social ascent and social descent? Such are the problems to be discussed now.

Their analysis is at the same time an analysis of the physical and mental differences of the different social classes. The answer to these questions may be given only by facts. Therefore, putting aside speculation and theoretical reasoning, turn now to the facts. In order not to disfigure the "pure facts" by reasoning, for the present we will not pay any attention to whether the differences are due to the factor of heredity and to a factor of environment, or whether they are wholly inherited or acquired. We shall study the situation as it is, regardless of this problem. Only when the study is finished, will we try to find which of the differences are due to each of these fundamental factors. Keeping this in mind, consider these data.

2. BODILY DIFFERENCES OF THE POPULATION OF DIFFERENT SOCIAL STRATA

The first problem will be: are there *bodily* differences between the population of the higher and lower social strata? If such differences exist, do they play a part in determining social position of the individuals? If they do play a part, are they permanent in the sense that under any social conditions and in any society a certain bodily trait favors a social lifting while another one facilitates a social degradation? If they are not permanent, if they fluctuate from society to society, what bodily characteristics and what circumstances help social climbing, and under which conditions do they lead to social sinking? V. de Lapouge said that "the bodily differences of the population of different strata of the same society often are greater than that of different races." [2] The statement seems to contain an element of truth. A series of researches shows that there are many bodily differences between the upper and lower social classes. The most important of them are as follows:

1. *Stature.*—As a general rule the upper social classes—the wealthy, the privileged, the professionals—have a stature higher than that of the lower social classes—the poor, the manual wage earners, the peasants, and social outcasts. This statement has been proved by so many and such different studies that we must accept it as quite certain. For the sake of brevity, only a few data out of the many which may be found in the references given in the footnotes are laid down here.

A. Niceforo measured the stature of 3,147 children of Lausanne. The results obtained are as follows: [3]

STATURE

Age, Years	Boys		Girls	
	Wealthy	Poor	Wealthy	Poor
7	120.0	116.1		
8	126.2	122.5	123.3	119.5
9	129.9	123.9	129.6	124.4
10	134.2	128.9	135.2	129.7
11	135.2	134.2	137.4	134.1
12	140.5	138.8	142.9	140.1
13	144.4	140.5	148.2	146.5
14	150.1	146.2	152.6	146.4

Similar results were obtained in Glasgow where 30,965 girls and 32,811 boys were measured. The children were divided into four classes: (*A*) the poorest, (*B*) the poor, (*C*) the good, (*D*) the best, according to the financial status of their parents. The results may be seen from the following table:[4]

HEIGHT

Boys, Age, Years	*A*	*B*	*C*	*D*
5.5 to 6.5	41.3	42.1	42.1	43.0
6.5 to 7.5	43.0	44.0	44.0	44.8
13.5 to 14.5	55.2	55.5	57.2	57.7

The measurement of girls gave similar results. In Italy the measurements of Pagliani gave the following data:[5]

Age, Years	Height of the Boys	
	Wealthy	Poor
11	133.6	128.5
12	137.0	132.5
13	142.5	138.6
14	150.6	140.0
15	157.2	148.6
16	163.8	151.2
17	164.0	151.4

Similar results were obtained in Russia by Prince Viazemsky, Grousdeff, and Dementieff,[6] in Bulgaria by Doctor Wateff,[7] in England by J. Beddoe,[8] M. H. Muffang, and Roberts, in France by M. H. Muffang,[9] in Germany by H. Schwiening, E.Rüdin, Rietz, F. A. Schmidt, Samosh, Schuyten,[10] and by many others mentioned further. In short, the measurements of the height of children of the higher and lower classes in different countries invariably show that the average height of the former is greater than that of the latter.

Still more numerous are the measurements of army recruits in different countries. They invariably show that the stature of recruits decreases from the recruits from the well-to-do classes to those from the poorer social strata. According to Livi, who measured 256,166 Italian recruits, the height of recruits taken from the professional and wealthy classes was 166.9; that of recruits from the small merchant class 165.0; that of the recruits from the peasant, artisan and common laborer classes fluctuated from 165 to 164.3.[11] Similar correlations for the Italian population were found by P. Ricardi and Pagliani;[12] for the French recruits and different classes of the French population by Bertillon, Villermé, Topinard, Carlier, Longuet, Manouvrier, V. de Lapouge, Muffang, Simon and Houloup, Collignon;[13] for Switzerland by Chalumeau;[14] for Spain by Oloriz;[15] for England by Beddoe, Roberts, Rawson and B. S. Rowntree;[16] for Russia by Anouchin, Erisman, Wiazemsky, Grousdeff and Dementieff;[17] for the United States by B. A. Gould, H. P. Bowditch and Alex Hrdlička;[18] for Germany by O. Ammon, Lansberger, Röse, Pfitzner, Koch-Hesse, A. Geissler, Weisenberg, Z. Hoesch-Ernst and Meuman;[19] for India partially by Sir H. Risley and Crooke;[20] for Poland by Talko-Hryncewitz;[21] to mention but a few investigations. It would be tiresome to list here all the data obtained by these investigators. It is enough to give two or three representative examples of the data. In England, according to Charles Roberts, the mean height of the adults of ages 20 to 30 is as follows:[22]

Occupations	Mean Height
General population	67.5
Professions	69.0
Commercial class, clerks, shopkeepers	68.0
Laborers working out-of-doors (agricultural, miners, sailors)	67.5
Artisans living in the town	66.5
Sedentary laborers (tailors, factory workers)	65.5
Lunatics	65.5
Prisoners	66.0

In the United States, according to Doctor Hrdlička:

> The American soldier averages in general between 171 and 172 centimeters; the native born soldier averages between 171.35 and 173.5 centimeters. The male college students, though a lower mean age, are between 171.2 and 175.2 centimeters. They are of superior stature to the native soldiers, due doubtless on the average to their better environmental conditions.[23]

Manouvrier studied the stature of the poor and rich districts of Paris. The lowest stature happened to be in the poorest district (XX) where the percentage of funerals at the cost of the municipality was highest. In Spain, according to Oloriz, the mean stature of the professionals is 163.9 centimeters, while that of the common laborers is only 159.8 centimeters. In France, according to Longuet, the mean height of the students is 168.7 centimeters, that of the officials and executives 167.4, that of the commercial class and shopkeepers 165.1, that of the common laborers 164.4. In India, on the bases of the Crooke data, the average stature of the highest and middle castes is 164.6, while that of the lowest castes (Dravidians) is 163.4 centimeters; Sir Herbert Risley adds that the dominant Indo-Arian type has higher stature than that of the conquered races, with the exception of the Turko-Iranian type which has a height either equal to or in some cases even greater than that of the India-Iranian type. Similar results were obtained by Kotelmann in his measurements of the students in Hamburg, by P. Hasse in Leipzig, by Landeberger in Poland, and by many others.

Without giving any additional data, I will add to the above only a remark concerning the stature of criminals, feeble-minded, truants, and dependents, on the one hand; and on the other, that of men of genius and talent, as two polar social layers. One of them is at the very bottom of the social pyramid, the other is at its very apex. As far as the average height of the criminals, inmates of asylums for idiots, feeble-minded and insane, is concerned, the measurements of Charles Goring, Charles Roberts, J. F. Tocher, Charles Davenport, B. E. Martin, R. Boyd, E. A. Doll, W. T. Porter, H. H. Goddard, W. Healy, Cyrus D. Mead, L. W. Kleine, and many other authors, show that their stature is somewhat below that of the total population. However, the exceptions among the criminals are numerous and require a further study of the problem.[24]

As far as the height of the men of genius and talent is concerned, we do not have the data about a great number of them. Nevertheless, the data supplied by Havelock Ellis about British men of genius, plus some less numerous data given by other authors, render very probable the statement that the average stature of men of genius is generally of the highest in comparison with that of their countrymen, and, at any rate, considerably higher than the average stature of a corresponding population. Among 362 British men of genius concerning whose stature it was possible to obtain data, 119 happened to be very tall, 74 were of average stature, and 83 were of low stature. Of 86 men of genius about whom it was possible to get quite accurate data, 50 were tall (more than 5 feet 9 inches), 12 were average, and 21 were low-average. "There really is an excess of such abnormally tall persons," says H. Ellis, having compared the curve of distribution of the heights among men of genius with that of the total population. "It is noteworthy that the men of genius who spring from the lower social classes tend to be abnormally tall." [25] No less interesting are the results obtained by E. B. Gowin concerning the height and weight of 2,494 contemporary prominent men in America. In height as well as in weight they excel American policyholders. The average height of prominent executives (railroad presidents, governors of states, presidents of large universities, etc.) is 71.4; prominent intellectuals, 70.7; lesser executives, 69.3; common policyholders, 68.5 inches; similar is the difference in regard to weight. Of other details of Gowin's study, the following table is also of interest.[26]

Dr. C. Röse came to similar conclusions.[27] Finally, studies of bright and dull children have shown that bright children (who in majority belong to the upper strata) are taller than the dull ones from the lower classes. The height of 594 gifted children studied by Dr. L. M. Terman and Dr. B. T. Baldwin is greater than the normal height of American children of the same sex and age. Seventy per cent of the gifted children belong to the upper classes.[28] Similar results have been found by B. T. Baldwin in

Class	Height Feet	Height Inches	Weight, Pounds
Bishops	5	10.6	176.4
Preachers in small towns	5	8.8	159.4
University presidents	5	10.8	181.6
Presidents of small colleges	5	9.6	164.0
City school superintendents	5	10.4	178.6
Principals in small towns	5	9.7	157.6
Presidents of State Bar	5	10.5	171.5
County attorneys	5	10.0	162.9
Sales managers	5	10.1	182.8
Salesmen	5	9.1	157.0
Railroad presidents	5	10.9	186.3
Station agents	5	9.4	154.6

his other measurements.[29] Similar are the results obtained by many other investigators.[30] I know few studies which did not find a correlation between social standing, brightness, and higher stature. On the bases of the above data, it is safe to say that *there is a tangible correlation between high stature and high social class, on the one hand; between a low stature and low social class, on the other hand, providing social classes of a given society are taken into consideration.*

There are reasons for believing that this correlation is characteristic, not only of present civilized societies, but also, it seems, of former and less-civilized societies. Different observations of ethnologists, anthropologists, and travelers, various historical records and legends note very often the difference in the stature of the dominant groups and leaders as compared with that of the lower classes in ancient or preliterate societies. Peshel indicates that among the Kaffres the average stature of the governing families is higher by 110 millimeters than that of the Kaffres' total population;[31] the same fact was indicated by Charles Darwin, in regard to the Polynesians; by Waitz in regard to the Arabs, Fijians, the Sandwich Islanders, Tahitians, Tongans, Jiacuts, and Chukchees;[32] and by several authors in regard to the Tasmanians, Tapajos, Greeks,[33] and to the different castes of India. The class of Spartiats in Sparta was, it seems, taller than the classes of subjugated Helots and Perioeki; the same is likely to be true in regard to the highest classes in Athens compared with those of the slaves and serfs, and in regard to the Roman patricians compared with the slaves and plebeians. That the nobility and wealthy classes in the Middle Ages were taller is witnessed by the nickname: *il popolo grosso* and *popolo grasso* with which these classes are usually characterized in the chronicles —especially in the Italian ones—of that time. In the past the warrior class was usually the dominant class; and the warrior class was also the tall and physically strong class, whether they were the Goliaths of primitive groups, or the hoplites of Sparta, or the Roman patricians, or the medieval feudal knights whose armor is a testimony that they were tall and strong people.[34] Add to this the travelers' descriptions of many chiefs of the preliterate tribes as the tall and physically superior men—the quality necessary for leadership in the primitive groups;[35] finally take the word "high" used for the designation of a high stature and at the same time "high classes" (especially in the Russian *vysoky,* German *hohe,* French *élevé*). This may point to the fact that these two categories of phenomena were very closely correlated in the past. On these bases it is probable that *the above correlation of tall stature with the upper social classes and low stature with the low social classes which exists in present civilized societies has also existed in the past and in the most different societies. In this sense it is a permanent correlation.*

This does not mean that every member of a low social class is therefore less tall than every member of a higher social class. It signifies what any statistical "average" and any statistical correlation signifies, no more and no less. Among other things, it designates also—and this has to be stressed for the sake of certain conclusions given further—that *the curves of the stature of the higher and lower classes are overlapping: though in average the stature of the upper classes is higher than that of the lower ones, nevertheless, a part of the members of the upper classes have a lower stature than a part of the members of the lower social strata.* This fact is very important in this as well as in subsequent comparisons. We shall see its significance further. Now it is enough to indicate the fact and to bear it in mind.

The discussion of whether the indicated difference in stature is the result of heredity or environment will be postponed. This analysis will be given further. Now let us continue our analysis of the bodily differences of the upper and lower social classes.

2. *Weight.* What has been said of the stature may also be said of the weight of the members of the upper and lower social classes. *On the average, the weight of the members of the first group is greater than that of the second.* This again has been proved by so many investigators, at different times and in so many different countries, that we must accept it as a quite tested scientific statement. For the sake of brevity no figures are given. Abundant data may be found in the sources quoted above to which I add several other sources.[36] Here again we find an overlapping of the curves of the weight of members of the upper and the lower classes similar to that of the curves of stature. We have also reason to think that this correlation between the greater weight and upper social classes, and between the lesser weight and lower social classes has existed within the societies of different times and countries. It seems to be a more or less permanent correlation also.

3. *Cranial Capacity, Size of Head and Weight of Brain.* Among bodily traits, the characteristics pertaining to the size and shape of the head, and to the weight of the brain have usually been regarded as among the most important. Many anthropological and sociological theories have tried to explain fundamental social and historical processes on the bases of the cranial differences of different peoples, races, and social groups. Instead of discussing the truth or the falsity of these theories let us proceed directly to the problem as to whether there are some cranial differences between the higher and the lower strata. The corresponding data may also give an answer to the question whether different "cranial philosophies" of history are true or not true.

The measurements of cranial capacity, size of head, the weight of brain, and the shape of head of the members of different social classes do not give a very certain basis for definite scientific conclusions. Nevertheless, they give a more or less valid basis for a tentative conclusion which will run as follows: excluding the purely pathological cases, *it is likely that on the aver-*

age the cranial capacity or size of head, and the brain weight of the members of the upper social strata are somewhat greater than that of the members of the lower social classes of the same society, stature, weight, sex, and age. This conclusion, it seems, is the most probable one from the data accumulated up to this time. However, as some of the data are given without consideration of the stature and the weight of the body, and as some measurements may be defective, therefore the conclusion is still only tentative, and still needs to be tested. Omitting many authors who, like Gobineau, G. Klemm, and H. S. Chamberlain, made statements similar to the above, without any valid measurements, the principal facts on which my statement is based are as follows:

Dr. Pfitzner found that the size of the head of the Strasburger upper classes is greater than that of the common Strasburger population.[37] Professor Matiegka measured the weight of the brains of 235 men in Prague who died at ages between 20 and 60 years. The results obtained are as follows:[38]

Social Classes	Weight of Brain, Grams
Unskilled laborers	1,410
Skilled (masons)	1,434
Doorkeepers, watchmen, carriers	1,436
Artisans, mechanics	1,450
Businessmen, salesmen, musicians	1,468
Physicians, university teachers	1,500

Here the gradation of brain weight is parallel to social stratification. Similar results were obtained by Peacock in Edinburgh and by Boid in London. The average weight of the brains of the dead wealthy men in Edinburgh was 1,417 grams, while that of the poor people was 1,354 grams, a difference so conspicuous that we are inclined to think that the measurements were somewhat defective.[39] On the other hand, the brains of prominent astronomers and mathematicians measured by Dr. Spitzka happened to be above average weight.[40] A. Niceforo, having measured fifty sons of masons and fifty sons of professors, physicians, and lawyers in Lausanne, obtained the following results:[41]

Age Groups, Years	Cranial Circumference		Probable Weight of Brain, Grams	
	Professionals' Sons	Masons' Sons	Professionals' Sons	Masons' Sons
10	528.0	523.3	1,334.58	1,326.75
11	533.0	524.8	1,352.88	1,335.45
12	535.5	524.9	1,358.07	1,335.45
13	536.4	528.6	1,358.07	1,335.45
14	541.8	528.4	1,371.12	1,337.19

Beddoe found similar results concerning the size of heads of professional Scotchmen and Englishmen compared with the common population.[42] Still more interesting and more numerous are the data given by Dr. F. G. Parsons. Summing up the results of his own and of other English Anthropometrists' measurements, (by J. Beddoe, Reid, Writh, Turner, M. Young, Fleure, Haddon, Shuster, Brown, Gladstone) he gives the following figures for length plus breadth of the heads of the various social classes in the United Kingdom:

Social Groups	Number of Cases Measured	Size of Head (Length Plus Breadth)
Criminals	3,000	342
General population	Several thousands	343 to 352
St. Thomas's Hospital students	153	345.7
Railroad engineers	118	346.0
King's College students	457	347.0
Cambridge undergraduates	1,000	347.5
Oxford undergraduates	959	349.0
King's College teaching staff	88	350.0
University College staff	25	350.0
Educated Scots	20	351.5
Educated Englishmen	40	353.0
British anatomists	29	354.0

In general, while the indices for the length plus breadth of the head of the population are fluctuating between 343 and 352, gravitating to 343 to 346, the same indices for the educated and privileged social groups are fluctuating between 344 and 357.5. "Most of the series of the teachers and students and learned assemblies are well up in the list," says Dr. Parsons.[43] On the other hand, we see that the index for criminals is the lowest in the table. A. MacDonald also found that out of 1,074 children of Washington, D. C., "children of the non-laboring classes have a larger circumference of head than children of the laboring classes." At the same time, bright boys have a larger circumference than the dull ones.[44] These results were confirmed by further study of 16,473 white and 5,457 colored children.[45] Still more conspicuous are the results obtained by Dr. C. Röse.[46] Of many interesting results of his measurements, only a few are included. His data have an additional value because of the very large number of cases studied.

Social Groups	Indices of the Head Size (the Sum of the Length and Breadth of Head) Centimeters
Infantry Regiment of Bautzen:	
Staff officers and lieutenants chief	35.0–35.32
Lieutenants	34.83
Volunteers	34.74
Under officers	34.69
Soldiers	34.32
Royal Ulanen Regiment in Hanover:	
Officers and under officers	35.10–35.16
Soldiers	35.01
Danish Battalion in Copenhagen:[1]	
Officers	67.01
Under officers	66.38
Soldiers	66.21
Regiment in Erlangen and Nurnberg:	
Officers and subofficers	34.77–34.96
Soldiers	34.45

(Similar results are obtained by the measurements of the heads of the officers and soldiers of several other regiments in Sweden, Denmark, and Germany.[47])

The sons of farmer owners	34.86
The sons of agricultural laborers	34.14
The soldiers from the professions	66.42[1]
The soldiers from the common people	66.1
The managers and employees and wage earners of the Chemischen Laboratoriums Lingner in Dresden:	
The president	36.20
Principal executives and chemists	35.27
Foremen	34.94
Clerks and laborers	34.73
General population of Dresden (recruits)	34.11
The managers and employees of the Dresden Street Car Directory:	
Board of directors	36.01
Managers	35.83
Clerks and employees	34.90
Conductors, watchmen, laborers(skilled and semi-skilled)	34.73
The Technische Hochschule in Dresden:	
Full professors	35.79
Associate and assistant professors	35.72
Instructors	35.64
Students	34.58
Dresden recruits generally	34.11

(Similar results are given by the measurement of the heads of the professors and students of the Technical Institut in Erlangen.)

The children of Dresden at the age from 6 to 14 years:	
From poorer classes	32.06
From wealthier and professional classes	32.23
The students of the secondary and high school in Dresden from 10 to 22 years of age:	
All students	33.61
From the upper classes (Adel)	33.92

[1] The sum of the length plus the breadth plus the height of the head.

These figures, followed by many similar data obtained by Dr. Röse, exhibit a striking correlation between social position of a group and an average head size of its members. In a similar way, Dr. Da Costa Ferriera, having measured the heads of 375 Portuguese, found that the size of the head of common laborers and artisans was considerably less than that of the members of the professions and students. The same correlation was obtained by Durand de Gross;[48] V. de Lapouge;[49] Dr. E. Rüdin;[50] Otto Ammon;[51] by M. H. Muffang, in his measurements of the peasants, students, professors, managers, and aristocracy of de Saint-Brienc in France;[52] by Talko-Hryncewitz in regard to the laboring classes, nobility and educated classes in Poland;[53] by André Constantin in his measurements of the soldiers and different ranks of army officers in France,[54] by Girard,[55] Binet,[56] Deniker,[57] Montessori,[58] G. Buschan,[59] Broca,[60] Debierre,[61] and Topinard,[62] in regard to different groups of population.

The data of Drake and Brookman show that the circumference of the head of the lower castes in India is also somewhat less (54.0) than that of the higher castes (54.2). Of many data given by the above authors, only a few are cited. Essential results of the measurements obtained by André Constantin of the size of the officers' and soldiers' heads are as follows:

Social Groups	Number of Cases Studied	Circumference of Head, Centimeters
Officers of artillery	129	56.11
Officers of infantry	129	56.07
Medical officers	38	55.84
Cavalry officers	32	55.80
Subordinate officers	665	55.30, 55.47, 55.50, 55.91[a]
Soldiers		55.20, 55.29, 55.36, 55.74[a]
Peasants		54.98, 55.60, 55.65, 55.55[a]
Liberal professions:		
Responsible positions	56	56.87
Subordinate positions	88	56.21

[a]From different regiments or localities.

Of the details of the study, it is worth mentioning that among officers the circumference of heads of sons of professors, officers, bankers, physicians, engineers, and business men averaged 56.65 centimeters, compared with 55.85 and 55.60 for the heads of officers in cavalry who came from the common people. On the other hand, not all officers from the higher classes happened to have large-sized heads. Four of them had a size of only 54.22

centimeters. This fact followed by another, namely, that some of the soldiers had a cranial capacity above that of the officers, indicated again the fact of overlapping mentioned above.[63]

Essentials of Dr. Pfitzner's data are as follows:[64]

Size of Head, Millimeters	Class A (Lowest Social Classes), Per Cent	Class B (Middle Social Group), Per Cent	Class C (Upper Social Group), Per Cent
Men:			
491–540......	35	31	17
541–560......	42	46	43
561–610......	23	23	40
Women:			
471–520......	43	33	21
521–540......	41	46	43
541–590......	16	21	37

One of the tables of A. MacDonald concerning the circumference of head of American children of non-laboring and laboring classes is as follows:[65]

Age Groups	Circumference of Head	
	Boys of Non-laboring Classes Inches	Boys of Laboring Classes, Inches
From 5 years 8 months to 6 years 6 months	20.23	20.04
6 years 7 months 7 years 6 months	20.46	20.35
7 years 7 months 8 years 6 months	20.53	20.50
8 years 7 months 9 years 6 months	20.68	20.57
9 years 7 months 10 years 6 months	20.80	20.67
10 years 7 months 11 years 6 months	20.88	20.74
11 years 7 months 12 years 6 months	21.02	20.82
12 years 7 months 13 years 6 months	21.05	20.96
13 years 7 months 14 years 6 months	21.33	21.12
14 years 7 months 15 years 6 months	21.54	21.27
15 years 7 months 16 years 6 months	21.67	21.66
16 years 7 months 17 years 6 months	22.00	21.80

Further, it is proper to state that, with a few exceptions of specific pathological cases, the cranial capacity of idiots, feeble-minded, and partially of prostitutes and criminals, it seems, is lower than that of the average population.[66] This means that the lowest social layers represented by these unfortunates have correspondingly the lowest average cranial capacity. On the other hand, the measurements of cranial capacity or brain weight of men of genius and talent—men almost all of whom occupied the highest social strata—show that the average weight of their brain is above that of the general population. According to Manouvrier, the average capacity of the skulls of thirty-five eminent men was 1,665 cubic centimeters as compared with 1,560 cubic centimeters general average. G. Buschan studied 98 brains of this group and compared them with 279 brains of the common population of the same age. The essential results of the comparison are as follows: Among prominent men 54.0 per cent had a brain weight greater than 1,450 grams; 9 per cent had greater than 1,700 grams, and 7 per cent greater than 1,750 grams; for the common group the same percentages correspondingly are: 25.0; 0.4; 0.0. Among prominent men there were none with a brain weight of less than 1,200 grams; while among the common people there were 3.5 per cent with a brain weight of less than 1,200 grams.[67] Similar results were obtained by Spitzka[68] and Dräseke.[69]

Dräseke gives a rather long list of the brains of prominent men, which in essence confirms the conclusions of Spitzka and Buschan. The weight of brain of the greater part of the prominent men in the list of J. Dräseke fluctuates between 1,600 and 1,400 grams. Some of them (Oliver Cromwell, Ivan Tourgueneff, Cuvier, Byron, B. Butler, William Thackeray) had brains which weighed above 1,658 grams; some (Gambetta, R. E. Grant, Bunsen, Menzel) had below 1,400 grams.[70]

Finally, to all these data must be added those which have disclosed a correlation between cranial capacity and intelligence. As the higher social classes perform almost exclusively intellectual functions, and as the performance of these requires a greater intelligence than does purely manual work, such as is done by the lowest classes, therefore, the data which establish the correlation between intelligence and cranial capacity, are, at the same time, an indirect corroboration of the larger cranial capacity of the higher social classes. At the present moment a considerable number of investigations are being made which give a positive answer to this question. Such are the greater part of the works quoted. Besides them, can be mentioned Bayerthahl,[71] Wingate Todd,[72] A. Ploetz,[73] E. Rietz,[74] Vaschiede and Pelletier, Parchappe, E. Huschke, Bischoff, and Rüdinger, who came to the same positive conclusions.

All these authors have tried to establish the existence of the correlation in various ways. Some of them showed that, proceeding from the lower organisms to the higher ones, with two or three exceptions, an increase in the relative weight of the brain in relation to the weight of the whole body is seen.[75] Others have indicated the fact that primitive and retarded races have correspondingly lower cranial capacity than civilized peoples. While, according to Buschan, among the Germans the per cent of those who have cranial capacity above 1,300 grams is 75 per cent, and among the old civilized Chinese 92 per cent, among the Hottentots it is only 16 per cent. While among the white race the per cent of those who have a cranial capacity below 1,200 cubic centimeters is less than 8 per cent and among the Chinese people about 2 per cent, the same capacity for the black race is 45 per cent.[76] Similar data were given by Broca, Topinard [77] and, for the whites and Negroes in the United States, by W. Todd.[78] Further, Broca, Topinard, Buschan, and Beddoe tried to show that the progress of culture has been accompanied with an increase of average cranial capacity of the European population.

Other authors tried to measure directly the cranial capacity of the intellectually superior groups and that of the intellectually inferior ones. As an example of the results obtained, I will cite data additional to those given above. Röse measured several thousands of children of the Dresden schools at ages from 6 to 14 years. The results are as follows:[79]

Groups According to Their School Records	Length and Breadth of Head, Centimeters
Very superior	32.27
Superior	31.97
Satisfactory	31.75
Inferior	31.14

Similar results were obtained by L. M. Terman and B. T. Baldwin in an anthropological study of 594 exclusively gifted children in California. Their cranial capacity is above the average norms throughout.[80] Of 56 men with records of superior intellectual ability who were measured by André Constantin, 38 had a head circumference of 57 centimeters and above; of these, 22 men had a head circumference of 57 centimeters; 11 of 58; 4 of 59; 1 of 60 centimeters. Of 88 men with a somewhat inferior intellectual record, only 35 had a head circumference of more than 57 centimeters.[81] Similar results were obtained by Beddoe in his measurements of 526 men: 60 of them who exhibited the highest intellectual ability had the largest heads. Ammon, Muffang, and other authors mentioned above came to the same conclusions. Less decisive results were obtained by Karl Pearson, P. Radosavljevich, and R. Pearl. In their studies they also found correlation between intellectual ability and cranial capacity, but it was only "slight," though "sensible." [82] The works which showed no correlation in this respect, or even negative correlation, are those of Giltschenco, Seggel, Eylrich and Loewenfeld,[83] of Cleeton and Knight,[84] Cattell and Farrand.[85] But it was properly indicated [86] that their material, as well as some of their methods in measuring, may be seriously questioned. The negative results obtained by Cleeton and Knight are not valid because they measured only 30 persons, who were, besides, a selected group. The above materials lead to the conclusion that the average head size of the higher social classes is somewhat greater than that of the lower social classes; at the same time, it is necessary to note that there is the fact of overlapping again.[87] Though the materials upon which these conclusions are based are not few in number, nevertheless these conclusions may be only tentative and must still be tested by further studies. If the correlation between size of head and intelligence exists, then a larger head has been a trait which necessarily belonged to the chiefs and aristocracy of the past societies, because, as we shall see, even the leaders of preliterary tribes were those who were more intelligent. In other words, the correlation is likely to be permanent or steady.

4. *The Shape of the Head.*—Perhaps there is no other bodily trait which has been given a greater importance and upon which have been based more fundamental theories than the shape of the head. Theories of the racial differences; theories concerning the Aryan and Nordic racial superiority; theories of social evolution, progress, and degeneration of a people; and so on, have been based principally on the significance given to the shape of the head, to dolichocephaly and brachycephaly. The most brilliant examples of such theories were given by Otto Ammon and Vacher de Lapouge,[88] not to mention less prominent authors and many superficial popularizers of these really prominent scholars and original thinkers.[89] According to these theories, dolichocephaly, with a cephalic index lower than 75 or 80, is one of the most important characteristics of *Homo Europaeus* or the Nordic race.[90]

The essential sociological conclusions to be derived from these theories may be summed up as follows: First, almost all progress of the European civilization is due to the blond Nordic dolichocephals; second, they have been the natural leaders of the people and its real aristocracy; they have composed the higher social strata of Ancient Greece, Ancient Rome and of medieval Europe in the period of their progress and prosperity; as long as the dolichocephalic type of a people and especially of their aristocracy exists, everything is going on perfectly well; if this type is multiplying, the result is a brilliant progress for the country. As soon as this racial type begins to be superseded by brachycephals, the country is bound to degenerate and decay. The cause of the decay of the Greek civilization was a decrease and disappearance of the dolichocephals among the Greek population, whose cephalic index increased from 76 to 81. The same may be said about the decay of Ancient Rome and other countries.[91] For the same reason, contemporary Europe, where this racial type is disappearing and where with the advent of democracy the upper strata of the societies are more and more occupied by the brachycephals, is doomed to decay.[92] The disappearance of the dolichocephals is due to the present social selection, which in different ways exterminates them and facilitates a greater multiplication and survival of the brachycephalic posterity. Such is the essence of this "philosophy of history." Of the detailed statements of this school, should be mentioned the contention that the city population is more Nordic than the country population; that it is the Nordic type, principally, that migrates from the country to the city; but, climbing the social ladder, it becomes less and less prolific and finally dies out. When in this way the dolichocephalic resources of a population are exhausted, the decay of a country is inevitable. Ammon and Lapouge, being unanimous in the principal points of their theory, at the same time differed in some details. While Lapouge was more pessimistic and considered Europe of the nineteenth century as already in a state of decay, Ammon continued to regard the situation more optimistically.

This theory has been outlined here as an example of the importance which has been given to the cranial index. Now if it is true, a considerable difference in the cephalic index of the higher and lower classes must exist. It must be expected, further, that the prominent men of genius and talent are to be dolichocephalic; also that the more energetic city population will be more Nordic than the country population. To what extent are these expectations warranted by the facts?

In spite of the common belief that the aristocracy of Europe has been composed of the dolichocephalic type and that the higher social classes have been predominantly long-headed, this opinion may be seriously questioned. First, the data concerning the past are very scarce and uncertain. Second, we certainly know that several prominent kings of the past, *e.g.*, Tiberius and some other Roman Emperors, were rather broad-headed. If it is more or less certain that the earliest prehistoric population of Europe, especially its lowest strata, were extremely long-headed,[93] we do not have any reliable facts on which to base an opinion that the aristocracy and the leaders of that time were still more dolichocephalic. The data given by Lapouge [94] and by some other authors concerning the Greek, Roman, and medieval aristocracy are extremely scarce and too uncertain to be a reliable basis for certain generalizations. A few skulls, whose bearers and their social position are unknown; a few references to pictures and statues, against which it is possible to set forth the opposite type of pictures and statues—this is practically all upon which is based the hypothesis of the long-headed aristocracy of ancient times! [95] In the third place, the assumption that long-headedness is necessarily connected with extraordinary energy, initiative, progressive mind, talent, and so on is still a mere hypothesis.[96] That dolichocephalism alone does not guarantee these qualities is shown by the fact that many primitive peoples, the Australians, Eskimos, New Caledonians, Hottentots, Kaffirs, Negroes of West Africa, and so on, have a very dolichocephalic cranial index—from 71 to 74 [97]—and yet, they do not exhibit these qualities at all.

Therefore, all that exists, as proof of the hypothesis of long-headedness, are the measurements of different groups of the contemporary population of Europe. It is true that much of the data obtained by Ammon and Lapouge and several other anthropologists seem to corroborate it. But other data, supplied partially by the same and other authors, contradict it. As a general result we must say that *the hypothesis is, at least, still uncertain and not proved.*

This may be seen from the following representative figures:

In the first place, Niceforo,[98] in his measurement of the well-to-do and poor children, found that in both groups there were both types and in this respect there was no significant difference. In the second place, among 594 of the most gifted children of California "various types of cephalic indices are found, but the majority of the children are of the mesocephalic type." Cephalic indices are as follows:

Age	Boys	Girls
7 years	81	83
8 years	86	82
9 years	81	79
10 years	81	80
11 years	80	80
12 years	80	80
13 years	80	79
14 years	79	80
15 years	80	81

From this it is seen that the most gifted chiidren of America (with I.Q. 151.33) are far from being dolichocephalic in their total.[99] In the third place, data given by Dr. Parsons show that the index of the higher social groups of the English population is by no means more dolichocephalic than that of the criminals or the general population. This is seen from the following figures:[100]

Social Groups	Cephalic Index
British criminals	78.5
Population of the nineteenth century	74.9 to 77.5
Higher and educated groups (intellectuals, professors, and students of Oxford, Cambridge, King's College, Royal Engineers, and so on)	77.6 to 81.9

Further, the index of the British population, since the eighteenth century, has been becoming more and more brachycephalic, though we cannot say that during the eighteenth and nineteenth centuries the English people became stagnant and less progressive than they had been before. In the fourth place, the result of the measurements of the American children by A. MacDonald is that "long-headedness increases in children as ability decreases. A high percentage of dolichocephaly seems to be a concomitant of mental dullness."[101] In the fifth place, the data obtained by

Dr. Röse, in spite of his own desire to corroborate the dolichocephalic myth, are quite contradictory and do not show any definite correlation. This is shown by the following data: [102]

Social Groups	Cephalic Index	Social Groups	Cephalic Index
Infantry Regiment in Bautzen:		*Pupils of real schools in Dresden*:	
Staff officers	81.4	10 years old:	
Chief lieutenants	86.3	All	87.1
Lieutenants	84.4	From the nobility	83.1
Volunteers	84.6	11 years old:	
Under officers	84.9	All	86.8
Soldiers	84.6	From the nobility	87.2
		22 years old:	
Konig- Ulanen Regiment in Hanover:		All	83.6
		From the nobility	85.4
Officers	80.2		
Under officers	82.5	*Technische Hochschule in Dresden*:	
Soldiers	82.4		
		Full professors	83.2
Liebgarde Cavalry Regiment in Stockholm:		Associate and assistant professors	83.2
Officers	81.9	Instructors	83.8
Under officers	79.8	Students	84.0
Soldiers	78.9	Recruits generally	85.2
Recruits in Copenhagen:		*Pupils of elementary schools in Dresden*:	
Sons of farmer-owners	81.6		
Sons of agricultural laborers	82.0	Very superior	85.8
		Superior	86.4
Recruits in Schwarzbourg:		Average	86.4
Sons of farmer-owners	83.0	Inferior	86.4
Sons of agricultural laborers	81.6		

These representative data, taken from many figures given by Röse, show that, if there is any correlation between higher social position and dolichocephaly, it is so indefinite and is contradicted by so many exceptions that we are entitled to disregard it as being non-existent.

In the sixth place, the measurements of the children of Liverpool by Muffang show that the cephalic index of the children of the higher social classes is less dolichocephalic than that of the children of wage earners.[103]

In the seventh place, Talko-Hryncewitz did not find any dolichocephalic tendency in the skulls of the Polish nobility and educated classes compared with that of the common people. The same results were obtained by Livi in Italy. Finally, the Spanish students, according to Oloriz, happened to be more brachycephalic than the common people.[104]

No other data of the same character will be cited. The above followed by the acknowledgment of Lapouge that "the necessary data about the cephalic index of the different social and occupational groups are lacking," [105] is enough to warrant the statement that *the dolichocephalic hypothesis is still a mere belief and nothing more.*

Somewhat stronger seems to be the situation of the second fundamental hypothesis of the correlation between dolichocephalism and the city population. Many data show that the city population in many places is more long-headed than the country population, and that those who migrate to the city from the country are more dolichocephalic than the members of the corresponding country population.[106] But even this statement cannot pretend to be a general rule, and Ripley, J. Beddoe, R. Livi, F. J. Craig, E. Houzé,[107] and other anthropologists have shown that there are many exceptions to it. In this respect Livi's hypothesis remains still valid. He states that as the cities attract the migrants from places more distant than the places which are near to them, therefore, where the surrounding city population is of a dolichocephalic type, the city population has to be more brachycephalic; where the surrounding city population is of a brachycephalic type there the city population will be more dolichocephalic.[108] That is all.

5. *Other Differences in the Head and Face.*—If in regard to the cephalic index we do not find any certain correlation between the long-headed type and higher social classes, and between brachycephalism and the lower classes, does this mean that, in regard to the head and face, there is no difference between these classes? I think that there is a difference, but it is somewhat more complex, and, thanks to the complexity, somewhat in-

tangible. It consists in the fact that *among the lower social classes, especially the lowest ones, there exists a greater number of the different anomalies of the head, such as prognatism, assymetry, plagiocephalism, and so on; furthermore, the facial angle and facial index in many cases are different;* but all this cannot pretend to be a general rule and must still be tested. The following figures may give an illustration of my statement: [109]

The Kind of Anomalies	Number of Cases Among Seventy Poor Children	Number of Cases Among Seventy Well-to-do Children
Plagiocephalism	40	32
Low, retreating forehead	5	3
Prognatism	15	7
Assymetry of face	22	16
Enormous jaw	8	3
Anomalies of ear	21	13
Other small anomalies of head	24	20
Total	135	94

In a similar way Niceforo studied 48 university students and 48 manual wage earners, and found out that the total number of anomalies in the group of students was 35, while among the wage earners it was 70.[110] Similar results were obtained by Zugarelli.[111] Very numerous data of this kind have been collected concerning the lowest social classes, the criminals and prostitutes. Of the prostitutes of St. Petersburg studied by Pauline Tarnowsky, 44 per cent had skull deformities; 42.5 had facial deformities, 42 ear anomalies, 54 teeth deformities.[112] Of 190 prostitutes of Breslau studied by Bohnhofer, 102 had the stigmata of degeneracy; similar results were obtained by C. Andronico; of 30 prostitutes of Chicago studied by E. S. Talbot, 16 had abnormal zygomatic processes, 14 assymetry of the face, 3 mongoloid head; 16 were epignathic, 11 prognastic.[113] Somewhat analogous were the results obtained by F. Marty,[114] A. W. Tallant, and G. E. Dawson. As to criminals, an abundance of deformities and ailments of the above kind among them—especially among the habitual and professional criminals—is a fact which is beyond doubt. It is true that Lombroso and his school somewhat exaggerated it and derived some conclusions not warranted by facts, but this exaggeration must not lead us to the opposite extremity of disregarding what was factual and true in Lombroso's studies, and what has been proved by many scientists—the opponents of Lombroso in other respects. Studies of Charles Goring, Healy, W. Scott, E. Ferri, Corre, Garofalo, Lacassagne, L. Manouvrier, H. Maudsley, Havelock Ellis, H. Kurella, A. Niceforo, Cliquet, A. Marro, F. Marty, and many other criminologists showed that deformities and different ailments are found more frequently in prisoners than in non-prisoners.[115] Finally, the facts collected by the authors just mentioned and by Villermé, Colignon, Lagneau, Seeland, Hervé, Dachkevitch, Bertillon, Marty, Dementieff, and others, lead to the conclusion that not only among social outcasts but generally among the lower classes different kinds of deformities and ailments of the head and face are more numerous than among the higher social groups. A corroboration of this will be given further when we discuss the health of the various social strata.

6. *Pigmentation.*—In connection with the Nordic hypothesis, it is almost generally accepted that the social and mental aristocracy of the Western countries has been more blond than the lower classes. "The upper classes in France, Germany, Austria, and the British Isles are distinctly lighter in hair and eyes than the peasantry," we read even in the book of W. Z. Ripley, [116] who is far from being a partisan of the "Nordic" theory. This statement in a still more exaggerated form has been made by V. de Lapouge, Otto Ammon, H. Chamberlain, and by many other followers of this hypothesis. As one of the variations of this general theory, we have been told that the more energetic population of the city is more blond than the country population. This has been a natural inference from the theory that the city population is predominantly the "Nordic" and that the Alpine race is a sedentary and predominantly rural race. Quite recently the theory was revived by H. Onslow who categorically assures us that "the ruling class was always fair complexioned," that the word "fair" means "bright and blond" and that "blondness" is a

characteristic of mental and social superiority.[117] To what extent is this contention true as far as it concerns different social classes of the same society? The answer is that its partisans have not supplied us with necessary and satisfactory proofs of their statements. In the first place, the hypothesis concerning the lighter pigmentation of the city population compared with that of the country population is quite wrong. "The tendency of the urban population is certainly not toward the pure blond, long-headed, and tall Teutonic type. It appeared to manifest a distinct tendency toward brunetness." Such is the real situation in the words of W. Z. Ripley, who summed up the fundamental results of the corresponding studies of G. von Mayr, Virchov, J. Beddoe, Carret, Bouchereau, Schimmer, R. Livi, and others.[118] Somewhat contradicting his previous statement, Doctor Ripley tries to explain the fact by saying that "it is not improbable that in brunetness, in the dark hair and eye, is some indication of vital superiority."[119] This sounds as subjective as the opposite statement of the adherents of "blondness," but the fact of greater brunetness of the city population remains and stubbornly refutes all myths of the predominant light-colored Nordic urban population created by its adherents. This additionally shows the fallacy of the general Nordic theory discussed above.

Now concerning the pigmentation of the higher and lower social classes. Putting aside the unbased guesses about the color of the aristocracy of the past or the quite incidental references to the pigmentation of the few men of historical prominence, which may be confronted by no less numerous opposite examples, let us turn to factual evidence. The oft-cited study of A. Niceforo gives the following results in this respect.[120] (See p. 243.)

The data contradict completely the criticized theory. The poor children have higher percentage of the fairs than have the wealthy ones. In Italy, R. Livi found that among the poor mountainous population and the peasants, the per cent of the light colored was considerably higher than among the city population and the wealthier parts of Italy.[121] Karl Pearson, having studied 1,000 Cambridge graduates and 5,000 school children, did not find any correlation between pigmentation and intelligence.[122] On the other hand, J. Jörger found that among

Age Groups, Years	Per Cent of Children with Fair Eye Color		Per Cent of Children with Fair Hair Color	
	Poor	Wealthy	Poor	Wealthy
7	19	18	26	21
8	18	18	26	20
9	17	17	25	20
10	16	17	24	20
11	16	15	22	18
12	16	15	23	18
13	16.4	14.8	22.1	17.2

the descendants and the members of such criminal and feeble-minded families as the Zero family there have been light- as well as dark-colored people.[123] J. F. Tocher, in a careful study of criminals and feeble-minded in Scotland, also did not find any difference in pigmentation between the inmates of prisons and asylums and the common population, with the exception that insane individuals exhibited a slight tendency to be lighter eyed and darker haired than the sane population.[124] A study of the Old Americans by Dr. Aleš Hrdlička showed further that the common opinion in regard to blondness of the Old Americans is also fallacious. About 50 per cent of them are halfway between the blond- and dark-haired, and one-fourth of the males are dark or dark-brown haired, and only 1 per 16 males and 1 per 14.5 females are blond haired.[125] In the United States, H. G. Kemagy studied 152 supersalesmen in order to find out whether twenty-six qualities, such as "positive," "dynamic," "impatient," "negative," "conservative," "slow," "deliberate," "thoughtful," etc., are connected with blondness and brunetness or not. The results of the study were negative: no correlation between alleged blond and brunet traits was found. Similar results were obtained by Dr. D. G. Paterson.[126] Finally, if men of genius are taken: their study, from the standpoint of pigmentation, also does not support the criticized theory. Of such more or less systematic studies, I know only one—that of Havelock Ellis. Other quite incidental indications of a few blond men of genius, which have been pointed out by H. Onslow, or Osborn,[127] do not have scientific value and may be confronted by many opposite examples. The results obtained by Havelock Ellis in his study of British genius are as follows: of 424 British men of genius concerning whose eye and hair color he obtained data:

71 were unpigmented (light).
91 were light medium.
54 were doubtful medium.
85 were dark medium.
115 were dark fully.[128]

These figures refute the alleged blondness of the British men of genius. It is natural to expect that the men of genius of other countries, whose population is darker than the British, would be still darker colored and the per cent of blond men of genius would be still lower than in England. More detailed data given by Havelock Ellis still confirm my criticism. In the following table 100 is taken as the index of the mean fairness, and all indices above as the indication of a greater blondness, while all figures below 100 are taken as the indication of an increasing darkness: [129]

Categories of British Men of Genius	Number of Men	Index of Pigmentation
Political reformers and agitators	20	233
Sailors	45	150
Men of science	53	121
Soldiers	142	113
Artists	74	111
Poets	56	107
Royal family	66	107
Lawyers	56	107
Created peers and their sons	89	102
Statesmen	53	89
Men and women of letters	87	85
Hereditary aristocracy	149	82
Divines	57	58
Men of genius of low birth	12	50
Explorers	8	33
Actors and actresses	16	3

This shows, first, that the royal family is very far from being at the top of the list; second, that the pigmentation of the hereditary aristocracy is dark and much darker than that of the created peers who came out of the middle classes; the third, that the statesmen and explorers—the men of energy—were dark; these facts completely contradict the one-sided interpretations of this table which were given by H. Onslow. The figures do not give any confirmation of the "blond theory" and its variations. Not so decisive but similar are the results obtained by M. A. Thomas concerning the pigmentation of the 181 most prominent men of the contemporary Canada. This is seen from the following figures:[130]

Number of Men	Color of Hair	Number of Men	Color of Eyes
12	Blond	124	Blond (blue, gray, green)
23	Light brown		
100	Medium brown or brown	36	Medium (brown)
40	Very dark brown and black	21	Brunet (dark brown black)
6	Red, reddish-brown and auburn		
Total 181		Total 181	

If according to color of eyes, there is a predominance of blondness among these, the most prominent men and women of Canada, in regard to color of hair the situation is reverse. Furthermore, a careful study of correlation between intelligence and pigmentation made recently by N. D. Hirsch, who tested 5,504 children in Massachusetts, did not show any noticeable correlation. "The I.Q. differences (of the blond, mixed and brunette types), within a national group, are small and inconsistent." Hirsch's study of I.Q. of different—Nordic and the non-Nordic European nationalities did not give also any correlation between the Nordic racial type and superior I.Q.[131]

The above is enough to show that this theory, in spite of its popularity, is a matter of belief but not of scientific study.

7. *Faces, Beauty and Proportions.*—Here I am going to discuss something which is intangible, and yet which seems to exist as a further difference between the upper and the lower social strata, taken as whole social groups. The ideal of beauty varies greatly from group to group; and yet, within the same society, in the same historical period, there is something common among all its social strata. Other things being equal, beauty, especially for a female, is a condition which facilitates her upward promotion in the social pyramid—either through marrying a man of better social position, or through becoming a highly paid mistress or actress or movie star, or "Miss America," or what not. Actresses and especially movie stars are highly paid. Often being of a low origin, they represent, in total, a group much more beautiful than the common unselected group of women. This means that in the present society in various ways there goes on permanent recruiting of beautiful women into the higher social strata. The same process in different ways seems to have proceeded in past societies. If such is the case, the beauty and handsomeness of the mother, being transmitted to her children, facilitate an accumulation of comeliness in the higher classes. Through this process of social selection—a variety of Darwin's sexual selection—the higher social layers come to be more handsome than the lower ones.

A similar process takes place in regard to males as well. Other conditions being equal, from two candidates for a position, the one who appears handsomer is likely to be preferred to another who is ugly. From two lovers or rivals, the more handsome is likely to be preferred as a husband or lover. Many "Apollos" of humble origin in this way have made their careers, and sometimes, especially in the history of Byzantium, obtained even the position of monarch. Ugliness has been, and is, a very great obstacle to social climbing. An ugly man of low origin is a man for whom all doors to promotion are locked, if he does not have any extraordinary ability. Since this process of recruiting handsome males and females into higher social strata, and leaving the less handsome in the lower classes, is a permanent one, it is natural that in the long course of time it has greatly contributed to the handsomeness of the upper classes. From the more handsome parents come more handsome children. This is one of the reasons why the upper classes must be, on the average, more handsome than the lower classes. The second cause for several aristocracies lies in the deliberate extermination of defective children of aristocracy. The Spartans give an example of this phenomenon. The third cause lies in the difference of occupation and environment of the different classes. The occupation of the higher classes is principally intellectual while that of the lower classes is manual work. Permanent intellectual activity gives to a face "an intelligent expression" and the more so the more "intellectual" is the work. The play of the facial muscles, their combination, the expression of the eyes, the attitude of body and so on, become quite different from those which are shaped by purely physical work. As a result, a man of intellectual occupation, being quite average in his innate handsomeness—since he acquires this intangible but very real "intelligent appearance"—appears more handsome than a man of the same innate handsomeness, but who does purely manual work. This kind of work gives to its bearer what is styled the appearance of "a hue man," or a proletarian; makes the skin of the face and body rude; often disfigures the body through accidents; and often causes many wounds, anomalies, and other defects. Add to this the fact that the better paid higher classes have the better hygienic conditions; better food; greater cleanliness; take and can take better care of their bodies; use, especially among women, more artificial means for their beautification, giving a greater time for this purpose; and finally, are better dressed.[132] As a result of all these causes, it is natural to expect a greater degree of handsomeness among the upper classes. The facts, it seems, warrant this expectation.

The first corroboration of this hypothesis is language itself. The words: "beautiful," "aristocratic," "well shaped," "noble," "fine," "handsome," "intelligent," are often used as meaning something identical or congenial. This is especially in regard to "aristocratic face," "aristocratic feet" and "hands," and "fine" proportions of the body.

A second corroboration, though it is somewhat indirect and subjective, is the impression which one receives from many pictures of the different members of the upper classes, in general dictionaries, historical works, in national galleries, in private albums, in private houses, newspapers, magazines, and from the living representatives of the different upper social groups. Certainly, there are individuals far from being handsome or "aristocratic looking" but in total, as a whole group, these pictures and living persons impress us rather favorably.[133] Even those of the men who could not be styled as handsome, nevertheless had and have faces which could be styled as "noble," strong, imposing, or impressive. The third corroboration is that "among the personal characteristics of the king or his substitute in early society, physical strength and beauty hold a prominent place."[134] Such is the short summary of a long series of facts collected by J. G. Frazer.[135]

The fourth corroboration has been indirectly given by Havelock Ellis. His British men of genius, with few exceptions, belonged to the higher social classes (aristocracy, professionals, middle class). A large proportion of them, according to Ellis, were notably handsome and imposing. Besides, even in those who were not handsome, there was one feature which was noted as striking and beautiful—this was the unusual brilliancy of the eyes.[136] It is impossible, of course, to extend the property of this selected group to the whole higher classes; nevertheless, in a lesser degree, the same may be said about them as about the classes performing principally intellectual functions.

The fifth (similar) corroboration is given by Doctor Terman's study of gifted children of California, who again, in more than 70 per cent of the cases, belong to the professional and commercial classes. Doctor Moore reports that 97.5 per cent of them are "normal," "bright" or "very bright" in appearance.[137]

Still more definite results were obtained by Niceforo. The figures have already been given which show that the number of defects and anomalies of the head and face among children from the poor classes was considerably greater than among those of the upper classes. Similarly, his measurement discovered a greater disproportion and disharmony of different parts of the body of children and adults of the poor classes. Their physiognomy had a less intelligent expression; the facial index was unfavorable for the poor, and so on.[138] Furthermore, considerable materials in this connection have been collected by different authors and published in special works about physiognomy.[139] Very proper is the observation of Dr. Robert Michels concerning the physical type of the different leaders in the present democracies who have climbed from the bottom of the lower strata to the apex of the social pyramid. "They constitute not only a psychical, but also a physical type." In general, they are very handsome. J. Jaurès, Guesde, Lagardelle, Karl Marx, Hervé, F. Lassal, Bebel, Turati, Liebknecht, C. Prampolini, E. Ferri, R. MacDonald, Vandervelde, Adler, and many others, are examples. "In Italy the heads of the leaders of the socialist parties are beautiful models of mankind and the best specimens of the race of the country." Of 33 socialist deputies in the parliament in 1902, 16 were "above the medium as regards appearance." [140] This is an illustration of the above-indicated "recruiting" of handsome people from the lower into the higher social strata. In this and in many other forms, the lower classes are impoverished in favor of the higher social layers. On the other hand, the lowest social unfortunates exhibit a great deal of what is styled as "utter ugliness," "animal," "brutal," "fearful," "terrible," "asymmetrical face," and so on. I speak of criminals, idiots, dependents, the feeble-minded, and partially the prostitutes. A glance at the album of Lombroso makes this clear. Low foreheads, enormous jaws, dull eyes, something bestial, unintelligent —such are the characteristics of these faces. This again does not mean that all the members of the higher and lower classes exhibit the indicated differences. It is certain that among the higher classes—especially in the period of their decay—we find many individuals far from comely; and contrariwise, among the lower classes and destitutes, we find males and females of an extraordinary beauty. The fact of overlapping in this respect is quite certain. But taken as whole groups, these classes, nevertheless, seem to exhibit the above-mentioned traits.

8. *Temporary and Local Differences.*—Besides these more or less constant bodily differences, there may be many other differences of a local and temporary character. They exist only in a

specific society and at a particular period. For instance, in a society composed of different races, as is the United States, the proportion of the black race within the upper classes is much less, and within the lower strata much greater, than that of the white race. The same is true for India where the darker races are situated almost completely within the lower caste. This difference of the upper and the lower strata is local. It does not exist within all societies composed of the people of the same race. There may be other similar temporary and local bodily differences. Furthermore, some investigators have found a greater disproportion of the parts of the body of the lower classes compared with the body parts of the higher classes. The figures concerning the relative length of the arm may give an illustration of this. Niceforo measured the length of arm span of 33 students and 33 manual wage earners. The results are as follows: [141]

Social Groups	Height	Arm Span
Students	170.9	171.5
Wage earners	167.0	172.7

Students are taller, and yet their arm span is shorter than that of the wage earners. Some other investigators did not, however, find such results. For this reason we must conclude that such differences are rather local. Measurements of other bodily traits, such as chest circumference, have given similar inconclusive results. The study of such local differences is outside the scope of this book. Therefore it is enough to mention their existence and to discriminate between the more or less constant and universal differences and those of a changeable, temporary and local character.

SUMMARY

1. The upper classes are taller, have a greater weight, greater cranial capacity, greater handsomeness and less serious and less numerous anomalies and defects than the lower classes. This phenomenon is more or less permanent and universal.

2. The correlation is, however, not perfect and shows a great deal of overlapping.

3. In regard to dolichocephaly and brachycephaly, and in regard to pigmentation, there is no constant and significant correlation between these characteristics and social status.

4. Side by side with the constant and general differences, there are others which are temporary, local and changeable from time to time, from group to group.

[1] Concerning physical and mental dissimilarity of individuals, see WAXWEILER, E., *Esquisse d'une Sociologie,* pp. 157 *ff.;* HANKINS, F. H., "Individual Differences," *Journal of Social Forces,* December, 1925.

[2] LAPOUGE, V. DE, *Les Sélections Sociales,* pp. 28 *ff.;* "De l'inégalité parmi les hommes," *Revue d'Anthropologie,* 1888.

[3] NICEFORO, A., *Les Classes Pauvres,* p. 21, Paris, 1905.

[4] ELDERTON, E. M., "Height and Weight of School Children in Glasgow," *Biometrica,* Vol. X, p. 296.

[5] See PAGLIANI's paper in *Annali di Statistica,* p. 228, 1878.

[6] VIAZEMSKY, N., *Ismenenia organisma v. periode sformirovania,* Vol. I, pp. 66 *ff.;* also, "Développement Physique des élèves russes, serbes, et bulgares," *L'Anthropologie,* Vol. XIX, pp. 579-594, 1908.

[7] WATEFF, DR., "Contribution a l'étude anthropologique des Bulgares," *Bulletin de la Société d'Anthropologie de Paris,* 1904.

[8] BEDDOE, J., "The Somatology of 800 Pupils of the Naval School," *Journal of Anthropologic Institute of Great Britain and Ireland,* 1904; MUFFANG, M. H., "Écoliers et étudiants de Liverpool," *L'Anthropologie,* Vol. X, pp. 21-41, 1899; ROBERTS, CHARLES, "The Physical Development of the Human Body," *Manual of Anthropology,* 1878.

[9] MUFFANG, M. H., "Écoliers et Paysans de Saint-Brienc," *Revue International de Sociologie,* pp. 795 *ff.,* 1897.

[10] SCHWIENING, H., *Über die Korperbeschaffenheit der Zumeinjährigfreiwilligen Dienst berechtigen Wehrpflichtigen Deutschlands,* Berlin, 1909.

[11] See LIVI, R., "Essai d'Anthropometrie Militaire," *Bulletin de l'Institut International de Statistique,* Vol. VII, pp. 273-306, Rome, 1894; "Report," *Bulletin de l'Institut International de Statistique,* Vol. XIII, pp. 76 *ff.,* and *Sullo sviluppo del corpo in rapporto con la professione,* Roma, 1897.

[12] RICARDI, P., *Statura e condizione sociale,* Firenze, 1885; PAGLIANI, *Lo sviluppo umanô per età, sesso e condizione,* Milano, 1879.

[13] BERTILLION, J., "Taille," *Diction. encyclop. des sciences médicales,* and "La Taille en France," *Revue scientifique,* 2-me sem., N. 16, 1885; Villermé, "Memoirs sur la taille de l'homme en France," *Annales d'Hygiéne publique,* Vol. I, Paris, 1829; TOPINARD, P., *Anthropology,* pp. 318-319, 390, London, 1878; CARLIER, "Les rapports de la taille avec le bien-être," *Annales d'Hygiéne publique,* 1892; LONGUET, article in *Annales de Démographie,* 1900; MANOUVRIER, "Sur la taille de Parisiens," *Bulletin de la Société d'Anthropologie de Paris,* pp. 156 *ff.,* 1888; DE LAPOUGE, *Les Sélections Sociales,* pp. 142-147, 356; MUFFANG, M. H., *op. cit.;* SIMON and HOULOP, "Professions, Tailles et Poids," *Normandie médicale,* 1913; COLLIGNON, series of papers in *Bulletin de la Société d'Anthropologie de Paris,* for 1890, 1894, and 1895.

[14] CHALUMEAU, "Influence de la taille humaine sur la formation des classes sociales," *Pages d'Histoire,* Génève, 1906.

[15] OLORIZ, *La talla humana en Espana,* Madrid, 1896.

[16] BEDDOE, J., *op. cit.;* ROBERTS and RAWSON, *Final Report of the Anthropologic Committee,* London, 1884; ROWNTREE, B. S., *Poverty,* p. 211, London, 1906.

[17] ANOUCHIN, *Geographicheskoie raspredelenie rosta moujscogo nacelenia Rossii,* St. Petersburg, 1889; ERISMAN, F., *Untersuchungen über de Körperliche Entwicklung des Fabrikarbeiter in Zentral Russia,* Tûbingen, 1899.

[18] GOULD, B. A., *Investigations in the Military and Anthropologic Statistics of American Soldiers,* pp. 121, 132, 134, 294-295, New York, 1869; HRDLIČKA, ALEŠ, "Physical Anthropology of the Old Americans," *American Journal of Physical Anthropology,* pp. 211-214, 1922; BOWDITCH, H. P., "Growth of Children," *Tenth Annual Report of Massachusetts Board of Health,* Boston, 1879.

[19] AMMON, OTTO, *Die natürliche Auslese,* pp. 118-127 and *passim;* LANDSBERGER, "Das Wachstum im Alter d. Schulpflicht." *Archiv für Anthropologie,* Vol. XVII; WEISENBERG, S., *Das Wachstum des Menschen;* LEXIS, "Anthropologie und Anthropométrie," *Handwörterbuch der Staatswissenschaften,* edited by CONRAD, B. I, pp. 535-536, 1908; GOTTSTEIN, A., "Anthropométrie," *Handwörterbuch der Sozialen Hygiene,* Vol. I, pp. 40-41, 1912; HOESCH-ERNST, Z., and MEUMANN, *Das Schulkind in seiner Körperlichen und geistigen Entwicklung,* Leipzig, 1906; GEISSLER, A., "Messungen von Schulkindern in Gohlis," *Zeitschrift für Schulgesundsheitspflege,* pp. 249-253, Leipzig, 1892.

[20] RISLEY, SIR HERBERT, *The People of India,* pp. 37-38, 1915; CROOKE, *The Tribes and Castes of Northern India,* 1896; *The Imperial Gazeteer of India,* Vol. I, pp. 292-293, 1907.

[21] TALKO-HRYNCEWITZ, "The Main Anthropometric Characteristics of the Common People and of the Cultured Classes in Poland," *Bulletin of the Polish Academy of Science,* Vol. LIX, pp. 543-553, Krakow, 1919.

[22] ROBERTS, CHARLES, "On the Uses and Limits of Anthropometry," *Bulletin de l'Institut International de Statistique,* Vol. VI, pp. 15-16, Rome, 1892.

[23] HRDLIČKA, ALEŠ, *op. cit.,* pp. 211-214.

[24] See GORING, CHARLES, *The English Convict,* London, 1913; ROBERTS, CHARLES, *op. cit.,* pp. 15-16; TOCHER, J. F., "The Anthropometric Characteristics of the Inmates of Asylums in Scotland," *Biometrika,* Vol. V, p. 347; DAVENPORT, CHARLES, and MARTIN, B. E., "The Deviation of Idiot Boys from Normal Boys in Bodily Proportions," *Proceedings of XLVII Session of American Association for the Study of the Feeble-minded,* Detroit, 1923; DOLL, E. A., "Anthropometry as an Aid to Mental Diagnosis," *Publications of the Training School, at Vineland, N. J.,* No. 8, 1916; PORTER, W. I., "The Physical Basis of Precocity and Dullness," Transactions of the *Academy of Science of St. Louis,* pp. 161-181, 1893; HEALY, W., *The Individual Delinquent,* 1915; GODDARD, H. H., "The Height and Weight of Feeble-minded Children," *Journal of Nervous and Mental Disease,* pp. 217-235, 1912; KLEINE, L. W., *Pedag. Seminary,* January, 1896; MEAD, CYRUS D., "Height and Weight of Children," *Pedag. Seminary,* Vol. XXI, pp. 394-406, 1914. GILLIN, JOHN L., *Criminology and Penology,* Chap. V, New York, 1926.

[25] ELLIS, HAVELOCK, *A Study of British Genius,* pp. 204-208, London, 1904.

[26] GOWIN, E. B., *The Executive and His Control of Men,* pp. 32, 320-327, New York, 1920.

[27] RÖSE, C., "Beiträge zur Europäischen Rassenkunde," *Archive für Rassen- und Gesellschafts-Biologie,* pp. 797-798, 1905.

[28] TERMAN, L. M., *Genetic Studies of Genius,* Vol. I, 1925, pp. 144-145, and Chap. VII.

[29] BALDWIN, B. T., "Physical Growth and School Progress," *United States Bureau of Education, Bulletin No. 10,* 1910; "The Physical Growth of Children from Birth to Maturity," *University of Iowa Studies,* Vol. I, p. 229.

[30] See SCHMIDT, F. A., and LESSENICH, H. H., "Uber die Beziehung zwischen korp. Entwick. und Schulerfolg," *Zeitschrift für Schulgesundsheitspflege,* pp. 1-7, 1903; SPIELREIN, J., *Uber Kindermessungen,* etc., *ibid.,* pp. 451-461, 503-513, 548-560, 1916; SAMOSCH, *Einige Bemerkenswerte Ergebnisse,* etc., *ibid.,* Heft 6, 1904; HERTEL, A., *Report of the Danish Commission,* 1882; STEWART, S. E., "A Study of Physical Growth and School Standing of Boys," *Journal of Educational Psychology,* pp. 414-426, 1916; STYLES, C. W., and WHEELER, G. A., "Heights and Weights of Children," *United States Publications, Health Reports,* Pt. II, pp. 2990-3003, 1915; SCHLESINGER, E., "Das Wachstum der Knaben und Jünglings vom 6 bis 20 Lebensjahren," *Zeitschrift für Kinderheil.,* pp. 265-304, 1917; YOUNG, J. E., "Supernormal Environment in its Relation to the Normal Child." *Transactions of the International Congress on School Hygiene,* pp. 17-30, Buffalo, 1913; see some other sources further.

[31] PESHEL, O., *Völkerunde,* pp. 85-86, Leipzig, 1881.

[32] WAITZ, *Anthropologie,* Bk. I, pp. 67-69.

[33] See SPENCER, HERBERT, *Principles of Sociology,* Vol. II, pp. 301, 333-334, D. Appleton & Company, New York, 1909; FRAZER, J. G., *Lectures on the Early History of the Kingship,* pp. 258-264, London, 1905; LOWIE, R. H., *op. cit.,* Chaps. XII to XIV.

[34] See SPENCER, HERBERT, *ibid.,* pp. 334-337.

[35] See some facts in DESCAMPS, P., *Les Pouvoirs publiques chez les Sauvages.*

[36] Besides the above references, see ROWNTREE, B. S., *Poverty,* p. 212; CHRISTOPHER, W. S., "Measurements of Chicago Children," *Journal of American Medical Association,* Vol. XXXV, pp. 683-687; SMEDLEY, F. W., *Child-study Report,* N3, pp. 11-40, Chicago, 1902; GRATSIANOFF, N. A., *Materials for Investigation of Physical Development in Childhood and Youth,* St. Petersburg, 1889; SACK, N., "Uber die Körperliche Entwicklung der Knaben," *Zeitschrift für Schulgesundsheitspflege,* pp. 649-663, 1893; DE BUSK, B. W., "Height, Weight, Vital Capacity, and Retardation," *Pedag. Seminary,* Vol. XX, pp. 89-92, 1913; RIETZ, "Körperentwicklung und geistige Begabung," *Zeitschrift für Schulgesundsheitspflege,* 1906; further, the studies of RÜDIN, E., *Archiv für Rassen- und Gesellschafts-Biologie,* p. 309, 1904; SCHMIDT, F. A., SAMOSH, and SCHUYTEN, mentioned above; TERMAN, L. M., *op. cit.,* pp. 144-145; DIKANSKY, M., *Uber den Einfluss der Sozialen Lage auf die Körpermasse von Schulkindern,* München, 1914.

[37] PFITZNER, W., "Sozialanthropologische Studien," *Zeitschrift für Morphologie und Anthropologie,* 1901 and 1902.

[38] MATIEGKA, "Uber die Beziehungen des Hirngewicht zum Berufe," *Politisch-Anthropologische Revue,* 1904; *Revue Scientifique,* 1903.

[39] NICEFORO, A., *op. cit.,* pp. 36-38.

[40] Though the brain weights of the prominent men show a considerable fluctuation, ranging from 2,231 grams (the brain of Oliver Cromwell) and 2,012 grams (the brain of Ivan Tourgeneff) to 1,290 grams (the brain of R. E. Grant), nevertheless, on the average, they are likely to be above the average brain weight of a corresponding population. See DRÄSEKE, J., "Gehirngewicht und Intellegenz," *Archiv für Rassen- und Gesellschafts-Biologie,* pp. 499-522, 1906.

[41] NICEFORO, A., *op. cit.,* p. 36. See there some interesting details.

[42] BEDDOE, J., *The Races of Britain,* p. 232, London, 1885; "Evaluation et Signification de la capacité crânienne," *L'Anthropologie,* 1903.

[43] PARSONS, F. G., "The Cephalic Index of the British Isles," *Man,* pp. 19-23, February, 1922.

[44] MACDONALD, A., *Man and Abnormal Man,* p. 19, Washington, D. C., 1905.

[45] *Ibid.,* pp. 35 *ff.*

[46] RÖSE, C., "Beiträge zur Europäischen Rassenkunde," *Archiv für Rassen- und Gesellschafts-Biologie,* pp. 689-798, 1905, and pp. 107 *et seq.,* 1906.

[47] RÖSE, C., *ibid.,* pp. 769 *et seq.* See here other data.

[48] GROSS, DURAND DE, "Excursion anthropologique dans l'Aveyron," *Bulletin de la Société d'Anthropologie,* p. 193, 1869.

[49] DE LAPOUGE, V., *Les Sélections Sociales,* pp. 357 *et seq.*

[50] RÜDIN, E., *op. cit.*

[51] AMMON, OTTO, *Zur Anthropologie der Badener,* Jena, 1889, and *Die natürliche Auslese beim Menschen,* Jena, 1893.

[52] MUFFANG, M. H., the quoted papers: *Écoliers et étudiants de Liverpool* and *Écoliers et Paysans.*

[53] TALKO-HRYNCEWITZ, *op. cit.*

[54] See CONSTANTIN, ANDRÉ, "Contribution a l'étude des correlations physiques et psychosociologiques de la circonférence céphalique," *L'Anthropologie,* Vol. XXIX, pp. 265-288, 1918-1919.

[55] GIRARD, "Sur l'expression numerique de l'intèlligence des espèces animales," *Revue philosophique,* 1905.

[56] BINET, A., "Recherches de céphalométrie," and "Anthropométrie scolaire," *Année psychologique,* 1900 and 1908.

[57] DENIKER, "Revue d'anthropologie," in *L'Année psychologique* for 1904, 1905, and 1906.

[58] MONTESSORI, "Sui caratteri antropometrici," *Archivio per l'antropologia e la etnologia,* 1904.

[59] BUSCHAN, G., *"Gehirn und Kultur,"* Wiesbaden, 1906.

[60] BROCA, "De l'influence de l'éducation sur le volume et la forme de la tête," *Bulletin de la Société d'Anthropologie de Paris,* 1892.

[61] DEBIERRE, "De l'influence du travail cerebral sur le volume et la forme du crâne," *Bulletin de la Société d'Anthropologie de Lyon,* 1884.

[62] TOPINARD, P., *Anthropology,* pp. 120-121, 229, 310.

[63] CONSTANTIN, ANDRÉ, *op. cit.,* pp. 268, 275-288.

[64] PFITZNER, W., "Der Einfluss der Socialen Schichtung auf die anthropologishen Charactere," *Zeitschrift für Morphologie und Anthropologie,* Vol. IV, p. 65, 1902.

[65] MACDONALD, A., *op. cit.,* pp. 76-77.

[66] See TOPINARD, P., *op. cit.,* pp. 120, 310. Indicated works of J. Beddoe, J. F. Tocher, Rietz, F. G. Parsons, G. E. Dawson, *Pedagogical Seminary,* December, 1896; TARNOWSKY, PAULINE, *Étude Anthropologique sur les prostitues,* 1887; BUSCHAN, G., "Kultur und Gehirn," *Archiv für Rassen- und Gessellschafts-Biologie,* pp. 691-692, Bd. I, 1904; PORTEUS, S. D., "Cephalometry of Feeble-minded," *Training School Bulletin,* pp. 49-72, 1919 and 1920.

[67] BUSCHAN, G., *ibid.,* pp. 689-701.

[68] See the article of SPITZKA, *Philadelphia Medical Journal,* May 2, 1903.

[69] DRÄSEKE, J., *Gehirngewicht und Intellegenz,* pp. 499-522.

[70] See also HAUSEMAN, *Über die Gehirne von Theodor Mommsen, Robert Wilhelm Bunsen, und Ad. V. Menzel,* Stuttgart, 1907. The average of brain weight among adult Europeans (20 to 60 years) is, according to P. Topinard and Deniker, 1,361 grams for men, 1,290 grams for women.

[71] BAYERTHAHL, "Über den gegenwärtigen Stand der Frage nach den Beziehungen zwischen Hirngrosse und Intellegenz," *Archiv für Rassen- und Gesellschafts-Biologie,* Vol. VIII, pp. 764-774, 1911; "Kopfgrosse und Intellegenz in Schulpflightigen Alter," *Zeitschrift für exper. Pädag.,* 1910, Heft 2 and 3.

[72] TODD, W., "Cranial Capacity and Linear Dimensions in White and Negro," *American Journal Physical Anthropology,* No. 2, 1923.

[73] See the notes of PLOETZ, A., in *Archive für Rassen- und Gesellschafts-Biologie,* Vol. IV, p. 396.

[74] RIETZ, E., *Körperentwicklung und Geistige Begabung, Zeitschrift für Schulgesundsheitspflege,* pp. 65-88, 1906.

[75] See the summed up data in the quoted paper of BAYERTHAHL, "Über den gegenwärtigen Stand der Frage nach den Beziehungen zwischen Hirngrosse und Intellegenz."

[76] BUSCHAN, G., *op. cit.,* p. 693.

[77] See TOPINARD, P., *op. cit.,* pp. 121, 229.

[78] According to W. Todd, the average cranial capacity for the male white is 1,391 cubic centimeters, for the male Negro 1,350; for the female white, 1,232 cubic centimeters, for the female Negro 1,221. TODD, W., *op. cit.,* p. 188.

[79] RÖSE, C., *op. cit.,* p. 760.

[80] TERMAN, L. M., *op. cit.,* p. 152.

[81] CONSTANTIN, ANDRÉ, *op. cit.,* p. 288.

[82] PEARSON, KARL, "On the Relationship of Intelligence to Size and Shape of Head, and to Other Physical and Mental Characteristics," *Biometrica,* Vol. V, pp. 120-122; PEARL, R., "Biometrical Studies on Man, Variation and Correlation in Brain weight," *Biometrica,* Vol. I, pp. 78-83; *Studies in Human Biology,* Pt. I, Chaps. I and II, 1924; RADOSAVLJEVICH, P. R., "Pedagogical Measurements of Pupils in Mostar," *Proceedings Fourth International Congress for School Hygiene,* pp. 541-550, Buffalo, 1913.

[83] EYLRICH and LOEWENFELD, *Über die Beziehungen des Kopfumfanges zur körperlange und zur geistlichen Entwicklung,* Wiesbaden, 1905; SEGGEL, "Verhaltniss von Schadel, etc.," *Archive für Anthropologie,* 1904. A somewhat negative answer of Dr. F. Boas is in the first place purely dogmatic, being not supported by facts; in the second place, it contradicts his own statements. *Cf.* pp. 28 and 29 of his *Mind of Primitive Man,* New York, 1911.

[84] *Journal of Applied Psychology,* Vol. VIII, pp. 215-231, 1924.

[85] CATTELL and FARRAND, "Physical and Mental Measurements, etc.," *Psychology Review,* pp. 618-648, 1896.

[86] See critical remarks of A. Ploetz and E. Rüdin in *Archive Rassen- und Gesellschafts-Biologie,* Vol. IV, pp. 396, 535.

[87] See about overlapping, the remarks of A. NICEFORO in his paper: "The Cause of the Inferiority of Physical and Mental Characters in the Lower Social Classes," *Problems in Eugenics,* pp. 192 *et seq.,* 1912.

[88] See AMMON, OTTO, *Anthrop. Untersuchungen der Wehrpflichten in Baden,* Hamburg, 1890; *Die natürliche Auslese beim Menschen,* Jena, 1893; *Die Gesellschaftsordnung und ihre natürlichen Grundlagen,* Jena, 1895; *Die Körpergrosse der Wehrpflichtigen im Grossherzogthum Baden,* Karlsruhe, 1894; LAPOUGE, V. DE, *Les Sélections Sociales; L'Aryen, son rôle social,* Paris, 1899. *Race et milieu social,* Paris, 1909. See a survey and criticism of these theories in HANKINS, F., *The Racial Basis of Civilization,* New York, 1926.

[89] As an example of such "popular" imitation of the brilliant works of these scholars, there may be mentioned GRANT, MADISON, *The Passing of the Great Race,* and STODDARD, LOTHROP, *Racial Realities in Europe* and *The Rising Tide of Color.*

[90] LAPOUGE, V. DE, *Les Sélections Sociales,* pp. 16 *et seq.*

[91] LAPOUGE, V. DE, *op. cit.,* pp. 64-80, 408 *et seq.*

[92] *Ibid., passim* and Chap. XV; AMMON, OTTO, *Die Gesellschaftsordnung, passim* and pp. 149 *et seq.;* all principal propositions of these authors are summed up in eleven Ammon-Lapouge's laws. See the "laws" in LAPOUGE, V. DE, *L'Aryen, son rôle social,* pp. 412 *ff.*

[93] See RIPLEY, W. Z., *The Races of Europe,* pp. 456-465, 1910.

[94] LAPOUGE, V. DE, *op. cit.,* pp. 40 *ff.,* 410 *ff.*

[95] See the reasonable critical remarks by HOUZÉ, E., "L'Arien et l'Anthropo-Sociologie," *Travaux de l'Institut de Sociologie;* and KOVALEVSKY, M., *Contemporary Sociologists* (Russian), Chap. VIII.

[96] The recent attempts to prove it by B. S. Bramwell gave only a mass of incidental and self-contradictory data which cannot prove anything and which, as we see further, are disproved by the facts. See BRAMWELL, B. S., "Observations on Racial Characteristics in England," *The Eugenic Review,* pp. 480-491, October, 1923. The same must be said about ONSLOW, H., "Fair and Dark," *The Eugenic Review,* pp. 212-217, 1920-1921.

[97] TOPINARD, P., *op. cit.,* pp. 240-242. My criticism of this hypothesis does not mean that I do not appreciate highly this part of the works of V. de Lapouge and Otto Ammon which deals with social selections. I certainly estimate it very highly, and in total find the books of these authors among the most suggestive and valuable contributions to sociology.

[98] NICEFORO, A., *op. cit.,* pp. 43-44.

[99] TERMAN, L. M., *op. cit.,* Table 38, pp. 148, 170.

[100] PARSONS, F. G., *op. cit.,* pp. 19-23.

[101] MACDONALD, A., *op. cit.,* p. 19.

[102] RÖSE, C., *op. cit.,* pp. 760, 769-792.

[103] MUFFANG, M. H., *Ecoliers et étudiants de Liverpool,* pp. 21-41.

[104] See indicated works of Talko-Hryncewitz, R. Livi, Oloriz.

[105] LAPOUGE, V. DE, *op. cit.,* p. 357.

[106] See the data in the quoted works of Otto Ammon, V. de Lapouge, C. Röse, W. Z. Ripley, Durand de Gross, and others.

[107] See the quoted works of these authors. CRAIG, "Anthropometry of Modern Egyptians," *Biometrica,* Vol. VIII, pp. 72-77; HOUZÉ, E., *op. cit.,* pp. 95 *ff.*

[108] See also WISSLER, CLARK, "Distribution of Stature in the United States," *Scientific Monthly,* pp. 129-144, 1924. Generally speaking, the discussed theory greatly exaggerates the achievements of the Nordic race and underestimates the achievements of other, especially Alpine, races. A more objective estimation may be found in DIXON, R. B., *The Racial History of Man,* pp. 514 *ff.,* 1923.

[109] NICEFORO, A., *op. cit.,* p. 55.

[110] *Ibid.,* p. 58.

[111] ZUGARELLI, "Osservazioni in torno all frequenza dei dati degenerativi somatici in rapporto con la condotta," *Nuova Rivista di psichiatria,* Napoli, 1894.

[112] TARNOWSKY, PAULINE, *op. cit.,* and *Les femmes homicides,* Paris, 1908.

[113] See CLARKE, WALTER, "Prostitution and Mental Deficiency," *Social Hygiene,* No. 3, pp. 364-387, 1915; LOMBROSO, C., and FERRERO, G., *La donna delinquente, la prostituta, e la donna normale,* 3d ed.; FOINITZKY, *The Female Criminal* (Russian); GRANIER, C., *La Femme Criminelle,* Paris, 1915.

[114] MARTY, F., "Récherches Statistiques sur le développement physique des delinquants," *Arch. d'anthropologie criminelle,* No. 8, pp. 178-195, 1898; TALLANT, A. W., "Medical Study of Delinquent Girls," *Bulletin of the American Academy of Medicine,* No. 13, pp. 283-293, 1912; DAWSON, G. E., *Pedagogical Seminary,* 1896.

[115] See LOMBROSO, C., *L'Homme criminel,* Vols. I and II and Atlas; LAURENT, E., *L'anthropologie criminelle,* Paris, 1893; FERRI, E., *Criminal Sociology,* Boston, 1917; GORING, CHARLES, *The English Convict;* HEALY, W., *The Individual Delinquent;* KURELLA, H., *Naturgeshichte des Verbrechers,* Stuttgart, 1893; MARRO, A., *I caratteri dei delinquenti,* Torino, 1887; MANOUVRIER, L., "Quelques cas de criminalité juvenile et commerçante," *Arch. d'anthropologie criminelle,* pp. 881-918, 1912; PARMELEE, M., *Criminology,* Chap. IX; SUTH-

ERLAND, E., *Criminology,* pp. 179-182; GILLIN, JOHN L., *Criminology and Penology,* Chap. VI. See there the literature.

[116] RIPLEY, W. Z., *op. cit.*, pp. 469, 548-550.

[117] ONSLOW, H., "Fair and Dark," *The Eugenic Review,* Vol. XII, pp. 212-217. See similar statements in BRAMWELL, B. S., "Observations on Racial Characteristics in England," *The Eugenic Review,* pp. 480-491, 1923.

[118] RIPLEY, W. Z., *op. cit.*, pp. 555-559. See here the facts.

[119] *Ibid.*, p. 557.

[120] NIÇEFORO, A., *op. cit.*, pp. 50-51.

[121] LIVI, R., report in *Bulletin de l'Institut International de Statistique,* Vol. VIII, pp. 89-92.

[122] PEARSON, KARL, "On the Relationship of Intelligence," *Biometrica.* Vol. V, p. 133.

[123] JÖRGER, J., "Die Familie Zero," *Archive für Rassen- und Gesellschafts-Biologie,* pp. 494-554, 1905.

[124] TOCHER, J. F., "The Anthropometric Characteristics of the Inmates of the Asylums in Scotland," *Biometrika,* Vol. V, p. 347.

[125] HRDLIČKA, ALEŠ, "Physical Anthropology of the Old Americans," *American Journal of Physical Anthropology,* No. 2, pp. 140-141, 1922.

[126] LAIRD, DR. A., *The Psychology of Selecting Men,* pp. 127-131, 1925.

[127] In *The New York Times,* 8, IV, 1924.

[128] ELLIS, HAVELOCK, *A Study of British Genius,* pp. 209-210.

[129] *Ibid.*, pp. 209-216. ELLIS, HAVELOCK, "The Comparative Ability of the Fair and the Dark," *Monthly Review,* August, 1901.

[130] THOMAS, M. A., "Hereditary Greatness in Canada," *Journal of Social Forces,* p. 309, December, 1925.

[131] See the figures in HIRSCH, N. D., "A Study of Natio-Racial Mental Differences," *General Psychology Monographs,* Vol. I, Nos. 3 and 4, pp. 333-337, 302-309, May and July, 1926.

[132] On the other hand, with the exception of the periods of decay, the aristocracies of ancient Greece and Rome, and the Middle Ages, paid the greatest attention to athletics and physical development, and had a manner of life—in the form of war, Olympiads, Tournaments, etc.—which called forth physical development. The same must be said about contemporary high classes. In colleges and universities their youth is carefully trained in various athletics and sports.

[133] See a series of facts in F. A. Woods' paper about the portraits of Early Americans in *Journal of Heredity,* May, 1920; WIGGAM, A. E., *The Fruit of the Family Tree,* 1924, Chap. XVI.

[134] FRAZER, J. G., *Lectures on the Early History of the Kingship,* pp. 258 *et seq.*

[135] See LOWIE, R. H., *op. cit.*, pp. 338 *ff.*

[136] ELLIS, HAVELOCK, *op. cit.*, pp. 217-218.

[137] TERMAN, L. M., *op. cit.*, p. 220.

[138] See NICEFORO, A., *op. cit.*, pp. 53-63.

[139] See "Physionomie," *L'Encyclopédie du XIX siècle,* 1872; QUETELET, *Anthropometrie,* Vol. III, Chap. X; DEMOLIN, E., *Comment la route crée le type social,* pp. 301-302.

[140] MICHELS, R., "Eugenics in Party Organization," *Problems in Eugenics,* pp. 232-237, 1912.

[141] NICEFORO, A., *op. cit.*, p. 64; CRAIG, J. I., *op. cit.*, pp. 70-78. See also NICEFORO, A., "Apropos de quelques comparaisons entre les mensurations obtenues sur les sujets appartenant à des classes sociales différentes," *Bulletin de la Societé d'Anthropologie de Paris,* 1911.

CHAPTER XI

DIFFERENCES IN VITALITY AND HEALTH OF DIFFERENT SOCIAL CLASSES

THIS chapter will sum up very briefly the fundamental differences of the lower and higher social classes as they appear in vitality and health.

I. DURATION OF LIFE AND MORTALITY

One of the criteria of vitality and health is the death rate and the duration of life. In this respect the upper social classes average a greater longevity and a lower mortality than the lower classes. This statement is well demonstrated by many investigations. Only a few figures, selected from those investigations indicated in the footnote sources, will be given.

In the first place, the studies of Casper, of Kemmerich, of Ploetz, and my own, showed that the average longevity of monarchs, princes, presidents, in the United States, France, and Germany, and Roman Catholic popes is above that of the population of the corresponding countries at the corresponding times. Moreover, the more prominent members of this ruling group, on the average, have had a greater duration of life than the less prominent rulers. Preëminence of the rulers above the general population in this respect is still more conspicuous, since their environment and activity are far from being favorable for a long life.[1]

In the second place, the study of the longevity of prominent men who in the greater majority have belonged to the upper social classes shows that their duration of life, and that of their fathers, have been far above that of the common population of the corresponding countries and times. Here are a few figures.[2] The greater number of these prominent men lived in the sixteenth, seventeenth, eighteenth, and nineteenth centuries.

In the third place, my study of American millionaires and captains of industry and finance showed that their longevity has also been above that of the general population of the United

Classes of Prominent Men	Number of Persons	Average Longevity, Years
Monarchs	272	53.6
Jurists, judges, lawyers	49	68.9
Statesmen, politicians	81	67.4
Army, navy, military men	75	67.1
Theologians, clergy	131	68.7
Artists, musicians, architects, painters	180	64.0
Scholars, scientists	290	67.3
Authors, poets, journalists	147	64.4
Roman Catholic popes	85	69.8
American millionaires	278	69.2
French literary men	854	67.3
Presidents of United States	24	69.9 or 70.0
Secretaries of the United States, Vice-Presidents and Presidents Pro Tem of Senate	216	64.0
Presidents of France, Germany	6	68.0
The most eminent women of all countries and times	670	60.8
American eminent inventors	252	74.7

States.[3] J. Philiptschenko's study of the longevity of the most prominent Russian scholars has given similar results. Their average longevity is 67.25 years, which is higher than the average longevity of the Russian population.[4] These facts show that the highest social groups and the real leaders in various fields of activity have a longevity considerably greater than that of the common people and lower classes.[5] Side by side with these studies of the longevity of the above exclusive groups, we have many studies of the longevity and mortality of the different economic and occupational classes. These studies show that the duration of life of the upper social classes is, on the average, far longer, and the mortality far lower, than that of the lower social strata.[6]

Of abundant data confirming this statement only a few which are representative and illustrative are given here. An idea of the longevity of monarchs and American captains of industry, inventors, eminent medical men, and statesmen is given in the following table in which their longevity is compared with that of the population of the United States, 20 years old, and above, who died in 1920:

Age Groups, Years	Frequency of Distribution of Ages, in Per Cent, Among					
	Monarchs Who Died in the Nineteenth and Twentieth Centuries at the Age of 20 Years and Above	United States Secretaries and Vice-Presidents	American Inventors	American Millionaires and Multimillionaires	491 American Eminent Medical Men	Those Who Died in United States in 1920 at Age of 20 Years and Above
20 to 29	2.9	...	0.8	2.2 (20 to 39)	...	10.3
30 to 39	2.9	0.4	1.6		3.4	12.4
40 to 49	11.8	1.9	4.1	4.7	9.2	12.9
50 to 59	20.6	19.0	15.0	11.5	18.1	15.7
60 to 69	29.4	30.6	27.5	27.0	30.1	19.3
70 to 79	20.6	31.5	23.6	34.1	27.3	18.8
80 and above	11.8	16.6	27.4	20.5	11.9	10.6
Total	100.0	100.0	100.0	100.0	100.0	100.0

In spite of a very considerable increase in the average expectation of life in the nineteenth and twentieth centuries, and notwithstanding the fact that the average expectation of life in the United States is much higher than in Europe, nevertheless, the duration of life of the monarchs, not to speak of the millionaires, the inventors, the medical men, the Secretaries of the United States Federal Government, is considerably higher than that of the general community of the people who died in the United States in 1920. The same result is obtained if an average duration of life of these exclusive groups is compared with the general average expectation of life whether at birth, or at the age of 20 years, or later. According to Casper, the following number out of 1,000 princes and 1,000 poor survive the ages. (See p. 261.) With still greater reason this may be said of the longevity of prominent men, generally, compared with that of the common people.[7]

Ages, Years	Princes	Poor
5	943	655
10	938	598
50	557	338
80	57	21
		and so on

If we take the mortality of children, the result is that the children of the monarchs have the lowest mortality, the children of the aristocracy and rich and privileged classes are next; and the highest mortality is among the children of the lowest and poorest classes of the city population. The following figures are an illustration:

Social Groups	Mortality of Children at the Age of 0 to 1 Year per 1,000 Born Alive
Royal families:	
Contemporary royal families of Europe	34.8[8]
Royal families of Europe from 1841 to 1890	65.0[9]
Population of Paris (1911 to 1913):	
I. The wealthiest group	51.0
II. Less wealthy group	69.0
III. Still less wealthy	107.0
IV. The poorest group	151.0[10]
Prussia (1880 to 1888):	
(Including the stillborn)	
Paupers and dependents	421.5
Servants	331.9
Common laborers	251.2
Independent (rentner, *selbstandige*)	242.4 to 215.9
Higher employees (private)	211.1
Government officials	203.1[11]
Christiania (1850 to 1879):	
Common labor	191.0
Petty commercial classes	188.0
Higher government officials	170.0[12]

In England the mortality of children of the common people under 5 years of age was in 1883 to 1885 five times greater than that of children under 5 years old of the professional and business classes.[13] Results for the adults of the different social classes are similar. The following figures are a representative illustration:[14]

Social Group	Per 1,000 of the Population of Each Specified Class in the Population of Bremen Who Died in 1911 at the Age:					
	0 to 1 Year	1 to 5 Years	5 to 15 Years	15 to 30 Years	30 to 60 Years	60 Years and Over
Rich....	48.9	2.8	1.7	1.2	6.2	50.7
Middle..	90.9	9.2	2.5	2.7	8.6	56.1
Poor....	255.8	26.2	4.0	6.6	13.6	50.9

Social Groups	Mortality per 1,000 Adults of the Corresponding Class
Paris (1911–1913, per 1,000 population of each class):	
I. The wealthiest group................	11.0
II. The less wealthy....................	13.0
III. Still less wealthy....................	16.0
IV. The poorest group....................	22.4[15]

France (1907–1908, per 1,000 living of each age):

	At the Ages of 35–40	40–45	55–60	60–65
Employers............................	10.0	12.5	27	37
Salaried persons........................	11.0	13.0	34	48
Work people........................	12.0	16.0	37	49

(Death per 1,000 living at the ages of	Employer 35–45	Worker 35–45	Employer 55–65)	Worker 55–65)
Farming class....................	7	8	21	30
Carpenters and joiners...........	7	10	30	43
Bakers..............................	11	18	37	58
Printers............................	8	22	26	56
Textile industry..................	4	11	13	41
Butchers...........................	17	29	41	86
Building trade....................	8	16	28	49[16]

England, Dublin (1883–1885, per 1,000 of population of 25 to 65 years old):

All classes	28.5
Professional and wealthy	15.9
General body of officials	18.36
Clerks and commercial assistants	19.69
Artisans and petty shopkeepers	23.4
General labor (except farm labor)	35.4[17]

Italy (ages from 15 to 60):

Professions	16.2
Commercial	17.7
Tailors	18.8
Porters, woodcutters	18.8
Other trades (manual)	29.9—29.2
Metal factory workers	32.8[18]

Since 1883 to 1885 the situation as to differences remained up to the years of the war, in essence, similar. According to the Report of the Registrar General, in England the professional and well-to-do classes continued to have a mortality considerably lower than that of common labor.[19]

Similar data have been published for Sweden by Wappäus and A. Vogt; for Germany by J. Conrad, Gebhard, and Schurtz; for Switzerland by Kummer and Niceforo; for Italy by Il Ramazzini; for Russia by Ballod and Novoselsky, not to mention many other authors,[20] some of whom are cited at the beginning of this chapter.

Several studies of the problem in the United States have given similar results. In spite of the fact that the standard of living of the American industrial wage earners at the present moment is pretty high, their mortality is still notably higher and their duration of life is still shorter by about eight years than that of the other social classes of this country.[21]

Not to add other figures, which are very numerous and convincing, it is certain on the basis of the above, that under existing conditions the vitality of the lower classes, as it is shown by their longevity and mortality, is considerably lower than that of the higher classes. Members of all classes are mortal, but not in the same degree.

The greater longevity of the upper strata and prominent men, compared with that of the lower classes, is easily understood. It is, on the one hand, the result of a more comfortable environment, on the other, the result of heredity and selection. The rôle of selection is especially important as it concerns that part of the upper classes which is composed of climbers from the lower classes. As a rule, only men with a high longevity have a chance to climb from the lower classes to the higher. The reason is that the climbing demands time. In order to manifest their ability, such men must spend many years in work and preparation before they are recognized and promoted or become prominent. If they die at an early age, they do not have time to show their talent, and therefore do not have a chance to cross any considerable vertical distance. They are eliminated before they reach a high position. The great men and the climbers generally "live a long time for the excellent reason that they must live a long time or they will never become eminent," [22]—such is the situation. It is seen from the following figures. The average of ascent to the throne for the non-hereditary monarchs is 48.5 years; for the Roman-Catholic popes 61.3; for the French, German, and American presidents correspondingly, 59.5, 59.0 and 55.0 years; the average number receiving the Ph.D. in America is 32.2; the leading American scientists got their recognition at an age from 30 to 44; the eminent American inventors made their invention at an average age of 34.9; the average age at election of Russian scholars as members of the Academy of Sciences is 48.5 years; among the poor-born American millionaires, the percentage of those who became rich at an age of from 21 to 30 is only 2.2; more than 60 per cent of them became rich at an age of 51 years and above. Among 222 secretaries of the government of the United States 94.1 per cent obtained their position at the age of about 40 years, 61.9 per cent at the age of above 50 years.[23] This means that those who died at ages earlier than these could not climb to the corresponding positions. They were eliminated before they could cross the distance. For this reason it is quite comprehensible that the age composition of the group actively engaged in the professions and government is more mature and has a lower percentage of young people than industry, or especially, agriculture. On the other hand, within each occupation, the upper strata are composed of people more mature than the lower layers.[24] An average age of the bishops, generals, higher officials, full professors, and so on, is higher correspondingly than that of ministers, soldiers, lower officials, instructors, and so forth.[25] This shows that longevity—different for different ranks—is an indispensable condition of social promotion for the non-hereditary—and partly for the hereditary climbers—hence a higher longevity of the upper classes is a result of selection, to a great extent. They have been supplied permanently, in the main, by people with a long duration of life. As far as longevity depends greatly upon heredity, the climbers with long longevity have transmitted it to their posterity. Such, in brief, is the explanation of the greater longevity of the upper classes compared with that of the lower ones.

2. HEALTH, STRENGTH AND VIGOR

A detailed discussion of the morbidity of the different social groups will not be entered into at this point. It is enough to point out that, though different occupational and social classes have different "occupational" illnesses, nevertheless, it is safe to say that, *in passing from the higher social strata to the lower ones, the general health of the corresponding classes is diminishing.* With relatively few exceptions, given principally by the farmer class, where its conditions are satisfactory, at the apex of the health pyramid of a society are its prominent leaders (men of genius and talent) and professional, wealthy and governing classes (except in periods of decay); next come various groups of the middle classes and agricultural classes; in the lowest strata is the proletarian class of the cities, and at the bottom, the feeble-minded, the idiots, the dependents, the destitutes, the criminals, and the prostitutes. In other words, *the social stratification of a society is positively correlated with the "health stratification" of the social groups of the same society.* Surely, here again there is a considerable overlapping; and the extent of it seems to fluctuate from society to society, from period to period; nevertheless, these facts do not disprove the general rule.

The first confirmation of this correlation is the comparative longevity and mortality of the higher and lower social classes.

The second corroboration consists of the facts of the physical development of the higher and lower social classes. Not only as to height, weight, cranial capacity, and better bodily proportions do the higher classes excel the lower ones; but in many other respects the physical development of the favored classes is generally better. "Whether the good development of the children of the favored classes is due to environmental influences, including diet and medical inspection, or to superior heredity, is a question that cannot be settled with the data at hand. The superiority in development is the common report of investigators"; such is the real situation.[26]

Even in regard to physical force and resistance to fatigue, where the poor and manual classes are supposed to be superior on account of their work and practice—even in these respects the children of the favored classes do not show inferiority. Such is, at least, the result of many experimental studies. The figures of Niceforo[27] give a representative illustration:

Age Groups, Years	Strength of Grasp (Right Hand) Measured by the Dynamometer in Kilograms		Resistance to Fatigue Measured by Ten Subsequent Pressures of the Dynamometer (Averages of Each Subsequent Ten Grasps)		
	Wealthy	Poor		Wealthy	Poor
7	10.0	8.6	Averages of the		
8	11.8	10.8	series of the first		
9	14.5	12.3	pressure	19.1	18.8
10	15.7	14.6	Second pressure	18.3	18.0
11	16.7	16.6	Third pressure	18.2	17.8
12	19.0	18.8	Fourth pressure	18.2	16.9
13	21.5	20.0	Fifth pressure	14.2	14.0
14	24.8	23.3	Sixth pressure	15.0	13.7
			Seventh pressure	14.7	13.2
			Eighth pressure	13.9	9.8
			Ninth pressure	12.3	8.7
			Tenth pressure	12.0	7.0

From these figures we see that the strength of grasp of the children of wealthy parents and their resistance of fatigue is greater than that of the children of the poor classes. Similar results have been obtained by several other investigators in Europe and America, *e.g.*, by F. W. Smedley, by B. W. de Busk, L. M. Terman, B. T. Baldwin, Moore, Schuyten, Barr, Miss Carman, E. A. Dull, and many others.[28] Other authors, *e.g.*, A. MacDonald, J. A. Gilbert, G. M. West, J. E. W. Wallin, did not find such a correlation.[29] Such contradiction is, however, normal because, as we have already seen and shall see, the overlapping in this respect, especially at the present time when purely physical strength plays a part much smaller than before in social life, must be especially great. The above data are given only to show that even in this respect, contrary to a popular opinion, the lower classes are, if not inferior, then, at least, not superior in comparison with the higher classes.

The third confirmation of the superior health of the higher classes is supplied by the studies of the health of the poor and lower classes, and especially by investigations of the health of paupers, dependents, inmates of the workhouses, asylums, and, partially, of prostitutes and criminals. It would be tedious to give here all the abundant data collected in this field. It is enough to point out the works of Charles Booth, B. S. Rowntree, A. L. Bowley, and many other investigators, to make unnecessary the presentation of such data.[30] In these works they are given in abundance. As an illustration, I will give only the following short table of B. S. Rowntree: [31]

Social Classes	General Physical Conditions, Per Cent				Defective Children
	Very Good	Good	Fair	Bad	(per 1,000 children)
The poorest.......	2.8	14.6	31.0	51.6	2.8
The middle.......	7.4	20.1	53.7	18.8	
The upper........	27.4	33.8	27.4	11.4	1.3

On the other hand, the permanent inmates of the workhouses and the habitual paupers and dependents, according to the best definition given them, are "those who are born without manly independence and are unable to do a normal day's work, however frequently it is offered to them." One of the principal causes of their failure is their inherited and acquired physical and mental defectiveness. The same may be said of a considerable number of criminals and prostitutes.[32]

Even the health of this large, and still increasing, social class which is styled as proletarian, or the class of industrial wage earners, is pitiful enough and certainly lower than that of the professional and well-to-do classes. And what is more important, in many places it has not been improving during the last few decades, but rather growing worse. The data which show that the health of the industrial workmen in the United States is lower than that of other principal social classes have been given by many authors, among them by L. J. Dublin, in the data of the Metropolitan Life Insurance Company.[33] In England, the corresponding facts have been disclosed by the study of the recruits during the war. The investigation disclosed a striking increase of the physical defects of this class from the large cities.[34] In Germany the study of the problem by many authors—even before the war—disclosed a similar situation in this class.[35]

Finally, within the proletarian class itself, the lower strata, represented by the poorest and irregularly employed groups of workers, "unsteady" and "professional casual" types, show a health which is poorer and physical defects which are more numerous than those of the "proletarian aristocracy," the better paid and more regularly employed industrial workers.[36]

From the above,[37] it seems safe to conclude that the higher social classes, in general, are physically healthier and superior to the lower ones, and that *social stratification, with some exceptions, is correlated and considerably coincides with "biological" stratification of the same population from the standpoint of physical superiority.* There is no doubt that in some fields (mental diseases, etc.) the upper strata are likely to be more defective than the lower. It is quite probable also that as a temporary and local phenomenon the aristocracy may be even more defective physically than the lower classes, especially in the periods of its decay and "effemination" in leisure and idleness. None the less, as a rule, the above correlation seems to be valid.

This again is due, besides better environment, to a great extent, to a permanent selection of the healthy people from the lower classes. Climbers, as a rule, must be strong people. Without endurance, energy, force, and health, they cannot achieve, and thereby become prominent and promoted. In this way, they permanently supply the upper classes with biologically vigorous elements. As health also depends considerably upon heredity, it is transmitted to the posterity of these climbers who remain within the upper strata. In brief, the above result is due not only to a better environment but to the fact that the population of the upper classes is selective.

3. THE CORRELATION IS LIKELY TO BE PERMANENT

To what extent may this physical superiority of the higher classes, disclosed by the study of the modern societies, be applied to the higher classes of past societies? In other words, is it a quality which belongs to the higher strata of all societies, or is it a characteristic of only a few modern social aggregates? The answer to this question can be only tentative. With this reservation, the most probable answer seems to be as follows: *With the exceptions of periods of decay, and specific extraordinary circumstances, the leaders and the higher classes of almost all societies seem to have been, on the average, superior physically to the lower classes. Among preliterate tribes and past societies an even closer correlation between social and biological stratification may be expected than among modern societies because of the greater importance of physical strength in such societies compared with the more advanced ones. In a period of decay this correlation becomes lower or even disappears; in periods of progress it is likely to increase.* Such is the answer which, in my opinion, is nearest to the truth.

The principal facts which corroborate this are as follows:

The height of the chieftains and of the higher classes of past societies was, it seems, on the average, greater than that of the lower social strata. Still more numerous and more valid facts may be given to show that the higher classes and the leaders of primitive and past societies were physically better developed than the subordinate subjects and classes. Necessarily so, else they could not have been the dominant and ruling classes. If they had been weak, they would have been subjugated and ruled instead of subjugating and ruling others. Ratzenhofer and M. A. Vaccaro, Oppenheimer, and Gumplovicz, not to mention many other names, properly show that domination in many cases was called forth by military conquest. In this way there appeared the dominant Aryans in India, the Spartans in Sparta, the privileged groups in Greece, the patricians in Rome, the Normans in England, a part of the nobility in Europe, nobility (Spanish) in South America, and so on. What does this mean? Necessarily that these conquerors were physically superior and, thanks to this superiority, could subjugate by force populations often more numerous than the conquerors. This is especially true for the past when military weapons consisted of only the physical force of the human body and the simplest arms. Under such conditions, the physically weak could neither conquer, nor subjugate, nor keep their dominion over the conquered masses and classes, often several times more numerous. Similarly, the physically weak could not become chieftains and rulers of their own tribe, unless they displayed an exceptional mental talent. Intelligence, of course, side by side with physical strength, played its part also; but, within the same society, intelligence is considerably correlated with physical superiority. Therefore, it is likely that the leaders and conquerors, being superior physically, often were mentally superior as well. In view of these conditions, it is comprehensible why the "aristocracy" of the past, as a general rule, had to be superior to the lower classes of the same society. The facts seem to warrant this deduction. The principal among them are as follows:

Concerning the *leaders of the preliterate tribes,* Herbert Spencer writes: "Naturally, in rude societies, the strong hand gives predominance. Bodily strength alone procures distinction among the Bushmen." The same feature has been found among the Tasmanians, the Australians, in South America, among the Fuegians, the native tribes of the Pacific Coast, the Andamanese, among tribes of American Indians, among the natives of the South Sea

Islands, among the Siou society, the Columbians, the Haidahs, among the Tapajos, the Bedouins and others.[38] A long series of corresponding facts have been given by J. G. Fraser, by Doctor Vierkandt,[39] by P. Descamps, E. Mumford, M. Kovalevsky, A. H. Post, M. A. Vaccaro, by J. Kohler, and by many others. "Savage hordes in the lowest stage of civilization are organized, like troops of monkeys, on the basis of authority. The strongest old male by virtue of his strength acquires a certain ascendancy, which lasts as long as his physical strength is superior to that of every other male." [40] Such in brief is the situation. The same conclusion is suggested by the athletic contest, existing among many groups, to get the position of a king or leader, or to get the king's daughter. Not only men but women of the higher classes of the preliterate tribes appear to have been physically superior compared with the females of lower social status.

The court lady (among African races) is tall and elegant; her skin smooth and transparent; her beauty has stamina and longevity. The girl of the middle classes, so frequently pretty, is very often short and coarse, and soon becomes a matron, while, if you descend to the lower classes, you will find good looks rare, and the figure angular, stunted, sometimes almost deformed.[41]

This has been found among many other preliterate groups.[42] The situation in Homeric Greece is depicted in the *Odyssey* and the *Iliad*. A great development of athletics and sports among the privileged classes of Greece, an excellent military and physical education of the Spartans so brilliantly depicted in Plato's *Republic* and *The Laws,* and in Thucydides' *The Peloponnesian War,* an artificial biological selection which existed among the Greek nobility; the miracles of physical courage, endurance and strength, showed by this group throughout the history of Greece, except in the time of decay; all this makes certain an excellent physical development of the Greek higher classes. The same must be said of the ancient Roman nobility. Concerning the ancient Germans, Tacitus' statement that they elected *"duces ex virtute,"* and many other sources, witness the same; about medieval Europe:

. . . everyone knows that maintenance of headship largely depended on bodily prowess. And even but two centuries ago in the

Western Isles of Scotland, every Heir, or young Chieftain of a tribe, was obliged in Honour to give a public specimen of his Valor, before he was owned and declared Governor.[43]

That the greatest care was given to physical health in ancient Hindu society, among its rulers and highest castes, is seen in many pages of *The Sacred Books of India.* The Arian invaders were in the first place fighters. To be able to subjugate and to keep their power among the subjugated aboriginals they had to be strong warriors. Therefore, it is natural that among them the commanders as a rule were only "those who are well up in Nîtisâstras, the use of arms and discipline, who are not too young, but of middle age, who are brave, self-controlled, able-bodied." [44] The Kshatriyas, as the soldiers, had to undergo a severe military and physical training. A different but no less severe (mental and) physical training was imposed upon the Brahmanas. In connection with this was introduced and practised an artificial eugenics to a degree scarcely known to present societies.[45] The nobility of the primitive and past societies had to be strong physically because its very business was warfare; hence an intensive and permanent physical training, athletics, sport, tournaments, and so on, even in time of peace. The same may be said of the medieval nobility. Its originators were the strongest, the bravest, the daredevil, self-chosen fighters, warriors, and brigands. Their posterity continued the manner of life of their forefathers, except in periods of decay. The newcomers from the lowest classes were replicas of these originators. The general picture is well depicted by A. Luchaire.

The noble was ever fighting. At this period war existed everywhere. War was the function, the profession of the noble; he was above all a soldier. In time of peace the occupation of the noble consisted in permanent physical training, hunting and the tournament. Because the tournament was a veritable military school, by these voluntary and regulated combats, one exercised and trained himself for that offensive and defensive strife which entirely filled the life of the noble. The hunt was also a battle, a school of war. Even the noble lady had the same military training and education. They also were fighters and soldiers, strong, healthy, and energetic. Again, many upstarts from the lowest classes were the strongest and bravest chiefs of the brigands. Being such, they rendered such important services that kings made them great personages, well paid and provided with titles and fiefs.[46]

Not only the nobility, but also the second privileged class of ancient and medieval societies—the priesthood—contrary to common opinion, exhibited the same physical vigor and strength. Lapouge says, and quite rightly:

The very severity of the monastic regulations concerning physical defects means that only the physically strong could stand it. It is necessary to keep in mind that if a part of the ordinary clergy had a comfortable life the majority of the medieval monasteries, religious orders and cloisters imposed such a physical régime as they do not dare to impose even upon the convicts in the galleys. The totality of the persons who submitted themselves to the ascetic life among the Buddhists and the Brahmanists were healthy and vigorous for the same reasons. The fakirs stood tortures which could not exist in Christian communities, and, if the fakirs endured them, this means that they had the necessary vigor and health.[47]

For my own part, I find that the longevity of the Roman Catholic popes and the highest clergy is longer even than that of prominent men, who generally have a duration of life far above that of the common people. The average duration of life of 85 Roman Catholic popes is 69.8 years, that of 131 prominent theologians, the greater part of whom lived in the Middle Ages, is 68.7 years. These figures are the highest in the Middle Ages, and even in the present time.[48] These data witness convincingly the vitality and the health of the clergy.

Finally, the exclusive vital energy displayed by the most prominent historical personages, by those men of action who by their executive activity—good or bad, it does not matter here—influenced the life of whole nations, is really wonderful. The energy of prominent monarchs and rulers—such as Clovis, Clothaire, Charles the Great, Louis VI, Philip II, Augustus, Louis IX, Charles V, Louis XI, Louis XIV, Napoleon I, in France; Osman I, Orchan, Amurath I, Bajazet I, Mahomet I, Amurath II, Mahomet the Great, Bajazet II, Solyman the Magnificent, in Turkey; Ivan III and Ivan IV, Peter the Great, Catherine II, in Russia; Charles V, Philip II, Charles III, in Spain; William the Conqueror, Henry II, Edward I, Edward III, and Edward IV, Henry V, Henry VII, Henry VIII, Elizabeth, Oliver Cromwell, William III, Victoria, in England; C. Cæsar, Augustus, Tiberius, Diocletianus, S. Severus, Constantine the Great, Theodocius the Great, Justinianus the Great, in Western and Eastern Roman Empire; Otto I, Henry III, Lothaïr the Saxon, Frederick I the Barbarossa, Frederick II, Rudolph I, of Hapsburg; Albert the Great, Maximilian I, Frederick III, Ferdinand I, Frederick the Great Elector, Frederick the Great, William I, in the Holy Roman Empire, Prussia and Austria; Washington, Lincoln, and Roosevelt, in the United States—appears as if it were inexhaustible. When their lives and activities are considered from a purely "energetic point of view," the wonder is how such an enormous amount of energy could be displayed by one human being. How different is the real life of these "shapers of history" from the fictitious pictures of the "lazy and idle kings" so often presented by radical propagandists! The same must be said of other—non-royal—"executives of history," even money makers and financiers. They all displayed a hurricane-like activity which can be produced only by a strong and vigorous human organism.[49]

From the above and many other considerations, it seems to be certain that the higher social classes have been, as a general rule, more healthy and stronger than the lower ones. Only in periods of degeneration of the aristocracy, examples of which are given by the French upper groups before the Revolution of 1789, by the courtiers of Charles I, by the Russian nobility of the end of the nineteenth and in the twentieth centuries, by the Roman plutocratic nobility of the end of the Roman Republic (first and second centuries B.C.),[50] only in such periods of social idleness and parasitism of the higher classes, does this rule seem not to be valid. In such periods the discrepancy between the social and the "biologic" stratifications of society appears to increase and the lower social strata may become equal, or perhaps even superior, physically, to the higher ones. But such aristocracy has its own destiny: it is doomed; it is overthrown; it is expelled from the higher social strata and sinks to the bottom of the social pyramid.

Such has been the usual outcome of such periods, and this regularity, in its own turn, but confirms the above general correlation of physical health and vigor with social stratification.

SUMMARY

1. The higher social classes are stronger physically and also healthier, and have a greater vitality, than the lower ones. The duration of life of the higher social strata is longer and their mortality is lower than that of the lower social layers. The health of the higher classes is better than that of the lower.

2. On the average, the higher social classes are superior physically to the lower classes.

3. These facts show that the social stratification is positively correlated with the stratification of the same population from the standpoint of health and strength and physical superiority.

4. This correlation seems to be permanent; it has existed in the most different societies of the most different times, with the exception of the periods of decay of the aristocracy or the whole society.

5. The above correlation means that, other conditions being equal, physical superiority has been the condition which has favored the social promotion of individuals and has facilitated their social climbing, while physical inferiority has facilitated the "social sinking" of individuals and their location in the lower social strata.

6. The above correlation is not absolute and does not mean that all individuals of the higher classes are physically superior to all individuals of the lower social classes. On the contrary, in every society an overlapping in this respect seems to exist. This overlapping, and consequently the correlation itself, are fluctuating from society to society, or in the same society at different times. When the overlapping becomes great, which means that the higher classes become less and less superior physically in comparison with the lower classes, this degeneration of the higher classes is followed by their overthrow and social degradation. Their place is occupied by newcomers from the lower classes who are superior physically to the degraded nobility.

7. In preliterate groups and in past society the above correla-

tions seem to have been greater than in modern society where physical strength and prowess do not play such an important part as in the past.

[1] See the data and analysis in SOROKIN, P., "The Monarchs and the Rulers," *Journal of Social Forces,* September, 1925; PLOETZ, A., "Lebensdauer der Eltern und Kindersterblichkeit, *Archive für Rassen- und Gesellschafts-Biologie,* Vol. VI, pp. 33-43; KEMMERICH, MAX, *Die Lebensdauer und die Todesursachen innerhalb der Deutschen Kaiser- und Königsfamilien,* Leipzig and Vienna, 1909. For the comparison of longevity in the past see MACDONEL, W. R., "On the Expectation of Life in Ancient Rome and in the Provinces of Hispania and Lusitania, and Africa," *Biometrica,* Vol. IX, pp. 366-380. See other references in my "The Monarchs and the Rulers."

[2] See the data and analysis in SOROKIN, P., "The Monarchs and the Rulers"; ELLIS, HAVELOCK, *op. cit.,* pp. 172-176; ODIN, A., *Genèse des Grands Hommes,* Lausanne, Vol. II, Tables V and VI, 1895; GALTON, FRANCIS, *English Men of Science,* New York, 1875; CATTELL, J. MCKEEN, "Families of American Men of Science," *American Men of Science,* 3d ed., 1921; SOROKIN, P., "American Millionaires and Multimillionaires"; CASTLE, C. S., *A Statistical Study of Eminent Women,* p. 75, New York, 1913. The data about the longevity of American secretaries of the United States, American inventors and American eminent medical men were collected by the members of my seminar: Miss Vida Elliot, Miss M. Tanquist, and Sanford Winston.

[3] See the data in SOROKIN, P., "American Millionaires and Multimillionaires," *Journal of Social Forces,* May, 1925.

[4] LIEPIN, T., LUS, J., PHILIPTSCHENKO, JUR., "Actual Members of the Academy of Sciences During the Last 80 Years," *Bulletin of the Bureau of Eugenics,* No. 3, p. 17, Leningrad, 1925.

[5] This correlation between a greater longevity and talent is corroborated by L. M. Terman's study of gifted children. The longevity of their grandfathers is at least 2.35 years or more in excess of the expected. TERMAN, L. M., *op. cit.,* Chap. VI, pp. 133-135. See also BINDER, R. M., "Health and Eugenics," *Eugenics and Race,* pp. 292-295, Baltimore, 1921. Dr. Castle's, mine, and several other authors' data show further that the longevity of the most eminent men and women is also higher than the longevity of the eminent people of a lower degree.

[6] See BALLOD, C., *Sterblichkeit und Lebensdauer in Preussen,* Berlin, 1907; PRINZING, FR., *Handbuch der Medizinischen Statistik,* 1906; HERSCH, L., "L'inégalité devant la mort d'après les statistiques de la ville de Paris, Effets de la situation sociale sur la mortalité," *Revue d'Économie Politique,* Nos. 3 and 4, pp. 54 *et seq.,* 1920; NICEFORO, A., *op. cit.,* pp. 80 *et seq.;* OLLENDORF, "Die Mortalität und Morbiditätsverhältnisse der Metalschleifer in Solingen," *Centralbl. f. Allgem. Ges.,* 1882; KÖRÖSI, *Influence du degré d'aisance, etc., sur la mortalité et les causes de décès,* Stuttgart, 1885; BERTILLON, J., "Mouvement de population et causes de décès selon le degré d'aisance à Paris, Berlin, Vienne," *Actes du Xe Congres International d'Hygiene et de Demographie,* Paris, 1896; ZIMMERMAN, *Beiträge zur Theorie der Dienst- und Sterbens-Statistik,* Berlin, 1886-1888; HUMPHREYS, N. A., "Class Mortality Statistics," *Journal of the Royal Statistical Society,* June, 1887; OGLE, W., "Summary of Several Male Life Tables," *Journal of the Royal Statistical Society,* pp. 648-652, 1887; BERTILLON, J., "Morbidity and Mortality According to Occupation," *Journal of the Royal Statistical Society,* pp. 559-600, 1892; *Report of the Registrar General of Birth, Death, and Marriages for England and Wales,*

Supplement to the *Sixty-fifth Annual Report;* MARCH, L., "Some Researches Concerning the Factors of Mortality," *Journal of the Royal Statistical Society,* pp. 505-538, 1912; NOVOCELSKY, C., *Smertnost i prodolgitelnost jizny v Rossii,* St. Petersburg, 1916; DUBLIN, L. J., "Health of the Workers," *Monthly Labor Review,* pp. 8-14, 1925; MAYR, G. VON, *Statistik und Gesellschaftslehre,* Vol. II, pp. 84 *et seq.,* Freiburg, 1897; SEUTEMANN, "Kindersterb. soziäler Bevölkerungsruppen," *Beiträge zur Gesch. d. Bevölk, in Deutsch.,* herausgeg; NEUMANN, VON F., Vol. V. Tübingen, 1894; WAPPÄUS, J., *Allgemen. Bevölkerungsstatistik,* Vol. I, pp. 199 *et seq.,* Leipzig, 1859. A good summary and many data see in MOSSE, M., and TUGFNDREICH, G., *Krankheit und Soziale Lage,* pp. 1-41 and *passim,* München, 1913.

[7] CASPER, J. L., *Beiträge zur Medizinischen Statistik,* Berlin, 1825; see the detailed data and analysis in my articles about American millionaires and the monarchs.

[8] SAVORGNAN, F., "Nuzialità e Fecondità delle Case Sovrane d'Europa," *Metron,* Vol. III, No. 2, pp. 217-218.

[9] SUNDBAERG, G., "Maisons souvraines de l'Europe," *Ekonomisk Tidskrift,* Vol. VI, pp. 195-237, 1909.

[10] HERSCH, L., *op. cit.,* p. 293.

[11] MAYR, G. VON, *op. cit.,* p. 284.

[12] WESTERGAARD, H., *Die Lehre von der Mortalität und Morbidität,* pp. 395-396, Jena, 1901.

[13] HUMPHREYS, N., *Class Mortality Statistics,* pp. 264 *et seq.*

[14] FUNK, "Die Sterblichkeit nach sozialen Klassen in der Stadt Bremen," *Mitt. des Brem. Stat. Amtes im Jahre,* No. 1, 1911.

[15] HERSCH, L., *ibid.,* p. 291.

[16] MARCH, L., *op. cit.,* pp. 525-526. "The difference between employers and workmen exists in all the occupations even in those where the employer engages in manual labor with his workmen," says March.

[17] HUMPHREYS, N., *op. cit.,* pp. 264 *et seq.;* see also the mentioned work of W. Ogle, the life tables of Dr. Farr, Angells' *Upper Class Tables,* the *Peerage Tables,* the data of Clay, those of Grimshaw, and so on.

[18] NICEFORO, A., *op. cit.,* p. 96.

[19] See *Supplement* to the *Sixty-fifth Annual Report of the Registrar General of Birth, Death, and Marriages for England and Wales,* and the data of the reports and the supplements for the later years.

[20] See WAPPÄUS, J., *op. cit.,* pp. 199 *et seq.;* CONRAD, J., *Samml. nat. stat. Abh. des staatw. Seminars zu Halle, herausgeg;* VON CONRAD, J., Vol. I, p. 2, Jena, 1887; RAMAZZINI, in *Giornile italiana di medicina sociale,* fasc. I to III, 1907; BERTILLON, J., *De la fréquence des principales causes de décès, etc.; Bericht über den XIV Intern. Kongress f. Hyg.,* Bd. III, 1, Berlin, 1908; PRINZING, F., *Handbuch der Medizinischen Statistik,* 1906; MOSSE., M., and TUGENDREICH, *Enleitung, in Krankheit und Soziale Lage,* pp. 1-23, München, 1913.

[21] DUBLIN, L. J., "Health of the Workers," pp. 8 *ff.*

[22] ELLIS, HAVELOCK, *op. cit.,* p. 173.

[23] SOROKIN, P., "The Monarchs and the Rulers"; PHILIPTSCHENKO, JUR., *op. cit.,* p. 14.

[24] See the figures in SCHWARZ, OTTO, "Das Soziale Schiksal in seiner Abhangigkeit von dem Alter," *Allgemeinen Statisches Archiv,* Vol. XIV, pp. 138-148, 1925.

[25] See some data in *Allgemeinen Statisches Archiv,* Vol. XIV, pp. 249-254.

[26] BALDWIN, B. T., *The Physical Growth of Children,* p. 229.

[27] NICEFORO, A., *op. cit.,* pp. 28-30.

[28] See the quoted works of these authors.

[29] See MACDONALD, A., *op. cit.*, pp. 26 *et seq.*; GILBERT, J. A., "Researches on School Children and College Students," *University of Iowa Studies in Psychology,* Vol. I, pp. 1-39, 1894; WEST, D. M., "Observation of a Relation of Physical Development," *Science,* N. S., pp. 156-159, 1896.

[30] See BOOTH, CHARLES, *Life and Labor of the People of London,* all volumes, especially the final volume; ROWNTREE, B. S., *Poverty,* London, 1906; see other data in HAMILTON, LORD GEORGE, "A Statistical Survey of the Problem of Pauperism," *Journal of the Royal Statistical Society,* December, 1910; GILLIN, JOHN L., *Poverty and Dependency,* pp. 55 *et seq.*, New York, 1922; PARMELEE, M., *Poverty and Social Progress,* pp. 46 *et seq.*, 1921; LIDBETTER, E. J., "Pauperism and Heredity," *The Eugenic Review,* October, 1922; POTTS, W. A., "Criminality from the Eugenics Standpoint," *The Eugenic Review,* Vol. XII, pp. 81-90.

[31] ROWNTREE, B. S., *op. cit.*, pp. 213-215.

[32] See besides the above works, MALZBERG, B., "Mental Defects and Prostitution," *The Eugenic Review,* Vol. XII, pp. 100-104; KELLEY, A., and LIDBETTER, E., "A Comparative Inquiry on the Heredity and Social Conditions," *The Eugenic Review,* Vol. XIII, pp. 394-406; CLARKE, W., *op. cit.*; GODDARD, H. H., *Feeble-mindedness,* pp. 1-18, New York, 1914; FURBUSH, E., "Social Facts Relative to Patients," *Mental Hygiene,* Vol. V, pp. 595-596; NELS, A., *The Hobo,* University of Chicago Press; GREGOR, A., "Rassenhygiene und Jugendfursorge," *Archive Rassen- und Gesellschafts-Biologie,* Vol. XIII, pp. 37-55; GREGOR, A., and GRUHLE, H., *Über die Ursachen der jugendl. Verwahrlosung und Kriminalität,* Berlin, 1912.

[33] See DUBLIN, J., *op. cit., passim.*

[34] See *Report upon the Physical Examination of Men of Military Age by National Service Medical Board from November 1 to October 31, 1918,* London; ANONYMOUS, "A Physical Census and Its Lesson," *British Medical Journal,* pp. 348-349, 1918; COLLIS, E. L., and GREENWOOD, MAJOR, *The Health of the Industrial Worker, passim,* London, 1921.

[35] WELLMAN, E., *Abstammung, Beruf und Heeresersatz in ihren gesetz. Susammenh.*, Leipzig, 1917; THURNWALD, R., "Stadt und Land in Lebensprocess der Rasse.," *Archiv für Rassen- und Gesellschafts-Biologie,* Vol. I, *passim;* CLAASEN, W., "Die Abnehmende Kriegstüchtigkeit im Deutsche Reich in Stadt und Land," *Archive für Rassen- und Gesellschafts-Biologie,* Vol. VI, pp. 73-77. See here several other papers dedicated to the same problem; further, a great deal of data were published by Abelsdorf and by many other authors in many volumes of the *Schriften des Vereins für Sozialpolitik* dedicated to the problem: "Auslese und Anpassung der Arbeiterschaft" in different industries.

[36] See the data in LESCOHIER, D. D., *The Labor Market,* chapter on "The Laborer," 1919; SOLENBERGER, A. W., *One Thousand Homeless Men,* Chap. IX; ROWNTREE, B. S., and LASKER, *Unemployment, A Social Study, passim.*

[37] A very careful and competent investigation of the comparative health and morbidity and mortality of different social classes is given in a volume: *Krankheit und Soziale Lage,* München, 1913. Edited by Profs. M. Mosse and G. Tugendreich and composed of papers of the most prominent specialists, the volume gives an excellent statistical and medical summary of the investigations of the comparative morbidity and health of different classes. All those who want to have detailed data in this field are referred to this volume.

[38] SPENCER, HERBERT, *Principles of Sociology,* Vol. II, pp. 332 *ff.*; see also CANDOLL, A. DE, *Histoire de sciences et de savants,* p. 124, Génève, 1885.

[39] See the facts in the works of VIERKANDT, A., *Führende Individuen bei den Naturvölkern,* Zeitschrift für Sozialwiss, Vol. XI, pp. 542-553, 623-639, 1908; FRAZER, J. G., *op. cit.*, pp. 258 *ff.*; LOWIE, R. H., *op. cit.*, Chaps. XII and XIII; KOVALEVSKY, M., *Sociology* (Russian), Vol. II, pp. 186 *et seq.*; VACCARO, M.

A., *Les bases sociologique du droit et de l'état;* Post, A. H., *Evolution of Law, passim,* Boston, 1915; Kohler, J., *Philosophy of Law,* pp. 96 *et seq.*, Boston, 1914; Descamps, P., *Les Pouvoirs publiques chez les Sauvages,* pp. 225-261; Mumford, E., "The Origins of Leadership," *American Journal of Sociology,* Vol. XII, pp. 220 *ff.*, 373 *ff.*, 516 *ff.*

[40] Leopold, L., *Prestige,* p. 59, London, 1913.

[41] Spencer, Herbert, *op. cit.*, p. 301.

[42] Frazer, J. G., *op. cit.*, pp. 260 *et seq.*

[43] Spencer, Herbert, *ibid.*, p. 334.

[44] *The Sacred Books of the Hindus,* edited by Basu, Mayor B. D., Vol. XVI, p. 50, Allahabad, 1914.

[45] See *The Sacred Books of the East,* Vol. XXXIII, *Narada,* Vol. XII, pp. 8-20, Oxford, 1889. See many similar eugenical devices in *Narada, Brihaspati, Laws of Manu,* Chap. III; *The Institutes of Vishnu,* and other sacred books of India. See also *The Cambridge History of India,* Vol. I, Chaps. II to IV, New York, 1922.

[46] Luchaire, Ach., *Social France at the Time of Philip Augustus,* Chaps. VIII to XI, pp. 10, 261-271, 315, New York, 1912.

[47] Lapouge, V. de, *op. cit.*, pp. 268-270.

[48] Sorokin, P., "The Monarchs and the Rulers."

[49] See proper remarks and facts in Gowin, E. B., *The Executive and His Control of Men,* Chaps. I-IV; Taussig, F. W., *op. cit., passim;* Sombart, W., *Der Bourgeois, passim.*

[50] See the facts and the sources in Sorokin, P., *Sociology of Revolution,* pp. 397 *et seq.*, J. B. Lippincott Company, 1925.

CHAPTER XII

SOCIAL STRATIFICATION AND INTELLIGENCE AND OTHER MENTAL CHARACTERISTICS

1. THE CONCEPTION OF INTELLIGENCE (GENERAL AND SPECIAL)

UNDER general intelligence is understood "the aptitude to modify conduct in conformity to the circumstances of each case,"[1] or "the ability of the organism to adjust itself adequately to a new situation," or "behavior that leads to better and better adaptation not only in man, but in the whole animal kingdom. It includes the capacity for getting along well in all sorts of situations."[2] With slight variation the same conception of intelligence is given by almost all contemporary psychologists. The same definition applied to a special form of intelligence is styled as a talent or genius and means the ability to perform excellently a definite task—whatever it may be—set forth by an individual. According to the nature of the task there may be a special genius or talent for scientific, æsthetic, moral, and various practical activities. We may talk about a man who has a talent for hunting, dancing, singing, making money, ploughing, ruling men, inventing, painting, even stealing, and so on. The best specialists in every kind of a specific activity are styled as men of genius or men of talent, the *élite* or the leaders in this specialty.[3]

It goes without saying that intelligence is the most important condition for existence, survival, and success for the individual, as well as for the social group. There is no need also to insist that according to their intelligence human beings are not equal. In this respect we have the greatest gradation of men from that of the highest genius to the idiot; from an inborn leader in a definite kind of activity to a man absolutely incapable of achieving anything in this field.

If such is the case, we have a problem: what is the relation between the phenomena of social stratification of individuals within a society and their distribution according to intelligence?

Are these two kinds of distribution correlated with each other? Such is the problem to be discussed now.

2. CORRELATION OF SOCIAL AND MENTAL DISTRIBUTIONS

My answer to the question is positive. Aside from the problem, whether the result is due to heredity or to environment, *the higher social classes, on the whole, are more intelligent than the lower ones.* This may be said of the general, as well as of the special—the most important socially—forms of intelligence. In other words, as a general rule, *the social and mental distribution of individuals within a given society are positively correlated. The degree of this correlation varies* from society to society, from one period to another. In the periods of the decay of the higher classes or of an entire society the correlation may decrease or even disappear. But such an abnormal situation leads to a revolutionary displacement in which the degenerate higher groups are overthrown and demolished. The abnormality of such catastrophes in the life of a society only confirms the general rule. As long as a society exists more or less successfully, its higher strata as a whole consist of men on the average more intelligent than the people of the lower strata.[4] Here again is overlapping which is to be found in any society. Part of the higher classes is composed of individuals less intelligent than part of the members of the lower social strata. But this overlapping does not invalidate the above general rule.

What facts corroborate these statements? Many. The principal ones are as follows:

Correlation of Physical with Mental Development.—First, indirect corroboration is seen in the probable existence of a correlation of physical and mental development. Above it has been shown that the higher classes are better developed physically than the lower ones. It has also been shown that, according to many investigations, physical development is positively correlated with mental development: those who are better physically on the average are more intelligent. *"In corpore sano mens sana"*: such is the fact in the well-known statement of J. A. Comenius. Hence, the conclusion: The higher classes are more intelligent than the lower classes. The syllogism is logically unavoidable.

Its first premise has been established above. Its second premise, the fact of the correlation of the physical and mental development, has been obtained by Porter, Talko-Hrinzewicz, Ellis, Gowin, Livi, Pagliani, Villermé, Roberts, Sack, Gratzianoff, Coy, Cleveland, Pfitzner, Röse, Venn, Hartwell, West, Hastings, Christopher, Smedley, Beyer, Zirke, Ploetz, Baldwin, Chapin, Schmidt, Graupner, Rüdin, Dräseke, Mateigka, Bayerthal, Rietz, Binet, Simon, Debusk, Stewart, Naccarati, Spielrein, Mead, Donaldson, Terman, Doll, Goddard, Porteus, Wylie, Pearson, Parsons, Constantine, Boddoe, and by many other prominent specialists in this field.[5] It is true that some few authors, like Gilbert, Cattell and Farrand, E. Heidbreder and Radosavljevich, did not find this correlation.[6] But their results are rather exceptions to the general rule and do not disprove it. If there were not such exceptions then we should have taken the correlation as quite "perfect," a fact which I do not pretend to prove. Taken alone, this correlation may not give a convincing corroboration of the higher intelligence of the upper social groups; taken together with other facts which point to the same phenomenon, it represents an additional corroboration and in this sense is worthy of mention.

The Number of Men of Genius produced by Different Social Classes of the Same Society.—The second corroboration of my statement is the number of geniuses and prominent leaders produced by different social strata of the same society. When different fields produce different crops of the best flowers and when the smaller fields yield a larger crop, we have the right to say that these smaller fields are more fertile than the larger ones. This is just the situation which we find in regard to the number and quality of the leaders produced by different social strata.

Among present European societies the most "fertile" social group in the production of the men of genius seems to have been the royal families. The same families are at the apex of the social pyramid. Investigation of Frederick Adams Woods has shown that here for about 800 individuals we have about 25 geniuses. "The royal bred, considered as a unit, is superior to any other one family, be it that of noble or commoner." [7] Granting that the data of Doctor Woods are greatly exaggerated we still have an abundant crop of men of genius from the royal families which has not been produced by any other social group.

According to Francis Galton, in the English population about 250 men out of every 1,000,000 become simply eminent and only one out of 1,000,000 becomes a genius. Even at the climax of their history, between 530 and 430 B.C. "the ablest race of whom history bears record"—the ancient Greeks—had produced only one illustrious man per 3,214 free-born men who survived the age of 50 years.[8] This gives a criterion by which to compare the intelligence of European royal families with that of other groups which are the most conspicuous in the production of a genius. My study of monarchs of different times and countries—a group considerably different from that of Frederick Adams Woods' royal group—showed that out of 352 monarchs 50, or 15.0 per cent, were the men of an unquestionable mental superiority; 272, or 76 per cent, were men of a very high average intelligence and 30, or 8.5 per cent, were under an average level.[9]

These data show that climbing to the position of a monarch, for the group of monarchs and royal families as a whole, has not been a mere matter of chance but has had a serious basis—mental superiority in the form of "executive genius."

Let us proceed further and take the share of other classes in the production of the leaders, of men of genius and talent. This share is seen from the following figures, obtained by a rather painstaking investigation of the indicated authors. (See p. 284.)

The figures show that the upper and professional classes composing only 4.46 per cent of the population, produced 63 per cent of the men of genius, while the labor, artisan, and industrial classes, composing about 84 per cent of the population, produced only 11.7 per cent of the greatest leaders of Great Britain. The per cent of British men of genius produced by common labor and artisans is especially low: 2.5 per cent for 74.28 of the total population. Here are taken British men of genius since the beginning of the history of England up to the twentieth century. During the nineteenth century, according to A. H. H. MacLean's Study of 2,500 Eminent British Men of the nineteenth century, the share of aristocracy during this period rather increased (26 per cent of all leaders instead of 18.5 per cent); the share of the

Social Status of the Most Prominent British Men of Genius	Number of Cases	Per Cent in the Total Number of British Men of Genius
Upper Classes	154	18.5
Church	139	16.7
Law	59	7.1
Army	35	4.2
Navy	16	1.9
Medicine	30	3.6
Miscellaneous professions	65	7.8
Officials, clerks	27	3.2
Commercials	156	18.8
Crafts	77	9.2
Yeomen and farmers	50	6.5
Artisans and unskilled labor	21	2.5
Total	829	100.0

PER CENT OF THE CORRESPONDING CLASSES IN THE TOTAL POPULATION OF ENGLAND [10]

Upper classes and professions	4.46
Commercial class	10.36
Industrial class	10.90
Artisans	26.82
Labor	47.46
Total	100.00

professions increased also (49 per cent instead of 44.5 per cent); the share of the labor class and the artisans decreased, in spite of an increased literacy and greater educational facilities for the lower classes in the nineteenth century.[11] According to the more detailed study of Frederick Adams Woods, during the first quarter of the nineteenth century the artisans and labor class produced only 7.2 per cent of the men of genius in England, instead of 11.7 per cent as during the preceding centuries; and during the second quarter of the nineteenth century only 4.2 per cent.[12] Thus, in spite of an increase of educational facilities the great mass of the British population was and still is even more than before, sterile in the production of geniuses. Francis Galton studied 107 of the most prominent British scientists of the nineteenth century. Out of 107 scientists 9 belonged to the nobility; 52 to the liberal professions; 43 to the British class of bankers, large merchants and manufacturers; 2 to the class of farmers; and 1 to the labor and artisan class.[13] All these data are so illuminating that there is no need for any further commentaries.

France.—Similar results have been received in France in regard to all French men of letters. The corresponding figures obtained by Odin in his careful study show the following number of prominent men per the same number of the population of various classes. The nobility (159) produced literary geniuses in France two and one-half times more than the high magistrature (62); six and one-half times more than the liberal professions (24); twenty-three times more than the bourgeoisie (7) and two hundred times more than the labor classes! (.8)[14] According to different periods the per cent of literary genius produced by different classes is as follows:

Social Classes	Periods				
	1700–1725	1725–1750	1750–1775	1775–1800	1800–1825
Nobility	31.0	26.7	20.6	13.6	18.3
High magistrature	50.0	52.6	50.0	54.9	53.1
Bourgeoisie	7.1	10.35	18.5	18.6	15.2
Labor class	11.9	10.35	10.9	12.9	13.4
Total	100.	100.	100.	100.	100.

A decrease in the share of nobility in 1775 to 1800 is a result of its extermination in the French Revolution. Nevertheless, in the period from 1800 to 1825 it shows again an increase of fertility in the production of genius. Of the most illustrious French scientists, according to the study of de Candolle, 35 per cent were produced by the French aristocracy, 42 per cent by the professions and the middle class, and only 23 per cent were from all other lower classes, which composed from two-thirds to three-fourths of the population.[15] Of the 100 most illustrious scientists of Europe 41 came from the nobility, 52 from the middle class, and only 7 from the labor classes.[16] "The class of the workingmen, peasants, lower employees, sailors, soldiers, and so on is the most numerous in every country. It composes from two-thirds to three-fourths of the whole population. And yet, from these classes is derived the smallest percentage of illustrious scientists in spite of all means of promotion through schools and other institutions."[17]

There are some serious reasons for thinking that the proportion of the men of genius yielded by the French lower classes, in other than scientific and literary fields of activity is still less than that in scientific and literary fields. In brief, France gives the same picture of sterility of the lower classes in her production of great men that has been given by England.

Germany.—Fritz Maas studied 4,421 of the most prominent German men of genius in various fields of activity (writers, poets, painters, composers, scientists, scholars, artists, pedagogues, statesmen, captains of industry and finance, military men, and so on) who were born after 1700 and died before 1910. His study shows that the higher classes (nobility, professions and the wealthy class of the big manufacturers and merchants) who have composed less than 20 per cent of the total population, produced 83.2 per cent of the men of genius, while the lower labor classes, which composed more than 80 per cent of the total population, have yielded only 16.8 per cent of the German leaders. Especially small has been the relative share of the proletariat, in spite of the rather large size of this class in the second half of the nineteenth and at the beginning of the twentieth century. The per cent of the men of genius who came out of this class has been only 0.3 per cent. This is seen from the following table. (See p. 287.)

These figures show a real sterility of this class in the production of genius. Better is the situation of the artisan class which produced 8.7 per cent of all genius; the peasant class produced 3.8

Type of Genius	Per Cent of Genius from the Proletarian Class in the Total Number of Geniuses
Poets	0.3
Authors	0.5
Musicians	0.0
Painters	0.3
Actors, players	0.0
Theologians	0.8
Philologists	0.4
Historians	0.0
Pedagogues	0.8
Jurists	0.3
Physicians and chemical scientists	0.6
Biologists	0.0
Statesmen	0.0
Agriculturists	0.0
Military men	0.0
Captains of finance and industry	0.0

per cent, and the class of petty shopkeepers, petty employees, and subordinate officials yielded 3.8 per cent. In total the picture is essentially the same as that of England and France. And again, in spite of an increase of the educational facilities for the lower classes during the nineteenth century, these classes do not show any marked increase in their productivity of genius. This is seen from the following data:

Social Classes from Which the Men of Genius Came	Per Cent of Genius from Each Class in the Specified Historical Periods According to the Year of Birth		
	1700 to 1789	1789 to 1818	1818 to 1860
Nobility	19.2	14.2	11.0
High magistrature and professions	53.3	55.8	60.0
Bourgeoisie (commercial class)	15.3	16.4	16.4
Labor classes	11.9	13.6	12.4

A decrease of the proportion of men of genius from the nobility here, as well as in the table of A. Odin in France, is the result of the decrease of this class in its size in the total population—the decrease which resulted from the revolutions of 1789 and 1848 and Napoleonic wars, in which a considerable proportion of nobility perished and its privileges, as a class, were annihilated. Among the labor classes there is no steady trend of an increase of their productivity of genius. In another detailed table, Doctor Maas shows that among the labor classes, during the period from 1700 to 1910, the share of the artisans remains constant; the peasantry shows a slight increase of its productivity; the proletariat, on the contrary, shows a decrease of its share in the production of genius.[18]

United States of America.—Similar studies in the United States have given the same results. According to the data of Prof. J. McKeen Cattell, the share of different classes from which the leading American men of science came and the proportion of these classes in the total population of the United States were as follows:

Social Classes	Per cent of Leading Men of Science from Each Class	Per cent of the Class in the Total Population of United States
Professions	43.1	3.1
Manufacturing and trade	35.7	34.1
Agricultural class	21.2	44.1

The majority of the leading scientists came from the upper and middle classes and not a single one was produced by the group of domestic servants or by the class of day laborers.[19] Dr. Stephen S. Visher studied the occupation of the fathers of 18,400 of the prominent Americans from *Who's Who* with the following results.[20] (See p. 289.)

While in the clergy and professions we have one notable person per every 32 and 70 persons, among the class of unskilled labor we have only one prominent man per 75,000 persons! The con-

Social Classes	Persons in Each Class per Notable	Notable Men per 10,000 Persons in Each Class
Laborers, unskilled	75,000	0.013
Laborers, skilled and semi-skilled	2,470	4.
Farmers	1,100	9.
Businessmen	124	80.
Professions (except clergy)	70	142.
Clergy	32	315.

trast is more than tremendous. Dr. Edwin L. Clarke, in his study of 1,000 of the most prominent American men of letters came to the following results:[21]

Social Class from Which Men of Letters Came	Number of Men of Letters from Each Class
Professional	328
Commercial	151
Agricultural	139
Mechanical, clerical, unskilled	48
Unknown	334
Total	1,000

Again the same picture: a numerically insignificant part of the total population—the professional and commercial classes—produced more than 60 per cent of all prominent men of letters in the United States.

My study of 476 American captains of industry and finance showed that 79.8 per cent of these leaders were produced by the commercial and professional classes; 15.6 per cent by farmers; and only 4.6 per cent by the skilled and unskilled labor class.[22] And here again the share of the labor class in the production of the geniuses of industry and finance is not increasing but decreasing.

Similar results were obtained by Charles H. Cooley. Doctor Cooley's study of 71 of the most prominent poets, philosophers, and historians of all times and countries has shown that 45 of them came from the upper and upper middle classes, 24 from the lower middle class and only 2 from the labor classes.[23] Out of 217 of the most eminent women of all countries and of all times only 5 came from the farmer class, and only 4 from the labor class.[24] Scott Nearing,[25] partially, and George R. Davies [26] and Dr. L. M. Terman quite recently came to a similar conclusion. The brightest children, with an average I.Q. of 151.33, studied by Terman and his collaborators happened to come out from the following social groups:

Occupation of Fathers of Gifted Children	Proportion among Fathers of Gifted Child	Proportion of Each Occupational Group in Population of Los Angeles and San Francisco
Professional	29.1	2.9
Public service	4.5	3.3
Commercial	46.2	36.1
Industrial	20.2	57.7
Total	100.0	100.0

Per Cent of Quota of Each Occupational Group among Fathers of Gifted Children

Professional	1,003
Public service	137
Commercial	128
Industrial	35

"In the industrial group only one man gives his occupation as 'laborer' which is 0.2 per cent of our fathers as compared with 15.0 per cent of the total *population* classified as laborers in the census report." [27]

Russia.—Jur. Philiptschenko's study of the contemporary Russian scientists, scholars and representatives of the arts and literature gave the following results:[28]

Occupation of Fathers	Per cent of Scientists and Scholars from Each Class	Per cent of Representatives of Arts and Literature from Each Class	Per cent of Great Contemporary Scientists and Scholars from Each Class	Per cent of Greatest Scientists and Scholars, Members of Academies of Science for Last 80 Years
Professions	36	44.6	46.0	30.2
Officials	18.2	20.0	8.0	15.5
Military	9.4	7.7	14.0	16.2
Clergy	8.8	1.8	10.0	14.8
Commercial	13.0	6.7	12.0	5.6
Agricultural[a]	7.9[a]	9.6[a]	6.0[a]	14.1[b]
Skilled and unskilled labor	2.7	9.6	4.0	3.5[c]
Not known	4.0			0.1
Total	100.0	100.0	100.0	100.0

[a] Including the landlords and gentry.
[b] Only the landlords and gentry.
[c] Including peasants.

The labor classes (agricultural and labor) compose even in contemporary Russia more than 90 per cent of the population; and yet they yielded quite an insignificant per cent of scientists and scholars, artists, literary men, and so on; this per cent is still less among the great men of science.

The sterility of the proletariat is witnessed also by the fact that its leaders even in the nineteenth and twentieth centuries, as a general rule, have been the individuals from the upper and middle classes. Such, at least, has been the situation in Europe. The contemporary socialist movement is always called to life "by non-workers; it is derived chiefly from 'the cultured classes,'" truly says R. Michels, one of the best specialists in the field.[29] Spartacus, Th. Münzer, Florian, Geier, Mirabeau, Roland,

Lafayette, Sieyes, Phil. Egalité, Saint-Simon, Fourier, R. Owen, L. Blanc, Blanqui, Lassall, Karl Marx, F. Engels, Kropotkin, Bakunin, and so on are the examples in the past. The same situation in essence exists at present in Europe as well as in Russia.

Data obtained by different investigators in different countries will not be given here. They only confirm the above results. The complete accordance of all these authors, even those who apparently have tried to obtain the results favorable for the lower classes (Odin, Maas, Clarke, Cooley, Philiptschenko), gives a quite certain basis to state that the intelligence of the higher classes has been far above that of the lower classes in all European societies. Passing from the bottom of a social pyramid to its apex a systematic increase of the number of men of genius is seen—an absolute, as well as a relative increase. It is as though two pyramids—that of social classes and that of men of genius—are turned in reverse direction: while the pyramid of social classes becomes larger and larger in proceeding from the higher to the lower social classes, the pyramid of men of genius becomes narrower and narrower. Its largest base is at the apex of the pyramid of social classes, and contrariwise. Such is the second corroboration of my hypothesis.

Intelligence of Different Social Groups According to Intelligence Tests.—The third corroboration of my statement is the results of intelligence testing of various social groups. Though the methods of mental tests are still imperfect and may lead sometimes to doubtful results, nevertheless, when properly made to a sufficiently large number of individuals and applied and controlled by school marks of the children and by other methods of intelligence estimation, they may give an approximate indication of the degree of native plus acquired intelligence.

At the present moment, abundant data from which to judge the intelligence of various social groups have been assembled. The general conclusion suggested by numerous intelligence tests is that the higher social classes are more intelligent than the lower ones. Of many data of this kind, only a few which are representative will be mentioned. Other figures may be found in the sources indicated in footnotes.

In the first place, take the results of the intelligence tests given the United States Army. These have shown that the intelligence of different groups of the population of the United States is very different. Designating as *A, B, C +, C, C —, D, D—*, the intelligences which are correspondingly: "Very superior," "superior," "high average," "average," "low average," "inferior," and "very inferior," we have the following per cent of each group in the United States Army: [30]

	Percentage Making Grade						
	D –	*D*	*C* –	*C*	*C* +	*B*	*A*
White draft................	7.0	17.1	23.8	25.0	15.0	8.0	4.1
Negroes....................	49.0	29.7	12.9	5.7	2.0	0.6	0.1

The table shows how intelligence is distributed among the population, how great are the differences in intelligence of the different parts of the population, and how small is the per cent of the people with "superior" and "very superior" intelligence, among the population of the United States and of any other country.

The same data show, further, that there is a close correlation between social stratification and intelligence: the higher social groups have exhibited the higher intelligence. This is seen in the following data. (See p. 294.)

According to median intelligence rating, in the lowest intelligence groups (*D—, D,* and *C—*) are principally the following occupational groups: common laborer, miner, teamster, barber. Occupational groups which have a higher intelligence *C* are: horseshoer, bricklayer, cook, baker, painter, blacksmith, carpenter, butcher, machinist, plumber, gunsmith, mechanic, auto-repair man. Occupational groups with the *C*+ intelligence "high average" are construction foreman, stock-keeper, photographer, telegrapher. railroad clerk, filing clerk, general clerk, army nurse, bookkeeper.

B— intelligence has been shown principally by the occupational groups such as: dentist, mechanical draughtsman, accountant, civil engineer, medical officer. *A*— intelligence has been discovered principally among engineer-officers. In the form of I.Q. the same is expressed in the following figures:[31]

Occupation	I.Q.	Occupation	I.Q.
Civil engineers	274	Bakers and cooks	106
Lawyers and teachers	252	Printers	99
Chemists	205	Carpenters	91
Postal employees	200	Metal workers	88
Artists	198	Leather workers	88
Clerks	175	Horsemen	75
Salesmen	170	Teamsters	72
Merchants	138	Barbers	65
Policemen	119	Laborers	63
Machinists	107		

These data show a rather close correlation between social status and intelligence. Unskilled and semiskilled labor have a very inferior and low average intelligence; skilled labor groups are principally in the group of "high average" intelligence; superior and very superior intelligence are only among high professional and high business classes.

The same parallelism of social and mental ranks has been found in different forms. First, the intelligence of the white officers was much superior to that of the soldiers: in the terms of mental age the mean for the whole white draft is 13.1 years, for the officers the mean is 17.3 years.[32] Second, the investigation disclosed "the prevalence of superior intellectual ability among officers and among privates rated as 'best' by their officers and the amazing prevalence of inferior intelligence among disciplinary cases and men rated by their officers as of 'low military value' or 'unteachable.'" More detailed gradation according to intelligence beginning with the superior and passing to the inferior is as follows: commissioned officers, O.T.S. students, sergeants, corporals, the best privates, white recruits, disciplinary cases, the poorest privates, men of low military value, unteachable men.[33] On the other hand, it is necessary to mention that the testing disclosed a considerable overlapping of intelligence of different social groups. For instance, among the O.T.S. students there were men with *D, D—*, and E intelligence, and among the soldiers and the low ranks there happened to be men with *A* and *B* intelligence. The same may be said about the occupational groups. Everywhere the fact of overlapping has been discovered. This, however, does not disprove the indicated fact of existence of a superior intelligence among the higher social strata and inferior intelligence among the lower strata.[34]

Other proof of superior intelligence of the higher social classes is given by the results of *intelligence testing of the children of different social classes.* At the present moment we have very numerous studies of this kind and their results in essence are almost unanimous. The children of the professional and well-to-do classes, as a general rule, show a much superior intelligence to that of the children of the labor classes. The following figures may be taken as representative. According to the study of Doctor Terman, the median I.Q. for the children of the semi-skilled and unskilled labor classes has been 82.5 while the median I.Q. for the children of the professional and high business classes has been 112.5. The per cent of the superior children with I.Q. 135 to 140 has been among the studied group, in the professional class—53, in semiprofessional—37, in the skilled labor—10, in the semiskilled and unskilled—0.[35]

Similar results have been obtained in his last study of gifted children. Some of the corresponding figures of this valuable study are given above.

The I.Q. of 13,000 children, at the age of 11 and 12 years, studied by J. F. Duff and Godfrey H. Thomson in England (left column) and the I.Q. of the children in the Isle of Wight, tested by H. MacDonald (right column) have been as follows (according to occupation of their fathers). (See p. 296.)

While of 597 of Duff's and Thomson's group of children from the professions and higher commercial classes 471 were above average mental level and only 126 below the average, among 1,214

Occupational Groups	England I. Q.	Isle of Wight I. Q.
Professionals	112.2	106.6
Managers	110.0	108.7
Higher commercial class	109.3	103.3
Army, navy, police, postmen	105.5	99.9
Shopkeeping class	105.0	100.7
Engineers	102.9	100.8
Foremen	102.7	103.1
Building trades	102.0	99.1
Metal workers, shipbuilders	100.9	99.3
Miscellaneous industrial workers	100.6	99.1
Mines, quarrymen	97.6	97.9
Agricultural classes	97.6	96.7
Laborers	96.0	96.0

children from low-grade occupations—from laborers—746 were below and only 468 were above the average mental level.[36] Similar results were obtained by S. Z. Pressey and R. Ralston. Of 548 children studied, the per cent of those children who were above the group mental median, was:[37]

	Per cent
For the children of professionals	85
For the children of executives	68
For the children of artisans	41
For the children of laborers	39

According to the study of J. W. Bridges and L. E. Coler, out of 300 children studied, the mental average of the children of different social groups has been as follows:[38]

Children from professional class	1.42
Children of traveling salesmen	1.26
Children of proprietors	1.21
Children of skilled workers	1.12
Children of unskilled laborers	0.83

The intelligence of the Indiana high school seniors, according to the social status of their fathers, has been as follows:[39]

Social Groups	Per cent of Children above Median Intelligence	Per cent Very High Intelligence (A +)	Per cent of Very Low Intelligence
Professional	60	4.4	1.3
Clerical	60	2.4	
Salesmen	56	2.8	0.3
Artisans	55	2.3	0.8
Executives	54	3.0	1.0
Farmers	43	1.5	1.2
Day laborers	47	1.4	1.7

The testing of 8,121 children of elementary and high school by Dr. M. E. Haggerty and H. B. Nash gave the following results:

Groups	Medium I.Q.	Per cent of Pupils 140 and Up (Bright)	With I.Q. 50 to 59 (Dull)
Professional	116	11.75	0.00
Business and clerical	107	6.04	0.01
Skilled	98	1.94	0.58
Semiskilled	95	1.15	0.95
Farmer	91	0.87	1.93
Unskilled	89	0.04	3.36

The data at the same time show again the fact of overlapping. It is especially considerable among the people of high school. What this means is that only the greatly talented children of the unskilled and farmer groups succeed in entering it.[40]

Similar results have been obtained by Burt, H. B. English, Miss A. H. Arlitt, A. W. Kornhauser, Douglas Waples, N. D. Hirsch, H. MacDonald, Sylvester Counts, E. Dexter, W. H. Gilby and Karl Pearson, L. Iserlis, W. Stern, Charles E. Holley and others. It is needless to multiply examples. It is enough to say that in the United States, Germany, England, France, almost all mental tests of the children have given similar results.[41]

Tests of the children's and students' intelligence unanimously exhibit the intellectual superiority of the children of the higher classes compared with that of the lower classes. Indicating this, at the same time it must be indicated that a considerable overlapping exists here, too. Some of the children from the higher classes have a very inferior intelligence while some of the children of the lower classes are very superior intellectually. But, as before, such phenomena are exceptions to the general rule.

The next indication of the correlation of social standing and intellectual level is given by mental tests of the intelligence of the adults of different social standing.

Besides the above data of the mental test of the United States Army, here are some figures representative for the results obtained by various investigators. Excluding for a moment the lowest groups of social destitutes, according to the data of Terman, intelligence of the adults varies, according to their social status, as follows:[42]

Social Status	Range of I.Q.	Average I.Q.
Unskilled labor	From 63 to 89	75.5
Semiskilled labor	From 74 to 96	85.2
Skilled or better	From 84 to 112	98.3

The table shows the correlation of social status and intelligence, and at the same time the fact of overlapping. In another study the following significant results were obtained:[43]

Social Status	Median I.Q.
Common laborer in a sawmill	77
Deliveryman for a grocery store	78
Teamster	78
"Extra" man in fire department	79
Policeman	81
Successful street-car conductor	83
Successful salesman	112

C. W. Waugh, having tested 82 street-car motormen, and conductors, 61 salesgirls, 7 railroad engineers and 4 department store buyers, obtained the following results:

	Median I.Q.
Salesgirls	84.5
Street-car men	85.6
Engineers	100.0
Buyers	106.0

Knollin and Leidlei tested 30 business men of moderate success and limited educational advantages and found their median I.Q. was 102; one-fourth of them had 107 I.Q.; one-fourth, 93.6.

Finally, the tests of college students' intelligence show that their intelligence is above the median for the people in general.[44] These data are in accordance with the results of the United States Army test, and at the same time, they show the parallelism of social standing and intellectual level.

If we turn now to the unemployed, the dependent, the paupers, the criminals, and the prostitutes we find still further confirmation of this parallelism. Recognizing that among these lowest social layers, especially among the criminals, are the individuals of comparatively high mental level, nevertheless it is probable that on the average their intellectual level as a group is inferior and among them there is an extremely high per cent of feeble-minded, imbeciles and idiots.

According to Knolling Usted's study, the median I.Q. of 154 "migrating unemployed" or "hoboes" is 89; one-fourth had I.Q. median 79. Similar results have been obtained by G. Johnson. Of 107 unemployed studied, 5.5 per cent have had a mental age below 10 years, 12 per cent below 11 years, the median I.Q. was 89, an intelligence not higher, at any rate, than that of unskilled labor.[45]

Dr. Terman's opinion is that among the unemployed there is about 10 per cent feeble-minded.[46] According to opinion of Dr. Goddard this per cent is still higher [47] (about 50 per cent for the inmates of almshouses). Dr. Pintner and Dr. Toops obtained the following results in two groups of the unemployed in Cities "A" and "B":[48]

Intellectual Level	City "A," Per cent	City "B," Per cent
Feeble-minded	28.7	7.5
Border line	29.8	25.0
Backward	23.7	32.5
Normal	8.5	20.0
Bright	4.3	15.0

A. M. Kelly and E. J. Lidbetter have given the following data concerning the intellectual level of the specified groups of wage earners and their children in London county:[49]

Occupation of Parents	Children		
	Normal	Mentally Defective	Insane
Skilled, earning from 30 shillings and more	14	2	8
In regular employment, 23 to 30 shillings	25	11	16
Unskilled, 20 to 25 shillings	15	18	18
Casual and out of work, under 20 shillings	4	25	20
Not known	2	4	1
Total	60	60	60

According to Stenquist the per cent of the feeble-minded among the dependent is 18.5, that of the backward, 62; according to Hall the per cent of the feeble-minded is 67; according to Bridgman it is 26; Haines, 17; Williams, 6; Mateer, 33.7. But even those authors who give the lowest per cent indicate that this per cent is much higher compared with the per cent of the feeble-minded in the general population and that the per cent of the "border line" and "backward" among the dependent is extremely high while the per cent of mentally superior is very low. Ann Butter's study showed that among Indiana paupers 25.9 per cent are feeble-minded; according to Charles A. Ellwood's study the majority of the inmates of almshouses are feeble-minded; Dr. John L. Gillin found that this per cent is not lower than 25, and that at least 10 per cent of those who are living at the cost of public outdoor relief are feeble-minded.[50] On the other hand Miss E. M. Furbush's study of patients with mental diseases in 46 State Hospitals of the United States shows that 13.9 per cent of first admissions for 1919 were dependent, 68.5 per cent were marginal, 17.6 per cent had resources sufficient to maintain self and family for at least four months.[51] These data confirm the correlation of poverty and mental defectiveness from another standpoint.

It is evident that in connection with industrial and economic crises, a considerable number of quite normal individuals may be thrown into the group of unemployed people and under such conditions the mental level of the unemployed group may rise considerably; and yet it is likely that with few exceptions those who become unemployed, even under such conditions, are mentally less bright than those who retain their job. As to the regularly unemployed and paupers and dependent, it seems that they, as a group, are definitely inferior, and the very reason of their being paupers and dependent is that they are physically or mentally inferior and, therefore, cannot obtain independent livelihood.

Concerning prostitutes and delinquents the situation is still worse. Here is the table which gives the percentage of aments among prostitutes, studied from this standpoint:

Institution	Number of Cases Studied	Per cent of Aments
State Board of Charities, Richmond, Virginia	120	83.3
Chicago Moral Court	639	62.0
Chicago Moral Court	126	85.8
Illinois Training School for Girls	104	97.0
Massachusetts Vice Commission	300	51.0
Massachusetts State Woman Reformatory	243	49.0
New York State Reformatory for Women	193	29.0
Bureau of Social Hygiene	100	29.0

Thus, "the most accurate and conservative studies thus far made indicate that about one-half of the prostitutes who come into the custody of city and state institutions are mentally defective." [52]

The following table, which sums up the results of Dr. T. H. Harris and Miss Elizabeth Greene's study of mentality of the normal, and dependent, and the delinquent groups, gives an idea of the distribution of intelligence among these groups: [53]

Diagnosis	Public School (White), Per cent	Public School (Colored), Per cent	Industrial School, Per cent	Penitentiary, Per cent	County Almshouses, Per cent
Superior	10.5	0.1	1.3		
Normal	60.6	24.0	21.8	14.6	17.8
Dull normal	11.4	38.2	24.6	28.3	1.6
Border line defectives	3.5	4.6	5.3	10.9	0.6
Mental defectives	2.5	8.9	8.5	11.8	24.2
Character defectives	9.1	16.3	19.4	9.2	0.3
Psychopathic personalities	1.5	4.3	10.6	16.9	2.2
Psychopathic neuroses	0.3	3.3	7.5	5.3	0.3
Mental disease	0.3	....	0.5	2.9	50.0
Epilepsy	0.1	0.4	0.3	0.2	1.9
Others	0.1		0.2		1.0
Total number of cases studied	4,163	676	944	1,386	314

A glance at the table exhibits conspicuously the differences in mentality of the normal groups and the groups of social destitutes. The racial differences appear to be less conspicuous than the differences between the above groups of the same white race. Similar results have been obtained by Dr. John E. Anderson in his mental survey of the Connecticut Industrial School for Girls. Of 311 female delinquents one-fifth were mentally defective; one-fourth, border line; one-fourth, dull; one-fifth, normal; one-twelfth, superior. These data compared with the intelligence of 94,004 drafted men of the United States Army mean a much higher per cent of the mentally defective and inferior and a considerably lower per cent of mentally superior.[54]

Professors R. Pintner and M. Parmelee very concisely sum up the results of the numerous studies of the delinquents' mentality in regard to feeble-mindedness among this group. The data are as follows. (See table below.)

Granting that some of these figures are exaggerated and granting even that the lowest figures in the table are nearer to the truth (though this supposition is not based upon any serious basis) nevertheless we have the percentage of feeble-minded among delinquents much higher than among the general population.[56]

Investigators have passed rather a long way and tested the intelligence of different social strata, beginning with monarchs and nobility and the most prominent leaders, and ending with social unfortunates. They have used different methods of testing and have tried to deal only with the objective facts and principally

Author	Per Cent of Feeble-minded Among the Delinquent Children
Hill and Goddard	93
Gifford	66
Bridgman	89
Otis	75
Pintner	46
Pyle	9 to 11
Bronner	36
Williams	75
Haines	28
Crane	39 to 72
Healy-Bronner	11
Fernald	20 to 24
Bowler	45
Hall	35
Kelley	20
Ordahl	23 to 45
Miner	7
Anderson	21
Healy	7
Hickson	84.49
Median (for these and some other authors)	36

Author	Per Cent of Feeble-minded Among the Adult Delinquents
Rowland	31
Massachusetts Report	51
Spaulding	44
Rossy	22
McCord	54
Weidensall	40
Fernald	41
Haines	20
Pintner and Toops	29
Ordahl	29
Terman and Knollin	17 to 25
Doll	16
Goring	10
Goddard	25 to 50
Tredgold	10
Median (for these and some other authors)	about 31 to 35[55]

with those which could be measured quantitatively. They have tried to avoid any speculation and theoretical reasoning, however helpful it might have been at times. The above shows that, whether they like it or not, the facts completely corroborate the statements given at the beginning of this chapter. Intelligence is distributed unequally throughout different social classes and groups of a society. It is spread more generously in the upper social classes and its amount, as well as its quality, decreases as we pass from the higher social strata to the lower ones.[57] This means that social stratification and intelligence are correlated. It means, further, that a high intelligence, as a general rule, is a condition which almost always is necessary for and always facilitates social promotion of an individual who happened to be born in the lowest strata. It signifies also that, other conditions being equal, the more intelligent part of the population rises to upper strata and tends to concentrate principally in the upper classes while the mentally inferior gravitates to and tends to concentrate principally in the lower social layers. Side by side with this general rule is seen also that the correlation of social position and intelligence is not perfect and has exceptions in the form of overlapping of the mental levels of the higher and the lower social classes. Part of the members of the higher classes have an intelligence much inferior to a part of the individuals from the lower classes. This fact is significant and has great importance, as will be seen further.

3. IS THE CORRELATION GENERAL AND PERMANENT?

Now, is the above correlation characteristic only for present European and American societies or is it a general rule, typical of almost all society of the past? In accordance with the above, it seems that it is a general rule for the majority of society of all times, except in their periods of decay. It seems also that the correlation has varied from society to society, from time to time. In some exceptional cases, under extraordinary circumstances, it may have been very low or even nil; but all this does not annihilate the generality of the correlation.

As to the *leaders and chieftains of preliterate. groups,* we have many testimonials to the fact that they, being physically superior, at the same time have been superior mentally. Among many tribes the elderly and old men are recognized as the leaders because of their greater experience and mental superiority. For the same reason the best hunters, fishers, warriors, and so on, are the leaders in many tribes. To the same mental superiority is due the fact of the leadership of the shamans, magicians, teachers, inventors, priests, physicians—a fact rather common among the preliterate, as well as among more advanced groups. "At the earlier stage of social evolution the supreme power tends to fall into the hands of men of the keenest intelligence and the superior sagacity," such is the summary of the study of Dr. Frazer.[58] "The leaders (among preliterate tribes) are always individuals of superior ability of the nature required to control the conditions of the association," properly sums up the situation.[59] To the same conclusions came Herbert Spencer, A. Vierkandt, P. Descamps and others who have studied the problem.[60] He who desires to ascertain the corresponding facts will find them in the works of these authors.

As to the leaders and higher strata of the more advanced

societies the above data concerning the intelligence of the monarchs and the proportion of men of genius produced by upper classes, strongly suggest the fact of their intellectual superiority, independently from the hypothesis, whether it was due to heredity or to environment.

Further, all careful investigators of India unanimously state the intellectual superiority of the higher castes of the Brahmins and the so-called Kshatriya, concerning the high intelligence of the leaders in ancient Great Societies, such as Egypt.[61]

Apparently such achievements as the creation of the Greek states and civilization or the Roman Empire and Roman civilization do not give any reason to style their creators as inferior. Meanwhile, it is known that at least their best and finest products were due to the work of individuals from the upper and middle social strata. During the Middle Ages, the nobility and the clergy manifested their mental superiority by the fact of creation of the medieval culture, which was in a considerable part created by the nobility and the clergy, a much higher culture than is generally supposed. Their mental ability is witnessed also by their production of a very high per cent of the men of genius. H. S. Taine said:[62]

> Whatever an institution (in this case the higher classes) may represent, the contemporaries, who observe it during many generations, cannot be considered bad judges; if they surrender to it their will and their property, they do so only in proportion to its merits. Man cannot be expected to be grateful for nothing, by mistake, and to grant many privileges without sufficient reason for doing so; he is too selfish and too envious for that.

But compulsion? and force? and lies and other methods of getting and keeping power and privileges? What is to be said about that? Such objections may be raised. Nothing, except the reminder of a very simple truth: in order successfully to use compulsion and to keep power over a much more numerous majority, and to practise successfully lies and prejudices and superstitions and what not; in order to climb up and to dominate the masses,—for all this, at least, a bit of brain and intellect is necessary, independent of the fact whether such actions are moral or not. If this were not so, mentally inferior individuals would dominate the superior ones because the former are more numerous. If the privileged classes have dominated the lower ones for centuries and, as many say, contrary to their desire, it is evident that they had the mental ability to do so. If this domination was absolutely unjust and harmful for the masses, as many say, then this is a still stronger witness in favor of mental superiority of the privileged and mental inferiority of the masses. Apparently, if many times more numerous masses were mentally equal or superior to their oppressors they necessarily would have overthrown their enslavers. If such is not the case, except in extraordinary periods of decay of the higher classes and their revolutionary liquidation, then evidently this hypothesis of the stupidity of higher classes and the superiority of the lower ones is absurd and not warranted by the facts. Thus, whether we admit the beneficial influence of domination by the higher classes (and for this reason a willing recognition of their superiority by those who have been ruled), or whether we accept the opinion of compulsory ruling and exploitation, in both cases we need the hypothesis of intellectual ability of the higher classes. Even such facts as deliberate extermination by the conquerors of the most capable within the conquered—the facts indicated by Vaccaro—even they witness, perhaps, a very bad and dreadful method from a moral standpoint, and yet, an ability to grasp the situation and an intelligence to apply the methods for the achievement of a task set forth by the conquerors. The moral side of the problem does not concern us here because we are discussing not morals but intelligence of different classes.[63]

On the other hand, as soon as the upper classes of any society have been weakened and have lost their energy, ability, and virility, they soon have been overthrown. Such is the situation before revolutions and also after revolutions. If a society does not perish then the superiors among the people climb up again and become the new upper classes.[64]

This fact confirms the hypothesis from another point of view. For these reasons, to which will be added many others, it seems to be probable that the discussed correlation is, so to speak, permanent and general.

4. SPECIFIC ABILITIES

From the above it follows that, besides general intelligence, specific abilities, such as money making, military and strategic talent, scientific, artistic, literary and organizing talents are more frequent within the upper strata, than within the lower classes. This is due not only to environment and training but to selection also; as a general rule, the men of the lower classes talented in these respects are automatically picked up and transposed to the upper strata. In this way, their posterity become the members of the upper classes and permanently supply them with such abilities. The proportion of each ability among all such abilities, however, is not constant within the upper strata. It varies according to circumstances. In time of war, men with military ability are recruited in greater proportion and climb more intensively than in time of peace. In such periods their proportion is likely to increase while the proportion of others of the *élite* may decrease. In time of peace and intensive economic activity the proportion of the talented money makers may increase while that of military men may decrease. In this way, the composition of abilities within the upper classes permanently fluctuates. In the period of decay all such abilities seem to decrease generally.

5. CHARACTER AND OTHER PSYCHOLOGICAL DIFFERENCES

Besides the above intellectual differences it is likely that there are other psychological differences between the upper and the lower classes. The more important among them seems to be as follows: except during the period of decay, *the upper strata are composed of persons possessed of strong ambitions, bold and adventurous characters, with inventive minds, with harsh and non-sentimental natures, with a sort of cynicism and, finally, with a will for domination and power.* These terms are not quite definite but are used on account of the absence of any better ones. The reasons for these statements, in brief, are as follows: In order to be a successful ruler or to become a boss or a captain of finance, or a great inventor and reformer, intellect alone is not sufficient. It is necessary also to have a corresponding character. A man without a persistent character, in spite of his talent, cannot become either a great scientist, or money maker, or ruler, or inventor, or leader generally. Except, perhaps, in the case of poetry, all these activities demand a great deal of stubbornness, persistency, and determination as prerequisites to success. Soft characters who cannot work steadily in their own line rarely achieve prominence, in spite of intellect. For the same reason a climber, whether in the field of government, or money making, or conquest, or colonization, or science, or arts, cannot be a man of routine. Either in his actions or in his theories he must care to find new ways and to go along them in spite of opposition and difficulties. In this sense he must be an adventurer, and must have a boldness in venturing what timid men do not dare to do. A sentimental man who is very sensitive and compassionate toward the sufferings of other men has less chance to climb or to keep his power than an identical man free from such sentimentality. Ruling or money making; conquest or pioneering; building of political empires or empires of business; spreading a religion by bomb, sword, violence; or performing the acts of severe justice; revolutionary propaganda or efficient keeping of social order; these and other functions of the upper strata demand for successful performance a great deal of severity, hardness and insensitiveness toward the sufferings of other men. It is in the nature of these functions. A sincere diplomat would be a failure. An entirely frank captain of industry or strategist is the man who ruins his own business or the whole army. An honest man who makes no brilliant promises is one who rarely can obtain any political success. Hence, insincerity, cynicism, manipulation of ideas and convictions are necessary prerequisites for successful climbing through many channels.

In this way, besides training and other environmental influences, the upper strata are selectively composed of people with these characteristics. And, indeed, they exhibit these traits conspicuously enough. In vain would one try to find among great political rulers, or the captains of industry, or the conquerors, or the actual reformers "soft," sentimental, human, timid, sincere, and entirely honest natures. At best they are very few. Genghiz-Khan or Napoleon, Attila or Tamerlan, Peter the Great or Mohammed, Torquemada or Pope Gregory VII, Charles V or Caesar, Savonarola or Zishka, Carnegie or the Rothschilds, Lenin or Mussolini, Oliver Cromwell or Frederick the Great, Spartan aristocracy or Roman patricians, the Venetian aristocracy or the first Spaniards in America, the first Merovingians or Carolingians; the founders of the medieval noble families or that of the Vanderbilt and Astor Empires—these and thousands of other "builders" have not been soft.

In some regards they have been cruel, severe, harsh, and heartless. Many of them, for the success of their business, sacrificed even their own children, murdered their friends, robbed empires. Other leaders, who do not exhibit so conspicuously the savagery of a lion, in its place exhibit in abundance a cynical cunning or the slyness of a fox. They are especially numerous among politicians and money makers of so-called "democracies." Aristides, Talleyrand, Lloyd George, Disraeli, Briand, and many leaders of the present political parties are in essence machinators who skilfully manipulate ideas and convictions and have an extraordinary talent to prove to-day that "A is B" and to-morrow that "A is non-B," and always in the name of "Humanity," "Liberty," "Justice," "Progress," and other excellent phrases. It does not matter here whether this is desirable or not. What matters is that it exists. And it exists because it is a matter of necessity; it is demanded by the nature of the business of the upper classes.

When the aristocracy of a society begins to decay, these traits begin to disappear within the upper strata. They become timid, human, soft, and sincere. If the numerous humanitarians of the present moment may be believed, these traits are those which ought to belong to the upper strata. Perhaps they should. But, fortunately or unfortunately, they belong to the upper strata only in the period of their sinking and never in the period of ascending or safe domination. And the longer an aristocracy has been free from them the longer it has been able to keep its power. As soon as it becomes humanitarian and honest and meek, it is doomed to be overthrown and to be superseded by the bold and harsh and cynical newcomers. The same may be said of the aristocracy of wealth. The "humanitarian offspring" of the stern founders of a business empire can only squander the money of their fathers, and enjoy life in humanitarian idleness. They are what G. Sorel rightly styles "degenerated capitalists." The above is very well summed up by Napoleon in his statement: "When the people say that the king is kind, this means that he is a poor ruler." G. Sorel, V. Pareto, R. Michels, N. Machiavelli, and many others well understood and successfully proved it.

The permeation of a dominant class by humanitarian ideas, which led that class to doubt its own moral rights to existence, demoralizes its members, makes them inapt for defence. No social struggle in history has ever been permanently won unless the vanquished has as a preliminary measure been morally weakened.[65]

Such has been the real situation.

Brahmin aristocracy is severe, and it existed for at least 2,000 years. The Spartan aristocracy was severe and cruel, and it existed during at least seven centuries until it biologically disappeared. The Venetian aristocracy was severe also and as long as it was severe and pitiless, it successfully kept its power. The early medieval nobility and the Normans were severe. And, in spite of many great revolts, they successfully suppressed them and kept their domination. On the other hand, as soon as an aristocracy became humanitarian and soft and afraid to use violence, it usually was overthrown. Such is the situation in all prerevolutionary periods. Aristocracy and the kings of the prerevolutionary periods are invariably soft, impotent, mild, liberal, humanitarian, and effeminated. As a result, they are put down.[66] Perhaps it is very pitiful that the real situation is such; and yet it is such, in spite of the virtuous theories of the humanitarians.[67]

SUMMARY

1. Except in the period of decay, the upper classes are composed of people with a higher intelligence than the lower ones.

2. Social stratification and distribution of intelligence among different strata are positively correlated.

3. The degree of correlation fluctuates from country to country, from time to time.

4. This correlation everywhere and at all times is not perfect. It does not exclude a considerable overlapping.

5. In the period of decay it greatly decreases and may disappear.

6. Except during a time of decay, the correlation is likely to be permanent.

7. Definite kinds of special abilities necessary for social organization and control seem to exist in a greater abundance among the upper than among the lower strata.

8. Except during the period of decay, the upper classes are richer with strong, ambitious, bold and adventurous characters; with hard, severe and non-sentimental natures; with insincere and cynical men. In the period of decay, this difference disappears. The upper classes become soft, sincere, humanitarian, timid and cowardly. Such aristocracy is usually put down and superseded by the newcomers of usual type of character.

[1] COMTE, AUGUST, *Positive Philosophy,* translated by MARTINEAU, p. 386, New York, 1855.

[2] PINTNER, R., *Intelligence Testing,* p. 55, New York, 1923.

[3] *Cf.* PARETO, V., *op. cit.,* Vol. II, pp. 1295 *ff.;* see SOROKIN, P., *Systema Sociologii* (Russian), Vol. II, pp. 225-232.

[4] *Cf.* AMMON, OTTO, *Die Gesellschaftsordnung,* pp. 127 *ff.,* Jena, 1895; SUMNER, W., *Folkways,* Chaps. I and II, 1906.

[5] Their works were indicated in the foregoing chapters. COY, G. F., "The Mentality of a Gifted Child," *Journal of Applied Psychology,* Vol. II, pp. 299-307; CHAPIN, F. STUART, "Extra-Curricular Activities of College Students," *School and Society,* Vol. XXIII, No. 581; NACCARATI, C., "The Morphologic Aspect of Intelligence," *Archives of Psychology,* No. 45, 1921.

[6] Their works were also indicated above. HEIDBREDER, E., "Intelligence and the Height-Weight Ratio," *Journal of Applied Psychology,* Vol. X, pp. 52-62, 1926.

[7] WOODS, FREDERICK ADAMS, *Mental and Moral Heredity in Royalty,* p. 301, New York, 1906; also *The Influence of Monarchs,* Chap. XVII, New York, 1913.

[8] GALTON, FRANCIS, *Hereditary Genius,* pp. 329-330, London, 1892.

[9] SOROKIN, P., "The Monarchs and the Rulers."

[10] ELLIS, HAVELOCK, *op. cit.,* pp. 78-80.

[11] *Ibid.,* pp. 80 *ff.*

[12] WOODS, FREDERICK ADAMS, "The Conification of Social Groups," *Eugenics, Genetics and The Family,* Vol. I, pp. 312-328, Baltimore, 1923.

[13] GALTON, FRANCIS, *English Men of Science,* p. 16, D. Appleton & Company, New York, 1875.

[14] ODIN, A., *Genèse des Grands Hommes,* Vol. II, Table XXXII, Vol. I, p. 541, Paris, 1895.

[15] DE CANDOLLE, A., *Histoire des sciences et des savants*, p. 279, Génève—Bale, 1885.

[16] *Ibid.*, p. 272.

[17] *Ibid.*, pp. 273-274.

[18] MAAS, FRITZ, "Über die Herkunftsbedingungen der Geistigen Füher," *Archiv für Sozialwissenschaft und Sozialpolitik*, pp. 144-186, 1916.

[19] CATTELL, J. MCKEEN, *American Men of Science*, 3d ed., pp. 783-784, 1921.

[20] VISHER, STEPHEN S., "A Study of the Type of the Place of Birth and of the Occupation of Fathers of Subjects of Sketches," in *Who's Who in America, American Journal of Sociology*, p. 553, March, 1925.

[21] CLARKE, EDWIN L., "American Men of Letters," *Columbia University Studies*, Vol. LXXII, pp. 74-76, 1916.

[22] SOROKIN, P., "American Millionaires and Multimillionaires," pp. 635-636.

[23] COOLEY, CHARLES H., "Genius, Fame, and the Comparison of Races," *Annals of the American Academy*, Vol. IX, p. 15, May, 1897.

[24] CASTLE, CORA S., *A Statistical Study of Eminent Women*, p. 82, New York, 1913.

[25] See NEARING, SCOTT, "The Younger Generation of American Genius," *Scientific Monthly*, January, 1916.

[26] DAVIES, GEORGE R., "A Statistical Study of the Influence of Environment," *Quarterly Journal of the University of North Dakota*, Vol. IV, pp. 212-236.

[27] TERMAN, L. M., *Genetic Study of Genius*, Vol. I. pp. 60 *ff.*

[28] PHILIPTSCHENKO, JUR., *op. cit.*, *Bulletin* No. 1, pp. 11-12, 28; *Bulletin* No. 2, pp. 11-12; *Bulletin* No. 3, p. 35.

[29] MICHELS, R., *Political Parties*, pp. 239-240, New York, 1915.

[30] *Memoirs of the National Academy of Sciences*, Vol. XV, "Psychological Examining in the United States Army," edited by YERKES, R. M., p. 707, Washington, D. C., 1921.

[31] *Ibid.*, pp. 821 *ff.*

[32] *Ibid.*, Chap. XVII.

[33] YERKES, R. M., "Eugenic Bearing of Measurement of Intelligence," *The Eugenic Review*, pp. 234 *ff.*, January, 1923. See here the instructive figures and diagrams.

[34] See the details concerning the results of the United States Army mental test in the works indicated; see also GODDARD, H. H., *Human Efficiency and Levels of Intelligence*, pp. 1-30, 1920; PINTNER, R., *Intelligence Testing*, *passim* and the chapters, "The Soldier" and "The Employees," and works indicated below.

[35] TERMAN, L. M., *The Intelligence of School Children*, pp. 56 *ff.*, 188 *ff*, 1919; see also "New Approach to Study of Genius," *Psychological Review*, pp. 310-318, 1922.

[36] DUFF, J. F., and THOMSON, GODFREY H., "The Social and Geographic Distribution of Intelligence in Northumberland," *British Journal of Psychology*, pp. 192-198, October, 1923; MACDONALD, H., "The Social Distribution of Intelligence," *British Journal of Psychology*, Vol. XVI, pp. 123-129.

[37] PRESSEY, S. Z., and RALSTON, R., "The Relation of the General Intelligence of Children to the Occupation of Their Fathers," *Journal of Applied Psychology*, Vol. III, No. 4, pp. 366-373.

[38] BRIDGES, J. W., and COLER, L. E., "The Relation of Intelligence to Social Status," *Psychology Review*, Vol. XXIV, pp. 1-31.

[39] BOOK, W. F., *The Intelligence of High School Seniors*, Chap. X, New York, 1922.

[40] HAGGERTY, M. E., and NASH, HARRY B., "Mental Capacity of Children

and Paternal Occupation," *Journal of Educational Psychology,* pp. 563-572, December, 1924.

[41] See other facts in the indicated books of L. M. Terman and R. Pintner. See also McDougal, W., "The Correlation Between Native Ability and Social Status," *Eugenics in Race and State,* Vol. II, pp. 373-376, Baltimore, 1921; English, H. B., "Mental Capacity of School Children Correlated with Social Status," *Yale Psychology Studies,* 1917; *Psychology Review Monographs,* Vol. XXIII, No. 3; Arlitt, A. H., "Summary of Results of Testing 342 Children," *Psychological Bulletin,* February, 1921; Kornhauser, A. W., "The Economic Standing of Parents and the Intelligence of Their Children," *Journal of Educational Psychology,* Vol. IX; Counts, G. S., "The Selective Character of American Secondary Schools," *The University of Chicago Education Monographs,* No. 19, pp. 36-37, and *passim,* May, 1922; Waples, D., "Indexing the Qualifications of Different Social Groups for an Academic Curriculum," *The School Review,* pp. 537-546, 1924; Gilby, W. N., and Pearson, Karl, "On the Significance of the Teacher's Appreciation of General Intelligence," *Biometrica,* Vol. VIII, pp. 94-108; Holley, Charles E., "The Relationship Between Persistence in School and Home Conditions," *passim, University of Chicago Press,* 1916; Isserlis, L., "The Relation Between Home Conditions and the Intelligence of School Children," *Publications of the Medical Research Committee of the Privy Council,* London, 1923; Yates, "A Study of Some High School Seniors of Super Intelligence," *Journal of Educational Research,* Monographs, No. 2; Stern, W., *Die Intellegenz der Kinder und Jugendlichen,* Barth, Leipzig; Hart, H., "Occupational Differential Fecundity," *Scientific Monthly,* Vol. XIX, p. 531; Dexter, E., "Relation Between Occupation of Parents and Intelligence of Children," *School and Society,* Vol. XVII, pp. 612-614, 1923; Murdoch, K., "A Study of Differences Found Between Races in Intellect and Morality," *School and Society,* Vol. XXII, Nos. 568-569, 1925; Hirsch, N. D., *op. cit.,* pp. 324-326; MacDonald, H., "The Social Distribution of Intelligence in the Isle of Wight," *British Journal of Psychology,* Vol. XVI, pp. 123-129; Pyle, W. H., *Nature and Development of Learning Capacity,* 1925.

[42] Terman, L. M., *The Intelligence of School Children,* pp. 273 *ff.*

[43] *Ibid.,* p. 274.

[44] *Ibid.,* pp. 275-284. See here other results. See also Pintner, R., *op. cit.,* Chap. XIX; Hollingworth and Poffenberger, *Applied Psychology,* D. Appleton & Company, New York; Flanders, J. K., "Mental Test of a Group of Employed Men," *Journal of Applied Psychology,* pp. 197-206, 1918.

[45] Johnson, G., "Unemployed and Feeble-mindedness," *Journal of Delinquency,* pp. 58-73, 1917.

[46] Terman, L. M., *The Intelligence of School Children,* p. 284.

[47] Goddard, H. H., *Human Efficiency,* pp. 67 *ff.*

[48] Pintner, R., *op. cit.,* p. 372.

[49] Kelley, A. M., and Lidbetter, E. J., "A Comparative Inquiry on the Heredity and Social Conditions," etc., *The Eugenic Review,* Vol. XIII, p. 402.

[50] See Gillin, John L., *Poverty and Dependency,* pp. 64-67; Parmelee, M., *Poverty and Social Progress,* pp. 46 *ff.;* see also Tredgold, A. F., *Mental Deficiency,* New York, 1914; Gillin, John L., *Criminology,* Chaps. VII, VIII.

[51] Furbush, E. M., "Social Facts Relative to Patients with Mental Diseases," *Mental Hygiene,* Vol. V, p. 596, 1921.

[52] Clarke, W., "Prostitution and Mental Deficiency," *Social Hygiene,* p. 387, June, 1915. "Of the disorderly house inmates about 50 per cent are feeble-minded; of court cases about 30 per cent are defective; of institutional cases about 50 per cent (of prostitutes) are feeble-minded." Malzberg, Benjamin, "Mental Defect and Prostitution," *The Eugenic Review,* Vol. XII, pp. 100-104;

see also TREDGOLD, A. F., *Mental Deficiency,* pp. 8 *ff.;* GODDARD, H. H., *Feeble-mindedness,* pp. 13-15; and above indicated works of Granier, Ferrero, and Pauline Tarnowsky. "From 30 to 60 per cent of prostitutes are . . . high-grade morons." Quoted volume of *Memoirs of the National Academy of Sciences,* p. 808.

[53] HARRIS, T. H., and GREENE, ELIZABETH, "Maryland Mental Hygiene Survey," *Eugenic News,* February, 1922.

[54] ANDERSON, JOHN E., "A Mental Survey of the Connecticut Industrial School for Girls," *Journal of Delinquency,* Vol. VI, No. 1, pp. 271-282, 1921.

[55] See PINTNER, R., *op. cit.,* Chap. XIII; also PARMELEE, M., *Criminology,* pp. 163-170; and the quoted works of H. H. Goddard, Charles Goring, E. Sutherland, A. F. Tredgold, Healy, John E. Anderson, L. M. Terman.

[56] In England, according to Goring, it is 0.5 per cent; according to L. W. Weber, 0.36 per cent; according to the Census of the United States in 1910 there were 204.2, in 1920, 220.1 insane in the hospitals per 100,000 of population, or about 0.2 per cent. See United States Department of Commerce. "Insane and Feeble-minded in Institutions," pp. 49 *ff.,* Washington, D. C., 1914; POLLOCK, H., and FURBUSH, E. M., "Patients with Mental Disease, etc.," *Mental Hygiene,* Vol. V, p. 145. More reliable data of *War Department of the United States,* "Defects Found in Drafted Men," pp. 393-394, Washington, 1920, show that of one hundred of the recruits at the age of from 18 to 30, there were found 1.15 per cent who had mental deficiency, neurasthenia, neuroses, hysteria, dementia praecox, psychosthenia, psychoses, and manic depressiveness. Compared with this 1.15 per cent, the percentage of the feeble-mindedness among delinquents, even according to the lowest figures in the table, are several times higher. See the data for other countries in the papers of WEBER, L. W., "Läst sich eine Zunähme der Geisteskranken feststellen," *Archiv für Rossen- und Gesellschafts-Biologie,* Vol. VII, pp. 704-721; and RÜDIN, E., "Uber den Zusammenhang zwischen Geisteskrankheit und Kultur," *ibid.,* pp. 722-748. This conclusion does not exclude such a possibility as the I. Q. of a part of the criminals being not lower than the I. Q. of a corresponding population. Among criminals there is always a part who are victims of circumstances or of a lack of integrity of character but not of a lack of intelligence. This, however, does not warrant a conclusion like that of Dr. Carl Murchison, that the criminals, as a group, are more intelligent than the non-criminal population. See MURCHISON, CARL, *Criminal Intelligence,* pp. 42 *ff.,* 1926.

[57] V. de Lapouge was right in saying that different strata of the same racial type differ from each other in intelligence no less than different races. Compare the above differences in I. Q. with differences of the white and the black races in I. Q. found by studies of Ferguson, Yerkes, Pintner, Hirsch, Peterson, Brigham, Sunné, Odum, Pressey, Arlitt, Derric, Pyle, Murdock, and others. See a concise summary of these studies in GARTH, J. R., "Revue of Racial Psychology," *Psychological Bulletin,* pp. 355-357, 1925.

[58] FRAZER, J. G., *op. cit.,* p. 83-84; LOWIE, R. H., *op. cit.,* Chaps. XII to XIV.

[59] MUMFORD, E., *op. cit., American Journal of Sociology,* Vol. XIII, p. 521,

[60] See the quoted works of Herbert Spencer, A. Vierkandt, R. H. Lowie, P. Descamps, J. G. Frazer, and E. Mumford; also GOLDENWEILER, A., *Early Civilization,* p. 271, 1922; CHAPIN, F. STUART, "Primitive Social Ascendancy," *Publications of the American Society of Sociology,* Vol. XII, 1917.

[61] See, for instance, BREASTED, J. H. A., *History of the Ancient Egyptians,* pp. 76-77, 80-81, 1911. Mental tests of the upper and the lower castes of India is a further corroboration of historical evidence.

[62] TAINE, H. S., *Origines de la France Contemporaine* (Russian translated), pp. 552-553.

[63] See Vaccaro, M. A., *Les bases sociologiques du droit et de l'état, passim* and Chap. IV.

[64] See Sorokin, P., *Sociology of Revolution,* pp. 307 *ff.*

[65] Michels, R., *Political Parties,* pp. 242-243; Pareto, V., *Les Systèmes Socialistes,* Vol. I, pp. 37-57; *Traité,* Vol. II, pp. 1659 *ff.*; Machiavelli, N., *Prince* and *Discourses on Livy, passim.*

[66] See the facts in my *Sociology of Revolution,* pp. 397 *ff.*

[67] From this standpoint, the future of the present money aristocracy and intellectual and political aristocracy is likely not to be very bright. If they are sufficiently sly, they are quite humanitarian and soft and are permeated with the spirit of the injustice of their privileges and fortunes. Is it strange, therefore, that in Russia and Italy they have already been put down; in other countries, in Germany and France, in Spain and even England, we see a growth in the groups of severe and bold men, in form of the Fascisti, the Monarchists, the Communists, the Syndicalists, the Ku-Klux-Klan (whose members are usually recruited from the lower classes). In spite of the opposite character of their purposes, they all are similar in their contempt for soft humanitarianism and liberal verbosity. They frankly prepare to put down all humanitarians, parliamentarians, and liberal babblers, including the moderate socialists. This is the essence of the contemporary crisis of parliamentarism and liberalism and democracy and moderate socialism. Their leaders, in the course of time, have become too humanitarian and soft. According to the above rule of history, their deposition is to be expected. Of course, there are still a few "hard-boiled" leaders of finance and politics, and they seem to be more numerous in the United States than in any other country. But it is uncertain whether their number will increase or decrease. Correspondingly, they may keep their domination or may be put down.

CHAPTER XIII

HEREDITY OR ENVIRONMENT, SELECTION OR ADAPTATION?

ARE the above bodily and mental differences of the upper and lower classes the result of environment or heredity or of both of these factors? This problem will not be discussed in detail. Generally speaking, it is as follows: *the discussed physical and mental differences of the upper and lower classes are the result of both factors: heredity and environment, selection and adaptation.*

I. THE INFLUENCE OF ENVIRONMENT AND PARTICULARLY OF OCCUPATION UPON THE HUMAN BEING AND HIS BEHAVIOR

That an environment influences the physical, as well as mental characteristics of a man, is a very old truth. Apart from the ancient Greek writers, it is enough to look through some of *The Sacred Books of the East,* especially those of Ancient China and India, to see that the sages and the people of those remote times knew well this influence and deliberately used it for practical purposes.[1] At the present moment we have plenty of material which shows that in the first place, many bodily traits may be and are modified by different environmental agencies. Take, for instance, the height and weight of the human body. We have seen above that the upper social strata are usually taller than the lower ones. If we take only such an environmental agency as that which affects nutrition it may account a great deal for the difference in the stature of different social classes. We know that the growth of the body depends very much on the definite kind of vitamins[2] consumed in the form of food; we know also that the nutrition of the upper social classes has been better generally and has contained more products rich with "the vitamins of growth" than that of the lower social classes.[3] Hence, a part, at least, of the difference between the statures of different social classes has been due to this factor.

During the last few years, we have observed a striking confirmation of this correlation on the largest scale in Russia and in some other European countries. In Russia the starvation of the people during the Revolution and the famine of 1921-1922 effected a considerable decrease in the height of the population. This has been witnessed by measurements of the children of Petrograd in 1922 [4] and by several other studies of the Russian population. The stature of a large group of adult Russians measured by Professor Ivanovsky before, during and after the famine of 1921-1922 diminished through the famine by 4.7 centimeters for the adult males and by 3.5 centimeters for the adult females; "but when diet improved, stature increased again until it reached the normal stage as food became sufficient." Likewise, the weight fell and increased again after the famine; even "the volume of the head (soft parts) and the length from the vertex to the chin have decreased." [5]

Similar effects have been found in Germany, in France, in Belgium, in Denmark during the years of famine and of the war and the corresponding quantitative and qualitative inferiority of nutrition of the population.[6]

The opposite phenomenon—an increase of the stature of the population—has been noticed by Otto Ammon in Holland, since 1872, in Saxony, in Italy, in Sweden, in France,[7] and in America in recent times (by Aleš Hrdlička). The authors are near to the truth in ascribing it to a favorable change in environment and to the improvement of the standard of living in these countries. The experiment of W. H. Lever, who built a special Garden City with the best hygienic conditions for his workingmen and their children to prevent their biological deterioration, noticed before, is also very significant. It is seen from the following figures, which give the data for the height and weight of the children of different classes compared with that of the children of workingmen who were put into the excellent conditions in this Garden City (Port Sunlight).[8] (See p. 319.)

The table shows that under good conditions the children of workingmen, who used to be less tall and heavy than the children of well-to-do classes, became rather taller and heavier than even the children of the wealthy class (though in this case one is not sure that the children of Garden City were not selected).

Classes of Children	7 Years Old		11 Years Old		14 Years Old	
	Height	Weight	Height	Weight	Height	Weight
Schools for wealthy children....	47.	49.3	55.5	70.	61.7	94.5
Schools for well-to-do children..	45.3	44.1	53.1	61.4	58.2	95.8
Schools for skilled workers' children..........................	44.3	43.	51.8	59.	56.2	75.8
Schools for poor children.......	44.	43.	49.7	55.5	55.2	71.1
Schools in Port Sunlight (Garden City)........................	47.	50.5	57.	79.5	62.2	108.

The same must be said of the differences in health, longevity, physical development and, finally, in mental level.[9] Better and more hygienic conditions of the upper classes, compared with those of the lower ones, account for a considerable part of the above differences. Better education of upper classes, the very nature of their professional work, a more intelligent environment, a series of facilities for mental development which are inaccessible to the lower classes, and so on, all should have caused a considerable difference in the mental level of the poor and wealthy, manual and intellectual occupational classes. Thousands of different facts demonstrate this beyond possibility of contradiction.

Among these environmental differences an especially important one is the rôle played by *the occupation of the different social classes.* According to the classical statement of Lamarck:

> dans tout animal qui n'a point dépassé le terme de son développement, l'emploi plus fréquent et soutenu d' un organ quelconque fortifie peu à peu cet organe, le développe, l'agrandit et lui donne une puissance proportionnée à la durée de cet emploi . . . au contraire, le défaut constant d'usage de tel organe l'affaiblit et le détériore, diminue progressivement ses facultés et tend à le faire disparaître.

If "function creates organ," then, on this basis, especially important is the rôle of occupational work in the modification of the human body and mind and behavior. Occupational work is, so to speak, permanent. It is repeated from day to day. It demands a permanent adaptation of body and mind for the performance.[10] In this sense its influence is durable, incessant, unavoidable, and, therefore, enormous.

Occupation practiced for a long time marks a whole organism and shapes it, making it conform to its nature. The rough skin of the hands of a manual worker and the tender one of an intellectual; the extraordinary development of finger muscles of a pianist and the corresponding muscles of a manual worker; the military "stand" of the body of a professional soldier and the different habitual poses of a sailor—these and a thousand similar formations of the body by occupational work are well known. Moreover, some anthropologists go so far as to admit the possibility of the modification of the form of head and its size under the influence of a permanent intellectual work or its lack.[11] Maybe they go too far[12] but this shows only that even such stable characteristics of a body are thought of as influenced by occupation and environment. Furthermore, there is no doubt that the death and birth rate and some other vital processes are noticeably determined by occupation. All this indicates the influence of occupation upon the human body and its health and physiological life.

It is also beyond doubt that the *occupation stigmatizes the movements and habitual posture of the body.* Everybody knows the wallowing walk of sailors or the rigid posture of military men, or the slow and stately movements and gestures of the priests (especially in Russia and Europe). The same should be said of one's *speech reactions.* Occupation stamps these very markedly. The character of pronunciation, construction of phrases, accent, occupational terminology, occupational "slang"—all this is marked by a man's occupation, being acquired in the process of the occupational work and adaptation to it.

Occupation modifies and often determines many exterior traits in one's face and appearance. The too-much powdered face of actresses and prostitutes, the tonsure of Roman Catholic priests, the long hair and beard of Greek-Orthodox ecclesiastics, the bronzed color of the faces of farmers and people working out-of-doors, and the pale facial color of many indoor occupational groups, such are a few examples of numerous facts of this kind.

Occupation often determines a man's dress and clothes. Different kinds of uniform, beginning with that of military men and the clergy and ending with the occupational dress of a nurse, and many occupational emblems and cockades are instances of this form of occupational influence.

With still greater reason this may be said about *the influence of occupation upon man's psychology.*

Any occupation requires not only physical but also psychological adaptation for its performance. From a musician, his occupation demands a special musical ability; from a painter, a sharp sense of color; from a scholar, intellectual ability; from a bookkeeper, accuracy; from an habitual murderer, an indifference to the sufferings of his victims; from a prostitute, a suppression of the usual repulsion at being handled by everybody. Without a corresponding physical accommodation, one cannot successfully perform his occupational work and either will be fired or will quit it himself. Therefore, all the psychological processes of any member of an occupation undergo modification, especially when one stays for a long time in the same occupation. *The processes of perception and sensation, attention, imaginative reproduction, and association bear the marks of a corresponding occupation.* We are sensitive in perception of objects connected with our occupation, and we are deaf and dull to the objects which are heterogeneous to it. In the same combination of stimuli, e.g., in the same landscape, the attention of a farmer is given to certain aspects while the attention of an artist or an historian or a geologist is paid to quite different sides of the picture. All have the same view, but everyone sees and perceives in his own manner determined by his specialty. Corresponding experiments performed in The Cerebral Institute in Petrograd verify this.[18]

Still greater is the occupational influence on the processes and on the character of one's evaluations, beliefs, practical judgments, opinions, ethics, and whole ideology. Occupational idiosyncrasy, "l'esprit de corps," occupational ideology and ethics, occupational solidarity and unions, and existence of psychological types of a soldier, a priest, a banker, a farmer, a judge, a teacher, a carpenter, are the evidences of this. A pharmacist perceives the world *sub speciæ* of drugs and medicaments; a judge perceives it *sub speciæ* of codes and laws; a minister, from the standpoint of religion, and a soldier sees it from his military viewpoint. It is natural that an industrial working man dealing with inanimate and mechanical machines and surrounded by the same automatic and lifeless environment of a modern factory step by step acquires the ideology of determinism, mechanical materialism, and atheism. It is comprehensible also why a farmer or a priest who deals with the living plants and animals or with human beings, with animation, the spirit and mystery of their behavior, are animistic, spiritualistic, and indeterministic.[14]

Further, occupation determines considerably the place and district of our dwelling, its character and type, its furniture and equipment. Occupation determines our budget of income and budget of time: the hours of our working, recreation, getting up, and going to bed. It influences the character of our meals, and recreations, that of our reading and amusements. It fashions our habits, our ethics, our manners, our etiquette. It determines considerably with whom we are associated, whom we meet, with whom we talk and are in contact. All this being taken into consideration makes apparent the enormous influence of occupation on the whole physical, mental, moral, and social nature of man.

It would be really miraculous if even innately similar individuals placed in different occupational environments, became identical physically and mentally. Only the occupational agency of environment has been outlined here but it is only one among many factors out of which the environment of the upper and the lower classes is composed. *Hence, the general conclusion is that a great many differences—physical, mental, moral, social and in behavior—among different social classes are due to the heterogeneity of environmental factors among which they are born, grow, live, and work.*

Does this mean that the environmental factor is enough to account for all differences among social classes—the facts of social differentiation and the social position of any individual? Not at all. This leads us to another fundamental factor—the factor of heredity and selection.

2. "OVERLAPPING," "UPSTARTS," AND "FAILURES" CANNOT BE ACCOUNTED FOR THROUGH ENVIRONMENT

In the first place, take those members of a society who show characteristics quite different from the class in which they were born and grew up, and who do not remain in the same social group, but change—from the son of a slave to a monarch; from the son of a beggar to a captain of industry; from a prince's son to a social destitute; from the son of an intellectual to a fool. How is it possible to account through environmental factors for these facts? Almost all the cases of overlapping of the physical and mental traits of the upper and the lower classes stressed above, represent this kind of phenomena. "Good luck" or "hard luck"? This is not an explanation. "Environment again"? But, if we admitted that for physical and mental development the environment of the lower classes is not favorable, and through this tried to explain their physical and mental inferiority, then, evidently, to avoid self-contradiction, we cannot look to the same unfavorable environment for an explanation of a genius born and brought up in this poor environment—and yet possessed of extraordinarily good health and intelligence. If an environment of a professional and well-to-do group is recognized as favorable for physical and mental development, then, evidently, a man born in these conditions who becomes a stupid and sick pauper cannot be explained through the same environmental factor. Such an attempt would be a self-contradiction. Some of the ardent environmentalists may say:

> Well, but within the same social class the environment is not mathematically identical for all families of the class. It may be that, as an exception, the environment of a poor family has been good, or that of an aristocratic and wealthy family has been bad. Hence, the exceptions and their explanation.

Such a statement goes too far, and, at the same time, it is too short-sighted. In the first place, we surely know of many great leaders born in very humble conditions, with lack of necessities, and education, and healthy moral and intellectual atmosphere who, nevertheless, in spite of all these obstacles, succeeded in overcoming them and became great leaders. We know also of instances of the opposite character where, from a very good family, with good family life, with the most positive spiritual and mental and moral facilities, came children with quite different qualities. These phenomena cannot be explained through the above environmentalist argument. It is fallacious also in the sense that it introduces a mysticism in explanation, on the one hand, and destroys the very basis of environmentalist theory itself on the other. Why? Because usually environmentalists explain many superior traits of the upper classes such as *A,B,C,D,E,F*, through (*a*) better economic conditions, (*b*), better standard of living, (*c*) better education, (*d*) better intellectual atmosphere, (*e*) social inheritance of a position, (*f*) easier promotion, and so on. The formula of their explanation is: $A = \mathrm{F}$ (a), $B = \mathrm{F}$ (*b*), $C = \mathrm{F}$ (*c*), and so on. In brief, they say *A,B,C,D,E,F* are functions or results of the causes or independent variables *a,b,c,d,e,f*. The same may be said about their explanation of the opposite characteristics of the lower classes.

In the fact of overlapping and appearance of the "white crows" in different classes, we have the situation in which the characteristics *A,B,C,D,E,F* being given, the causes *a,b,c,d,e,f* are lacking (the cases of many "upstarts" and great leaders from the poor classes). And contrariwise, the causes *a,b,c,d,e,f* being given, the functions *A,B,C,D,E,F* are absent (the cases of many failures from the upper classes). One of two things: either we hold the validity of the environmental formula, and then it is evident we cannot explain through it the cases of the "white crows" and all cases of overlapping stressed in the previous chapters; or, if we try to do so, we destroy the formula itself. Such an attempt would mean that the qualities *A,B,C,D,E,F* are not the results of the conditions *a,b,c,d,e,f*. Thus the admitted explanation of the superior traits *A,B,C,D,E,F* through a better environment is denied and, as a result, the whole environmental theory is destroyed. In this case it is possible to say: if the traits *A,B,C,D,E,F* are not necessarily the results of the environmental conditions *a,b,c,d,e,f*, then these characteristics of the upper classes also may not be a result of their environmental conditions *a,b,c,d,e,f*, and they may be the result of their innate traits.

The discussion shows the fallacy of hyper-environmentalism and its logical self-destruction. If we hold the formula, we cannot explain through it the cases of overlapping. If we try to do so, we destroy the formula and open the way for an exclusive hereditary explanation of the superiority of the upper classes.

3. THE DIFFERENT FATES OF INDIVIDUALS WITH IDENTICAL OR SIMILAR ENVIRONMENTS CANNOT BE EXPLAINED THROUGH ENVIRONMENTAL THEORY

A second category of facts difficult for a satisfactory environmental explanation presents itself when individuals from the same environmental conditions or from the same family have quite different personalities and happen to obtain quite different social positions. In England, there were thousands of individuals who lived approximately under the same conditions as Oliver Cromwell, or Charles Darwin, or Faraday; in the United States, there were thousands of lads who had approximately the same and even much better conditions than had Lincoln; in Russia, there were hundreds of thousands of peasant lads who were in similar or in much better conditions than was M. Lomonosoff. And, yet, out of these thousands only Oliver Cromwell became the Dictator; only Charles Darwin became a great scientist; only Lomonosoff, in spite of the greatest obstacles, became one of the noted scientists of the world in the eighteenth century. What is the cause? Why such exceptional "luck"? Environment? Alas! No one of the excessive environmentalists has given us an explanation of how an environment may account completely for such "miracles." All that we have in this respect is the vague and purely dogmatic statements about "fortunate environment" without any attempt to show in what this exceptional "fortune" consisted and why many more "fortunate" people did not become Darwins. The same may be said about hundreds of thousands of similar, good and bad, "miracles."

This is especially true in regard to the present democratic countries, such as the United States and some European countries. Here, theoretically, everybody may become what he pleases. There are no juridical or religious or moral or social "taboos" against anybody becoming an Edison, Ford, Carnegie, Lincoln, Washington, A. G. Bell, Emerson, Benjamin Franklin or what not. And, yet, only these few personalities became what they are, in spite of the fact that their starting conditions were often much harder than those of millions of other individuals. Why such luck again? I fear that no environmentalist could answer the question in a satisfactory way. At any rate it is up to them to give an explanation which they have not as yet given.

4. MEN OF GENIUS AND IDIOTS CANNOT BE EXPLAINED THROUGH ENVIRONMENT

The third series of phenomena which could not be accounted for through the environmental factor is *the extreme types of human beings*: the men of genius and the greater part of the mentally defective, feeble-minded, and idiots. At the present moment, it seems to be certain that the greater part of these types are the product of heredity. Without a corresponding innate basis, it seems to be impossible to become a genius of the highest rank. The same factor seems to be responsible for the majority of cases of feeble-mindedness. It is true that an exclusively unfavorable combination of circumstances may hinder the development and manifestation of a potential genius and may still aggravate an innate disposition to a mental disorder, or even create it in some exceptional cases. But if in this negative respect the environment plays a rôle that may be efficient, it is relatively impotent in the production of positive genius, as in the transformation of a born idiot into a normal person. This statement has been sufficiently corroborated by the abundant data obtained by Francis Galton, Karl Pearson, and their numerous followers. Bad heredity and an abundance of defective relatives of the mentally defective; an abundance of men of talent among the relatives of men of genius; researches which show a close correlation between physical and mental traits of parents and children, and other relatives; such facts as a lack of an increase of men of genius from the lower classes during the nineteenth century, in spite of the fact that their environment, standard of living and educational facilities improved markedly during this period —these and many similar facts make it seem to be certain that in the production of such extreme types of human beings the principal rôle is played by heredity but not by environment. Its rôle in such cases is rather a subsidiary but not a primary one.[15] In order to become a Sir Isaac Newton, or Napoleon, or Jack Dempsey, or Nurmi, or Michelangelo, or Phidias, or Aristotle, or Confucius, or Shakespeare, or, on the other hand, to become an idiot, it is necessary to be born as Newton or other geniuses were born, or as an offspring of "The Tribe of Ishmael," The Jutes, the Kallikaks, "The Nams," "The Zero," and other negative hereditary families. Francis Galton says:

> I acknowledge freely the great power of education and social influences in developing the active power of mind, just as I acknowledge the effect of use in developing the muscles of a blacksmith's arm, and no further. Let the blacksmith labor as he will, he will find there are certain feats beyond his power.

Numerous experimental investigations completely prove the innate diversity of abilities among human beings of the same race. Such, for instance, are the study of Dean C. E. Seashore, concerning the ability of discrimination of differences in pitch,[16] F. L. Wells' experimental study of ability of tapping among ten individuals;[17] many industrial researches concerning the *efficiency* of work of different, but equally trained, workers;[18] the experiments of Dr. G. S. Gates of Columbia University, and so on. They show that abilities are distributed differently among human beings and—what is more important—that equal practice leads not to a decrease of the differences, but rather to their increase: through practice, the less capable gain something but those who are more capable at the start gain still more. Thus practice and environment cannot diminish the difference. Education does not diminish but increases rather the physical and mental differences among individuals. It is not so much a factor of leveling as that of aristocratizing a society.[10]

If this is true in regard to such simple operations as addition and number checking, or heel trimming, or ironing a shirt, or typewriting, it is to be expected the difference is still greater in much more complicated activities and achievements, such as science and art, literature and music, governing and economic organization, invention and military operation. The leaders in such activities must be born with a corresponding innate capacity to be great leaders. No education and no environment can make a man a great genius unless he is equipped with a corresponding innate "presence of God." The above quotation from an old Chinese statement and a similar idea brilliantly developed by V. de Lapouge seem to be quite correct.[20]

5. THE BEGINNING OF SOCIAL STRATIFICATION ITSELF AND INEQUALITIES AMONG PRIMITIVE TRIBES CANNOT BE ACCOUNTED FOR THROUGH ENVIRONMENT

The next category of social phenomena which cannot be accounted for completely through an environmental factor is the fact of social stratification itself and creation of a different social environment for different social classes and groups. The extreme environmentalists like to emphasize on all occasions the difference in social environment of different classes and races and say that, if the environment were similar, there would not have been any racial or social superiority and inferiority. I wonder why they do not push the problem further and ask why some races or some social groups of the same society, living often in a geographic environment almost identical with or even less favorable than that of other racial or social groups, have succeeded in creating a civilization and favorable social conditions, while those other races or groups could not do this. Moreover, being put in the favorable social environment made by the "creative groups," they have not been able to push their civilization further nor even to keep it on the level received by them. Why is it that in the same geographic environment one people creates a brilliant civilization while another people does not show this ability? Why is it so? Civilizations or favorable social environments do not fall from heaven. They must be created before the harvest of their crops. Whence, then, this difference and how explain it from a purely environmental viewpoint?[21] It must be explained because we surely know many well-studied facts where the outlined situation existed. Take, for instance, many preliterate tribes. There is no artificial inequality. The environment is nearly identical for all members of the group. Their education and training, their "economic status," their position at the start, are similar. And, yet, some of the members succeed in rising to leadership, become chieftains, headmen, obtain great authority and influence, while other individuals do not rise above the general level.[22] Such growth of leaders and social inequality cannot be accounted for by differences in environment because they do not exist here in noticeable form. The only answer is the innate differences of the members of the tribe which manifest themselves in the facts of social ascendency and social differentiation. This may be said even of those leaders of preliterate tribes whose influence is based on their wealth.[23] It is well known that in many cases the wealth of such individuals has not been inherited but obtained by themselves. Why have they succeeded in accumulating and, as a result, got the influence, while other individuals of the same tribe could not do it? The environmental hypotheses cannot help here again. The same may be said of many other cases of this and other kinds. Why, for instance, would not the Roman aristocracy and population, which after the first and second centuries A. D. began to be composed of the lower classes of different race and stock, continue the work of their predecessors, in spite of the fact that the newcomers received a brilliant civilization and were put in the environment created by their predecessors? Why did not the environment help them to continue the work of their predecessors and to push Roman culture further and further? The environmental theory may say something in explanation, but, it seems to me, it never can give a complete account of the decay without the help of hereditary and racial factors. In accordance with O. Seek, V. Pareto, Sensini, Fahlbeck, L. Woltmann, and T. Frank, we are urged to think that:

> What lay behind and constantly reacted upon Rome's disintegration was, after all, to a considerable extent, the fact that the people who built Rome had given way to a different race. The lack of energy and enterprise, the failure of foresight and common sense, the weakening of moral and political stamina, all were concomitant with the gradual diminution of the stock which, during the earlier days, had displayed these qualities.[24]

Other similar facts will not be presented here.[25] They will be dealt with later.

From the above we must conclude that *there are many phenomena of social stratification and social distribution of individuals, and many differences among the individuals, as well as among the groups, which cannot be accounted for satisfactorily by the environmental hypothesis. To be explained they need the hereditary factor. For this reason it is certain that a part, at least, of these differences among the upper and lower social strata, as well as social stratification itself, are the result not only of environment but of heredity, not only of adaptation, but of selection as well.*

6. THE "REACTIONARY" NATURE OF THE EXTREME ENVIRONMENTAL THEORY

Among some sociologists at the present moment there is an opinion that the "environmental theory" is progressive and promising while "the hereditary theory" is "conservative" and leads to justification of the privileges of the minority and does not give any hope for an increase of social equality. This is the reason, (of which these sociologists are often unaware), which incites them to be favorable toward an extreme environmentalism and unfavorable toward "heredity." This opinion, like many popular opinions, is utterly wrong. If the theory of omnipotent environment were true then there would not be any hope for the lower strata. If the rôle of heredity is almost nil, then, according to the theory, the better environment of upper classes should have produced better and better men while the bad environment of lower classes should have made them worse and worse. The discrepancy between the strata should increase more and more. No genius from the lower classes and no stupid man from the upper strata could appear because a bad environment of the former and a good environment of the latter would have made impossible such "miracles." There could not be any hope for the lower classes, even in improving their environment because, destined to be stupid by virtue of their environment, they never would be able to force the more intelligent upper classes to improvement and would have no chance to defeat them, while for "the greedy and predatory" upper strata (according to these theories) there could not be any reason to help the lower classes to put down their own privileges. Thus, the theory, being pushed to its logical consequences, dooms all members of the lower classes in all generations to be inferior slaves, without any hope and prospect, and all members of the upper layers to be forever the superior masters and leaders. Such is the logical conclusion of this "progressive" and "liberal" theory of an omnipotent environment.

The real life, in this and in many similar cases, happens to be much more liberal and generous. Through its mystery of fortunate and unfortunate combination in the germ cells it has made possible the appearance of the great leaders from the bottom of the social pyramid, in spite of unfavorable environment, and, on the other hand, through the same factor of heredity it has produced many failures among the upper strata. This shows that the factor of heredity has often been more "democratic" and less caste-limited, than the factor of environment. I am really glad that the situation has been and is such. The above makes clear the fallacy of an excessive environmentalism. Objectively, it is even more "reactionary" than the opposite theory of omnipotent heredity in its most excessive and "reactionary" interpretations. *Sapienti sat.* Let "liberal" and "progressive" sociologists go easy with the fashionable excessive "environmentalism." This "child" cannot give the results which they naïvely expect from him.

Now, when social stratification in its forms, height, and profile; social mobility in its forms, variations and fluctuations, its channels and controlling mechanism; and finally, the qualities of the people who dwell in different social strata have been studied, we may turn to the causal part of our study—to the causes of stratification and circulation.

[1] "By nature, men are nearly alike; by practice they get to be wide apart." "There are only the wise of the highest class, and the stupid of the lowest class who cannot be changed." Such is one of many statements of the ancient thought of China, and Confucianism. See *Lî-Kî, passim* and Bks. I, VII, and VIII, *The Sacred Books of the East,* Vol. XXVII.

[2] See the data and experiments in Apert, Dr., *La croissance*, pp. 81 *ff.*, Paris, 1921; Jackson, Clarence M., *The Effects of Inanition and Malnutrition upon Growth and Structure,* Pt. II and pp. 457-461, *passim,* 1925.

[3] See GROTJAHN, A., *Über Wandlungen in d. Volksernährung;* SCHMOLLER, G., *Staats und Socialwissensch. Forschungen,* Vol. XX, Heft 2, Leipzig, 1902; KLEPIKOFF, S. A., *Nutrition of the Russian Peasantry* (Russian); SLOSSE and WAXWEILER, E., *Recherches sur le travail humain dans l'industrie,* 1910; the data for other countries concerning the nutrition of different social classes may be found in WEBB, AUGUST, *The New Dictionary of Statistics,* pp. 156-165, 273-289, London, 1911. For the past, see D'AVENEL, *Le méchanisme de la vie moderne,* pp. 156 *ff.*, Paris, 1908.

[4] See the data in SOROKIN, P., *Sociology of Revolution,* p. 219.

[5] See the details in IVANOVSKY, A.: "Physical Modifications of the Population of Russia Under Famine," *American Journal of Physical Anthropology,* No. 4, 1923.

[6] See HEIBERG, P., "The Increased Cost of Living and Heights of Recruits," *Meddeleeser, Danmarks Anthr.,* Vol. II, No. 2, 1920; APERT, DR., *op. cit.,* p. 91; *Vrachebnoje delo,* p. 628, February, 1921; HRDLIČKA, ALEŠ, *op. cit.,* p. 228; AMMON, OTTO, *Die Natürl. Auslese,* pp. 118-127.

[7] See also HOUZÉ, E., *op. cit.,* pp. 108-110; CARRET, J., *Étude sur les Savoyards,* Chambéry, 1882.

[8] SCHALLMAYER, W., *Verebung und Auslese,* p. 88, 1910.

[9] See *e.g.,* ARMITAGE, F. P., *Diet and Race,* 1922, in which he tries to show that color, cranial forms, and other bodily traits depend on the kind of food consumed.

[10] *Cf.* IMBERT, *Mode de Fonctionnement économique de l'organisme, passim,* Paris, 1902; DE MOOR, "La plasticité organique du muscle," *Travaux de l'Institut de physiologie,* Institute of Solvay, Vol. I, v, fasc. 3, 1902.

[11] Dr. C. Röse, contrary to Otto Ammon's opinion, thinks that dolichocephaly of the city population and that of many intellectual professions is not a result of selection but of more intellectual occupation and work. RÖSE, C., *op. cit.,* pp. 747 *ff.*

[12] The conclusions of Dr. F. Boas and Dr. C. Röse were met with a serious criticism by many prominent physical anthropologists and statisticians, such as C. Gini and especially Professor Sergi, and therefore are still to be tested. See SERGI, "Influenza delle ambiente sui caratteri fisici dell 'uomo," *Rivista italiana di sociologia,* pp. 16-24, 1912.

[13] See SOROKIN, P., "The Influence of Occupation on Human Behavior and Reflexology of Occupational Groups (Russian), *Russian Journal of Psychology, Neurology, and Experimental Psychology, No. 2,* 1922.

[14] See LANGEROCK, "Professionalism," *American Journal of Sociology,* Vol. XIII, pp. 776-781; BOGARDUS, EMORY S., *Fundamentals of Social Psychology,* Chap. XXIV; DEMOLIN, E., *Comment la route crée le type social* and *Les Français d'aujourdhui, passim,* 1898; BAUER, A., *Les classes sociales,* and series of papers and discussions concerning the occupational types and influence of occupation in *Revue international de sociologie* of 1900 and 1901. As an example of occupational psychology of farmers, see WILLIAMS, J. M., *Our Rural Heritage,* 1925; for that of leisure class; VEBLEN, THORSTEIN, *The Theory of the Leisure Class;* TAUSSIG, F., *Inventors and Money-Makers,* 1915; SOMBART, *Der Bourgeois.* A deep insight into the problem has been disclosed by many ideologists of revolutionary syndicalism and Guild Socialism such as G. Sorel, E. Berth, Lagardelle, Proudhon, Leoné, and others. *Cf.* LAGARDELLE, *Le socialisme ouvrier;* SOREL, G., *Les Illusions du Progrès,* and *Reflexions sur Violence;* BERTH, E., *Les Méfaits des Intellectuels;* GRIFFUELHES, *L'action Syndicaliste;* PROUDHON, *L'idée générale de la révolution en XIX siècle,* Paris, 1873.

[15] The corresponding literature is so enormous that it is useless to mention many very valuable works.

[16] SEASHORE, C. E., *The Psychology of Musical Talent.*

[17] See papers of WELLS, F. L., *American Journal of Psychology,* 1908 and 1912.

[18] See *The Reports of the Industrial Fatigue Research Board,* Nos. 10 and 22, Great Britain.

[19] See the remarks of Lapouge completely corroborated by experimental studies. LAPOUGE, V. DE, *op. cit.,* pp. 101 *ff.* To the same conclusion lead all contemporary mental tests.

[20] LAPOUGE, V. DE, *op. cit.,* Chap. IV.

[21] See GOBINEAU, A. DE, *Essai sur l'inégalité des races humaines,* Vol. I, Chaps. I to VIII, Paris, 1853, where Gobineau gives an unsurpassed criticism of all shortcomings of the one-sided environmental theory. In spite of the one-sidedness of his own theory his criticism appears to me quite valid and brilliant. A detailed criticism of the one-sided environmentalism will be given in my *Contemporary Social Theories.*

[22] See the facts in the quoted works of E. Mumford, A. Vierkandt, Herbert Spencer, A. Goldenweiler, P. Descamps, and R. H. Lowie.

[23] See the facts in the works of P. Descamps, A. Vierkandt, and M. Kovalevsky.

[24] FRANK, TENNEY, "Race Mixture in the Roman Empire," *American History Review,* Vol. XXI, p. 705.

[25] Many of them are given in Gobineau's quoted work, in LAPOUGE, V. DE, *Les Sélections Sociales,* and recently in HUNTINGTON, E., *The Character of Races, passim,* New York, 1924.

Part Four

FUNDAMENTAL CAUSES OF STRATIFICATION AND VERTICAL MOBILITY

CHAPTER XIV

THE FUNDAMENTAL CAUSES OF SOCIAL STRATIFICATION

1. THEORY OF A NATURAL ORIGIN OF SOCIAL STRATIFICATION

SINCE social stratification exists within every organized human society, apparently its existence is due to the conditions which are prevalent wherever social life exists. In other words, in addition to particular and temporary factors in social stratification which shape its specific forms, there must exist "causes"[1] which are universal and intimately connected with the phenomenon of "living together" of human beings. What are they? In their concrete forms these causes are numerous and different, but they may be grouped into a few general classes. Such classes are: first, the very fact of living together; second, innate differences of individuals, due to the differences in the complements of their chromosomes; third, differences in the environment in which individuals are placed since the moment of their conception. Let us take up these three main causes for consideration.

2. "LIVING TOGETHER" AS A PERMANENT FACTOR OF SOCIAL STRATIFICATION

More or less permanent living together is possible only under the condition of the organization of behavior and interrelations of members of a group. Organization means a differentiation of the members into the strata of (1) the governing men and (2) those who are governed. Without any "controlling center," whatever is its name, no permanent organization and "living together" are possible. As soon as such controlling center emerges, social stratification appears, no matter what the name of this center. Be it the delegation, elected leader, representative body, "the monarch by will of God," or a chief by "will of the people," this does not matter. What matters is the controlling power of the ruling men and the dependence of others on this power. Since it appears, social inequality is given. From this, as from a kernel, other forms of social stratification follow. Social stratification is a permanent feature of social organization, as the latter is an intimate trait of any permanent living together. In this sense, "Oligarchy is a fatal and inevitable characteristic of any society, any group and party."[2] However, if the individuals were innately identical, and their environment were the same, the factor of living together by itself would not have been able to produce the immensely conspicuous forms of social stratification which are found in history. If such has not been the case, it has been due to an interference of the other permanent factors of stratification. Such factors are the innate differences of individuals and the difference in their environment. In the conditions of "living together" they have been the agencies which created and are creating all conspicuous forms of social stratification.

3. INNATE DIFFERENCES OF INDIVIDUALS, AS A PERMANENT FACTOR OF STRATIFICATION

At the present moment we certainly know that innate physical and mental qualities of individuals are different. Under such conditions, it would have been miraculous if there had not appeared a social differentiation and stratification. If, on a billiard table, we have billiard balls of different sizes, try to distribute and redistribute them, as one may, nevertheless, they will be unequal in all cases of distribution. If we have individuals with different qualities and capacities the fact of their inequality will be manifested in stratification. Distribute them as you like, put them under any conditions, nevertheless, in any group, be it a preliterate tribe, a gang of criminals, a Christian community, a Communist faction, an arch-democratic society, a "levelers'" sect, the fact of inequality of its members, in this or that form, has been, is, and will be manifested. Whether we style the fact as inequality and stratification, or prefer to style it by other high-sounding phrases, this does not matter at all.[3] What matters is that under such conditions there will be leaders and led, the influential, the rulers, and the ruled, the dominating group and the dominated. This is what constitutes the kernel of stratification. Contrary to Ward, it is as natural as any division of labor. Such is the general rule to which there is no exception whatsoever. I do not know any social group, even among all "levelers'" groups, in which a real equality of individuals has been realized, in which all its members have had an equal amount of influence, an equal social position, an identical behavior. Never has such a group existed and no one can point to a single example of it, unless one takes "speech reactions." Real equality is still a myth which has never been realized. No social reconstruction can overcome the fact of stratification, unless individuals are made equal innately. For this, an equalization of the chromosomes is necessary, a task which may be performed only by an Omnipotent Being. All that any social reconstruction may do, therefore, is to redistribute the billiard balls on a table in a different way and to label them with different names (such as "equality"), in some cases to diminish or increase their inequalities where such inequalities are due not to innate differences, but to environmental conditions. And that is all.

Innate differences (polymorphism and dimorphism) of individual organisms among *animal societies* of bees, ants, jackals, monkeys, and so on, call forth a differentiation of their members into different social classes, castes, and strata. The same factor is responsible for the emerging among them of their leaders and rulers.[4]

The same is true in regard to *preliterate tribes.* The stratification of a primitive society into more privileged and dominant masculine groups and disinherited female groups; into socially stratified age groups, beginning with the group of the oldest and ending with the youngsters; an emergence above the general level of headmen and chieftains and more influential and privileged primitive aristocracy; all this has been called forth, in the first place, by natural inequalities, in body and mind, of the members of these groups.[5]

Animal and primitive groups in this respect are especially important because the differentiating rôle of environment, especially of the anthropo-social environment, plays very little part. Consequently, if even here social stratification is found, though in a less developed, and yet, in a quite clear form, this means that it may be due only to the natural differences of their members.

The same basis continues to be the factor of social stratification in all more advanced and more complicated societies, with this difference that, parallel with their complication, there have appeared secondary causes of inequality which, being produced by the primary factor, in their own turn create new bases for further social stratification, and in this way lead to greater and greater stratification of social organization until it reaches the tremendous proportions which exist and have existed in great and complicated societies.

4. ENVIRONMENTAL DIFFERENCES AS A PERMANENT FACTOR OF SOCIAL STRATIFICATION

Even without innate differences of individuals, the differences in their environment are enough to produce a social stratification under the condition of "living together." The different environments may produce social stratification in the following ways: in the first place, through favorable and unfavorable conditions. Individuals placed in favorable circumstances have a greater chance to promote themselves than individuals who have to overcome many impediments to reach the status of the more fortunate members of society. A primitive man who by chance happens to obtain a better place for fishing is in a more favorable condition to promote himself than another who, by chance, is unlucky in his place of fishing. A mining pioneer (*e.g.,* Senator Clarke) by chance coming to a spot rich in gold has much greater chance to become rich and influential than another miner who has "hard luck." An individual born within a rich and intelligent family has a better starting point for his life race than another born in a poor and ignorant family.

In the second place, different environments may lead to the same result through direct and indirect *modification* of human and mental traits. One environment facilitates a vigorous exercise of the body and the mind; inventiveness, self-control, and so on. Another environment may facilitate the opposite traits. This may be said of geographic, as well as of the anthropo-social environment. As a result, in the course of time, innately identical individuals may be very considerably changed. On the bases of their acquired differences they become different; the difference, as in the case of innate differences, produces an inequality in the struggle for life, for control, for obtaining the necessities of life, for domination and influence. This usually results in a form of stratification.

In these two ways different environments call forth the phenomena of differentiation of individuals and lead to social stratification. As the environment of different individuals and groups rarely has been quite identical, therefore, this factor has been operating permanently throughout history. Innate differences and different environments, in the conditions of living together, are always in operation; hence the appearance of social stratification becomes still easier. These factors are quite enough to produce all the principal forms of social inequality. In everyday life we may see that boys' gangs, a crowd of grown-ups, a pioneer colony, a class of school children, a band of outlaws, a society of "levelers," the population of a new settlement, in brief, all groups composed of a new people, without any previous ranks and hierarchy, as soon as they continue to live together, almost immediately show a differentiation into leaders and the led, influential and non-influential members, the aristocracy and the "plain people," with many different intermediary strata.

It is needless to quote specific cases simply because the outlined "semi-spontaneous stratification" is a phenomenon which we meet practically in every group of men who have lived together any length of time. Thus, we come to *the theory of "spontaneous and natural" origin of social stratification which contends that for its appearance any special catastrophic or extraordinary factors are unnecessary.* The permanent operation of the above two factors, which really exist at all times and in all societies, is quite enough to call forth social stratification.

5. CRITICISM OF THE MILITARY THEORY OF SOCIAL STRATIFICATION

It is easy to see that the above "natural theory" of stratification differs considerably from the fashionable theory of Gumplowicz, Ratzenhofer, Oppenheimer, and many others who have tried to explain the origin of social stratification almost exclusively as due to the war. Conquerors become the aristocracy; the conquered the lower strata; to keep their superiority the conquerors issue obligatory rules of conduct known as law, and in this way juridically secure their privileges, influence, leadership, and high positions. I do not say that this hypothesis is quite wrong. But I do say that it is insufficient. Its insufficiency consists in that a *local, temporary, and facilitating condition—war—in this theory is put in the place of a universal, permanent, and necessary cause of social stratification.* War is surely a condition which greatly facilitates the origin and the growth of social stratification. And Herbert Spencer, probably, better than anybody else, has shown that.[6] But is the war an indispensable condition for the establishment of social stratification? Not at all. Stratification exists not only among the militant but also among peaceful societies, not only in time of war, but in periods of peace also. In infinitely numerous and various groups, such as a new settlement, a gang of boys, a class of children, a rural community, wherein without any war and warfare, there exists stratification into the leaders and the led with their various ranks of prestige, authority, influence, and privileges, and this seems to develop spontaneously. These reasons are enough to contend that the war factor is not a necessary condition for the origin and existence of social stratification. It is true, further, as the war theory states, that in many countries and at different periods the aristocracy has been established through war, and through the same factor a free population has been degraded to the status of slaves and serfs. But in all such cases we have not so much an establishment of aristocracy or slavery as the *substitution* of one aristocracy or slavery for another. The Dorians, the Romans, the Aryans, the Spanish, the Portugese, the Teuton, or the Norman Conquerors, establishing their social domination and privileges in conquered societies, did not originate social stratification but simply changed its forms. Stratification in the conquered countries had existed before their conquests. The conquerors only put down this native aristocracy and placed themselves in their position; they did not create this stratification for the first time. The war factor is an efficient temporary and local condition which *facilitates* social stratification but is not a fundamental, necessary, and universal factor in it. If war had not existed at all in the history of mankind, stratification, nevertheless, would have appeared through the working of the above fundamental factors.

6. WAR AND OTHER FACILITATING AND HINDERING CONDITIONS OF SOCIAL STRATIFICATION

The above shows that, aside from the fundamental and necessary causes of social stratification, there are many other conditions which facilitate or hinder the growth of social stratification. It is not my task here to give a detailed enumeration and analysis of all these conditions. It is enough to say that *all conditions which contribute to an increase of innate heterogeneity of a people, or to differences of their environment, or to an increase of antagonisms among individuals or groups are conditions which facilitate an* increase *of social stratification.* Some of them, such as an enlargement of the size of a group and an increase of the heterogeneity of its population, have been discussed in the first part of this book. *All conditions which contribute to an increase of similarity of the people, or to the similarity of their environment, or to their solidarity, facilitate a* decrease *of social stratification.* Such are the general characteristics of the two classes of conditions. What they are in each individual case is a *questio facti* and must be factually studied in each case.

SUMMARY

1. There are permanent and fundamental causes of social stratification, which, under conditions of living together, permanently operate in the way of creating social stratification.

2. These causes are: innate differences of individuals and differences in their environment.

3. They are quite sufficient to produce all the principal forms of social stratification.

4. War is not an inevitable or universal primary factor of social stratification. It is only a condition which facilitates its origin or growth.

5. Besides war there are other concrete conditions which facilitate or hinder an increase of social stratification. Among the facilitating conditions especially important are: an enlargement in the size of a group and an increase in the heterogeneity of its population.

6. As it is improbable that in the future the innate qualities of individuals or their environment will be identical, a complete abolition of social stratification is improbable.

[1] Practically, in the field of social phenomena, we very rarely have one-sided "causal relation" with a cause as a condition preceding in time and with "an effect" resulting later on from the cause. Social phenomena are "interdependent" but not one-sidedly dependent.

Therefore, instead of applying the formula: "cause and effect" here we must apply the formula "variable-function." In the majority of the cases such a formula may be reversed: what we make the "independent variable" and what the "function" depends completely on the purpose of investigation. Such substitution gives the possibility of analyzing more properly the functional relations of interdependent phenomena. It has all the positive qualities of an analysis according to "cause and effect" without its inconveniences. Even in the physical and natural sciences such a substitution has begun to take place and is becoming common. It is reasonable also because formula "variable-function" is free from a metaphysical flavor of cause as something which acts, produces, creates its effect. I use the terms "cause," "factor," and "effect" in the sense of "variable" and "function." See Cournot, A. A., *Traité de l'enchainement des Idées, etc.*, Vol. I, *passim*, Paris, 1861, and *Considérations sur la Marche des Idées*, etc., Vol. I, Chaps. I, II, and *passim*, Paris, 1872; Mach, E., *Erkenntniss und Irrtum, passim*, 1906; Pearson, Karl, *The Grammar of Science*, Chap. III; Hayes, *Introduction to the Study of Sociology*, Chap. II, 1920, and *Sociology and Ethics*, Chap. IV, 1921; Pareto, V., *op. cit., passim* and Chaps. I and XII; Poincarè, H., *La Science et L'hypothèse*, pp. 110 *ff.*, Paris, 1908; Tschuproff, A. A., *Ocherky po teorii Statistiki, passim*, 1912; *Grundbegriffe and Grundprobleme der Korrelationstheorie*, Berlin, 1925; Keslen, H., *Hauptprobleme der Staatrechtslehre*, pp. 1-94, Tübingen, 1911; Duhem, P., *La théorie physique, son objet et sa structure*, Paris, Chévalier et Rivière Cie.; Weber, M., *Gesammelte Aufsätze zur Wissenschaftslehre*, pp. 112 ff., 87 *ff.*, 420-425, 1922.

[2] See Michels, R., "La Crisi psicologica del socialismo," *Rivista italiana di sociologia*, pp. 374-375, 1910; also his *Eugenics in Party Organization*, pp. 232-233, and *Political Parties, passim*. "An iron law leads to the formation of an oligarchy in all groups and parties, regardless of the nature of the doctrines they profess, whether monarchic, aristocratic, or democratic. Leadership may at first be spontaneous; it is superseded by professional direction, and at last leaders become bureaucratic masters of routine, irremovable. At some future time the socialists may possibly be successful, but socialism (as a theory of equality) never," properly says Michels.

[3] From this viewpoint the attempt of L. Ward to prove that natural differences of men do not produce stratification is quite speculative. He eliminates inequality through a mere substitution of "low-sounding" for "high-sounding" phrases. See Ward, L., "Social Classes in the Light of Modern Social Theory," *American Journal of Sociology*, Vol. XIII, pp. 617-627; see also Howerth, Ira W., "Is There a Natural Law of Inequality," *Scientific Monthly*, Vol. 19, pp. 502-511.

[4] "Even in the animal world, there are certain eminent individuals which in comparison with the other members of their species show a superiority of capability, brain power, and force of will and obtain a predominance over the other animals," says Perty. This is a general rule. I quote from Park, Robert E., and Burgess, Ernest W., *Introduction to the Science of Sociology*, 2nd ed.,

p. 809. See the facts in the works: PETRUCCI, *Origine Polyphyletique des sociétés animales;* WHEELER, W. M., *Ants, Their Structure, Development, and Behavior,* and *Social Life among Insects,* New York, 1923; ESPINAS, A., *Des Sociétés animales,* Paris, 1878; WAGNER, W., *Bio-Psychology* (Russian), Vols. I and II, Wolf Company, St. Petersburg; BREHM, TIERLEBEN, in different volumes; MUMFORD, E., *op. cit.,* pp. 224 *ff.;* LEOPOLD, L., *Prestige,* pp. 16-62. Many corresponding facts are given in the works of Charles Darwin, L. Morgan, and P. Kropotkin.

[5] See, besides the quoted works of Herbert Spencer, A. Vierkandt, E. Mumford, P. Descamps, and others, SCHURZ, H., *Alterklassen and Männerbunde,* Berlin, 1902; RIVERS, W. H. R., *Social Organization,* New York, 1924; LOWIE, R. H., *Primitive Society,* New York, 1920; SIMS, N., *Society and Its Surplus,* pp. 207 *ff.,* 1924.

[6] See SPENCER, HERBERT, *Principles of Sociology,* Pt. V, *passim.*

CHAPTER XV

THE FACTORS OF VERTICAL CIRCULATION

1. PRIMARY PERMANENT FACTORS

SINCE vertical circulation in some degree exists in every society it follows that among its factors, besides local, temporary, and specific conditions, there must be conditions which operate in all societies, in all periods. Correspondingly, the factors of vertical circulation may be divided into: (*a*) primary or general, and (*b*) secondary, or local and temporary, which facilitate or hinder mobility.

Among the primary factors are: (1) demographic factors, which lead either to the dying out of the upper strata or to their relative diminution in the total population; (2) dissimilarity of parents and children; (3) change of environment, especially of the anthropo-social environment; (4) defective social distribution of individuals within social layers.

2. DEMOGRAPHIC FACTORS OF VERTICAL CIRCULATION

Under this heading are meant all forces which call forth sterility, lower differential birth rate, or higher mortality of the upper classes. In the course of time they cause either an extinction of the aristocratic families, or a decrease of their proportion in the total increased population of a society. In both cases such a situation creates a kind of "social vacuum" within the upper strata. As the performance of the functions carried on by the upper strata continues to be necessary, and as the corresponding people cannot be recruited any longer from a diminishing upper population, it is natural that this "vacuum" must be filled by the climbers from the lower strata. Such in essence is this factor of vertical circulation.

It is not certain that the fecundity of the upper strata is always and everywhere lower than that of the lower strata. But it is possible to say that such a phenomenon has taken place within many societies and at different periods. Besides, it seems possible to contend that in some way, not exactly known to us, almost any aristocratic family sooner or later dies out either biologically or socially, in the sense that its descendants cease to be noticeable as the continuators of a given aristocratic family. Though biological and social extinction of a family are quite different, and social extinction may take place without biological extinction, for our purposes social extinction is as important as biological. An illegitimate male son of a monarch born from a peasant girl and remaining within a peasant class is a peasant, but not a prince; socially he is not a continuator of a royal family. These reasons make this cause so general that it may be put into the class of primary factors of circulation.

Here are some representative facts.

At the present time in Western countries the birth rate of the upper strata in general is less than that of the lower classes. This is true in regard to economic, political and intraoccupational and interoccupational stratification. Here are representative figures:

PRUSSIA, 1907 [1]

Occupational Groups and Their Strata	Number of Children Born (in Wedlock) per 100 Married Men
Agriculture:	
Farmers, owners, and managers	15.5
Higher employees	15.9
Clerks	22.2
Laborers	23.8
Industry and mining:	
Owners and managers	16.4
Higher employees	from 11.2 to 15.1
Unskilled and skilled laborers	21.4
Commerce and insurance:	
Owners and managers	13.4
Higher employees	12.4
Laborers	19.6

Breslau, 1905[2]

Occupational Groups	Average Number of Children in Marriages of More Than 25 Years' Duration	
Entrepreneurs	4.97	
Higher and middle officials	4.50	
Subordinate officials	5.45	
Private employees	4.73	
Skilled laborers	5.70	
Unskilled laborers	5.95	
Economic classes:		
Paying rent:		
Up to 250 marks	5.58	
From 251 to 500	5.52	
501 to 750	4.71	
751 and over	4.02	
House owners	4.74	
	Number of Childless Marriages per 1,000 Marriages of Each Class with Duration of	
	From 0 to 5 Years	Over 25 Years
Social classes:		
Entrepreneurs	117	97
Higher employees	99	72
Laborers	97	82

BAVARIA [3]

Social Strata	Average Number of Children per Father
General population	3.1
Higher officials	2.3
Middle officials	2.4
Lower officials	3.3

FRANCE 1906 [4]

Per 100 families of each specified class in the marriages with duration from 15 to 25 years, the number of children was as follows:

Annual Emolument in £	Less Than 20	20 to 40	40 to 60	60 to 100	100 to 160	160 to 240	240 to 400	400 and over	Total
Employees [a]	277	241	259	245	223	231	229	238	237
Laborers	329	321	293	280	254	234	—	—	307
Among Marriages Which Lasted for More than 25 Years the Number of Sterile Cases per 1,000 Marriages of Each Specified Class:									
Employees		95 [b]	86	99	113	101	111	109	101
Laborers		70 [b]	74	91	98	100	—	—	78
Proportional Number of Families with More than Seven Children:									
Employees		56	53	41	33	26	23	52	44
Laborers		95	86	76	55	50	.....	.....	88

[a] The term "employees" designates the entrepreneurs and higher employees.
[b] Less than 40.

These data show that fertility decreases and sterility increases as we pass (1) from the lower intraoccupational strata to the higher strata; (2) from the manual unskilled strata to the more intellectual, skilled, and better paid occupations; (3) from the poorer economic classes to the more wealthy; (4) from the lower social classes to the higher ones. There are some deviations from this regularity but they do not annihilate the general rule. Quite similar is the situation in other European countries. Here are some further data:

ENGLAND AND WALES (1911)[5]

Social Classes	Children Born per 100 Families	Children Surviving per 100 Families
Upper and middle classes	213	187
Intermediate	248	211
Skilled labor	278	231
Intermediate	285	236
Unskilled labor	317	253

SCOTLAND[6]

Occupational Classes	Average Number of Children Born in Families of Completed Fertility in Each Class
General population	5.49
Occupational groups with fertility above the average fertility of the population, consisting chiefly of manual laborers (unskilled and semiskilled) in different trades and farmers and fishermen	from 7.04 to 5.91
Occupational groups with fertility below the average fertility of the population, commercial dealers, merchants	from 5.44 to 4.77
Publishers, booksellers	4.75
Private means	4.71
Commercial occupations	4.63
Men of the navy	4.48
Civil mining engineers	4.43
Chemists, druggists	4.38
Clergymen	4.33
Artists, musicians, dramatists	4.27
Schoolmasters, teachers	4.25
Literary, scientific men and women	4.09
Advocates, solicitors	3.92
Physicians, surgeons	3.91
Army officers	3.76

UNITED STATES OF AMERICA 1923[7]

Social Classes	Average Number of Children	
	Born per Family	Living per Family
Foreign-born parents (Immigrants)	4.0	3.4
Native-born white Americans	3.0	2.8

UNITED STATES OF AMERICA 1923[7]

Occupational Groups and Their Strata	Average Number of Children in 1923 per Pair of Parents, Including Children Who Died	Average Number of Living Children per Pair of Parents, 1923
Mining:		
Mine operators (young) [a]	4.0 to 4.2	3.6
Mine foremen, overseers	4.4	3.8
Mine operators, officials, manufacturers	3.5	3.2
Mine chemists, assayers, metallurgists	2.0	1.9
Manufacturing:		
Factory laborers (young)	3.8 to 3.4	3.2 to 2.9
Factory foremen, overseers	3.2	2.9
Factory managers, superintendents, manufacturers, factory owners, officials	2.5	2.4
Technical engineers	2.2	2.0
Trade:		
Laborers (young)	3.2	2.7
Retail dealers	3.0	2.7
Bankers, brokers	2.2	2.1
Designers, draftsmen, inventors	2.0	1.9

Occupational Groups and Their Strata	Average Number of Children in 1923 per Pair of Parents, Including Children Who Died	Average Number of Living Children per Pair of Parents, 1923
Personal service:		
Janitors, sextons	3.9	3.3
Porters	3.1	2.6
Hotel keepers, managers	3.1	2.8
Restaurant, café keepers	2.7	2.5
Public service:		
Garbage men, scavengers, laborers (young)	3.6	3.1
Guards, doorkeepers	4.2	3.6
Policemen	3.0	2.7
Officials, inspectors (city and country)	3.1	2.8
Officials, inspectors (state and United States)	2.4	2.2
Clerical occupations:		
Messengers, office boys	2.7	2.4
Agents, collectors	2.2	2.1
Stenographers, typists	2.0	1.9
Bookkeepers, cashiers	2.0	1.9
Transportation (water):		
Longshoremen, stevedores	4.0	3.3
Captains, masters, pilots	2.7	2.4
Professional service:		
Actors, showmen	2.1	1.9
Architects	2.1	2.0
Artists, sculptors	2.0	1.9
Authors, editors	2.3	2.1
Lawyers, judges, justices	2.3	2.2
Teachers	2.2	2.0
Clergymen	3.5	3.2
Physicians, surgeons	2.3	2.1

[a] Their marriage has not lasted as long as that of more qualified older groups; therefore the number of their children is lower than it would be if the marriage had lasted longer.

These figures show again that among the immigrants who in general are of a lower stratum than the native born parents, the fertility is higher than among the higher social stratum of Americans. Still more conspicuous are the data for the inter- and intraoccupational strata. They show that in general within all occupations the highest strata are the least fertile. Among the occupations, the professional men and the clergy are the least fertile. There are, of course, some exceptions, but they do not nullify the general rule.

Norway.—The census of families in Norway in 1920 has given similar results. The average number of children per marriage which lasted 18 years or more is 6.52. High officials, professionals, and rich people have the lowest number of children (4.24). Fishermen, agricultural laborers, farmers, and factory laborers have the highest number of children, 8, 9, and more.[8]

I shall not present other similar data which indicate the same phenomenon, *viz.*, the lower fertility of the upper intraoccupational and interoccupational, economic and social strata compared with that of the lower layers of the population. With all due allowances in regard to the duration of marriage and other conditions, at the present moment this is an ascertained fact typical of all countries of Western civilization.[9]

In the above figures, large class divisions exist. If more detailed groups of prominent men of the upper classes are taken, the conclusion is still more warranted. Here are the facts. In the first place the study of the *royal families* by F. Savorgnan, Sundberg, P. Jacoby, and M. Kemmerich has shown that, in general, their fecundity is lower than that of the common population of their countries at a corresponding period. Besides, the percentage of childless marriages among these families is higher than that among families of the common people.[10] The study of prominent men of science, literature and other men and women of genius, by Francis Galton, R. Steinmetz, J. McKeen Cattell, Havelock Ellis, C. S. Castle, J. W. Philiptschenko and M. Thomas, has shown the same low fecundity and a high sterility.[11] The studies of the *aristocracy, nobility, peerage, and prominent statesmen and other notable families* by Francis Galton, Fahlbeck,

G. Hansen, F. Savorgnan, Havelock Ellis, Furlan, J. Bertillon, and others, have given similar results.[12] Finally the same is true in regard to the strata of the rich classes, higher officials, and professionals,[13] with some exceptions as to clergymen and a narrow circle of rich families. But, again, the celibate clergy, by virtue of celibacy, is childless (at least socially). And even the richest relatively fertile families show in the second and later generations after becoming rich, the same tendency to a low fertility and high social sterility.[14] In brief, numerous studies of fertility and sterility of many specific upper groups corroborate the general statement in regard to the lower birth rate and greater degree of childlessness of the upper strata.[15] To this it must be added that, according to L. Flügge, the new ascending men show a decrease of fertility greater than the old aristocracy. Flügge explains this through the hypothesis that the old aristocratic families which had climbed gradually became "immune" while the new arrivals did not have, as yet, the time necessary to acquire immunity. Whether this is so or not, the indicated fact is worth mentioning and is often observed.[16] To what extent the phenomenon of lower fertility and higher sterility of the upper classes is common for all times it is difficult to say certainly. Several studies show that this discrepancy between the fertility of the upper and the lower classes fluctuates. For instance, in the English population, the difference has been considerably less at the middle of the nineteenth century than at the beginning of the twentieth century. While in the period of 1851-1861 the total fertility of the upper and middle class in England was only 11 per cent below the mean, and that of the unskilled labor class only 3 per cent above the mean, in 1891-1896, the fertility of the upper and middle class was 26 per cent below the mean and that of the unskilled labor class 13 per cent above the mean.[17] Among the German royal families, according to Kemmerich, fertility and sterility fluctuated in the following way. (See p. 355.)

If the figures are reliable, they show that within the royal families, fertility and sterility fluctuate considerably in time, and from dynasty to dynasty. Several other studies show similar oscillations. It follows from this that the difference between the fer-

Periods of History	Average Number of Children per Family	Average Per Cent of Sterile Marriages
From time of Charles the Great to 1300	2.3	33[a]
From Rudolf Hapsburg to 1450	4.5	25[a]
From Frederick III to 1600	5.5	18[a]
From 1600 to 1790	4.2	18[a]
From 1790 to 1908	4.0	18[a]

[a] Approximately.

tility of the upper and the lower strata may fluctuate. It seems to be probable, nevertheless, that the lower fertility of the upper strata is, if not a permanent phenomenon, at least common for many societies and many periods.[18]

Although, as we have seen, the mortality of the lower classes has been considerably higher than that of the upper strata, nevertheless, it does not compensate for the lower rate of increase of population of the upper strata. Some previously given data show this. The indicated sources give many additional corroborations of this statement.[19] *In spite of lower mortality the members of the higher strata, owing to their lower fertility, increase often less rapidly than the members of the lower ones.*

To the factor of lower fertility must be added that of a *high death rate by violence* which takes place in regard to some groups of aristocracy (royal, executive, and military), and which leads to the extinction of many aristocratic families, and, through that, creates a "social vacuum." Here are some illustrations of the statement.[20] (See p. 356.)

These figures show that some upper groups have a death rate by violence, at least, in some periods, much higher than that of the common population represented here by the data of the United States in 1921. The figures are only illustrative, of course; and yet they show what is going on within many upper groups at some periods of history. The social position of monarchs, executives, and politicians is generally connected with a great danger of death by violence. The position of a military aristocracy, both

Social Strata	Per Cent of Death by Violence in Total Number of Deaths
Monarchs, total [a]	31.9
Roman Empire	66.3
Byzantium	34.9
Turkey	25.0
England	22.5
Holy Roman Empire, Austria, Prussia	21.1
Russia	26.9
Germany (from 800 to 1300) [b]	20.0
Germany (from 1300 to 1450) [b]	25.0
Prominent military men	20.0
Presidents of United States and France	12.1
Presidents of Bolivian Republic	40.0[c]
Prominent statesmen, political leaders	10.0
Roman Catholic Popes	9.0
Population of United States in 1921	7.2[d]

[a] For 423 monarchs of different countries and periods.
[b] For all members of the German Kaiser's and Royal families.
[c] Approximately.
[d] Suicide, and all deaths by violence.

in the past and the present (the strata of commanding officers) in the period of war, dooms it to greater extermination than the average mass of population or soldiers. As we shall see, long wars have caused the greatest "social vacuum" in the upper social strata, and, through this, called forth an extraordinarily intensive infiltration of successful men from the lower classes into the higher ones. The above reasons: *lower fertility, higher sterility, and high rate of the death by violence are universal enough to be important factors of the social circulation.*

The enormous significance of this for the phenomenon of social circulation is easy to understand. According to the computation of Lapouge, if there were two social classes numerically equal, and of these the one had three and the other had four surviving children per family, then, at the end of the first generation, the total population would consist of 43 per cent of the first and 57 per cent of the second class; at the end of the second generation the proportions would be 36 and 64 per cent, respectively; and after about 300 years the proportions would be respectively 7 and 93 per cent.[21] This brings out clearly the significance of the lower fertility of the upper classes. This, together with violent death, leads to the situation that an increase of additional high positions due to an increase of the population and size of a society cannot be filled exclusively from the higher classes; it creates a kind of "social vacuum" in the upper strata and makes necessary an infiltration of newcomers from the lower classes. Hence the upward current of vertical circulation.

The following data clearly show this.

The number of the Spartiats before the Persian war was about 8,000; in 420 B.C. it decreased to 6,000, in 371 to 1,500, about the time of Aristotle to 1,000; in 244 B.C. there were only 700 Spartiats, of which only 100 were the full-right Homoioi.[22] In Rome, since 164 to 136 B.C. the number of full citizens diminished from 337,452 to 317,933; as to the patricians, to the time of Cæsar, there were only about 15 patrician families surviving; all others were extinct. Even the equestrian and noble families which climbed at the time of Cæsar and Augustus were extinct at the time of Claudius. In order to have 300 senators, already in 177 B.C., 177 plebeians were raised to this dignity. Similar extinction of the higher social group took place in Athens. The number of privileged full citizens in Athens was about 15,000 to 16,000 at the beginning of the Peloponnesian war; after the catastrophe in Sicily, about 9,000; at the end of the third century B.C., about 5,000 or 6,000; about the time of Sulla, 2,500.[23]

Such extinction was the result of low fertility[24] and great losses of the upper strata due to wars.

The same phenomenon took place later in history. By the fifteenth century, almost all aristocratic families of the time of the Crusades were extinct. According to K. Bücher, the notable families of the Middle Ages very rarely existed longer than one century.[25] The aristocratic families of France, as has been shown by Benoiston de Chateauneuf, on the average, did not exist longer than 300 years.[26] In England, of 500 old aristocratic families of the fifteenth century, hardly any exist to-day; the remnant that does exist consists only in the names of the families granted to men of a quite different origin. Almost all present peers who bear the names of these old families were created and granted titles and names much later. Of 394 peers who were in England in 1837, 272 were created after 1760. Of 1,527 baronetcies created from 1611 to 1819, only 635 remained. All others were extinct.[27] In Augsburg, of 51 senator families from 1368 to 1538, all except 8 died out. In Nuremberg, of 118 patrician families, 63 died out in the period from 1390 to 1490. In Berne in the period from 1717 to 1787, of 381 families, 148 died out.[28] In Geneva, of 133 notable families in 1789, after 60 years 41 families were extinct.[29] Of 1219 aristocratic families of Sweden, 946 (77.6 per cent) died out in a period of 100 years; 251 families, during 101 to 200 years; 21 families, during 201 to 300 years; only one family existed longer than 300 years. Of 1,547 families, 84 per cent died out in the third generation; only two families reached the ninth generation; and none longer.[30] Fahlbeck has shown that sterility is systematically increasing parallel to the increase of generations: in the first generation the per cent of childless marriages was 13.72; in the second 63.68. In Russia, to the time of Feodore Alexeevich, the old *boyar* families were almost completely extinct.[31] In Amsterdam, of 201 notable merchant families, 142 died out during three centuries, from the sixteenth to the nineteenth centuries. Of these 142 families, 30 were extinct within 0 to 100 years, 39 within 150 years, 43 within 200 years. The situation among the notable families in Hamburg has been similar.[32] A like extinction of the aristocratic families took place in Venice.[33] We see the same now and in the past among the royal or half-royal families, not to mention other upper families. Of 59 *mediatisieren* families in the Almanach de Gotha, within the last century five families died out completely, and one in the male line.[34]

These examples, a few of many similar ones, show how the "social vacuum" is permanently created through the permanent dying out of the upper families. If we now take the periods of wars and social upheavals, the dying out will appear much greater and still more conspicuous.

The losses among the aristocracy of ancient Greece—Sparta and Athens—and among the Roman patricians—the nobles and equestrians—were enormous during the periods of long and great wars, such as the Persian, the Peloponnesian, the Carthaginian, and other wars; and during the periods of civil wars and social revolutions. They wiped out an enormous part of the upper classes and created a vast "social vacuum" in the upper strata During the Middle Ages, the same story was repeated many times. Such wars as the Crusades, or the Hundred Years' War, played havoc within the circles of nobility. Of 2,800 chevaliers who started from Cypres in the Crusades, only about 100 returned. "These wars swallowed the flower of the French nobility." [35] The result of such upheavals as the French Jacquerie, or many other revolutions, was still worse. Every battle in the Middle Ages carried away hundreds or thousands of the members of the upper strata.[36]

The same process is going on up to this time. Modern wars, among them the last war, carried away a per cent of commanding officers considerably higher than that of the soldiers. During the Franco-Prussian War the losses per 1,000 officers were 89; per 1,000 soldiers 45.[37] The same is true of other wars, including the World War and the present upheavals. The Russian Revolution, which wiped out almost the entire nobility and upper strata, is a typical example. Since such is the case, it is natural that during such periods the infiltration of newcomers from the lower strata into the higher ones is especially intensive.

The above sufficiently corroborates the statement concerning the demographic factors of social circulation. Whatever may be the concrete causes of lower fertility, higher sterility, and an exceptionally high mortality (during some periods) of the upper social classes, these demographic conditions make social mobility necessary and inevitable. *And the greater the difference in the number of surviving children of the upper and the lower strata, the more intensive the vertical circulation caused by this factor will be.* For this reason an ascending current in the present population of England must be stronger than it was about 1851-1861, because, as we have seen, the difference in the number of surviving children of the upper and the lower classes at present is greater than it was before. The same seems to be true in regard to several other countries. As this difference varies from time to time, it follows that, in the past, the periods of increase of the difference should have been the periods of an intensification of the vertical circulation, providing this factor were not checked by opposite factors.

3. DISSIMILARITY OF PARENTS AND CHILDREN AS A FACTOR OF VERTICAL CIRCULATION

Since the publication of the works of Francis Galton, especially of his *Hereditary Genius,* it has become customary to think that talented parents beget talented children, while stupid parents beget stupid children. The reason for this is seen in the factor of heredity. At the present moment, there seems to be no doubt that this rule is, in many cases, true. But is it a rule which is universal and does it not know any exceptions? It seems not. We certainly know many cases where the children of prominent parents happened to be below normal, and the children of quite average parents quite prominent. Dr. A. Marro rightly says.

While one has seen children inheriting from their parents qualities by which parents have become eminent, other children, on the contrary, do not correspond at all to this expectation. One is painfully surprised to see the sons of Hippocrates quite stupid, and one is struck with astonishment in noting that from the race of Socrates and Aristotle there has not arisen the least spark of science, that Charles V, Peter the Great, and Napoleon I had only foolish sons.[38]

A similar admission is made by Francis Galton himself. "It has often been remarked that the men who have attained pinnacles of celebrity failed to leave worthy successors," says Galton.[39] It is possible to give hundreds of historical cases of this kind. The majority of the failures from the eminent families give an abundant source of material for its corroboration. On the other hand, it is possible to indicate hundreds of historical cases where the children of quite average parents have turned out to be eminent men of genius: Shakespeare, Beethoven, Schubert, Faraday, Pasteur, Lincoln, and the greater part of the self-made men, achievers and climbers—these supply examples of this fact.

Whatever may be the causes of this phenomenon, the fact of the dissimilarity of the parents and the children in many cases is beyond doubt. And, it seems to me, the number of such cases is not so small as was formerly believed. If they appear to be rare, this is due to the fact that the attention of the investigators for the last few decades has been turned almost exclusively to the opposite facts: the biologists, the eugenists, and other investigators have looked for and registered very carefully every fact of similarity of the children and their parents, and have somewhat disregarded the opposite facts. Hence, the impression that the facts of dissimilarity are few and scarce. Meanwhile, the opposite is to be found in almost every study of heredity. I do not know a single investigation of such cases where the correlation between the qualities of the parents and the children would be perfect. In the best cases, even in such comparatively simple traits as stature, pigmentation, the color of hair or eyes, not to mention other traits, the correlation happens to be approximately 0.5.[40] In regard to other traits it was much lower. Similarly, there scarcely may be found any study of this kind which would not indicate the fact of "overlapping." The presence of overlappings and the indicated difference between the theoretically perfect and the actual coefficient of correlation are found in all statistical studies of heredity. This means that *the fact of dissimilarity of parents and children is also permanent and universal.*[41]

In the causation of the dissimilarity, probably both heredity and environment participate. As to the factor of heredity, it interferes through the fortunate and unfortunate combination of the genes of both parents. The genes are so numerous that their combinations in the offspring of the same parents are rarely identical. Consequently, some traits may appear in parents and be lost in their offspring, and *vice versa.*[42] This can happen especially easily in the inheritance of the highest abilities of a parent by his child. Here a remark of Galton appears to be quite reasonable:

> The highest order of mind results from a fortunate mixture of incongruous constituents, and of such that naturally harmonize. These constituents are negatively correlated, and therefore the compound is unstable heredity . . . and very easily may be disintegrated and give instead of a genius a lunatic or an insane person.[43] This,

perhaps, may explain the fact that the per cent of feeble-minded and insane has been often higher among the posterity of men of talent than among common people.[44]

On the other hand, a fortunate combination of the constituents may result in the birth of a talented child from average parents. This may explain the appearance of eminent men among the average, common people. Hence, the dissimilarity due to this biological factor. Parallel with this factor, the factor of the prenatal and postnatal environment in various ways may call forth dissimilarity of the children from their parents. A series of facts which show the modifying rôle of environment has been given above. As an example, take the influence of the environment of the financial and political aristocracy upon their posterity. It was noticed long ago that the later generations of a great founder of a dynasty and that of a self-made captain of industry often have shown a trend toward physical and mental degeneration, or, to speak more mildly, to a greater and greater deviation from the type of their ancestor. Differing with P. Jacoby, I do think that this is not a universal rule typical of every kind of political, economic, or intellectual aristocracy;[45] I think that in many cases such a degeneration has been due not only to environment, as Jacoby thinks, but to an unfortunate combination of genes also. Nevertheless, in many cases such a deviation is a fact due to the specific environment of the upper strata.

My study of monarchs and rulers has shown that in regard to the longevity of monarchs of the same dynasty there is a trend to a shortening in the later generations. The only hypothesis which is in harmony with the corresponding facts is the detrimental influence of the environment of the monarchs.[46] In the second place, the study of American millionaires has shown also that often the third and later generations of the offspring of a self-made captain of industry more and more deviate from his type. Instead of accumulating money, they successfully squander it; instead of a busy career, they lead a life of *dolce far niente,* hunting for pleasure.[47] Though differing with Veblen, I believe that such "degeneration" is not a general phenomenon, and in some cases may be due to the factor of heredity. However, Veblen seems to have been right in his contention that many such facts have been due to environmental factors.[48] Inheritance of wealth gives to the descendants of self-made millionaires the possibility of being idle and not exerting their energy and potential ability in a hard money-making business. The same inherited money permits them to satisfy all their desires—in the first place, the sensual ones. This leads to effemination and soft-heartedness. In this way, step by step, the later generations may deviate more and more from the type of their forefathers and finally become a sort of lazy, degenerated, and parasitic absentee-owner.

In the third place, genealogical studies of the descendants of royal families supply many examples of the same degeneration. Such examples are given in the families of Augustus, Constantine the Great, the Alcmeonidæ, the Pisistratidæ, Dionysius, the Tyrant of Sicily, the Cyrus of Persia, the Seleucus of Syria, the Lagidæ of Egypt, and the Ottomans of Turkey. We find similar facts in the dynasties of the Merovingians, and the Carolingians; the later generations of these dynasties exhibit a pitiful picture of weak, insane, and helpless nonentities, quite different from the great founders of these dynasties. Even in more modern royal families such cases are not absent. P. Jacoby, in spite of his one-sidedness, has given a long series of facts of this kind in the dynasties of the Savoy-Sardinia, the Medici, the Anjou, the Aragon, the Bourbon, the Valois, and others.[49]

The existence of many "failures" among the descendants of the great rulers and aristocracy and an increase of their number in the later generations seem to have been due not only to the factor of unfortunate marriages, but to the environmental factors also, including such environmental conditions as licentiousness, idleness, drunkenness, venereal diseases, debauchery, not to mention the extraordinary physical exertions, and mental and nervous strain often inseparable from the position and duties of monarchs and aristocracy. Under such conditions, it would have been miraculous if such an environment had not influenced the posterity of the great leaders.[50] Hence, the dissimilarity of the children from their parents.

And here again the theory of L. Flügge is likely to be true. It contends that on the average the descendants of rapidly ascending climbers are likely to be "degenerated" more and more quickly than the descendants of the old aristocratic families, whose founders climbed gradually and in the course of time acquired a kind of immunity. The great exertions and strenuous lives of the many contemporary successful men are likely to influence their posterity unfavorably. The leisure and luxury of the posterity itself may facilitate disastrous results. Whether this hypothesis is true or not as a general rule, there is no doubt that many contemporary families of the "financial, social, and intellectual aristocracy" in the second, third, and fourth generations show conspicuous physical weaknesses, insanity, psychoses, and neuroses. A considerable part of them sink back in the social scale in the third and fourth generations; another part become notorious by the social scandals of the descendants; the offspring of another part lead the lives of idlers and seekers of pleasure, and so on. I could enumerate dozens of such cases among the richest American families. L. Flügge,[51] P. Jacoby, and several other writers give a considerable number of data from Europe. At least as a partial phenomenon the hypothesis seems to be warranted by facts. If such is the case, then it follows that within present societies it facilitates more and more rapid social circulation up and down the scale. Since the posterity of the present upper families degenerates more rapidly, the discrepancy between their qualities and social position appears more rapidly also and leads quicker to the social sinking of the upper families and to the ascent of the still more recent ones from the bottom of society.

A common result of dissimilarity between fathers and children is the discrepancy between the social position of individuals and their inner and acquired qualities, necessary for a successful performance of the functions of the position. If a father is quite fitted for his position, his dissimilar son may be unsuitable for it. And the greater the dissimilarity, the more necessary becomes a voluntary or a compulsory vertical shifting of individuals.[52]

The shifting of individuals is carried on in three principal ways. In the first place, *through the preventive shifting of individuals, performed through the machinery of social testing and selection of the individuals.* Its essence consists in the fact that the children, before obtaining their social position, are tested and are either barred or promoted, according to the results of the test. The stupid children from a family of high social standing cannot pass through school and be graduated (the cases of misuse are not interesting for us now). The profligate persons could not pass the test of the medieval Church, as a rule. The same may be said about an occupational test. As a result, in spite of their birth in a high stratum, many failures of this kind may be prevented from obtaining a high position. In this way many would-be successors to a throne have been eliminated; many would-be heads of industrial corporations have been put aside from a responsible position. Many sons of prominent scholars are barred from graduation or the position of a professor. Many candidates are beaten in elections. Many sons of high officials have been excluded from responsible official ranks. In brief, in any society there are many sieves which perform this eliminating function. It is true that in this way only a part—and sometimes a small one—of the unsuitable individuals are sifted and barred or promoted. But this part is enough to produce a strong or weak stream of vertical circulation.

In the second place, *there is a repressive way of shifting of individuals from the social stratum in which they have been born. It is performed through a repressive social pressure.* Their unsuitableness for the position leads to a failure in the fulfilment of duties. A poor performance calls forth either dismissal or degradation of such a person; or, if a man is a manager of his own business, his poor management causes its failure; the business is ruined, the man himself is put down. If the man is an executive of a church, a school, an army, or an empire, his failure leads to disorganization of the institution. Owing to the disorganization many people begin to suffer. Suffering urges them to get rid of such a leader. This creates a social pressure which often puts down the leader and promotes a lower-born person. In this way many failures from the upper strata have been put down, and many "risers" from the lower classes promoted.

In the third place, *individuals being placed by their birth in a position for which they are unsuited, become dissatisfied and begin to try to change it in the way which is dictated by their "natural proclivities.*" An inborn ruler or a great thinker, born from slave parents, tries to obtain a position which permits an adequate expression. For many an inborn slave, born in the position of a ruler, power is a burden; such persons try to get rid of it or hold the power only nominally in the form of "reigning without ruling," or, at least, do not hold steadfastly to their position and easily give way to anybody who craves it.

In these three ways: *through preventive sifting of unsuitable individuals by the machinery of social selection, through repressive shifting after failure under the influence of social pressure,* and *through personal efforts of improperly placed individuals, the factor of dissimilarity between parents and children causes a permanent stream of the vertical circulation, and does not permit all children to hold the position of their parents or that in which they are born.* Such is the second cause of vertical circulation.

The corresponding facts are so common that there is no need to indicate them extensively. It is enough to say that the greater part of the self-made men and climbers, who have risen under normal conditions, corroborate the above. Be it Henry Ford, Carnegie, Edison, Lincoln, Gregory the Hildebrand, Napoleon or S. Severus, or tens of thousands of others, great and small "climbers," the larger part of them have risen because they happened to be considerably dissimilar from their parents, one of the differences being their dissatisfaction with the position in which they had been born. On the other hand, millions of failures from the upper strata, who have been put down, are again the victims of their dissimilarity from their parents. Were they quite similar to their fathers, such "rising" or "sinking" would not take place in many cases.

4. CHANGE OF ENVIRONMENT, AND ESPECIALLY OF THE ANTHROPO-SOCIAL ENVIRONMENT AS A FACTOR OF VERTICAL CIRCULATION

An individual or a group may be unfit for the successful performance of their social functions not only through their own fault but because of the change of the environment in which they act. A man with the specific talent for strategy may climb up very rapidly in time of war, and may not promote himself in time of peace. A fine artisan may rise in a society with a system of handicraft industry, and he may not have any chance in a society of machine production. A purely physical force often has been the cause of leadership in primitive societies, but it has much less importance in present society. An exclusive honesty and asceticism led to a social rise in the Middle Ages, and the same qualities are likely often to ruin a man under existing conditions. A few decades ago the manufacturers of bicycles had a chance to become rich men; a continuation of the same business now is a way to bankruptcy. A talented royalist writer is likely to be honored in a monarchic society; and the same talent devoted to monarchy is likely to lead the writer to a prison in a revolutionary republican society. The same may be said of almost all forms of human activity. These examples show that the social position of an individual depends not only on himself, but also on his environment. Besides the natural selection which with the change of environment leads to a survival of the fittest, and to the extinction of those unfitted for the changed environment, there is also a social vertical shifting of the individuals caused by the change of the anthropo-social environment. Any considerable change of it results in a social redistribution of individuals: those who, through the change, are put in a favorable position begin to rise or continue to hold their high positions; those who cannot or do not wish to adapt themselves to the change, are likely to go down.[53]

As the social environment of human beings is always changing,[54] *and the rate of change is especially intensive now, this means that within social life there is a permanent factor of vertical circulation.* It incessantly operates within a society and incessantly produces social redistribution of its members. Any invention, any change in the methods of production, in *mores,* beliefs, standards, literary and dress fashions, in science and arts, in the means of transportation—in brief, in any field of social life—may ruin one group of individuals, and promote another. The same is true in regard to changes in geographical environment. An earthquake may ruin one city and may be beneficial to another. An unfavorable climate which leads to a bad crop in the United States may be beneficial for the Canadian farmers. Some changes may be favorable for the promotion of honest men, some for dishonest; some for the ascetic, some others for the licentious; some for the conservative temperament, some others for the progressive. In short, the variety of changes of environment have caused a promotion of the most different types of human beings. Through this factor, whole social layers, fitted for their positions under certain conditions, may become quite unfitted under other ones, and *vice versa.*

A few historical examples are sufficient to illustrate this.

A change of social environment, which led to the legalization of the Christian Church by Constantine the Great, caused a social promotion of the Christians, who before had been persecuted, and a sinking of the non-Christians, who before had been promoted. An increased rôle of money since the thirteenth and fourteenth centuries in England called forth a social rise of the money-making class, and facilitated social sinking of the landed aristocracy. The immense rôle played by the discovery of America in the field of social shifting is well known. The same may be said of the commercial and industrial revolutions, and finally of any change of the geographical and the anthropo-social environment.

All factors which facilitate change are factors facilitating vertical social shifting, and vice versa.

5. DEFECTIVE SOCIAL DISTRIBUTION OF INDIVIDUALS AND THE LAG IN SHIFTING AS A CAUSE OF THE EXTRAORDINARY VERTICAL CIRCULATIONS

Though the previous three factors of social circulation operate permanently, nevertheless, their work has been, it seems, not so intensive, nor so perfect qualitatively, in many cases, as it should be. From a quantitative viewpoint, its almost permanent defect has consisted in that only a part, and sometimes an insignificant part, of the "non-suitable" individuals have been shifted in time, while another part—and often the majority—of the non-suitable men have been left in positions for which they have not been fitted.

The institute of juridical or factual inheritance of social position, into which the individuals have been born, has always hindered timely and proper shifting of all non-suitable individuals to places corresponding to their innate and acquired qualities. It is certain that even in the United States, among present dwellers in the economic, occupational, or political strata, there is a considerable proportion of unsuitable individuals. It is not a very rare picture to see a mediocre man placed above a man of ability, and an incapable person giving orders to a more capable one. Such discrepancy between the social position of individuals and their physical and mental qualities has been shown above in the part devoted to the study of the population of the different strata. Though there is a correlation between social status and many physical and mental qualities of the social classes; yet, in regard to the physical and other traits everywhere, the fact of overlapping has been met. The characteristics of the upper strata are not common to all their members, and at the same time are found among the members of the lower classes. And, contrariwise, the traits typical for the majority of the lower classes are found also among a part of the upper classes. This is an evident manifestation of defectiveness in the social distribution of individuals or that of the existence of a lag.

Even in the most mobile society the membranes which separate one stratum from another are not so permeable as to permit an infiltration of all capable "newcomers," or an ousting of all "unsuitable" dwellers born within a stratum. The testing, selecting, and distributing agencies shift only a part of the unsuitable persons. Another part, owing to various causes, continues to stay where it is born. *In brief, one of the permanent defects of any society is a lag in the distribution of its members according to their qualities, and an existence within each social stratum of individuals not suited to their social position.*[55] Such is the defect from a quantitative point of view.

From the *qualitative standpoint,* an almost permanent defect of social distribution of individuals has consisted in a looseness of correspondence between the type of the people desirable for each stratum at a certain period and the type of people who have really been selected for each stratum by the machinery of social distribution of individuals. A permanently changing social life demands a variation of the type of men suitable for each class under changing conditions. In war time the interests of a society demand leaders of one type; in peace time, leaders of another type. In a period of social disorganization, in order to prevent anarchy, the Mussolini type of man may be needed; the same type may be unsuited to a peaceful and normal society. In the periods of great moral decadence which menaces the existence of society, the leaders of a severe ascetic type, pitilessly repressing licentiousness (inquisitors), may be proper. In a morally normal society, they may become a nuisance. An ideal machinery of social selection and distribution must be so flexible as to be able to change the type of people for each stratum as soon as it is necessary. Such flexibility, however, does not exist. It is difficult often to change the machinery for the production of a standard type of automobile; how infinitely more difficult it is to change often the infinitely more complex machinery of social testing and distribution of individuals. As a result, *there almost always is a lag between the "human flour" sifted through this machinery for different social strata and between the "flour" which is necessary because of the new changed conditions.* A type of people who in previous conditions were quite fitted for a certain stratum, now, under the new conditions, may be out-of-date or unsuitable. This lag has existed to a degree in all societies and continues to exist up to this time.

The above quantitative and qualitative lag in timely and complete shifting of unsuited individuals may lead to their accumulation in all strata in greater and greater proportion. As a result, the social functions of all strata begin to be poorly performed. This results in a disintegration of the whole life of a society. Its members begin to suffer. Suffering produces a greater and greater dissatisfaction. If such a situation continues, there comes either a slow decay of the society, or a revolutionary explosion. The latter often takes place. In the conflagration of revolution, the social building is burnt. Together with the destruction of the upper social strata, its inhabitants, as a group, are put down. At the same time, the leaders and most talented or energetic men from the lower classes climb up, in the form of leaders of a revolution and its dictators. In this consists the work of the first stage of the revolution.

If society does not perish in the course of this surgical operation, which sometimes happens, then comes the second period of revolution, which begins to recover from the destruction which took place during the first period. As in the first period there is no mechanism of control of social distribution of individuals, it is natural that many people from the lower classes who do not have any ability for a successful performance of the functions of the upper strata, succeed in climbing into this upper strata. They, differing from the more able newcomers, are put down in the second period. On the other hand, in the wholesale ousting of the occupants of the upper strata in the first period, side by side with the unsuitable groups, many able individuals are put down. In the second period of revolution these more capable ones begin to climb again. In other words, the second period of revolution is marked by a "reverse circulation." As a result, to the end of the second period of revolution, there is a new aristocracy, composed of talented newcomers and talented members of the previous aristocracy, and a new lower stratum composed of the previous lower classes, minus its "climbers," and minus a part of the previous aristocracy incapable of the performance of the functions of the upper strata. In this bloody way, revolution may destroy great defects in the prerevolutionary distribution of individuals, cut out the "swellings" composed of the unsuitable people in all layers; and redistribute the members more properly. This work done, "the revolutionary policemen of history" may go away. The society with a more proper redistribution of individuals begins its new life. Further, in the course of time, owing to the same quantitative and qualitative lagging in the timely and complete shifting of its unsuitable members, they again appear in all strata and again may accumulate in dangerous proportions. Such being the case, the interference of revolution becomes again inevitable. And again the same tale is repeated. Such is the "ever-revolving circle" of history.

In this way, the defective social distribution of individuals, being unstopped or weakened in time, leads to a sudden, compulsory, and violent social redistribution of individuals, through the medium of revolution. The reader may find the factual corroboration of this theory in my *Sociology of Revolution.* The prerevolutionary society in ancient Rome and Greece, in the Middle Ages, before the English Revolution of the seventeenth century, before the Russian Revolution, before the great French Revolution, exhibit conspicuously the abnormal defectiveness of social distribution of its members: in the upper strata is found a great proportion of effeminate, idle, and incapable individuals who, according to their qualities should be put within the lower strata; in the lower layers is an extraordinary accumulation of the energetic "climbers" barred from climbing to the upper position. The degenerated aristocracy is incapable of fulfilling its business of social control; the pushers underneath undermine the existing régime from the bottom. The result is a revolutionary explosion and its consequences.[56]

6. SECONDARY, LOCAL AND TEMPORARY FACTORS OF SOCIAL CIRCULATION

Besides these permanent factors of vertical circulation of individuals there are many other secondary conditions which may facilitate or hinder vertical mobility. Their detailed analysis is not the subject of this book. In regard to their nature, it is possible to make the following generalizations. Secondary, local, and temporary factors of social circulation include:

1. All concrete factors which facilitate an increase in the difference of the number of the surviving children of the upper and the lower classes;

2. All factors which facilitate an increase in a dissimilarity of parents and children;

3. All concrete conditions which facilitate an increase in discrepancy between the qualities necessary for a successful performance of a social function and the innate and acquired qualities of the people who occupy corresponding positions (qualitative and quantitative defects of social distribution of individuals).

All conditions opposite to the above are factors which hinder an intensification of vertical social mobility.

SUMMARY

1. Among many factors of vertical circulation, there are several which are permanent and universal (primary).

2. The most fundamental among them are: (*a*) the demographic factor; (*b*) the dissimilarity of parents and children; (*c*) a permanent change of environment, especially of the anthropo-social environment.

3. These factors permanently break the existing equilibrium of the social distribution of individuals and make vertical circulation inevitable.

4. None the less, their work is not so intensive and so perfect as to shift in time and in an appropriate direction all unsuitable persons. Hence, the existence in all societies of a quantitative and qualitative lag in the vertical circulation of individuals.

5. When the lag becomes too great, and the proportion of unsuitable persons in all strata accumulates to too great a degree, there is facilitated the explosion of revolution and a violent redistribution of individuals among the different strata. Sometimes the society perishes in this surgical operation; sometimes, through revolution, the lag is diminished and more or less normal distribution of individuals is reestablished. Before turning to the effects of mobility, the social mobility of present Western societies should be studied in greater detail.

[1] *Zeitschrift des Königl. Preussisch, Statist. Landesamts,* Jahrgang, 1912.

[2] *Breslauer Statistik,* Bd. 28, II, Breslau, 1909. See many other data in MANSCHKE-REGENBOURG, R., *Beruf und Kinderzahl;* SCHMOLLER, G., *Jahrbuch für Gezetgebung,* 40 Jahrgang, Heft 4, pp. 259-329, 1916.

[3] "Die Familienverhältnisse der Bayrischen Staatsbeamten," *Archiv für Rassen- und Gesellschafts-Biologie,* Bd. 13, 1918-1921.

[4] "Statistique des Familles," *Statistique générale de la France,* 1906; MARCH, L., "The Fertility of Marriage According to Profession and Social Position," *Problems in Eugenics,* pp. 208-220, 1912.

[5] STEVENSON, T. H. C., "The Fertility of Various Social Classes in England and Wales from the Middle of the Nineteenth Century to 1911," *Journal of the Royal Statistical Society,* p. 410, May, 1920.

[6] DUNLOP, J. C., "The Fertility of Marriage in Scotland, a Census Study," *Journal of the Royal Statistical Society,* Vol. LXXVII, pp. 275-277, 1913-1914. See in both papers other detailed data.

[7] Compiled from *Birth, Stillbirth, and Infant Mortality Statistics, 1923,* pp. 171 *et seq.,* Table 10, Washington, D. C., 1925.

[8] BOURDON, JEAN, "La statistique des familles Norvégiennes au Recensement de 1920," *Journal de la Société de Statistique de Paris,* No. 12, p. 324, 1925.

[9] See data in the following works: GINI, C., "Il diverso accrescimento delle classi sociali," *Giornale degli economisti,* January, 1909; BERTILLON, J., "La natalité selon le degré d'aisance," *Bulletin de l'Institut International de Statistique,* Vol. XI, and "Statistique des successions en France," *ibid.,* Vol. XVIII; STUART, "Natalité selon le degré d'aisance," *ibid.,* Vol. XIII; GINI, C., *I fattori demografici dell'evoluzione delle nazioni,* Torino, 1912; STEWART, JOHNSON, "The Relation Between Large Families, etc.," *Journal of the Royal Statistical Society,* pp. 539-550, 1912; HOLMES, SAMUEL J., *The Trend of the Race,* Chap. VI, New York, 1921; WILLCOX, W. F., "Differential Fecundity," *Journal of Heredity,* Vol. V, pp. 141-148, 1914; PEARSON, KARL, "On the Effect of a Differential Fecundity on Degeneracy," *Biometrika,* Vol. VII, 1910; SAVORGNAN, F., "Da Fecondita delle aristocrazie," *Metron,* Nos. 3 and 4, 1925; MAY, R. E., *Zur Frage des Geburtenrückgangs;* SCHMOLLER, G., *Jahrbuch für Gezetzgebung,* 40 Jahrgang, pp. 37-76, 1916; POWYS, A. O., "Data for the Problem of Evolution in Man," *Biometrika,* Vol. VI; HERON, D., *On the Relation of Fertility in Man to Social Status,* London, 1906; MOMBERT, P., *Studien zu Bevölkerungsbewegung in Deutschland,* Karlsruhe, 1907; PEARL, R., *The Biology of Population Growth,* Chap. VII, New York, 1925.

[10] See SAVORGNAN, F., "Das Aussterben der adeligen Geschlechter," *Jahrbuch für Soziologie,* Bd. I, pp. 323 *et seq.;* JACOBY, P., *Études sur la sélection chez l'homme,* Pt. I, and *passim,* Paris, 1904; KEMMERICH, M., *op. cit., passim.*

[11] See ELLIS, HAVELOCK, *op. cit.,* pp. 152-166; CATTELL, J. MCKEEN, *op. cit.,* pp. 793-794; GALTON, FRANCIS, *English Men of Science,* pp. 27 *et seq.,* New York, 1875; STEINMETZ, S. R., "Der Nachwuchs der Begabten," *Zeitschrift für Sozialwiss.,* Bd. 7, Heft 1, 1904; PHILIPTSCHENKO, JUR., *op. cit.,* Nos. 1 to 3; THOMAS, M., *op. cit.,* p. 310; CASTLE, C. S., *op. cit.,* pp. 50-51.

[12] ELLIS, HAVELOCK, *op. cit.,* p. 164; GALTON, FRANCIS, *Hereditary Genius,* pp. 123 *et seq.,* London, 1892; FAHLBECK, *La Noblesse de Suède,* pp. 173 *et seq.;* HANSEN, G., *Die Drei Bevölkerungsstufe,* pp. 175 *et seq.,* München, 1889; FURLAN, "La Circulation des élites," *Revue International de Sociologie,* p. 385, 1911; BERTILLON, J., *La dépopulation de la France,* pp. 102 *et seq.,* 139-140, Paris, 1911; SAVORGNAN, F., "La Fecondita delle Aristocrazie," *Metron.,* Nos. 3 and 4, 1925.

[13] DUBLIN, L. J., "The Higher Education of Women and Race Betterment," *Eugenics in Race and State;* BAKER, R. E., and ROSS, E. A., "Changes in the Size of American Families," *University of Wisconsin Studies,* No. 10; NEARING, N. S., "Education and Fecundity," *Publications of the American Statistical Association,* Vol. XIV, pp. 156-174.

[14] See SOROKIN, P., "American Millionaires and Multimillionaires."

[15] Of many data one or two illustrations only are given. While the per cent of childless marriages among the general population of Scotland has been about 10 per cent, it is for the peerage about 16 per cent, for 548 married men of English genius about 19 per cent; while at the end of the nineteenth and the beginning of the twentieth centuries the per cent of childless marriages in the common population of Europe was about from 7 to 12 per cent; for the royal families, 22 per cent; for the half-royal families, 18.2; for the Swedish nobility, 18.1 to 22.8; for the Hungarian nobility, 25.8; for the wealthy Netherland classes, 16.2; for the English peerage, 16.4; for the intellectuals of Copenhagen, 15.0; for the American well-to-do families (Vassar girls), 19.4.

[16] See FLÜGGE, L., *Die Rassenbiol. Bedeutung des Sozialen Aufsteigens und das Problem der immunisierten Families,* Gottingen, 1920.

[17] STEVENSON, T. H. C., *op. cit.,* pp. 416-417; see here other details.

[18] The exceptions to this rule seem to exist principally in polygamous societies,

where the chances for procreation of the upper classes are greater than in monogamic groups.

[19] See also SCHALLMAYER, W., *op. cit.*, pp. 243-248.

[20] SOROKIN, P., "The Monarchs and the Rulers," *Journal of Social Forces*, March, 1926; for details, KEMMERICH, MAX, *Die Lebensdauer und die Todesurachen innerhalb der Deutschen Kaiser- und Königsfamilien*, Leipzig, 1909; *Mortality Statistics, 1921*, p. 23, Washington, D. C., 1924.

[21] LAPOUGE, V. DE, *op. cit.*, p. 350.

[22] SEEK, OTTO, *Geschichte des Untergangs der antiken Welt*, Vol. I, pp. 340-341, Berlin, 1910.

[23] BELOCH, *op. cit.*, pp. 71-72.

[24] Julius Cæsar had only one daughter, who died before his death; Augustus had only one daughter, who was abnormal; Tiberius, one son; Caligula did not leave any posterity; Claudius had one son, who was killed; Nero, Galba, Otho, Vitellius, Domitian, Trajan, Nerva, Hadrian, and Antoninus Pius did not leave any posterity. The aristocratic families were similarly unfertile and sterile.

[25] As I indicated, their illegitimate descendants, and those descending through the female line, might exist, but social existence of such families, which is the only thing here important for us, was discontinued.

[26] See *Memoires de l'Académie des Sciences Morales et Politiques*, m-4, Vol. V, p. 753; CHATEAUNEUF, BENOISTON DE, "Durée des familles nobles en France," *Annales d'Hygiène*, January, 1846.

[27] DOUBLEDAY, THOMAS, *The True Law of Population*, pp. 33 *ff.*, 57 *ff.*, 1843; BOUGLÉ, C., *La démocratie dévant la science*, pp. 81-82.

[28] FURLAN, "La Circulation des élites," *Revue internationale de sociologie*, 1911, pp. 850-860.

[29] DE CANDOLLE, A., *Histoire des sciences et des savants depuis deux siècles*, pp. 156-157, 1885. See other facts in HANSEN, G., *op. cit.*, pp. 175 *et seq.*

[30] FAHLBECK, *La Noblesse de Suède*, p. 173 *et seq.*

[31] PLATONOFF, *Lectzii po Russkoi Istorii*, p. 437.

[32] KOHLBRÜGGE, J. H. F., "Stadt und Land als biologische Umwelt," *Archiv für Rassen- und Gesellschafts-Biologie*, Vol. VI, pp. 631-632. See here other data.

[33] JACOBY, P., *op. cit.*, p. 431.

[34] SAVORGNAN, F., *op. cit.*, p. 339. For the past, see many facts in JACOBY, P., *op. cit.*, pp. 315-430.

[35] See MARTIN, H., *Histoire de France*, Vol. IV, pp. 237 *et seq.*

[36] See KOLABINSKA, *op. cit.*, pp. 50 *et seq.*

[37] MULHALL, *The Dictionary of Statistics*, p. 818, 1903.

[38] See MARRO, A., "The Influence of the Age of the Parents upon the Psychophysical Character of the Children," *Problems in Eugenics*, p. 119.

[39] GALTON, FRANCIS, and SCHUSTER, E., *Noteworthy Families*, p. xv, London, 1906.

[40] See PEARSON, KARL, *The Scope and Importance to the State of the Science of National Eugenics*, pp. 27-29, London, 1909.

[41] *Cf.* CONKLIN, E. G., *The Direction of Human Evolution*, pp. 128 *et seq.*, New York, 1922.

[42] CONKLIN, E. G., *op. cit.*, p. 129; SCHALLMAYER, W., *Vererbung und Auslese im Lebenslauf der Völker*, p. 133, 1910.

[43] GALTON, FRANCIS, *op. cit.*, pp. xv-xvi.

[44] See the data in my "The Monarchs and the Rulers,"; WOODS, FREDERICK ADAMS, *The Influence of Monarchs; JACOBY, P., op. cit., passim;* PHILIPSCHENKO, JUR., *op. cit., passim.*

[45] See JACOBY, P., *op. cit.*, pp. 615-618, *passim;* see also KEMMERICH, MAX, *op. cit., passim.*

[46] See SOROKIN, P., "The Monarchs and the Rulers."

[47] See SOROKIN, P., "American Millionaires and Multimillionaires," pp. 639-640.

[48] See VEBLEN, *The Theory of the Leisure Class, passim.*

[49] See the facts and analysis in JACOBY, P., *op. cit.*, pp. 313-430; MOUGEOLLE, P., *Les problèmes de l'Histoire,* pp. 201-223, Paris, 1880.

[50] This is true not only in regard to the very top of a social cone but also in regard to a large upper and middle social stratum; not only for the present but, as many ancient writers witness, also in regard to the past.

"Passing their life in luxury, lying on comfortable beds, using abundantly perfumes of all kinds, and feeding themselves with the most refined food, the Sybaritas lose the force of their body and the ability to sustain any fatigue," says Diodore.

Q. Metellus, speaking to the Roman Senate, after the destruction of Carthage, said, "I do not know whether this victory is going to be harmful or beneficial for the Republic; if it is beneficial through giving us peace, it may be dangerous because it put away Hannibal whose invasions of Italy awoke the sleeping Roman virtue; there is a reason to fear that this indefatigable rival eliminated, Italy may fall asleep again."

"When a Republic reaches the degree of power and prosperity in which there is nothing which may menace it, the people cannot more enjoy their happiness; luxury and pleasure begin to corrupt their mores," says Polybius.

Similar observations are given by Xenophon concerning the Persians, by Seneca concerning the Romans, by Machiavelli about all peoples. Here is Machiavelli's generalization:

"It may be observed that the provinces amid the vicissitudes, to which they are subject, pass from Order into Confusion, and afterward recur to a state of Order again: for the nature of mundane affairs not allowing them to continue in an even course, when they have arrived at their greatest perfection, they soon begin to decline. In the same manner, having been reduced to Disorder, and sunk to their utmost state of Depression and Ruin, unable to descend lower, they, of necessity, reascend; and thus from Good they gradually decline to Evil; and from Evil again return to Good. The reason is that Valor produces Peace; Peace, Repose; Repose, Disorder; Disorder, Ruin; so from Disorder, Order springs; from Order, Virtue; from this Glory and Good Fortune." The whole theory has been excellently summed up by the poet in the following way:

"There is the moral of all human tales;
'Tis but the same rehearsal of the past:
First freedom, and then glory—when that fails,
Wealth, vice, corruption, barbarism at last,
And history with her volumes vast
Hath but one page."

MACHIAVELLI, N., *History of Florence,* The Colonial Press, p. 225.

[51] See FLÜGGE, L., *Die Rassenbiologische Bedeutung des Sozialen Aufsteigens und das Problem der immunisierten Familie*s.

[52] From this standpoint in a caste-society it cannot be so intensive as in a modern democratic society because the prohibiting of intercaste marriages is likely to diminish the chances of any dissimilarity of the children and parents and because of a great specification of training and stratification of education for each caste: such a society trains the son of a Brahmin to be a Brahmin and the son of a Sûdra to be a Sûdra. This means that in a caste-society both

factors—heredity and environment—tend to make the children more similar to their parents than in a modern society with its common cross-marriages and its public schools training similarly the pupils of all classes and groups.

[53] Brooks Adams rightly says, "Nothing is commoner than to find families who have been famous in one century sinking into obscurity in the next, not because the children have degenerated, but because a certain field of activity which afforded the ancestor full scope, has been closed against his offspring. Particularly has this been true in revolutionary epochs, such as the Reformation; and families so situated have very generally become extinct." ADAMS, BROOKS, *The Law of Civilization and Decay,* p. vii and Chap. VI, New York, 1897. In a specific form this has been shown clearly by V. Pareto. He distinguishes two fundamental types of men: "rentiers" who have rigid types of behavior, do not have an ability of combination, machination, and innovation, and are conservative and steady in their habits and conduct; and "speculators" who are versatile in their behavior, able in the art of combination, machination, and innovation, and somewhat cynical in their flexibility. The Spartan aristocracy was composed principally of the first type; the Athenian and democratic aristocracy, principally of the second. There are social conditions which favor the ascendancy of the "rentier" type of men; and there are other conditions under which the "speculator" type climbs successfully. These periods fluctuate; correspondingly fluctuates also the composition of the upper classes from the standpoint of the predominant type of "rentiers" and "speculators." When an environment which previously facilitated climbing of the rentier type of men changes, the change brings a sinking of this type of men and a climbing of the opposite type, and *vice versa.* Hence, an ever-revolving rhythm of the "rentier" and "speculator" types of government and aristocracy. See PARETO, V., *op. cit.,* Vol. II, pp. 1427 *ff.* and Chaps. XII-XIII.

[54] See OGBURN, W., *Social Change, passim;* NOVICOV, *Les Luttes entre sociétés humaines,* chapter on "La loi de l'accélération," Paris, 1896.

[55] See SENSINI, G., "Teoria dell'equilibrio di composizione delle classe sociali," *Rivista italiana di sociologia,* September and December, 1913; see many facts in LORIA, A., *Les Synthèses economiques,* Paris, 1911, and in his "The Psycho-Physical Élite and the Economic Élite," *Problems in Eugenics,* Vol. I, pp. 179-184. A. Loria, however, goes too far in his negative attitude toward a correlation between the social position and psychological qualities. Facts do not warrant his extremism.

[56] See SOROKIN, P., *Sociology of Revolution,* Pts. III and V.

Part Five

PRESENT-DAY MOBILE SOCIETY

CHAPTER XVI

HORIZONTAL MOBILITY

AFTER the general characterization of social stratification and vertical mobility just outlined, turn to an analysis of contemporary Western societies from the standpoint of social circulation. Such an analysis will give us, in addition to a description of many typical traits of the societies in which we live, a deeper insight into the phenomenon of vertical circulation.

It goes without saying that *our epoch is a period of intensive social mobility*. Perhaps the most conspicuous characteristic of Western societies has been an intensive social circulation since the end of the eighteenth century. Our societies are mobile societies *par excellence*. And moreover, it seems possible to contend that *the horizontal, and to a certain extent the vertical, mobility of Western societies has been increasing since the end of the eighteenth century*. At the present moment Western peoples remind one of a pot of boiling water in which the water particles move up and down, to and fro, with great rapidity. To this is due the illusion that our democratic societies are as though not stratified, in spite of the fact that they are actually stratified. To this is due our other illusion that present democracies tend to equality, while objectively they are as unequal as any autocratic society. Great mobility, with its intensive transposition of the individuals, makes such an illusion natural and inevitable. So much for a general introduction to the subject. Now consider the facts, and, in the first place, show the tendency of an increase of horizontal mobility since the second half of the nineteenth century.

1. AN INCREASE OF TERRITORIAL CIRCULATION OF INDIVIDUALS WITHIN WESTERN SOCIETIES

The mobile character of present society manifests itself, first of all, in an intensive and increasing *territorial* circulation of its members. It is often said that "with an advance of civilization society passes from a nomadic to a settled or sedentary manner of living."[1] This statement is likely not to be quite true. At least, in contemporary Western societies its members become less and less attached to the place where they are born; a greater and greater number of individuals change the place of their abode; the number of such changes is increasing more and more; and the spatial distance crossed by the individuals during their life becomes greater and greater. In the past (or in an immobile society at present) the majority of individuals died where they were born. Territorial migration was limited to a comparatively narrow circle around the place of birth. Consequently, a territorial community was composed almost exclusively of people born in the same neighborhood. The number of strangers within each community was nil or quite insignificant. Shifting from place to place was a comparatively rare phenomenon. Quite a different picture is presented by present Western societies. Railways, automobiles, steamers, aëroplanes, and other means of transportation are responsible for the intensive and increasing territorial mobility of our societies. In this respect society really becomes more and more mobile; its members, more and more migratory, the population of a territorial community more and more composed of people born in different places; people born in the same community are more and more scattered throughout the most diverse places on this planet; the population of a neighborhood, more and more shifting. A few figures are enough to corroborate the above statements.

India may serve us as an example of a relatively immobile society. Here the situation has been as follows:

> Owing partly to their conservatism and dislike of change, and partly to the disadvantages which the caste-system imposes on the Hindu when separated from their own social group, the people of India are very disinclined to leave their own social group, and at the time of census (1901) more than nine-tenths of them were resident in the districts where they had been born. Even of those who were numerated elsewhere, the great majority were found only a very short distance from their original home and were not emigrants in the ordinary sense of the term.[2]

As to the emigration from India abroad it is almost nil. Out of more than 300,000,000 population of India in 1909 to 1910, 11,644 individuals emigrated abroad; in 1919 to 1920, 221; in 1909 to 1910, 6,909 individuals returned to India; in 1919 to 1920, 3,783.[3] China presents a somewhat similar picture.

If we take present-day Western societies the picture is quite different. In the United States the per cent of the people whose residence at the time of census was in the same state where they were born is, for 1920, only 67.2 per cent; for 1910 and 1900 correspondingly, 66.5 and 68.3 per cent; the remaining percentage of the residents was composed of foreign born and people born in other states. These figures of migration, as the *Census Report* properly indicates, are much lower than the real per cent of interstate migration.[4] Nonetheless the contrast with India is great. If we could have the figures for the intercounty migration there is no doubt that the contrast would have been still greater. Further we have seen how insignificant is emigration from India: it is less than 0.003 per cent. We can find nothing comparable in Western countries. At the end of the nineteenth century the per cent of immigrants as well as emigrants from all Western countries was much higher.

The following figures may give some idea of the territorial migration in European countries: Per 1,000 population of the following cities at the end of the nineteenth century the number of persons who were born in the same city was, in Antwerp, 661; London, 629; Hamburg, 543; Rome, 446; Christiania, 425; Berlin, 424; Paris, 349; Vienna, 345.[5] This means that at least one-half of their population was born outside of the city. In the country population the per cent of people residing at the place of their birth is somewhat higher; nevertheless, in Bavaria, already in 1890 the per cent of those born in the same community where they were residing was only 64.4.[6] In Austria, in 1890, this per cent was 65.2; in France, in 1891, 57.2;[7] in Sweden, in 1900, 58.2; in 1910, 56.2.[8]

These figures show clearly an incomparably greater territorial mobility of Western societies since the second half of the nineteenth century as compared with that of immobile societies like India.

But that is not all. As previously mentioned, the territorial mobility of Western societies has been increasing since at least the second half of the nineteenth century. This may be shown, in the first place, by statistics of foreigners settled in different European countries. For the sake of brevity only the principal data which corroborate this statement are given.

PER CENT OF FOREIGNERS IN THE TOTAL POPULATION OF THE SPECIFIED COUNTRIES

Country	Date	Per Cent	Date	Per Cent	Date	Per Cent	Date	Per Cent	Date	Per Cent
France [9]	1851	1.0	1881	2.9	1901	2.6	1911	2.9	1926	6.0
Germany	.....	.....	1880	0.6	.....	.....	1910	1.9		
England	.....	.....	1881	0.3	.....	.....	1911	0.7		
Denmark	1850	2.0	.....	.....	.....	.....	1911	4.0		
Austria [10]	1869	1.1	1880	1.6	.....	.....	1911	2.1		
Sweden [11]	1860	0.2	1880	0.4	1900	0.7	1910	0.9		
Switzerland [12]	1850	3.0	1880	7.4	1900	11.6	1910	14.7		
United States of America [13]	1850	11.2	1880	13.3	1900	13.6	1920	13.2		

With the exception of the United States, in all countries the per cent of foreigners, more or less permanently dwelling in the country, shows a steady tendency toward an increase. The years of the World War naturally diminished international infiltration, but since 1920 it resumed its previous tendency and is likely to progress in this direction,[14] until it will reach its point of saturation if such point exists. The population thus becomes more and more internationalized. There is no need to say that the number of foreigners who visit a foreign country is much greater than the above figures. For instance, in 1910 the number of foreigners who visited Italy, according to the railway and steamer tickets, was no less than 2,595,223.[15]

Notwithstanding a decrease of immigration for the last few years, in connection with the World War and a restriction of immigration, the tendency of an increase has been very clear. From 1820 to 1924, 35,974,703 immigrants came to the United

THE NUMBER OF IMMIGRANTS TO THE UNITED STATES BY DECADES

1820 to 1830	151,827
1831 to 1840	599,125
1841 to 1850	1,713,251
1851 to 1860	2,314,824
1861 to 1870	2,377,279
1871 to 1880	2,812,191
1881 to 1890	5,246,613
1891 to 1900	3,687,564
1901 to 1910	8,795,386
1911 to 1920	5,735,811
1921 to 1924	2,344,599

States from other countries and continents.[16] This is a case of international territorial migration scarcely precedented in history.

In the past any individual, like Marco Polo or Herodotus, who succeeded in visiting other countries or in circumnavigating the globe, was a sort of a rare marvel; now, millions of individuals trot from country to country, from continent to continent. Absolutely and relatively, compared with the population, their number has enormously increased. The geographic distance crossed by an individual during his life now is much greater than before. In brief, territorial mobility of population judged from the standpoint of international migration has increased enormously. As a result, in present-day cities it is difficult to find any large factory where people recruited from different local places and from abroad also, do not work side by side. The same may be said about territorial migration within a country. It shows also a definite trend of increase.

If the proportion of people who reside in a definite place but were born in another section of the same country is taken, this proportion also shows a steady and systematic increase since the second half of the nineteenth century. In Sweden in 1860, the proportion of people who were born in some other department than that of their residence was 7.0 per cent; in 1890, 13.5; in 1910, 17.4 per cent;[17] in Switzerland, the per cent of people who resided in a canton[18] other than that of their birth was, in 1850, 7.3; in 1900, 13.9; in 1920, 18.5; in Bavaria, the per cent of the people residing in Bavaria but born outside of it, (in other German states) was in 1875, 1.2; in 1890, 2.4; in 1900, 3.0; in 1910, 2.9.[19] The data from France, Austria, and Germany are similar.[20]

As a result, the workers in the same factory are recruited from wider and wider territorial area and become more and more heterogeneous from the standpoint of their birthplace. The following data are representative in this respect: Of 1,200 working men in a cable factory in Berlin, only 8.7 per cent were born in Berlin; 88.6 per cent were born in different parts of Germany; and 2.65 per cent were foreigners.[21] Among 72 workers of another factory in Berlin only 36 were Berliners and 3 were foreigners, the others being born in different parts of Germany.[22] Among 140 employees of the third factory in Berlin 55 were Berliners and 3 foreigners; the remainder were from all parts of Germany.[23] Among 230 employees of a Siemens-Schuckert factory in Vienna only 80 were from Vienna and 9 were foreigners, the remaining number from other parts of Austria and Hungary.[24] According to birthplace the employees of a Bavarian factory in 1894 and 1908 were distributed in the following way:[25]

Distance from the Place of Work to the Place of Birth, Kilometers	Per Cent of Workers According to Their Birthplace	
	1894	1908
0 to 10	69	47.7
11 to 30	9.4	11.3
31 to 100	9.5	9 2
101 to 400	6.1	12.4
400 and over	6.1	13.4

This table shows an increase of territorial mobility from 1894 to 1908. In this respect it is representative. Among the employees of a textile factory in Speyer, 17.6 per cent were born in Speyer, 3.4 were foreigners; the remnant was born in different places of Germany.[26] Among the workers of 61 years and over in a Bavarian factory, the per cent of those who worked all the time in the same geographical place was 36.1; who worked from 2 to 5 places was 41.2; from 3 to 9 places, 16.0; at 9 and more places, 6.7.[27] Similar data give other studies.[28] These data are representative. They show how great is the present territorial mobility and interpenetration of people born in different places and countries. If a still more microscopical analysis is made the territorial mobility in still more conspicuous forms may be seen. Dr. R. D. McKenzie's study [29] of Columbus, Ohio, and Seattle, Wash., shows that in Columbus only 58.6 per cent of the registered electors of 1917 re-registered in 1918, the difference being due principally to territorial shifting of the electors. In the Seattle Chamber of Commerce (1920) 20.9 per cent of the members were members less than one year; 39.4, between one and two years; about 50 per cent, between two and three years. Finally, an increase of territorial circulation of individuals is shown also by the statistics of passenger traffic. Here are some representative data:

LONDON [30]

Years	Population	Millions of Passengers Carried	Journeys per Head of Population
1902........	6,661,000	1,106	166
1912........	7,310,000	2,035	278
1922........	7,573,465	2,922	386

BELGIUM [31]

Years	Thousands of Passengers Carried by State Railways	Thousands of Passengers Carried by Interurban Railways
1913....................	206,541	101,502
1922....................	227,926	177,067

NEW YORK CITY

Years	Number of Passengers Carried by the Street-car Lines
1868	about 50,000,000
1890	about 500,000,000
1921	more than 2,500,000,000

CHICAGO

Years	Number of Annual Rides per Capita on the Surface and Elevated Lines
1890	164
1910	215
1921	338

In addition, the rides per capita on steam and electric suburban lines almost doubled between 1916 (23) and 1921 (41). The number of automobiles in Illinois increased from 131,160 in 1915 to 833,920 in 1923. Meanwhile, the population of Chicago increased from 1912 to 1922 less than 25 per cent (23.6 per cent). A traffic count in Chicago, at the corner of State and Madison streets, showed that at the rush period 31,000 people in an hour, 210,000 men and women in 16½ hours passed the southwest corner.[32] In London, May 4, 1891, the number of people who entered London City was 1,186,096, the number [33] of carts, 92,372. Ancient Rome in the days of her greatest triumphs scarcely could count such a number of people passing through her gates. Finally, the shifting from room to room, from apartment to apartment in the present big cities seems to have been increasing, too. "The masses of beings who inhabit (them) become veritable nomads who pass from room to room and from house to house," rightly says Dr. Bruhnes.[34]

The data show that territorial mobility in present Western societies is very great, and is more and more increasing. Correspondingly, an attachment to a definite place becomes shorter and less substantial. The population becomes more and more migratory.[35] Under such conditions the phrase "dear mother country" or "my beloved birthplace" or "my home" are likely to become weaker and weaker. Since man to-day stays one year in one place; another year, in another place; later shifts to a third, and so on, it is natural that he cannot have the deep attachment toward his birthplace and the local patriotism which are inevitable in a man who stays throughout his life where he was born. Instead of "my country" or "my dear native place" we more and more have *ubi bene ibi patria.* Such territorial mobility has many effects which we will discuss later.

2. AN INCREASE OF THE HORIZONTAL CIRCULATION OF SOCIAL THINGS AND VALUES

Another very conspicuous and important expression of the increasingly greater territorial mobility of present-day Western societies is the comparatively great circulation of social things and values. Under this term I mean anything, material or spiritual, which is created or modified by conscious or unconscious human activity. Newspaper news, or Communist ideology, or a chopped stone implement, or an automobile, or bobbing of hair, or birth control, or money, or cultivated land—all are social things according to this definition. A more intensive and more rapid circulation of social things and values means practically the same thing that a more intensive circulation of individuals means. Interpenetration of the former is a substitute for territorial interpenetration of the latter. If a definite custom from one social group penetrates into another this is in a sense equivalent to a penetration of the members of the first group into the second. Thus, if we have in present Western society an increase in territorial migration of individuals and circulation of social things and values, this means an increase of horizontal mobility in double proportion.

The mobility of social things and values, like that of individuals, may take two principal forms: *horizontal* and *vertical.* When a social thing, for instance, a bathtub or radio, is used by a more and more numerous population of the same class, regardless of the country, this is an example of its horizontal expression.

When a social thing, used within a definite social layer, *e.g.*, a definite fashion or ideology or dance, crosses the class boundary and begins to be spread within other social strata, we have its vertical circulation. Let us present the facts which show an increase of the horizontal circulation of social things and values. An approximate measurement of horizontal mobility of social things may be obtained, in the first place, by statistics of letters and objects mailed, the number of telegrams dispatched, the number of telephone conversations held; in the second place, by the amount of exports and imports of material objects; in the third place, by the amount and rapidity of the interchange of different spiritual values, such as ideologies, beliefs, and fashions. The available data concerning these phenomena do not leave any doubt as to the increase of the horizontal circulation of these social things and values. The following data show this clearly:[36]

Country	Number of Letters per Head of Population		Number of Objects Mailed per Head of Population	
	1875	1913	1875	1913
Germany	12.7	79.9	16.1	112.6
Austria	7.4	47.2	9.7	60.4
Belgium	10.9	38.9	18.4	104.9
France	14.9[a]	47.8[a]	23.1[a]	91.2[a]
England	37.6[a]	95.9[a]	44.9[a]	127.5[a]
United States	22.8[a]	89.2[b]	29.2[a]	164.1[b]
Italy	4.0	15.3	7.6	43.7
Sweden	5.0	31.6	5.3	41.7
Japan	1.6	28.6[a]	1.6	35.1
Russia	0.48	8.4	0.77	11.5
British India	0.67	2.9	0.69	3.3
Egypt	0.7[a]	3.9	1.04[a]	5.9
The Congo	0.00048	0.1[a]	0.001	0.0

[a] 1880. [b] 1916

The table shows clearly the increase and at the same time conspicuously stresses a great difference in this respect between the Western countries and such countries as the Congo, Egypt, India, or even Russia. The circulation of letters and other objects mailed in these Eastern and half-Western countries is incomparably less than in the dynamic Western societies. The total number of telegrams dispatched in 1860 on the earth was 5,484,330; in 1910, 219,965,021; in 1913, 499,402,082. The number of inter-urban telephone conversations was in 1896, 69,970,227; in 1913, 691,291,770.[37] As to the number of telephone conversations within a city, the data for Chicago show that it increased by 55.7 per cent from 1914 to 1922. The same is true in regard to the number of letters delivered.[38] The data of Chicago are representative for a great majority of the cities and communities. Add to this the radio and other devices for communication and contact, and the increase of the horizontal mobility of social things and values will be still greater.

The same conclusion results from the statistics of intranational and international circulation of different material objects. It is enough to take the statistics of international exports and imports to see an increase of international circulation of material objects. According to the data of A. de Foville, the total value of the exported and imported merchandise in the world was in 1870, fifty-seven billion francs; in 1903, one hundred and twenty-five billion francs; according to a somewhat different computation of M. A. Neymarck the total value of the *Valeurs mobilières négociables* in the world was in 1895, four hundred and fifty billion francs; in 1910, about eight hundred; in 1912, about eight hundred and fifty billion francs.[39] Since that time the tendency to increase has continued, with the exception of the abnormal years of the World War.[40] Thus, the material objects and social values circulate among present Western societies, as well as within each of them, more intensively and rapidly than in non-mobile societies; and besides, we see that during the last few decades there has been manifested a decided trend toward an increase in the amount and rapidity of the circulation.

Finally, if we take the circulation of the news, ideas, beliefs, fashions, ideologies, emotional attitudes, customs, standards, and other social values, it becomes more and more intensive, more rapid, and spreads over a wider and wider area. In a few days or hours the news of anything happening in one part of the planet is transmitted throughout the world and made known to hundreds of millions of people. By radio and cable, speeches, sermons, news, and so on are broadcasted through the world. Through newspapers, journals, and so on, the same is done with a degree of success of which the past did not even dream. Movies and photographs bring to our eyes the remotest phenomena and depict them as though we were viewing them. As a result, any new discovery is known everywhere within a week; any important event in one part of the earth is influencing and is influenced by pressures from all groups and parts of the planet. Therefore, it is not to be wondered at that while in the past there was necessary a period of several hundreds or thousands of years for the diffusion of a definite value (custom, belief, ideology, religion) within a rather limited area or for its penetration from one group to another one, now this diffusion is achieved within a few months, or for the whole world within a few years. The historians of arts compute by thousands of years the periods of a substitution of one style for another in the past. According to W. M. F. Petrie, an average span of time for a change of a style in the ancient Egyptian Art was about 1,330 years.[41] In Greece, according to H. B. Walters, the periods of the domination of principal types of the ancient pottery was as follows: Pre-Mycenæan period was about 1,000 years; Mycenæan, 700; Græco-Phoenician period, 400; Hellenic period, 350; even their detailed modification such as different phases of the "red-figured vases," or modifications of the Etruscan pottery demanded a time span from several decades to several centuries.[42] Mougeolle computed that to spread civilization from a warm zone to a moderate one demanded a span of time of about 6,000 years, while to spread from moderate to cold regions only about 2,000 years was necessary.[43] At the present time a radical change in the arts, in painting and sculpture, and in literature and music happens within a few decades, and often within a few years. The nineteenth century alone witnessed a succession of at least from four to six quite different schools in literature and painting and music and even architecture. Futurism and ultra-futurism arose, developed, spread throughout Western societies and died within some fifteen to twenty-five years. Small modifications are happening within a few weeks and months. As to the fashions and fads, their rapid circulation and change are well known. Professor Bogardus' data show that about 80 per cent of all fads live less than one year; the majority of them live even less than six months. Only a quite insignificant per cent of them live two or three years.[44] The same may be said about many ideologies, beliefs, fashions, tastes, and other values. For Christianity to be spread throughout a part of Europe, a period of seven or nine centuries was necessary.[45] At least two centuries were necessary for the diffusion of Islam in a limited area composed of the Islamism of the sixth to eighth centuries. In our day, for a diffusion or spreading of Communism throughout the world five or six years have been enough. Correspondingly, the life cycle of almost all social values, ideologies, fads, beliefs, fashions, and what not have become much shorter. Within five to ten years appeared and disappeared the hatred between the Germans and the Allies. Within five to ten years the fame of a fashionable writer, composer, preacher, or singer, appears and declines. To-day, a semigod adored; to-morrow, forgotten. There are exceptions, of course, but they only confirm the rule.[46]

We are led to the same conclusion by the rapidity and importance of inventions in Western societies within the nineteenth and twentieth centuries. They have been so numerous and so important and so quickly follow one another, that the most important device at the present moment is likely to be outdistanced within a few years and, therefore, to be short-lived.[47] Bicycles appeared and are already gone; different phonographs are displaced by the radio; the models of automobiles change almost every year; the same is true of aëroplanes, electric motors, different machines, and so on.

As a result, the means of broadcasting and diffusion of any social thing and value have increased enormously. This has provoked the most rapid diffusion, penetration, and circulation of social values in present societies. Hence, their enormous horizontal mobility.

To sum up: present Western societies are marked by the most intensive territorial migration of individuals, and by intensive circulation of social things and values. This phenomenon is likely to increase. It breaks down the territorial isolation and originality of men, cultures, mores, habits, and of the social physiognomy of territorial groups. These societies remind one of a mad "merry-go-round" in which men, objects, and values incessantly move with a mad rapidity, shift, turn round, clash, struggle, appear, disappear, diffuse, without a moment of rest and stability. Compared with immobile societies in all these respects they offer a contrast to them no less striking than that of boiling water or a waterfall to a quiet pond or lake. Other forms of horizontal circulation within Western societies will now be taken up.

3. HORIZONTAL INTRAOCCUPATIONAL CIRCULATION OF INDIVIDUALS

A further important form of the horizontal circulation is a shifting from one job or factory or occupation to another of the same kind. Among such shiftings there are many which do not represent any noticeable change in the vertical direction. These kinds of the intraoccupational circulation or labor turnover, therefore, are not vertical but horizontal, intraoccupational mobility. This is the reason why they are analyzed here.

The statistics of present labor turnover in Western societies show that such horizontal occupational turnover is very intensive at the present moment, and seems to have been increasing during the last few decades. Here again is seen a great contrast to the immobile societies. The following data—few out of many similar—may give an idea of what is going on in this field within Western societies at the present moment.

United States of America.—A careful investigation of labor turnover by P. F. Brissenden and E. Frankel gives the following facts concerning the length of service typical for a considerable number of industries. (See p. 395.)

To this it may be added that out of 439 individual employees who worked less than 1 week, 21 served less than one day; 94, 1 day; 57, 2 days; 111, 6 days. During the years of the war one worker changed 87 jobs during 23 months and 6 days; another, 7 jobs during 5 months and 4 days; the third, 16 jobs during 7 months and 10 days; the fourth, 20 jobs during 10 months and 19 days.

The authors find that in 1917 to 1918 the average proportion

Length of Time of Service	On Payroll at End of Year (Active)		Separated from Service During Year	
	1913–1914	1917–1918	1913–1914	1917–1918
One week or less	....	2.3	....	17.7
Over one week to two weeks	....	2.5	....	10.4
Two weeks to one month	....	4.1	....	12.4
One month to three months	....	9.8	....	20.3
Three months or less	13.1	18.7	52.0	60.8
Three to six months	7.4	8.4	15.6	12.6
Six months to one year	8.3	12.6	13.7	10.5
One to two years	12.1	14.6	8.1	7.1
Two to three years	11.1	9.2	4.0	2.7
Three to five years	15.0	8.8	3.4	3.0
Over five years	32.9	27.8	3.3	3.2
Total	100.0	100.0	100.0	100.0

of those who among the active workers worked less than 1 year was about 40 per cent; those who worked more than 1 year was about 60 per cent. In general, "throughout the 10-year period (from 1910 to 1920), for every equivalent 3,000-hour worker in the aggregate work force, there were on the average more than two labor changes per year." In addition it must be said that, according to the authors, in the years of industrial prosperity labor turnover tends to increase, in the years of depression, to decrease; it is greater among the non-skilled than the skilled laborers; greater in the poorly organized factories than in the well-organized ones; and greater among men than women.[48]

These data show how great is the horizontal occupational turnover in the United States. Generally, labor turnover of 100 per cent is thought of as average; a turnover of 200 per cent is not rare; it sometimes rises to 400 per cent.[49]

The data for other European countries are perhaps somewhat lower but in essence are similar to those of the United States. E. L. Collis and Major Greenwood have constructed the following typical table for England. Of 1,000 entrants in war time there remained among the factory workers after 1 month of service, 917; after 2 months, 868; after 3 months, 826; after 4 months, 791; after 5 months, 757; after 6 months, 730. For peace time, after 6 months, the number of those who remained is 658.[50] For Germany we have a series of very careful and minute studies. Here are some representative data taken from these investigations:

In a textile factory in München among its workers at ages of 14 to 21 who worked for about three years, the per cent of those who changed their job for another of the same kind[51] from one to two times was 59.3; two times and more, 40.7; among the workers at ages 22 to 30, who were working about 11.5 years, 77.2 per cent changed their job from one to five times; 22.8 per cent, five times and more; among the workers at ages 41 and over, who were engaged in work about 36.5 years, 69.8 per cent changed their job from one to five times; 16.4, from six to nine times; 13.7 per cent, nine times and more.[52]

.In a Vienna machinery-production factory, of the employees who were engaged in the same occupational work for 3 years 38.5 per cent changed their job for the same kind from one to two times; 19.2, from three to four times; 42.3, four and more times; among those who were engaged in this occupation for 9 years 31.0 per cent changed their job from one to four times; 48.3, from five to eight times; 20.7, eight times and more; among those who were working in the same occupation for 16 years, the corresponding figures are: 20, 30, and 40 per cent; for those who were working for 40 years in their occupation, corresponding figures are 23, 36.7, and 40.0 per cent.[53]

In a Vienna automobile factory, the per cent among its employees of those who were serving less than 6 months was 16.4; less than 1 year, 3.9; from 1 to 4 years, 32.4; and 5 years and more, 47.3.[54]

In a Luckenwalder hat factory of its employees at ages 14 to 21 years, who were engaged in this pursuit for 3½ years, 80.9 per cent changed their job from one to five times; 19.1, from six to twelve times. The corresponding figures for the employees at ages 31 to 40 years, who were working for 21.5 years, are: 61.9 and 38.1.[55] Similar are the data for other studies of this type.[56]

This gives an idea of the intensiveness of horizontal occupational shifting of the greater part of the population of the Western society. The German studies, as a general rule, show also that the shifting of the qualified and better paid workers is somewhat less than that of the poorly paid unskilled laborers. It is to be expected that the horizontal intraoccupational circulation of other more qualified occupations is somewhat less than that of laborers. But even this seems to be not very large. The group of teachers in the United States may serve as an example. The study of Dr. L. D. Coffman shows that the median number of years of teaching for the teachers—men and women—of rural schools is 2; for the town schools, 12 for men and 6 for women. Dr. Elmer showed that the length of service of women clerical and secretarial workers in Twin Cities is as follows: 14.2 per cent remain less than 6 months; 28.2, 6 months to 2 years; 33.9, from 2 to 5 years; 24.1, over 5 years.[57] This is far from being very long or continuous.

Not multiplying these examples, the conclusion may be reached that horizontal intraoccupational shifting in present-day Western societies is very intensive, and, as some data show, has been increasing during the last two or three decades. In this respect present society seems to become less and less stable or more and more dynamic.

4. INTERFAMILY HORIZONTAL CIRCULATION

When a husband or a wife gets a divorce and remarries again, this phenomenon is one of interfamily circulation. In a great number of cases such interfamily shifting of an individual is not followed by a noticeable change of his position in a vertical direction. For this reason it is possible to regard the interfamily circulation as a form of the horizontal shifting. There is no need to say that the family institution has probably been the most important social group. Its social functions have been the most important also. "What the family is, such will society be," rightly say Confucius and the Le Play School.[58] For this reason, the movement of the interfamily circulation has especially great significance. What is going on in this field in Western societies? *A steady and rapid increase of the interfamily circulation of individuals.* In more emphatic terminology, this means a disintegration of the family institution and a weakening of the family bonds between husband and wife. The process is common to all Western societies. It is manifested in a rapid increase of divorce. The principal data in this respect are as follows:[59]

Countries	The Average Number of Divorce Cases Per 100,000 Married Couples in the Years:			
Switzerland	1886–1891 188	——	1906–1915 242	——
Denmark	1896–1905 96	——	1906–1915 153	——
Hungary	1876–1885 32	1886–1895 33	1896–1905 57	1906–1915 152
Germany	1886–1895 80	1896–1905 95	1907–1914 133	——
France	1886–1895 69	1896–1905 102	1908–1913 115	——
Holland	1875–1884 25	1885–1894 49	1895–1904 63	1905–1914 91
Belgium	1876–1885 21	1886–1895 41	1896–1905 63	1909–1912 80
Sweden	1876–1885 28	1886–1895 34	1896–1905 47	1908–1913 68
Norway	1887–1894 20	1896–1905 41	1906–1915 61	——
Finland	1876–1885 13	1886–1895 19	1896–1905 27	1906–1915 44
Luxembourg	——	——	1896–1905 21	1909–1912 41
England and Wales	1876–1885 7	1886–1895 7	1896–1905 9	1907–1914 10
Scotland	1876–1885 13	1886–1895 17	1896–1905 25	1906–1915 31
Austria	1886–1895 3	1896–1905 4	1909–1912 8	——
Ireland	1876–1885 0.01	1886–1895 0.01	1896–1905 0.17	——
Serbia	1887–1894 65	1896–1905 65	——	——
Rumania	1896–1903 109	——	——	——
Australia	1896–1905 64	1906–1915 71	——	——
New Zealand	1886–1895 23	1896–1905 64	1906–1915 106	——
Japan	1899 834	1904–1913 706	——	——

United States of America (population to one divorce):

1870	1880	1890	1900	1906	1916	1922
3,517	2,551	1,881	1,363	1,185	884	731

Married population to one divorce:

1,233	935	676	500	433	356	303

Russia (per 1,000 existing marriages among the Greek-Orthodox population:

1867–1871	1872–1876	1877–1881	1881–1886	1920–1922	1923
1.3	1.5	1.4	1.7		

Number of marriages consecrated in the same year to one divorce:

				11.7	12.9

During the years of the World War the movement of divorces was somewhat checked in the belligerent countries, but after its termination it assumed its tendency to increase and in some countries has made an enormous upward jump.[60]

A more detailed analysis of these divorce phenomena shows, as a general rule (which, however, has some exceptions), that interfamily shifting is more intensive (divorce rate is higher) among the city than among the country population; among childless married couples than among the couples with children; among heterogeneous married couples, that is, where the husband and wife belong to different race, or nationality, or religion, or culture, or occupation, or have different economic status, or greatly different age, than among homogeneous couples; among atheists than among religious people; among Liberal Protestants than among the Roman Catholics or the Greek-Orthodox people. The divorce rate is the lowest among the clergy and among those engaged in agriculture, and the highest among actors, showmen, musicians, and several other professions. In some countries it is higher among the well-to-do classes than among the poor population.[61]

It is not my purpose to discuss the enormous significance of this increase of interfamily mobility. I will say only that it is probably the most important social process of the present time in its positive or disastrous effect. My purpose is only to indicate the increase of interfamily circulation, and to show that it is not an isolated fact but one among many similar processes of increase in horizontal circulation. The Western man successfully "liberates" himself from the ties which used to attach him to his birthplace, to his country, to his occupation and work place and, finally, to his family. During the last few decades these ties have been becoming more and more loose and the "free" men began to shift more and more intensively along the horizontal dimensions of the social space.

5. HORIZONTAL SHIFTING OF CITIZENSHIPS AMONG INDIVIDUALS

Since territorial, family, and intraoccupational mobility of present Western societies is intensive, it is to be expected that it has to be accompanied by a considerable horizontal circulation of the individuals from state to state, from one religious group to another, from one political party to another, and generally from one ideological group to another. These large social groupings cannot be stable and their size cannot be unchangeable when more basic and more primary groupings, such as territorial, family, and occupational groups are mobile. The facts seem to corroborate this expectation. In the first place, within present societies we see a considerable interstate shifting of individuals. Under interstate shifting is meant not a territorial migration of the individuals from state to state, which does not mean a change of citizenship, but the shifting of citizenship. This is a phenomenon quite different from the mere international migration discussed above.

As to shifting of citizenship, the nineteenth and the twentieth centuries show that during this period, especially since 1914, such shifting has been considerable. In this respect our epoch is also extremely dynamic. This is manifested by a considerable fluctuation in the number of the independent states, in their territory and in the number of their citizens for the last century. For the sake of brevity, the principal changes in this field since 1870,[62] and particularly since 1914 only, will be mentioned. If the political map of Europe only is studied, it will be seen that since the end of the eighteenth century it has been radically modified several times. It had one form before the French Revolution and Napoleonic wars. It was radically changed during the Napoleonic wars. After the overthrow of Napoleon it was considerably remodeled again. Later on the changes continued to take place in the form of a creation of independent Rumania, Greece, Serbia, Bulgaria, and Montenegro, not to mention other less important alterations. As a result of these alterations millions of people who had been before the citizens of one state became the citizens of another one. Some new states came into existence; others disappeared. From 1870 to 1914, we have a consolidation of 35 states of Germany into one German Empire; alteration of the boundaries of France, Germany, Italy, Austria, Russia, Turkey, China, Japan, and the Balkan states. Note the disappearance of the Orange Free State, the transfer of Egypt, Tunis, and Korea from one government to another, a cardinal modification of the structure of the British Empire, not to mention other changes.[63] Finally, since 1914, there came into existence, at least 10 new independent states (Czecho-Slovakia, Egypt, Esthonia, Latvia, Lithuania, Finland, Poland, Hungary, Danzig, three states in Arabia); one state (Montenegro) completely disappeared; while some others, such as Georgia, appeared and disappeared, still others, as Austria-Hungary, Russia, and Turkey, were radically altered. To this it must be added that the area and the number of citizens of the states have been changed also, as a result of an encroachment of the territory and population of the conquered by the victorious states. The following figures depict a part of these alterations:[64]

Countries	Area (in English Square Miles)		Number of the Population	
	1913–1914	1921–1925	1911–1915	1921–1925
British Empire	11,429,078	13,355,426	424,775,160	449,583,000
Russia	8,417,118	7,041,120	182,182,600	132,000,413
France	207,054[a]	212,659[a]	81,201,509[b]	94,836,702[b]
Germany	1,236,600[b]	182,213[c]	76,991,985[b]	59,852,682[c]
Italy	110,555[a]	119,624[a]	35,238,997[a]	38,775,576[a]
Turkey	710,224	494,538	21,273,900	13,357,000
Austria	115,882	32,369	28,995,844	6,535,759
Hungary	125,609	35,875	20,886,987	7,980,143

[a] Without colonies. [b] With colonies. [c] Germany lost all its colonies.

The figures show what an upheaval has happened in regard to the area and population of different states since 1914. There is no need to say that these changes have been due not so much to the fluctuation of the birth and death rate of the population as to the encroachment of the areas and the population of the conquered states by the conquerors.

Within some eight or ten years the political map of the world has been radically altered; the alteration is still going on, and is likely to go on in the future. The sacredness and unchangeableness of state boundaries and citizenship become impossible in present dynamic societies and exists only on paper or is defended only in so far as it is profitable for a certain country. As soon as it is not profitable, treaties are broken; guaranties are discarded not only by Germany but by the Allied states too. The flexibility of the primary horizontal groupings necessarily leads to a fluctuation of the interstate boundaries also. This very fact manifests again the dynamic and mobile character of present-day Western societies.

6. INTERRELIGIOUS CIRCULATION

With still greater reason we may say that our society is dynamic also in regard to the shifting of the individuals from one religious group to another. The changes in the religious attitude of a population accumulate gradually. Such periods of accumulation may appear as quite static. In fact, the accumulated changes, having reached their point of saturation, suddenly burst forth and manifest themselves in the most conspicuous religious revolutions and in the greatest fluctuation of the size and character of existing religious groups. As examples of such periods may be cited the period of appearance and spreading of Buddhism in India and China; Mohammedanism in Arabia and other countries; Christianity in Ancient Rome and Europe; the periods of the Renaissance and the Reformation in Europe, and finally, the present period of the growth of "the religion of Atheism," of "Scientific Religion," the religions of "Humanitarianism," "Socialism," "Communism," and so on. "Atheism," "Communism," "Humanitarianism," "the religion of Reason," "the Scientific Religion," are also religions as they have all the principal characteristics of religion. From a purely scientific standpoint as a means of social control they are much less efficient, and as a system of ideas, are no less "superstitious" than the historical religions which they try to despise for "prejudices and superstitions."[65] Such periods come from time to time as a manifestation of a long period of gradual accumulation of changes in religious attitudes. Such periods are marked by a very intensive shifting of individuals from one religious group to another, by a disappearance of one existing religion and by the appearance of new ones.

It is quite likely that present Western societies are approaching such a stormy period. Some of them, like Russia, have already entered it. In other societies, decades of "anti-religious" propaganda of Rationalists, Humanitarians, Socialists, and radical writers, together with many changes in the whole social life, seems to have undermined many previous beliefs and weakened the religious convictions of the present population and the dogmas of previous religions generally. In this way they have prepared a religious crisis, which in part already exists, and in part is going to take place in the future whether we like it or not. (As far as my personal opinion is concerned, I regret it enormously.) But the fact of some decadence of the existing Christian religions seems to be beyond doubt. In the first place, the growing class of the proletariat already is marked by an atheistic, mechanistic, and materialistic attitude. In the second place, socialism in its dominant forms of the Marxian and similar varieties, is openly atheistic. It directly challenges any spiritualistic religions, styling them as "the opium of the people." Fervent Communist persecution of religion and ardent atheist propaganda are only more conspicuous manifestations of what is typical for the dominant varieties of Socialism generally. In the third place, the attitude of the non-socialist radical thinkers, writers, scholars, and scientists either is near to atheism, or represents an animosity toward the Christian Religion, or has a taint of mockery toward it (take, for instance, the attitude of Anatole France, or George Bernard Shaw, or H. G. Wells, or many other fashionable writers), or, in the best case, represents a religion quite different from what Christianity and the Christian Church have been and are in reality.[66] In the fourth place, many contemporary "rationalist" varieties of Christianity according to the interpretation of their ministers show such a deviation from the historical forms of the Christian Religion, its dogmas, beliefs, services, and ceremonies, that it is more proper to term such "Christian" churches and organizations as "the religion of the New Republic" or that "of the Nation," or that of the religion of George Bernard Shaw, H. G. Wells, H. L. Mencken, and so on, than that of Christian religion. And the very character of the present religious services in many churches represents practically nothing more than a college classroom, when a talented or non-talented professor is lecturing about some philosophical, ethical, political, and social topic. The only difference is that before and after the lecture there is a bit of music and singing which are absent in the college classroom. Finally, an increase of the people who do not belong to any of the existing religious organizations is somewhat evidenced by the statistics. This is seen from the following figures which, however, reflect the reality only very imperfectly: [67]

Country	Per Cent of the Population Without Any Religious Affiliation (sans cult)	
	1900	1910
Austria	0.02	0.07
Hungary	0.01	0.01
Italy	0.11	2.52
Switzerland	....	0.22
Bavaria	0.02	0.06
Denmark	0.15	0.30
Holland	2.26	4.97
Norway	0.59	0.47
Czecho-Slovakia	....	20.00
Union of South Africa	39.30	50.50
British Australia	0.18	0.22
New Zealand	1.21	1.46

United States of America: of a total population of 100,757,735 in 1916, the membership in all religious denominations was 41,926,854 or about 41.6 per cent of the whole population; of a total population of 110,663,502 in 1923, the membership in all religious denominations was 48,224,014 or about 43.4 per cent of all the population.[68]

What per cent of those who have not belonged to any denomination or have been atheists or freethinkers in the United States these data cannot answer. We have many reasons to think that the European figures represent only a small fraction of the real number of atheists or "freethinkers" or irreligious persons.[69] And, yet, even as they stand, they show that in the majority of Western countries the proportion shows a trend to increase. If such is the case this means that the number of persons who do not enter, or who leave, the existing religious bodies tends to increase.

Side by side with this we see also a permanent shifting from one religious body to another. The statistics of countries, like the United States where religious freedom has been somewhat greater than in Europe and where corresponding statistics have been more carefully computed, show this to some extent. From 1890 to 1916, 17 denominations which had existed in 1890 disappeared, and 31 new ones came into existence. Of those which continued to exist, some increased their membership; some decreased. For instance, the South Baptist Convention increased by 111.6 per cent; National Baptist Convention, by 117.8 per cent; Adventist Christians, by 173 per cent; Free Baptists, by 362 per cent; while the membership of the Primitive Baptists decreased by 17.9 per cent; that of Evangelical Protestants, by 50.3 per cent; that of Spiritualists, by 48.3 per cent; that of Cumberland Presbyterians, by 56.3 per cent; and so on.[70]

Some fluctuation of the size of the different religious bodies is shown also by statistics of European countries.[71] Here again we have every reason to suppose that the figures do not adequately reflect the real changes in the religious attitudes of the population. But even as they stand the figures manifest the existence of interreligious circulation.

It is possible to think that the real interreligious circulation at the present moment is much greater than the above figures show. Separation of the church from the state and religious freedom, together with the general mechanistic trend of our civilization, seem to have made interreligious shifting during the last century much more intensive than it was in the Middle Ages. And there are some reasons to expect that in the near future the changes in the religious attitude of the Western population accumulated during the last century, will manifest themselves openly in a great regrouping of, and circulation of, the population among different religious bodies.

7. INTERPOLITICAL PARTY CIRCULATION

Shifting from one political party to another, disappearance of some of the existing parties and appearance of new ones, and fluctuation in the size or membership of the parties in present Western societies exhibit an exclusively high degree of dynamism. Within a few years, sometimes within a few months, the political parties of a European country change radically. Political bodies remind one in this respect of a kind of soap bubble which quickly grows and just as quickly bursts, or a kind of hotel which is entered by a multitude to-day and is forsaken to-morrow. Millions of citizens permanently circulate from party to party. Instability in this field is especially great and alterations especially rapid and considerable. As a result, within a few months or in the best case, within a few years, the victorious party is defeated by another, which, in its turn, is defeated by its competitors. But few data are sufficient to show this.

In the United Kingdom, since 1846 to 1924, there have been 27 changes of government in the form of changes in the Cabinet; the longest period was 7 years and 2 months, the shortest, 6 months. This gives 2.9 years as an average duration of the Cabinet.[72] This means that on an average within 2.9 years the majority of the population changes its political sympathies and votes for a different party. This means that within this time span the conservative party had to give way to a liberal party, and *vice versa.* Since 1924, the situation has become still more complex, due to an increase of the Labor party. In France, between 1870 and 1911, the Cabinet was changed 49 times: the longest period being 2 years, 9 months, and 11 days, and the shortest, 20 days. This gives 9 months as the average time for the existence of the Cabinet in France.[73] This means that in an average time of 9 months the political affiliation of the majority of the French population changes, and that millions of the voters swing from one party to another. Parallel with this great interparty shifting of the population the political parties themselves show a permanent change in the form of the decay of one party and appearance of another. The following table which gives the composition of the French House of Representatives, according to the parties from 1868 to 1912, may give an idea of the great flexibility in this field.[74] (See p. 407.)

The table shows such a great variety of political parties and such a change of their membership from legislature to legislature,

Political Parties	Legislatures										
	National Assembly	I	II	III	IV	V	VI	VII	VIII	IX	X
Action Liberal											31
Bonapartists	30	75	99	45	65						
Boulangists						44					
The Left Center		48		39		40					
Conservative									33		
Constitutionalists		22							3		
The Right Party							59				19
The Extreme Left		98		46							
The Democratic Left											77
The Republican Left		193		168						82	
Independent											23
Legitimists	200	24									
Liberal					64						
Monarchists			103	45	73						
Moderate Republicans	100				275	216					
Nationalists								101	45	16	
Orleanists	200	54									
Progressive									140	60	79
Radicals	100				107		122	104	228	269	113
Radical-Social						110		75			149
Rallies							35	38	50		
Reactionaries								44		80	
Republican			314					254			
Government Republicans							311		48		
Royalists						166					
Socialists							49	56	45		33
Socialists Independent										29	
Socialists United										55	73
Republican Union				204							
Total Number of the Deputies	630	514	516	547	584	576	575	581	589	591	597

that its meaning is clear without any further commentaries. It is representative for the majority of European countries. They have had similar alterations in the political composition of their parliaments and similar great changes in the number of the votes for different parties in successive elections. During the last few years the situation has not improved but rather has become worse. It is enough to take the results of the last two or three elections in the majority of European countries to see that they have been quite different, and that the circulation of the population from party to party has been rather increasing than decreasing. At the same time the number of parties has increased to such an extent that observers do not exaggerate much in saying that every hundred voters endeavor to establish their own party. In order to see this it is enough to examine the *Statesman's Year Book* from 1918 to 1925, and to look at the corresponding data. They confirm the above conclusively. Every election brings a substantial alteration in the composition of the parties and in their success: yesterday's victorious party to-day has been defeated and to-day's conqueror is likely to be defeated to-morrow.[75]

Even in the United States, with the two-party system, the shifting of the population from party to party within four years (from presidential election to presidential election) has been considerable. This may be seen from the following figures:[76]

Years	Popular Vote for Presidential Electors				Electoral Vote for President		
	Republican	Democratic	Socialist	Miscellaneous Independents	Republican	Democratic	Progressive
1888...	5,444,337	5,540,050	....	146,897			
1900...	7,219,530	6,358,071	127,519	50,232			
1904...	7,628,834	5,084,491	436,184	114,753	336	140	
1908...	7,679,006	6,409,106	434,649	111,693	321	162	
1912...	3,483,922	6,286,214	926,098	4,126,020	8	435	88
1916...	8,538,221	9,129,606	598,516	41,894	254	277	
1924...	15,725,003	8,385,586	27,650	4,826,471	382	136	

The figures show that in the United States also, millions of voters shift from party to party within a few years.

Without any further data the above shows that present Western societies are very mobile in this respect.

8. GENERAL CONCLUSION CONCERNING HORIZONTAL MOBILITY OF WESTERN SOCIETIES

The preceding suggests that in all principal forms of horizontal mobility, present Western societies exhibit a very high degree of dynamism. In many fields the horizontal shifting of the population seems to have been increasing. The most conspicuous characteristic of present Western societies is indeed their great mobility. This has an enormous significance and, through its effects, puts definite stigmas on present societies. As we shall see later, a great many characteristics of our civilization are due to the effect of this intensive mobility.

It is proper to note that I do not regard this trend of increase in mobility as a permanent and eternal trend. Probably, having reached its point of saturation it will stop and may even be superseded by the opposite trend. Such reversals have happened many times in the past. They may happen in the future. And several facts, among them the Japanese statistics of divorces, show how interfamily mobility, after having reached an exclusively high intensiveness, may begin to decrease and go down. We know also many cases where the labor turnover has decreased but did not increase during the last decade. Russia has shown that atheism, having reached an enormous proportion in the period of 1917 to 1922, has since that time begun to decrease. These facts suggest that the contemporary tendency of present-day societies may be replaced by an opposite one. Anyhow, we live in a mobile age, in an age of shifting and change.

[1] See BÜCHER, K., *Industrial Evolution* (Russian translated), Vol. II, pp. 170 *et seq.*

[2] *The Imperial Gazetteer of India*, Vol. I, pp. 467-468, 497.

[3] *Statistical Abstract for the United Kingdom Relating to British India*, p. 203, 1919-1920.

[4] *State of Birth of the Native Population*, Table I, Washington, D. C., 1922.

[5] MAYR, G. VON, *Statistik und Gesellschaftslehre*, Vol. II, p. 121, 1897; for all largest German cities in 1890, the per cent of those who were born in the city of their residence was only 43.73. *Ibid.*, p. 123.

[6] *Ibid.*, p. 122.

[7] *Ibid.*, p. 124.

[8] *Stat. Arsbok for Sverige*, pp. 13-14, 1919.

[9] BERTILLON, J., *La dépop. de la France*, p. 45; *Annuaire International de Statistique*, pp. 136 *et seq.*, 1916; *Journal de la Société de Statistique de Paris*, pp. 162-163, May, 1925.

[10] *Annuaire International de Statistique*, pp. 136 *et seq.*

[11] *Stat. Arsbok for Sverige*, pp. 13-14, 1919.

[12] *Statistisches Jahrbuch der Schweiz*, p. 45, 1923.

[13] *Fourteenth Census of the United States Population*, p. 613.

[14] See MORELLET, JEAN, "Les mouvements migratoires européens," *Revue des Sciences Politiques*, pp. 404-451, July to September, 1925.

[15] STRINGHER, "Sur la balance des paiements entre l'Italie et L'étranger," *Bulletin de l'Institut International de Statistique*, Vol. XIX, pp. 104-106.

[16] *Annual Report of the Commissioner General of Immigration*, p. 122, 1924.

[17] *Stat. Arsbok for Sverige*, pp. 13-14.

[18] *Statistisches Jahrbuch der Schweiz*, p. 45, 1923.

[19] *Statistisches Jahrbuch für den Freistaat Bayern*, p. 17, 1919.

[20] See MAYR, G. VON, *op. cit.*, Vol. II, pp. 121-125.

[21] "Auslese und Anpassung der Arbeiterschaft," *Schriften des Vereins für Sozialpolitik*, Bd. 134, p. 6, Leipzig, 1910.

[22] *Ibid.*, pp. 177-179.

[23] *Ibid.*, pp. 184-186.

[24] *Ibid.*, p. 255.

[25] "Auslese und Anpassung der Arbeiterschaft," *Schriften des Vereins für Sozialpolitik*, Bd. 135, Dritte Teil, p. 172, Leipzig, 1912.

[26] *Ibid.*, p. 215.

[27] *Ibid.*, p. 175; Vierter Teil, pp. 33-37; Teil I, pp. 65, 203-205.

[28] See other data in other volumes of the same series of "Auslese und Anpassung der Arbeiterschaft" for 1910-1912 and 1914-1916.

[29] MCKENZIE, R. D., *The Neighborhood*, p. 160, 1923.

[30] *London Statistics*, Vol. XXVIII, p. 242, 1921-1923.

[31] *Annuaire Statistique de la Belgique et du Congo*, p. lxxi, 1922; Bruxelles, 1924; for Denmark, see *Statistics Aarbog*, pp. 77-79, 1922.

[32] BURGESS, ERNEST W., "The Growth of the City," *Publications of American Sociological Society*, Vol. XVIII, pp. 85-97.

[33] MAYR, G. VON, *op. cit.*, Vol. II, p. 357.

[34] BRUHNES, J., *Human Geography*, p. 543, Rand McNally Company, Chicago.

[35] President L. D. Coffman rightly says that "the present home is a building in front of a garage."

[36] *Annuaire International de Statistique*, pp. 130-131, 1920. See here the data for the number of the telegraph and telephone bureaus, the length of the telephone and telegraph lines, and so on.

[37] *Annuaire International de Statistique*, pp. 130-131, 1920.

[38] BURGESS, ERNEST W., *op. cit.*, pp. 94-95.

[39] FOVILLE, A. DE, "Les éléments de la balance économique des peuples," *Bulletin de l'Institut International de Statistique*, Vol. XV, pp. 202 *et seq.* See also NEYMARCK, M. A., "La statistique internationale de valeurs mobilières," *ibid.*, Vol. XX, p. 1297.

[40] See *Statistical Yearbooks* of different countries and *Yearly Reports of the United States Department of Commerce.* For the sake of brevity, the figures will not be given here.

[41] See FAURE, ELIE, *History of Art*, Vol. I, Synoptic Tables, Harper &

Brothers, 1921; PETRIE, W. M. F., *The Revolutions of Civilization*, pp. 47, 84, and *passim*, 1911.

[42] WALTERS, H. B., *History of Ancient Pottery*, Vol. I, pp. 237-244, 402-403; Vol. II, pp. 279 *et seq.*, London, 1905.

[43] MOUGEOLLE, *Statistique des civilizations*, p. 259, Paris, 1883. See here other facts. See also NOVICOV, J., *Les luttes entre sociétés humaines*, pp. 187-196. J. Novicov formulated even a special "law of acceleration" which, according to him, is a permanent historical tendency. In accordance with the above I do not think that the existence of such a law is proved. For instance, the period of existence of one of the eight types of the Egyptian art does not show that the span of time between the change of the earlier periods was longer than at the later periods. Between the third and the fourth periods the span was only 650 years, while between the fifth and the sixth periods it was 1,900 years, between the seventh and the eighth (latest periods), 1,690 years, and so on. PETRIE, W. M. F., *op. cit.*, p. 84. The facts given by J. Novicov to corroborate his "law" are too few and not convincing. My statement concerning the trend of an acceleration within present Western society ought not be understood in the sense of a permanent and eternal universal tendency. I do not have such pretensions. The trend may be quite temporary and may be superseded by an opposite one in the future.

[44] BOGARDUS, EMORY S., *Fundamentals of Social Psychology*, pp. 159-160.

[45] See historical atlases which show the area of the successive diffusion of Christianity or Islam.

[46] *Vide*, about a rapidity of social change at the present moment, OGBURN, W., *Social Change*, pp. 103 *ff.*

[47] See *e.g.*, BYRN, E. W., *The Progress of Invention in the Nineteenth Century*, *passim* and Chaps. I and II, New York, 1900.

[48] BRISSENDEN, P. F., and FRANKEL, E., *Labor Turnover in Industry*, pp. 38-39, 117-122, 134-135, and *passim*, 1922.

[49] *Ibid*, *passim*; LESCOHIER, DON, *The Labor Market*, Chap. IV; LAIRD, D. A., *The Psychology of Selecting Men*, pp. 26 *et seq.*; WILLITTS, J. H., "Steadying Employment," *Annals of the American Academy of Political and Social Science*, May, 1916.

[50] COLLIS, E. L., and GREENWOOD, MAJOR, *The Health of the Industrial Workers*, pp. 361-371, London, 1921. *Vide*, also WEBB, S., *Prevention of Destitution.*

[51] *Stellenwechsel* in difference from a change of geographical place (*Ortswechsel*) or from a change of occupation (*Berufswechsel*).

[52] "Auslese und Anpassung der Arbeiterschaft," *Schriften des Vereins*, Bd. 133, pp. 132-133, Leipzig, 1910.

[53] *Ibid.*, Bd. 135, Teil I, pp. 201 *et seq.*, Leipzig, 1911.

[54] *Ibid.*, p. 57.

[55] *Ibid.*, Bd. 135, Teil IV, pp. 36-37, Leipzig, 1912.

[56] See other volumes of this exclusively valuable series.

[57] COFFMAN, L. D., *The Social Composition of the Teaching Population*, pp. 28 *et seq.*, New York, 1911; see also *Annual Report of the United States Department of the Interior*, pp. 1277-1301, 1904; ELMER, M. C., *A Study of Women in Clerical and Secretarial Work*, p. 16, 1925; see also BILLS, M. A., "Social Status of the Clerical Worker," *Journal of Applied Psychology*, pp. 424-427, 1925.

[58] Confucius and the Le Play School probably more than anybody else understood the great rôle of family, and deeper than any others, analyzed its social functions. See *The Sacred Books of the East*, Vol. III; *The Texts of Confucianism*, *passim*, and especially *The Hsiâo King or Classic of Filial Piety*,

Vol. XXVII, *The Lî-Kî, passim,* particularly Bks. I and VIII; Vol. XXVIII, Bk. XVI.

LE PLAY, *Constitution Essentielle de l'Humanité passim;* PINOT, R., "La Classification des espèces de la famille établie par Le Play est-elle-exacte?" *Science Sociale,* 19 Année, 1er Fasc., pp. 44 *ff.;* DEMOLINS, E., "Comment on analyse et comment on classe les type sociaux," in the same Fascicule, *Science Sociale, passim;* VIGNES, M., *La Science Sociale d'après les Principes de Le Play et de ses Continuateurs,* Vol. I, Chaps. I and II, *passim,* Paris, 1897; DEMOLINS, *Anglo-Saxon Superiority, to What It Is Due, passim.* See other works of Le Play's Sociological School.

See also COOLEY, CHARLES H., *Social Organization,* Chap. III. "Filial piety is the root of all virtue, and the stem out of which grows all moral teaching. It commences with the service of parents; it proceeds to the service of the rulers (or of a society as we should say now); it is completed by the establishment of character. For teaching the people to be affectionate and loving there is nothing better than filial piety; for teaching them the observance of propriety there is nothing better than Fraternal Duty; for changing their manners and altering their customs there is nothing better than family education." These statements of Confucius are true not only for China but also for past and present societies. And the Le Play School (H. de Tourville, E. Demolins, R. Pinot, Rousiex, and others) made it quite clear with their analysis and classification of the types of family and corresponding types of society.

[59] The data are taken from the following sources: *Annuaire International de Statistique,* pp. 117-118, 1920; Bureau of the Census, *Marriage and Divorce,* Washington, D. C., 1925; *Narodnoije Khosaistvo Sojusa S. S. R.vtzyfrakh,* pp. 33-34, Moscow, 1924.

[60] See the data, analysis and the sources in SOROKIN, P., "Influence of the World War Upon Divorces," *Journal of Applied Sociology,* November and December, 1925.

[61] See, besides official statistical publications of different countries, the works: MAYR, G. VON, *Statistik und Gesellschaftslehre,* Vol. III, pp. 201 ff.; JACQUART, C., *Le divorce et la séparation de corps,* Bruxelles, 1909; Bosco, A., *I divorzi e le separazioni personali dei conjugi,* Rome, 1908; BERTILLON, *Étude demographique du divorce,* Paris, 1883; BÖCKH, R., "Statistik der Ehescheidungen in der Stadt Berlin," *Bulletin de l'Institut International de Statistique,* Vol. XI; YVERNES, M., "Les divorces et les séparations de corps en France," *Journal de la Societé de Statistique de Paris,* pp. 101 *ff.,* 1908; *United States Department of Commerce and Labor, Marriage and Divorce,* Washington, D. C., 1909; LICHTENBERGER, J. P., *Divorce,* New York, 1909; WILLCOX, W. F., "The Divorce Problem," *Columbia University Studies,* Vol. I; ELLWOOD, CHARLES A., *Sociology and Modern Social Problems,* Chap. VIII; DRACHSLER, J., "Intermarriage in New York City," *Columbia University Studies,* Vol. XCIV, pp. 16 *ff.;* BRANDT, LILIAN, "Family Desertion," *L'Année sociologique,* Vol. 11, pp. 475 *ff.,* 1905.

[62] See the data for the whole nineteenth century in SOROKIN, P., *Sistema Soziologii,* Vol. II, p. 386; *Annuaire International de statistique,* pp. 4 *et seq.,* 1916; LEVASSEUR, E., and BODIO, "Statistique de la superficie et de la population," *Bulletin de l'Institut International de Statistique,* Vol. XII; JURASCHEK, "Flächeninhalt und Bevölkerung Europas," *ibid.,* Vol. XIV.

[63] *Vide* the details in CALDECOTT, A., "International and Inter-Racial Relations," *The Sociological Review,* pp. 13-23, 1910; see also the treaties in international law, such as F. List's treaties.

[64] Compiled from *Statesman's Yearbook* for 1914 and 1925.

[65] See about the character of the religious regroupings in SOROKIN, P., *Sistema Soziologii,* Vol. II, pp. 431-435; GUIGNEBERT, *L'évolution des dogmes,*

pp. 143 *et seq.*, and *passim*, Paris, 1910; ELLWOOD, CHARLES A., *The Reconstruction of Religion;* LE-BON, G., *Psychology of Socialism;* KIDD, B., *Social Evolution;* MACHIAVELLI, N., *Discourse on T. Livi;* SUMNER, W. G., "Religion and the Mores," *American Journal of Sociology*, Vol. XV, pp. 577-595.

[66] Besides several facts which corroborate this statement, it is confirmed by possibly the best statistical study in this field made by Prof. J. H. Leuba. His study of the belief in God and immortality among the students of American colleges, among American scientists and scholars has given the following results: Among college students, 43 per cent "think themselves morally independent of the existence of God." Among the freshmen, the per cent of the believers in immortality is 80.3; among the sophomores, 76.2; among the juniors, 60.0; among the seniors, 70.1. Among scientists, the per cent of non-believers in God and immortality is 58.2. It is interesting to note that the per cent of non-believers is greater among the greater than among the lesser scientists and scholars. Further, it is greater among historians and sociologists than among biologists and especially among representatives of the physical sciences. These data obtained in a careful investigation seem to be typical for the present religious attitude of the intelligentsia of Western societies. See LEUBA, J. H., *The Belief in God and Immortality*, pp. 202-203, 212-216, 250-253 and Chaps VII-X, Boston, 1916. 125,000 answers to a recent National Religious Poll in the United States yielded the following results: 91 per cent of all who replied believe in God; 88 per cent, in immortality; for the replies of New York population corresponding figures are: 73 and 64. If the figures are representative they conspicuously stress what is said in the text.

[67] *Annuaire International de Statistique*, pp. 152-157, 1916, and pp. 94-95, 1920.

[68] *Religious Bodies, 1916*, Pt. I, pp. 29 *et seq.*, Washington, D. C., 1919; *Statistical Abstract of the United States*, pp. 4 and 59, 1924.

[69] This is corroborated by many facts; among them see the characteristics of the present desperate conditions of Protestantism in Europe by Rev. Dr. George Stewart in *The Literary Digest*, Dec. 5, 1925. More careful and detailed studies of communities and especially of the city population disclose a much higher per cent of atheists. R. D. McKenzie's study of Columbus, Ohio, has disclosed a very considerable proportion of atheists in the different wards of the city. See MCKENZIE, R. D., *op. cit.*, pp. 589 *et seq.* See also the quoted volumes: "Auslese und Anpassung der Arbeiterschaft," *Schriften der Vereins für Socialpolitik*, which show a high per cent of atheists among the proletariat of Germany; also the quoted work of Leuba.

[70] See other data in *Religious Bodies*, Pt. I, pp. 30 *et seq.*

[71] See *Annuaire International de Statistique*, for 1916 and 1920.

[72] *Statesman's Yearbook*, p. 9, 1925. See here the details.

[73] E. CHARTIER, LE, *La France et son Parlement*, p. 83, 1911. See here the details.

[74] *Ibid.*, p. 310.

[75] See *Statesman's Yearbook* for the last few years.

[76] *Statistical Abstract of the United States*, pp. 141-142, 1924.

CHAPTER XVII

VERTICAL MOBILITY WITHIN WESTERN SOCIETIES

I. THE INTEROCCUPATIONAL AND INTRAOCCUPATIONAL MOBILITY

WITHIN our societies vertical circulation of individuals is going on permanently. But how is it taking place? What is its intensiveness? What are its forms and trends? Does it have a gradual or a sudden character? In brief, what are the characteristics of this process of which very little is known? Individuals have been speculating too much and studying the facts too little. It is high time to abandon speculation for the somewhat saner method of collecting the facts and studying them patiently. Unfortunately in this respect very little has been done. The task now before me is not unlike that of a physiologist who, though he has studied but a few small spots in the circulatory system, must yet on this basis construct the whole process of blood circulation of the organism. Such an enterprise may naturally lead to many mistakes. And yet, since the necessary material is absent, somebody must venture to construct such a theory in order to stimulate further studies of the process. In this sense, my hypothetical construction may be beneficial. At any rate, there is no alternative. With this reservation and warning, let us proceed to the study of the *vertical mobility* within our present societies. By this term is meant any change in the occupational, economic or political status of individuals which leads to a change of their social position. The analysis should begin with the interoccupational and intraoccupational circulation of individuals, which is very different from the simple fact of labor turnover or purely territorial mobility discussed heretofore.

Definite change of occupation, not merely change of territorial place within the same occupational position, almost always is connected with a change in the social position of an individual. This is the reason why interoccupational mobility is considered as a form of vertical but not of horizontal mobility. The same may be said of a change of rank within the same occupation. The points to be discussed now are as follows: To what extent is the occupational status of a man determined by that of his father in our societies? What is the intensiveness of interoccupational circulation? Has it been increasing or decreasing during the last few decades? Where, and among what occupational groups, are the children of fathers belonging to the same occupation scattered? From what occupational groups are recruited the members of each occupational group? Is interoccupational mobility sudden or gradual? What is its velocity? Are there some occupations among which the circulation of their members is especially intensive, or in which such an "occupational affinity" does not exist? A satisfactory analysis of these and similar problems may give sufficient insight into the physiology of present societies. The discussion will begin with an analysis of the transmission of occupation from a father to his children.

2. TO WHAT EXTENT DOES THE OCCUPATIONAL STATUS OF THE FATHER DETERMINE THAT OF HIS CHILDREN? TWO TYPES OF SOCIETY

In regard to the transmission of occupation from the father to his children, it is possible to imagine two opposite types of society: one in which all children (100 per cent) "inherit" the occupational status of their father; another in which no child inherits it. Among present existing societies, hardly any one of either type in its pure form is found. None the less, some societies are nearer to the first type, others to the second one.

Indian caste-society is an example of the type with an exclusively high transmission of occupation from father to son. Factually and juridically the father's occupation determines that of his son. Social inheritance of occupation from the father by his sons is one of the most characteristic traits of the India caste-system. "Community of occupation is ordinarily regarded as the chief factor in the evolution of caste. Almost every caste professes to have a traditional occupation." [1] "Castes are social aggregates which have the privilege of monopolizing hereditarily the performance of a definite occupation." [2] "Caste is an occupa-

Countries	Number of Cases Studied	Number of Cases in Which Son's Occupation Is Identical with, or Similar to, that of Father	Percentage of Transmission of Occupation from Father to Son	Occupational Group Studied	Place and Time of Study	Author
United States of America.....	299	79	26.1	Students of summer session	Minneapolis, 1925	P. Sorokin
	142	32	22.5	Business men, miscellaneous group	Minneapolis, 1926	P. Sorokin and M. Tanquist [9]
	1,207	296	24.5			
	130	23	17.7	Alumni of University of Minnesota		O. M. Mehus
	62	39	62.9	Prominent naval officers, United States, England		Charles Davenport [10]
	24,442	?	2.7 to 49.5, according to occupation	Employed boys of New York	N. Y. State, 1920	H. C. Burdge [11]
	248	178	72	American millionaires	1924	P. Sorokin [12]
	2,069	1,461	70	Farmers' sons of New York	1924	E. C. Young [13]
	1,580	954	60	Farmers' daughters of New York	1924	E. C. Young
	757	525	69.3	Farmers' sons	1924	E. C. Young
	201	169	84.1	Farm operators	1923	R. L. Gillett [14]
	572	364	63.7	Farmers' sons and daughters, Minnesota	1925	C. Zimmerman

England.......	4,196		From 5.6 to 61.7 according to occupation Average 37.5	Scholars of evening continuation schools in Lancashire	1912	S. J. Chapman and W. Abbott [15]
	1,550	506	32.6	Men from *Who's Who*		E. Perrin [16]
	1,550	513	33.1	Men from *Dictionary of National Biography*		E. Perrin
Italy..........	3,127	1,629	52.1	Men of different occupations in Rome	1908	C. Gini and F. Chessa [17]
Germany......	1,361	775	56.9	Students of German universities, 1887 to 1890		J. Conrad [18]
	3,150	930	29.4	Prominent leaders of Germany of the eighteenth, nineteenth and twentieth centuries		Fritz Maas [19]
	134	67	50.0	Mannheim families		F. Chessa [20]
	841	354	42.0	Employees of Krupp factories	1906	Ehrenberg and Racine [21]
			from 8.9 to 60.9	Children of operators of different factories in Germany	1910 to 1916	H. Hinke, M. Morgenstern, R. Sorer, R. Walleroth, A. Syrup, M. Bernays [22]
France........	97	identical 24 similar 49	24.7 50.5	Different families	1900	A. Coste [23]
	62	32	51.6	Different families	1900	Charles Limousin [24]
Russia........	122	65	53.3	Russian prominent scientists	1923	Philiptschenko [25]

tional *milieu:* a son of a blacksmith must become only a blacksmith; a son of a soldier, a soldier; a son of a priest, a priest."[3] All Hindu religions and juridical codes unanimously prescribe this duty as one of the most important.[4] Though this is not precisely the real situation, and there have been cases of changes of occupation,[5] nevertheless they have been relatively scarce. An analogous, though somewhat milder, situation has existed in many other societies: in Ancient Egypt, in China, in Rome of the third, fourth, and fifth centuries A. D., in Byzantium, in ancient Peru, among many preliterate tribes, in the Middle Ages, and so on.[6] In all these societies, at least at some period, the transmission of occupation from generation to generation in the family has existed, and consequently the occupational status of the father determined—factually or juridically—that of his children.

The present Western societies, in which the occupational status of parents plays a much more moderate part in determining that of their children, are a contrast to this type; in other words, in our societies, *the percentage of hereditary transmission of occupation from the father to his children is much lower than in the above social aggregates.*[7] The occupational status of a family continues still, to some extent, to determine that of its children, but its rôle seems to be less important now than it has been in the "immobile" societies.[8] The juridical and factual freedom of children in choice of occupation in Western societies seems to be much greater than in a caste and other immobile societies.

An idea of the present situation may be given by the following figures. They are fragmentary, but, nevertheless, they show the real situation to some extent:

These data are very fragmentary; the methods of defining the identity or similarity of occupation differ with different authors; further, some of them have studied the occupations of all the children of the father, while some others have taken only one son of the father. All this naturally causes a considerable difference in the figures and makes their validity very questionable. And yet, as a very rude index of occupational continuity, they may serve. The inferences which may be drawn from them are as follows: *Within present Western societies the transmission of occupational status seems to be in all occupational groups much less than* 100 *per cent; its maximum seems to be at about 70 per cent; its minimum at about 3 to 10 per cent. The average index of transmission fluctuates between 20 and 60 per cent. This means that the contemporary occupational groups are far from being rigid, and the membranes between them far from being impenetrable.*

The next question is whether the transmission of occupational status is equal in all occupational groups or fluctuates from group to group. If it fluctuates, in what occupations is it higher and in what lower?

The first question must be answered negatively: the percentage of transmission strongly fluctuates from group to group. This inference is given by practically all the mentioned studies. Here are a few examples. (See the tables on pp. 420 *et seq.*)

The table shows a great fluctuation of inheritance of occupation in different social groups. Another point in the table is worthy of mention. F. Chessa in his *Trasmissione Ereditaria dei Professioni* came to the tentative conclusion that "hereditary transmission of occupation is stronger in those occupations which demand a greater technical experience and specialization or a more or less large amount of money for their performance than in the occupations which do not demand either of these conditions." Concerning the liberal professions, Doctor Chessa states that hereditary transmission of occupation is relatively higher in the professions which are "connected with social honor and privileges," are durable and stable, or demand an intensive intellectual effort, than in the professions which do not have these characteristics.[33] Similar opinions were expressed by some members of the Paris Sociological Society at the meeting devoted to the discussion of the problem.[34] The data of the Minneapolis group, as well as those of some other groups in the preceding table, it seems, corroborate these statements.[35] They, however, are still only very tentative and need to be tested by further studies.

3. IS THERE ANY TREND IN TRANSMISSION OF OCCUPATION FROM THE FATHER TO THE CHILDREN?

Has the transmission of occupation from the father to the children been increasing or decreasing during the last few generations? Because of absence of data the question cannot be an-

Occupation of Father	Per Cent of Transmission of Occupation from the Father to His Son					
				Minneapolis Groups		
	Data of E. Perrin (1,500 Persons in the English *Who's Who*) [26]	Data of Chapman-Abbott (4,196 Students of Evening Continuation Schools in Lancashire) [27]	Data of Burdge (24,442 Boys in New York State) [28]	For One Son	For All Independent Sons	
					Group "a"	Group "c"
Professional........	30.0	[a]	7.7	90.0	84.4	39.9
Clerical...........	[a]	49.1	49.5	[a]	[a]	51.8
Business...........	28.4	27.4	13.9	22.6	34.8	
Government service	56.8	5.6	0.8	[a]	[a]	
Army and navy executive positions	[a]	[a]	2.7	[a]	14.3	
Farmers, landowners	9.3	[a]	[a]	3.8	29.6	40.0
Unskilled labor.....	[a]	10.9	21.0	[a]	33.3	21.4
Miscellaneous trades and artisans.....	25.0	18.9	6.5	[a]	22.2	32.1
Building trades......	[a]	24.2 [b]	8.0	[a]	[a]	
Woodworking.........	[a]	[a]	6.4	[a]	[a]	
Metal trades.........	64.3 [c]	33.3	34.0	[a]	[a]	
Clothing...........	14.2 [d]	[a]	4.2	[a]	[a]	
Mining.............	[a]	36.0	[a]	[a]	[a]	
Clay, glass, stone...	[a]	[a]	6.9	[a]	[a]	
Printing...........	[a]	[a]	13.0	[a]	[a]	
Transportation.....	[a]	[a]	10.8	[a]	[a]	
Food preparation....	[a]	[a]	6.6	[a]	[a]	
Textiles...........	12 to 60.0 [e]	61.7	13.4	[a]	[a]	
Leather...........	50.0 [f]	[a]	13.9	[a]	[a]	

[a] Corresponding data are either absent or too few to have any validity.
[b] Together with woodworking.
[c] For Vienna Maschinenfabrik.[29]
[d] For a German wool-hat industry.[30]
[e] For different German textile factories.[31]
[f] For Offenbachen Leather Factory in Germany.[32]

swered in a general way. The data are fragmentary, but some of them will be given here without any definite generalization regarding their significance. In the first place, some data were collected by me and by some of my students. They concern Minneapolis students of the Summer Session (1925 to 1926), regular students, Minneapolis business men, and some other groups of the Minneapolis population. They give the following results: In the first place, the *data show a definite tendency toward a decrease of "hereditary"*[36] *transmission of occupation*[37] *from the father to his children as we pass from the generation of the great-grandfathers to the generation of the propositi.* This trend is seen from Tables I and II in which the term "identical," as applied to occupation, is used in the narrow sense of this word. The occupation of a father and his children is styled "identical" when both of them are "farmers," or "grocers," or "fishermen," or "clergymen," or "teachers," or "university and college professors and instructors," and so on. Table I shows the percentage of transmission of occupation from father to *one* of his sons in each generation, beginning with the great-grandfather of the propositus and passing to his grandfather and father, and ending with the propositus himself. Table II shows the percentage of transmission of occupation from the grandfathers to *all* their independent sons gainfully engaged in pursuits, compared with the percentage of transmission of occupation from the fathers of the propositi to the independent propositi and their independent brothers gainfully engaged in occupational pursuits. This is done in order to be certain that the trends of the first table are not due to the fact that from each family only one son in each generation is taken.

The table shows that while 72 per cent of the grandfathers of the propositi of my groups had the same occupation as that of the great-grandfathers, only 38.9 per cent of the fathers of the propositi have had the same occupation as that of the grandfathers; this percentage still diminishes to 10.6 for the propositi themselves. A great decrease of "hereditary" transmission of an occupational status in the later generations is clear from these figures. Similar results were obtained by Miss Tanquist in her study.

TABLE I

Generations	Number of Families Studied			Number of Families in Which Son's Occupation Was Identical with that of Father			Percentage of Transmission of Occupation from Father to His Son		
	a	*b*	*c*	*a*	*b*	*c*	*a*	*b*	*c*
Paternal great-grandfather (and grandfather).......	93 [d]	23	214	67	16	164	72.0	69.5	59.4
Paternal grandfather (and father)................	131	49	353	51	22	135	38.9	44.9	38.2
Father (and propositus)....	136 [e]	59		9	6		6.6	10.1	
	85 [f]		329	9		42	10.6		12.7

[a] My group.
[b] Miss Tanquist's group, No. 1.
[c] Miss Tanquist's and my group, No. 2.
[d] The number of families in the earlier generations is less than in the later ones because some of the propositi could not give any information about their great-grandfathers, and in a few cases even about their grandfathers.
[e] Including the families with the propositus—a dependent student.
[f] Excluding the families with a student-propositus (dependent).

In Table II there is taken not one but *all* grandfathers' sons gainfully engaged, on the one hand, and *all* independent sons of the fathers. The results of this "wholesale" comparison of transmission of occupation from the grandfathers to their children, and from the fathers of the propositi to their sons are as follows. (The corresponding data concerning the generation of the great-grandfathers in regard to all their sons could not be obtained.)

It is to be expected that the percentage of transmission of occupation is higher when we take all sons, as is the case in Table II, than when we take only one father's son, as is the case in Table I. Notwithstanding this natural difference, both tables show a considerable decrease of transmission of occupation from a father to his sons in the later generations. The same tendency is shown by the data of Miss Tanquist. To these data I may add that of 93 families for which I have the corresponding data

TABLE II

Generations	Number of Independent Sons Gainfully Engaged			Number of Sons Whose Occupation Is Identical with that of Their Fathers			Percentage of Transmission of Occupation from Father to Son		
	a	*b*	*c*	*a*	*b*	*c*	*a*	*b*	*c*
Grandfather (and his sons gainfully engaged)......	330	168	1,248	122	49	480	37.0	29.2	38.4
Father (and his sons gainfully engaged)..........	350[d]	142		79	32		22.6	22.5	
	299[e]		1,207	79		296	26.1		24.5

[a] My group.
[b] Miss Tanquist's group, No. 1.
[c] Miss Tanquist's and my group, No. 2.
[d] Including the sons who are dependent students.
[e] Excluding the dependent students.

for all generations, beginning with the great-grandfathers, there are only two cases (or 2.1 per cent) in which the great-grandfather, grandfather, father, and propositus have had the same occupation; and there are 23 cases (or 24.7 per cent) in which the same occupation has been held throughout three subsequent generations: great-grandfather, grandfather, and father, or grandfather, father, and propositus.

The study of the Mannheim families has given the same results: the percentage of transmission of occupation from the great-grandfather to their sons was 67.0, while for the generations of the fathers and propositi, it was only 42.5.[38] The study of the movement of farm population in New York State by E. C. Young has given the following percentage of men and women born and brought up on farms and entered in occupations other than farming: for 1800 to 1829 the percentage for men was 6, for women 13; systematically increasing, the percentage for 1890 to 1899 is 39 for men and 44 for women. The study of the Minnesota farmers by C. Zimmerman has shown that while among the farmers 85.5 per cent have farmer-fathers, among their children at the age of 18 years and above, only 63.7 per cent entered farming occupation.[39] This seems to point indirectly to the same trend, a decrease of the inheritance of the fathers' occupations by his children.

These and a few other data show a definite trend of a decrease of inheritance of occupational status. Such general facts as the removal of feudal and juridical obstacles to a change of occupation after the end of the eighteenth century; the industrial revolution; the growth of the division of labor; the perfecting of the means of transportation; an increase of horizontal mobility, and other great changes seem to indicate the same trend. However, the data are too few and concern principally the farm population which has been generally shifting in a progressive proportion toward other occupations; therefore, until more numerous data are collected, no general conclusion can be made. This cautiousness is still more valid in that my study of the American millionaires has shown a somewhat opposite trend: among the deceased generation of the millionaires, only 49 per cent had occupations identical with, or similar to, those of their fathers, while among the living generation of the millionaires, this per cent rises to 72.[40] This suggests that within the same society there may be groups in which inheritance of occupation goes down, while within other groups it increases. This probably is the most correct picture of what is going on in reality. The trend of a decrease of inheritance of occupation means that the occupational status of the population is less and less determined by the occupational status of the father or family; that the caste-tendency decreases; that occupational groups become more and more penetrable; that the general structure of society becomes more and more elastic and flexible; that the occupation of a man is more and more determined by factors other than the family. The opposite trend means the opposite phenomena.

4. INTENSIVENESS OF INTEROCCUPATIONAL SHIFTING IN THE LIFE OF ONE GENERATION

Turn now to the intensiveness of interoccupational shifting within the life of one generation. The principal data unanimously indicate that the present rate of shifting from occupation to occupation is intensive enough. Dr. L. J. Dublin's and R. J.

Vane's study of the wage earners among the policyholders of the Metropolitan Life Insurance Company has shown that 58.5 per cent of them had another occupation at the moment of death than at that of the issuance of the policy. This means that within a few years more than half of these people changed their occupation at least once.[41] Of 24,442 employed boys in New York City at ages from 16 to 18 years 23.6 per cent had no change; 25.7 had one change; 22.8, two; 12.1, three; 6.4, four; 3.3, five; 1.5, six; 1.0, seven; 1.2, eight; 2.4, nine; and more; 50 per cent of the boys held their jobs for less than 6 months.[42] Data concerning 46 Minneapolis business men are as follows: 43.4 per cent of them did not change their occupations; 28.3 changed once; 10.9, twice; 15.2, three times; 2.2, four and more times. The data collected by O. M. Mehus covering 407 alumni of the University of Minnesota who were graduated between 1910 and 1915, have shown that within a period of from 10 to 14 years only 42.5 per cent of them did not change their occupation; 39.5 changed once; 11.5, twice; 5.6, three times; 0.4, four and more times. In total, the percentage of those who changed their occupation at least once in the last two cases is very near the results obtained by Dublin and Vane. Among German factory workingmen, the principal data are as follows: among the workers of one factory, 75 per cent of the men and 45 per cent of the women remained in the same occupation (though in different factories); the remaining percentage changed their occupation at least once.[43] For some other factories we have more detailed data. Among the workers at the ages from 14 to 20 years, 68.9 per cent had no change; 26.4, one change; 4.7, two changes. Among the workers of 41 years and above, 20 per cent had no change; 43.3, one change; 31.7, two changes; 5.0, three and more changes.[44] In another factory for similar age groups of the wage earners, the corresponding data are as follows: no change, 30.1 per cent; from one to three changes, 69.9 per cent; for the age group of 41 years old and above, no change, 8.3 per cent; from one to three changes, 80.8 per cent; from five to ten changes, 11.1 per cent.[45] For still another factory, the percentage of those who did not have any change of their occupation is 55.0 per cent; for those who changed for a similar occupation, 14.2; who changed once for quite a different occupation, 16.7; who changed from two to four times, 12.5; who changed four times and more, 1.6 per cent.[46] Somewhat similar are the data on other factory wage earners.[47]

Further data are given by Austrian and Bavarian occupational statistics. In Austria, from Dec. 31, 1907, to Dec. 31, 1910, 2,661,333 persons, or 9.31 per cent of the gainfully engaged population, changed its occupation (including the newcomers and the retired). According to fundamental occupational groups, in agriculture and forestry, the per cent is 8.64; in industry and artisanship, 19.68; in commerce and transportation, 13.74; in professions and public service, 13.56; in the army, 84.25; in private service, 15.53; and among dependents, 3.60. Side by side with these interoccupational shiftings, many changes took place in the movement from stratum to stratum within each occupation.[48]

For a three-year period, the general index of shifting, 9.31 per cent, is rather high.

The results of the Bavarian census show that in the period from July 31, 1914, to Dec. 31, 1916 (war time), 20 per cent of all gainfully engaged population changed its occupation. For men the percentage is 27, for women 10.8. Here we have the percentage of shifting much higher than that in Austria. This is due probably to the World War.[49]

Further studies show that the factor of the war in general called forth an enormous displacement from occupation to occupation.[50]

In spite of the somewhat fragmentary character of these and some other data, they show that interoccupational shifting within present Western societies is relatively high. In the course of an individual life, it seems that only a small percentage of the population remains in one occupation; the majority change their occupation at least once; a very considerable part changes twice and more.

There is no need to say that the rate of shifting varies strikingly from occupation to occupation, and from one stratum to another within the same occupational group. As to the comparative interoccupational mobility of different occupational groups, the quoted studies suggest the following tentative inferences:[51] *other conditions being equal, first, within the same occupation the more qualified and better paid strata shift less intensively than the less qualified and more poorly paid groups; second, members of occupations which disappear shift more intensively than members of occupations which develop and prosper; third, unskilled labor is more mobile than skilled labor; business and professional groups (their higher strata) are likely to be still more stable even than the group of skilled labor. In a country where agriculture does not rapidly disappear, the occupational mobility of those engaged in agriculture is likely to be low; in a country where agriculture dies out, the shifting of agriculturists to other occupations is likely to be high.* Such seem to be the general rules; they have, however, numerous exceptions. Finally, in each concrete case, the intensiveness of shifting depends *considerably upon the age of the people engaged in an occupation.* Other conditions being equal, shifting is likely to be greater among young people who have recently entered an occupation and are in the process of finding a suitable occupation, and among people at the age of 40 years and over, part of whom become "independent," part retire, and part must shift to easier occupations on account of their age, energy, and health.[52]

Let us now ask what has been the trend in this field? Has the interoccupational shifting within the life of one generation been increasing or decreasing? The data necessary to give the answer are absent. Two or three samples are given which answer the question somewhat positively. Here is an example, concerning Minneapolis business men and their fathers:

Generations		Number of Changes of Occupation in the Life of a Generation, in Per Cent					
		No Change	One Change	Two Changes	Three Changes	Four and More	Total
Group "A"	Fathers	57.2	32.6	8.2	2.0	....	100
	Sons	43.4	28.3	10.9	15.2	2.2	100
Group "C"	Fathers	68.8	24.9	5.8	0.3	0.2	100
	Sons	64.6	29.6	4.5	1.1	0.2	100

Though the occupational career of the sons is far from being finished, while that of their fathers is practically terminated, nevertheless, the interoccupational mobility of the sons is considerably greater than that of the fathers. Some general considerations make such a trend probable. It also is in harmony with a decrease in the transmission of occupation discussed above. But all this is too uncertain to provide a solid basis for a general conclusion. The above trend appears to me as probable and representative for a considerable part of the population; however, this is a mere hypothesis which has to be tested by further investigations on a large scale.

The above shows also that the membership of almost all occupational groups at the present moment is composed of two different elements: one relatively stable and permanent; another permanently changing, entering an occupation for a time and then going out of it. If the above data are representative, then this second element is, and tends to be, more and more numerous. This means that the population of the occupational groups becomes fluid, like water entering a pond from one side and going out from another. Being true in regard to an occupational group, this is true also in regard to large social classes. For instance, in 1913 the influx of newcomers into the German proletariat was about 1,707,000 men, or about 9.26 per cent of the total number of the proletarians. In the same year, 985,000 proletarians left their rank and went to another social class. If there were no growth of this class, its population within 15 years would have been completely changed.[53] This illustrates well the shifting character of the present occupational groups and social classes. Later on the results of such a mobility in the different fields of social life will be discussed.

5. DISPERSION OF THE SONS OF FATHERS WHO BELONG TO THE SAME OCCUPATION THROUGHOUT DIFFERENT OCCUPATIONAL GROUPS, AND RECRUITING MEMBERS OF THE SAME OCCUPATIONAL GROUP FROM DIFFERENT SOCIAL GROUPS AND STRATA

Where are the sons of the fathers of the same occupation going? What other occupation, besides that of their father, do they principally enter? Is there a conspicuous gravitation and

TABLE SHOWING OCCUPATIONAL MOBILITY OF 407 UNIVERSITY GRADUATES (1910 TO 1915) WITH RESPECT TO OCCUPATION OF FATHERS

Occupation of Father	Occupation of Son or Daughter																					
	Farmer		Merchant		Lawyer		Minister		Doctor		Engineer		Teacher		Dentist		House-wife		Miscel-laneous		Total	
	Number	Per Cent	Number	Per Cent	Number	Per Cent	Number	Per Cent	Number	Per Cent	Number	Per Cent	Number	Per Cent	Number	Per Cent	Number	Per Cent	Number	Per Cent	Number	Per Cent of 407
Farmer	5	5.9	2	2.3	14	16.6	3	3.5	10	11.9	5	5.9	20	23.8	2	2.3	3	3.5	20	23.8	84	20.6
Merchant			3	7.5	5	12.5	1	2.5	3	7.5	6	15.0	5	12.5	3	7.5	1	2.5	13	32.5	40	9.9
Lawyer			1	4.3	5	21.7							2	8.6			6	26.	9	39.1	23	5.7
Minister			1	5.2	2	10.5			4	21.			6	31.5					6	31.5	19	4.7
Doctor									6	45.9			2	15.3			1	7.6	4	30.6	13	3.2
Engineer					1	8.3			1	8.3	2	16.6	2	16.6	1	8.3	1	8.3	4	33.3	12	2.9
Teacher	2	18.1											2	18.1					7	63.6	11	2.7
Dentist													3	100.							3	0.7
Miscellaneous			7	3.4	22	10.8			14	6.9	13	6.4	28	13.8	12	5.9	25	12.3	81	40.	202	49.6
Total	7	1.7	14	3.4	49	12.	4	1.	38	9.3	26	6.4	70	17.2	18	4.4	37	9.2	144	35.4	407	100.

MINNEAPOLIS GROUPS, GROUP "A"

Fathers' Occupations	Number of Families	Sons' Occupations									
		Farmers	Professions			Students of Universities and Colleges	Business, Trade, Manufacturing Bankers, Merchants, Storekeepers	Executive Positions	Skilled Artisans	Unskilled and Semiskilled	Total
			Teachers and Principals of Elementary and High Schools	University and College Teachers, Editors, Publishers	Physicians, Veterinarians, Pharmacists, Clergy, Engineers, Artists, Lawyers, Officials						
Farmers	55	*43*	40	3	15	18	23	4	7	10	163
Professions:											
Teachers of elementary and high schools	2	...	*1*	1	2	1	...	...	...	...	5
University and college teachers, editors, etc.	1	...	...	...	...	*1*	...	...	...	...	...
Physicians, clergy, artists, engineers, lawyers, etc.	23	1	10	6	*18*	14	2	2	...	2	55
Business, commerce, manufacturing, banking, merchandizing	33	1	19	4	9	8	*24*	1	7	4	77
Executive positions	6	1	1	2	1	1	1	*1*	...	...	8
Skilled artisans	15	3	5	2	6	6	3	1	*6*	1	33
Unskilled, semiskilled	4	...	1	...	1	2	1	...	1	*2*	8
Total	139	49	77	18	52	51	54	9	21	19	350

GROUP "B"

Fathers' Occupations	Sons' Occupations							
	Number of Families	Farmers	Semi-skilled	Skilled	Semi-professional and Small Business	Professional and Big Business	Unskilled	Total
Farmers	191	*220*	29	85	147	52	15	548
Semiskilled	22	4	*17*	14	15	1	2	53
Skilled	110	7	34	*102*	66	13	15	237
Semiprofessional and small business	160	12	14	37	*131*	50	10	254
Professionals and big business	33	1	2	5	20	*18*	....	46
Unskilled	19	1	7	13	11	1	*9*	42
Total	535	245	103	256	390	135	51	1,180

SCHOLARS OF EVENING CONTINUATION SCHOOLS IN LANCASHIRE AT AGES FROM 15 TO 30 YEARS [54]

Fathers' Occupations	Number of Families	Number of Male Occupied Children	Percentage of Male Children Engaged in Various Occupations								
			Textile	Metal	Building, Woodwork	Mining	Tradesmen	Clerical	Public Authority	Unskilled	Miscellaneous, Mainly Skilled or Business
Textile	538	976	*61.7*	8.9	3.9	......	4.7	10.4	......	4.0	4.4
Metal	387	633	33.3	*33.3*	4.4	......	6.5	4.8	......	4.3	5.4
Building, woodwork	230	400	33.5	13.5	*24.2*	1.2	5.2	9.5	1.0	5.0	6.7
Mining	192	424	33.2	7.5	3.0	*36.0*	4.5	4.	......	5.9	5.4
Tradesmen	274	475	22.5	12.6	5.0	......	*27.4*	18.7	1.9	5.0	5.7
Clerical	78	114	17.5	12.2	1.7	......	3.5	*49.1*	......	......	14.0
Public authority	92	160	38.7	15.6	3.7	......	6.8	21.8	*5.6*	1.8	5.0
Agents, travelers	84	133	26.3	10.5	6.0	4.5	7.5	19.5	1.5	6.7	17.2
Unskilled	234	465	48.0	12.6	4.3	2.6	3.2	8.8	2.8	*10.9*	6.4
Miscellaneous trades (skilled or business)	143	238	37.8	13.8	5.0	......	7.1	13.4	......	2.9	*18.9*
Railway	74	98	39.8	11.2	4.0	......	6.1	22.4	......	4.0	11.2
Unclassified	53	80	28.7	15.0	2.5	......	5.0	25.0	......	3.7	18.7
Total	2,379	4,196	4.00	14.5	6.0	4.3	7.7	13.1	1.2	5.0	8.2

"affinity" between different occupations? Is it manifested in the form of an intensive "exchange" or "circulation" of their members between the related occupations? If such is the case, what occupations are related? On the other hand, from what social strata are recruited the members of the same occupational group? In what proportions? With what intensiveness? Such are the further questions connected with the problem of interoccupational mobility. In order to answer tentatively all these important ques-

Population of Rome (1908) on the Basis of the Data of the Marriage Statistics [55]

Fathers' Occupational Class	Sons' Occupational Class				
	Unskilled	Skilled	Middle Class	Upper Class	Total
Unskilled	*263*	458	104	55	880
Skilled	78	*772*	158	151	1,159
Professions and business (middle class)	19	125	*97*	116	357
Upper class	17	138	84	*497*	731
Total	377	1,488	443	819	3,127

Mannheim Families [56]

Fathers' Occupations	Sons' Occupations					
	Commercial	Artisans	Professions	Common Labor	Agriculture	Total
Commercial	*12*	3	5	6	1	27
Artisans	10	*10*	2	20	6	48
Professions	3	1	*2*	......	......	6
Common labor	2	9	1	*30*	1	43
Agriculture	2	......	......	5	*3*	10
Total	29	23	10	61	11	134

24,442 NEW YORK BOYS AT AGES FROM 16 TO 18 YEARS[57]

Fathers' Occupations	Sons' Occupations (in Per Cent)																
	Professions	Clerical	Business	Executive Positions	Government Service	Building Trades	Metal Trades	Woodwork	Clothing Trades	Clay, Glass, Stone	Printing	Transportation	Food Production and Preparation	Textiles	Leather	Miscellaneous Manufacturing	Unskilled Labor	Total
Professions	*7.7*	37.5	6.4	1.7	0.6	4.1	23	0.3	0.6	1.7	1.7	4.7	0.1	1.3	1.2	1.0	6.4	100
Clerical	3.3	*49.5*	4.8	1.0	0.6	3.7	19	0.9	....	1.6	1.9	4.2	0.4	1.4	1.0	1.3	5.4	100
Business	2.6	40.8	*13.9*	1.6	0.4	2.3	15	0.5	1.2	2.2	2.4	5.1	0.7	1.0	1.5	1.2	7.6	100
Executive positions	2.4	34.8	7.2	*2.7*	0.3	3.3	20.6	0.8	0.5	2.6	2.4	7.6	0.7	1.5	1.1	1.2	10.3	100
Government service	1.9	42.4	6.6	1.2	*0.8*	3.8	16.3	0.4	0.5	2.9	3.9	7.0	1.1	1.5	1.6	0.7	7.4	100
Building trades	2.6	28.7	4.4	1.7	0.3	*8.0*	24.5	1.3	0.8	2.6	3.5	5.7	1.1	1.5	1.4	1.7	10.2	100
Metal trades	2.9	23.6	3.9	1.8	0.2	3.7	*34.0*	1.2	0.5	2.1	4.6	4.7	1.2	1.5	1.4	1.1	11.6	100
Woodwork	2.3	28.4	5.5	2.5	0.2	3.9	24.4	*6.4*	0.5	2.5	2.5	3.6	0.7	2.0	1.4	2.5	10.7	100
Clothing	2.3	39.0	9.7	1.4	0.4	2.7	15.5	0.5	*4.2*	4.5	3.1	3.3	0.9	1.5	1.0	2.0	8.0	100
Clay, glass, stone	3.5	35.0	3.3	0.6	0.6	3.3	20.8	1.5	0.4	*6.9*	4.6	5.4	1.0	1.9	1.9	1.0	8.3	100
Printing	1.2	39.6	5.8	2.3	....	2.0	20.2	0.3	1.2	1.7	*13.0*	3.2	0.3	0.6	0.9	1.4	6.3	100
Transportation	2.4	29.3	3.8	2.2	0.4	3.8	25.2	1.0	0.4	2.4	3.8	*10.8*	0.7	1.3	1.8	1.4	9.3	100
Food production	2.1	25.6	6.8	1.5	0.3	3.7	23.1	1.2	0.7	2.7	3.5	7.2	*6.6*	1.4	2.3	1.9	9.4	100
Textiles	2.3	20.9	5.8	2.0	....	3.8	18.6	1.5	2.3	5.2	2.9	4.7	....	*13.4*	6.1	1.2	9.3	100
Leather	2.9	22.7	5.7	1.8	0.4	1.6	23.3	1.4	1.4	1.9	3.9	4.7	1.4	2.7	*13.9*	2.2	8.1	100
Miscellaneous manufacturing	4.1	30.6	6.7	1.4	0.2	3.8	20.0	0.4	0.8	1.8	4.3	5.2	1.0	1.6	1.7	*6.5*	9.9	100
Unskilled labor	1.8	20.9	4.5	1.3	0.5	4.2	22.8	1.5	1.2	3.0	3.2	6.2	1.6	2.4	2.6	1.3	*21.0*	100
Total	2.6	31.0	6.5	1.7	0.4	4.0	22.4	1.1	1.0	2.7	3.5	5.9	1.3	1.7	1.9	1.6	10.7	100

tions of "social physiology," data of my own and of some other investigations are given. They may throw light upon these problems. The tables answer these questions. (See pp. 429-434.)

There is no use introducing other similar tables, such as the data of Perrin, concerning the occupational status of the fathers of 3,000 men from the English *Who's Who* and *Dictionary of National Biography;* Fritz Maas' data concerning the fathers' occupations of the prominent men of Germany; Fisher's data concerning the occupation of 18,000 persons from the American *Who's Who;* Philiptschenko's similar data concerning the occupations of the fathers of the Russian scientists, scholars, literary men, artists and students; the data of Edwin Clarke, J. McKeen Cattell, A. Odin, and others.[58] In essence they give something similar.

The tables, the mentioned sources, and other material indicated further, give a sufficient basis for a series of inferences. They are as follows:

A. Within present Western societies, children of fathers of the same occupation, and often children of the same family, are dispersed among the most different occupational groups. This is clearly shown by all horizontal lines of the tables. This is corroborated by numerous studies of different authors. Part of the data have been given above in the discussion of the "hereditary transmission of occupation." Since only a part of the children inherit their fathers' occupations, this means that the remaining part enter other occupational groups.[59]

B. Each of the occupational groups at the present moment is recruited from the offspring of the most different groups. This is shown by the vertical columns of the tables. There are numerous other data which indicate the same fact. Here are some of them: The occupational group of teachers in the United States is composed of the offspring of the following occupational classes.[60] (See p. 436.)

I have given above figures showing from what social classes have been recruited American men of science, American literary men, and other notables; English, German, Russian, and French men of science and genius. If we take American money makers

Occupation of Parents	Of Men Teachers, Per Cent	Of Women Teachers, Per Cent
Farmers	69.7	44.8
Professional	7	7.5
Business men	6.2	15.3
Artisans	8	16.4
Laborers	7	11.3
Public officials	0.8	1.8

as an occupational group, we have the following occupational groups from which they have been recruited:[61]

Occupational Groups	Fathers of Deceased American Millionaires	Fathers of Living American Millionaires
Farmers	56	18
Merchants, manufacturers, bankers, financiers, business men	119	186
Physicians	5	2
Teachers and college men	5	2
Engineers	1	4
State officials	9	9
Lawyers, judges	3	7
Workingmen	16	4
Seamen	1	1
Clergymen	10	7
Military men	3	4
Artists, players	0	2
Editors, journalists	0	2
Total	228	248

Among the American farmers in Seneca County, New York, 15.9, and in Minnesota, 14.5 per cent came from other than agricultural occupations.[62] In Livingston, Philadelphia, and Condor counties, from 18 to 30 per cent are the sons of fathers of other than farming occupations;[63] 36.6 per cent of the fathers of the workingmen and women of a Speyer textile factory were artisans and craftsmen; 26.3, peasants; 19.4, factory workers; 5.3, textile factory operators; 0.2, merchants, officials and so on.[64] For the fathers of the operators of another factory (Wollhutindustrie in Luckenwalder) the corresponding data are as follows: 18.2 per cent of the fathers are factory workingmen; 28.9, textile-factory operators; 22.8, artisans; 9.3, farmers; 7.9, agricultural laborers; 10.7, merchants,professionals,and business men; 1.6,not known.[65] The occupations of the fathers of 195 automobile-factory workers in Vienna are: 63 of the fathers were factory workers; 84, artisans and small enterprisers; 23, farmers and farm laborers; 19, state and private employees and officials; 6, professionals and business men.[66] For another machine factory in Vienna, the data are as follows: 15.4 per cent of the fathers were in the same occupation; 13.1, skilled workmen; 20.8, artisans; 13.1, farmers; 16.9, small business, subordinate officials, teachers, and professionals; 14.6, unskilled labor.[67] Other data concerning the working class are similar.[68]

The same may be said of the occupational groups of the high state and municipal officials,[69] professors (of the German and Austrian universities),[70] employees of public and private corporations,[71] and other occupational groups.

A series of investigations in Italy has disclosed similar facts. Each of the studied occupational groups turned out to be recruited from children of fathers who belonged to different occupational groups.[72] Similar facts have been disclosed by the studies of fathers of the factory workers in Russia and Belgium.[73]

There is no use in lengthening the list of these data. It is possible to state certainly that this statement is true for almost all occupational groups of present Western societies. Varying in degree, each of them is recruited from the children of fathers of different occupational status. This is nothing but another side of the fact of the scattering among different occupations of children whose fathers belong to the same occupation—the fact indicated above.

C. The preceding two propositions mean that *in present Western societies different occupational groups are strongly interwoven, and the cleavages between them are considerably obliter-*

ated, or, more accurately, are somewhat indefinite and not clearly cut. Indeed, since one son of a family is an unskilled laborer, another a business man, and the third a physician, it is not easy to decide to what group such a family belongs. On the other hand, since the offspring of the same family or of many families of the same occupational status enter the most different occupations, the cleavages between occupations are thereby considerably obliterated, their "strangeness" toward each other is weakened; their social heterogeneity and repulsion diminished. As a result, the precipice between occupational groups becomes less than it is in a society where such dispersion of the children of fathers who belong to the same occupation does not take place, or is a very rare phenomenon. This means that there is a fallacy in the statement of many theorizers of class struggle who continue to talk about the present social classes as though they were still a kind of caste. They forget completely about the fluid composition of present occupational groups. However, a part of the truth is in their statement. What is it? The answer is given in the next propositions.

D. In spite of the above-shown dispersion among different occupations, the "hereditary" transmission of occupation still exists, and, on the average, it is still high enough. It is likely also that the fathers' occupation is still entered by the children in a greater proportion than any other. It is enough to glance at the horizontal and the vertical columns of the tables to see that in the majority of cases the sons enter the occupation of the fathers in a greater proportion than any other one; on the other hand, that each of the occupations (vertical columns) is recruited principally from the sons of the fathers who have such an occupation. This means that a part of the population, during one or two or more generations, still remains in a régime like a caste-system. Shall we wonder, therefore, that this part has habits, traditions, standards, mores, psychology, and behavior similar to that of a caste-society? Shall we wonder that the cleavages between such "rigid" parts of each occupation are quite clearly cut—economically, socially, mentally, morally, and even biologically? Under specific conditions, such a part of the population may give a real basis for the existence of a class psychology and class antagonisms. To this extent the partisans of the class struggle may have a reason for their theory and aspirations. As an illustration of this, the following fact may be mentioned. Among the German proletariat, the narrow-proletarian psychology and ideology—in the form of social-democratic and communist affiliations—have existed principally among those who have been "hereditary proletarians" or used to remain within this class throughout their life.[74] The same may be said of any "hereditary and non-shifting part" of any occupation.

E. The next basis for the aspirations of partisans of class theories is given by the fact which may be generalized as follows: *The closer the affinity between occupations, the more intensive among them is mutual interchange of their members; and*, vice versa, *the greater the difference between occupations the less is the number of individuals who shift from one group to another.* The tables and other data given previously show that the children of common laborers enter principally occupations of unskilled and skilled labor. Only a relatively small part of them succeed in entering the higher professional occupations, becoming managers and owners of big business enterprises. On the other hand, the children of the professionals and successful business men, in a great majority, enter the professional and business and privileged occupations. Only a small part of them become artisans, skilled, and especially unskilled, laborers. Here we see how "like begets like." Look, further, at the data concerning the fathers of the factory workers in Germany. Only an insignificant part of these laborers have come from the big business and professional classes. Peasants, artisans, and factory workers—such are the classes from which the great majority came. Since such is the case, it is natural that there are cleavages not so much between occupational groups in the narrow sense of the word, as between bigger social subdivisions going on along the lines of the "affine" and "non-affine" occupational subdivisions. In a class composed totally of the affine occupational groups, *e.g.*, of different groups of unskilled and semiskilled labor, there appears and exists a community of interests, habits, morals, traditions, and ideologies considerably different from those of another class composed totally of other affine occupational groups, *e.g.*, of different professional and business groups. These differences, being rein forced by differences in the economic status of such classes, create a basis for what is styled as the present class-differentiation, with its satellites in the form of the class antagonisms and class friction. Thus far the partisans of the class struggle may have a basis for their activity and propaganda.

6. INTEROCCUPATIONAL AND INTRAOCCUPATIONAL ASCENT

The above is closely correlated with the next trait of contemporary interoccupational circulation. *This is the permanent vertical interoccupational and intraoccupational circulation going on within present Western societies.* By this the fact which has been implicitly discussed throughout this chapter is especially stressed. The fluid part of all occupational groups, which shifts from occupation to occupation, or from "promotion" and "demotion" within the same occupation, moves not only horizontally but vertically also. Strong or weak, ascending and descending currents permanently run throughout the occupational structure of present societies. As a result, *among the most privileged occupations or the highest positions of an occupation, we always find individuals who climbed from the lowest occupational strata, and,* vice versa, *among the lowest occupations there almost always are "failures"—descendants of the highest occupational groups.* The proportion of such "upstarts" and "failures" varies from group to group, from place to place, from year to year; but it is a permanent phenomenon of present societies. In periods of revolution and upheaval, such "climbing" and "sinking" takes on a mass character.[75]

As an illustration of the above, other data will be presented here.

United States of America.—Among 885 leading men of science, 10.1 per cent are the sons of clergymen; 7.5, the sons of physicians; 8.3, the sons of teachers; 21.2, the sons of farmers.[76] Socially, as well as economically, the majority of these cases represents a social ascent from the lower occupational positions to the higher ones.

Among 1,000 leading men of letters, 139 have been farmers' sons; 48, the sons of mechanical, clerical, and unskilled occupational groups.[77] These cases are to be regarded also as a social promotion.

Among 248 living American millionaires, 18 are sons of farmers; 4, the sons of laborers; 7, the sons of clergymen; 1, the son of a seaman.[78]

Of all presidents of the United States, 48.3 per cent came from farmers, laborers, and humble professional families.[79]

Of 45 state governors in 1909, 41 were sons of farmers or other humble families. Of 56 cabinet officers (from 1869 to 1903) 47 were farmers' sons. Of 47 railway presidents, 55.4 per cent, again, were country boys. Of all members of the House of Representatives and of the Senate of the United States in 1909, 69.4 per cent were also country-bred boys.[80]

Among 18,356 notables in *Who's Who* in America, in 1922-1923, 23.4 per cent were farmers' sons; 0.4, sons of unskilled laborers; 6.3, sons of skilled laborers.[81] This again may be regarded as a social ascent.

If we take contemporary prominent men in general, we are told that in the seventh volume of Appleton's *Cyclopedia of American Biography,* published in 1901, are included nearly two thousand notices of Americans who have become prominent during the decade that had passed since the first appearance of Appleton's *Cyclopedia of American Biography,* in 1889.[82]

In *Who's Who in America* for 1924 to 1925, there are 2,774 new biographies which were not in the edition of 1922 to 1923. In comparison with the first edition of *Who's Who* in 1899, the number of biographies increased from 8,602 to 25,357, in spite of the fact that since 1899, 9,409 names were omitted owing to death.[83] This shows, to some extent, a permanent "metabolism" of the group of notables; some of its members die out or drop out, and their places are permanently filled by newcomers.

Here are shown the most conspicuous examples of the ascending current. Less conspicuous, but much more general and more important, are mass phenomena of social climbing. They are shown in different forms: in the first place, in the form of the social ascent of new immigrants from lower occupational positions to higher ones; in the second place, in the form of the climbing of tenants and agricultural laborers to the position of farm owner; in the third place, in the form of social promotion of laborers to higher positions within the same occupation or to higher occupations. In this form, the ascending current on a large scale has been flowing throughout the history of the United States, or at least from the eighteenth century to the present day. Here are some data:

The occupations of immigrants from 1890 to 1910 were as follows: 1.4 in professional occupations; 20.2, skilled laborers; 23.4, farm laborers; 35.9, unskilled laborers; 19.1, in other occupations.[84] This shows that a great majority of the immigrants entered the lowest occupations in this country. At their starting point in America they have had, economically and socially, much lower positions than the native-born population. Part of them, however, within their life, and the majority in the second generation, rise to the level of the native-born population of the United States. This is shown by the following data:[85]

PERCENTAGE OF EACH SPECIFIED CATEGORY OF THE MALE BREADWINNERS 18 YEARS OF AGE AND OVER IN THE FOLLOWING OCCUPATIONAL PURSUITS:

Categories of the Population	Unskilled Labor	Miners	Iron and Steel Workers	Textile Operatives	Building Trades	Clerical Pursuits	Salesmen	Professions	Agriculture	Servants	Teachers (Women)
Native born of native parents.....	8.0	1.5	0.8	0.8	5.0	3.4	3.8	64.1	47.3	18.2	10.8
Native born of foreign parents (second generation) .	8.6	2.3	1.9	1.5	6.3	5.7	4.8	17.7	25.9	21.5	7.5
Foreign born (first generation of immigrants).......	14.4	5.1	2.1	2.2	6.2	2.0	2.5	14.4	21.2	37.8	2.0

The table shows clearly the occupational and social ascent of the second generation of the immigrants: it strongly approaches the occupational status of the native born from native parents. Its percentage in the unskilled and low-paid occupations greatly decreases compared with that of the first generation of the immigrants; while the percentage in more qualified and better-paid occupations (clerical, professions, salesmen, agriculture, teachers) considerably increases. All in all, these figures show that the immigrants in the second generation reach almost the occupational status of the native born of native parents. This ascent, judged from the economic standpoint and from the standpoint of the standard of life, is completely corroborated. The corresponding data will be given further.[86] From the above table of H. C. Burdge, we see that only 21.0 per cent of the children of unskilled laborers entered unskilled occupations; all others entered semi-skilled, skilled, business, and professions. Among them, 29.0 per cent entered professions, clerical, business, executive, and governmental service. Similar facts are given by other tables.

As an example of intraoccupational ascent the data concerning the different stages may serve: farmers' boy, hired laborer, tenant, and farmer-owner. W. S. Spillman's study of 2,112 Midwestern farm owners shows that 20 per cent of them started their career as farm boys and passed successively the stages of hired laborer and tenant before becoming farm owners; 13 per cent started as farm boys, became hired men and, finally, farm owners; 32 per cent passed the stages of farm boys and tenants before becoming farm owners. And only 34 per cent passed directly from the stage of farm boy on the home farm to the level of farm owner.[87] Somewhat similar results are given by other investigations.[88]

The picture given by some other countries varies somewhat in detail, but in essence it is similar to that of the United States of America.

England.—The data concerning men of genius in England show that 11.7 per cent of them in the past, and from 7.2 to 4.2 per cent in the first half of the nineteenth century, came out of the labor and artisan class. These cases undoubtedly represent the fact of social ascent. Among the English peerage, baronetage, and aristocracy also, a considerable proportion are people who came from the middle and lower strata and who have risen to very high positions of social service. The same may be said of a considerable number of the highest state officials who, like Lloyd George, Ramsay MacDonald, and many others, successfully climbed to the highest position from the lower social strata. During the last two or three decades, such ascent and "ennobling" seem to have been especially intensive. One of the characteristics of the English aristocracy, during the last two centuries especially, has been that it has been permanently "refreshed" by an infusion of the blood of newcomers from the lower classes. During the last decade such ascent assumed an especially strong character. It is enough to read the yearly list of the king's grants and rewards to see what a considerable number of the newcomers are promoted from the lower to the higher positions each year. Among such names there regularly are people of very modest and humble origin. These cases illustrate the process of conspicuous social climbing.

Side by side with this are numerous ordinary processes of social ascent which go on incessantly on a large scale. From the Chapman table we see that only 10.9 per cent of the children of unskilled labor entered unskilled occupations; all others entered other, more qualified, trades, among them: 3.2 per cent became tradesmen; 8.8, clericals; 2.8, public service; 6.4 entered business and skilled occupations. In general this is undoubtedly social promotion. The same author in another study found that among 63 managers and employers in cotton manufacture, 48, or 76 per cent, have risen from the position of operator in which they started; among 88 employers in the building trade, this percentage was 63; among the directors of the spinning companies, 73 per cent; among other 45 mill managers, 84 per cent; among the managers in another city, the percentage was 13 among the managing directors, and 42 among the managers; among the assistant managers, 67. On the basis of these data the author concludes that "there exists a free channel of no insignificant dimensions through which the directing classes are continually recruited from the wage-earning classes."[89] The concrete figures of the climbers may vary from group to group, but the current itself is active from the bottom to the top of English society.

Germany.—Maas' study has shown that among German leaders in various fields of activity who were born after 1860, there have been 12.4 per cent who came of the labor classes.

Most's study of 479 higher governmental and communal officials in Germany has shown that 34 of them came of the middle official families; 14, from the lowest official ranks; 20, from teachers of the lowest rank; 19, from artisan families; 1, from a labor family.[90]

Of 2,186 university and college professors and Privat-Docents in Germany and Austria, 90 were sons of the officials of the lowest ranks; 74 were sons of teachers; 52, sons of artisans.[91] All these cases are examples of social climbing.

The investigations of J. Conrad, Franz Eulenburg, A. Reinhardt, and the Baden School statistics, concerning the social composition of the students of the universities of Halle, of Leipzig, and of Wurtemberg, in essence give similar results: in the first place, they show that the percentage of the students from the labor and lower classes has been increasing as we approach our time; *e.g.*, in Wurtemberg University, from 1871 to 1911, this percentage increased from 49.7 to 56.7; in the second place, more than half of the students at the end of the nineteenth and the beginning of the twentieth centuries were recruited from social strata such as the labor class, farmers, teachers, artisans, and subordinate officials. As these students after graduation become candidates for the highest positions, these cases are again facts of social climbing.[92]

Among 1,653 persons who between 1898 and 1921 passed the law examination in Baden and were candidates for the high state and communal positions, 139 were sons of teachers of lower ranks; 164, sons of middle officials; 77, of lower officials; 45, of the saloon and hotel keepers (*gastwirte*); 104, of artisans; 5, of common laborers. Of 6,373 *Badishen Lehrerseminaristen* who passed the examinations from 1905 to 1919, 895 were the sons of artisans; 64, of common laborers; 806, of skilled workers, of private and public officials of the lowest ranks.[93]

In the labor occupations, the same facts are seen. Among 4,374 skilled employees studied in the printing trade, 392 were sons of common laborers.[94] Among their grown-up children from 7.47 to 12.4 per cent entered the professions. Among 750 independent. children of skilled workers in Berlin factories: 35 became merchants and salesmen; 4, teachers; 6, bookkeepers; 14, clerks; 15, government officials; 3, dentists.[95] Among the *Deutsche Techniker*—the social stratum higher than the labor class—we have from 7.96 to 18.96 per cent of people whose fathers were common laborers.[96] Among the "employees" in Germany and Austria (clerks, shop assistants, teachers, and other subordinate salaried personnel) there is also a proportion who came from the "lower working classes."[97]

Finally, all quoted studies of industrial laborers in Germany show that among their children from 2 to 10 per cent go to the professions and more qualified occupations, on the one hand; on the other, among the working-class aristocracy there invariably is a percentage of the people who are the sons of unskilled common laborers.[98]

Russia.—Philiptschenko's study of the University and College students in Petrograd, Russia, in 1923-1924, has given the following data concerning the occupation of their fathers and paternal grandfathers:[99]

Generations	Per Cent in Each Specified Occupational Group						
	Qualified Profession	Government Service Military Men	Clergy	Employers, Landowners	Peasants	Common Labor	Total
Fathers of the students......	20.4	32.4	6.8	11.9	19.3	9.2	100
Paternal grandfathers.......	8.9	12.1	9.7	21.7	33.9	13.7	100

These data show a definite social rise of the students' fathers compared with the grandfathers; the percentage of the fathers among the groups of peasants and common laborers is much less, and among the group of the qualified professions and officials is much higher than the corresponding percentages among the grandfathers.[100]

Among contemporary literary men, artists, and musicians in Petrograd there were 9.6 per cent who came of the class of common labor; among contemporary scientists and scholars in

Petrograd, this per cent is 2.7.[101] These facts represent again a phenomenon of social climbing. Among the members of the Russian Academy of Science for the last 80 years, 2.1 per cent rose from the peasantry.[102]

Some data concerning France, Italy, Russia, and other European countries give a general picture very similar to the above.

The survey shows that in present Western societies under normal conditions a permanent ascending—interoccupational and intraoccupational—current has been active. The above data give, to some extent, a quantitative indication of the intensiveness of this process. As an example of intraoccupational ascent may be mentioned the data of the occupational census in Austria, which show that in agriculture, industry, commerce, and transportation, a high per cent of independent (*selbständige*) farmers and promoters come from the ranks of hired laborers and apprentices. In agriculture 50 per cent, in industry 88 per cent, in commerce and transportation 50 per cent of the *selbständige* come out of the lower intraoccupational layers.[103]

7. INTEROCCUPATIONAL AND INTRAOCCUPATIONAL DESCENT

Side by side with the ascending current is a descending one. Its existence is shown everywhere. It is enough to glance at the above tables to see that. It is enough to study the occupational status of the fathers of the members of almost any semiskilled and unskilled occupational group to verify its existence.

The Burdge tables show that 6.4 per cent of the children of professional fathers; 5.4 per cent of those of the clericals; 7.6 per cent of those of the business men; 10.3, of those of the executives; 7.4, of those of the officials, became unskilled laborers. This means a fact of occupational degradation. From the table of Professor Chapman we see that from 1.8 to 6.7 per cent of the children of the skilled, semiskilled, business and clerical fathers entered unskilled labor. Similar facts are given by my table.

For the sake of brevity, I will present here only a few data. More of them may be found in the above-quoted works.

Among 2,943 factory operatives in Berlin studied by Wellman, there were found 339 sons of fathers who belonged to the professions, entrepreneurs, business men and officials. These cases represent a clear fact of intraoccupational and interoccupational sinking. Among 4,374 employees and operatives in the printing industry in Germany, Adelsdorf found 186 sons of fathers with high social standing (prominent professionals, capitalists, business men, and so on). Besides, there were 482 sons of less prominent professionals, business, and merchant fathers; and 1,228 sons of employees and officials and artisans of the lower ranks. If the last group may not be regarded as a case of interoccupational descent, the first two groups seem to give such a case. Among 886 operatives of a Pforzheimer *Bijouterarbeiter,* Jourdan found that 4.9 per cent among the men laborers, and 7.3 per cent among the women operatives, came from the professional, official, and business classes.[104] Among 2,939 skilled workers, studied by Adelsdorf, 14.5 per cent came from the professional, official, business, and executive classes.[105] Further, of 251 cases studied by F. Syrup, there were two cases of clear social descent. Similar facts are given by all studies of the quoted series: "Auslese und Anpassung der Arbeitershaft."

Descending occupational displacement is shown by the American data published by Dublin and Vane and by that of the American Occupational Census analyzed from this standpoint by J. St. J. Heath. Within a few years between the time of issuance of policy and the death of the policyholders, 4 per cent of the painters, 7 per cent of the tailors, 13 per cent of the carpenters—all skilled workers—were driven to unskilled labor.[106] Heath's study of occupational displacement between the census of 1891 and 1901 has led to the conclusion that "a considerable number of artisans are driven from a skilled to an unskilled trade through the pressure of economic forces."[107] In periods of business depression, such a displacement usually takes on very large proportions.[108]

As the greatest social degradation may be taken the cases in which people of qualified occupation and social standing become prostitutes and criminals. Statistics of these "occupations" show that among these classes there are not only people of unskilled and skilled labor, but professionals and business men also. In Germany, *e.g.,* per 100 persons indicted for crimes in 1895, 1.5 per cent were of the officials and professionals.[109] In Italy, per

100,000 professionals, capitalists, pensioners, in 1891 to 1895, there were 288.58 convicts in these classes.[110] The same may be said of prostitution.

In brief, whatever occupational groups are taken, in each are found traces of the existence of the descending current. There are cases where man sinks only from one occupational stratum to the next lower one. There are cases where an individual falls from a relatively high occupational layer to the lowest one. Concrete cases of such "sinking" are known to everybody. In this or that proportion, they happen in everyday life.

8. UNDER NORMAL CONDITIONS, THESE "UPS" AND "DOWNS" GO ON GRADUALLY AND IN AN ORDERLY FASHION, BEING CONSIDERABLY CONTROLLED BY A SOCIAL MECHANISM OF SELECTION AND DISTRIBUTION OF INDIVIDUALS

Except in periods of great upheavals, like the World War or revolutions, the above "ups" and "downs" occur gradually and almost imperceptibly. The considerable vertical displacement of a family or an individual demands, as a rule, in the quickest case, several years, or, more often, one, two or three generations. This is due to the fact that the ascending or descending displacements do not take place without the testing and training of individuals. A climbing fellow must show his ability. Many years of training or work are necessary to acquire it. Hence, the gradual and relatively slow "social promotion" of the climbers. The same is true of the sinking men. Being born in a qualified position, they automatically occupy a place similar to that of their parents. With a rather average ability and work, they may very easily keep it. Social inertia works in their favor. An extraordinary moral or mental failure is necessary for such men to be ousted and displaced. Their first "failure" usually is not enough to produce their degradation. A persistency and recidivism in failure is necessary to call forth such an effect. For all this naturally takes years and years. This explains partly why "ups" and "downs" come gradually.

It must be added that there are many other causes which hinder a sudden and quick vertical displacement. Among them the fundamental rôle is played by a complex of social conditions styled briefly juridical or factual inheritance. Inheritance of wealth, the social position of a family, its traditions, its reputation, all continue to play—juridically and psychologically—a very considerable part. In the speech reactions of a democratic society, they boast that they judge a man only according to his personal qualities. This is true only to some extent. The social standing of a family, its titles, reputation, wealth, its relatives, and so on, still play a very great part in a man's reputation independent of his personal qualities. Among the American upper four hundred, a titled prince of average personal quality is usually preferred as a bridegroom to a brighter, but non-titled, man. The same, with a slight variation, may be said of thousands of similar facts. That titles are highly appreciated in America simply follows from the fact that during recent years hundreds of pseudo-princes and dukes and counts and barons and viscounts have appeared in this country. If there were no demand, evidently there would not have been such an abundant supply, and *vice versa*. For the above reasons it is natural that a considerable proportion of the vertical social displacements through a considerable social distance demand a time span of two or three generations. Another part of such displacements happen within the life of one generation, but demand also a considerable number of years. Here are some facts which illustrate and corroborate these statements. In the first place, many of the above tables show that the greater part of the population which shifts from occupation to occupation, shifts into the next "affine" occupational groups, or enter their parents' occupation; only a relatively small percentage enters occupations very "different" from that of their fathers. This means that a majority do not jump suddenly from a lower occupation to a higher one, omitting the next steps, but move gradually from one step to the next one. In the second place, such graduation has been disclosed by the above data concerning the first and the second generations of the immigrants to the United States. Very similar is the picture given by the studies of the immigrants from the country to the city in several continental studies.

According to Otto Ammon, we have the following picture of

the destinies of the three generations of immigrants from the country to Karlsruhe:[111]

Generation	Per Cent of Each Generation in:			
	Lower Classes	Middle Classes	Professional (*Studierten*)	Total
Immigrants	82	14	4	100
Their sons	41	49	10	100
Their grandsons	40	35	25	100

The figures show a slow upward movement from generation to generation.

Another example is given by Ehrenberg and Racine's study of the three generations of the Krupp Corporation's employees. The social ascent of the second generation in comparison with the first may been seen from the following data:[112]

Generations	Per Cent in Each Specified Occupational Class		
	A. Masters, Merchants, Officers, Professionals	*B.* Foremen, Skilled Workers	*C.* Unskilled, Common Labor
First (176 fathers)	11.9	37.5	50.6
Second (841 independent children)	23.5	64.0	12.5

P. Mombert has given several data which show that the relatively high social positions are filled principally by people from the "middle social positions," and the "middle positions" are filled by climbers from the "lower strata." This shows the graduation of the vertical circulation. Here are some of Mombert's data (in a shortened form). He studied the fathers and grandfathers of 75 higher and 113 lower officials of railroad, post, and telegraph. The results are as follows:[113]

Occupations	Higher Officials		Lower Officials	
	Grand-fathers, Per Cent	Fathers, Per Cent	Grand-fathers, Per Cent	Fathers, Per Cent
High professionals and big business men	6.6	12.0	0.9	0.9
Middle officials, teachers, small business men	70.6	52.0	61.1	31.0
Skilled labor, subordinate employees	20.0	34.6	33.6	61.9
Unskilled	2.8	1.4	4.4	6.2
Total	100.0	100.0	100.0	100.0

The figures show that among the fathers and grandfathers of the higher officials the percentage of the higher occupational groups is considerably greater than among that of the lower officials, while among them the percentage of the unskilled and skilled labor is considerably higher than among the parents and grandparents of the higher officials. This shows that the higher officials more than the lower officials are recruited from higher occupational groups.

Among the independent children of 4,000 skilled and partly unskilled printing operatives, 39 per cent became merchants and salesmen; 21, clerks; 8.9, skilled printers; 31, skilled workers in other trades.[114]

What has been said of the social ascent in the time span of the two or more generations may be said of the social descent.

Side by side with such relatively slow vertical shifting, there are many cases where individuals succeed in crossing a considerable vertical distance within the life of one generation. But even in such cases, many years are necessary before such crossing is accomplished. This is especially true of the upward movement (the downward one, it seems, is somewhat easier). If there were no inheritance of the social status of the family, and if the capacity and ability of the individuals and their chances were equal, then in such an ideal society the following rule would be valid: the greater the vertical distance to be crossed, the longer is the time necessary for its crossing. Then the social distance itself could be measured by the time span necessary for its crossing. As these conditions are absent, therefore the reality shows great deviations from this rule. And yet the reality shows that even in the best conditions, as a rule, there are necessary years and years to "cross a considerable vertical social distance." Here are some facts which illustrate and corroborate this statement:

Berlin's statistics of the occupation of immigrants to the city from the country in 1885 show that from 1 to 15 years, and more, were necessary in order that immigrants might climb considerably up the occupational ladder. While among the immigrants who were in Berlin only 5 years or less, there were only 12 per cent entrepreneurs, and only 5.5 per cent of entrepreneurs who employed more than 5 workmen; among the immigrants who were in Berlin more than 15 years, there were 40.9 per cent of entrepreneurs, and a much greater per cent of large employers.[115] Still more general data are obtained from the statistics of occupation in several countries. They show, first, that the average age of the higher strata (employers and independent) in each occupation is higher than the lower strata (employees and laborers); they show, further, that the average age within professions and business is higher than in agriculture; finally, they show that the percentage of young people is the highest in agriculture and the lowest among the qualified professionals.[116] All this is direct and indirect corroboration of the statement.

Perhaps more conspicuous are the following data which show the age at which hereditary and non-hereditary men ascended to the specified positions. (See p. 454.)

These figures show: first, inheritance of social position by monarchs, as well as by other groups, furnishes the possibility of climbing to a social position at an earlier age (less than one year) than a non-hereditary climber can reach the position. Second, to inheritance of social position is due the fact that the hereditary monarchs, farmers, millionaires, and so on, get their

Average, Minimum, and Maximum Age at Which the Specified Positions Were Reached by Hereditary and Non-hereditary Climbers[117]

Categories of Groups	Average Age at Ascent to Throne, Years	Minimum Age, Years	Maximum Age, Years
Monarchs:			
All (300) monarchs	31.1	0 to 1	80
Non-hereditary monarchs	48.5	25	80
Roman Catholic popes (all elected)	61.3	18	100
French presidents	59.5	47	74
German presidents	59.0	48	78
American presidents	55	43	68
American millionaires:			
Started poor	from 40 to 60	25	61 and above
Started rich	from 20 to 40		
American college men:			
Age of getting Ph.D.	30.2		
Age of gaining reputation by leading men of science	from 30 to 44		
Members of Russian Academy of Science	48.5	27	72
American farmers:			
Age at which they become owners of farms	26.5 [a]		
	36.0 [b]		

[a] Sons of prosperous farmers.
[b] Poor hired men.

social position at an age considerably earlier than does a corresponding non-hereditary climber. Third, the non-hereditary climbers, even such as the owners of farms, reach their position after many years of work and at a relatively mature age.

9. From the above, it follows that *within the same occupational division the average age of the higher intraoccupational strata is likely to be higher than in a lower one.* If this rule is not universal, at any rate, it has a general character. The average age of ascent of the Roman Catholic popes is likely to be higher than that of the cardinals, the cardinals' ages at ascent higher than those of the bishops; the bishops', than those of the priests. The same may be said about the ages of the appointment of generals, colonels, and subordinate officers in an army and about the

ages of men receiving the degrees of Bachelor, Master, and Doctor in scientific fields.

Here are some other data:

AGES OF DIFFERENT CATEGORIES OF GERMAN OFFICIALS [118]

Age Groups, Years	Highest Officials, Per Cent	Middle Officials, Per Cent	Lower Officials, Per Cent
Less than 50	60.9 years	73.6	71.3
50 to 54	15.1	11.3	14.9
55 to 59	10.9	7.6	8.3
60 to 64	8.5	5.7	4.0
65 and over	4.6	1.8	1.5

10. The next statement, which does not need any corroboration, is that *different individuals move in the vertical direction at different velocities.* Some are not able to move at all; some cross a great distance in a period of time in which other individuals can cross only a short distance.

11. On the basis of the propositions of "5" and "8" it seems possible to make the following statement as approximately true: If we subdivide the occupations into the following groups: qualified professional and big business; less-qualified professionals and small business; semiprofessional and clerical; skilled; semiskilled and unskilled; then *the greater the number of the strata to be crossed, the less the number of the ascendants.* The real frequency of the distribution of the ascendants seems to be not very different from this rule—the rule which will be met again in the frequency of distribution of the ascendants from one economic stratum to another.

12. On the basis of some of my data, I am tempted to indicate the following fact which, however, is not a general rule and takes place only within some occupations. Within such occupations *the middle occupational strata seem to be more stable than the extreme ones; the proportion of the children born within the middle strata who shift to another stratum seems to be less than the shifting proportion of the children from the upper and*

lower occupational classes. Here are some data. The quoted study of Ehrenberg and Racine concerning the Krupp employees shows that among the sons of fathers who belong to Class A (*Meister, Kaufleute, Beamte,* and *Studierte*) only 50.9 per cent remained in the same class; among the sons of the lowest class C (*Ungelernte, Arbeiter, Tagelohner,* and *Hilfsarbeiter*) this percentage is only 18.8; while among the middle class B (*gelernte und angelernte Arbeiter, Vorarbeiter*) the percentage is 70.1. This shows that from the middle stratum a considerably less percentage shifted away than from either extreme groups. Those who shifted from class A went downward to the lower classes B and C; those who shifted from class C went upward to classes B and A; those who shifted from class B went in both directions, to classes C and A. This suggests another rule: somewhat opposite to the "rich become richer and the poor become poorer"; in social shifting, *for the highest occupational strata the chances to go down are much greater than the chances to go up, while for the lowest occupational strata the rule is reversed.* In the field of economic vertical circulation, we will meet the same rule. Both rules are not general; but they are worth mentioning to show the non-generality of the popular statement that "the rich become richer."

13. *These "ups" and "downs" go on quite differently in periods of great social upheaval, especially in time of revolution. Here they have a sudden and anarchic character, are free from graduality, proceed more rapidly, and have a mass character.* The validity of this statement has been shown before.[119] In time of revolution the "ups" and "downs" are anarchic and do not have a really selective character in the first period of revolution. In time of war or reform movements they are also intensive, but, unlike time of revolution, have usually an "orderly" and "tested" character.[120]

14. FALLACY OF THE ONE-SIDED EUGENISTS AND RADICALS

The fundamental inference from the above is that the present occupational and social strata biologically represent a conglomeration of people recruited from the most different classes. Among the "aristocratic" or "upper" strata there are many offspring of fathers and grandfathers who belonged to the lower classes. And, *vice versa,* the strata of the skilled and unskilled laborers contain a considerable percentage of "failures" from the upper layers. Within two or three generations, a considerable part of the population of each stratum biologically changes. The practical significance of this is evident. Only two inferences will be briefly mentioned here.

If the present upper classes represent a *mixtum compositum* recruited from the capable people of all classes, it is rather fallacious to depict them as the offspring of long-existing aristocratic families who for many generations have been separated from the common people, as many eugenists and many radicals do. Neither the attacks of the radicals against the "caste-aristocracy," nor the exaggerated eugenical dithyrambs to the upper classes as the offspring of a long-existing hereditary aristocracy seem to be warranted by the facts. Such aristocracy composes a small fraction of the present upper classes. On the other hand, since the class of the proletariat is recruited principally from the failures of the upper strata[121] and from the less intelligent elements of the lower classes incapable of ascent, the real significance of such slogans as "the dictatorship of the proletariat" is evident. With the exception of a small talented section within this class, this means the dictatorship of people who are less intelligent and capable, who are failures, who have many defects in health, in character, in mind, and who do not have an integrity of human personality. The inevitable result of such a dictatorship is disintegration of a society controlled by such "leaders," and aggravation of the situation of the proletariat itself, in the first place. He who wants these results may long for a "dictatorship of the proletariat." It certainly leads to these results.

[1] *The Imperial Gazetteer of India,* Vol. I, p. 314.

[2] Mazzarella, "Le forme di aggregazione sociale nell' India," *Rivista italiana di sociologïa,* pp. 216-219, 1911.

[3] Bouglé, Charles, *Essais sur le régime des castes, passim,* 1908, and *La Démocratie devant la science,* p. 151. See also Senart, *Les castes dans l'Inde,* Paris, 1896.

[4] See *e.g., Laws of Manu,* Vol. X, pp. 74 *et seq.; Apastamba,* I.I.I. 1-11; II, 5, 10, 4-11.

[5] *The Imperial Gazetteer of India,* Vol. I, p. 314.

[6] See Spencer, Herbert, *Principles of Sociology,* Pt. VII, Chap. XIV; Maunier, R., "Vie religieuse et vie économique," *Revue International de Socio-*

logie, January, 1908; BOUGLÉ, CHARLES, "Remarques sur le régime des castes," *L'Année Sociologique,* pp. 4 *et seq.,* 1900; CHESSA, F., *Trasmissione Ereditaria delle professioni,* pp. 1-23, Torino, 1912; LOWIE, R. N., *op. cit.,* pp. 345-357.

[7] Several writers, among them R. Maunier, have concluded that there is an historical trend toward a disappearance of the hereditary transmission of occupation from the father to his sons. "When the first occupations differentiated, they regularly assumed the form of an exclusive monopoly of a definite family. . . . As we proceed towards more civilized societies, the intensiveness of occupational differentiation among families diminishes." Monopolization and the prohibition against changing an occupation disappear. Correspondingly, inheritance of occupation from the father by his children tends to disappear also. MAUNIER, R., *op. cit.,* pp. 33-36. Though, as I will show further, within Western societies during the last century there seems to have existed a trend toward a decrease of inheritance of occupation, nevertheless, I do not think that the above "eternal" trend really exists, nor that its existence has been proved. As I mentioned above, in India at the earliest stages of its history the caste-system seems not to have existed. It appeared only later on. In the history of ancient Rome, the rigid hereditary attachment to an occupation appeared not at the earlier but in the latest stages of Roman history. The Guild system of the Middle Ages assumed a rigid hereditary character, not at the beginning, but rather at the end of the Middle Ages. These facts, not to mention many others, are enough to question Maunier's "eternal trend." Therefore, the trend of a decrease of transmission of occupation from the father to his children, which is to be discussed further, must not be understood as a real perpetual tendency. It may be only a temporary trend which in the future may be superseded by the opposite one.

[8] This is one of the further symptoms of the increasing atrophy of the social functions of the family.

[9] Unpublished study and Master's thesis of M. Tanquist prepared in my seminar. Preliminary results.

[10] DAVENPORT, CHARLES, "Naval Officers," *Publications of the Carnegie Institute,* pp. 10-19, Washington, D. C., 1919.

[11] BURDGE, H. C., *Our Boys,* p. 327, Military Training Commission, 1921.

[12] SOROKIN, P., "American Millionaires and Multimillionaires," p. 635.

[13] YOUNG, E. C., "The Movement of Farm Population," *Cornell University Agricultural Experiment Station Bulletin* No. 42, pp. 16-21.

[14] GILLETT, R., "A Study of Farm Labor in Seneca County," *Agricultural Bulletin* No. 164, Albany, 1924; ZIMMERMAN, C., The *Migration to Towns and Cities, American Journal of Sociology,* Vol. XXXII, pp. 452-453.

[15] CHAPMAN, S. J., and ABBOTT, W., "The Tendency of Children to Enter Their Fathers' Trades," *Journal of the Royal Statistical Society,* Vol. LXXVI.

[16] PERRIN, E., "On the Contingency Between Occupation in the Case of Fathers and Sons," *Biometrika,* Vol. III, pp. 467-469.

[17] CHESSA, F., *op. cit.,* p. 28.

[18] CONRAD, J., *Die Deutsh. Universitäten für die Universitätsaustellung in Chicago,* Berlin, 1893.

[19] MAAS, F., *Über die Herkunftsbedingungen der Geistigen Führer,* p. 169.

[20] CHESSA, FRITZ, *op. cit.*

[21] EHRENBERG and RACINE, "Kruppshe Arbeiterfamilien," *Archive für exacte Wirtschaftsforschung,* 6 Erg. Bd., 1912.

[22] The quoted volumes of "Auslese und Anpassung der Arbeiterschalft," *Schriften des Vereins für Sozialpolitik.*

[23] See *Revue International de sociologie,* pp. 52-53, 118-119, 1900.

[24] See *Revue International de sociologie,* pp. 52-53, 118-119, 1900.

[25] Philiptschenko, *op. cit., Bulletin* No. 1, p. 28.

[26] See PERRIN, E., "On the Contingency Between Occupation in the Case of Father and Sons."

[27] CHAPMAN, S., and ABBOT, W., "The Tendency of Children to Enter Their Fathers' Trades," *Journal of the Royal Statistical Society,* Vol. LXXVI, pp. 599-604.

[28] BURDGE, H. C., *op. cit.*, p. 327.

[29] SORER, R., "Auslese und Anpassung in einer Wiener Maschinenfabrik," *Schriften des Vereins für Sozialpoltik,* Bd. 135, p. 254.

[30] HERRMANN, E., "Auslese und Anpassung der Arbeiterschaft in der Woolhutindustrie," *Schriften des Vereins für Sozialpolitik,* Bd. 135, p. 60.

[31] BERNAYS, M., "Auslese, etc.," *Schriften des Vereins für Sozialpolitik,* Bd. 133, pp. 232-233.

[32] MORGENSTERN, M., "Auslese, etc.," *Schriften des Vereins für Sozialpolitik,* Bd. 135, pp. 57-58, Leipzig, 1912.

[33] See CHESSA, F., *Trasmissione Ereditaria dei Professionel,* pp. 64-65.

[34] The opinions of René Worms, Delbet, Limousin, Monin, and Zizek. See *Revue international de sociologie,* pp. 52-57, 118-125, 198-199, 1900.

[35] In another form they are corroborated by Dr. L. J. Dublin's data for occupational shifting within the life of an individual in the United States. The average percentage of industrial policyholders who were in the same occupation at the moment of their death as that they had held at the moment of issuance of policy is 41.5 per cent; for the "professionals" it is 71.4; for the skilled workers it is considerably higher than for the unskilled ones. See DUBLIN, L. J., and VANE, R. J., "Shifting of Occupation," *Monthly Labor Review,* pp. 37-38, April, 1924. See further Sec. 4 of this chapter.

[36] "Hereditary" everywhere means "social transmission" of occupation from the father to the son, not the "biological inheritance."

[37] Under "occupation" everywhere is meant principal occupation.

[38] CHESSA, F., *op. cit.*, p. 120.

[39] YOUNG, E. C., *op. cit.*, p. 39.

[40] SOROKIN, P., "American Millionaires and Multimillionaires," p. 635.

[41] DUBLIN, L. J., and VANE, R. J., "Shifting of Occupations Among Wage-earners, etc.," *Monthly Labor Review,* pp. 137-138, April, 1924.

[42] BURDGE, H. C., *op. cit.*, p. 198. Here the figures are higher, partly because the data do not differentiate between a change of occupation and simple labor turnover.

[43] "Auslese und Anpassung der Arbeiterschaft," *Schriften des Vereins für Sozialpolitik,* Vol. 135, Dritte Teil, pp. 54-56.

[44] *Ibid.*, pp. 174-175.

[45] *Ibid.*, Bd. 135, Vierter Teil, p. 36-37.

[46] *Ibid.*, p. 208.

[47] See other volumes of the same series.

[48] LEOPOLD, M., "Statistik des Berufswechsel," *Allgemeinen Statistisches Archiv,* Bd. 14, Heft 1 and 3, p. 131; SORER, W., *Zählung des Berufswechsels in Osterreich, ibid.*, Bd. 10, 1916-1917.

[49] LEOPOLD, M., *ibid.*, pp. 126-127; *Beiträge zur Statistik Bayerns,* Heft 89.

[50] See some data in the work of M. Leopold and other sources indicated here.

[51] See the figures in the quoted sources.

[52] See BÖHMERT, W., "Das Berufschicksal der Arbeiter" and "Angestellten nach Uberschreitung des 40 Lebensjahres," *Zeitschrift der Arbeiterfreund,* 1913; SCHWARZ, O., *op. cit.*, pp. 138 *ff.*

[53] LURIE, *Sostav Proletariata,* pp. 5-6, Petrograd, 1918.

[54] CHAPMAN, S. J., and ABBOT, W., *Journal of Royal Statistical Society,* Vol. LXXVI, pp. 599-604, 1912-1913.

[55] GINI, C., and CHESSA, F., *op. cit.*, p. 28.

[56] CHESSA, F., *op. cit.*, p. 120.

[57] BURDGE, H. C., *op. cit.*, p. 327.

[58] See their works quoted above and further.

[59] See also HOAG, E. F., *The National Influence of a Single Farm Community,* Washington, D. C., 1921. The work gives a microscopic picture of the dispersion of people from a farm community.

[60] COFFMAN, L. D., *The Social Composition of the Teaching Population,* p. 73, New York, 1911.

[61] SOROKIN, P., "American Millionaires and Multimillionaires," p. 635.

[62] GILLETT, R. L., *op. cit.*, p. 59; ZIMMERMAN, C., *op. cit.*

[63] YOUNG, E. C., *op. cit.*, pp. 46-47.

[64] "Auslese und Anpassung der Arbeiterschaft," Bd. 135, Teil III, p. 206.

[65] *Ibid.*, Bd. 135, Teil IV, p. 30.

[66] *Ibid.*, Bd. 135, Teil I, pp. 73-74.

[67] *Ibid.*, Bd. 135, Teil I, pp. 188-192.

[68] See other volumes of the same series. See further the quoted works of Abelsdorf, Wellman, Rassback, Jourdan, Günther, P. Mombert, O. Most, and others.

[69] See MOST, O., *Zur Wirtscharts- und Sozialstatistik der Höheren Beamten in Preussen, passim,* Leipzig, 1916.

[70] See EULENBURG, FRANZ, *Der Akademische Nachwuchs,* 1908; MOMBERT, P., "Zur Frage der Klassenbildung," *Kölner Vierteljahrshefte für Sozialwissensh.*, I Jahrgang, Heft 3, pp. 40-44, and *Die Tatsachen der Klassenbildung;* SCHMOLLER, G., *Jahrbuch für Gesetzgebung,* etc., pp. 93-122, 1920.

[71] GÜNTHER, AD., *Die Deutsche Techniker,* Vols. I and II, Leipzig, 1912; BUELENS, J., *Les Employés en Allemagne,* Anvers, "Veritas," 1913, and *Les Employés en Autriche,* Anvers, 1914.

[72] See GINI, C., *I fattori demografici;* CHESSA, F., *op. cit., passim.*

[73] See KOVALEVSKY, M., *Le régime économique de la Russie,* p. 207, Paris, 1908; *vide Étude statistique des familles ouvrières,* p. 109, Bruxelles, 1909.

[74] See LURIE, *Sostav Proletariata,* p. 9; see also the series "Auslese und Anpassung der Arbeiterschaft," *Schriften des Vereins für Sozialpolitik.*

[75] See SOROKIN, P., *Sociology of Revolution,* Pt. III.

[76] CATTELL, J. MCKEEN, *American Men of Science,* 3d ed., p. 784.

[77] CLARKE, *op. cit.*, p. 74.

[78] SOROKIN, P., "American Millionaires and Multimillionaires," p. 635.

[79] SOROKIN, P., "Monarchs and Rulers."

[80] SPILLMAN, W. J., "The Country Boy," *Science,* pp. 405-407, Sept. 24, 1909.

[81] FISHER, S., *op. cit.*, p. 553.

[82] Appleton's *Cyclopedia of American Biography,* preface, Vol.. VII.

[83] *Who's Who in America,* preface, 1924-1925.

[84] *Reports of the United States Immigration Commission,* Washington, D. C., 1911, Sixty-first Congress, Third Session, *Senate Documents,* Vol. VII, p. 101, 1910-1911.

[85] *Ibid.*, pp. 780-819.

[86] See many other instructive details in the same publication, and in *Twenty-third Annual Report of the Commission of Industrial Statistics of the State of Rhode Island,* pp. 332 *et seq.*, Providence, 1910. . . . See also accurate remarks of LESCOHIER, DON, *op. cit.*, pp. 251 *et seq.*

[87] SPILLMAN, W. S., "The Agricultural Ladder," *The American Economic Review,* Vol. IX, No. 1, *Supplement,* pp. 171 *et seq.*

[88] See ELY, R. T., and GALPIN, CHARLES J., "Tenancy in an Ideal System of Landownership," *ibid.*, pp. 180-212; YOUNG, E. C., *op. cit.*, Pts. II and III; GILLETT, R. L., *op. cit.*, pp. 58-64; HOAG, E. F., *The National Influence of a*

Single Farm Community, pp. 35 *ff*., Washington, D. C., 1921; ELMER, M., *op. cit.*, p. 37.

[89] CHAPMAN, S. J., and MARQUIS, F. J., "The Recruiting of the Employing Classes from the Ranks of the Wage-earners in the Cotton Industry," *Journal of the Royal Statistical Society*, pp. 293-306, 1912. This and the further material show the fallacy of such a statement as this: "In Europe, the boy is as a rule brought up to follow his father's occupation; he does not try to rise above his class." CALHOUN, A., *A Social History of the American Family*, Vol. III, p. 132. In America generally they exaggerate the "European feudalism and caste-régime."

[90] MOST, O., *op. cit.*

[91] EULENBURG, FRANZ, *Der Akademische Nachwuchs.*

[92] See CONRAD, J., *Des Universitätsstudium in Deutschland wahrend der letzten 50 Jahre*, Jena, 1884; EULENBURG, F., *Die Entwicklung der Universität Leipzig in den letzen 100 Jahren;* REINHARDT, A., *Das Universitätsstudium der Wurtemberger seit der Reichsgrundung.*

[93] MOMBERT, P., *Zur Frage der Klassenbildung*, pp. 40-44.

[94] ABELSDORF, W., *Beiträge zur Sozialstatistik der Deutschen Buchdrücker*, Tübingen, 1900.

[95] WELLMAN, *Abstammung, Beruf und Heerersatz*, Leipzig, 1907.

[96] See GÜNTHER, AD., *Die Deutschen Techniker;* see MOMBERT, P., *op. cit.*, p. 107.

[97] See BUELENS, J., *Les Employés en Allemagne*, and *Les Employés en Autriche.*

[98] See the volumes of "Auslese und Anpassung der Arbeiterschaft," *Schriften des Vereins für Sozialpolitik.*

[99] PHILIPTSCHENKO, *op. cit., Bulletin* No. 2, pp. 30-36.

[100] PHILIPTSCHENKO, *op. cit., Bulletin* No. 2, pp. 30-36.

[101] *Ibid.*, no. 2, pp. 11-12.

[102] *Ibid.*, no. 3, p. 35.

[103] LEOPOLD, M., *op. cit.*, p. 131.

[104] See MOMBERT, P., *op. cit.*, p. 103.

[105] ABELSDORF, W., *Die Wehrfähigheit zweier Generationen*, etc., Berlin, 1905.

[106] DUBLIN, L. J., and VANE, R. J., *op. cit.*, pp. 40-41.

[107] HEATH, "Underemployment and the Mobility of Labor," *Economics Journal*, pp. 202-211, 1911.

[108] See LESCOHIER, DON, *op. cit.*, pp. 23 *et seq.*

[109] MAYR, G. VON, *Moralstatistik*, p. 819.

[110] PARMELEE, M., *op. cit.*, p. 82.

[111] AMMON, OTTO, *Gesellschaftsordnung*, p. 145.

[112] EHRENBERG and RACINE, *op. cit.*

[113] MOMBERT, P., "Zur Frage der Klassenbilding," pp. 42-44. See here other data.

[114] Paper of HENKE, HANS, "Auslese und Anpassung der Arbeiter in Buchdrückgewerbe," p. 192, Leipzig, 1910.

[115] BRÜCKNER, "Die Entwicklung der grossstadtischen Befolkerung," *Allgemeinen Statisches Archiv*, Vol. I, p. 645.

[116] "Im grossen und ganzen gelangt die Untersuchung zu dem erfreulichen Ergebnis, das der Prozentsatz der Selbständigen in den drei Berufsabteilung (the Selbständigen, the Angestellten and the Lohnarbeiter) mit dem Alter regelmassig zunimmt." Such is the conclusion of Dr. Schwarz, who has studied the correlation of the age and occupational position. This is true in regard to the successful climbers, but cannot be applied to those who do not climb. Having reached a definite age (40 to 50 years old), they are exhausted

and often go down (factory workers and common laborers). See SCHWARZ, O., *op. cit.*, pp. 138-145.

[117] See the sources in SOROKIN, P., "The Monarchs and the Rulers," *Journal of Social Forces,* March, 1926; SPILLMAN, W. S., *The Agricultural Ladder,* pp. 170-179; HOLZINGER, K. J., "Higher Degrees of College Professors," *Journal of the American Statistical Association,* Vol. XVIII, p. 879; CATTELL, J. MCKEEN, *American Men of Science,* 2nd ed., pp. 575-581; SOROKIN, P., "American Millionaires and Multimillionaires"; see also GILLETT, R. L., *op. cit.,* pp. 59-62.

[118] *Allgemeinen Stat. Archiv,* Bd. 14, pp. 249-254; see also SCHWARZ, O., *op. cit.,* pp. 138-145.

[119] See facts and detailed analysis in SOROKIN, P., *Sociology of Revolution,* Pt. III, Chap. XV, Par. 5.

[120] See the quoted work of M. Leopold, which gives the statistical material of great occupational displacements during and after the World War.

[121] See about this in a very careful study of the failures from the upper strata in connection with their defects of character and integrity by JONES, D. C., "An Account of an Inquiry into the Extent of Economic Moral Failure," *Journal of the Royal Statistical Society,* pp. 520-533, 1913.

[A few days ago Professor W. A. Anderson sent me the results of his study of intra- and interoccupational mobility of 319 graduates of North Carolina State College. The results are practically identical with my own published in *The Publications of American Sociological Society,* Vol. XX, pp. 236-240.]

CHAPTER XVIII

VERTICAL MOBILITY WITHIN WESTERN SOCIETIES (*Continued*)

SHIFTING ON THE ECONOMIC LADDER

LACK of necessary data does not allow the answering of the questions raised by the principal problems of present-day economic mobility in general. All that it is possible to cite are a few fragmentary data which may or may not be typical.

1. TRANSMISSION OF ECONOMIC STATUS FROM FATHER TO SON

The index of identity for the economic status of father and son depends on the statistical subdivision of income groups. If such subdivisions are very detailed (*e.g.*, \$500, \$600, \$700, etc.) the percentage of transmission of economic status will be lower than in a case where the subdivisions are less detailed (*e.g.*, \$500, \$1,000, \$1,500, etc.). This statistical factor does not have a serious significance in all compared cases but it influences the percentage of transmission if the subdivisions are different. This must be kept in mind in the interpretation of later data.

My studies of the group of students and professors at the University of Minnesota and of Minneapolis business men disclosed the results given in the following table. (See p. 464.)

In the student-professors' group, the income groups are less than \$500, from \$500 to \$3,000, \$3,000 and more; in the miscellaneous group the subdivisions are more detailed: less than \$700, from \$700 to \$1,200, from \$1,200 to \$2,000, from \$2,000 to \$5,000, \$5,000 and more. The difference in subdivisions is responsible for the difference in the percentage in identical status in both groups.

The table shows that, in contrast to the inheritance of occupational status, no trend toward a decrease of the transmission of the

STUDENTS' AND PROFESSORS' GROUPS

Generations	Number of Cases Studied	Number of Cases in Which Son's Economic Status Is Identical with That of Father	Percentage of Identical Economic Status of Father and Son
Paternal grandfather and father.....	127	82	64.6
Father and propositi...............	123	82	66.6
Father and all his sons (independent)	414	305	73.7

TANQUIST-SOROKIN'S MISCELLANEOUS GROUP

Generations	Number of Cases Studied	Number of Cases in Which Son's Economic Status Is Identical with That of Father	Percentage of Identical Economic Status of Father and Son
Paternal grandfather and father.....	349	113	32.3
Father and propositi...............	424	145	34.2
Father and all his sons (independent)	1,150	444	38.6

economic status from father to son exists here as we proceed from the generation of the grandfathers to that of the propositi. This means that changes in the economic status of father and son have not been increasing during three generations, within the group studied. The next data concern American millionaires and multimillionaires. They are as follows:[1]

ECONOMIC STARTING POINT OF AMERICAN MILLIONAIRES

Generations of the Millionaires	Started Life Poor		Started Life Neither Poor Nor Rich		Started Life Rich		Total	
	Number	Per Cent	Number	Per Cent	Number	Per Cent	Number	Per Cent
Deceased generation..	111	38.8	90	31.5	85	29.7	286	100.0
Living generation....	72	19.6	102	27.7	194	52.7	368	100.0

This table testifies again rather in favor of an increase than of a decrease of the hereditary transmission of economic status within the group studied. The figures show an increase of rigidity of the rich American class. The percentage of those who started their career poor is twice as high in the deceased as in the living group. The percentage of those who started their career rich is also almost twice as high in the living as in the deceased group.

For England we have F. G. D'Aeth's study of the economic status of 254 sons of 85 fathers. Income groups are as follows:

18 shillings a week	£300 a year
25 shillings a week	£600 a year
45 shillings a week	£2,000 and more a year
£3 a week	

Of 254 independent sons of these fathers, 185 have an economic status similar to that of their fathers. This gives 72.8 per cent of the transmission of economic status from father to sons.[2] The percentage is very near to this for the sons of the Minneapolis students-professors' group.

To what extent these data are representative I cannot say. If it is taken into consideration that the intensiveness of shifting from one economic status to another seems to tend toward an increase in periods of economic "booms" and social upheavals; and if it is agreed that since the end of the nineteenth century and up to 1915 such "booms" have practically ceased in the history of the United States because of diminution of the natural resources of the country and the increase of the population, then, perhaps the above results do not appear altogether strange and improbable.

2. SOME TENTATIVE HYPOTHESES

In this field, however, the final index of transmission of economic status is not very important because within the life of one generation the economic status of almost any individual fluctuates continuously to some degree. The complex character of the present economic processes calls forth the incessant "ups" and "downs" of an individual along the ladder of wealth and poverty. There are not many people whose real income has remained unchanged during a few months or during a few years. Slight or great variations are quite normal phenomena. To measure all these fluctuations quantitatively seems to be impossible on account of lack of data and the very complex character of the fluctuations. It is much more important to formulate some regularities in this field, if such regularities exist. On the narrow basis of the material collected by me and by some others, I venture to state the following proposition as a tentative hypothesis:

1. *Shifting from one economic status to another as it affects the number of the shifted people, as well as the rapidity and intensiveness of the process, tends to increase in periods of social upheaval, war, political and social revolutions, and rapid industrial and commercial transformations due to great inventions, discoveries and the like.*

The first corroboration of this statement is found in the conditions during the World War and the revolutions incident to it. Within four years, from 1914 to 1918, in Russia almost all the well-to-do and rich classes were made poor while a great many poor became rich. "Who has been nothing has become everything" (as "The International" runs), and *vice versa.* Within four years the entire classes of landlords and well-to-do farmers, entrepreneurs, merchants, bankers, business men, well-to-do or high-salaried state and private officials, employees, intelligentsia, and professionals, not to mention the nobility and gentry—in brief all the higher economic layers—were cut off and turned into poor people. On the other hand, a great many Communists, new business men, profiteers, swindlers, and underhanded dealers, who before the war and the revolution had not been anything, now became *nouveaux riches.*[3] This is a real social cataclysm or economic shifting in practically all European, and partly even in so tremendous, but still extraordinary, has been the vertical economic shifting in practically all European, and partly even in American societies, during the last ten years.

In the first place, it manifested itself in the European Agrarian Revolution which in Esthonia, Latvia, Lithuania, Poland, Rumania, Czechoslovakia, Bulgaria, Greece, Jugoslavia, and partly in Germany led to an annihilation and impoverishment of the class of landlords. Their estates, buildings, implements, and cattle were taken from them, either without any remuneration or by giving in exchange a half-fictitious one many times lower than the normal value of their loss. In this way within a few years no less than 125,000,000 acres of land were taken and given to other than their previous owners. This means that, beside the sudden impoverishment of a whole class, there was an enrichment of the people who were benefited by the reform.[4] Such an "earthquake" does not occur in normal periods within a short period of time.

Side by side with this great displacement of landed property, we have witnessed many other extraordinary shifts of economic values from individual to individual and from group to group. During the World War many rich people became bankrupt, while many profiteers and "shrewd" dealers became rich. On the other hand, the fluctuations of income of a great many people seem to have become much greater. Later on, in connection with the revolutions and the depreciation of money in several countries, the vertical shifting along the economic ladder became still more intensive; some groups were ruined; some others profited enormously. As a result, during these years, the shifting of wealth, the sinking of some groups and the climbing of others was extraordinary. Here are some illustrations and facts. As an example, take Germany. In the first place, the annulment of the State and Communal bonds led to enormous financial losses to all private persons who had invested their wealth in this manner. In the second place, payment, with the depreciated money, of mortgages which before the World War amounted to fifteen billion gold marks, represented another form of shifting of an enormous amount of wealth from one group to another. In the third place, the restriction put on house owners led to great losses for them and to an extraordinary enrichment of those, including many foreigners, who bought the houses literally for nothing. In this way in Berlin about one-fourth of all the houses passed into new hands. In the fourth place, all persons and corporations that paid their financial obligations with the depreciated money profited greatly thereby at the cost of their creditors. The total amount of such obligations in Germany was about five billion gold marks.[5]

Add to this swindling on money exchange, the strongest fluctuations in the value of paper money, various bonds, and so on; then take into consideration the fact that hundreds of thousands of people participated in the brokers' game, and a picture of this greatest economic mobility will become somewhat clearer. Is it any wonder, therefore, that many people within these few years rose from nothing to positions of captains of industry and finance, while many others were ruined? A few figures demonstrate the point. The net income of the Krupp corporation from 1913 to 1914 increased from 33,900,000 to 86,400,000 marks. The Köln-Rottweilschen firm whose net income was 4,400,000 marks in 1913, in 1915 had 14,500,000. Similar "ups" came to many other firms. It was not a rare phenomenon for the net income of a firm to surpass its capital. The Gasapparat-and-Gusswaren-A.-G. Mainz whose capital was 1,300,000 marks, in 1915 had an income of 3,600,000 marks.[6]

Shall we wonder that within these years many, who did not have anything before, or had very little, became millionaires and multimillionaires? And some of them had time after their extraordinary success to fail again. Names like Otto Wolff, Ottmar Strauss, Hugo Stinnes, Otto Markiewicz, Hugo Herzfelds in Germany; like C. Castiglioni, Siegmund Bosel, and Bronners in Austria, and the captains of industry and finance in other European countries give conspicuous examples of these mad "ups" and "downs" in the field of economic mobility. On the other hand, many previously rich people—the princes and members of many royal families in the first place—were ruined.[7] Similar shifts occurred within other belligerent and neutral countries. Besides the shiftings of wealth within a country, this condition has manifested itself in the form of extraordinary shifts from country to country. This may be seen from the figures on p. 469, which give an approximate idea of what has happened in this respect.[8]

From the above and similar data it is possible to say that these years of upheaval have been followed by extraordinary economic "ups" and "downs" in European and American societies.

For the United States we have a somewhat microscopic picture of this extraordinary "dance" of incomes. The conclusion of Edward White corroborates my statement:

During this period (of the Great War) incomes were affected more violently because of the unprecedented economic upheaval than is general in a normal time.[9]

Countries	The National Wealth in Billions of Dollars	
	1912–1913	1920–1921
United States of America	188	375
England	73	73
Germany	83	58
France	58	51
Italy	22	20.5
Belgium	11.5	10.3

The author gives data concerning the fluctuation of the incomes of 1,240 persons whose income for one or more years between 1914 to 1919 was $300,000 or over. As the total number of such persons during these years was 1,636, it follows that the author's sample is well representative. The first result of this careful study is that the aggregate income of these 1,240 persons increased from $333,871,933 in 1914 to $765,418,107 in 1916 (climax) and went down to $460,357,496 in 1919—the fluctuation being far from normal. The net results which show the character of the fluctuation are as follows:

Of twenty-three persons, each of whom for 1914 reports a deficit, in 1916, one reported a net income exceeding one million dollars; and nine reported incomes between $500,000 and $1,000,000. In the group of 59 persons reporting in 1914 net incomes not exceeding $10,000, 5 reported in 1916 net incomes in excess of one million dollars each. The number of individuals reporting under $100,000 decreased from 561, in 1914, to 264, in 1919; in contrast to which the returns of individuals reporting between $100,000 and $300,000 and between $300,000 and $1,000,000, increased respectively from 338, in 1914, to 437, in 1919, in the first class, and from 234 to 483 in the second. Those reporting a million and over were 57 in 1914, and 56 in 1919.

How the aggregate income of each of these income groups changed is shown by the following table. (See p. 470.)

The table shows that the income of the group of persons who in 1914 reported less than $100,000 shows the most remarkable

NET INCOME SHOWING FOR EACH YEAR BY PERCENTAGES THE RATIO OF INDIVIDUALS GROUPED ACCORDING TO SIZE OF NET INCOME FOR 1914 TO THE AMOUNT REPORTED IN 1914

Income Class	1914	1915	1916	1917	1918	1919
Under $100,000	100	439	886	811	586	632
From $100,000 to $300,000	100	174	276	238	191	162
From $300,000 to $1,000,000	100	154	182	137	100	92
$1,000,000 and more	100	107	129	118	76	78
Aggregate	100	160	229	196	143	138

expansion. In 1916 it reached 886 in comparison with 100 for 1914. None of the other income-class groups show even a close approximation to the expansion of the income of this group.

Finally, the following tables show the dispersion of the members of each income group throughout the income classes from year to year:[10]

DISPERSION OF THE GROUP OF PERSONS OF A SPECIFIED INCOME CLASS THROUGHOUT THF RANGE OF INCOME CLASSES IN THE SEVERAL YEARS

Group of Persons Whose Incomes in 1914 Were Not in Excess of $100,000

Income Class	1914	1915	1916	1917	1918	1919
Under $100,000	561	332	122	87	150	159
From $100,000 to $300,000	......	161	240	201	225	189
From $300,000 to $1,000,000	......	63	172	255	183	205
$1,000,000 and more	......	15	27	18	3	8
All	561	561	561	561	561	561

Group of Persons Whose Incomes in 1914 Were Between $100,000 and $300,000

Income Class	1914	1915	1916	1917	1918	1919
Under $100,000	......	31	11	16	46	63
From $100,000 to $300,000	388	243	139	98	140	175
From $300,000 to $1,000,000	......	104	209	261	191	143
$1,000,000 and more	......	10	29	13	11	7
All	388	388	388	388	388	388

Group of Persons Whose Incomes in 1914 Were Between $300,000 and $1,000,000

Income Class	1914	1915	1916	1917	1918	1919
Under $100,000	......	......	......	......	20	34
$100,000 to $300,000	......	22	15	27	52	67
$300,000 to $1,000,000	234	187	168	174	144	115
$1,000,000 and more	......	25	51	33	18	18
All	234	234	234	234	234	234

Group of Persons Whose Incomes in 1914 Were $1,000,000 and Over

Income Class	1914	1915	1916	1917	1918	1919
Under $100,000	......	......	1	2	7	8
From $100,000 to $300,000	......	......	2	1	5	6
$300,000 to $1,000,000	......	4	3	10	13	20
$1,000,000	57	53	51	44	32	23
All	57	57	57	57	57	57

The table shows how great were the "ups" and "downs" for each of the groups within 1 or 2 years. Within one year, 15 individuals in the group "under $100,000" climbed to the group of "$1,000,000 and more." And within 3 years 7 of the group of $1,000,000 and more "sank to the group of $100,000 and less." The whole table shows how intensive generally the shifting of the persons of all classes from stratum to stratum was. In connection with an economic expansion during 1914 to 1916 the general trend for all groups was upward; during 1917 to 1919 this was replaced by the opposite downward movement. Later on we shall use the table for other purposes.

The increase of economic mobility in a period of contemporary social upheaval is typical for all such periods: a study of revolutions,[11] of wars, of great social movements, of commercial and industrial revolutions, due to great inventions or discoveries, sufficiently corroborates this generalization. All such epochs have been marked by an extraordinary shift of wealth from group to group; by an extraordinary economic impoverishment of many previously rich people, and by an extraordinary climbing of the economic ladder by many newcomers who honestly or dishonestly take advantage of the opportunity.

2. The second generalization runs as follows: *The greater the economic distance to be crossed by an individual the less is the number of such "jumpers" (up or down).* This fact has been disclosed by the data collected in Minneapolis, and is shown by the following table. In this table by "ordinary" shift is meant a transition from one income group to the next one. By "extraordinary" shift is meant the transition from one economic level to a third when the intervening step is skipped. By "extraordinary shift of the second degree" is meant the transition from the given income group to the fourth when two next steps are skipped:

Groups	Total Per Cent of Economic Shifts in the Life of Each Group	Per Cent of Ordinary Shifts	Per Cent of Extraordinary Shifts	Per Cent of Extraordinary Shifts of the Second Degree
Fathers of the students group [a].	100.0	91.5	8.5 [c]	
Propositi [a]	100.0	92.8	7.2 [c]	
Group No. 2 [b]	100.0	70.0	30.0 [c]	
Business Men [b]	100.0	76.0	18.0 [d]	6.0

[a] As ordinary shifts in these groups are taken transition to the next income group among the income classes; "less than $500," "from $500 to $3000," $3000 and over"; "extraordinary" shift means a jump from the existing level to the third in either direction.

[b] Income classes for this group are as follows: "less than $700," from $700 to $1200," "from $1,200 to $2,000," "from $2,000 to $5,000," "$5000 and over." The difference in the absolute percentage of "ordinary shifts" between the first two and the third and the fourth groups is due to this difference in income group divisicns.

[c] All extraordinary shifts without specification of degree.

[d] Only extraordinary shifts of the first degree.

The table shows very clearly the validity of the generalization. Its second corroboration is given by the above table of Mr. White concerning the dispersion of 1,240 persons It is enough to look at the table to see that in each of the four classes the number of the ordinary shifts is greater than that of the extraordinary, and the number of the extraordinary shifts of the first degree is greater than that of the extraordinary shifts of the second degree. It is true that there seem to be a few exceptions in the years 1918 and 1919, but they are rather a result of the fact that the base point (1914) in the table is taken as "immovable" for all years. Between 1914 and 1916 many of the persons of the group "under $100,000" succeeded in shifting to a higher income group; therefore, their further movement during the next years to still higher groups was an ordinary but not an extraordinary shift. In the table, however, the base point is still "the situation as it was in 1914." Hence, there are very few exceptions. That this consideration is valid is shown by the analysis of the shifts from 1914 to 1915. We do not find any exception to the rule. The corresponding data rearranged in percentages give the following figures:

Income Groups in 1914	Total Number of Persons	Total Number of Shifts	Total Per Cent of Shifts
Under $100,000	561	239	100.0
From $100,000 to $300,000	388	145	100.0
From $300,000 to $1,000,000	234	47	100.0
$1,000,000 and over	57	4	100.0

Income Groups in 1914	Ordinary Shifts		Extraordinary Shifts, First Degree		Extraordinary Shifts, Second Degree	
	Number	Per Cent	Number	Per Cent	Number	Per Cent
Under $100,000	161	67.4	63	26.4	15	6.2
From $100,000 to $300,000	135	93.1	10	6.9	0.0	0.0
From $300,000 to $1,000,000	47	100.0	0.0	0.0	0.0	0.0
$1,000,000 and over	4	100.0	0.0	0.0	0.0	0.0

The third corroboration of the proposition is given by the study of D'Aeth already referred to. Of 254 sons of 85 fathers, 185 have the father's economic status, 69 sons have an economic status different from their fathers. They shifted to other income groups. Of these 69 shifts, 48 represent "ordinary" shifts; 15, "extraordinary shifts of the first degree"; 4, "extraordinary shifts of the second degree." [12]

Many indirect indications of this type are given by the German studies quoted above of the working class and other occupational groups: they show that the majority of the sons have an economic status similar to that of their fathers, and that only a small percentage of the sons have succeeded in making an extraordinary economic shift. To what extent the proposition is generally true at the present moment cannot be certainly decided. This must be the task of further studies in this field.

3. The preceding rule means that the *majority moves along the vertical line of economic stratification gradually, without sudden jumps and skipping of the next steps in either direction.* It seems that a considerable length of time is necessary for the majority of those climbing or sinking, say two or three generations, to cross a considerable economic distance. Under normal conditions *only an insignificant minority of "the lucky or unlucky fellows" make successful jumps over a considerable economic distance.* But even then in order to climb a great distance or ruin a large estate years and years are necessary.

The first proposition is well illustrated by the social ascent of immigrants in the United States. As a rule, it is only in the second generation (native born from foreign parents) that they succeed in approaching the economic standard of the native population. This is seen from the figures on p. 475.

We have a similar picture if we compare the earnings of the same sex and age groups of the native population and of the immigrants of the first and of the second generation as to the rents paid by the three classes, their standards of living and so on. In all these respects, the first generation of immigrants occupies the lowest position; but the second generation shows a decided progress which practically makes its economic status identical with that of the native born of native parents.[13] The figures show that for the mass of population a length of time of at least one generation is necessary for the ascent of a noticeable but still

Categories of Population	Per Cent of Male Heads of Families Earning Each Specified Amount per Year				
	Under $100	$100 to $200	$200 to $300	$300 to $400	$400 to $500
Native born of native parents..............	0.3	1.1	2.5	5.7	10.2
Native born of foreign parents..............	0.0	0.6	2.5	8.6	14.4
Foreign born...........	1.1	4.3	9.7	19.0	19.8

Categories of Population	$500 to $600	$600 to $700	$700 to $800	$800 to $900	$900 to $1000	$1000 and over
Native born of native parents..............	15.3	15.0	20.5	7.5	8.0	14.0
Native born of foreign parents..............	14.4	14.1	15.8	6.1	9.8	13.7
Foreign born...........	16.2	11.8	9.7	2.8	2.9	2.8

moderate economic distance. It appears to me that the picture given by the table is representative of the ascending and descending economic shifting of a large mass of the population.

An example of the extraordinary rise of a few is given by the career of American millionaires and multimillionaires who have started life poor. But even in these cases, as may be seen from the following figures, it has required many years to cross the great distance from the bottom or from the middle economic strata to the position of captains of industry. (See p. 476.) The table shows that only 2.2 per cent of the millionaires who started poor became rich between the ages of 21 and 30. More than 70 per cent of them became rich at the age of 41 years or more. For those who started in the middle or already rich class, the time of climbing is correspondingly shorter because the economic distance to be crossed by them is shorter than for the born-

The Age at Which Americans, Starting Poor or in Middle Class, Became Rich; or Starting Rich, Became Responsible Managers of Large Enterprises[14]

Groups of Millionaires	From 21 to 30 Years, Per Cent	From 31 to 40 Years, Per Cent	From 41 to 50 Years, Per Cent	From 51 to 60 Years, Per Cent	From 61 Years and Over, Per Cent	Total, Per Cent
Started poor..........	2.2	23.4	38.7	24.0	11.7	100
Started middle.........	5.9	33.7	39.6	18.2	2.6	100
Started rich...........	26.9	52.8	19.7	1.2	0	100

poor millionaires. Here are the most successful climbers of the type of Carnegie, Rockefeller, Ford, and so on. If even they had to work 30 or more years to reach the apex of the financial pyramid, it is certain that men of smaller caliber took a much longer time to cross a considerable economic distance.

What has been said of economic ascent may be said also of economic sinking. Though, in general this may proceed somewhat more rapidly than ascent, nevertheless, under normal conditions the majority of people also sink gradually, often during two and three generations. Only a few individuals fall with the rapidity of a stone through the air. But again, they seem to compose only an insignificant proportion of the total mass of the sinking population.

A further interesting result disclosed by my study of the Minneapolis groups is as follows: comparing the economic status of the sons and the fathers of different income groups, we see that *"the middle" economic status is more stable than either "extreme."* The percentage of sons with a status identical to that of their fathers is considerably higher in the "middle strata" than among the well-to-do and the poor. Correspondingly, the proportion of shifts among the extreme groups is higher than among the middle group. This is seen from the following groups. (See p. 477.)

In all groups, throughout two generations, "the middle" income classes are less variable or more stable than the others. The number of the cases, however, is too limited to even suggest that

Economic Status of Fathers (Income Classes)	Economic Status of Sons			
	Total Number of Cases Studied	Number of Cases in Which Sons' Economic Status Is Identical with That of the Father	Per Cent of Identity of Economic Status of Father and Son	Per Cent of Shifts of Sons to Other than Father's Economic Status
Students and professors group:				
Under $500..........	18	3	16.7	83.3
$500 to $3,000........	329	277	*84.2*	*15.8*
$3,000 and more......	67	39	37.3	62.7
Minneapolis business men:			0.0	100.0
Under $700..........	4	0	35.7	64.3
$700 to $1,200........	14	5	*50.0*	*50.0*
$1,200 to $2,000.......	30	15	25.4	74.8
$2,000 to $5,000......	55	14	22.2	77.8
$5,000 and over.......	18	4		
Minneapolis group No. 2:			20.7	79.3
Under $700..........	29	6	40.7	59.3
$700 to $1,200........	135	55	*53.3*	*46.7*
$1,200 to $2,000.......	370	196	19.9	80.1
$2,000 to $5,000......	222	44	9.4	90.6
$5,000 and over.......	32	3		

this rule is general. It is simply indicated in order that it may be tested.

5. A further result of the Minneapolis study is that *when the sons' economic status becomes different from that of the fathers, the sons of the lowest economic classes rise, the sons of the middle groups in almost equal proportion rise and fall, and the sons of the highest income strata principally fall.* In the above table, 83.3 per cent of the sons of the poorest class in the students group, who shifted to other than the fathers' economic status, went up to the higher income group. The same is true of the sons of

the poorest group in the group of Minneapolis business men. On the other hand, in both groups, the shifted sons of the highest income groups all went down. Finally, out of 15.8 per cent of the shifted sons of the income group, "$500 to $3,000," 8 per cent went down and 7 per cent went up. The same may be said of the shifted sons of the income group, "$1,200 to $2,000": half of them went down; the other half went up. Results for the shifted sons of the income group, "$2,000 to $5,000" are similar: 40 per cent of them sank, 34 per cent climbed higher. To what extent these results are general cannot be said. If the data are representative they mean that in case of a shift for the sons of the poor classes the chances of rising are much greater than for a continued fall, while for the sons of rich people, the chances are reversed.

6. The above data permit it to be said certainly that *within present Western societies two opposite currents of economic circulation—the ascending and descending—are permanently active.*

7. The next certain inference from these data is that *each economic stratum of Western societies is composed not only of sons of fathers who belong to this stratum, but in a considerable proportion of newcomers—the offspring of all other poorer or richer families. Accordingly, the richest class is composed not only of children of rich parents but of children of poor parents, also; while among "the poorest proletarians" there is a part composed of the offspring of rich parents.*[15] Even the class of wealthiest men of contemporary America or Europe is not an exception to this rule. Some data concerning American millionaires and multimillionaires have been given above. Hence, it is not accurate to depict present economic classes as "hereditarily rich" or "hereditarily poor." Each of them, to some degree, is like a water reservoir from which permanently flows a downward current of economic failures and into which is permanently pumped a current from the lower levels. As a result, the composition of each class is fluid, changeable, and unstable, at least in part. This factual situation somewhat contradicts many radical denunciations of the "leisure class" and their glorification of the proletarian class, as though the classes were closed and hereditary. As I remarked above, in regard to the occupational classes, such statements may

be true only in regard to a part of each of these classes, and even of them for only a few generations. Only an insignificant part of each economic class remains in the same class during many generations. Such cases strongly suggest that people who are poor or rich during five or more generations are in the place proper to their innate qualities.

Present society is a field of incessant battle among millions of people who are trying to rise. In climbing each of them presses on all the others. Those who under the existing circumstances are weaker, owing to innate weakness or to the less favorable conditions, are stopped and very often put down. Those who are stronger, go up and up, until they reach the apex of the economic pyramid. But even then they cannot have a feeling of security; in order not to be ousted they must continue their fight.[16]

This dynamic character of present economic mobility calls forth many important effects. Later we shall see that many characteristics of the poor, as well as of the wealthy classes of present society, are closely correlated with economic mobility in present societies.

[1] SOROKIN, P., "American Millionaires and Multimillionaires," p. 636.

[2] D'AETH, F. G., "Present Tendencies of Class Differentiation," *The Sociological Review,* pp. 269-276, 1910.

[3] See the facts and the details in my *Sociology of Revolution.*

[4] See SCHIFF, WALTER, *Die Agrargesetzgebung der Europäischen Staaten vor und nach dem Kriege, Archiv für Socialwissenschaft und Sozialpolitik,* Heft 2, pp. 469-529, 1925.

[5] See the details in LEWINSON (MORUS), R., *Die Umschichtung der Europäischen Vermögen,* pp. 1-34, Berlin, 1925.

[6] *Ibid.,* pp. 44-45.

[7] See *ibid., passim* and Chap. VII.

[8] ALBERTI, MARIO, "Tables Relating to Reparations," *Associazione Bancaria Italiana,* Milano, 1924.

[9] WHITE, EDWARD, "Income Fluctuation of a Selected Group of Personal Returns," *Journal of the American Statistical Association,* Vol. XVII, pp. 67-81.

[10] *Ibid.,* p. 78.

[11] SOROKIN, P., *Sociology of Revolution.*

[12] D'AETH, F. G., *op. cit.,* pp. 272-274.

[13] See many other data in Reports of the United States Immigration Commission, Sixty-first Congress, Third Session, *Senate Documents,* Vol. VII; *Immigration Commission,* Vol. I, pp. 298, 364 *ff.,* 1910-1911.

[14] SOROKIN, P., "American Millionaires and Multimillionaires," p. 638.

[15] An idea of dispersion of people, whose fathers belong to the same income class throughout different economic classes, is given by the following table concerning group No. 2 already studied:

Economic Status of Fathers	Number of Fathers	Economic Status of Sons					
		Less than $700	$700 to $1,200	$1,200 to $2,000	$2,000 to $5,000	$5,000 and Over	Total Number of Sons
Less than $700....	14	*6*	11	9	3	0	29
$700 to $1,200.....	58	6	*55*	48	25	1	135
$1,200 to $2,000...	137	10	69	*196*	80	15	370
$2,000 to $5,000...	86	8	31	109	*44*	30	222
$5,000 and over....	16	1	2	11	15	*3*	32
Total..........	311	31	168	373	167	49	788

[19] In the light of the facts given it is scarcely possible to agree completely with the following statement, which is very common at the present moment: "Keeping riches once gained is easier than ever before. The rich by inheritance have a position which they can lose only by a destructive tendency amounting almost to madness." WATKINS, *Growth of Large Fortunes,* p. 159; DALTON, HUGH, *Some Aspects of the Inequality of Incomes in Modern Communities,* p. 283, London, 1920. It is enough to look at the above table showing the fluctuations of the great incomes of the United States in 1914 to 1919 to see that this statement is one-sided. It is difficult to call hundreds of the captains of American industry in these years mad people; and yet, many of them from the income group with an income of $1,000,000 and more sank down into groups with an income of less than $300,000 and even less than $100,000. I think the opposite statement of Leroy Beaulieu, or de Tocqueville, or Charles H. Cooley, is nearer to reality.

[W. A. Anderson's mentioned study yielded the results similar to my own. But as regards the hereditary transmission of the economic status from the grandfather to the father and to the son it gave an opposite result. This may be due to the fact that his income-group division is too small: only $100.]

CHAPTER XIX

VERTICAL MOBILITY WITHIN WESTERN SOCIETIES

(*Concluded*)

POLITICAL CIRCULATION

ALMOST all the principal statements concerning occupational and economic circulation seem to apply to political circulation within present Western societies.

1. INTENSIVE POLITICAL CIRCULATION IN PERIODS OF UPHEAVAL AND AT THE PRESENT TIME

In the first place, *political circulation is especially intensive in periods of great social upheavals, such as war, revolution, and great reform movements.* In the first period of revolution it usually has an anarchic character—a result of the shifting not being controlled by the normal mechanism of social selection and distribution of individuals. We would naturally suppose that political circulation during recent years has been especially intensive. The facts prove this beyond doubt. Within the last few years we have witnessed the deposition or assassination of many heads of the government and hereditary dynasties in Russia, Germany, Austria, Portugal, Turkey, Persia, Hungary, Greece, Bulgaria, Poland, China, and Abyssinia, Afghanistan, Albania, and several states in Arabia and in South America. All this has happened within the last 15 (mostly within the last 8) years. There are few epochs which rival our time in this respect.

This "wholesale" overthrow of monarchs and heads of the government means also the overthrow of a considerable group of the previous court aristocracy. With the deposition of their leaders they also lost their high position in the political pyramid and became common laborers, artisans, servants, clerks, and what not. Furthermore, in countries where the dynasties have not been overthrown, many fundamental changes within the highest government classes have, nevertheless, taken place: the responsible managers of governmental affairs in the form of prime ministers, members of cabinets, and so on, have been recruited from strata and families considerably different from the social circles from which they were recruited before. As a result, side by side with this great "political sinking" of previous rulers, we have an ascent of new "people" who often come from the lowest or the middle social strata. Instead of the Romanovs we have a group of Soviet dictators almost all of whom come from the class of artisans, small professionals, small business men, industrial workers and peasants. Instead of the Hapsburgs we have Dr. Hainisch, as the President of Austria, a man from the class of entrepreneurs. Dr. Masaryk is a son of a poor artisan; Admiral Horthy comes from a stratum which though relatively high is yet much lower than that of many aristocratic families of Hungary. Instead of the Hohenzollerns in Germany there was Dr. Ebert, the President, a son of a saddle maker; Paul Loebe, the Reichstag Speaker, a son of a carpenter. In place of other monarchs of German states we see new people mostly from the middle social layers. Instead of the Osmans in Turkey, we have Mustapha Kemal Pasha, a man from a middle social stratum, who under normal conditions would scarcely have any chance of occupying the throne of the Osmans. Instead of the hereditary Shah of Persia we have a new Shah, Risa Khan, a few years ago a simple soldier and a stableman. Similar changes have occurred in the other indicated countries. In the place of the Chinese Emperor, we see a crowd of independent dictators, some of whom, as the Lord of Manchuria, have risen from the condition of a simple robber. In Greece several radical changes have occurred during recent years: in 1913 the King, George I, was killed; Constantine reigned only from 1913 to 1917, and then was superseded by his brother. In 1920 he returned, but in 1922 was deposed again and died in exile. His son George II ascended the throne in 1923, but in the same year was deposed. The process is still going on.

Side by side with these "ascents and descents," which have been going on with a motion-picture rapidity are seen no less important changes in other countries. Italy is ruled by Mussolini, a son of a blacksmith; in England, we have seen the cabinet of the Labor Party composed in greater part of newcomers from the labor or middle class. In France we have had Herriot's government composed again of the newcomers. In Germany we have had the Social Democratic governments recruited again in considerable part from the same labor class or from the middle classes —a stratum quite different from that from which the government was recruited before the revolution. Similar processes have taken place in Czechoslovakia, Austria, Hungary, Belgium, the Netherlands, Denmark, Norway, Sweden, Bulgaria, Poland, Esthonia, Latvia, Lithuania, and some other countries. With the exception of the monarchs in some of them, everywhere the previous rulers were driven out and superseded by new people from the new social classes. Moreover, in several countries even these newcomers have risen and sunk back, while the previous classes or the nearest to them have returned again.

Labor governments, either in the form of a Communist dictatorship or Socialist, Radical, and Labor cabinets, appeared and disappeared in Hungary, Bavaria, Saxony, Germany, Bulgaria (Stambolisky's dictatorship), England, Sweden, Poland, Esthonia, Czechoslovakia, and some other countries. And all this has happened within a few years! Truly, these are times in history which move with the rapidity of a motion picture. This is not all. This "mad" circulation has only been a symptom of a more fundamental regrouping within the social and political strata. In a schematic form these earthquakes have occurred as follows: The period from 1914 to 1917 was one of sinking of the previously high political classes; the years from 1917 to 1921 were, in continental Europe, years of a great political ascent of the class of industrial laborers. This was manifested in the establishment of cabinets with a majority or under the leadership of the Labor or Socialist parties in Germany, many German States, Austria, Belgium, and some others. Almost all Communist, Socialist, and Labor governments of that period were established in the name of the proletarian class, and were recruited to a considerable extent from this class or from the circles of its ideologists. The pretensions and power, the authority and ascent of these cabinets were based mostly on the force of this class. By 1923 to 1926 this stage had passed in many countries of continental Europe. Whatever may have been its causes, one fact is certain; these governments did not give to the masses what they had promised to them, and therefore they lost some of their admiration and support. The years following 1921, in many agricultural countries, were years of political ascent of the peasant and farmer class. After the tide of the proletarian class came a rising wave of the agricultural class. Their leaders, their parties began to play a great part—sometimes a dominant one—and after 1921 and 1922 cabinets were led by peasant-farmer leaders in Esthonia, Latvia, Lithuania, Poland, Bulgaria, Hungary, Czechoslovakia, Rumania, Jugoslavia, and partly in Germany and France.[1] This class took the place of the class of the proletarian government which has failed to show either a conspicuous creative ability or ability to manage successfully affairs of state. The peasant-farmer class still continues to hold power in some countries. In some others it drove out the proletarian government, and entered into a national agreement with the classes of land owners, capitalists, and previous aristocracy. Together they have established a non-socialist government and put in power men like Hindenburg or Admiral Horthy, or even Pashich or Radich. In some countries, as in France, this class is still waiting the time when "cartels," socialist, and similar governments will fail completely. In Russia it is forcing the Soviet rulers step by step to give up their Communism and is preparing to bury them in the future.

In this schematic way, it is seen that during these years circulation in the political field has been going on with an extraordinary rapidity and over the widest range. The political aristocracy has been recruited from the lowest classes, and the classes themselves, at least temporarily, have changed their relative positions in the whole social pyramid. But, as I mentioned, we see already the first processes of the future consolidation and "reverse movement." Many "newcomers" already have fallen from power, many previous aristocrats have climbed back again. The process is still going on. Its final outcome will probably be that a part of the previously degenerated aristocracy will remain in the lower strata; the talented part will climb up again, and with the talented part of "the newcomers" will compose the upper political strata of the future. What will be the name of this aristocracy and of the future rulers—whether monarchs, presidents, representatives, senators, servants of the people, public servants—all this is a detail which may be important from some other viewpoint but which is a trifle from the standpoint of an objective sociologist. Before our eyes is repeated what has been repeated many times in the tragic comedy of human history. So much for extraordinary political circulation in periods of upheaval.

2. THE GRADUAL CHARACTER OF POLITICAL CIRCULATION IN NORMAL TIMES

In contrast to this, in normal periods political circulation seems to act more gradually. The majority of the ascending families ascend step by step, sometimes through two and three generations. This is confirmed by the data concerning 479 high officials in Prussia. Only a few individuals jump suddenly over a great "political distance." In this respect the above rule, *"the greater the political distance to be crossed, the less is the number of such jumpers,"* may be applied to this type of circulation, too. The graduality of shifting in this field, even in the cases of the most successful jumpers, is witnessed by the fact that they reach their high positions usually at an advanced age. The above figures indicating the principles concerning monarchs, presidents, and popes may be applied to prime ministers and ministers and generally to high state officials. This is shown by the above data concerning the age of the German high officials. As a general rule, the climbers rarely reach such positions earlier than the age of fifty years.[2] For the sons of high officials the age is naturally lower. Only in periods of upheaval do we see a considerable lowering of the age. According to Gowin, the average age of leaders at such periods is about from 34 to 41 years.[3] This means that even the few lucky jumpers must work years and years to climb high along the political ladder.

3. INHERITANCE OF POLITICAL STATUS WITHIN PRESENT SOCIETIES

As in the case of occupational and economic positions, in this field before the World War, in the monarchic, as well as the republican European countries, there existed to some degree, hereditary transmission of socio-political status from father to the sons. In monarchies and monarchical democracies hereditary transmission applied to the various ranks of the princes, various ranks of nobility and aristocracy, and many "titled ranks." Actually, it existed also in republican countries: the sons of prominent statesmen and highest officials used to occupy if not quite identical, at least similar social ranks, whatever their names.[4] Out of 479 Prussian high officials about 400 were from high social strata. The elective system of appointment does not always check the monopolization of a high position within the narrow circle of a few families. The elective position of the Roman Catholic Pope and of cardinals during several centuries was really monopolized within the families of Segni, Visconti, Colonna, Medici, Borgia, Orsini, and Gaetani, some of whom were consanguineous. Of 29 presidents of the United States we already have had four cases in which the presidents were close relatives. With still greater reason it is possible to say this of socio-political positions which are not so exclusive. It is difficult to measure these phenomena quantitatively, but I am inclined to think that "the inheritance" of socio-political position in general is higher than that of occupation or economic status, in the democracies, as well as in non-democratic monarchies. The following words of a talented French journalist written on the occasion of the appointment of M. Beranger as French Ambassador to the United States seems to present the situation satisfactorily:

> Under the old régime a person belonging to the aristocracy through this very fact was supposed to be fit for occupying any of the highest positions. Birth in the nobility opened for him the way to all high places. We had a revolution in order to change this situation. But it happens that nothing has been changed. As before, we have dukes, barons, marquesses, and counts who distribute among themselves all the important political places. The only difference is that now they belong not to the royal court but to that of the parliament. Having no special merits they are appointed to such positions only because of their birth within parliamentary circles. In this way there has appeared a new aristocracy in all respects similar to that of the old régime.

In this statement the real situation is somewhat exaggerated;

and yet it stresses well the fact of "an inheritance of political status" within present societies.

It would be very profitable to study quantitatively the real degree of transmission of this status within present democracies. But unfortunately the necessary data are absent and the study encounters the greatest difficulties. For the same reason it cannot be said whether there has been a definite trend toward an increase or a decrease of such inheritance during the last few decades before the war and revolutions. It is certain that the transmission has decreased during the period since 1915. But, as indicated, such a decrease is a characteristic of a period of upheaval and is not typical for a normal time. Frankly, I do not know whether we are drifting toward an increase or a decrease of inheritance of socio-political positions.

4. DISPERSION AND RECRUITING OF THE MEMBERS OF A POLITICAL STRATUM

The above, however, must not hide from us another side of the situation, the fact that *part of the children of fathers of the same socio-political rank occupy different political strata; and the fact that the members of each politico-social layer are recruited, at least in part from children of fathers of the most different political positions.* It is enough to note the highest responsible statesmen in the Western monarchies and republics before the World War to see that among their ranks there are "climbers" from humble families: David Lloyd George in England; Count S. Witte, in Russia; K. Kramarge in the old Austria; Viviani, in France; several presidents of the United States and France, are conspicuous examples of such climbers who succeeded in reaching the highest governmental positions (as prime ministers and presidents) in spite of their humble origin. There is no doubt that the number of such people within high socio-political circles was considerable. On the other hand, among the people who did not have any political distinction or importance, there also were individuals who had been born in a high political stratum. The posterity of many presidents, ministers, high officials, prominent statesmen sometimes within two or three (sometimes even within one) generation are lost among political nullities. Nobody knows where they are; they do not play any rôle, and do not have any important position. They simply become plain citizens and nothing more. Some quantitative data of this kind have been given in the chapter devoted to the analysis of the descending current in interoccupational circulation.

5. AVENUES OF CLIMBING

Among the ways of climbing used by such jumpers within present societies, the most common channel seems to be political activity in the form of work within political parties. Such seems to have been the career of the greater part of the extraordinary risers in democracies. This kind of activity is usually accompanied by journalistic and partly by juridical and scholastic occupations. In its essence all this is the "ability of speech making," whether in the form of writing or oratory. Hence, as I have already mentioned, such jumpers are, as a rule, good orators and prolific writers (quantitatively). If in periods of war or national danger people with a military talent rise to power, in peaceful periods people with verbosity have the principal chances of succeeding in democracies.[5] This is especially true of jumpers who begin their careers as extremist leaders of the masses, as anarchists, socialists, communists, and so on. A great many contemporary statesmen have begun their careers on the extreme left, and risen in this way; then as they rose they have become more and more moderate and finally finished as relatively conservative people. Clemenceau and Viviani, Briand and Millieran, Scheidemann and Noske, Ebert and Lloyd George, Vandervelde and Mussolini, and thousands of other people have passed through such "transformations." The career of a clever fellow in present societies is easier if he starts it within the socialist and extremist ranks than if he begins in conservative circles. In the last case, if he is of low origin, he is likely to be treated by the conservatives with a kind of superiority and then only very slowly may be promoted to only a moderately high position. Having him within their ranks they do not fear him and therefore do not care much about him. Quite different is the attitude of an extremist. He is independent and may be dangerous. Therefore, the ruling aristocracy is ready to "buy" him for a higher price. They willingly offer him a higher position, as soon as it is possible to make him "their own." Hence, the paradox of present societies: for an ambitious man of low standing it is more profitable to start a political career as an extremist than a moderate; it is more profitable to be a "socialist and communist" than "a conservative"; to be a radical than a non-radical. If in the past to be extremist or "socialist" meant to be ready to sacrifice many worldly things for "high ideas," now the situation is rather the reverse: to be a socialist now means to take the quickest, most comfortable, and surest way of climbing and getting the desired power and other worldly things. This paradox, perhaps, explains why at the present moment we see so many sons and daughters of prime ministers and peers in England (*e.g.,* Mr. Baldwin, Jr., Lady Cynthia, daughter of the late Lord Curzon, etc.) and the sons of the political aristocracy in other countries, who have suddenly turned into "laborers" and even half communists. Whatever may be the reasons for these "converts" they surely do not act stupidly from the standpoint of their careers.[6]

It is not my purpose to evaluate all this. One thing, however, is clear: for a continuation of social prosperity such an exclusive success of "speech makers" and their abundant presence in responsible ranks of the government is scarcely necessary and useful.[7] It is scarcely a good thing to make "extremism" more profitable than moderation. "Oratorical talent" is a good thing; but for the building of a country it is more necessary to have real ability *to do* things than merely to talk them over. Creative engineers, business men, farmers, or specialists probably are as necessary as lawyers, journalists, politicians, and the superficial writers in political and economic matters who fill now in abundance the field of politics and even high political ranks.

[1] If we take the data of the *Statesman's Yearbooks* for 1914, 1918, 1921, and 1925 (the data very incomplete and only approximately depicting the situation), we have among the deputies of the houses of representatives of the fourteen countries in 1914, about 15 per cent of the Socialist, Syndicalist, and Labor parties; this per cent in 1918 to 1921 (including the communists) rises to 25 to 26 per cent in 19 European countries, and remains in the same level for 1923 to 1925. The percentage of the representatives of the agrarian, peasant, and farmer parties for the fourteen countries (excluding Russia) is about 8 for 1913 to 1914; about 13 for 1918 to 1921; and about 20 for 1923 to 1925. In spite of the inaccuracy of these data (the real strength of the peasant-farmer

parties seems to be higher) they reflect the rise and stagnation (factual decline) of the Socialist and Workers parties, and a continued growth of the peasant-farmer political groupings.

[2] Such are data given by the age of the prime ministers and ministers in the *Statesman's Yearbook* even for these years.

[3] See GOWIN, B. E., *Correlation between Reformative Epochs and the Leadership of Young Men,* 1909.

[4] *Vide,* GONNARD, R., "Quelques considerations sur les classes," *Revue Economique International,* Aug. 10, 1925. See above given data concerning the number of the ranks of peerage, baronetage, and so on in England and other countries. See also COOLEY, CHARLES H., *Social Organization;* pp. 213 *ff.*, 229 *ff.*

[5] *Cf.* ARISTOTLE, *Politics,* Bk. II, Chap. V.

[6] The indicated fact is only a detail of a more general trait of contemporary society. Among Socialists and Communists who try to undermine capitalism we find a considerable proportion of capitalists, bankers, rich people, and people of high social standing. They subsidize the Socialist and similar organizations with money. Such a "paradox," however, may be explained easily. Many of the capitalists make a good profit in this way. Some others get also something in the way of social and political promotion. See the facts and the explanations in MICHELS, R., *Political Parties.*

[7] See remarks on this by DEMOLINS, E., *Anglo-Saxon Superiority,* pp. 201-235.

Part Six

THE RESULTS OF SOCIAL MOBILITY

CHAPTER XX

THE EFFECTS OF MOBILITY ON THE RACIAL COMPOSITION OF A SOCIETY

IN THE chapters dealing with the causes of mobility the phenomenon of vertical mobility has been taken as "a function" or a "result," and its causes or its "independent variables," have been searched for. Now the functional equation will be reversed: the phenomenon of vertical circulation will be taken as "an independent variable" and we shall try to find its "functions," the social phenomena which fluctuate with its fluctuation. It goes without saying that such phenomena are very numerous. The purpose is not to give an exhaustive enumeration of all such "functions" of vertical circulation, but only a brief sketch of those which are permanent and important. In the first place, the effects of the vertical mobility on the racial composition of the population must be studied.

1. UNDER THE CONDITION OF LOWER PROCREATION OF THE UPPER STRATA A MOBILE SOCIETY PERMANENTLY WASTES ITS "BEST" POPULATION

If it be true that (1) in a mobile society its upper strata are composed of people physically and mentally superior to the population of the lower classes; (2) that the rate of procreation of the upper strata is lower than that of the lower layers; (3) that better parents leave better offspring; (4) and, finally, that a relative or absolute "vacuum," created through the lower procreation of aristocracy and through the sinking of its failures, continues to be filled by the best elements recruited from the lower societies; then, in such a society, vertical mobility apparently leads to a permanent waste of its best elements. The data given in earlier chapters show that these "ifs" have existed in many societies. The "ifs" being given, the conclusion appears as logically inevitable. In a simplified form the process goes on as follows: A lower procreation of the upper classes and sinking of some of their "failures" creates a "vacuum" within the upper classes. It is filled by recruiting talented people from the lower layers, usually from the next lower stratum below the aristocracy. These people who have climbed to the highest positions, in their turn, sooner or later become less prolific. Their place again is filled by the best from the classes still lower. These climbers, like their predecessors, become again less prolific. In this way, the upper strata suck and waste the best from the lower strata. If they return something to the lower strata, it is as a rule, only the "degenerates," the "failures," the "wrecks," which do nothing more than contaminate and aggravate the lower classes. Whether this waste must lead to a final depletion of the population or not, we will discuss later. Meanwhile, let us say that what we have described in theory is only a simplified scheme of what has been going on in reality.

The real process of "wasting" is much more complicated. *Its first stage has consisted in the territorial migration of population from the country to the city.* Since the growth of the cities, they have almost completely monopolized the function of social promotion of individuals. Royal or republican courts, authorities, and offices of the "ennoblement," the staffs of armies, high church authorities, political institutions, colleges, theaters, art and literary institutions, manufacturing, or artisanship, commercial and banking enterprises—in brief, almost all channels of social promotion have been concentrated in the city. Unless he migrates to the city, a man of a humble origin in the country has almost ceased to have any chance to climb. Even if in a few cases a man, while staying in the country, has succeeded in making money or doing something prominent, such a man, in order to become really prominent, has to get the sanction of the city authorities. A rich peasant is still only a peasant; a wonderful country poet without the sanction of the city press and the city is still only the poet of "his neighborhood," not known to the world. This explains why, during the last four centuries, at least in Western societies, and since the great growth of city life, in ancient Rome, or Greece, or other ancient civilizations, permanent or temporary city dwelling became an inevitable step in climbing the social ladder. This explains also why the upper strata has been recruited almost exclusively from people who have either been born, or, at any rate, have stayed for a period more or less long in cities. Such being the case, it is comprehensible that, for all who have been born in the country in humble conditions, migration to the city has been a necessary step in the way of social promotion. Up to the second half of the nineteenth century, the city population was not self-supporting. Its mortality was greater than its birth rate. Since the cities did not disappear and continued to grow, this is due only to a permanent migration of the country population to the cities.[1] This means that the city population in the past represented in its majority migrants from the country in the first, second, or later generations. *The second step in the way of social ascent has consisted in the permanent sifting of rural migrants by the city machinery of social selection and distribution of individuals.* Part of the migrants have succeeded in entering at once, or within one generation, the relatively higher social strata of the city; another part has entered the class of the working people and proletariat.[2] While the upper strata of the city aristocracy have been dying out or sinking, the vacancies have been permanently filled by country migrants or by their offspring in the second and subsequent generations. They, after an ascent, have undergone the same fate, and the vacancies left by their extinction or sinking have been filled by new waves of the rising offspring of new country migrants. In this way, *the city has been draining the country population; and the upper strata, the best elements of the lower classes.* This means that the upper strata of Western societies for the last few centuries, in a considerable part have represented partly the first, but principally the second and the subsequent generations of rural migrants. At the end of the eighteenth century, the aristocracy of the Middle Ages was almost burned out. What remained was exterminated during the wave of revolutions at the end of the eighteenth century. After that time, the upper strata, with very few exceptions, began to be filled by new people; by new rural migrants, and by the offspring of previous rural migrants.

Into the place of the previous aristocracy of birth came the aristocracy of wealth, and talent, and political ability. But that has been burned out with an even greater rapidity than the upper classes before it. Whether we take the richest families or the prominent families which occupied the upper classes of European societies at the beginning of the nineteenth century, we find that their offspring now either do not exist, or are degraded, or compose only quite an insignificant part of the total of the upper classes. The composition of the occupational, financial, and political aristocracy now changes probably with a greater rapidity than one century ago.[3] During the last 60 or 80 years European societies have been "digging" their upper strata in an extensive proportion from the middle classes. Since the beginning of the twentieth century, we see that they have gone still deeper and begun to dig from the classes of the proletariat and peasantry. "The shovel of the machinery of social selection of individuals" has been going deeper and deeper and has now almost reached the bottom of the society. Evidently, if the existing upper or even middle class had had in abundance the leaders who could successfully perform the functions of the upper strata, such a "deep digging" of the *élite* would not have been necessary and scarcely would have taken place. If it has taken place this suggests that the existing upper and middle classes are burnt out with a rapidity which makes "the deeper digging" an absolute necessity. We see a somewhat similar process in the history of the United States. The offspring of the old Americans (Americans before 1790) have had a fertility much lower than the immigrants. This is one of the causes why they are already in minority in this country.[4] Though in general, in comparison with the first generation of immigrants, they have been occupying a higher occupational, economic, and political status; nevertheless, as we have seen, the second generation of the immigrants approaches this status. Many families of the old Americans are already extinct; part are sunk; part are surrounded by the newcomers in the highest social strata. The rapidity of burning out the best material has been grasped already in a popular statement that prominent American families rise and sink back within three generations. The statement exaggerates the situation; nevertheless, it stresses an excessive rapidity of rising and dying out or sinking back. All fields of social life in the United States at the present moment are drawing their upper layers from all social strata. To everybody is given a chance to become somebody. This means a real democracy. Under the condition of differential fertility, this means also a rapid burning out of the best human fuel of the country.

From the past, a classical example of the same wasting of the best human material in a mobile society is given by ancient Rome and Greece. The earliest ages of these societies were relatively immobile. Aristocracy was the aristocracy of birth. Later on, however, they entered the mobile stage also. In Rome, after the reform of Servius Tullius, and after 499 B. C. (*leges Valeriae et Horatiae, lex Canuleja,* still later, *leges Liciniae Sextiae*), the aristocracy of birth was succeeded by that of wealth. Patrician families began to disappear; the upper classes began to be recruited from wealthy plebeian families—nobles and equestrians. These families dying out or sinking, after the end of the Republic, the upper classes began to be filled by climbers from still lower strata—the freemen, slaves, and barbarians. In this way "the shovel of social selection" dug deeper and deeper until it reached the very bottom of the social pyramid.[5] A somewhat similar picture is given by the history of ancient Greece. This wasting is a very serious disadvantage of the mobile societies, as far as the above four conditions are present. A relatively immobile society may be free from such disadvantages. The general conditions of an immobile society do not lead to an artificial diminution of the posterity of its higher castes. On the contrary, their general trait is to have as many children as is possible. This is one of the fundamental religious commands and the earnest desire of the upper families. The institution of polygamy, which is rather common among such societies, facilitates the possibility of having numerous offspring for the upper classes. Thus it is that, in spite of 2,000 years of an exclusive supremacy of the Brahmin caste in India, the caste does not have any trouble in this respect and is far from being extinct. It still exists and still keeps its unquestioned superiority. It has not been burnt out. It has not been put down. It has not been diluted. We may or may not dislike the caste-system, but the fact that it does not burn out its best human material is its characteristic correlated with immobility, and is probably one of the causes of the long existence of such a society. The rapid progress of the mobile societies is paid for very highly. They must burn their best human fuel and waste the highest form of wealth—their best brains and best capacities. This fuel burns brilliantly and drives societies with a wonderful rapidity. Immobile societies move very slowly; they are stagnant; but they are less wasteful of their best human fuel.

2. DOES THE WASTING OF THE BEST HUMAN MATERIAL LEAD TO A FINAL DILUTION OF THE POPULATION OF MOBILE SOCIETY?

The answer depends on whether the waste of the upper classes is or is not greater than the production of talents within the lower classes. If the production is not less than the waste, and it may be continued indefinitely, then apparently a mobile society is not doomed to a final depletion of its best stock. If the production is less than the waste and the sources of the lower classes in regard to a fortunate combination of genes are limited, then evidently the permanent waste leads to an exhaustion of the best human material, and to racial depletion. Theoretically, both hypotheses are possible. And at the present moment we cannot decide the question *certainly* in either way. Nevertheless, in a hypothetical way, the supposition of exhaustion seems to be more probable. Let us briefly discuss the principal arguments *pro* and *contra.* The first argument of "the optimists" is that differential fecundity is a temporary phenomenon; that with the expansion of birth control the birth rate of the lower classes will fall down also; that in this way, the discrepancy of procreation of the lower and the upper strata will disappear and negative selection will be stopped.[6] The argument appears to be fallacious. In the first place, it is doubtful whether the discrepancy between the fertility of the upper and the lower classes will disappear. The facts, as we have seen from the data of T. H. C. Stevenson, show an increase but not a decrease of discrepancy for the last 50 years in England. Other data given in Chap. XV exhibit the discrepancy very clearly also. There is not proof of a decrease of the discrepancy[7] even in France where birth control has been practiced for a long time. Therefore, the belief in its disappearance is still a mere speculation not based on any factual material. In the second place, even admitting the validity of this belief, I do not see how a universal low birth rate may stop the deterioration of the population. Contrary to the common opinion, I am inclined to think that it will lead from bad to worse. My reasons are as follows: As eugenics exists still only on paper, and there are not great hopes that it will be practiced efficiently in the future, the universally low birth rate, accompanied by a low mortality, means an elimination of the factor of natural selection and an increase of the chances for survival and procreation of weak individuals. Under the condition of a high birth rate and a high mortality, in less civilized societies such weak elements are eliminated. Therefore, as a rule, only relatively strong elements are surviving.[8] In the relatively healthy conditions of civilized societies, under the conditions of low mortality and low birth rate, the chances for the procreation of weak elements greatly increase. As a result, the contamination of the stock is likely to increase also. If heredity is not a phantom, as we have reason to believe, then the possible results of such a situation are at hand. They lead to racial deterioration. I am even inclined to think that, under such conditions, race depletion is likely to come sooner than under the condition of a differential fecundity;[9] if only the lower classes procreate intensively, such a procreation, accompanied by a relatively high mortality, would eliminate the comparatively weak elements from these classes, and would give more chance for a "fortunate combination" of the genes, which produces strong and talented men. Up to this time, I have been speaking of the relatively strong elements, meaning by them the vitally strong people. But as far as it has been shown before that intelligence and health are somewhat correlated, the higher vitality means also a higher intelligence. A diminution of the proportion of strong people among the population means also a diminution of the proportion of intelligent people. The higher vitality means also a higher intelligence. For this reason, the above considerations may be applied to the survival of the talented and more intelligent people also. These, in brief, are the reasons why the arguments in favor of lowering birth and death rates appear to me fallacious and not very hopeful. I willingly admit that such a situation may temporarily facilitate an increase in the standard of living, a decrease of the chances of war, and many other beneficial results. But with such results in these respects, it seems it cannot stop the deterioration of the stock and the impoverishment of the funds of a nation. In this respect it may be rather disastrous. Finally, there is another point. A society with a generally low birth rate is in danger of being engulfed by and becoming a minority among peoples with a high birth rate. In the period from 1908 to 1913, a yearly increase of the population per 1,000 inhabitants was for France, 0.9; for Belgium, 7.7; for Switzerland, 9.5; for Sweden, 10.4; for England and Wales, 10.4. Now for the less industrial countries such as Russia it was about 18; Rumania, 18.4; Bulgaria, 18.6; Serbia, 14.5; Portugal, 14.1.[10] Such a difference in the rates of increase of population, being continued during one or two centuries, will lead to a situation in which the offspring of the low-procreating population become a small minority in the total population of the earth and even within the low-procreating countries themselves. The difference is responsible for the fact that from 1900 to 1910 in Czechoslovakia, the Czech population increased by 8.49 per cent, while the German population increased only 1.96 per cent.[11] The low birth rate of France is responsible for the fact that its population, before our eyes, is more and more supplanted by that of other peoples and nations. During 6 years, from 1919 to 1924, at least 800,000 foreign laborers entered and remained in France; at the beginning of 1925 there were 2,100,000 permanently resident foreigners, who composed 6 per cent of the whole population of France.[12] Owing to the low birth rate, France must admit them and must facilitate immigration to France, as has been shown by the recent French law on immigration. In this way the French population, however talented it may be, is step by step supplanted by Italians, Poles, and others; if such a situation is continued during one or two centuries, the French will compose only a minority in France. Whether this is good or bad does not matter. What matters is the fact that an annihilation of the differential birth rate within one society does not annihilate but rather increases the differential fertility among different societies. Low birth rate in one society, while there are others with a high birth rate, directly or indirectly leads to an engulfment not only of the talented part of the unfertile society, but also of the whole population of such a society in other societies. The chances that within a few decades it will be possible to introduce birth control among all native peoples of Asia, Africa, and Australia are insignificant. Therefore, through the low birth rate Western societies prepare their "decay" and engulfment by other more fertile nations.[13] Contemporary France shows all the pitiful effects of the general low birth rate and stagnation in the increase of the population.[14] The French are far from being able to check the exhaustion of the best elements of France. So much on this point.

2. The second argument of "the optimists" consists in an indication of improved biological balance of the city population and a general increase of life expectation in the civilized countries. Since the end of the nineteenth century the birth rate of the city population has become higher than its mortality rate. During the last few decades, the general expectation of longevity has increased also. From these facts they conclude that the city population, and that of industrialized countries generally, can maintain its biological balance without any degeneration or depletion.[15] Is this argument valid? Can these facts check the waste and impoverishment of the "racial fund" of a mobile society? I do not think so. In the first place, the improvement of balance has been reached not through a selection or an increase of birth rate but exclusively through a decrease of the mortality, and of children's mortality, especially, due to the improvement of sanitary conditions of the city. Such an improvement represents again nothing but the elimination of natural selection. For this reason, all previous considerations are applicable to this case also. The improvement has not been followed either by a weakening of the differential fertility among the city population, or by an increase of birth rate, or by a real eugenic selection.[16]

3. The third and most fundamental argument of the optimists is of course the hope in education. Being inclined to neglect the factor of heredity, they say that through an ideal education (I wish I might see it), it is possible to compensate for all losses of the negative selection. This, however, does not eliminate the fact of the wasting of the best elements. This also does not

remove the waste itself and the losses. In fact, let the best elements be put through "the ideal education," they probably would shine still brighter than people of average heredity. Education is really a great thing and I highly appreciate its importance. This, however, does not prevent my skepticism as to its omnipotent rôle. No education can make out of an idiot, a bright man; out of a man of average heredity, a genius.[17] It somewhat raises the mental level of an average man, and that is all. Besides, the existing system of education is pretty impotent as character education. It is not known certainly whether it facilitates moralization or demoralization, socialization or antisocialization. It surely increases skepticism and the analytical frame of mind, but these things though fine in a due proportion, in an exaggerated amount may be disastrous and lead to sophistication, nihilism, cynicism, hesitation, impotence, and similar results. With an increase of education suicides increase, crimes do not show any sign of decrease, and mental diseases increase also. Social unrest grows. Maybe education is not responsible for all this; but it is evident that it has not been able to check these evils. This means that the efficiency of education is limited and warns us not to trust too much to it.

4. To the above consideration, may be added one reason of a socio-historical character. In order that a society may exist during many centuries and thousands of years, it is apparently necessary that there be some more or less talented leaders or a considerable number of men who may successfully cope with the problems of social control and social organization. The long-existing societies or groups, like China, India, or the Jewish nation, are all societies with a very high birth rate and a high mortality. On the other hand, several historical societies, such as ancient Rome or Greece, as soon as they had entered the period of low birth rate, began to show symptoms of decay and social and mental unfertility. The double parallelism of these phenomena suggests that the high birth rate seems to be an essential condition for the long existence of a society while a low birth rate is a satellite of decay. As far as a long existence plus a brilliant culture, as of China, India, and the Jews, presupposes the existence of the brilliant group of the leaders, this suggests

that their high fertility has been an essential condition for the production of these capable people. On the other hand, the lack of such elements in the most brilliant population of Rome and Greece, after the period of their infertility, suggests that this, perhaps, was due to the exhaustion of the "positive racial fund" of these nations facilitated by their low birth rate. Such a hypothesis is in accordance with the facts. And, together with other considerations, it makes probable the conclusion that, sooner or later, a wasting of the best elements of a mobile society is likely to lead to the final depletion of the population. In spite of my belief, this hypothesis is, however, still not proved definitely, and must be tested. I would be the first to be glad were the hypothesis wrong.

3. EXHAUSTION OF THE ÉLITE AND THE DECAY OF NATIONS

If the above conclusion is valid, it somewhat explains many facts of the decay of cultures and societies. Ancient Rome and ancient Greece supply the classical examples of this phenomenon. If the existence of talented leaders is a condition necessary for the existence and progress of a society, and if mobility leads to an exhaustion of their reserves, it is natural that sooner or later such a society must come to decay and must give way to other societies which have succeeded in accumulating the potential *élite* under conditions of comparative immobility, high procreation, and a severe elimination of weak elements, and many similar conditions. This means that a mobile society, however brilliant its civilization may be, is likely to come to decay and must give way to "barbarians." In this way, the old theory of the appearance, growth, and decay of societies—the theory set forth by Confucius and Plato, by Florus and Seneca, not to mention many others—seems to be not quite fictitious. This standpoint has a specific interest to the present time. On the one hand, many symptoms of social disorganization and decay within present Western societies are seen. On the other hand, the miraculous awakening of Japan and the Eastern peoples generally is noted.[18] And, perhaps the voices which interpret this situation as the decay of Western societies and as the coming to the scene of history of new "barbarians" or of the oldest nations, which for centuries have been sleeping, are not quite false. Three hundred years of peace, under the Shogunate of Takugava, together with a comparative immobility of the Japanese society, have permitted Japan to accumulate an extraordinary number of the *élite*. Such a condition made possible its miraculous regeneration within some 50 years, a regeneration absolutely unthinkable if there had not been such an accumulation of an exclusively superior human material. Many of the Asiatic peoples have been in similar conditions. Living for centuries under "barbarian conditions," with high birth rate and high mortality, they have undergone the process of natural selection and cleansing of their racial funds. Put into contact with the high European civilization, they very quickly acquire its desirable traits. In this way, in a short time, they may be able to become serious rivals; and, who knows, perhaps even the successors of the leading nations of the European societies. I repeat again, this is still an hypothesis, but an hypothesis which may be not quite fallacious and which seems to be in harmony with real historical events. However it may be, one thing seems to be clear: if we desire the continuation of our civilization, differential fertility and a generally low birth rate are scarcely favorable conditions for this purpose.

[1] Up to the second half of the nineteenth century this statement cannot be questioned. It is admitted even by R. Kuczynski, and J. H. F. Kohlbrügge, the most serious critics of G. Hansen's theory. See the data and corresponding theories: HANSEN, G., *Die Drei Bevölkerungsstufen;* KUCZYNSKI, R., *Der Züg nach der Stadt,* Stuttgart, 1897; WEBER, A. F., *The Growth of Cities;* KOHLBRÜGGE, J. H. F., "Stadt und Land als biologische Umwelt," *Archive für Rassen- und Gesellschafts-Biologie,* pp. 493-511, 631-648, 1909; BÜCHER, K., *Industrial Evolution;* PÖHLMAN, R., *Die Übervölkerung der Antiken Grossstädte,* pp. 16-17, 115, Leipzig, 1884. See here other literature.

[2] At the present moment it seems to be impossible to sustain either the theory of G. Hansen, who tried to prove that rural migrants, as a rule, enter a relatively higher social stratum than the majority of the city-born people, or the opposite theory of Kuczynski. The truth, as it has been shown by several later studies, seems to lie between these opposite theories. See "Auslese und Anpassung der Arbeiterschaft," all volumes; *Statistisches Jahrbuch für den Bayern,* p. 33, 1919; WEBER, A. F., *op. cit.,* Chap. VII; HOUZÉ, E., *op. cit.,* pp. 93 *ff.*

[3] Taking into consideration the low fertility of prominent men, this is to be expected. Among French contemporary celebrities an exclusively high per cent are childless. Thiers, Jules Ferry, Gambetta, Lepère, Spuller, Waldeck-Rousseau, Goblet, Floquet, Challemel-Lacour, and many other statesmen and men of talent did not have children at all. Among others, 445 celebrities (94 artists

and actors, 133 literary men, 111 statesmen, 23 great captains of industry and finance, 33 highest military officials, and 51 different notables) had only 575 children born. Bertillon, J., *La dépopulation de la France,* pp. 130-140. According to the study of L. J. Dublin, "half of the educated women in the United States do not marry; and those who do, follow the American fashion of raising very small families." The average number of children per married graduate is 1.4 and per graduate only 0.7 of a child; while per married woman of native parentage it was in 1918, 2.7; per woman of foreign parentage, 4.4. The author rightly says that "the continuation of these conditions means the extinction of valuable stock and a gradual dilution of our best blood." The same is true in regard to graduate college men, as the statistics of the graduates of Harvard, Yale, and of other universities show. The same is true in regard to all Western mobile societies and their upper strata. See other data in Holmes, S., *The Trend of the Race,* pp. 136-139; Schallmayer, W., *op. cit.,* pp. 234 *ff.*

[4] See Rossiter, W., *Increase of Population in the United States,* pp. 96-97, Washington, D. C., 1922; also Hrdlička, Aleš, *Old Americans,* Chap. VII, 1925.

[5] See the details in the works of Seek, Otto, *op. cit., passim;* Fahlbeck, *La décadence et la chute des peuples, passim;* Frank, J., *Race Mixture, passim;* Sensini, *Teoria del Equilibrio, passim;* Lapouge, V. 4e, *op. cit.,* Chaps. III and XIV; Pareto, V., *op. cit.,* Vol. II, pp. 1694 *ff.*

[6] This argument is very common. As an example of it see the article by MacIver, Dr. R. M., "Living Standards and Birth Rates," *The New Republic,* Dec. 2, 1925; Cox, Harold, *The Problem of Population,* London, 1922; Pearl, R., *The Biology of Population Growth,* pp. 176-177.

[7] I know only the data of the Zürich city population for 1920, which show a fertility of unskilled labor near to that of the upper classes. But even these data are still in favor of unskilled labor. See Ehrler, Dr., *Der Einfluss der Geburtenrückgangs auf die Familiengrösse;* Schmoller, G., *Jahrbuch für Gesetzgebung,* Heft 4, p. 191, 1925. The figures concerning the fertility of various classes in London for the period of 1911 to 1921 given by de Jastrzebsky do not support his claim. See de Jastrzebsky, T. T. S. "Changes in the Birth-rate and in Legitimate Fertility in London," *Journal of the Royal Statistical Society,* pp. 26-46, 1923.

[8] The principal arguments in favor of a eugenical character of natural selection in less civilized societies are as follows: Comparison of the death rates of the different age groups in civilized (England) and less civilized societies (Russia, Hungary, Bulgaria, Servia, and ancient Rome) shows that the mortality of the children in less civilized societies is much higher than that in civilized societies. But the mortality rates of the people at the age of 30 years and older in civilized societies is rather higher than in less civilized ones. This difference suggests that only relatively strong elements may survive in less civilized societies. Thanks to their greater vitality they, in spite of unhealthy conditions, can show a lower death rate at higher ages, than the corresponding age groups of civilized societies. Since in spite of healthy conditions in civilized countries these age groups die at a rate higher than the corresponding groups in the less civilized countries, this means that they are "the physical weaklings" who have survived only because of the healthy conditions of civilized societies. Under less favorable conditions they would be eliminated at an early period and could not have a chance to leave a posterity as they do in civilized societies. See the figures and the facts in the works: Ploetz, A., "Lebensdauer der Eltern und Kindersterblichkeit," *Archive für Rassen- und Gesellschafts-Biologie,* Vol. VI, pp. 33-43; Prinzing, Fr., "Kulturelle Entwick-

lung und Absterbeordnung," *ibid.*, Vol. VII, pp. 579-605; MacDonald, W. R., "On the Expectation of Life in Ancient Rome," *Biometrica*, Vol. IX, pp. 366-380; Pearl, R., *The Biology of Death*, Chap. IV, and *passim;* Snow, E. C., "The Intensity of Natural Selection in Man," *Draper's Company Research Memoires*, Vol. VII, pp. 1-43, 1911; Pearson, Karl, "A First Study of the Inheritance of Longevity," *Proceedings of the Royal Society*, Vol. LXV; Biometrika, Vol. I; Darwin, L., "Some Birth Rate Problems," *The Eugenic Review*, Vol. XII, p. 157; Huntington, E., *The Character of Races*, pp. 185 *ff.*, 336 *ff.*, Chap. XXII, 1924; Schallmayer, W., *op. cit.*, pp. 168 *ff.*, 189 *ff.*

Recruiting statistics give a second series of data. They show that the per cent of the defective recruits in civilized countries, such as France and Germany, has been considerably higher than that in less civilized countries, like Russia, in spite of the fact that the Russian standard of fitness for recruiting was not lower than in the former countries. Besides, the same statistics of recruits in France and Germany show that for the last years before the war, in spite of the lowered demands for fitness, the percentage of defective recruits was increasing but not decreasing—the phenomena going on parallel with that of a decrease of birth rate and mortality. On the other hand, official study has shown that the city population, where the mortality during recent years has been partly lower than in the country, has greater defects than the country population. These facts are very significant. See the figures and data: Claassen, W., "Die Abnehmende Kriegstüchtigkeit im Deutschen Reich in Stadt und Land," *Archiv für Rassen- und Gesellschafts-Biologie*, Vol. VI, pp. 73-77; the articles of the same author, *ibid.*, Vol. VIII, p. 786, Vol. X, p. 584; Reisner, H., *Rekrutierungsstatistik*, *ibid.*, Vol. VI, pp. 59-72; Schallmayer, W., "Eugenik, Lebenshaltung und Auslese," *Zeitschrft für Sozialwiss.*, Vol. XI, Heft 5 to 8, 1908; *Report upon the Physical Examination of Men of Military Age by National Service Medical Board*, London, 1920; United States War Department, *Defects Found in Drafted Men*, Washington, D. C., 1920. It is necessary to add to this those forms of negative social selection in civilized societies which have been so brilliantly depicted by Lapouge. The military, the religious, the political, the moral, the juridical, and the economic conditions of contemporary civilized societies are unfavorable to the survival of superior elements of the population and favorable to the survival of inferior elements. Lapouge somewhat exaggerated the negative side of contemporary social selections; nevertheless, his principal contention is likely to be true. Lapouge, V. de, *op. cit.*, Chaps. VII to XV.

[9] H. Hart tried to compute the degree of lowering of I.Q. as a result of differential fertility. His conclusion is that average I.Q. of American family has been 94.3; that of the children 93.7. "Differential fecundity is having a rather slight, but unquestionable depressing effect upon the mental-test ability of the rising generation in the United States." The conclusion of the author can be only tentative and must be tested, but it seems to be not improbable. Hart, H., *op. cit.*, p. 531.

[10] *Annuaire International de Statistique*, pp. 2-3, 1917.

[11] See Niederlé, L., *La Race Slave*, Paris, Alcan, 1911.

[12] *Journal de la Société de Statistique de Paris*, pp. 162-163, May, 1925.

[13] *Cf.* Steinmetz, S. R., "L'avenire della razza," *Rivista Italiana di Sociologia*, pp. 485-509, 1910; Lapouge, V. de, *op. cit.*, *passim*.

[14] See Bertillon, J., *La dépopulation de la France*, *passim*.

[15] See the quoted works of R. Kuczynski, J. H. F. Kohlbrügge, A. F. Weber.

[16] Even the improvement itself may be partly due to the continued migration of country people to the city. We do not know what would have happened to the city population had there not been the permanent influx of country people;

we have not had a case in which the city population has been isolated from the country migrants. On the other hand, besides the above data of recruit statistics, there are many cases in which it has been found that the second and third generations of country migrants to the city were weaker and more defective than their parents. This is especially true of factory workers. See the series "Auslese und Anpassung der Arbeiterschaft," the studies of R. Sorer, M. Bernays, F. Syrup, F. Schumann, and others whose data show that the second generation of factory workers are biologically worse than their fathers. Similar data were obtained by W. Abelsdorf (*Die Wehrfahigkeit Zweier Generation,* Berlin, 1905) concerning the employees of the printing industry, and by Tapezirer concerning the employees in the metal industry (*Metallarbeiter und Buchdrucker*). Further, the studies of W. Claassen and some others have shown that venereal diseases, as far as the statistics are reliable, have been increasing. We must say the same about cancer and in part about tuberculosis (for some countries) and, finally, about heart and mental diseases, not to mention many other illnesses. The adequacy of the figures to the real situation may be questioned. But we do not have other factual data which would permit opposite statements. At the best, few of them show that the third or the fourth generations of city dwellers are not worse than those of the country population. See Houzé, E., *op. cit.,* p. 93. These and many other facts make it very doubtful whether the alleged improvement in the health of the city population may be really inferred from the simple fact of a decrease of childhood mortality and of an increase in expectation of life due to the improvement of the sanitary conditions of the cities. See the figures and data: Schallmayer, W., *op. cit.,* Chaps. VII and VIII; Weber, L. W., "Läst sich eine Zunahme der Geisteskranken feststelen," *Archiv für Rassen- und Gesellschafts-Biologie,* Vol. VII, pp. 704-721; Rüdin, E., "Über den Zusammenhang zwischen Geisteskrankheit und Kultur," *ibid.,* pp. 722-748; Claassen, W., "Ausbreitung der Geschlechtskranheiten in Berlin 1892 bis 1910," *ibid.,* Vol. X, pp. 479-483, and his paper in Vol. VIII; Gruber *und* Rüdin, E., *Fortplanzung, Vererbung, Rassenhygiene,* München, 1911; Pollock, H., and Furbush, E., "Patients with Mental Disease, etc.," *Mental Hygiene,* p. 145, 1921; Collis, E. L., and Greenwood, Major, *The Health of the Industrial Worker,* pp. 129 *ff.,* 155 *ff.,* London, 1921; Sadler, W. S., *Race Decadence,* London, 1923; Cumming, "Social Hygiene and Public Health," *Journal of Social Hygiene,* February, 1924; Dublin, L. I., "The Problem of Heart Disease," *Harper's Magazine,* January, 1927.

[17] I gave the data that in spite of an increase of educational facilities for the last century the per cent of men of genius from the labor classes has not increased.

[18] See Prince, A. E., "Europe and the Renaissance of Islam," *The Yale Review,* April, 1926.

CHAPTER XXI

THE EFFECTS OF MOBILITY ON HUMAN BEHAVIOR AND PSYCHOLOGY

1. BEHAVIOR BECOMES MORE PLASTIC AND VERSATILE

WHEN a man remains throughout his life in the same occupational, economic, and political status, his behavior inevitably becomes very rigid and non-flexible. Under the yoke of permanent performance of the same work, in the same social and economic conditions, the body and mind, and the whole behavior, acquire a definite rigidity. Habits become "second nature." On this account the behavior of people of the same status approaches uniformity, while that of people in different social positions becomes widely divergent. A quite different picture is given by the behavior of the members of a mobile society. Since they pass from occupation to occupation, from one economic and political status to another, the establishment of very rigid habits is hindered because a form of behavior suitable for one occupation becomes unsuitable for another. A change of status requires a corresponding accommodation of body, mind, and reactions. A change of economic standards produces the same result. Besides, behavior in a mobile society has to be more versatile, changeable, and capable of greater variation and modification. Contrariwise, a man who passes from one occupation to another (say, from agricultural laborer to minister or teacher) who cannot correspondingly modify his responses and actions, and adapt himself to the new position, is likely to be discharged. In this way a greater versatility and plasticity of human behavior is a natural result of social mobility. It is enough to compare from this standpoint the behavior of a Hindu and an American. A native Hindu may be excellently adapted to the performance of his traditional occupation; but, if he is suddenly moved to a quite different occupation, he is lost. Among Americans every day we see successful, almost casual, shifting from one position to quite another. The proposition is so self-evident that there is no necessity further to dwell upon it. As a more detailed inference from this general statement, the following differences are worth mentioning in the behavior and psychology of the populations of relatively immobile and mobile societies.

2. INCREASE OF MOBILITY TENDS TO REDUCE NARROW-MINDEDNESS AND OCCUPATIONAL AND OTHER IDIOSYNCRASIES

When a man throughout his life works at the same occupation and has the same economic and social status, his mind is decidedly marked by the stigmas of his social position. Whether he wants to or not, he is doomed to think and to look at the world through the glasses of his "social box." As he does not have a chance to get into another position, he naturally cannot understand the "standpoint" of those in other positions, and is doomed to evaluate, to think in the terms, from the viewpoint, and with the interest which is given to him by his permanent social status. All its virtues and idiosyncrasies are reflected in his opinions, beliefs, ideology, standards, and morals. He cannot get rid of them. He cannot properly grasp any different standpoint. His "seclusion" within his social box keeps him from acquiring a broad mind, flexible and versatile "viewpoints," larger mental vistas. *L'esprit de corps* here becomes inevitable; its stigmas, the most conspicuous.

Another picture is given by the mind of a man who passes from occupation to occupation, from poverty to riches, from subordination to domination, and *vice versa*. Such a shifting means passing through different "social atmospheres," breathing different social air, experiencing different standards, habits, morals, ideas, customs, and beliefs. He acquires different "mental vistas" and "viewpoints." He obtains a knowledge of the manner of life in different social boxes. The psychology of poor and rich, that of a laborer and a dentist, that of a subordinate and commander becomes familiar to him in the way of direct experience. Is it to be wondered at that his mind becomes also more plastic, broader, and more open; his mental horizon, larger; the idiosyncrasies, less conspicuous; *l'esprit de corps,* less intensive? Corroboration of these statements may be found everywhere. If we want to know the characteristic attitudes of a farmer, we do not go to a man who has been a farmer for a few months, but we go to one who is a farmer for life. On the other hand, take a man of any occupation who has followed it for a lifetime—be he a dentist, a fisher, a soldier, a professor, a factory operative—he will necessarily exhibit the narrow-mindedness, idiosyncrasies, and *l'esprit de corps* of his social status more conspicuously than a man who has passed through several different positions. As an illustration *en masse* we can mention the German factory workers, whose social-democratic ideology and affiliation have been found principally among "hereditary" proletarians who themselves and whose fathers have been for life factory workers. Those who have adopted this position only temporarily, show a much smaller proportion of socialist affiliation than the permanent proletarians.[1]

3. MOBILITY TENDS TO INCREASE MENTAL STRAIN

The necessity of being more versatile and able to adapt oneself to different social strata leads to an increase of mental strain in the population of a mobile society. It is much easier to adjust one's mind and body and reactions to one occupation or status than to many and different occupations. Having adapted himself to his occupation for life, a member of an immobile society may do his work and live his life under the spell of inertia and routine. For him it is not necessary permanently to make over new ideas and to make newer efforts to adapt himself to changing conditions. A member of a mobile society must do this unceasingly. Any change of occupation or social-economic status requires from him new efforts and new work. This increases the activity of the nervous system, and causes a permanent mental strain.[2] Then there is the possibility that one cannot successfully keep his position and may be ousted. Is it strange, therefore, that the life of Western societies is a very strenuous and nervous one? Living in such a mobile environment, we often are not aware of its incident strain. But prominent people like Rabindranath Tagore, used to living in an immobile society, like India, declare that our society is mad in its mobility and futile strenuousness.

4. MOBILITY FACILITATES INVENTIONS AND DISCOVERIES

G. Tard properly noticed that an invention is a "lucky marriage" or combination of two or more ideas in a mind of an inventor. Such a "marriage" may be intentional; it may be and has often been a matter of chance. A mobile society gives a much greater chance for such lucky combinations than an immobile one. Since, in the former society, people and things are more mobile and changeable, this means that the environment itself gives here a more diversified and more numerous combination of ideas, values, and things productive of inventions in the minds of the people. In an immobile society, with its permanent and monotonous environment, there is no such incentive for invention, as well as no such favorable combination of conditions which may suggest the ideas of invention. For this reason, it is to be expected that in a mobile society the stream of inventions is greater, and that it must increase with an increase of mobility unless it is checked by degeneration of the population. The facts completely corroborate the statement. The nineteenth and twentieth centuries in Western mobile societies have been marked by an extraordinary crop of inventions, and in the latter the greater number. Among the causes for such phenomena, social mobility seems to have been one playing a significant part.

5. MOBILITY FACILITATES AN INCREASE OF INTELLECTUAL LIFE

G. Tard, E. De-Roberty, Draghicesco, and J. Izoulet,[3] not to mention many other names, have shown that any new idea represents a combination of different previous ideas. According to them, for such a combination there is necessary the social contact of different individuals with different ideas. Consequently, periods when we have an especially intensive meeting of different peoples with different cultures, are marked by a cross-fertilization of ideas, by an intensification of intellectual life, and by an intensive creation of new economic, religious, philosophical, scientific, æsthetic, and moral values. On the basis of this generalization it is logical to infer that an increase of mobility facilitates an intensification of mental life and the creation of new values. At least, at its first stages.[4] Increase of mobility means an intensification of interchange of ideas, a clashing and crossing of values of different strata with different cultures, an increase of chances for a cross-fertilization of minds. So much for deductive reason. The facts seems to corroborate this expectation. In ancient Greece the climax of intellectual life was reached just in the period of an increase of social mobility and of social upheaval (normal and revolutionary): Herodotus, Socrates, Plato, Thucydides, Sophocles, Aristophanes, Xenophon, Phidias, Aristotle, the founders of Stoicism and Epicureanism, not to mention other names, lived in such a period. In Rome, Cicero, Seneca, Vergil, Epictetus, Horace, Lucretius, and the greatest jurisconsults, lived also in "a shifting epoch." In the same shifting period appeared and grew Christianity. Confucius and Lao-Tze, the founders of Confucianism and Tao-ism, lived in a period of social disorder and of great circulation. Mencius, the most prominent follower of Confucius, lived in a similar shifting and disorderly period. The periods of the Renaissance and Reformation were again periods of extraordinary normal and revolutionary circulation in Italy and other European countries. From the end of the fourteenth to the sixteenth century

> . . . we behold a rapid social transformation in Italy, an enormous intellectual activity. On all sides old traditions, forms, and institutions were crumbling and disappearing to make way for new ones.

Scholastic methods were superseded by the natural sciences; in architecture and painting we see the appearance of such giants as Brunelleschi, Donatello, Masaccio, Michelangelo, Raphael, Leonardo da Vinci; in political sciences we observe the appearance of Machiavelli, Guicciardini; in poetry, new people like Ariosto; among the preachers, men like Savonarola. At the same time, the period was of one of the greatest shifting. "The fifteenth century was rightly styled the age of adventurers and bastards." [5]

The same may be said of the Reformation. It is strange therefore that

> . . . previous to the thirteenth century Italy produced no great painters. In the thirteenth century seven were born; in the fourteenth, seven; in the fifteenth, thirty-eight (and among them such as

Perugino, Botticelli, Pinturicchio, Leonardo da Vinci, fra Bartolomeo, Giorgione, Raphael, Michelangelo, Correggio, Titian); in the sixteenth, twenty-three, of whom fourteen fall in the first half. In the seventeenth, eighteenth, and nineteenth centuries a few scattered painters, none of them of very high merit.[6]

It is interesting to note further that excessively mobile periods in the history of France are marked also by a greater number of prominent men of letters who were born and lived during and immediately after such periods. In the fourteenth century the highest number of births of men of letters falls in the period from 1376 to 1400 (annual average number being 0.86, instead of 0.50, 0.78, and 0.56 during the first three-quarters of the century). The period, as we know, was very tempestuous; from 1358 to 1425 we had the Jacquerie, the Revolution in Paris, the English-French wars, the revolutions of the Caboshiens, and their struggle with the Armagnacs, and so on.

The next period, in which the annual number of births of prominent men of letters reaches the highest level, unprecedented before, is the period from 1591 to 1605. (The annual number of births is 14.54, instead of 7.70 to 11.24 from 1561 to 1590.) We know that the second part and the end of the sixteenth century in France were the periods of great upheaval; like the religious wars, many revolts, the Bartholomew Massacre, "the Catholic League," and so on. Finally the highest number of births in all periods from the fourteenth century to 1830 is shown in the years from 1801 to 1815. (The annual number of births is 52.10 for 1801 to 1805, and 53.72 for 1811 to 1815; then the number drops to 43.58 for 1816 to 1820; 36.64 for 1821 to 1825; 37.04 for 1826 to 1830.)[7] The great French Revolution and Napoleonic wars with their greatest mobility seem to be responsible for such a record. A similar picture is given by the prominent men of letters in the United States. The stormy and shifting period from 1791 to 1811 gives the highest number of prominent men of letters born from 1701 to 1851. This is seen from the figures on p. 514.[8]

An increase of the men of genius during and after revolutions and wars has been manifested many times.[9]

Finally, looking at the number of eminent men and women born

Distribution of 1,000 American Literati Born Prior to 1851, by Period of Birth

	Period before 1701	1701–1710	1711–1720	1721–1730	1731–1740	1741–1750	1751–1760	1761–1770	1771–1780	1781–1790	1791–1800	1801–1810	1811–1820	1821–1830	1831–1840	1841–1850
Absolute number	6	4	3	7	8	8	18	14	34	49	103	122	178	140	169	137
Per million of white population								10	15	15	23	20	22	13	11	7

between 700 B.C. and A.D. 1850, and studied by J. McK. Cattell and C. S. Castle, it is easy to see also that they appeared in much greater number in mobile periods and in the periods of great social upheaval than in the periods of social stagnation or immobility.[10] As the last centuries have been centuries of intensive mobility within Western societies, it is natural that we should witness in them a tremendous intensification of intellectual life, an intensive creation of new ideologies, theories, systems, inventions, and discoveries. Such things are in complete harmony with my proposition. Permanent shifting incessantly creates new situations which demand new responses; the constant friction and clash of different ideologies gives an impetus to ever newer combinations; these extraordinary combinations of circumstances in our ever-changing social life suggest new ideas and intellectual constructions. Hence appears the enormous intellectualism of our epoch, the brilliant progress of science and the arts, philosophy and social thought.

6. MOBILITY FACILITATES ALSO AN INCREASE OF MENTAL DISEASES

If mobility favors an increase of broad-mindedness, larger experience, intellectualism, inventions, and discoveries, it also facilitates an increase of many opposite phenomena. In the first place, an increase both of mobility and mental diseases seems to exist in a close correlation. Great mental strain and versatility of behavior, demanded by life in a mobile society, are so exacting that they cannot be met by many individuals. Their nervous systems crumble under the burden of the great strains required of them. Hence arises the increase of mental diseases and nervousness, psychoses, and neuroses shown by the statistics of all Western countries. The data may be questioned, but the critics of these statistics cannot offer any other data for corroboration of their opposite optimistic conclusions. For the above reason, personally, I think that the statistics of mental diseases, which show their permanent increase, in essence correctly reflect the reality. In England per 100,000 population in 1859 there were 159 patients with mental diseases; in 1908, 360. In the United States per 100,000 of the population in 1880 there were 81.6 patients with mental diseases in the institutions; in 1910, 217.5; in 1920, 220.1.[11] Similar data exist for other European countries. The mobility of present society appears to be one of the causes of these mental wreckages. Increase of mental diseases is the reverse side of an intensification of the mental strain within our societies.

7. MOBILITY TENDS TO INCREASE SUPERFICIALITY, TO DECREASE SENSITIVENESS OF THE NERVOUS SYSTEM

If on the one hand the mobility broadens the mind and makes mental life more intensive, on the other hand it facilitates superficiality. Charles H. Cooley properly remarks:

> Outside of his specialty, the man of our somewhat hurried civilization is apt to have an impatient, touch-and-go habit of mind as regards both thought and feeling. . . . We are trying to do many and various things, and are driven to versatility and short cuts at some expense to truth and depth.[12]

Time and patience are necessary in order to know anything thoroughly. One who stays in a definite location for a long time is likely to know it much better than a tourist who stays in the place for one or two days. Besides, if an individual knows that he has to stay in a given place for life, he is vitally interested in the study of his environment. The tourist does not have such an incentive. He is interested only in so far as the place is suitable for providing pleasure. In just such positions are the members of immobile and mobile societies. Since the members of a mobile society are in one occupation, locality, economic status, or position to-day, and shift to another social position to-morrow, they become like tourists. They do not stay for a long time in one "social box"; they are not going to remain there for a lifetime; therefore they do not care about and cannot study their environment seriously. Why should they burden themselves with such additional effort since they are going to shift? They try to know their temporary "box" only as much as is necessary for a passable performance of their function. We more and more acquire the superficial psychology and attitude of a tourist. Like him, our minds are "broad": we know everything; we have seen all the countries of the world; we are ready to judge of anything. But, like a tourist's "broad-mindedness," our "broad-mindedness" is often an absence of any mind, and reminds one rather of a bag filled with many different things, beginning with potatoes and onions, and ending with a few sentences of Plato and Lenin, the manners of Gloria Swanson and Valentino, and distorted sentences of the last copy of *Liberty* or *The Nation*. All this is incongruously mixed up and represents a hodgepodge of superficiality. Read the majority of contemporary books. How rarely you find among them the discriminating depth and care and attention and concentration, which is so conspicuous in the books of the old masters who lived in less mobile societies. If incidentally such books appear, they never become the "best sellers." Not only the writers, but the readers, too, do not have time to read such delicate things. Our textbooks and "reading books" are especially characteristic. They are nothing but modified tourists' guides. They give all that in a tourist's hurried way may be necessary and may be consumed. But no more. Good in this respect, they are as superficial as the *Tourists' Guide*. Often composed of the distorted fragments of different authors, they embody all the tourists' superficiality and "open-mindedness" of our superficial education.[13] We are led to the same superficiality in another way. Owing to the division of labor our *direct* experience is relatively narrow. Most of our information is obtained in an *indirect* way, not from *things* but from books and papers. We are people who live in a "paper environment" predominantly. Between us and the real world there is everywhere a paper world. We look, see, judge what is shown and how it is shown by the papers which we read; 99.9 per cent of foreigners have not seen, touched, smelled, experienced anything from Bolshevism, Fascism, to Chinese events—in fact anything—directly. They know only what has been said in the papers. They read in these fragmentary, sensational, always superficial, usually partial, and often incongruous bits of information. Is it to be wondered at that the ideas of these 99.9 per cent about all phenomena outside of their direct experience are often superficial and absurd? Is it strange that many intellectual "book and paper eaters" very often produce theories which are "absurd" for anybody who really knows the situation? This may explain why in many cases a plain citizen from the street has a more accurate judgment of events than many a prominent intellectual whose mental vistas are misguided by their confinement in "the paper environment."

In connection with this superficiality, there is another trait of contemporary Western psychology which is also closely correlated with mobility. This trait is an increase in the insensitiveness of our nervous system. Our nervous system must be wrecked completely, if it were sensitive to all the innumerable phenomena which surround us in our permanent mobility. It could not have stood physiologically if it did not develop an insensitiveness toward many stimuli. They are so numerous and so changeable that it is a matter of necessity to be insensitive in regard to many of them. In the way of adaptation to our mobile environment, we have developed this insensitiveness to a considerable degree. A suicide or murder, or fire, which in a less mobile society calls forth great excitement and expression, does not touch us much. We quietly read about them every day without any excitement. We pass by such phenomena in the street. "It is not my business; let those who are in charge take care"—such is our psychology. The same attitude is shown by us in thousands of other cases. Our nervous system, for the sake of its preservation, has become thicker or less sensitive. This is manifested in many forms; and in its turn has produced many typical social phenomena. In the first place, "the necessity of advertisement"; in the second place, "the necessity of sensations"; in the third place, "the rudest methods for impression on the minds of fellow men." Something delicate and noiseless cannot reach people's minds in our noisy and moving environment. Their insensitive nervous system remains "deaf" toward such things. Hence the present advertisements which try to be as large as the sky, as lurid as hell, as noisy as a thunderstorm, and as persistent as stubbornness itself. They do not intend to impress you in some "delicate psychological way"; no, they are purely mechanical, created as though not for a sensitive nervous system but for a nerveless cord which has to be impressed by the rudest methods. If somebody wishes to draw public attention to something, he must exaggerate and hyperbolize the thing to an enormous extent, and must present it in the most "impressive" form. Only in this way may one be made to listen. Maybe this is good, maybe it is bad, but one thing is certain: it is a matter of necessity in our shifting, noisy, and "booming" society.

8. MOBILITY FAVORS SKEPTICISM, CYNICISM, AND "MISONEISM"

Under conditions of superficiality and the greatest complexity of numerous and often opposite theories and ideologies, the mobile character of present social life facilitates also a skeptical attitude and a lack of very firm faith and convictions. On the other hand, it facilitates the phenomena of an intellectual misoneism. The members of an immobile society placed in their rigid "boxes" breathe and learn, as a rule, only a definite course of ideas, opinions, beliefs, and values. They have little chance to listen to many ideologies and to learn different beliefs. Naturally, their mental luggage is definite; their convictions are firm; their faith is strong and inflexible. There are few chances for criticism and almost none for weakening one ideology by another. Very different is the situation in a mobile society. Horizontally and vertically circulating individuals, placed in a stream of circulating theories and ideas, learn, listen to, read, and breathe the most different ideologies and opposite opinions. Each of them criticizes all of the others; each of them shows the weak points of all others. An individual who has a firm conviction that his theory is all right, faces its criticism and is shown its defects. Under such conditions it is most difficult to have an enthusiastic faith in a dogma, a firm conviction in the accuracy of a theory, an unwavering belief in the righteousness of an ideology. All this is undermined by criticism and analysis of other theories.[14] As a result, relativism takes the place of firm conviction; skepticism, that of fanaticism; disbelief, that of firm faith. We see all this around us. Firm convictions, especially among the intelligentsia, are weakening. Skepticism, sometimes even cynicism, is spreading. Relativism begins to reign supreme in sciences and intellectual constructions. It finds its supreme expression in Einstein's theory of relativity. The typical idols of the intelligentsia become men like George Bernard Shaw or Anatole France, with their cynicism and mockery of any value, beginning with God and ending with the family and morality. The proletariat is openly atheistic in a great proportion. The capitalists show often wonderful "manipulations" without firm convictions. If the devil himself promises them a large profit they are ready, at least in part, to enter into friendly cooperation with him. The capitalists' negotiations with the Soviet rulers is a corroboration of this hypothesis. They willingly merchandise even the jewels on which the blood of the victims may be seen. Endless criticism of any value step by step undermines all dogmas and beliefs, all sanctities and values. As a result, the intellectuals become the victims of their own criticism: they become impotent in action, the Hamlets, the wavering crowd of skeptics not capable of any action because they do not have any firm and sacred conviction. In the best case they are good only for echoing the impulses of the dissatisfied elements of a society or for a "justification" of the pretensions of their superiors. Under similar mobile conditions, such an inundation of skepticism and of destructive criticism has occurred several times in the history of different peoples. Such was the era of the sophists in Greece, which coincides with the epoch of mobility and which gave us such sophists as Gorgias, and such "practical pupils" as the Thirty Tyrants. Mobility facilitates an increase of such superintellectualism. The motto of our epoch is: "Everything is relative in this world, except the absolute character of this statement." Intellectuals of our epoch are a mixture of Protagoras, Gorgias, Socrates, and Montaigne. The fanatics are the minority.

Within the less educated masses mobility facilitates somewhat different mental characteristics. Confronted with an extreme complexity of different intellectual schools and currents, and having no time either to digest all this or to be busy with fine reflections and discussions, they, for the sake of the integrity of their mental life, often proceed along a different way. Max Nordau well understood this phenomenon. In order not to be lost in this complexity and not to be poisoned with its destructive effects, such masses

. . . settle the problem in another way. They simply give up (all this complexity and its civilization). For humanity has a sure means of defence against innovations which impose a destructive effort on its nervous system, namely, "misoneism," that instinctive, invincible aversion to progress.[15]

Maybe it is better to understand under "misoneism" a partly intentional, partly unintentional avoidance of all theories which only aggravate the perplexities of life, break up mental harmony and peace, and in this way, disorganize the human soul and undermine the bodily health. It expresses itself in a sudden dogmatism of the masses; in the phenomena of mass adherence to a theory which gives them simplicity and harmony, enthusiasm and firm conviction. Being inoculated with such a theory they become deaf and blind toward anything else, and they stick to it as to a shelter from all sophistication and intellectual troubles. Communism and anti-evolutionism, Fundamentalism, Christian Science, and Adventism, Fascism and "Humanitarianism," "Ku-Klux-Klanism," and the Billy Sunday followers are examples of such phenomena. They are the reactions of the masses against this intellectual complexity. Sticking to their theories they become as firm as any fanatic, as inimical to all arguments and sophistication, as that democratic crowd, led by Anitus and Melitus, which condemned to death a great intellectual and a great skeptic, Socrates. Reading the evolution trial at Tennessee, one could not help seeing the similarity of the situation to that of the trial of Socrates. In both cases the accusation was against intellectualism in its destructive manifestation; in both cases the accusers were the democratic people and honest plain citizens who tried to check the demoralizing rule of the "skeptical" mind. In both cases, the verdict was against intellectualism. These facts are only the symbols of hundreds of similar facts which take place in mobile society. Each of these effects, dangerous if taken separately, may, however, neutralize one another, and give an equilibrium in which criticism and skepticism may stimulate intellectual life, while misoneism may give a basis for social stability. Properly combined, they may give a basis for a synthesis of progress and order, which represents the most desirable form of social change.

9. MOBILITY DIMINISHES INTIMACY AND INCREASES PSYCHO-SOCIAL ISOLATION AND LONELINESS OF INDIVIDUALS—MOBILITY AND SUICIDE—MOBILITY AND THE HUNT FOR SENSUAL PLEASURE—MOBILITY AND RESTLESSNESS

It goes without saying that the state of loneliness is something undesirable and that of isolation is something painful for the great majority of people. Besides, as the facts of imprisonment in lonely cells show, they are psychologically and biologically harmful. We need to be bound by close social ties with other fellow men. This proclivity means not so much the necessity of a formal and mechanical contact with other human beings, as something more: the necessity of a close *intimacy* with other men, the desirability of a real community of feeling, an urgent need of a unity of understanding, a close friendship, an intimate "living together." The purely mechanical and formal contact with other men does not give this intimacy and does not cure the "loneliness" so dreaded by the majority of men. Among a crowd of people we often feel ourselves quite lonely; among the multitude of contacts, we remain wholly "a stranger." [16]

An increase or a decrease of mobility is a condition which influences considerably the chances of such intimacy. A Russian proverb says: "To know a man intimately, one must eat several bushels of salt with him." As salt is consumed in a very small quantity, the eating of several bushels supposes plenty of time necessary for reaching a nobly intimate level with a man. As a rule, it is impossible to become intimately acquainted in a few meetings. If such is the situation, then, under the conditions of an immobile society it is easier to be bound intimately with somebody than in a mobile society. Permanency of social position in an immobile society means also a permanency of the people among whom one lives, and an entire possibility of knowing them intimately. In a mobile society, where its members are shifting from group to group, from place to place, the chances for intimacy are much less. Before one acquires an intimate knowledge of his fellows, and establishes intimate relations with some of them, he is shifted to another group, from this to a third, and so on. As a result, the chances for intimate relations become less, and the socio-psychological loneliness of individuals is likely to become greater. In spite of his fellows and clubs, one remains "a stranger"; his psychological isolation persists; formal meetings and the usual "How do you do?" "Hello!" and community of occupation cannot always break the psychical walls which surround an individual. His loneliness remains with him. As already mentioned, contemporary man more often cuts off the ties which bind him to his native place, occupation, party, state, religion, family, citizenship, and so on. He becomes less and less attached to anything and to anybody. He begins to remind us of one down driven by the wind in the air. He becomes "free," and, as a consequence, lonely as a socially unattached atom.

A decrease of intimacy in a mobile society manifests itself also in other forms. *People become less intimate not only in their mutual interrelations, but in their interrelations with things also.* A medieval artisan was in "intimate" relations with the things which he produced. They bore on themselves the imprint of the personality of their producer. The producer himself was an artist, who put on the things the marks of his talent, who invested the thing with his tastes and art, his mind and skill. Hence, the extraordinary artistic character of medieval, Chinese and ancient Japanese objects. Now, with the division of labor, with the present system of mass-machinery production, where each man performs only one of thousands of operations necessary to produce the whole object, the object and the man are isolated also. There cannot be any feeling of a creative artist. There cannot be the marks of personality on the things produced. There cannot be any intimacy of the producer with the object.[17] All that there is represents only monotonous automatic work, drudgery,[18] in which man plays only the part of machinery which deals with other machinery. The whole of this civilization of ours is stamped by an impersonal character. Our business corporations, factories, firms, publishing houses, all these are great impersonal marks. The products produced are "standardized," impersonal, anonymous, stripped of any psychology, any soul. They are comfortable, but "gray and faceless," like our soulless "How do you do?" and "Fine weather, is it not?" The above considerations are conspicuously corroborated by the statistics of suicide. Durkheim's excellent study has shown that the fundamental factor of suicide is increase or decrease in the social ties of an individual. Any phenomenon which tends to increase his social isolation and loneliness favors an increase of suicide, and *vice versa.*[19] The phenomena of social mobility and suicide run parallel. Throughout the nineteenth century horizontal and vertical mobility has been increasing within European countries; suicide within these countries has been increasing also. In cities mobility is greater than in the country. In cities suicide is higher than in the country. A single person or widowed person does not have family shelter against social isolation; therefore he is more lonesome. Single and widowed persons also show a higher per cent of suicides than married ones. The periods of social upheaval result in a great shifting of the mass of individuals. At the end of such upheavals they find themselves in quite a new social position, among quite new and often inimical persons, while they are already isolated from their previous friends. As a result, their social isolation and loneliness are likely to increase greatly. Hence, it is to be expected that the curve of suicide at the end of such upheavals goes up. Statistics corroborate the expectation. In this way, psychologically, sociologically, and statistically the correlation between mobility and isolation, between isolation and suicide, seems to be very probable and really tangible.[20]

Finally, it seems to me, *there is also a functional relation between mobility and the phenomenon which may be styled as a hunt for pleasure, on the one hand, and as a psychological restlessness, on the other.* It is scarcely erroneous to admit that our epoch in Western societies is marked by an increase of the "hedonistic" trend and Epicureanism. It is manifested in the progress of a materialistic conception of life and ideologies, in the direction of human efforts to an increase of comfort, in a reinforcement of the social struggle for economic objects, in a domination of wealth, in a money criterion of all values, in an increase of sexual freedom, in a hunting for pleasure in different forms, in jazz and dancing, and in many similar facts. Side by side with this, we have observed an increase of social restlessness. It has been expressed not only in the growth of strikes, disorders and revolutions, but in other forms also: our fellow men appear to us as though they had lost something and were permanently looking for it. Young and old are restless. The old thing which has been styled mental peace and quiet has practically disappeared. Neither in religion nor in philosophy, nor in ethics, nor in politics, nor in business does it exist; there is no trace of a deep peace; all and everything is in the process of a reconstruction whose end is not seen. Everywhere they are "seeking for something lost," trying new and newer experiments—endless seeking and apparently hopeless seeking, like the work of Sisyphus.

There is no doubt that the causes of this are numerous. But among them, it seems to me, some rôle is played also by mobility through its facilitation of loneliness. If it is unbearable, is it not natural to try to break it by mad dancing, by mad rushing into a crowd (theaters, unions, factions, clubs), by the hope to secure intimacy in the way of hasty marriages, hasty love affairs, numerous dancing embraces, through imitation of "intimacy actions" among a host of quite "new friends"? People remind one often of those heroes who have lost their "Blue Bird" and are forever trying to catch it; but in vain: psychology cannot be deceived. All these means do not give the desired intimacy and do not break the loneliness. They give nothing but a short-lived "satisfaction" of this mental hunger for intimacy and deep psychological community. Like alcohol for a drunkard, they for a moment satisfy; but soon the hunger becomes still greater and more urgently demands its satiation. Hence, permanent restlessness, flapperism, dancing, craving for excitement, and similar phenomena. People are looking for what has been taken away by mobility. All this "looking for" has been growing side by side with family disorganization. The phenomena are parallel. It is to be expected. The family has been the surest shelter against loneliness. Now it is disintegrating. It does not serve the numerous crowd of divorced people; it does not serve people who have married hastily; it does not serve those who have not been married; it does not serve those who are driven away from their families by the stream of mobility. The proportion of such categories of people has been increasing. Is it strange, therefore, that the hunt for pleasure and restlessness have been increasing also? For these "hungry hearts" and "restless souls," at least, social mobility is partly responsible. They are a scum produced by the social stream of circulation.

10. MOBILITY FACILITATES DISINTEGRATION OF MORALS

More intensive shifting from place to place—in vertical and horizontal directions—hinders considerably an inculcation of rigid habits and stable morals. In an immobile society such an inculcation may be made much more successfully because each social box has its own rigid habits and because the position of an individual within such a box is permanent. In a mobile society, the members, being only "temporary dwellers" in a box, and permanently "butterflying" from position to position with their different standards and morals, cannot be inculcated with rigid and definite habits, and the habits themselves cannot have the same degree of stability as those inculcated in an immobile society. Hence, the greater moral stability of the members of a mobile society; hence, the demoralization nowadays; hence, a high level of criminality at the present time. Many sociologists, such as E. Durkheim, John Dewey, Charles H. Cooley, E. A. Ross, Robert E. Park, and Ernest W. Burgess, W. Thomas, and Znaniecki, Emory E. Bogardus and E. Sutherland,[21] quite rightly have shown a correlation between an increase of horizontal mobility and these phenomena. With a still greater reason, it is possible to insist on the correlation between disintegration of morals, criminality, and demoralization, on the one hand, and vertical mobility on the other. In a mobile society an

> individual is now subjected to many conflicting schemes of education. Hence, habits are divided against one another; personality is disrupted; the scheme of conduct is confused and disintegrated.[22]
>
> We are dependent for moral health upon intimate association with a group of some sort, usually consisting of our family, neighbors, and other friends. It is the interchange of ideas and feelings with this group that makes standards of right and wrong seem real to us. When we move to town or go to another country or get into a different social class, a common result is a partial moral isolation and atrophy of the moral sense. If the causes of change are at all general we may have great populations made up largely of such displaced units, a kind of "anarchy of spirits" among whom there is no ethos or

settled system of moral life at all, only a confused outbreak of impulses, better or worse.[23]

The discussed correlations are corroborated by several statistical as well as historical facts. In Columbus, Ohio, it has been found that the correlation between mobility and juvenile delinquency by wards is 0.39.[24] In Chicago, the average period of residence of the families of 30 delinquents in their present locality was 2.3 years, while this average for the families of 30 non-delinquents of the same social status living in the same part of the city was 5.25 years.[25] Still more conspicuous corroboration of the statement is given by historical correlation. I hope I have been able to show that the periods of revolutions, which represent periods of an extraordinary vertical mobility, regularly have exhibited an extremely high demoralization, "a real anarchy of spirit and conscience," an utter bestiality, cruelty, and wholesale criminality.[26] No other epochs give to us such a demoralization. Such a thing is natural from the standpoint of this correlation. More than that, besides the periods of revolution, the same trend of demoralization and disintegration of morals is conspicuously exhibited by many epochs of intensive vertical mobility. For the sake of brevity, only one example which is representative for such periods will be given. As already mentioned, the period from the fourteenth to the sixteenth centuries in Italy was a period of extraordinary vertical circulation. It was accompanied by brilliant intellectual activity and utter demoralization. With the disintegration of the previous social groups "each individual was left to his own guidance, was solely ruled by personal interest and egotism; hence, moral corruption became inevitable." The whole of Italy was corrupted. The moral perversion of the upper strata, composed partly of bastards, partly of the old aristocracy, was horrible.[27] The Renaissance and the Reformation, besides revolutionary explosions, have exhibited similar tendencies. In ancient Greece, the centuries of an increase of vertical mobility were those of moral decay. Similar parallelism is given by the history of ancient Rome.

For this reason it is not strange that, in spite of an increase of education, improving the standards of living, and the work of many social agencies, criminality within Western societies has not been decreasing within the last few decades.[28] In some societies, as far as statistics show, it has rather been increasing. This means that an intensive social mobility, in its horizontal and vertical forms, has been one of the factors which has been checking the efficiency of anticriminal forces.

[1] See the factual illustrations of this in the works: WILLIAMS, J. M., *Our Rural Heritage, passim;* GROVES, N. E., *Rural Mind;* LURIJE, *Sostav Proletariate;* SOMBART, W., *Der Bourgeois;* TAUSSIG, F. W., *Inventors and Money-Makers;* the series of occupational essays in *Revue International de Sociologie* for 1901-1902; BAUER, A., *Les classes sociales,* and works quoted above in Chap. XIII; MUNSTERBERG, *G., The Americans.*

[2] *Cf.* COOLEY, CHARLES H., *Social Organization,* Chap. X.

[3] See especially DE-ROBERTY, E., *Sociologie de l'action,* 1908; DRAGHICESCO, *Du rôle de l'individu dans le determinisme social,* and *L'ideal createur;* IZOULET, J., *La cité moderne.*

[4] Several facts make us think that a happy cross-fertilization of ideas is especially noticeable at the first stages of an increase of mobility. If it is continued for a very long time, a corresponding intensification of the intellectual values produced may not follow.

[5] VILLARI, *The Life and Times of N. Machiavelli,* introduction.

[6] COOLEY, CHARLES H., *Genius, Fame, and Comparison of Races,* p. 31.

[7] See ODIN, A., *op. cit.,* Vol. II, Table II.

[8] CLARKE, E. L., *American Men of Letters,* pp. 38-39; also COOLEY, CHARLES H., *Genius, Fame, and Comparison of Races,* pp. 37-39.

[9] See my *Sociology of Revolution,* Pts. III and IV; see also MAISTRE, J. DE, *Œûvres complètes,* Vol. I, pp. 35-36.

[10] Study from this standpoint the tables and the diagrams in CASTLE, C. S., *op. cit.,* pp. 30-38. Preliminary results of my study of prominent leaders suggest that they are more "mobile" than common people. It is also significant that Dr. C. Murchison's study has shown that among criminals the more mobile criminals have a superior intelligence than the less mobile ones. Murchison, C., *Criminal Intelligence,* pp. 49 *ff.*

[11] See quoted works of WEBER, L. W., "Läst sich eine Zunähme der Geisteskranken festellen"; RÜDIN, E., *Über Zusammenhang zwischen Geisteskrankheit und Kultur;* POLLOCK, H., and FURBUSH, E., *op. cit.* See also the actual number of idiots, cretins, and persons with mental diseases in principal European countries in *Annuaire International de Statistique,* pp. 162-166, 1916. The data shows that from 1880 to 1910 the number of such persons has been growing more rapidly than the population.

[12] COOLEY, CHARLES H., *Social Organization,* p. 99.

[13] See the remarks of DEMOLINS, E., *Anglo-Saxon Superiority,* pp. 12 *ff.*

[14] *Cf.* LEUBA, J. H., *op. cit.,* Chap. X.

[15] NORDAU, MAX, *Degeneration;* CARVER, T., *Sociology and Social Progress,* p. 710.

[16] *Cf.* HAYES, E. C., *Sociology and Ethics,* pp. 136-138.

[17] *Cf.* SIMMEL, G., *Philosophie des Geldes,* pp. 357-386.

[18] See PATRICK, G. T. W., *The Psychology of Social Reconstruction,* Chap. V and *passim,* 1920.

[19] See DURKHEIM, E., *Le suicide, passim,* Paris, 1912.

[20] See figures in E. Durkheim's quoted work.

[21] See SUTHERLAND, E., *Criminology,* pp. 128-133; THOMAS, W., and ZNA-

NIECKI, F., *The Polish Peasant,* Vol. V, p. 167; MCKENZIE, R., *The Neighborhood.*

[22] DEWEY, JOHN, *Human Nature and Conduct,* p. 130.

[23] COOLEY, CHARLES H., *Social Progress,* pp. 180-181.

[24] MCKENZIE, R., *op. cit.,* p. 166.

[25] SUTHERLAND, E., *op. cit.,* p. 131. See also BRUHNES, J., *Human Geography,* p. 543. J. Riis in his study of the movements of the population of New York City has shown that the bands of *apaches* are nearly always composed of men without any fixed home and even without any family. See RIIS, J., *How the Other Half Lives.*

[26] See the facts in SOROKIN, P., *Sociology of Revolution,* Pts. I and III.

[27] VILLARI, *op. cit.,* pp. 3-14.

[28] See the figures: VON MAYR, G., *Statistik und Geselschaftslehre,* pp. 683-710; for the United States, see SUTHERLAND, E., *op. cit.,* Chap. II.

CHAPTER XXII

THE EFFECTS OF MOBILITY IN THE FIELD OF SOCIAL PROCESSES AND ORGANIZATION

1. MOBILITY, UNDER SOME CONDITIONS, FACILITATES A BETTER AND MORE ADEQUATE SOCIAL DISTRIBUTION OF INDIVIDUALS, THAN IN AN IMMOBILE SOCIETY

IN THE ideal mobile society individuals must be distributed according to their capacity and ability, regardless of the position of their fathers. Such a social distribution where everybody is placed at his proper place, seems to be the best. At least since ancient India and China, through Plato and Aristotle, up to the present democracies, this type of social distribution of individuals has been recognized as the most desirable. And, it seems, only an ideal mobile society can realize it. In an immobile society, only extremely fortunate racial purity may to some extent approach such a type. But even as such a purity cannot prevent the appearance of children dissimilar to their parents, therefore, even an exclusively fortunate immobile society has to deviate from the ideal rule. In an ideal mobile society such children are at once shifted to the positions corresponding to their ability. However, in order that such a rule may be realized, definite conditions are necessary. Among them the most important are: *an equality in the starting point of children and an equality of chance.* As we cannot know *a priori* who are talented and the nature of these talents, we must test them. In order that the testing be fair it is necessary that children start from the same point, equipped more or less equally, and given equal chances in their "life race." Only under such conditions of equality may be determined those among them who are "good runners." Otherwise, the result may be fallacious and misleading. The second fundamental condition is the *adequacy of the testing institutions and methods.* This consists in that the methods of testing must test those talents and abilities which really are necessary for a successful performance of a definite social function. If we decide a man is suitable for the position of a ruler because he has a good style (as in China), the method may scarcely be recognized as adequate: for a successful ruler the style is of little importance. If we decide that any student who receives good grades *eo ipso* is suitable for any prominent leadership, we may be mistaken again. If we decide that all tall people are suitable for the position of a military strategist, the method of testing is inadequate again. This explains what is meant by an adequate method of testing. Both of these conditions have scarcely been realized to a full degree in any of the mobile societies. Therefore, none of them can boast of a realization of the ideal distribution of individuals. All of them have been defective. For this reason it is somewhat difficult to decide whether mobile or immobile societies have been nearer to their ideal rule of social distribution of individuals. We know some mobile societies, and the United States of America may serve as an example, in which the social distribution of individuals has been very satisfactory. But we know also some immobile societies, like India, where social distribution has been not altogether bad. The objective fact of an unquestionable supremacy of the Brahmins during 2,000 years; is a very convincing test of their adequacy for their social position, regardless of whether we like the caste-system or not. Surely, stupid men, without money and organization, cannot keep such exclusive domination for so long a time. And surely, too, it is absolutely childish to try to explain such a fact through "prejudices" and "superstitions." No prejudice, if it does not perform something useful, can exist even 100 years.

On the other hand, we know some mobile societies with highly incapable grafters and irresponsible adventurers and demagogues at the top, and some immobile groups with a degenerated hereditary aristocracy. This explains the difficulty in deciding definitely which of these types of societies, as they really have existed, is nearer to the realization of the above "golden rule of social distribution of individuals." However, in regard to present time, it seems that, in general, within mobile societies deviation from the rule is less than within relatively immobile societies. Since, in mobile societies, there is the system of "open positions," there is a greater competition for the higher places among the aspirants.

Through this the relatively weaker individuals are eliminated or ousted by the relatively stronger ones. A strong stream of mobility resembles a strong current which sweeps or drives away all those trees which are rooted weakly. In this way, the weak posterity of prominent parents is driven down; strong men of humble origin climb up; and as a result, the whole social structure is permanently cleansed from the inappropriate dwellers of its different stories. On the other hand, within relatively immobile societies, the present aristocracy is considerably "worn out." It does not represent the earlier generations of strong men, whatever their origin, but their latest posterity, already contaminated by unfortunate cross-marriages, weakened by detrimental conditions, licentiousness, luxury, venereal diseases, spoiled by a *dolce far niente,* and privileges without the corresponding responsibility. At the same time, within the lower strata there may be many talented people. Inheritance of social position hinders the depression of unworthy aristocracy and the elevation of talented upstarts from the bottom of the pyramid. For these reasons it is possible to think that within present societies the normal vertical mobility (not that of an anarchical or revolutionary time which is quite blind and unselective), in spite of the non-realization of the two mentioned conditions, facilitates a more appropriate social distribution of individuals.

2. MOBILITY FACILITATES AN ECONOMIC PROSPERITY AND A MORE RAPID SOCIAL PROGRESS

Since, in a mobile society, individuals are placed better, they are likely to be more efficient than the less fortunately placed individuals of an immobile society. Thanks to these and some other factors, mobile society progresses more rapidly than an immobile one. This statement is corroborated by history. The fact that mobile periods generally have been marked by great intellectual development has already been mentioned. As far as economic prosperity is concerned, a correlation between the periods of mobility and an increase of economic prosperity has been indicated by V. Pareto.

When in a country where the classes had been separated for a long time, they suddenly mix together; and the social circulation becomes suddenly intensive, such periods are marked by a considerable increase of economic prosperity of the country. As examples may serve Athens in the time of Pericles; Republican Rome, after the victory of the Plebeians; France, after the Revolution of 1789; England, in the time of Cromwell; Germany in the time of the Reformation; Italy after 1859; Germany after 1870.[1]

The United States of America, after the Civil War, gives an additional illustration. The correlation exists, however, only to a definite point; having reached it, a further increase of mobility seems not to be followed by a further increase of prosperity. A stronger stroke on a piano key and pedal is followed by a louder sound. But there is a "point of saturation" beyond which no increase of the stroke's force is followed by an increase of the sound. Such is the situation here: The increase of mobility after Pericles was followed by a decline in the prosperity of Greece; similar cases are numerous in history. In this as in other social processes there exists a limit beyond which the correlation disappears.

3. MOBILITY AND SOCIAL ORDER

As to the influence of mobility on social order and social stability the situation is very complex. On the one hand, mobility exerts quite positive effects on social stability. A better social distribution of individuals favors social stability. In the first place, when an individual is placed in a function to which he has an inclination, he is psychologically satisfied. He enjoys his job. For this reason he is far from ready to revolt against the existing régime. In the second place, the greater efficiency of properly placed individuals gives a greater possibility of procuring all the necessities for the population as a whole, and in this way removing the deep causes of social disorders and riots. In the third place, the open doors of a mobile society offer a great chance for the majority of leaders and ambitious persons to rise. Instead of becoming leaders of a revolution, they are turned into protectors of social order. Occupying relatively high positions, they do not have a serious motive for annihilation of the existing régime; their interests are rather opposite. In a way mobility permanently robs the revolutionary factions of their possible and capable leaders. Furthermore, in contradistinction to the later generations of an hereditary aristocracy, the generations which become soft hearted, "humanitarian," and inclined to hesitate in their rights and privileges and finally become impotent in their actions, the new "climbers" do not have these weak traits. Having climbed through their personal efforts, they are sure of their rights; they are not soft hearted; with all their mind and energy they are ready to protect themselves and the social order. If it is necessary, they will not hesitate to apply force and compulsion to suppress any riot. (Mussolini is one of the examples of this type of men). In this way they facilitate the preservation of social order. In the fourth place, an increase of inventions helps to raise the standards of living of the whole population of a mobile society. This is a condition which works for stability, too. The absence of hereditary privileges and artificial preferences decreases the validity of the arguments of dissatisfied people; instead of being heroes they are regarded as failures. Shifting of the population from stratum to stratum and the corresponding experiences are likely to weaken hatred and envy between different social groups. A man who has been both a millionaire and a workingman is not a complete stranger to both groups. He may evidence a "like-mindedness" in regard to either one. He is likely to be more moderate even in his dissatisfaction, than a man who is a stranger to a different social class. Through these and similar factors social mobility works in favor of social stability. But the picture has another side also.

In the first place, it has been indicated that mobility facilitates demoralization and generally weakens the rigidity of many socially necessary habits. This leads to an undermining of social order. In the second place, a decrease of intimacy and intensiveness of social ties leads to the same result. In the third place, a decrease of intimate relations with things and the drudgery of everyday work increases a desire for breaking the monotony and getting rid of it.[2] In the fourth place, the rigidity of an immobile society is a great stabilizing factor; since the social position of every individual is predetermined before his birth, the individuals accept this predestination as a kind of necessity. An individual quietly occupies that "box" in the social building in which he is born. He does not try to change it by any means. He does not strive to climb at any cost. He does not fear to be outdistanced. Quite different is the situation within a mobile society. Its members neither socially nor psychologically have this "psychology of predestination." They try to climb up. They are ambitious. They fear to be outdistanced. Correspondingly, they do not have either patience or satisfaction with their position. He who is below wants to go up. He who is in the upper strata wants to climb further or dreads to be put down. Hence, there is a mad rush to put down all obstacles irrespective of whether it leads to social disorder or not. Hence, an increase of the "centrifugal tendencies" of present society. This naturally does not favor social stability. All this leads to a continuous fight among individuals, groups and factions of a mobile society. This psychology becomes especially dangerous in the period of a general economic depression or in that of a social crisis. The suffering masses do not accept passively their situation. They try to improve it by all means, though at the cost of other groups. When legal forms of fight fail, they are ready to turn to violence. Hence, strikes, disorders, and revolutions break out. They mark the history of the majority of modern societies.

To the same result we are led by the difference in the nature of authority in a mobile and immobile society. In the first society, the authority is based on "the will of the people." It does not have any mystical elements nor any supernatural prestige. The masses like it—when they are satisfied. As soon as there is a situation from which they begin to suffer, they are prone to drive the authorities by mild or by rude methods. In this process the prestige of the authorities and leaders diminishes, instability increases, and the result is confusion, or social tremors, or a social earthquake. History seems to corroborate this conclusion. Modern mobile societies, whether in France, or Germany, or Italy, or in the United States of America, not to mention many republics of South America, have had revolutions and disorders within the last 150 years. Some of them, like France, have shown an extreme degree of instability or irritability. The history of ancient Rome and the Greek societies, like Athens, after the period of entering a mobile stage, shows the same high instability. Athens during 200 years, according to Aristotle, had 11 different constitutions, several revolutions, and many disorders. Rome's history after the end of the second century B.C. is a history of continuous instability and anarchy. From this standpoint the somewhat pessimistic views of J. de Maistre, J. Legge, and H. S. Maine[3] are not very far from the truth. The opinions of the great contemporaries of the ancient mobile society, such as Plato, Aristotle, Polybius, and Thucydides, in this respect are still more characteristic: they unanimously state that any mobile society in the form of a democratic society is unstable and is doomed to continual social upheavals.[4] As a contrast to that instability, the history of India or China in the past records only great but rare social upheavals.

The history of contemporary modern societies is relatively very short, and yet the present situation is far from being stable. Many voices, led by O. Spengler, already cry that the present culture and societies are decaying. The behavior of the "proletarian class" (manual as well as intellectual) has exhibited an extraordinary degree of irritation, and a proclivity to disorders on account of any and every cause and under the most trifling pretexts. By this is not meant that mobile societies are necessarily unstable. It indicates only the fundamental facts and reasons which do not allow one to conclude that mobile societies are more stable and have a greater chance for long existence than immobile ones. Such a statement is not warranted by fact. Whether the opposite contention, as a general rule is true or not, I cannot say.

4. MOBILITY, LONGEVITY, AND CONTINUITY OF THE CULTURE COMPLEX

Another problem near to the problem of the relation between mobility and stability is that of the influence of mobility on the longevity and continuity of the culture complex. By this is meant a unique combination of many social and cultural characteristics which in their totality compose "a socio-cultural face" of a society or give to it its social individuality. When we talk of the Greek and Roman or the Hindu cultures we do not think of any specific trait, but of the totality of all important cultural characteristics in their specific combination. Though political régime or political independence constitutes one of these characteristics, nevertheless, a specific culture complex may continue its existence, in spite of changes in a political régime or a loss of political independence. The Roman culture complex continued to exist after the transition from the Republic to monarchy; the Greek culture complex did not disappear after the subjugation of Greece by Philip of Macedonia. India has seen very many invasions during the last 2,000 years, and yet its culture complex exists up to this time. As long as such a culture complex exists we say that the corresponding society exists, though it may be politically dependent. It is interesting to ask, what is the influence of mobility on the longevity of such culture complexes? Does it facilitate or abbreviate them? The problem seems to be answered negatively: mobility is a factor which shortens the longevity of a culture complex, weakens its continuity and facilitates its disintegration and through this, the long existence of a society or social institution.

An increase of horizontal mobility means a dispersion of the people of a definite community throughout different localities and the infiltration of a community by people recruited from other places with other standards. This facilitates the disintegration of a local culture complex; it transforms a specific local culture into a kind of a mixture of the components of the most different cultural traits. As a result, the local type of a culture complex is likely to disappear and to be superseded by an incongruous mixture of all kinds of culture which cannot have any style or individuality, except that of mechanical mixture. Very similar are the effects of vertical mobility. If any social stratum has a permanently fluid population recruited from different social strata, it is natural that "the type" of a stratum is difficult to preserve under such conditions. Each of its members brings different habits and morals; such differences, step by step, obliterate the "style" of a group through mechanical mixture of different components and more and more disfigure it. As the members do not stay for a long time within the group, they cannot be properly inculcated with its cultural characteristics. The result is the disintegration of the cultural style of the group and disruption of its continuity. The more fluid is the population of a social form, and the more heterogeneous are the groups from which it is recruited, the sooner and the stronger "the form" is changed and disfigured.[5] These considerations explain the discussed proposition. We find its corroboration not only in the history of different social institutions, but in the history of whole societies or the great culture complexes. The history of the Greek and Roman civilizations, on the one hand, and that of the Hindu and Chinese societies on the other, may serve as the examples. The intensive mobility of the first societies is partly responsible for the rapid disintegration of the Greek and Roman culture complexes. Though their components certainly entered the medieval culture, nevertheless, as unique combinations of cultural traits, both civilizations, and correspondingly, both societies, had already ceased to exist by the early centuries of the Middle Ages. They disintegrated and were obliterated. Great vertical and horizontal mobility at the beginning of the Middle Ages ended their existence. Quite a different picture is given by the relatively immobile societies of India and China. In their history they have experienced also many invasions, subjugations and other upheavals, and yet, they have been able to preserve their culture complexes and social physiognomy throughout thousands of years. They have not been completely disintegrated. They exist up to this time. The evolution of their civilizations has not been discontinued. This vitality and persistency of their culture complexes, at least, is partly due to their relative immobility.[6]

5. MOBILITY FACILITATES ATOMIZATION AND DIFFUSION OF SOLIDARITY AND ANTAGONISMS

In an immobile society the social solidarity of its members is concentrated within the social box to which they belong. It rarely surpasses its limits because the social contact of an individual with the members of other different "boxes" is very weak and rare. Under such conditions the members of different boxes are likely to be strangers or to be in quite neutral relations. But within each box the ties of solidarity of its members are most intensive; for the same reason that the solidarity of the members of an old-fashioned family is strong. They have a complete understanding and a complete community of interests, or a complete like-mindedness, elaborated in the closest face-to-face contacts throughout a life span. The same may be said of hatred and antagonisms. All these socio-psychical phenomena are "localized" within and "centered" around a definite social box. In a mobile social body a "delocalization," and "atomization," and diffusion tend to take place. Since an individual belongs to different social groups and shifts from one box to another, his "area" of solidarity is not limited within one box. It becomes larger. It involves many individuals of different boxes. It ceases to "concentrate" within one box. It becomes "individualized" and selects not "boxes" but persons, or social atoms. The same may be said of the attitudes of hatred and antagonism. At the same time the phenomena of solidarity and antagonism are likely to lose their intensiveness. They become colder and more moderate. The reason for this is at hand: an individual now is not secluded for life in his box. He stays for a shorter time within each box; his face-to-face contacts with the members of each social group become shorter, the number of persons with whom he "lives together," more numerous: he becomes like a polygamist who is not obliged and does not invest all his love in one wife, but divides it among many women. Under such conditions, the attachment becomes less hot; the intensiveness of feeling, less concentrated.

In the social field this calls forth two important changes. In the first place, the map of solidarity and antagonisms within any mobile society becomes more complex and curved than in an immobile one. It is relatively clear in an immobile society. It goes along the lines separating one caste, order, or clear-cut stratum from another. The vertical and horizontal trenches are in general simple and conspicuous. In periods of social struggle, slaves fight with slaves against masters; serfs against their lords; plebeians, against patricians; peasants, against landlords. Much more complex is the map of solidarity and antagonism in a mobile society. Since the boxes are less clearly cut off from each other, and since each of them is filled by a fluid population from different strata, the lines of solidarity and antagonism become more whimsical, and assume the most fanciful character. During the

World War the citizens of the United States showed a considerable difference in their attitudes toward the belligerent countries. Anglo-Saxon, French, and Slavic citizens sympathized with the Allies; the German-Americans, with the Central Powers. The unity of the citizenship did not prevent this splitting. If, further, is taken into consideration the difference in religion, political aspiration, economic and occupational status, the lines of solidarity and antagonism for and against the War appear to be most fanciful. People of the same nationality, or of the same religion, or occupational status, or economic status, or children of the same family, very often happen to be in opposite factions.

In the second place, the lines of solidarity and antagonism in a mobile society become more flexible and more changeable. A man, who yesterday was an antagonist of a definite measure, to-day becomes its partisan because his social position has been changed. Shifting from one social position to another calls forth a similar shifting of interests and solidarity. Fluidity of social groups facilitates the same result. Therefore, it is not strange when we see that yesterday's foes are to-day's friends. The group, which last year was an enemy to be exterminated, to-day turns out an ally. In the contemporary interrelations of groups and whole countries this flexibility of the map of solidarity and antagonism is conspicuous. Germany a few years ago was a mortal enemy. Now she is a good friend of many previously inimical countries. A few years ago, who dared say that von Hindenburg would be elected President of Germany? He was elected. The attitude of the German people was completely changed. And the same may be seen everywhere, even in the psychology of an individual. One's sympathies and antipathies now change very rapidly. The old "hatred and feud to death" of "faithfulness to the death" are rare phenomena now. They become legends, like marriage faithfulness and the vow. "Butterfly" individuals more and more become butterflies in their hatred and love, solidarity and antagonism. Woe to a diplomat who sincerely relies on the promise of an ally to be forever his companion in war and peace! Woe to an individual who thinks that his fellow is to be faithful to him forever! Such phenomena have gone out of fashion.

6. MOBILITY FAVORS AN INCREASE OF INDIVIDUALISM FOLLOWED BY A VAGUE COSMOPOLITANISM AND COLLECTIVISM

The nineteenth and twentieth centuries have been marked, within Western societies, by an increase of individualism, by a weakening of patriotism, and, at the same time, by somewhat indefinite forms of socialism and "international solidarity." The whole of contemporary civilization with its "inalienable rights of man" is stamped by individualism. An increase in the pacifist movement and propaganda, an increase in the antipatriotic and anti-nationalist attitudes of Socialists, Syndicalists, Communists, Anarchists, Liberals, and finally of a part of the intelligentsia and the proletariat, manifests a conspicuous weakening of patriotism. The establishment of the First, Second, and Third Internationals and their relative success, the growth of international and cosmopolitan propaganda, are manifestations of the third-mentioned phenomenon. The causes of such phenomena are complex; but among them the factor of mobility seems to have played a considerable part. In essentials the correlation between mobility and these trends is as follows: The indicated increase of horizontal mobility mechanically weakens the attachment to a definite place or country. An intensive shifting from place to place does not permit an individual to have this exclusive love for "his native place" which is so common in the people who live and die at the place of their birth. Our shifting individuals inevitably begin to have the psychology of *"ubi bene ibi patria."* Since they have become, so to speak, "globe trotters," it is natural they cannot be patriots to the degree characteristic of the population of an immobile society.

Mobility facilitates an increase of individualism because it destroys this "seclusion for life in one social box" typical of an immobile society. When a man is for life attached to his "box," a knowledge of the box is enough to know the characteristics of the man. On the other hand, the man feels himself not so much as a particular personality, but only as a cell or a component of the group to which he belongs.[7] Under such conditions, the "boxes" but not the individuals are the social atoms or units. When the "boxes" are less definite and rigid, when their population is fluid, when an individual passes from position to position and often belongs to several overlapping groups, his attachment to the box becomes less intensive; his characteristics cannot be decided through his temporary position; in order to know him one must take him as an individual and study his personality. This participation in many groups, shifting from one group to another, and impossibility of identification with any one group makes an individual something separate from a social box; awakens his personality, transforms him from the component of a group to an individual person. As he is shifting from group to group, he now must secure rights and privileges for himself, not for a specific group, because he himself does not know in what group he will be to-morrow. Hence the "Declaration of the Rights of Men" but not that of a group. Hence the demands of liberty of speech, religion, freedom, self-realization for a *man,* but not for a group. Hence the equality of all individuals before law; and individual responsibility instead of that of a group, as is the case in an immobile society. A mobile society inevitably must "invest" all rights and responsibilities in an individual but not in a group. For the same reasons, in a mobile society, in order to know a man we cannot rely any more on the information that he is a member of a given group. Such information was more or less satisfactory in an immobile society. Under the conditions of intensive circulation, to say that "Mr. Smith is a business man, or mechanic, or clerk," means almost nothing because Mr. Smith yesterday might be a minister and to-morrow may become a millionaire or a senator. We need to know his whole curriculum. We must know his character and intelligence, his life and shiftings. His family status, as such, does not give much information for our purpose either, because children of a humble family often go up, and *vice versa.* This explains the reason of individualism as a mark of a mobile society; it shows also why the members of a mobile society must have a much more intensive feeling of personality and individuality than the members of an immobile group. So much for this point.

The above partly explains also the diffusion of a somewhat vague internationalism and the collective trends of our time. Butterflying from country to country, from stratum to stratum, an individual inevitably becomes a kind of comet which is permanently moving without any attachment to a definite solar system. He has many temporary places but does not have any permanent one. Naturally, he becomes, as he likes to appear to himself, "a citizen of the world," a cosmopolitan, an internationalist. This is not so much his virtue as a matter of necessity. His solidarity becomes diffused; it now concerns many places; it does not have the intensiveness of a narrow solidarity of an immobile society. Being larger in size, it is cold, dull, and theoretical. We love the whole world, not loving particularly any real human being. We talk of the welfare of mankind, not taking any particular care of anybody. The farther we go in this direction, the more we lose sympathy and devotion toward the living man. One of the results of this is a depreciation of a man's life. In an immobile society the life of a member of a "box" was sacred. Murder of a member was felt to be a great sacrilege. Now, when we meet thousands of people without entering into an intimate "living together" with them, man becomes a kind of theoretical and arithmetical abstract unit, lifeless, soulless. His murder we resent but rather theoretically, without any deep emotion, like a murder in a moving picture. This weakening of resentment is manifested not only in the impossibility of pitiless revenge and feud for the murderer (as it was in the past), but in the great leniency with which we treat murderers. Moreover, when a mass murder of thousands of human beings is performed in the name of "Liberty," "Revolution," "Progress," "Communism," and other "gods" of our epoch, many people do not resent at all such wholesale slaughtering; the slaughtered thousands of human beings are nothing but abstract arithmetical units. Step by step we become generous toward the whole of mankind, and rather cruel toward a living man. It is not strange, therefore, that many of the most enthusiastic partisans of internationalism and "mankind" show in their behavior contempt toward a real man. In the name of half-fictitious conceptions of "proletariat," or "international," or "mankind" they sacrifice thousands of human lives for their purely theoretical conceptions. Revolutionary internationalists, like the Communists, give plenty of examples of this kind.[8]

It has already been indicated that complete social isolation or loneliness is unbearable for the majority of people. It has been mentioned also that mobility facilitates such an isolation. Detached from an intimate oneness with any group, losing even family shelter against loneliness, modern individuals try by every means to attach themselves to some social body to avoid their isolation. And the more the family is disintegrated, the stronger is this need. Some enter labor and occupational unions; some try to fight their isolation through an affiliation with political parties; some, through a participation in different societies, clubs, churches; some through a mad rush from one dancing hall to another. Some try to belong at once to many and often opposite groups. All these "collectivist tendencies" are nothing but the other side of individualism and isolation, created by mobility. They are attempts to substitute for the previous lost "boxes" something similar to them. To some extent all these unions, clubs, societies, and so forth, serve this purpose. But only to some extent. Shifting does not permit one to attach himself to such groups strongly. Hence arise the trends to go further in this direction. This trend is conspicuously manifested in the social schemes of Communists, revolutionary syndicalists, and guild socialists. They contemplate a complete engulfment of an individual within the commune, or syndicate, or a restored guild. They unintentionally try to reëstablish "the lost paradise" of an immobile society, and to make an individual again only a "finger of the hand" of a social body. The greater is the loneliness, the more urgent the need. I fear, however, that until social mobility is diminished, such attempts, even being realized, cannot give what is expected of them. In the best case they may create a kind of a compulsory "social box" which will be felt to be a prison by its members. In conditions of social mobility such a cell will be destroyed by its prisoners. In order to realize the program it is necessary to diminish the mobility. If we are entering such a period, then in some form these schemes may be realized. Are we entering one? I cannot confidently say. Some symptoms are in favor of such an hypothesis. But they are not quite clear as yet; the topic is too big to be discussed briefly, and the writer too much likes the mobile type of society to prophesy its funeral; therefore, he prefers to finish the discussion right here. Whatever may happen in the future, our mobile period is far from ended. And if our aristocracy would try to be a real aristocracy, strong in its rights and duties, creative in its achievements, less sensual in its proclivities and free from parasitism; if it would raise its fecundity; if the channels of climbing are open to every talent among the lower strata; if the machinery of social testing and selection is properly reorganized; if the lower strata are raised to levels as high as possible; and if we are not permeated by the ideologies of false sentimentality and "humanitarian impotency," then the chances for a long and *brilliant* existence of present mobile societies are great and high. Let history do what it has to do; and let us do what we ought to do without wavering and hesitation.

[1] PARETO, V., *op. cit.*, pp. 1655-1656.

[2] See PATRICK, G. T. W., *The Psychology of Social Reconstruction, passim,* 1921.

[3] See MAINE, SIR HENRY SUMNER, *Popular Government, passim,* 1886; MAISTRE, J. DE, *Œuvres complètes,* Vol. I, p. 226 *ff.*, 375 *ff.*

[4] See PLATO, *Republic,* Bks. VIII and IX; ARISTOTLE, *Politics,* Bks. III and V, Chap. V.

[5] G. Simmel's statement that "the social forms can remain identical while their members change" may be true only as far as the changing members are similar. If they are dissimilar and heterogeneous, no maintaining of an identity of social form is possible. See SIMMEL, G., "Comment les formes sociales se maintiennent," *L'Année sociologique,* Vol. I, *passim.* See the criticism of this theory in my *System of Sociology,* Vol. I, pp. 331-335.

[6] The problem of longevity of a society and its culture complex has been studied very little. Trying to understand the causes of a long existence of the Chinese and the Hindu societies and cultures, I came to the following conclusions: In the first place, it has been due to a severe natural selection (high birth and mortality rates) which have been eliminating the weak elements and facilitating the survival of the best part of the population. To this factor it is due that the Chinese and the high classes of India are of the most talented. This little is known; nevertheless, it is true. Besides many data the recent mental and moral tests of different nationalities by V. C. Murdock have shown that the Chinese occupy one of the highest places in this respect. See MURDOCK, V. C., "A Study of Differences, etc.," *School and Society,* Vol. XXII, Nos. 568-569. See also SCHALLMAYER, W., *op. cit.*, Chap. XI. SYMONDS, P. M., *The Intelligence of the Chinese in Hawaii, ibid.*, Vol. XIX, 1924; WOLCOTT, C. D., *The Intelligence of Chinese Students, ibid.*, Vol. XI, 1920; WAUGH, K. T. A., *Comparison of Oriental and American Student Intelligence, Psychological Bulletin,* Vol. XVIII, 1921; YOUNG, K. T., *The Intelligence of Chinese Children,* Vol. V, 1922; TERMAN, L., *Genetic Studies of Genius,* Vol. I, pp. 56-57; for the intelligence of various castes of India *vide*: HERRICK, D. S., *A Comparison of Brahman and Panchama Children, Journal of Applied Psychology,* Vol. V, pp. 252-260; WAUGH, K. T., *op. cit.* In the second place, there seems not to have existed differential fertility. The greatest duty of all, and especially of the upper strata, has been to have many children, especially sons,

This has been facilitated by the polygamy of the upper strata which has been permitted juridically and practiced factually. Both of these causes prevented the wasting of the best elements of the populations. Besides, in India a great rôle seems to have been played by the rigid prohibition of intercaste marriages. This seems to have prevented contamination of the race of Brahmins, and has led to a fortunate inbreeding of high racial stock. A practice of a severe but very efficient eugenics has facilitated this result. The severest social selection of the Brahmins of the high orders which they have had to undergo in the form of severe educational testing, and the severest training, which inculcates the most rigid habits and inflexible morals, are further conditions. As a result of this severest biological and social selection and the most efficient training of the mental, as well as volitional and emotional characteristics, the highest caste became something which might be exterminated physically, but could not be broken in any other way, neither through rewards and pleasure, nor through torture and suffering. They are invincible and unconquerable. In this way, the culture complexes of India became stagnant but vital. In China (see SCHALLMAYER, W., *op. cit.,* Chap. XI) a pure "inbreeding" did not play any important rôle. Besides the above biological factors, a great social selection and minute training in habits and as a part of this, ceremonialism, together with "filial piety," and other measures of Confucianism, have given great stability to Chinese society, and an ability to withstand all invasions and subjugations without complete disintegration of the society and its culture complex. All political and military storms, which in many societies often lead to disintegration, could not destroy these societies. These social storms have passed on their surface, like winds on a deep sea, without destroying the basic institutions of these civilizations.

Present mobile societies in this respect appear to me as unstable. Biological selection works within them in a rather negative way. Social selection is somewhat loose, and incidental, especially in regard to the character of the people. Habits and morals are plastic but not very stable. Self-control, in the form of a powerful control of the lower affections and sensual pleasures, is not very efficient. Ceremonies and persistency of habit inculcation exist in a low degree. The family institution is being disintegrated. Religious influences become less efficient. Measures of compulsion and punishment are put away as rude and barbarian. All that we have is education. In it are invested all our hopes. I hope they are justified. But I cannot help thinking that such a basis of social stability and social longevity is somewhat fragile. I hope I may be quite wrong in my skepticism.

[7] DURKHEIM, E., *La division du travail social,* and BOUGLÉ, CHARLES, "Revue générale des théories récentes sur la division du travail," *L'Année sociologique,* Vol. VI; PALANT, *Les antinomies entre l'individu et société, passim.*

[8] The attitude of a great many foreign "intellectuals" toward the Red Terror shows this also. They praise enthusiastically the lofty phraseology and the fictitious "humanitarianism" of the Communists but they do not even mention fifteen millions of lives, at least, sacrificed to this God of "humanitarian communism." They do not pay and do not want to give any attention to these victims. This fact is a very conspicuous illustration of my statement. It confirms the rule that the enthusiastic caretakers of mankind usually are very careless and rather cruel toward a real human being.

Appendix: SOCIAL AND CULTURAL DYNAMICS*

*Chapter Five from Volume Four of *Social and Cultural Dynamics*

GENESIS, MULTIPLICATION, MOBILITY, AND DIFFUSION OF SOCIOCULTURAL PHENOMENA IN SPACE

I. The Problem of Uniformities in Sociocultural Change

The preceding chapter established two general uniformities in the change of any total culture, namely: that the change proceeds differently in sociocultural systems and in congeries; and that in systems all the compartments change together in any important movement. The propositions valid for the systems are inapplicable to the congeries, and vice versa. Now we can take a series of further steps and inquire: Are there more specific and more definite uniformities in the change of the systems as well as in that of the congeries? If so, what are they?

Guided by the concept of the four main directions of any change or process — spatial, temporal, quantitative, and qualitative [1] — we can inquire: (1) Are there some uniformities in the genesis, multiplication, mobility, and spread of sociocultural phenomena *in space?* (2) Are there any *time* uniformities in such a change? (3) Are there any *quantitative* uniformities in the field? (4) Finally, are there any *qualitative* uniformities?

It goes without saying that the empirical sociocultural world is in an incessant flux. *Spatially* — the cultural objects and values are continually moving and changing their positions in physical and social space. *Qualitatively* — they change in thousands of ways: the new becomes old; the strong, weak; the bright, dull; and so on. *Quantitatively* — they now increase, now decrease, now remain constant; be they certain crimes, fashions, beliefs, styles, or what not. From the standpoint of *time* — they change now synchronously, now with some lag; now with accelerating, now with retarding velocity. The problem is to find what, if any, uniformities exist in these changes.

As to the question concerning the existence of uniformities in sociocultural change, it has already been answered positively, through re-

[1] See *Dynamics,* Vol. I, chap. iv.

jection of the contentions of the Atomistic and Anti-Uniformist position (see Chapter Three). On the other hand, one should be careful to avoid the blunder of the manufacturers of pseudo uniformities produced so easily and in such a profusion in the past as well as in the present. In order to avoid this common error, an investigator should be overcautious rather than exuberant in his claims for uniformities. This overcaution means, first, one should be as critical as possible in regard to the validity of any uniformity claimed by its discoverers. Only the uniformities that stand a rigid test are valid uniformities. Second, even in regard to valid uniformities, one should not exaggerate either their rigidity, their universality, or their unexceptionableness. The point is that most — and possibly all — uniformities in sociocultural change are never quite rigid, without exception, and amenable to a precise mathematical formulation. They are rather of a prevalent rule or pattern, almost always having exceptions. As such, they are notably different from the more precise uniformities in the physicochemical changes. Furthermore, sociocultural uniformities of change are rarely, if ever, absolutely *universal or unlimited,* valid for any culture-complexes of any time. As a rule, they are *limited uniformities,* valid only for certain cultural configurations of a given period or area.

A large number of uniformities have been set forth as unlimited or universal, like the statements: "All sociocultural phenomena originate, grow, and decay"; "In the course of time they all undergo progressively increasing differentiation and integration"; "All are accumulative in their change and display a progressively accelerating tempo of change"; "All have a dialectical rhythm of thesis, antithesis, and synthesis in their change."

Put in such an unlimited form, they almost always exceed the legitimate limits of their validity, and turn into pseudo uniformities. A limited formulation of the same uniformities is expressed in the form: "Only a certain class of the sociological systems, but not congeries, originate, grow and decline"; "Only within certain time and space limits do certain sociocultural systems (but not congeries) display increasing differentiation and integration, and, the limits reached, they reverse the trend"; "Only the sociological systems of a certain kind change according to the Hegelian three-phase rhythm, while others have different rhythms (two-phase, four-phase, and so on)"; such a limited formulation makes them more valid and accurate. Therefore, in a study of the uniformities of sociocultural change, it is exceedingly important to point out the limits of their validity, and, as a rule, to avoid unlimited formulas.

Viewed in this modest setting, a number of approximate uniformities are certainly observable in sociocultural change. Let us now turn to their study.

II. Uniformities in Mobility, Multiplication, Displacement, and Circulation of Cultural Phenomena in Space

We shall begin our study of uniformities with those given in the field of genesis, multiplication, mobility, and spread of cultural phenomena in space (physical and social). Aristotle has brilliantly demonstrated that local motion or displacement of the phenomenon (the subject of the change) in space is the primordial, primary, and simplest form of change. All other motions or changes — quantitative or qualitative — are derivative from it and cannot occur without a local displacement, or motion in space. It can exist without other forms of change, while the others cannot occur without it.[2] So far as this form of change embraces not only motion in space, but also what in mechanics is called displacement, it is the simplest form of change, from the standpoint of mechanics.[3] After this form of change is studied, we shall pass to the more complex — qualitative and quantitative — change of culture in time.

It goes without saying that sociocultural phenomena are changing their positions in physical as well as in social space. They incessantly migrate, circulate, and shift from place to place, from one group to another, one class to the other, to and fro, up and down, in the differentiated and stratified sociocultural universe.[4] An automobile and Lenin's Communism; short skirts and bobbed hair; bathtub and radio; jazz and lipstick; the theory of evolution and a Beethoven symphony; protective tariff and theosophy — these and practically all

[2] See Aristotle, *The Physics* (Loeb Classical Library edition, New York-London, 1929), Bk. VIII, chaps. vi, vii, viii, ix; pp. 338 ff.; "De Mundo," chaps. iv, v, vi; *The Works of Aristotle,* translated under the editorship of W. D. Ross (Oxford, 1931), Vol. III.

[3] "Displacement differs from motion in that it excludes the notion of time." L. Lecornu, *Le mécanique. Les idées et les faits* (Paris, 1918), p. 19; P. Appel et S. Dautheville, *Précis de mécanique rationelle* (Paris, 1921), chaps. i, ii; J. C. Maxwell, *Matter and Motion* (London, 1882), p. 20.

[4] See an outline of social space in my *Social Mobility.* In that work I concentrated on the mobility and circulation of individuals and social groups, paying little attention to that of sociocultural things and values. Here I am dealing — very concisely — with some of the aspects of the latter problem. A systematic conception of sociocultural space is given in my forthcoming *Sociocultural Causality, Space, Time.*

cultural objects and values shift from the United States to China; from Vienna to Sydney and Calcutta; from Detroit to Moscow; from the upper classes to the lower; from the city to the country; from the nobility to the proletariat; or vice versa. The sociocultural universe is like an ocean with a multitude of ice-cakes incessantly floating and drifting upon it; now slowly, now tempestuously; now in small pieces, now in giant icebergs (big systems), and again in whole ice-fields (vastest supersystems).

This spatial migration and circulation of cultural phenomena embraces a series of different processes: (1) *A spatial migration of a given cultural object,* a certain automobile or religious relic or rare book, that moves from one place to another in its material form. Having moved from A to B, it is no more at A and is now at B. Such a phenomenon always means a pure migration of materialized value in its objectified shape. (2) *Multiplication and spatial spread (migration) along certain routes, in certain directions, and over certain inhabited areas, of certain cultural phenomena.* In contradistinction to a mere spatial migration of a given object, this process is more complex: it involves not only a mere spatial migration, but a multiplication of a given cultural value in many copies, and a distribution (migration in many directions) of these copies over certain areas of population.

In this case a cultural value remains at A, and does not disappear from there, as in the previous case, while other copies of it move from A to B, C, D . . . N. What is called *diffusion* always means this second process, implying multiplication of the same cultural value in many copies, and the spread of these copies. This process has two forms: multiplication of the value in *one center* and spread from that center — for instance, the manufacture of cars at Detroit and their spread from Detroit; and multiplication in *several centers* and spread from these centers. The gospel of Communism may be spread through pamphlets manufactured in Moscow only, and, through Moscow Communist agents only, sent over the world. But it also may be spread through pamphlets manufactured in different centers (Moscow, China, America, etc.), and distributed through the local agents of those areas.

A cultural value may be broadcast by radio from one station, or circulated by one newspaper only; or from many stations and by many newspapers. The net result in both cases (one and several centers) is multiplication, migration, and diffusion of the value over certain populated areas. Subsequently we shall deal mainly with the spatial migration of cultural phenomena of the second type, involving multiplication.[5]

The main problems to be considered here are as follows: (1) *What are the roads or lines along which the social things and values move or drift* in social space, *horizontally,* from group to group, man to man, one inhabited place to another; and *vertically,* from one stratum to another, from the lower to the higher class, or vice versa? (2) What are the *directions of* this movement? Is it one-sided, say, from the city to the country, from "civilized" to "uncivilized" people, from the upper to the lower classes, or is it a two-way current? If so, do both streams carry similar values, or are they different? If they are different, in what does this difference consist, and is there any uniformity in it? (3) In each given society, *what social classes are the main innovators (creators) and importers of new cultural values into its culture; are they mainly the upper and middle classes, or are they predominantly the lower classes?* What uniformities, if any, are shown in this field? (4) Do cultural objects and values travel only in the form of singular traits or the simplest elements of culture? Or do they shift also by the groups of congeries and by small and vast cultural systems? (5) What happens to *the cultural elements, congeries, or systems in the process of their circulation? Do they change? Do they break into pieces? Do they consolidate with one another, in this process of drifting? Do they clash and destroy this or that "floating" section?* (6) As a special case of this general problem, *what happens when two vast cultural continents come into contact with one another, as a result of either spatial expansion of one or both, or a "continental migration" of one?* (7) Considering that, on the basis of common observation, some cultural object-values have a great "success" and become "best-sellers" in their multiplication and spread *urbi et orbi,* while others remain "sedentary," "poor sellers," at the place where they appear and either do not multiply or spread, or do so very modestly — we can inquire what the reasons for it are. Why does one book, composition, or picture become a "best-seller" while another does not? Generally, why do some value-objects move fast and multiply, achieving success everywhere, while others do not? As a specific case of that, why does it happen that a given object-value,

[5] However relevant is the distinction between diffusion, borrowing, imitation, and other related processes, for our purposes it is unessential; therefore we shall pay little attention to these differences, covering by the terms diffusion, migration, spread, all these varieties, but specifying other distinctions more relevant for our purpose.

being "unsuccessful" in a given culture area, is highly "infective" in another? Why does it not move and spread at a given period, while it does so at another period, often a long time after its creation, and vice versa? What are the reasons for such contrasts? (8) When a given cultural value multiplies and spreads in social space, *are there some "normal curves" of such a growth and spread?* If there are, what are they? (9) When cultural values (congeries and systems) of one culture come into contact with another culture, *what kind of values penetrate and spread first in the infiltration:* are they economic, technological, political, religious, or some other one of the values? Is there any uniformity in this field? (10) Finally, *where and how do new cultural values, particularly great systems and supersystems, originate,* and *do the centers of their genesis shift in social space from area to area, from society to society?* This last question logically should be the first, because in order to shift and spread from place to place, cultural values must be somewhere originated and created; however, for the sake of convenience, it will be discussed last.

Those are the main questions to be discussed in this chapter. They do not exhaust the important aspects of the circulation and multiplication of social values and objects in social space, but they embrace a considerable part of these aspects and can serve as an easy introduction to the main problems of this work.

III. Routes of Travel of Cultural Objects, Phenomena, Values

Putting aside for the moment the social and other conditions to be discussed further, let us state that man-made or man-modified objects and values travel along the lines of man's travel, communication, and contact. This uniformity is evident and needs no proving. Any cultural value-object moves either directly by the agency of a human being or by the man-made means of *contact and communication.* Therefore the lines of the roads traveled by men and used as the means of communication are the lines of travel of the cultural object-values. A path in the mountains, a caravan road in the desert, a highway for wagons, horses, or cars; rivers, lakes and sea routes navigated by canoe, boat, or ship; railroads and routes of airplanes; lines and networks of telegraph, telephone, radio; such are the main channels through which the value-objects move, travel, and spread *horizontally* from place to place, man to man, group to group, in social space. The channels of communication and contact are likewise the lines of circulation of the value-objects *vertically*, from one stratum of society to another. Such channels are the agency through which the people of the lower and higher classes meet one another directly, or where they come in touch with the objects and values of each stratum. Such a channel may be the household of the lord, for his valet, servants, and tenants; and these, in turn, for the still lower classes.[6] It may be a library or church, the store, community fair, community playground, theater, movie, radio, if they are attended or patronized or possessed by various classes; it may be the battlefield, or any other *locus* where the different strata meet together. It may be a set of any object-values

[6] The servant class "acted as somewhat of a buffer between classes, and were one of the most important forces in acquainting the lower classes with the ideas and habits of those above them. The fact that the servants of the rich were constantly recruited from the laboring classes, and as often sank back into them, made for a large amount of contact between the servants and their less fortunate brethren. In this capacity they were one of the chief agencies for spreading the upper-class luxury among the lower classes." E. L. Waterman, *Wages and Standard of Living of English Labor, 1700–1790* (Radcliffe Thesis, 1928), pp. 7–10, also pp. 276 ff.

This observation is stressed again and again by practically all competent investigators of the vertical displacement of the standard of living, of fashion, dress, certain manners, beliefs, etc. In the phenomenon of "aping one's betters" the role of the servant class has been particularly conspicuous. In other cases, for instance, of imitation and vertical displacement of luxuries from the aristocracy to the bourgeoisie, the migration of the fashions, habits, etc. of the aristocratic classes to bourgeoisie, and from it to the lower classes, or vice versa, has proceeded again through the contact-lines and agents that were the "go-betweens" for these classes.

See facts and data in regard to vertical migration of words, phrases, expressions, slang, etc., in R. de la Grasserie, *Etude scientifique sur l'argot et le parler populaire* (Paris, 1907), pp. 2 ff., *et passim;* A. Niceforo, *Essai sur les langages spéciaux, les argots et les parlers magiques* (Paris, 1912); in regard to various habits, luxuries, dress, fashions, beliefs, etc., A Challamel, *History of Fashion in France* (translated from French) (London, 1882), pp. 38–40, 57, 64, 126, 167, *et passim;* G. Hill, *A History of English Dress* (London, 1893), Vol. I, pp. vi ff., *et passim;* K. R. Greenfield, "Sumptuary Law in Nürnberg," *Johns Hopkins Studies,* Vol. 38, No. 2, 1918, pp. 49–51; F. E. Baldwin, "Sumptuary Legislation and Personal Regulation in England," *Johns Hopkins Studies,* Vol. 44, 1926, pp. 21–33, 38 ff.; C. Booth, *Life and Labor of the People of London* (London, 1897), Vol. IX; John Wade, *History of the Middle and Working Classes* (London, 1834), pp. 20–26; P. Kraemer-Raine, *Le Luxe et lois somptuaires au moyen-âge* (Paris, 1920), pp. 9–10, 19, 24 ff., 51 ff., 93 ff., *et passim;* W. M. Webb, *The Heritage of Dress* (London, 1907), chap. xv.; C. C. Zimmerman, *Consumption and Standard of Living* (New York, 1936). Finally, G. Tarde, in his *Laws of Imitation* (translated by Parsons, 1903), made several sound generalizations in this problem. See Chapters Six and Seven.

The enormous role, in the vertical migration of culture patterns and elements, of such agencies as movies, radio, and newspapers, through which different social strata, upper and lower, come into contact with fashions, patterns, forms of conduct of the different classes, is evident, and needs no comment. The same is true of school, church, and other channels of vertical circulation of individuals, discussed in my *Social Mobility,* Chapter Eight.

used by one class but exposed to the perception of the other classes (palace, house, museum, etc.). The costume, bathtub, radio, carriage, hair-bob, song, doctrine, belief, and what not of one group exposed to the perception of persons of the other classes, would tend to be "imitated" by those who came in touch with them most frequently, unless there were special taboos, prohibitions, and other conditions of dis-affinity, of which something will be said later. Other conditions being equal, the *cultural objects and values circulate up and down also in a given stratified society along the lines of most frequent communication and contact of the members of different strata.*

Wherever the given cultural element (value or object) is originated, from that *locus* it tends to spread, and it travels along *the lines of communication and contact* which radiate from that center; and only later, more slowly, and less successfully, does it move in the regions and areas which are isolated, not connected, or connected less closely by the lines of communication and contact with that center, no matter how near or remote from it they are territorially. Whether the cultural element be a language, belief, cult, theory, custom, norm, material object — automobile, merchandise — even a disease,[7] or what not, it flows along these lines and "inundates" or spreads among the population living in the areas crossed by or adjacent to these lines of communication, travel, and contact. Along these lines the stream flows often hundreds and thousands of miles, leaving untouched or barely affected the populations much nearer to the center geographically, if they are not connected with it by the lines of communication and contact, or connected much less thoroughly. This explains why, in the

[7] Movement and spread of epidemics of plague and other infectious diseases follow the same rule and give particularly illuminating material for our purposes. See detailed and rather carefully mapped routes of the spread and movement of the great and small epidemics, horizontally, from place to place and vertically, from stratum to stratum, in the following works: E. A. Wesley, "The Black Death of 1348," *Proceedings of Liverpool Literary and Philosophical Society,* Vol. 60, 1907; C. Creighton, *A History of Epidemics in Britain,* 2 vols. (Cambridge, 1891–93), Vol. I, chaps. iii, iv, *et passim;* Vol. II, *passim;* M. Greenwood, Jr., "On Some of the Factors Which Influence the Prevalence of Plague," *Journal of Hygiene,* Plague Supplement, 1911, Vol. I, chap. 45; M. Greenwood, "Factors That Determine the Rise, Spread, and Degree of Severity of Epidemic Diseases," *XVIIth International Congress of Medicine,* 1913, sec. 18, pp. 49–80; W. G. Bell, *The Great Plague in London in 1665* (New York, 1924), *passim* and pp. 39 ff.; J. Brownlee and M. Greenwood, "Epidemic," *Encyclopaedia Britannica,* Vol. VIII; "Plague," *ibid.,* Vol. XVII.

For the spread of a recent innovation of the radio amateurs in the United States, see R. V. Bowers, "The Direction of Intra-Societal Diffusion," *American Sociological Review,* December, 1937, pp. 826–836 (though the character of the census data with which Bowers operates does not permit any very accurate analysis).

past, the new cultural elements spread mainly along the paths, caravan routes and other roads, and in the maritime regions which were on the maritime routes; why, in the past as well as in the present, the city has been a much more efficient center for sending as well as for receiving the new cultural elements than an *isolated rural area:* the number, convenience, and length of the lines of communication, contact, and travel of the city are generally much greater than those of the rural area;[8] why the many isolated, mountainous, desert, or forest populations have been passed by and untouched by an enormous number of such cultural streams and therefore remained more "stationary" and "unchangeable" in their culture; this explains these and thousands of other phenomena.

Any theory which claims that the cultural elements tend to spread concentrically from the center of their origin, moving to the first

[8] Concrete examples of this are given by the routes of diffusion and travel of a new religion (for a given country). A study of the diffusion of the Oriental and foreign cults in the ancient Græco-Roman world (the cults of Cybele, the goddess of Mâ-Bellona, Isis, Osiris, Mithra; the cults of Syria and Persia, and others) shows they spread first and most among the urban population, along the lines of the maritime routes, in maritime cities and ports, and among those classes who, like legionaries, merchants, intellectuals, government officials, were in direct contact with or on the route of travel of these beliefs and religions. See the facts in J. F. Toutain, *Les cultes paiens dans l'empire romain,* 3 vols. (Paris, 1907–20), Vol. I, chap. i, Vol. II, pp. 30, 58, 65, 159, 255, 266; Vol. III, pp. 103, 109, 113, 183, 425, 438; F. V. Cumont, *Oriental Religions in Roman Paganism* (Chicago, 1911), pp. 53, 56, 83, 201, 281; F. V. Cumont, *The Mysteries of Mythra* (Chicago, 1910), pp. 34, 40, 45, 63, 69; M. I. Rostovtzeff, *Mystic Italy* (New York, 1927), pp. 7–11, 30–31. See the general treatment in P. Sorokin and C. Zimmerman, *Principles of Rural-Urban Sociology* (New York, 1929), pp. 48 ff., and chaps. xvii, xviii. Sorokin-Zimmerman-Galpin, *Systematic Source Book in Rural Sociology,* 3 vols. (Minneapolis, 1930–31), Vol. I, pp. 233–259; Vol. II, pp. 373–380.

What is said of the routes of migration of beliefs can be said, with a respective modification, about practically any other cultural object, value, or phenomenon. An example of the routes of diffusion of tobacco or coffee can be found in R. U. Sayce, *Primitive Arts and Crafts* (London, 1933), chaps. 6, 7; of other traits in W. I. Thomas, *Primitive Behavior* (New York, 1937), chap. xvi.

For the same reason, in the maritime and steppe regions the given cultural trait spreads along the coasts and the border regions of the steppe or desert, with the lines of communication going in different directions and reaching the coast as well as the inside and borderline settlements of steppe or desert. A good example of this is given in the diffusion of language in such areas. Greek navigators spread Greek, in the past, along the shores of the Mediterranean; the Malayan navigators, over the region of the Malayan archipelago; so also did the Polynesian sea-travelers. Berbers, Turks, Arabs, and other nomadic people diffused their languages in and along the borders of the steppes or deserts they inhabited and traveled over. A. J. Toynbee rightly remarks that "because 'Britannia rules the waves' — or did rule them for a century or so — English has latterly become a world language." A. J. Toynbee, *A Study of History* (Oxford University Press, 1934), Vol. III, p. 391.

adjacent concentric area around the center, then to the next, and then to the next, and so on,[9] is fallacious in general, and can be accurate only for cases where the lines of communication and contact from that center radiate with equal frequency and convenience in all directions, and when the culture of all the groups around the center is identical, and where a series of certain other conditions is present. Such a situation is, for the past as well as for the present, a rare exception rather than the rule; therefore the theory can in no way claim to be a general rule.

The same can be said of the theories claiming that in the course of time the cultural stream proceeds from south to north, or from the East to the West, or from the West to the East; from mountains to plains, or from plains to mountains.[10] If the *lines of contact and communication* lie in such a direction from the center of origin of a given cultural element or system, as sometimes they do, then such a direction of the stream of the cultural values occurs; if they lie in the opposite or different directions, as more often they do, then the direction becomes opposite or different from the assumed one. No uniformity exists.[11]

[9] Recently C. Wissler insisted particularly upon such a "law of diffusion." "A culture trait spreads over contiguous parts of the earth's surface, and so does a somatic trait. The universality of this phenomenon is obvious. We may, therefore, formulate these observations as law, that anthropological traits tend to diffuse in all directions from their centers of origin." C. Wissler, *The Relation of Nature to Man in Aboriginal America* (New York, 1926), pp. 182–183. Even in application to the traits of the "primitive cultures," with which Dr. Wissler deals mainly, his generalization has been shown to be wrong. Still more fallacious is it in application to the areas of "complex cultures." See its factual criticism in R. Dixon, *The Building of Cultures* (New York, 1928), pp. 69 ff.; F. Boas, W. D. Wallis and several other anthropologists have given in their reviews of Wissler's work further factual criticism of the theory. In application to complex cultures, his "law" is almost entirely void. Only in the conditions indicated in the text on this page it finds itself realized once in a while. See E. C. McVoy. "Patterns of Diffusion in the United States," *American Sociological Review*, April, 1940.

[10] See S. C. Gilfillan, "The Coldward Course of Progress," *Political Science Quarterly*, 1920, pp. 393–410; V. Stefansson, *The Northward Course of Empire* (New York, 1922); P. Mougeolle, *Les problèmes de l'histoire* (Paris, 1886), pp. 97–106; *Statique des civilisations* (Paris, 1883), *passim;* R. Mewes, *Kriegs- und Geistesperioden im Völkerleben* (Leipzig, 1922), chap. 32; F. Stromer-Reichenbach, *Deutsches Leben... Was ist Weltgeschichte* (Lhotzky Verlag, 1919); E. Sasse, "Zahlengesetz der Völkerreizbarkheit," *Zeitschrift d. Königl. Preuss. Stat. Bureau*, 1879.

[11] See general criticism of these theories in my *Contemporary Sociological Theories*, pp. 106 ff. See also some critical remarks in G. Mosca, *The Ruling Class* (New York, 1939), pp. 8–13. The controversy of the direction of civilization and art from the East to the West (E. Smith, De Morgan, Montelius, Hoernes, Sophus Müller, Mewes, Sasse, and others), or from the West to the East (S. Reinach and others) has been one of the most sterile and fantastic. Both opposite claims, and also the claims of the northward or southward movement of culture in the course of time, do not stand the slightest test of facts or of logic. See W. Deonna, *L'archéologie* (Paris, 1912), Vol. II, pp. 193 ff.

IV. Directions of the Streams of the Cultural Elements

The problem of the routes of travel of cultural elements is different from that of the direction of this travel: along any physical route man can move either from A to B or from B to A. They say in mechanics any direction has two "senses." In the multidimensional social space, any "route" of movement of cultural objects and values has also at least two "senses," from A to B and from B to A. The question arises therefore: do the cultural streams move with equal rapidity and strength from A to B and from B to A, along a given social route, or do they move only one way from A to B and never from B to A? Do, for instance, the cultural streams move regularly from "the more to the less civilized groups" and rarely or never from the less civilized to those more civilized? Does the stream flow regularly from "the city to the country," or does it go in both directions?

In the vertical circulation does the cultural stream flow always from the upper — the rich, the aristocratic, the privileged, the educated — toward the lower classes (the poor, the ruled, the disfranchised, the uneducated), or does it flow simultaneously in both directions? What is generally the situation in regard to any route between two social centers united respectively in social space by a line of communication and by a flow of cultural objects and values? Can some relatively general rules be formulated here?

There is no doubt again that in the concrete multiplicity of these processes, there is a variation of the situation in various cases. In spite of this, it is possible to formulate a few propositions which sum up the most frequent uniformities in the field.

A. The first of such propositions is that the *direction of any current of cultural values running from one locus in social space to another is hardly ever one-way: it is almost always two-way;* if it flows from A to B (from the city to the country, from the more civilized to the less civilized cultural areas, from the aristocracy to the slaves, from a castle to the peasants' huts, from the United States to China, from the rich to the poor, from a given group or area to another) there normally is also a counter-current from B to A; from the country to the city, the savages to the civilized, the slaves to the aristocracy, and so on.

B. Second, *the character and the nature of the cultural objects carried by both currents depend upon many circumstances.* Specific important cases here are as follows: (*a*) The stream from the urban-upper-civilized centers carries mainly the "finished" and "formed" objects and values which as "finished" enter the culture of the rural-uncivilized-lower classes; while the opposite current consists mainly of the raw and unfinished material to be shaped and molded in the urban-upper-civilized centers. So far as "finished and formed" mean, in most of the cases, a cultural *system,* and "unfinished and raw" signify mainly *congeries,* the above proposition can be formulated in the sense that from the urban-civilized-upper centers flow mainly cultural *systems,* which as systems enter the centers by infiltration, while from the rural-uncivilized-lower centers flow mainly values which as *congeries* enter the upper-civilized-urban cultures, no matter whether they are systems or congeries in their native culture. For this reason, the first stream exerts more efficient effect upon the culture of the lower-rural-uncivilized centers than the second does upon the culture of its inflow. In this sense and for this reason, the first stream may be regarded as more powerful than the second. (*b*) If both centers do not have the rural-urban, upper-lower, civilized-barbarian contrast in their cultures, then the above difference in the content of the two streams does not occur and the nature of the objects and values circulated is determined by many local conditions; respectively, the contrast in the remodeling efficiency of the streams in regard to the culture which each of them enters, does not take place, at least as conspicuously as in the case "a." (*c*) The efficiency of each stream however may be quite different, regardless of the finished and raw forms of the values, if one current is backed by *force* and is imposed coercively upon the culture of the other center, while the latter does not have such a backing. The coercive imposition may here play the role of a factor which gives an additional advantage to the current coming from the culture of the conquerors and "great powers."

A few comments upon these propositions are not out of place. Why normally does any current going from A to B have a counter-current running from B to A?

The reason for the first proposition is that if such a current exists, the centers are in a process of interaction or in a contact. Any contact, with the exception of that between the dead (say the works of Plato, Beethoven, Shakespeare, etc.) and the living, is almost always two-sided: if one party conditions tangibly the change of the other, the second also influences, to some extent, the first party, no matter whether the party is man, group, or a cultural complex or conglomeration. If the products of one area flow into the other, something — products, money, or services of men — of the produce and culture of this other area has to flow into the first. Any commerce is the giving of something for something, exchange; therefore, by virtue of this axiomatic proposition, applicable not only to economic goods and trade in a narrow sense, but to practically any contact or commerce or interaction, the two-way movement of the streams is a logical necessity. The factual data corroborate it, *urbi et orbi*. Whatever are the centers between which there is a stream of the cultural values flowing, the stream always consists of two currents, one flowing from A to B, the other from B to A. Human agents, the press, radio, telephone, manufactured products, money, mores, and values of the city, incessantly flow to the country; from the country flows incessantly the stream of rustics, farmers, agricultural products, and other raw materials, beliefs, mores, tastes and so on, to the city. In most cases this stream is probably not so powerful as the first; and yet, its presence is unquestionable.[12] If missionaries, army men, business men, and other human agents of a more civilized country bring into a less civilized one elements of the culture of their own country and introduce them there, the same agents, remaining in the "less civilized" country, cannot escape being influenced by it, to some extent, and of importing into the more civilized country some elements of the culture of the less civilized country: some of its merchandise, ivory, metals, minerals, art-objects, mores, values — material and immaterial. Whether we take the history of the contact of the United States of America and China, Europe and China, England and India or Melanesia — Europe or America, on the one hand, and any of the so-called "backward peoples and cultures" on the other — everywhere this phenomenon is evident, tangible, and unquestionable.[13]

The same is true of the past. If Athens or Rome, in their golden days of expansion, spread and introduced their cultural values to many countries, they were, in turn, the recipients of the wealth, agricultural produce, human material, art-objects, and cultural values of these countries. The Roman world, beginning with the first century B.C., was inundated by the population, wealth, mores, beliefs, and other cultural elements of these, especially of the Oriental countries, to such

[12] See Sorokin-Zimmerman-Galpin, *Source Book,* quoted, Vol. III, particularly.

[13] As an example see the detailed historico-sociological analysis in G. H. Danton, *The Culture-Contacts of the United States and China* (New York, 1931); H. D. Lampson, *The American Community of Shanghai* (unpublished Ph.D. thesis, Harvard University, 1935).

an extent that the culture and population of the Græco-Roman world itself were greatly changed. The same happened in the Middle Ages between the cultures of the East and West, when contact was established. With a proper modification, the same can be said of the vertical streams. No aristocracy coming in contact with slaves can escape being "infected" with some of the elements of the culture of the slaves. Controlling them, it is, in turn, in some form and to some degree, conditioned and controlled by the slaves.[14] If the lower classes receive continually a stream of cultural objects and values descending upon them from the upper classes, the culture of the upper classes is also a recipient of the cultural elements of the lower classes, such as folk-songs, fairy tales, legends, patterns of ornamentation, jazz music and the spirituals, various beliefs and mores, not to mention human beings and the economic services and values supplied by these strata to the upper-class culture. The streams may not be equal, but both are there.[15] Even the caste-society, where such a two-way movement is least possible, is not exempt from this rule; even there the elements of culture of the Sudras or the outcasts flow upward into the stratum of the Brahmins. Still truer is this in regard to other, less rigidly stratified societies and cultures.[16]

As to the second proposition, one is tempted, at first glance, to formulate it in quantitative terms, in the sense that the stream from

[14] G. Tarde rightly remarks: "When two men are together for a long time, whatever may be their difference in station, they end by imitating each other reciprocally, although of the two, the one imitates much the more, the other much the less. The haughtiest country gentleman cannot keep his accent, his manners, and his point of view from being a little like those of his servants and tenants. For the same reason many provincialisms and countrified expressions creep into the language of cities, and even capitals, and slang phrases penetrate at times into drawing-rooms." G. Tarde, *The Laws of Imitation* (New York, 1903), pp. 215 ff.; see also pp. 371 ff.

[15] A concrete example is given again by the study of the circulation of the fashion of dress. If the lower classes or the rustics or the aborigines often imitate the upper-urban-civilized dress, these classes use the raw material produced by the lower-uncivilized-rural classes; sometimes even the patterns of the dress of these classes. This happens especially in the periods of a decline of the upper-urban-civilized strata. See the facts in this last case in W. M. Webb, *The Heritage of Dress,* quoted, pp. 223 ff.

[16] As mentioned, only the stream flowing from the dead or from the past to the present or the future is not influenced by the opposite stream, from the living to the dead, from the present to the past. But even such a stream in its perambulations is greatly conditioned by the living, the present, and the future: we cannot influence Plato, Aristotle, or Homer, but whether the cultural values created by them penetrate our culture, and if so, what interpretation is given to them by a given culture, and what evaluation they find there, is certainly determined by the presence of the given culture; and with its change, the values undergo a respective change. In this sense, the living present modifies the creation of the past and controls it, to a tangible extent.

the upper classes or the city or the "more civilized" country is stronger, greater, ampler, and carries a greater number of objects and values than the opposite current. However, such a proposition is very questionable. The point is that we do not have any measuring stick for saying that a thousand lipsticks, or a hundred pounds of nails, or ten radios flowing from the city to the country or from the civilized country to the "savages" is a greater quantity than a hundred bushels of grain, or potatoes, or nuts, or ten leopard skins, or one ton of elephant ivory which enters the city, the civilized country, from the rural area or the savage culture. Still less can we "measure" and say that the spread of the Christian religion by the missionaries among the natives is a more voluminous, larger, greater quantity than an introduction by the missionaries into the civilized country of some of the tunes, or art-objects, or "idols," or treasures of the savages. For these reasons such a quantitative proposition is untenable.

Instead, the proposition given above seems to be much nearer to the reality. It says that the stream from the upper to the lower classes, from the city to the country, from the more to the less civilized center, consists mainly of the *finished* objects and values or systems that enter it and function there as finished products, as systems, while the opposite stream brings mainly the *unfinished or raw* material, or congeries, which is to be finished and shaped, turned into a system in the city, the upper class, the civilized center. This material in the opposite (lower, rustic, and "savage") cultures may be functioning as finished, as system, but in the culture of the upper, urban, and civilized centers it becomes mainly a raw material or congeries to be reshaped, polished, and turned into a system. Indeed; the city or the upper classes or the civilized country send mainly the "finished products" — from nails, lipsticks, knives, plows, sewing machines, gasoline, kerosene, sugar, candy, tractors, up to the books, newspapers, radios, a religious creed, political ideology, scientific theory, certain games (baseball, football, bridge, crossword puzzles), songs, fads, fashions, and what not. Whether the values are "material" or "immaterial," they consist mainly of these "finished" forms, small or large systems, ready for use and "consumption" without any essential remodeling, manufacturing, or conversion into something entirely different. And vice versa. The opposite stream brings into the city, aristocracy, civilized country mainly that which is raw material for these centers, which they remodel, manufacture, give new form, new shape, new meaning and value. Whether the raw material consists of the slaves, serfs, unskilled labor imported from certain countries; or of manganese, iron, gold, wheat, fruits, furs, ivory; or of certain folk-tunes, customs, ornamentation, patterns of drawing, sculpturing, dancing; or a certain belief, conviction, ceremony, or ideology — practically all these are rarely used in their "native" form, but are molded, manufactured, machine-turned, reshaped, remodeled in these cultures into a system, into something very different from what they were in their native "raw" form. This does not preclude a part of the currents from the city, the aristocracy, the civilized country from consisting also of "raw" material for the other countries, though some of these materials may be used as finished products in the upper classes, or urban and civilized centers. But such a return is ordinarily a minor part of the current; in this sense, it is an exception, not the rule.

When the proposition is properly understood, it makes clear several things which jump to the attention of an observer of these currents; it makes comprehensible even the temptation to put the matter in the above quantitative terms. If the products and values of the upper-urban-civilized centers enter the lower-rural-savage cultures mainly in finished form, or systems, they are not lost there for an observer; as finished individualities they are visible all the time; they visibly enter and circulate there, and visibly modify, reintegrate or disintegrate the native-rural-lower cultures. In other words, they travel as a strong, powerful, and vigorous stream which is not lost, but which rushes into, and changes effectively, the cultures of their inflow. Hence the temptation to put the matter in these terms: such a stream is more voluminous quantitatively and more powerful operationally, than the opposite current. The latter is, in a sense, lost in the higher-urban-civilized centers. Since it brings mainly the raw material which is reshaped in these centers and is given a new form, or a form for the first time — which is made in the image and likeness of the forms of these centers — it becomes "invisible" in its entrance and circulation. It does not add visibly any new heterogeneous element to these cultures; it seemingly does not reshape and reintegrate them; it is just a material which is molded into new systems by these centers, along their own patterns. Hence the impression that the stream is less ample and powerful than the opposite stream. In a sense, such an impression is justified: the current does not exert indeed such kinetic effects as the opposite current. The proposition thus explains this accurately and satisfactorily. Any investigator and observer of the "influence" of the city upon rural culture, of the United States and Europe upon the Tasmanians, Melanesians, even upon China and India; of upper-class culture upon that of the lower strata of the same society, can hardly question its validity; the existing data support it amply.[17] In the light of the proposition, it is comprehensible why, from the standpoint of an observer, the cultural stream flowing from the upper classes molds and influences, or — in G. Tarde's terminology — is "imitated" by, the culture of the lower classes, more than the opposite current shapes the culture of the upper classes; why the same is true of the currents flowing from the urban to the rural, from the more civilized to the less civilized cultures. The reason is the difference between the streams consisting of the "finished" and "raw" objects and values.

The rule naturally has exceptions. One of these is that *in periods of decline of the urban centers, of the upper classes, of the given civilized culture, the content of the streams may be changed: the streams coming from these centers may carry the objects and values which may be accepted in the centers of their destination not as a finished but as a raw or decadent material, while the content of the opposite streams may be perceived as the finished.* In such periods, in Tarde's terminology, the urban, upper, civilized centers begin to "imitate" the culture of the rural, lower, less civilized countries.[18] Hence the "lower" stream becomes more powerful than the other. But even in such cases — and they have occurred indeed from time to time — the exception is rather fictitious, because the rule that the current consisting of the finished products tends to be more powerful than that of the raw material, continues to operate here as well as under normal conditions. The exception concerns only the change of the place to which the currents carry the finished and the raw products. Otherwise, the rule remains unchanged.

[17] In the period when the Oriental — Chinese, Arabic, etc. — cultures were more civilized than the European, Europe borrowed from them mainly finished products, such as the alphabet, Arabic numerals, anatomical charts, block printing, the mariner's compass, silk, tea, porcelain, playing-cards, gunpowder, scientific astronomy, even Aristotle.

[18] G. Tarde states that in the periods of decline of the upper class, the lower classes imitate it especially strongly. This statement is rather fallacious. See G. Tarde, *The Laws of Imitation, op. cit.*, pp. 224 ff. A. J. Toynbee rightly outlines the fact but wrongly ascribes it to the state of the *total* disintegration of the civilization. Meanwhile, the given aristocracy of the culture often declines and is replaced by a new one, without any fatal and irremediable disintegration of the respective society or culture. See A. J. Toynbee's transformation of the imitation (Mimesis) in such periods in his *A Study of History* (Oxford University Press, 1934–39), Vol. IV, pp. 131 ff., Vol. V, pp. 20 ff., 430 ff., 441 ff., Vol. VI, pp. 86 ff.

Here are a few examples of this uniformity. In the declining period of the Roman aristocracy, the upper classes, beginning with the emperor, developed such an imitation.

Amid all the elaborate luxury and splendour of indulgence there was a strange return to the naturalism of vice and mere blackguardism. A Messalina or a Nero or a Petronius developed a curious taste for the low life that reeks and festers in the taverns and in the stews. Bohemianism for a time became the fashion. . . . The distinguished dinner party, with the Emperor at their head, sallied forth to see how the people were living in the slums. . . . In the fierce faction fights of the theatre, where stones and benches were flying, the Emperor had once the distinction of breaking the prætor's head.[19]

Nero aspired to become the popular artist of the mob; Commodus, Caracalla, Caligula, Gratian, and other emperors imitated the Roman proletariat or "barbarians" in their dress, amusements, sport, tastes, and many manners, beliefs and superstitions.[20] So did the aristocracy generally. A wave of "vulgarization and proletarianization" arose within the upper classes.

Later on, with the increased decline of the upper classes, especially after the end of the third century A.D., many cultural values of the pagan aristocracy fell down in the scale of values and were either discarded, or, when moved down to the lower classes, were used not so much as a finished product but rather as raw material. This concerns, first, the pagan religion, philosophy, and science, still fostered within the upper classes and among pagan intellectuals. In the rising tide of the Christian culture, which originated and grew mainly from within the lower classes (up to the moment of legalization of Christianity and later on), and from Oriental sources, the elements of the pagan religion and philosophy either died out or entered the Christian religion only as raw material to be used in a refashioned form by the early Christians and early Church Fathers. On the other hand, the Christian beliefs moved up from the lower to the upper classes[21] and entered these

[19] S. Dill, *Roman Society from Nero to Marcus Aurelius* (London, 1905), pp. 73 ff.

[20] *Ibid.*, pp. 74 ff.; Otto Seek, *Geschichte des Untergangs der Antiken Welt* (Stuttgart, 1921), Vol. III, p. 301. See other facts in A. J. Toynbee's *A Study of History*, Vol. V, pp. 452 ff.

[21] "Up to that period all progress in religious thought had proceeded from the highest circles of the [Graeco-Roman] society. . . . The Oriental cults, on the other hand, emanated and diffused from the dregs of the population. In Rome the first followers of Isis were the demoralized and prostitutes. The worship of the Great Mother and of Mithras was recruited first from slaves, pirates, and soldiers. . . . The leadership in religion slipped from the hands of the upper classes . . . and the lower classes now

upper strata as the finished system, admitting of no substantial remodeling and reforming.[22]

The same can be said of many other cultural values of the upper classes of the decaying Roman Empire in the centuries from the fourth to the eighth A.D. They also were either discarded, or, as they went down into the masses, became just raw material for the finished products of these classes. A similar reversal of the cultural currents occurred in the periods of decline of a given aristocracy in other cultures: Chinese, Babylonian, Hindu, and others.[23]

The eves and the periods of great revolutions give further corroboration to the statement. On the eve of a revolution, the upper classes usually begin to import from the lower classes or from the "savages" many of their values, and try to use them as the finished product. The fashion of Rousseauan idyllic pastoralism, shepherdism, the sugar-coated *paysans* in the French nobility of the pre-Revolutionary period, even its "aping the dress fashion of peasants," is a typical example of that.[24] Likewise, a fashion of "primitive exoticism" and "primitivism," generally pervading the upper classes of such a period, illustrates the

---

imposed their superstitions upon the upper ones. . . . Even philosophy . . . now was contaminated by the popular religion and soon began either to defend or explain the very thing which, some time before, philosophy had fought and undermined." O. Seek, *Geschichte des Untergangs der Antiken Welt*, *op. cit.*, Vol. III, p. 138.

Similar transformation and reversal of the current occurred in the field of scientific theories. See P. Duhem, *Le système du monde* (Paris, 1914), Vol. II, pp. 395 ff.

[22] In order to see that, one has to read carefully all the main works of the Ante-Nicene Church Fathers, up to St. Augustine. They display this phenomenon quite clearly. See, for instance, in the volumes of *The Ante-Nicene Fathers* (Buffalo and New York, 1887–1891), "The Epistles" of St. Clement, of Mathetes, of Barnabas; "Apologies" of Justin Martyr; "Against Heresies" of Irenaeus (Vol. I); in Vol. II, Tatian's "Address to the Greeks"; Clement of Alexandria's "Exhortation to the Heathen"; "the Instructor," and "the Stromata"; Athenagoras's "A Plea for Christians"; in Vol. III, Tertullian's "Apology"; "The Prescription against Heretics" and other writings of Tertullian; in Vol. IV, Minucius Felix's work; and especially Origen's "De Principiis," and "Against Celsus." In the works of Lactantius and especially of St. Augustine (*Confession*, and *The City of God*) they are also evident. They all use as either negative, or as raw material, some of the elements of the pagan religion. On the other hand, they all set forth Christian beliefs as a finished product (system) not to be changed or touched by anybody or anything. This process continued later on, in the early medieval centuries. See H. O. Taylor, *Mediaeval Mind,* 2 vols. (London, 1922), chapters describing how the heritage of the upper classes of the Graeco-Roman world was modified and reinterpreted symbolically and used as raw material.

[23] See some of the facts in A. J. Toynbee, *op. cit.*, Vol. V, pp. 554 ff.

[24] See A. Challamel, *History of Fashion in France* (London, 1882), pp. 216 ff. "In 1780 the ideal of fashion was the peasant costume," *ibid.*, p. 171. During and after the Revolution "bourgeoisie became more independent of the fashions of the upper classes." *Ibid.*, pp. 208 ff.

same phenomenon.[25] Contemporary jazz and swing, in music; imitation of the archaistic and primitive patterns in painting and sculpture (Epsteins and their like); the obsession of literature and the theater with the topics and values of either the poorest classes, or criminal groups, or primitive and exotic tribes, or the dregs of society,[26] is another example of the same phenomenon, ominous for, but symptomatic of, the present decline of our upper classes. As we shall see in the next paragraph, when the upper classes begin to imitate the values and patterns of the lower classes, or the more civilized those of the less civilized groups, such a reversal of the normal situation of imitation by the lower classes of the values of the upper ones is one of the best symptoms of the beginning of the end of the upper or civilized groups' superiority and position. History gives a large number of cases of this kind.

If the difference of type — rural-urban, upper-lower, civilized-uncivilized — does not exist between the cultures of the two centers, the described contrast of the "finished" and "raw" material and its consequences does not exist, either. Two similar rural areas, or primitive tribes, or even two cities, may "exchange" their cultural objects and values; these may be different — for instance, one center may send coal and iron; the other, oil and gold; or one center may send the skins and meat of sheep, the other, corn; or one, apples, the other, potatoes. The objects are quite different, but not having generally the above difference between finished systems and raw objects and values (congeries), the difference here does not give any tangible advantage of efficiency to either type.

[25] An abundant testimony for that in French pre-Revolutionary society is given by *Mémoires de L. de R. Saint-Simon* (Paris, 1829–30), *Mémoires de Madame Campan* (Paris, n. d.) and other memoirs of the period; also in H. Taine's *Les Origines de la France contemporaine: l'ancien régime* (Paris, 1876); or E. and J. de Goncourt, *La société française sous la terreur* (Paris, 1854) and *Histoire de la société française pendant la révolution* (Paris, 1854); or F. Funck-Brentano, *L'ancien régime* (Paris, 1926). The spread of "exoticism," "primitivism," etc., in Russian aristocracy before the Revolution is well exemplified by Rasputinism and similar currents widely diffused.

[26] See the facts of vulgarization and barbarization of arts, growth of archaistic and primitivistic imitation of it, blossoming of exoticisms, tendency to move from the kingdom of God, and the noble values and types, to common types of values and persons, and then to the "caveman," criminal, prostitute, street urchin and other subsocial types as personages of literature, painting, music, drama, and other arts of the overripe Sensate phase, in *Dynamics,* Vol. I, pp. 89, 260, 298, 308, 338, 367, 485–88, 500, 592, 596, 618, 641–42, 647, 650–53, 656, 678 ff., *et passim.* See the facts of a similar trend of "physio-dirty" interpretation of man, culture, and values in the science, philosophy, and ideology of the declining stage of the overripe Sensate culture in Vol. II, pp. 115 ff., 206 ff., 230 ff., 288, 470 ff., *et passim.* See also A. J. Toynbee, *op. cit.,* Vol. V, pp. 450 ff.

Finally, the case "c" has in view mainly *the instances of conquest and coercive imposition of certain cultural objects and values by the conquerors upon the culture of the conquered.* Whether the conquerors are the Arabs, the Asiatic legions of the Mongols, the Aryans in India, the Dorians in Greece, the Spaniards in South America, the Normans in England, the Italians in Abyssinia, or the Europeans in many native areas of their conquest — if and when they impose and enforce certain (positive or negative) values and objects upon the culture of the conquered, the imposed cultural stream, backed by force and enforced for a period of time, may be more efficient than the opposite stream of the culture of the conquered upon that of the conquerors. If the latter do not settle amidst the conquered people, but continue to have their own country from which they control the conquered culture through agents; the disparity in the comparative efficiency of the two streams may be very considerable. If they settle in the country of the conquered, as a small island in the sea of native population, then the disparity is smaller; in the long run it may even disappear and the conquerors may even be engulfed by the native culture. But even in that case, during the first period of their domination, their dictatorship gives an additional efficiency to the stream of their culture in comparison with the stream of the culture of the conquered.

With a slight variation, the same can be said of the conquest by one class of a given population of its other classes, typified by the phenomena of deep and great revolutions and counter-revolutions. The triumphant revolutionary class, different from the overthrown governing class, brings with its victory a set of its own values and objects, imposes them by coercion upon society, including the previous aristocracy, and in this way makes them efficient and functioning. If it is overthrown by the counter-revolution, a new earthquake of cultural elements and values occurs, which eliminates a number of these new cultural elements and values and reinstates many of those that were overthrown by the revolutionaries. In brief, *force* has always been a very important factor in this field, and remains so up to the present time. It makes "finished" the values of the conquerors, which otherwise would be "raw," and it makes "raw" the values that otherwise would be "finished."

Among millions of cultural elements and systems that follow this rule, the rise and decline, spread and shrinkage, of a given language gives a typical example. With the expansion of the Arab conquests, the Arabic language spread and became dominant in North Africa, in Mesopotamia, in Persia (greatly modifying the native language), and over practically the whole zone of Arabic conquest, as the language of Scripture and learning, at least. So also did Christianity in regard to the Latin language, establishing it as that of the clerics and educated. In England, after the conquest by the Normans, Norman-French "became the official language for two centuries, but was then gradually ousted by English." [27]

A striking example can be seen in the history of French. What was originally the language of the Isle of Paris extended itself with the power of the kings of France, as the language of the official classes, of the gentry, of the army, of the law courts, and, so far as Latin was not employed, of the Universities and schools and of the Church. When the French Revolution threw the power of the king of France into new hands, the language of the new Republic (including Napoleon's empire) ramified more widely among the people. The common use of French extended even in areas like Brittany and Alsace, where the people spoke a very different language.[28]

So it was also in Spain with the Castilian language given successful domination as the ruler's dialect. So it was with Latin, with the spread of the Roman *imperium* and colonization. So it was with English, with the growth of the British Empire. And as A. S. Woolner has shown convincingly, so it was with a great many languages of the past — Egyptian, Greek, Sumerian, and several Semitic and Indo-European languages. With the rise of an empire and its power, the area of each of these respective languages spread over the conquered territories and areas, either entirely replacing the native languages, or becoming the language of the aristocrats, of the court, of learning, of the administration. With a decline of the empire and power, or with the advent of new conquerors, the preceding imposed language also declined and was replaced by that of the new conquerors.[29] What has been said of language can be said of religion [30] and, with proper

27 A. S. Woolner, *Languages in History and Politics* (Oxford University Press, 1938), p. 12.

28 *Ibid.*, p. 12.

29 See the facts, *ibid.*, *passim.*

30 With the political and military rise of the Sumerian, or Babylonian or Assyrian societies, respectively, their gods and the gods' names changed, and were raised or demoted in the hierarchy of the gods: the Nippur Bel was supplanted by Marduck of Babylon, and this by Asshur in Assyria. When each of these societies was dominant (mainly through their military conquests) their local god became the sovereign of all other gods, especially of the subjugated societies, and its cult and name spread over and supplanted, to a degree, the cults and names of the deities of the subjugated societies.

modification and reservation, of almost any cultural traits or any system of cultural values — art, religion, science, law, mores, etc. Force has played an important part in all such cases. The history of conquest and of the coerced diffusion of the culture of the conquerors imposed by the Dorians, Aryans, Romans, Persians, Mongols, Arabs, Spaniards (in America), Europeans (in North America), bears testimony to that.

Instead of by open military coercion, the same role can be played by the intervention of authoritative force with a veiled pressure.

As happened in the vote of the Council of Nice in favour of the Athanasian Creed, or in the conversion of Constantine to Christianity, or as happens in any important decision following upon the deliberations of a dictator or assembly. In this case, the vote or decree, like the victory, is a new external condition which favours one of the two rival theses or volitions at the expense of the other and disturbs the natural play of spreading and competing imitations.[31]

As a form of such pressure, money (bribery, abundant advertising, etc.), threats, promises of various remunerations, infliction of various punishments (for instance, for listening to foreign radio broadcasts in Germany, or reading foreign newspapers), and dozens of other pressure forms function. With a proper modification, the above applies to all such external measures aiming to aid the diffusion of one and to suppress that of other, rival, cultural values.

A peculiar combination of the preceding three rules — namely, that the cultural products of the upper-urban-civilized societies enter the lower-rural-uncivilized cultures as finished products; and that the situation may be reversed in the periods of decline of the upper-urban-civilized groups; and that, due to the backing of force, the conquering group may impose its culture upon the conquered — is presented by the cases when *a "less civilized" conquering group borrows the more*

So it was in Egypt also, with the rise and decline of each of the Egyptian empires and with the military success of each of them, in regard to the defeated and subjugated populations and their local deities. So also with the Greek deities: in the process of expansion of Greek power, their Pantheon spread over the subjugated and colonized areas. In these and other cases, "the relations between the gods were simply a transposition of political facts into theological terms." A. J. Toynbee, *A Study of History*, Vol. I, p. 116; Vol. V, pp. 527 ff. With a military subjugation of many societies by the Christian culture, the Christian God and Christian saints have been imposed upon an enormous number of groups, peoples, and tribes who were forced to abandon their deities, cults, and beliefs. The same is true of the imposition of the Western or Eastern Christianity, of the Roman-Catholic or Protestant creed by the respective victorious Christian nations upon the defeated Christian nations. The famous *cuius regio eius religio* is one of the formulas summing up the described situation.

[31] G. Tarde, *The Laws of Imitation*, *op. cit.*, pp. 169–170, and 368 ff.

perfect cultural values of the conquered. Such cases are rather numerous and therefore the peculiarity deserves to be mentioned. Thus conquering Romans adopted the Greek equipment of the cavalryman,[32] as well as the Greek gods under Latinized names: Zeus as Jupiter or Jovis, Heracles as Hercules, Persephone as Proserpine, Hestia as Vesta and so on. Ottomans (Turks) borrowed the Western firearms; the Parthians, administrative organization of the Seleucid Greeks; conquering Persians adopted the Median and the Egyptian dress, breastplates, and other cultural values of the conquered peoples. The victorious Manchu took many cultural values of the vanquished Chinese. Peter the Great borrowed certain military techniques of the conquered Swedes. The conquering Incas adopted several material values of the conquered peoples of Quito and of Chimu.[33] So also did Athenian conquerors in regard to many cultural values of the societies they brought under their control.

Our tobacco-smoking commemorates our extermination of the red-skinned aborigines of North America. . . .
Our coffee-drinking and tea-drinking and polo-playing and pyjama-wearing and taking of Turkish baths commemorates the enthronement of the Frankish man-of-business in the seat of the Ottoman Qaysar-i-Rum.[34]

Likewise, after a successful revolution, the victorious revolutionaries adopted many of the cultural values of the conquered former aristocracy and upper classes: in their material plane of living, in their dress, in manners, in forms of their political, military, and economic organization, in their art and ideology; in those particular fields in which the values of the previous upper classes appeared to be superior to the values of the lower classes and revolutionaries.

Similarly, the rural classes many times adopted the values of the decaying urban culture. For instance, during the Russian Revolution, when within two or three years the cities and their populations were enormously decreased, while the rural classes rose to a better position, an enormous number of diverse urban values, from pictures, pianos, fine furniture, jewels, up to books, dress, manners, and mores, shifted to the villages and were adopted there.

A similar process took place during other cases of the decline of the cities and a safer, more comfortable, and "victorious" position of the rural sections. This special case represents a peculiar mixture of

[32] See Polybius, *Histories,* Bk. VI, chap. 25, pp. 3–11.

[33] L. Baudin, *L'empire socialiste des Inka* (Paris, 1928), p. 61.

[34] See A. J. Toynbee, *op. cit.,* Vol. V, pp. 439 ff.

the three above uniformities, and, in view of its frequent recurrence, is mentioned specifically.

V. A Lag in Entrance of the Finished Products into the Culture of the Lower-Rural-Less Civilized Classes

If the proposition concerning the finished (system) and raw products (congeries) is valid, it means that the *upper-urban-civilized centers create and adopt these cultural values earlier than the lower-rural-less civilized population; that so far as they are "new" and "finished"*[35] *they appear first in the upper-urban-civilized groups and from these, they move and reach, with some lag in time, the lower-rural-less civilized groups.* In other words, the stream of the new and finished values flows, normally, downward and only after some lag in time does it reach and enter the culture of the lower-rural-less civilized groups. The upper-urban-civilized classes are, as a rule, the centers from which emanates the diffusion of the new and finished products. *Only in the periods of decline of these classes or groups, as mentioned before, is this uniformity reversed or broken.* In such cases the lower classes become the center of the emanation of the new values as the finished products, and the declining upper-urban-civilized strata adopt them with some lag.[36]

The reasons for such a uniformity are at hand. Since the upper-urban-civilized centers have a more developed and farther reaching

[35] As "unfinished" congeries the values may originate with the lower classes and go upward, as a "raw material," to be finished and put into a system.

[36] I stress the "finished" character of the value. The upper-civilized-urban groups regularly take some values of the lower-less civilized-rural groups as the raw material to be turned into finished products. As such, they are created and adopted first by the upper-civilized-urban groups and then, with some lag, spread downward (those values which can generally diffuse within the lower strata). In the light of this specification, such facts as the borrowing of the elements of the popular art of the lower classes by the grand art of the upper classes; as the utilization of the popular beliefs and rituals by the crystallized religion of the upper classes, and so on, represent no contradiction or exception to this rule. So far as they are taken as a raw material to be molded and finished, and so far as only after such finishing do they spread first within the upper and then lower classes, they follow the uniformity pattern formulated. In this formulation our proposition reconciles the theories of the aristocratic and popular origin and evolution of art as well as of other cultural values. Specifying, further, that in the periods of decline of a given aristocracy-civilized-urban group the process reverses; and that, in populations with blurred and chaotic lines of social stratification, the direction of the movement also becomes blurred and chaotic, it takes care of all the facts apparently contradictory to the proposition. See, for the objections and supposedly contradictory facts in the field of art, E. Pottier, "*Les origines populaires de l'art,*" *Recueil E. Pottier* (Paris, 1937); W. Deonna, *L'archéologie, sa valeur, ses méthodes* (Paris, 1912), Vol. II, pp. 82 ff.; C. Lalo, *L'art et la vie sociale* (Paris, 1921), pp. 139 ff.

network of communication and interaction with more numerous, remote, and different cultures of various countries, these classes and centers are exposed to them more and earlier, become naturally the first recipients of these values, and adopt them first, before the lower-rural-less civilized groups have any notion of them or contact with them. Hence, the uniformity of the downward direction of such a stream and the lag in its arrival in the lower-rural-less civilized areas and populations. The rule is well corroborated — and sometimes strikingly — by the data of history. With the exception of the periods of decline or the intrusion of the factor of physical coercion, it is the upper-urban-civilized groups who have been "innovators," not the lower-rural-less civilized groups or classes. The ruling class, the merchants, the clergy, the intellectuals, and professionals, by the nature of their occupation, move and travel more than the lower or rural classes; the first are exposed to the varying cultures of different areas more than the second; they adopt them earlier than do the second. Hence the rule, which is somewhat contradictory to the current opinion, according to which the upper classes are supposed to be "conservative" while the lower classes are thought of as innovators. Nothing can be more fallacious than this.[37]

Whether we take scientific theories, religious beliefs, moral norms, art-values, forms of social and political organization, technological changes, up to the material standards of living — kind of food, drink, sports and play, patterns of dress, and what not — all these values originate (being invented or borrowed from other cultures) in the upper-urban-civilized groups, and from those, with some lag, shift toward the lower-rural-less civilized groups. As mentioned, a few exceptions from this rule are found, but the rule as a rule remains.

History of the vertical diffusion of dress patterns or various elements of the material standard of living shows typical examples of that. Even nowadays, any new fashion or value, like the automobile, radio, telephone, movie, etc., originates in the metropolitan centers (Paris, New York, London, etc.), and is adopted by the upper strata; from there it moves to the stores of other big cities, and with some lag reaches the smaller towns, diffusing at the same time, downward;

[37] Therefore all the theories that claim (unreservedly) that "great innovations never come from above; they come invariably from below just as trees never grow from the sky downward, but upward from the earth" (C. G. Jung, *Modern Man in Search of a Soul,* London, 1933, p. 243) are evidently untenable. Such a situation is true only in regard to the periods of decline of the given upper classes; or in regard to the raw material taken from the lower classes. Otherwise, the general rule is opposite to that.

with a notable lag it reaches the rural parts, and, still later, passes to the population of the less civilized countries. Even now, in spite of a rapid system of communication, the fashion that is already outdated in the big metropolitan centers, in their upper classes, often is only beginning to reach the population of the rural areas. A lag of several weeks or months is a normal phenomenon even nowadays.[38]

In the past, with less developed systems of communication, it was much longer and much more conspicuous. With a considerable lag, the dress of the upper classes reached the bourgeoisie, and then the lower classes. The same is true of such novelties as tobacco, tea, white bread, sugar, and what not. Examples: In France, the conquering Franks had their costumes adopted, first, by the ruling classes of the native Gauls, and then by the lower classes.[39] From Charlemagne's courtiers the fashions and fine imported articles of Italy and the Orient spread among the noncourtiers and then to the middle classes. From feudal courts, fashions diffused downward.[40] Crusaders learned new fashions in the East, which, after their return, were spread among the upper classes and then, later, went downward to the lower classes.[41] From the aristocracy the fashions passed regularly to the bourgeoisie, and from it to the lower classes, becoming less expensive and less ornate.[42] The same is true of other countries.[43]

What is said of dress and objects of the material standard of living [44]

[38] Some two decades ago, it took about one year for a fashion to move from Paris to New York, and from six to eighteen months to move from New York to other inland towns. Now the shift is faster and takes less time. See P. H. Nystrom, *Economics of Fashion* (New York, 1928), p. 36.

[39] A. Challamel, *History of Fashion in France* (London, 1882), pp. 36 ff.

[40] P. Kraemer-Raine, *Le luxe et les lois somptuaires au moyen âge*, pp. 10 ff., 21, 31 ff., *et passim*.

[41] Challamel, *op. cit.*, p. 40.

[42] *Ibid.*, pp. 57 ff., 64 ff.

[43] See the details in H. Baudrillart, *Histoire de luxe*, 4 vols. (Paris, 1878–80), Vol. II, pp. 340 ff.; also in the quoted works of P. Kraemer-Raine, pp. 42 ff., *et passim;* P. Nystrom, *op. cit.*, pp. 35 ff.; John Wade, *op. cit.*, pp. 20–26; K. R. Greenfield, *op. cit*, pp. 49 ff.; G. Hill, *op. cit.*, Vol. I, pp. vi ff., *et passim;* E. Waterman, *op. cit.*, pp. 7–10, 95 ff., "This process of 'aping one's betters' does not go on between the highest and lowest classes, but is the imitation of the next higher class above. . . . One emulates those whom one might possibly become, without too great a stretch of the imagination." *Ibid.*, pp. 276–277. This graduality is a replica of the graduality of the climbing and descending of the individuals along the social ladder pointed out and documented in my *Social Mobility*, pp. 449 ff.

[44] In recent decades, such cultural objects as automobiles, radios, movies, oil burners, electricity, telephone; or such bio-social traits as bobbed hair, lipsticks, use of bathtubs; forms of dancing, entertainment, cocktail parties; playing the stock market; even use of the contraceptive means of birth control, a diminishing birth and death rate and an

can be also said of almost any cultural value, such as a language,[45] scientific theory, religious creed, art-value, ethical norm, rules of etiquette, and what not.[46] Only after a lag of several decades, even centuries, did Christianity reach and begin to diffuse among the rural classes of the Roman empire.

The most stubborn resistance (to Christianity) comes from the country people, the *pagani*. . . . The word *paganus* means a dweller in the country, *pagus*. It has now been demonstrated that the hostility of the peasantry to Christianity gave the meaning of "pagan" to *paganus*. This seems to date from the first half of the fourth century, and it gradually becomes general in the second half.[47]

So also, with a lag, from the top to the bottom of the social ladder, and from the urban to the rural classes, went the diffusion of Renaissance free thinking, of the Reformation, of the atheistic and "enlightened" philosophies of the eighteenth century in Europe; of socialism, communism, and atheism in Europe, in pre-revolutionary and revolutionary Russia. Similar was the process of the diffusion of Buddhism, Mohammedanism, and other religious creeds.[48]

The same is true of scientific and other theories, political and other ideologies, and moral norms.

---

increasing divorce rate, and thousands of other "novelties," luxuries, comforts, patterns, followed the rule of the uniformity discussed, in spite of somewhat "blurred" lines of social stratification in recent democratic societies. In the rough terms of eighteenth-century England, the "aping of one's betters" continues (except in periods of decline of the existing upper classes). It is due, not only to the factor of income and economic accessibility, but to the deeper reason of the greater and wider network of communication and contact of the upper-urban classes in comparison with that of the lower-rural classes.

[45] According to Sydonius Appolinarius, Latin was first spoken in Gaul by the Gallic nobility and then spread among other classes. In ancient France, French was first spoken by the upper classes; and "in each province there was and still exists a *bilinguisme;* the people guarded their ancient language while the nobles and bourgeoisie adopted the new language. In Bretagne, in Provence, the people still speak their dialect and bourgeoisie alone talk French." R. Maunier, "Invention et diffusion," *Melanges D. Gusti* (Bucharest, 1936), pp. 6–7.

[46] In Shanghai and in China, "the cultural blending of the white and the yellow races that has gone forward has come through the large number of the upper strata of the natives (Chinese) who have visited and studied in foreign lands and have brought back varying degrees of that culture." H. D. Lamson, "The Eurasian in Shanghai," *American Journal of Sociology,* March, 1936, pp. 642 ff. See also R. T. LaPiere and Cheng Wang, "The Incidence and Sequence of Social Change," *ibid.*, November, 1931; G. H. Danton, *op. cit., passim.*

[47] C. Guignebert, *Christianity, Past and Present* (New York, 1927), pp. 175–76.

[48] See the facts and sources in Sorokin-Zimmerman-Galpin, *A Systematic Source Book,* quoted, Vol. II, pp. 373 ff.

With a lag of several years, even decades, Darwinism and the theory of evolution, Marxism and Spenglerism, have reached the lower classes; and even now, only in their most primitive form. A more complex scientific theory takes, even at present, several years to reach the lower, rural, less civilized countries. Even the radical political and revolutionary ideologies, which supposedly originate within the lower classes, originate and are nursed first in the upper or middle classes and from these diffuse, with a lag, among the lower classes. The radical Sophist theories of Trasymachus, Georgias, and Athenian revolutionaries were originated within the ruling classes of Athens, and the Athenian revolutions of either Ten or Thirty Tyrants were led by the members of the upper classes but not by those of the slaves, unfree, or lower classes. Similar ideologies and movements in Rome originated and were led by the Gracchi and other members of the upper strata of Roman society. The radical philosophy of the Encyclopedists was created and nursed within the nobility of France. The creators and leaders of the revolutionary ideologies and movements in Europe of the nineteenth century were, again, mainly the members of the upper and middle classes, not of the lower classes. Saint-Simon and his school, Fourier, K. Marx, F. Engels, F. Lassalle, Bakunin, Kropotkin, J. Jaurès, G. Washington, and so on, they and thousands of other leaders, down to Lenin and Trotsky, belonged either to the upper or the middle classes of the respective societies. Sometimes such ideologies and movements are germinated for decades within the upper and middle classes before they reach the lower strata. In this later stage some of the leaders of the revolutionary movement are the members of the lower classes; but they are almost absent in the earlier stage of germination, and even in the later period are a minority rather than a majority.

Not different is the situation in the field of art and art-style. At any given period, in any complex culture, there coexist so-called "grand art" and "popular art," the latter often very different from the grand or aristocratic art. Several investigators have claimed that it is the grand or aristocratic art that regularly borrows from the popular art and, consequently, that the popular art leads while the grand art lags.[49] When, however, the problem is studied more carefully, it shows four things: First, when the grand art of the upper classes borrows something from the art of the lower classes, it borrows it as a raw material to be remolded and finished. Second, in the periods of decay of given

[49] See, for instance, E. Pottier, *Les origines populaires de l'art, op. cit.;* see also, partly, W. Deonna, *L'archéologie, op. cit.*, Vol. II, pp. 82 ff.

upper classes, the art of the lower classes indeed often leads while the decaying art of the declining upper classes becomes raw material for it. Third, in a society with the blurred lines of demarcation of social stratification (like ours), the crisscross of the currents becomes also blurred and multidirectional. Fourth, and the most important fact, is that so-called popular art, in most cases, is but a modified and disfigured grand art of the upper classes that existed before and passed downward with some lag and continues to exist there, while the grand art of the upper classes has already moved to a different form. In other words, a great deal of so-called popular art is but a disfigured survival of the previously existing art of the upper classes.

> The popular music is but a survival of the ancient and forgotten technique [of the grand art]; popular song is but a survival of the *modes antiques*.[50]
>
> As a rule, so-called popular art is but a survival and deformation of the previous art which was aristocratic and savant when it lived its proper life. . . . It is a survival of this art that fell into oblivion in its original milieu. . . . Like fashion, so-called popular art moves from up downward and not from the bottom upward. . . . Many of our popular "tunes" are the children of the refrains of the popular operas of the eighteenth century. . . . Most of our rustic dances are ancient dances of the court and aristocracy. . . . Popular poetry is an incorrect translation of the works of ancient poets—professionals.[51]

In brief, the uniformity of the phenomenon discussed is reasonably certain in the field of art also. It manifests itself in practically all the compartments of culture, providing that the respective cultural trait or value can generally be adopted by the lower-rural-less civilized groups (see further, section seven of this chapter). A few exceptions, like the case of the upper classes in the period of their decline, or an interference of the factor of rude force, exist there. But this does not nullify the rule.[52]

[50] W. Deonna, *op. cit.*, Vol. II, pp. 41–42.

[51] C. Lalo, *L'art et la vie sociale, op. cit.*, pp. 142–146. See there other facts. See also A. D'Ancona, *La poesia popolare italiana* (Livorno, 1906); L. Descaves, *L'imagier d'Epinal* (Paris, 1920).

[52] "Thus, whether the social organization be theocratic, aristocratic, or democratic, the course of imitation always follows the same law. It proceeds, given equal distances, from superior to inferior," says G. Tarde, who formulated this uniformity possibly better than anyone else. He gives a large body of factual corroboration of it in Chapter Six of his *Laws of Imitation*. He further remarks that a given class imitates the superior class nearest to it and the imitation tends to decrease with an increase of social distance between the social strata. See pp. 232 ff., and 224 ff. Among many facts of special interest given by G. Tarde is his remark that *even such a cultural activity as politics goes*

In the light of this uniformity, it becomes clear that the great tides of transformation of culture from Ideational to Idealistic or Sensate form, or vice versa, also originated in their "crystallized forms" within the upper-urban-more civilized strata and then, with some lag, in a simplified form, diffused downward — often, in the past, requiring several decades and even centuries for a passage from the upper to the lower rural classes. In this sense, each of these forms of culture has not been limited to the upper class of Græco-Roman or Western society, but has spread also over its middle and lower classes.

VI. Importers and Earliest Recipients of a New Cultural Value

In a more generalized form the preceding proposition can be formulated as follows:

Other conditions being equal, and assuming that various groups in a given population are equally congenial or indifferent to a new cultural value, *the persons and groups that are exposed to it most and earlier than the others tend to be the first importers and recipients of it. The persons and groups who are less exposed to it and come later into contact with it, tend to lag in acceptance and use of a new cultural value.*

For this reason, besides the upper classes, such groups as *merchants and traveling salesmen, missionaries, scholars and scientists, "intelligentsia," travelers, adventurers, journalists, government officials, groups and persons who indirectly* — through reading, hearing, or

also downward and the lower classes begin to discharge political activities after the upper classes, the great lords and ladies, cease to be interested in it... Hence the passage of the political régime from aristocracy to democracy. Ibid., p. 231. Generally, "the innumerable card players that we see in the inns of today are unwitting copyists of our old royal courts. Forms and rules of politeness have spread through the same channels. Courtesy comes from the court, as civility comes from the city. The accent of the court and, later on, that of the capital, spread little by little to all classes and to all provinces of the nation. We may be sure that in times past there were a Babylonian accent, a Ninevite accent, a Memphite accent, just as there are today a Parisian accent, a Florentine accent, and a Berlin accent [or Harvard and Oxford accents imitated by the 'inferiors']." *Ibid.*, pp. 217 ff.

G. Tarde stresses also the innovating role of the upper classes in starting a diffusion of a cultural value. "The principal role of a nobility, its distinguishing mark, is its initiative, if not inventive, character. Invention can start from the lower ranks of the people, but its extension depends upon the existence of some lofty social elevation, a kind of social water-tower, whence a continuous waterfall of imitation may descend. . . . As long as its vitality endures, a nobility may be recognized by this (innovating) characteristic. (When it ceases to perform this role, it is a sign that 'its great work is done' and it is declining)." *Ibid.*, pp. 221 ff.

otherwise coming in contact with a new value — *become acquainted with it; these groups have usually been the importers and first recipients of such values in the past as well as in the present* (providing *their culture is not inimical to those values*). Whether in introduction of, say, Buddhism in China, Oriental cults in Rome, Christianity in the Western world, or some new "foreign" and "imported" merchandise — such as a material commercial value, a new fashion, or new style of art; new philosophical, scientific, juridical or moral value — such novelties fairly uniformly are introduced by one or several of these social groups for the reason that they are exposed to them earlier and more thoroughly than many other groups (peasants, laborers, sedentary artisans, professions having limited contact with the rest of the world, etc.). For the same reason, *men* more frequently than *women* lead in the acceptance of such values (because man more frequently discharges the functions of the "secretary of foreign relations" than woman, who still discharges mainly the functions of "secretary of the interior," and therefore is less exposed to the new values than man). The same would be applicable to *age groups:* the age groups less exposed would tend to lag, those more exposed to lead, in the importation and acceptance of a given value. Which age group in which society is the leader in this respect is a matter of fact. Within the limits of the reservations and qualifications made, the uniformity manifests itself in many — great and small — historical facts.

A. As the rural classes generally are less exposed (have less contact with, and narrower and less remote horizons of, foreign cultural values) than the urban classes to the new and foreign values, they lag, as a rule, in acceptance of such values, in comparison with the more exposed urban groups. This lag shows itself in almost all fields of cultural values. In religious values, for instance, it comes out in the form of a subuniformity such that, all in all, the rural population, as compared with the urban, has regularly a smaller proportion of persons affiliated with religions other than the native religion of the society, and lags in its acceptance of a new and foreign religion, in comparison with the more exposed urban groups. In Rome, the *pagani* (rural population) lagged for a century or two in the acceptance of Christianity (as a new and foreign religion) in comparison with the urban exposed groups. In the United States, the "native religion" is Protestantism, while Catholicism, Judaism, Greek Orthodox, Buddhism and other religions are "foreign." In the total rural population, the proportion of people affiliated with the native religion is still notably higher, and with foreign religions notably lower, than in the total urban population. So also is it in England. In Poland the native religion is Catholicism; therefore the proportion of people affiliated with the Roman Catholic religion is notably higher among the rural population than among the urban. And so on, in practically any country.[53]

B. Studying the actual importation and diffusion of various religions in different societies, we can see the validity of the proposition. For instance, in the ancient Græco-Roman world, the foreign Oriental religious cults of Cybele, the goddess of Mâ-Bellona, Isis, Osiris, Mithra, astrology, the cults of Syria and Persia, Judaism — all these were first imported and accepted by the city groups, such as legionaries, merchants, foreign immigrants, scholars, intellectuals and writers, governmental officials, and the like. Some of these cults did not succeed at all in being adopted by the rural classes.[54] With a proper modification, the same can be said of many other cultural values. The rural classes usually lag, in comparison with the more exposed urban classes, in contracting, in importing, and in accepting such values.

C. The proposition is supported also by many observations concerning the "acculturation" of primitive peoples. Many an anthropologist has noted that women in such groups are more "conservative" than men in the process of acculturation, that is, in contacting and accepting a value of Western culture. The reason for that is, in most cases, not an inherent mystical "conservation" of the female organism, but the fact of a less exposure of women to the new values.[55] The concrete groups that are importers and first acceptors of the new value vary from society to society; but in each society they will be the persons and groups first and most exposed to the new value (when their culture is not inimical to it).

[53] See the statistical figures and other data in Sorokin-Zimmerman, *Principles of Rural-Urban Sociology* (New York, 1929), pp. 420 ff.; Sorokin-Zimmerman-Galpin, *A Systematic Source Book in Rural Sociology* (Minneapolis, 1931), Vol. II, pp. 373 ff.

[54] See the facts and the details in J. F. Toutain, *Les cultes païens dans l'empire romain*, 3 vols. (Paris, 1907–1920), Vol. I, chap. i, pp. 247, 266; Vol. II, pp. 24–30, 58, 65, 159, 255; Vol. III, pp. 102–109, 113, 183, 425, 438, *et passim;* M. I. Rostovtzeff, *Mystic Italy* (New York, 1927), pp. 7–11, 30–31; F. V. Cumont, *Oriental Religions in Roman Paganism* (Chicago, 1911), pp. 53, 56, 83, 201, 281, *et passim;* F. V. Cumont, *The Mysteries of Mythra* (Chicago, 1910), pp. 34, 40, 45, 63, 69; C. A. Guignebert, *Christianity, Past and Present* (New York, 1927), pp. 175 ff.

[55] See, for instance, M. Mead, "The Changing Culture of an Indian Tribe," *Columbia University Contributions of Anthropology*, Vol. XV, 1932; I. Schapera, "The Contributions of Western Civilization to Modern Kxatla Culture," *Transactions of the Royal Society of South Africa,* Vol. XXIV, 1936.

VII. Mobility and Displacement of Cultural Elements, Congeries, Subsystems and Systems, and Great Creative Centers of Culture

Cultural migration takes place in the form of multiplications and spatial mobility of: *the singular cultural elements, the congeries of such elements, small systems, and vast cultural systems, or even the total culture of a given group.*

The cultural objects and values drift and multiply like pieces of ice torn from big icebergs and like icebergs and large ice-fields. Who has not observed during the last few years, for instance, a Russian *samovar* or *vodka* or an *ikon* in the United States? Torn from the Russian cultural system, they have drifted into the American cultural continent. Who does not know about the combs, nails, watches, ready-made dresses, knives, guns, lipsticks, or even chewing gum, or cars, movies, radios, manufactured in the United States and sold in the village or city shops of China and India, and of many other countries? Some of these objects and values were again torn from the total cultural setting of Western culture and, as isolated elements, drifted to and settled in cultural continents essentially different from that in which they originated. And vice versa; in the United States one sees a Chinese lady's dress, Chinese art-objects, certain of their mores and values, which, in isolated form, have flowed to America and entered its culture. The case is so evident and is met so often, that there is no need to insist upon it. It suffices to say that it occurred in the past and is occurring in the present. In the remotest prehistoric periods, many species of cultivated plants and the methods of their cultivation were widely spread from the centers of their origin.[56]

Likewise, in later prehistoric periods, "a South Russian pin is found in a neolithic tomb in Denmark, British spear-heads in graves . . . in Holstein . . . Syrian vases in First Dynasty tombs in Egypt, and Egyptian slate-palettes in Byblos, before 3000 B.C."[57] Similarly,

[56] See E. D. Merrill, "Plants and Civilization," in *Independence, Convergence, and Borrowing* (Harvard University Press, 1938), pp. 22–43.

[57] V. G. Childe, "A Prehistorian's Interpretation of Diffusion," *ibid.*, pp. 10–11. See in this volume a large number of other phenomena of migration of single cultural elements. Likewise, in the works of anthropologists, such as R. Dixon's *The Building of Culture* (New York, 1938); C. Wissler, *Man and Culture* (New York, 1923); R. U. Sayce, *Primitive Arts and Crafts* (London, 1932); W. Wallis, *Culture and Progress* (New York, 1930); W. I. Thomas, *Primitive Behavior,* quoted; and many others, there is given a large mass of the facts and data of the migration of cultural elements. The fact of migration of single cultural elements does not oblige me to subscribe to a one-

several traits of the Sumeric culture went as far as Europe and India; the Aramaic alphabet and Phœnician script reached India and China;[58] some art-styles of Hellenic culture appeared in China and India; the Egyptian cultural traits traveled the longest distances in various directions from Egypt. Many isolated cultural traits of Western culture can be found at the present moment in the remotest village of Asia or Africa.[59]

No less certain is the fact that *cultural elements travel also in the form of a congeries of such elements or congeries of systems.* From Russia to many other countries there traveled, during the last two decades: *vodka,* the *samovar,* Communism, Planned Economy (with Five or Four Year Plans), Dostoievsky, a song — "Volga Boatman." This assortment is a congeries of cultural elements and systems. In thousands of other forms, such migrations of congeries have always been taking place from area to area (horizontally) and from one cultural stratum to another (vertically). One of the reasons why such travel by congeries is taking place is due to the fact that different human agents and groups of the same country or area are often interested in different and little related cultural objects and values of another given area. Therefore some are "importing," say, folk-songs, while others import wine, or certain mores, costumes, or beliefs. As a result, the country of the "importation" receives a congeries, as a total result of the importation by all the above groups and persons. The same can be said of the movement of the congeries from the upper to the lower strata, or vice versa. Again the case is so well known that there is no need to discuss it farther.

Finally, culture travels and diffuses in the form of small and vast cultural systems. Factory-system; machine shops; system of telegraph and telephone communication; railroad and airplane transportation; Prussian or French army organization; Christian religion; Buddhism; Communist ideology; Parliamentarism; Totalitarianism; American system of Education; Planned Economy; Classicism, Romanticism, the Renaissance,[60] "Great State System";[61] these and thou-

---

sided diffusionist theory. Migration takes place when a given element originates in one place as well as when we have two or more independent inventions and convergence.

[58] See H. Jensen, *Geschichte der Schrift* (Hanover, 1925), pp. 11 ff., *et passim;* R. B. Dixon, *The Building of Cultures,* quoted, pp. 136–141; T. F. Carter, *The Invention of Printing in China and Its Spread Westward* (New York, 1931), *passim.*

[59] A. J. Toynbee, *A Study of History,* Vol. III, pp. 129 ff.

[60] In Europe "the Renaissance" originated in Italy in the fourteenth century (omitting different Renaissances of the Carlovingian time and of the twelfth century); from there

sands of other cultural systems have been traveling during recent decades from country to country, crossing sometimes enormous distances. In the past as well as in the present, various cultural systems have been frequently "borrowed," "transplanted," "imitated," introduced, or have just drifted from one cultural continent to another. In some cases, for instance, in the case of the Japanese "reform" in the second half of the nineteenth century, a whole set of cultural systems of Western culture was transplanted and rooted in the Japanese culture. A similar "wholesale" borrowing of Chinese systems occurred in Japan in the seventh century. "Diffusion" of the Egyptian, Greek, Roman, Buddhist,[62] Chinese, or Hindu cultural — small and vast — systems in and over many cultural islands and continents in the past, as well as the spread of Western cultural systems over the whole world, during the last three centuries, are further examples of the same phenomenon.

Finally, once in a while we have a phenomenon of movement of a total culture. Concretely the processes assume two different forms. (*a*) When a large group of either peaceful migrants or conquerors enters and settles in a different cultural continent — for instance, the Dorians in subjugated Greece; the Aryans in India; the Spaniards in South America; the Europeans in North America; the Greek and the Romans among many cultures of their colonies; the Arabs among their conquered populations; the Europeans among the peoples of Asia, Australia, Africa; and recently, the Italians in Abyssinia — in these cases the conquerors or colonizers bring with them not only a set of separate cultural traits or systems but almost the whole culture of their own country. In such cases it is transplanted in its totality and planted amidst, or face to face with, a different culture. (*b*) Another variety of the shift of a considerable part of a culture

---

it spread during the next two centuries to France, England and Germany (modifying itself in the process of migration, according to the rule discussed later).

[61] For instance, migration and adaptation of the Egyptian Great State system in Imperial Rome. "It exercised a formative influence on the tradition of European State administration through its inheritance by the Hellenic monarchies and the Roman Empire. . . . The Empire of the fourth century . . . may be regarded as nothing less than an adaptation to the Mediterranean World of a system that has been inherited by the Caesars in Egypt as the successors of the Ptolemies and the Pharaohs." M. I. Rostovtzeff, *A History of the Ancient World* (Oxford University Press, 1926), Vol. II, pp. 325 ff.

[62] "Mahāyāna Buddhism came *in toto* (to China), and was accepted by the Chinese believers — almost *in toto*." Hu Shih, "The Indianization of China," *Independence, Convergence, and Borrowing in Institutions, Thought, and Art* (Harvard University Press, 1937), p. 22, quoted. See also W. F. Albright, *From the Stone Age to Christianity*, quoted, pp. 159–160, 226. K. S. Latourette, *A History of the Expansion of Christianity*, 3 vols. (New York, 1939).

is found when a notable part of a given total culture spreads over larger and larger areas, peoples, and societies. An expansion of a considerable part of Egyptian, Græco-Roman, Arabic, Minoan, Sumeric, Babylonian, or Western cultures, supplies the examples of this type. Many of the culture's systems and congeries inundate the areas and peoples where it did not exist before; sometimes it drives out the previous culture; sometimes, as we shall see, it enters a kind of alliance with it or coexists with it as a congeries-system side by side within the same geographic space, like the culture of the European settlement in the Chinese or Asiatic cities coexisting adjacently with the culture of the native parts of these cities. Since the spreading culture invades the new areas in a large part of its totality, all such cases approach, to some extent, the expansion and migration of culture almost *in toto*. Again, this type of culture-migration occurred in the past as well as it is occurring in the present. It occurs on a large scale when a given country borrows it, like Japan's borrowing of a large part of Chinese culture in the seventh century, and that of Western culture in the nineteenth; like the borrowing of a considerable part of Western culture by Russia under Peter the Great. It happens also when a large group of migrants, conquerors, or settlers, moves in and settles amidst the population of a different culture, and through that plant their culture *in toto* on a large scale, in vast areas. It occurs also on a small scale in the form of a migration of one or few individuals — a few aliens — to a different cultural continent. Though the individuals are few, and the social area of the transplanted culture is small, nevertheless, in so far as the migrants bring with them their own culture in its totality, or a greater part of it, such small-scale migration of culture belongs to the class of the shift or travel of culture as a whole.

The above dealt mainly with migration of cultural elements, complexes, and cultures horizontally. When it is viewed in a *vertical* aspect, the situation and the main forms remain essentially the same. (*a*) Bathtubs, bobbed hair, short dresses, the waltz, white collars, some of the rules of etiquette, and so on — each of these separate cultural elements migrated from the upper class to the lower; from the city to the country. In thousands of forms, a similar circulation of the cultural elements along the vertical ladder has been taking place in the past as well as in the present. (*b*) Likewise, the cultural systems also shift up and down in any society. Whether the system be radio-car-movie, jazz-dancing-crooning-going to places-doing things, the theory of evolution, "share-the-wealth plan," the Townsend plan, Christian Science, baseball-football, bridge-party, Emancipation of Women and Birth-Control complex, or any of thousands of other systems — they move up and down. (*c*) Finally, the migration of the culture of aristocracy or of the proletariat, in their greater part, occurs also. First, in the form of the social revolution, when the aristocracy is uprooted and thrown into the social sewers along with its culture; and when a considerable part of the previous dwellers of the lower strata climb up and establish at the top of the social pyramid a greater part of their previous culture. Second, in the form of the spread of the high standard of living of the upper classes throughout the lower ones; or, vice versa, of lowering the higher standards of living to the level of the poor classes. It is true that here the quality of the rising or declining standard of living remains different, but its essential patterns tend to be similar in the upper and the lower classes. The aristocracy may have Lincoln cars, expensive radios, luxurious mansions, summer estates, colorful and expensive parties, more refined manners, private schools and colleges for their children, and so on. The lower classes duplicate these with their Chevrolets and Fords, cheaper radios, rented houses; similar, though less expensive, summer vacations; similar bridge and drinking and dinner parties; dresses and costumes of the same pattern, though less expensive; public schools and State colleges for their children; similar manners, though less refined and polished; in brief, when the lower classes reproduce a number of essential patterns of the culture of the upper classes, though their copy is less expensive, such cases represent a vertical shift of the culture of the upper classes downward, into the stratum of the lower classes. When the opposite shift, namely, a lowering of the standard of living of the upper classes, takes place, and when the dwellers of the upper classes begin to reproduce in the essentials the main patterns of the culture of the lower classes, we have the upward migration of the culture of the lower classes in its greater part. In periods of great social calamities, such phenomena occur.

Such, in brief, are the main forms of the horizontal and vertical migrations of culture from this standpoint.

VIII. Spatial Shift of the Great Creative Centers of Culture

As a special case of the above shift and migration of cultural systems and combinations of systems from area to area, country to country, society to society, the shift of the great creative centers of culture is to be mentioned specifically. In view of its theoretical and practical importance, it deserves a little more detailed characterization, together with an outline of the problem of where cultural values and systems generally, and the great systems particularly, are created, and how the centers of their creations shift in social space.

In order that cultural values may shift, multiply, and spread in social space, their originals somehow and somewhere have to be invented, created, or discovered. Otherwise, there would be nothing — no value, pattern, machine — to migrate, multiply, and spread in the areas of the populations. Hence the problem: *how and where do new cultural values originate, especially new great cultural systems and supersystems?* Are there some uniformities in regard to the place of their origin? Are the creative centers of the great systems the centers that simultaneously create the great systems in *all* fields of culture, or do they each create only one or a few specific systems of culture? Do the main centers of creation of great cultural systems shift in time from country to country, from society to society? If they shift, does such a shift mean the wholesale shift of the creativeness in all fields of culture, from place to place; or is the shift limited to only one or two fields of culture, rarely, if ever, assuming a wholesale character? If a given country ceases to be the center of creativeness in one or a few fields of culture, is the loss of its leadership irrevocable and irretrievable, or may it possibly, after some time, regain the leadership of creativeness in the same or in another field of culture? Such are the main problems to be dealt with in this section.

As for the first question, concerning the place of origin of the simple cultural congeries and simple systems — such cultural values incessantly originate everywhere that interacting human beings with mental life (however primitive) are found. Such a group, be it a primitive tribe or even the patients of an insane asylum (except, perhaps, complete idiots), has some rudiments of mental processes: some images, ideas, beliefs, norms, patterns, or some meanings. These meanings and their congeries are objectified by such a group in this or that kind of vehicle; in their language, actions, and various objects. To a certain extent, some cultural congeries and even simple cultural systems are continually generated in any of such groups. We do not know any primitive group which does not have some meanings objectified in some vehicles — religious and magical beliefs, and their vehicles; norms of taboo, patterns of art, scientific notions and their vehicles.

In other words, the generation of simple cultural congeries and systems is coextensive with the social life of mankind as its inseparable concomitant; therefore it is found *urbi et orbi* within the human universe.

The same answer holds true for the generation of the simple cultural systems. We do not know any completely illogical or nonlogical human group. All of them display an ability to put together not only a congeries of meanings, but many consistent systems of meanings of the simpler kind. All of them are able to make the simplest judgments: A is B or A is not B, "this fish is eatable," "this snake is poisonous," "this man is my uncle or brother or father," "this is permitted," and so on. Even the most primitive human groups known display an ability to make much more complex logical propositions, ethical norms, patterns of art. Such simple cultural systems are generated everywhere that human groups are found.

The difficulty begins when we face the problem of the place of genesis in regard to new, complex, and great cultural systems and supersystems. They are not found everywhere; many tribes and groups do not have them or, if they have, they were imitated, borrowed, imposed by, or taken from some other groups. Furthermore, common observation shows that only a few individuals among the multitude of our own society create such new systems. Hence the real problem: *Why do some groups or individuals create such new and great systems (in science, religion, ethics and law, art and technology, forms of social organization) while other groups and individuals do not create them?* Why have not an enormous number of so-called primitive peoples created such great systems, while some other groups — so-called "historical" groups, like the Egyptians, Sumerians, Babylonians, Persians, Hebrews, Chinese, Hindus, Arabs, Greeks, Romans, Europeans, Americans, and others [63] — have been

[63] A. J. Toynbee finds, all in all, twenty-one different historical groups that created twenty-one different civilizations: the Western, two Orthodox Christian (in Russia and the Near East), the Iranic, the Arabic, the Hindu, two Far Eastern, the Hellenic, the Syriac, the Indic, the Sinic, the Minoan, the Sumeric, the Hittite, the Babylonic, the Andean, the Mexican, the Yucatec, the Mayan, the Egyptian, plus five "arrested civilizations" (that did not develop real civilizations): Polynesian, Eskimo, Nomadic, Ottoman, and Spartan. See his *A Study of History, op. cit.*, Vol. I, pp. 132 ff., Vol. IV, pp. 1 ff. Whether we take this list of the civilizations that have been able to develop great and new cultural systems or take any other list, is unimportant for our purposes. What is important is that not all the human groups have been able to develop great sociocultural systems ("civilizations" in Toynbee's sense) and that most primitive tribes remained on a lower level from this standpoint, and happened to be, in Toynbee's terms, either "abortive" or "arrested" civilizations.

able to do so? Likewise, why, within any historical society, have only a few individuals (historical persons) created some new and great sociocultural systems, while the majority have not done that?

The adequate answer to this problem can hardly be given at this present stage of our knowledge. In considerable part it still remains a mystery. However, a few operative conditions can be pointed out. They are mainly of three kinds: (*a*) *"fortunate" biological heredity of the creative persons or groups;* (*b*) *an urgent need of the creation of a new system for a given group in the given environment;* (*c*) *cross-fertilization of two or more cultural systems and subsystems in a given group* (*or individual*) *facilitated by the fact of their being in the area of an intensive mobility, circulation and cross-current of streams of different cultural values* (*systems of meanings and vehicles*).

We reject the exaggerated claims of various "hereditarists" and "racialists," geneticists, eugenists, biologists, biometricians, physical anthropologists, etc., who regard the factor of heredity as the most important, necessary and sufficient cause of genius and idiocy, of creativeness and uncreativeness, and try to account for everything in human history by this factor. An overwhelming part of their claims does not stand the test and is invalid.[64]

From this, however, it does not follow that the hereditary endowment of all human beings is identical, that there are no hereditary differences between men of genius and idiots; or that there are no special hereditary aptitudes for creativeness in special fields (mathematics, music, or poetry, etc.). According to the existing body of evidence, a fortunate hereditary endowment is a necessary condition for a person or a given group to become the creators of the new, and especially the great, cultural systems. From inborn idiots or mediocrities we can hardly expect the creation of such systems — in science, religion, ethics, law, philosophy, art, technology, and the forms of political, social, economic, or military organization; and such persons and groups have hardly created such systems.[65] Except in periods of decay, the potential creators, more fortunate in their hereditary endowment, seem to occur more frequently within the upper strata of a given society than in its lower strata; [66] among males more frequently than among females. Likewise, there may be some differences in this respect among the most divergent racial groups, particularly

[64] See the data, evidence, and literature in my *Social Mobility*, cited, chaps. x–xiii; and in my *Contemporary Sociological Theories*, chap. v.

[65] See *ibid.*, the data and evidence for that.

[66] See the evidences in the same works and chapters.

the blacks and the rest of the primitive races. The inter-racial differences, however, are much less than many claim; and they consist not so much in general creative ability or a lack of it, as in the special aptitudes of different racial groups for certain forms of creativeness, and the lack of it in others.[67] To sum up: those groups and persons who happen to be endowed with a more fortunate heredity necessary for creativeness of the great systems, have a greater chance to realize this potentiality than the groups and persons equipped with a poorer or less creative heredity. This condition is necessary, though not sufficient, for the creation of great sociocultural systems.

It is probable that a large number of the so-called primitive peoples belong to the groups endowed with a poorer heredity necessary for creativeness of great sociocultural systems, while those historical groups which have demonstrated such a creativeness have in all probability a more fortunate heredity. Though necessary, the factor of heredity is, however, insufficient in itself to produce actually the great cultural systems. In any society at any time, there have been a number of potential men of genius, potential creators, who, however, did not realize their potentiality. In order to realize it, a corresponding sociocultural environment is necessary. Two conditions of this environment are especially important. First of these is that the society in which the potential creators exist has *an urgent need for the creation of a new cultural system that can satisfy it*. Other conditions being equal, the more vital the need, the greater the stimulus is given to all the potential creators to satisfy it through an invention, synthesis, or discovery of the system needed, such as a technological device, moral code, art-system, or any other sociocultural system. This explains why a series of technological devices, like their most ingenious navigation system, was created by the Polynesians or Eskimos; domestication and cattle breeding by the pastoral peoples; invention of efficient military technique by the peoples in need of military activity; or the creation of a system of unifying religion like Judaism by the groups who were dispersed or in danger of being engulfed by other

[67] See *ibid.* A recent attempt of A. J. Toynbee to deny entirely the role of hereditary and racial factors in the presence or absence of creativeness is unwarranted. He himself gives a proof of that: he contends that only an insignificant minority in every society is creative while the majority ("the Internal and partly External Proletariat") is uncreative. If this is so, then what is the reason for the creativeness of the minority? Since it lives in the same environment as the majority, the environment evidently cannot account for the difference. If it cannot, then there remains only the factor of hereditary endowment of the creative minority. The existing body of the evidence in the problem does not permit us to accept also the too sweeping generalization of A. J. Toynbee.

societies; and so on, in any field of cultural life. That this factor of social urgency is real is demonstrated not only positively, as in the above cases, but also negatively, especially by the fact of a lack of creativeness, in a given society, of such systems as are not needed by it. Mountain-dwelling people did not and do not invent the technology of a skillful seafaring or sea-fishing race; and vice versa; seashore inhabitants do not create the ingenious technique of mountain climbing, the cultivation of various crops adapted to mountain conditions, and a number of other techniques needed by a mountaineer society. Pastoral, nomadic peoples of the steppes or deserts do not invent technical systems of stone-building, plowing, and hundreds of other technical devices fit for the inhabitants of, say, rocky mountains, and unfitted to, and unneeded by, such societies. What is said of technological inventions can be said of the nontechnological cultural systems, such as ethical norms, religious beliefs, scientific knowledge, art-systems, and what not. The native forms of each of such systems are always more or less adapted to the local needs of a given society. When and where we meet a great system in any of these fields of culture, we always find that it is meeting the urgent need of the society. Such is the second important condition.[68]

The third condition vital to the creation of great sociocultural systems is *the presence or absence of the different cultural cross-currents in a given society which serves as a meeting place of these cross-currents.* Other conditions being equal, the societies and the individuals that are the focal *locus* of such cross-currents have a greater chance of becoming the inventors of the great sociocultural systems than the societies which are not in such *loci.* The experience of a single society or individual is always limited. If it is not enriched by the experience of other societies or individuals, its fund of meanings and of their systems is always poorer than when it is enriched by a flow of the experiences — meanings and systems of meanings — of other societies and individuals. In that case, it has not only its own fund for a further synthesis, but also the fund of experience — usually much richer — of other societies and individuals. In that case, the possibilities of a new synthesis of the native and foreign elements

[68] This urgent need of a given society embraces indirectly the geographic conditions in which it lives. However, these geographic conditions, as such, play only an indirect and comparatively secondary role in the creativeness of the great cultural systems. From this standpoint, a great role ascribed to them by many, including recently A. J. Toynbee, is enormously exaggerated. See the role of the geographic conditions in my *Contemporary Sociological Theories,* chaps. ii, iii.

of the culture greatly increase for such a society or individual. We have seen in Chapter Two that the first — and most important — phase of creation of any new sociocultural system consists in a lucky marriage of two or more systems of meanings in the mind of an inventor. The steam-engine is but a lucky synthesis of the meaning and properties of a wagon and of steam energy. Christianity is but a great synthesis of Judaism, Hellenism, the cult of Mithra, and some other Oriental systems of meanings. Christian religious music, in the form of the Ambrosian and the Gregorian Chant, is again a synthesis of the patterns of Greek-Syrian, Alexandrian music. When this Christian music came into contact with the native music of various regions of Europe (Celtic, Teutonic, etc.) we received a brilliant new synthesis in the form of the *ars nova* in France and Italy, then in the form of the great Flemish music (Joquin de Pres and others), great Italian and Spanish music (Palestrina, de Lasso, Vittoria), then later on the French, and still later the great German music, culminating in Bach, Mozart, and Beethoven. Kant's system of philosophy is a great synthesis of Hume and Descartes, not to mention other philosophical systems; and so on. Any new great system is always a consistent synthesis of two or more great systems that existed before. With the presence of the potential creators in a given society,[69] with the social need of a new creation, the societies and individuals that are at the crossroad of a number of different cultural currents have richer material for their synthesis, have more patterns from which to choose, a more diverse combination of elements, more varied systems of meanings. They are situated better in this respect than the societies and individuals that have only their own fund. Hence, this third, and possibly the most important condition, so far as the creation of great sociocultural systems is concerned.[70]

An inductive verification of this hypothesis of the three above conditions seems to corroborate it well. (*a*) Various great systems (political, religious, artistic and others) created — whether in Egypt, Sumeria, Babylon, Creto-Mycenae, Greece, Syria, Persia, India, China, Arabia, Europe, or America — were created in areas which, in the

[69] The mentally inferior and mediocre persons and groups often are lost in such rich cross-currents and do not create anything except a purely eclectic congeries. In our theory, the presence of the potential creators is specifically reserved. Such creators, by definition and fact, can and do make a real synthesis of the diverse elements, and unity out of a rich plurality.

[70] See a developed form of this argument in my *Social Mobility,* chaps. xx, xxii. See there the data and the literature.

period of creation, were "highways" for the traffic of various cultural currents, not areas shut off from the rest of the cultural world. (*b*) Such creative societies rarely create great systems in all fields of culture at the same period, but do so mainly in that particular field for which, at a given period, it is a "meeting-place" of various currents. An area in which mainly currents of various religious systems meet, tends to create its great system mainly in the religious field; when it is the meeting-place for mainly artistic, scientific, philosophical, or political currents, it creates mainly in those respective fields. This means that most of such "historically creative" societies rarely create great systems in all fields of culture, or rarely do so in the same period of their history, but distinguish themselves by the creation of only one or a few great systems in one or a few fields of culture, during their total historical existence, or at each period of their history. It is hard to find in the whole history of human culture one society that created equally great systems in all main fields of culture in the same period of its history or even in its total life-span. The fields in which the given society distinguishes itself by creation of its one or few great systems are usually the fields in which its need for the system is particularly urgent, and in which the society is the meeting-place of various cross-currents of this specific system of culture. For a period of several centuries the Hindu population created mainly the great religious and philosophic systems; so also did the Hebrews, or the Iranic population before the sixth century B.C., or the Chinese of the sixth century B.C. During such a period the contributions of these populations in other fields of culture were more modest, so far as the creation of great systems is concerned. Sparta, Persia of the period of Cyrus-Darius-Xerxes, Assyria, and Rome distinguished themselves mainly by creation of great systems of military and political organization; Rome, in addition, by the system of law. Greece, of the centuries from the sixth to the second B.C., distinguished itself mainly by creation of the great systems in science-philosophy-arts, and much less in the field of religion or ethics. The Western population, during the centuries from the fifteenth to the twentieth, distinguished itself mainly by creation of the great scientific-technological-artistic systems and much less by those in other fields of culture (religion or ethics). This means that we have had hardly a society or populated area equally creative in all fields of culture at all periods of its history. Ordinarily any creative society creates, at any given period of its history, mainly in that field of culture in which its need for a great system is particularly great, and in which it is, at such a period, a meeting-place of various cultural currents. If, at another period, its need in the great system changes and it becomes the meeting-place of the cross-currents of another cultural sector — say, scientific instead of religious, or artistic instead of economic — its creativeness may shift and manifest itself in the creation of great systems in this new field.

(*c*) Farther on, our general proposition is also corroborated by the fact that many creative societies had been uncreative until they became the focal point for various cultural currents, and became creative after turning into such a meeting-place. And vice versa, when such areas ceased again to be the meeting-place of cultural cross-currents, their creativeness often declined, and soon they fell into "historical oblivion." (*d*) Furthermore, in a large area which is emerging as a creative territory the creation often appears first in such regions of the area as become first, in comparison with other regions, the meeting-place of cultures, like Ionia in Greece.[71] (*e*) For this same reason, as we have seen, the cities are more creative in regard to new systems than the country; the upper and mobile classes, with wider, longer, and more developed systems of communication and contact, are more creative than the lower, and especially the rural, classes.

(*f*) For the same reason, of many potential creators in a given society the actual creators become mainly those who are not deprived of the advantage of being at the "crossroads" of various cultural currents in the field of their creation. Among the total number of inventors and creators of great cultural systems in all the fields of culture, the percentage of the "isolated" creators who discovered and created some important system from A to Z, "all by themselves," without knowledge of what had been done in that particular field by others, without any contact with different cultural currents that had the elements of their synthesis, is very small, almost insignificant. Most of the creators in science, religion, ethics and law, or art, or the builders of the great state-business-cultural empires and organizations, were well versed in what had been created by others in their field and in what was done in the adjacent fields; they lived and swam in the currents around them, and in that swimming they con-

[71] See some details in H. E. Barnes and H. Becker, *Social Thoughts from Lore to Science* (New York, 1938), Vol. I, pp. 152 ff., and chap. iv; H. Becker, "Forms of Population Movement: Prolegomena to a Study of Mental Mobility," *Social Forces*, Vol. IX, 1930, pp. 147–160, 351–361.

ceived their synthesis and invention. At the present time, it is hardly conceivable that a person who did not study, say, physics or mathematics at all, and did not know what had already been done in these fields in the past and by his contemporaries, could discover anything new and great indeed in physics or mathematics. At best, some potential genius might, under these conditions, rediscover something by himself that was discovered a long time ago, but that would be about all that he could do. A discovery of America, for example, centuries after it was discovered by Columbus, would not make of the discoverer a new Columbus, or the creator of a new theory or system. The same, with some variation, can be said of the creators in other fields of culture, even in art and technological inventions. Fairly popular ideas of poets, painters, musicians, and inventors, who, supposedly without any technical preparation and knowledge of the past and present status of their art or technology, by sheer inspiration create a great poem, great symphony, or great picture, or invent something startlingly new — such ideas are mainly pure mythology, romantic and appealing but not corresponding to the reality at all.[72] Such creators may be the outsiders to the existing "professionals" in these fields, but they usually are well informed and trained in the field of their creative activity.

To sum up: *the main centers of the creativeness of the great cultural systems tend to be those societies which have a sufficiently good hereditary endowment, which have an urgent need for the creation of such systems to solve a vital need, and which happen to be situated in the areas that are the meeting-place of various cultural streams.* As a consequence of their creativeness, in this or that field of culture, such societies become "historical," and as long as they perform this function, they are the centers of the specific field of human culture and human history, the bearers of the "torch of progress" in their field in the historical drama. Out of thousands of various human groups and societies, this privilege of becoming "historical" has been reserved to only a small portion of the societies, and within each of these, to a small minority of its members. Respectively the total

[72] A more detailed study of the role of our third factor must distinguish between the various cultural currents that are congenial, uncongenial, and indifferent to one another. The probability of a fruitful synthesis is hardly the same in these three cases. However, here we cannot go into an analysis of this problem. Briefly, the problem has been touched in other paragraphs of this chapter. Some thoughtful elucidation of it is given in several works, particularly in the quoted main works of G. Tarde, and in the biosocial theory of E. De Roberty.

great drama of culture is played, at any given period, only on the stages of such creative populations and areas. At any given period, the number of such "historical theaters" is limited to a comparatively few societies. "Political creativeness" is played now in the theater of Egypt, now of Assyria, Sumeria, or Persia, now of China or Rome, now of Europe or America. "Philosophical creativeness" is unfolded now in India, now in Greece, now in Europe. "Religious creativeness" is displayed now in India, Persia, China, and Syria, now it is shifted to Greece, Rome, Africa, and from there to Europe and Arabia. "Art-Creation" is staged now in Egypt, now in Persia and India; from there it is shifted to Greece, and from there to Europe. Technological inventiveness is centered now in China or Egypt, now in Arabia, now in Europe and America; and so on.

In other words, the leadership in creativeness of great cultural systems shifts in social space from area to area or from society to society. Sometimes, if a given society distinguishes itself by creation of a great system in one field of culture, its leadership passes to another in this one field only. Sometimes, if a given society is a leader in several fields of culture, the leadership may shift to other societies in several of these fields. A concrete example of the first case is given by the *field of science and technological inventions*. On pages 148–150 of Volume Two of *Dynamics* are given the data of the number of scientific and technological inventions in Greece, Rome, Arabia, and the main European and American countries. They show in detail the periods when each country distinguished itself in this field, and when its creativeness declined and passed to other countries. The Golden Age for Greece was the period of 600 to 201 B.C., after which the leadership passed to Rome, which held it from about 100 B.C. to 400 A.D. From 800 to 1300 A.D., Arabia became "the star" in this field. From then up to the present time, Europe became the leader. Among various European countries, again, there were specific periods when each of them had an effervescence of creativeness before its decline, when Italy, France, England, or Germany was the leader. At the beginning of the twentieth century, for instance, the preceding importance of France and England shows a relative decline; Germany holds its own, while the United States of America, and in much lesser degree Russia and Japan, display a remarkable rise of their creativeness in this field.

The same phenomenon is observable, especially clearly, in the shift of the centers of military-political and economic creativeness. At any period of the world's history, the creation of *great political and military systems* — empires — is centered in only a few territorial and populational areas. For many of the earliest centuries it is centered in the Orient: in Egypt, Sumeria, Assyro-Babylonia, India, Persia, or China; now one, now another, of these centers playing the most important role, and then being succeeded by another country as the main star. Then the centers shift to Creto-Mycenæ, then Greece, then the Roman Empire. Then they shift to Arabia, from there to Europe; in Europe, from one country to another, now the Charlemagne Empire, now the Spanish Empire, now France, now the Hapsburg Empire, now the British, Russian, or German Empire playing the leading politico-military role. Later on, and especially at the present time, the centers of creativeness of such an empire are shifting, before our eyes, to America, to Japan and generally to the region of the Pacific Ocean, from the Mediterranean, the Baltic and generally European regions. And so the process goes on.

In different concrete forms, but along the same pattern, the centers of building of *the great economic empires* have similarly been shifting, from region to region, country to country, population to population. The main centers of economic creativeness at one period of human history may be centered in India or Cathay or Hammurabi's empire; at another, in Iran, Syria, or Minoan culture; at another they are located in Greece and Rome; still later on, in Arabian countries, then in Europe, then in America, and so on, within each big region shifting from people to people, from subregion to subregion, from city to city. Another example of such a *shift of the musical centers* in world history is well described by C. Lalo, who rightly puts this special shift in the framework of a much more general shift of the centers of creativeness in social space.

Localization of art in space is submitted to complex laws. This phenomenon of localization manifests itself more or less in all creative social fields. When a given region or a group discharges certain functions with a sufficient intensity of its control, the given function atrophies almost everywhere else; the movement and even creative production in that field seemingly stop in all other regions or groups. [This is exaggerated.] Like a centralization of a certain industry in a certain region . . .

Art forms a kind of artistic capital: sometimes one city, sometimes a vaster national milieu; seemingly everything converges to that center and all the solidary regions become its tributaries. The sentiment grows that only in that center reside the forces from which movement and life generate,

Such, for instance, was Bayreuth for all the Wagnerians at the climax of Wagner's fame. Contrary to racial theories that ascribe artisticity to some nation, for instance, to Italy, and aesthetic insensitivity to others, for instance, to England,

> history denies such beliefs: England played the leading role in the origination of harmony; France in the development of polyphony; Germany has been, during the last two centuries, a musical nation *par excellence*. Balzac denied any musical capacity to the Dutch; and yet, the Flemish led the musical development of the whole of Europe, without any contest, for two centuries. . . .
> Throughout history we see, side by side with this localization or centralization of superior art, the phenomenon of a displacement of this center when seemingly after an exhaustion of the creative force in one country, it cedes the leadership to another. . . . It is a fact that the center of musical art in the Occident has been successively: Asia Minor and Archipelago; Sparta; Athens; Milan; Rome; the Rhenish countries; France (Paris first, then Flanders); Rome again; then Germany. Musical art then is subject to a double evolution: in time and in space.[73]

In one of the preceding paragraphs of this chapter the same phenomenon of shift of the dominant *languages* from country to country in the course of time has been shown. In a large part of the inhabited area of this planet, the language most spoken becomes now Egyptian or Persian, now Greek or Roman, now French, German, Russian, or English. This shift of the domination from language to language proceeds more or less parallel with a shift of the political and cultural power from nation to nation.

With slight modification the same can be said of the shift of the centers of creativeness in philosophy, religion, arts, technological inventions, ethical and juridical systems, and finally, of political power, and of the systems of economic and social organization. No single population or nation has the monopoly of leadership in any of these fields forever. Having accomplished its task, sooner or later it loses its importance and is replaced by another society or nation, though, later on, it may again regain the leadership in the same or a different field of culture.

Sometimes, when a given society happens to be the leader in several fields (but not in all fields) of cultural creativeness, its leadership may shift to other societies simultaneously, in several fields. An example of that is given by the leadership of Italy in the early Renaissance

[73] C. Lalo, *L'esquisse d'une esthétique musicale scientifique* (Paris, 1908), pp. 318–19.

and by the loss of its leadership — in philosophy, science, all main forms of art (music, sculpture, literature, architecture, drama), in economics and, partly, in politics — in favor of Spain, France, the Netherlands, England, and Germany. Roughly speaking, in the fourteenth and fifteenth centuries, in all these fields, Italy leads all the other countries of Europe; in the sixteenth century the leadership in some of the arts and in economics and politics passes mainly to Spain; in the seventeenth, in some of these fields, to France and England and the Netherlands; somewhat later it passes in some of these fields to Germanic countries; finally, in the late nineteenth and the beginning of the twentieth century, in several arts, like literature, music, theater, it began to pass to Russia. Earlier, a similar thing happened to Greece. Being the leader of Europe and Asia Minor in many fields of culture — in almost all arts, philosophy, science, ethics, politics — during several centuries, after the second century B.C. it lost its place in most of these fields.

The same phenomenon can be observed on a much narrower scale: in the rise and decline of various cities or regions in the same country, as leaders in the creativeness of this or that great system. In the long-existing countries, the capital, the metropolis, the main seats of science, religion, philosophy, art, law or economics also shift from city to city, region to region, university to university. The center of one or of several creative fields is now Memphis, now Thebes, now Saïs and Alexandria in Egypt. Now it is Ionia, Sparta, Athens, Rhodes, Pergamon, or Alexandria in Greece, and the Hellenic world. Now it is Rome, now Naples, Bologna, Milan, Venice, or Rome again, in Italy. Now it is Vienna, Munich, Berlin, among the Germanic peoples. Now it is Kiev, Vladimir, Novgorod, Moscow, St. Petersburg, now Moscow again, in Russia. Now it is Charleston, Boston, Philadelphia, New York, Chicago or Los Angeles, in America; and so on. Such a shift of the centers of creativeness in one or more specific fields of culture within the same country is a smaller replica of the bigger shifts of the centers of creativeness from country to country.

To sum up: *the shift of the centers of creativeness proceeds mainly in one or more specific cultural systems (religious, military-political, scientific, musical, economic, and so on); only once in a while, if a given country happens to be the center of creativeness of several cultural systems (artistic, philosophic, scientific, and economic), does it lose its leadership in all or several of these fields in favor of either a new successor who assumes the leadership in all these fields, or, what is more frequent, in favor of several countries, each of which "inherits" the leadership in one of the fields of the previous leading country. This second case happens, however, much more rarely than the first type.*[74]

[74] A. J. Toynbee sets forth an interesting theory that in the period of growth of a given civilization it expands and migrates *in toto,* and is the center of creativeness in *all* fields of culture. In the period of decline, it disintegrates, and, like a white light decomposed by a prism into its constituent seven colors, it shifts and migrates, not *in toto,* but in decomposed parts: either its art or its religion or its economics or its politics migrate and diffuse, but not the whole civilization, as in the period of its growth. Set in such a form, the theory is hardly acceptable. First, Toynbee's "civilization" is not a unified system but a congeries of systems. As such, it neither grows nor declines nor disintegrates, because congeries cannot grow or decline or disintegrate, for the very simple reason that they never have been integrated as a real unity. Since this is so, no ground is given for a distinction of the periods of growth and decline of such congeries, and, therefore, for the above difference in the manner of their expansion and migration in the periods of "growth and decline." Second, any total civilization-culture can diffuse *in toto* in only one way — by its members migrating and settling as conquerors or immigrants amidst a different culture. Such a transfer of the total culture from area to area remains, however, limited to the groups of the conquerors or immigrants, and hardly ever spreads in its totality among the native populations amidst which the conquerors or immigrants settle. Just as in the imposition of Western culture upon the peoples of India, or the spread of technologico-scientific-economic aspects of Western culture over an enormous number of peoples, these peoples, be they Japanese, Chinese, Hindus, or Polynesians, did not accept the Western culture in its totality, but still retain their own religion, art, ethics, forms of family, social institutions, mores, and so on. Still truer was it in the past. Therefore it is hardly possible to contend that civilizations in the period of their growth spread in their totality among the peoples and areas of different cultures. Neither in the period of growth nor decline does such a phenomenon occur.

It does not occur for the reason that hardly any of the existing civilizations has been the leader in *all* fields of culture, and therefore induced the other peoples to accept it in its entirety, as Toynbee claims in regard to the periods of growth of civilizations.

Each of the "historical" civilizations at any given period of its history has been a leader in the creation of one or, more rarely, a few fields of culture, but never in all. Not even Greek or Western culture was the leader at any period of its whole history in *all* fields of culture.

For instance, the role of Greece as a creative center of the great religious system was very modest and in no way led the world. Therefore its religion did not diffuse widely. Likewise, Greece, as the builder of a great political empire, did not exist at all, up to the time of Alexander the Great Before the sixth century, B.C., Greece did not lead in the field of art generally, except, perhaps, in the field of music (Terpander), but even there its influence remained local. Likewise, Greece did not distinguish itself as a leader in the creation of the great law systems. The same is true of Western culture. If throughout the Middle Ages it distinguished itself by the development, organization, and realization of the great religious system — Christianity — during those centuries it was not the leader in science, technology, Sensate art, philosophy (as distinct from religion), nor in building the world political and economic empires (even Charlemagne's empire was parochial, on the scale of the previous Oriental empires), nor in many other fields.

However, once in a while it does happen. It assumes most frequently the form of *a shift of the center of the great military and political power from society to society, sometimes* (by no means always) *associated with a shift of the center of the creativeness in some other field of culture, mainly in art, technology and science, or economic power. When a given country grows as a military-political empire, such a growth is sometimes followed by its artistic, scientific, technological, or economic effervescence; when it begins to decline politically and militarily, such a decline is often followed by a decline of creativeness in the field of other cultural systems, particularly artistic, technological, scientific, and economic.*

Egypt in the periods of the climax of the Old, the Middle, and the New empires, was at the same time the center of the artistic, scientific, technological, and economic resplendence. In the periods of the decline of each of these empires, its resplendence in these fields declined.

Later on, after the thirteenth century, Europe became the center of creativeness in science, philosophy, technology, economics, Sensate art, but ceased to be the center of creativeness in the field of religion, or in several other fields. If this is true of the possibly most "encyclopedic cultures" — Greek and Western — still truer is it of the other civilizations and cultures. None of them, at any period of their existence, be it the period of "growth" or "decline," was the center of creativeness in all fields of culture. Therefore, it could not and did not charm other peoples by all parts of its total culture and these parts did not diffuse widely. For this reason, when each of them lost its leadership it was not a loss of leadership in all fields of culture but only in one or a few fields. Hence, the invalidity of Toynbee's theory, with its distinction of the periods of growth *in toto,* and decline *in toto* of a given civilization. No such distinction can possibly be made.

In a more accurate formulation, A. J. Toynbee's hypothesis can mean only two things: first, that a migration or diffusion of a given total culture occurs only in the form of migration and settlement in a new area of its members, such as conquerors or immigrants and colonizers. In that case, the total culture transplanted remains confined to the migrants and does not spread *in toto* over the peoples of different cultures among whom the migrants settle. Such transplantation occurs not only in the period of growth of a given civilization but also in its decline, in Toynbee's sense. Second, it is applied also to the case when a given society happens to be the leader in more than one field of culture (but never in all fields). In such case, we have the situation discussed in the text. Such a situation is very different from Toynbee's picture and does not mean at all that a civilization peacefully leads and spreads in its totality in the period of its growth, and decomposes and spreads fragmentarily in the period of its decline.

A. J. Toynbee's hypothesis appears, at the first glance, somewhat convincing, due to the widely spread opinion that the countries which are great military-political empires, are, at the same time, the leaders in all fields of culture. Such an illusion is certainly not warranted by the facts and Toynbee himself gives many evidences to the contrary. Some of the great political-military empires — Assyria, Sparta, Turkey, or the empires of Genghis Khan, Tamerlane, or even Rome or Carthage — have created mainly their own political and military systems, and almost no other great cultural system. See A. J. Toynbee, *A Study of History,* Vols. I, V, VI, *passim,* and especially Vol. V, pp. 194 ff.

Similarly the empires of Sargon or Hammurabi were at their time the centers of arts, economic creativeness, science, and technology. So also were the empires of Cyrus, Darius, Xerxes; the empire of Asoka and of Solomon; the Minoan empire at its climax; Athens and Greece generally of the fifth century B.C.; the Roman Empire of Caesar-Augustus and of the Antonines; Byzantium of Justinian; the empires of Kublai-Khan, Charlemagne, Queen Elizabeth and Anne, Louis XIV, Charles V of Spain, Catherine II of Russia, and so on. With the decline of some of these empires, their resplendence and economic creativeness often declined also.

This association in the shift of the political with either economic, artistic, or scientific creativeness is in no way, however, universal. There were many cases of a rise of the political and military empires not followed by a great effervescence in arts or sciences or any other field of culture. Sparta, at the period of its greatest military power, remained essentially sterile in almost all other fields of culture. So also did Carthage (except in the economic field). So also, in many periods, did Assyria and Babylon. The great ephemeral empires of Genghis Khan or Tamerlane hardly distinguished themselves by any great creations in most of the fields of culture. Even Rome during its most important growth as a political and military empire (from roughly the fifth to the first century, B.C.) remained "rustic" and rugged. The same can be said of the Turkish Empire at its climax and of several empires created in India.

On the other hand, many of the great cultural systems were created in small countries, or in the periods of a decline of the political and military empire of a given country. The great religious systems, like Confucianism, Taoism, Buddhism, Jainism, Christianity, Prophetic Judaism, Pythagoreanism, Orphism, and some others, were created and emerged either in a period of political anarchy and disintegration, or came out of the small countries, and even then when such countries were in the period of decline. Great philosophical systems, like Platonism, Aristotelianism, Neo-Platonism, Stoicism, Epicureanism, Neo-Pythagoreanism, were created in Greece, in the period of its decline as a political power and empire. Likewise, great philosophical systems of Europe — the philosophy of the great Scholastics, or of Descartes, or of Kant — were created not in the most powerful empires of Europe and not at the period of their political or military climax. Even the great artistic works of the Italian Renaissance (in painting, sculpture, architecture, music, literature) were not created in the most powerful empire of Europe at that time, nor in Italy at the most powerful period of its political and military history. Kant, Schiller, Goethe, Lessing, Herder, and other great creators of the philosophical, artistic, and scientific disciplines among the Germans, did not emerge in the period of the most powerful German Empire; if anything, they emerged when there was almost no great German Empire at all.[75]

Even scientific discoveries and technological inventions do not always blossom in the most powerful political and military empires, and at the climax of their power. It is enough to glance at the movement of these discoveries and inventions by countries, from period to period (see *Dynamics,* Volume Two, pages 148 ff., and Chapter Seven of this volume), and to confront the figures with the political and military history of each of the specified countries, in order to see that some effervescence of scientific and technological creativeness took place in the periods when a respective country was politically and militarily at a low ebb, or that it occurred in the small countries which in no way were the great political and military empires.

These considerations and facts validate the statement that the association discussed is in no way a universal uniformity. It is not even a typical rule: exceptions to it are possibly as numerous as the cases of the association. Finally, it has been shown in the preceding volumes of *Dynamics* that the spatial centers of Ideational, Idealistic, and Sensate supersystems of culture also shift from society to society, from area to area. Each of these forms of the supersystem existed now in India, now in China, now in Greece, now over the whole of Europe.

In a less fully developed form, the same phenomenon can be seen among so-called primitive peoples. The total culture of some of them, for instance, the Zuñi Indians, is nearer to the primitive Ideational; while the total culture of others, for instance, the Trobrianders or the Dobu, is nearer to the primitive Sensate. Each of such great supersystems, having existed for some time in a given population, eventually declines to give place to its rivals or to the mixed eclectic systems, and the center of such a declining system shifts to some other area or society.

[75] See additional facts in A. Coste's *Les principes d'une sociologie objective* (Paris, 1899), chaps. ii, xxii; *L'expérience des peuples* (Paris, 1900), chaps. i, ii. Coste, like A. J. Toynbee, exaggerates the negative association of the political greatness with "ideological" creativeness.

If, finally, we ask why the same society does not keep forever its creative leadership in one or a few of the fields of culture, or its given supersystem, and cedes it to other societies, the general answer is: first, possibly because of the impoverishment of its heredity endowment (through negative selection, and many adverse forms of social selection,[76] and other factors); second, because its urgent need for the keeping of the great system passes; third, because it ceases to be the meeting-place for cross-fertilization of various cultures; fourth, as will be developed later, in Chapters Fourteen to Sixteen, because of the general principle of limit that makes an eternal leadership of any empirical society improbable and hardly possible.

Such, in brief outline, are the important characteristics of the spatial shift of the creative centers of culture.

IX. Transformation of Cultural Objects and Values in the Process of Migration

In the preceding paragraphs the multiplication and circulation of the cultural objects and values has been outlined without any mention of whether they remain unchanged in the process of migration or undergo alterations and transformations. Now it is time to stress that in the process of circulation from one cultural center to another, they rarely enter the different culture without a tangible transformation. The essential uniformity here can be described in the following propositions:

A. When a cultural object or value — be it a simple element or a cultural complex or system — moves from one cultural center to another, (*a*) it may remain essentially unchanged if the culture of its immigration is similar to the culture from which it departed; (*b*) it changes if the cultures of immigration and departure are different; and the greater the contrasts between these, the greater the transformation of the migrating cultural value or system in the process of its migration and incorporation into the culture which it enters; (*c*) if the cultures of departure and of arrival are profoundly different, certain cultural systems of the first cannot penetrate and be rooted in the second culture at all. Even cultural congeries absolutely uncongenial to the culture of immigration find enormous difficulty in rooting themselves in a new culture.

The propositions thus claim that practically no cultural object or value can remain the same — in its meaning, use, and functions —

76 See my *Contemporary Sociological Theories*, Chapters Five, Six, and Seven.

when it passes to an essentially different cultural atmosphere or configuration; and that the change or transformation is proportional, so to speak, to the magnitude of difference between the culture from which it departs and the culture which it infiltrates.

B. *If we hold the difference between two cultures constant, then the magnitude or profundity of the transformation of the migratory cultural phenomenon depends upon its nature, especially in cultural systems and particularly upon the degree of its complexity, delicacy, and intricacy. Other conditions being equal, the more complex, refined, intricate the cultural system is and the greater ability, qualification, and training it requires for its adequate understanding and use, the more profoundly it transforms in the process of its passage from culture A to culture B, and in that of its infiltration and incorporation into B.*

The propositions are meant to be applicable to the migrating single cultural elements, to their congeries and systems; and even to the cultures *in toto*. It appears to be applicable to their horizontal as well as their vertical circulation. The propositions are important enough to deserve at least a brief elaboration. Begin with its first part.

It will be conceded that more or less complex cultural values and objects cannot be incorporated into an alien culture without their serious modification. A complex scientific theory, like that of relativity, or the theory of evolution, or the quantum theory, or high-grade idealism, materialism, determinism, indeterminism, the dialectic method, Kant's epistemology, Vico's philosophy of history, or an enormous number of other physical, chemical, biological, sociological, psychological and other theories and ideologies, cannot be "put into the heads" of savages, or of even our own laymen and nonspecialists, without a most fundamental simplification, transformation, and disfiguring of these values in the way of their "popularization" and "vulgarization." Such "simplifications" and "popularizations" are invariably a substantial disfiguring and alteration of these values and the change is the greater, the lower and more primitive the mental level of the group for which their popularization is intended. The Darwinian theory of evolution becomes in the mind of the masses a mere idea that "man comes from a monkey." Still more primitive is the popularization and "adaptation" of still more complex theories.[77]

[77] Even the comparatively simple results of our study of time-budgets published in Sorokin-Berger's *Time-Budgets of Human Behavior* (Harvard University Press, 1939) reached the readers of newspapers in the form: "Eight minutes for Love!" Many

If such is the situation in regard to different strata and their cultures in our own society, it is still more conspicuous in regard to the societies with profoundly different cultures. All this will be conceded and hardly questioned, so far as complex cultural values, and especially systems, are concerned. It will be conceded also in regard to complex and delicate "material values," like the handling, use, and running of a very delicate piece of machinery or system of machinery, which requires a highly trained specialist to operate it successfully.

But the proposition may be questioned in its validity in regard to simple cultural values, objects, and congeries, like, for instance, nail, rubbers, cheese or other form of food, clothing, lipsticks, rouge, simple utensils — pots, knives, axes, guns — or in regard to the simple "immaterial" values like the multiplication table, this or that poetry and prose, this or that simple belief, style, manner, custom, idea. It may be said that nail or rubbers remain nail or rubbers in the United States and among the native Melanesians, Tasmanians, or Fijians. Likewise, that belief in the immortality of the soul, or the multiplication table, or a simple proposition of physics or biology remains the same in both cultures. At first approach, it seems it does. It is enough, however, to study the situation a little more carefully to realize that it does not. Unless a given object or value in its generic form was already an element in the given culture, any new simple object or value that enters it from another and different culture undergoes a modification and transformation, to some extent and to some degree, either in its functions, use, or structure. Here is a fact which clarifies what is meant by that. In the pre-revolutionary days of Russia, the peasants of Vologda Province, of the Iarensky and Ustsy-

interpretations of the theories of my *Dynamics* happen to be unbelievably surprising to me! A similar change happens to any more or less complex theory or cultural system. This is the reason why all the attempts in the nature of "Science Service" have resulted in such a simplification and distortion of complex scientific theories that one often wonders whether such a service disseminates more pseudo science or science. In the light of the propositions discussed, it is clear that these shortcomings are not the fault of the popularizers, but that of the objective situation and immanent cultural conditions: one cannot explain adequately even the Copernican system to a child four years old, or to a man perfectly ignorant of the ABC of the mathematical and natural sciences. When my son at the age of 2½ years asked me: "Who brings the Moon?" I attempted, but failed, to explain to him the ABC of the motion of the moon around the earth. Finally, exasperated, I said: "Santa Claus!" This explanation was perfectly successful! In thousands of ways this "Santa Claus" or its equivalent, is all that remains from many systems of ideas, beliefs, art-values, norms, when they pass from the few specialists into the culture of the masses.

solsky counties — which were totally unindustrialized — had, as a kind of a luxury, a pair of rubbers. Rubbers remained, physically, of course, rubbers, as they were manufactured by the rubber factories in other parts of Russia. But, instead of their usual function, among these peasants the rubbers changed their function — and consequently their meaning, their value, and their cultural nature — fundamentally. First, they never were used when the weather was bad or wet, or the roads were dirty and muddy. Second, they were used only on holidays and other important occasions and festivities: weddings, village festivals, etc. Third, even then, if the weather and the ground were not perfect — dry and not muddy — they were carried in the hands but not worn on the feet. Usually they were used mainly on hot and dry summer holidays; and rarely, if ever, on cold, wet, and muddy days, when they function in an industrial society. Thus, physically, rubbers remained rubbers, but as a cultural object, they entirely changed in their meaning, functions, use, and value, when they migrated from the industrial regions to the purely agricultural region of peasants, hunters, and fishermen, with a culture different in many respects from that of the Western industrialized culture.

With a proper modification, the same can be said of practically any simple material object which comes as new from one culture to another. Though the generic idea and object of a nail (at least a "wooden" nail) is familiar and is a part of many "primitive" cultures; nevertheless, when iron or steel manufactured nails reach such cultures, in their cultural meaning, use, value, functions, nails experience a tangible transformation in their new "home." With still greater reason, the same can be said of many new objects of food, clothing,[78]

[78] Here the proverbial case of a savage chief who put on a top-hat, being otherwise perfectly naked, in meeting some European persons, gives an idea of the change. Again I remember the case when a salesman who spent the night in the house of my peasant aunt in the same region of Vologda Province left a piece of cheese in the house. It was a novelty. We saw how he ate it. When we tried it, it appeared impossible. We thought that perhaps it had to be baked, so we baked it; it became still less eatable. We gave it to the dog — and the peasant dogs were incessantly hungry — but the dog did not eat it. Finally, the piece was thrown out and we wondered how such an impossible thing could be eaten by such a fine gentleman as the salesman appeared to be. Here the new food was rejected and could not even enter and be incorporated into the culture of the peasants. In other cases, a new food may enter; but in its use and functioning it undergoes some change, like the above case of the rubbers. The use of wine and alcohol in the United States in the era of prohibition is another familiar case: instead of using them "normally" as, for instance, French or Scotch people do, they became something exotic, used wildly, associated with "Whoopee!"; "Fall down and go boom!"; with "night clubs" and gang-criminality!

and other forms of material cultural objects. If they are alien indeed to the culture into which they infiltrate they cannot help undergoing a tangible modification, especially in the case of complex instruments, machines, tools, utensils, etc. This concerns the horizontal as well as the vertical circulation. And the greater the contrast between the two cultures in question, the greater is the modification, even in regard to the same cultural object or value.[79] If such is the situation with the simple material objects, the proposition will hold still truer in regard to simple "immaterial" values, whether the value is a simple idea, belief, tune, custom, style, taste, or something else. The idea of the earth going around the sun and of the moon going around the earth is not the same in the mind of a scientist in the field; in that of a pupil of an elementary school; in that of an illiterate peasant; and in that of a savage. It has and will have several differential connotations and shadings in these minds — and cultures — in spite of the fact that it may be learned from the same textbook by all these persons (except the specialist, who has connotations and specifications that cannot be put into an elementary text). With a proper modification the same can be said of almost any other simple cultural value, if it is fundamentally new to a given culture. It may be a multiplication table (for the cultures which do not and cannot count much higher than a few scores and which count differently); or the idea of "nature," "God," "matter," "spirit," "mind," "right and wrong," "useful and harmful," "decent and indecent," "beautiful and ugly"; or the value of a tune, painting, manner, custom, or appreciation of a certain style, certain object, certain pattern. All these undergo a greater or less change when they pass from one stratum to another (vertically), and from one culture to another (horizontally).

[79] An excellent evidence of this is given by the daily reading of a newspaper. The paper, say the *New York Times,* is the same. But different readers read in it different parts. Some read mainly the sports section; others, book reviews; others, political news; others, the art section and so on. Chinese follow with especial care the news about China; Japanese about Japan; the French about France, etc. There are readers who look only at the pictures and cut them out; and so on and so forth. The paper physically is the same. But culturally it appears to be a multitude of different papers, as many and as different as there are different cultural groups, with as great contrasts in their cultures.

The same can be said about any book, picture, symphony, ethical norm, and so on. Aristotle's *Politics* is a very different thing for a freshman and for a competent professor of philosophy or sociology. Beethoven's *Missa Solemnis* is something quite different to a Chinese, Trobriander, European, and American; to a musician, and a farmer or businessman who is ignorant of great music; to an Atheist, Protestant, and Catholic. And so on, endlessly.

In a heterogeneous culture which they infiltrate they look seemingly the same as in their native culture, and yet they are different.

With still greater reason, the proposition can be emphasized in regard to the complex cultural systems. Christianity, Communism, Confucianism, Fascism, Darwinism, Parliamentarism or any other complicated system of ideology, religion, scientific theory, philosophical *Weltanschauung* — each of these is deeply different among the intellectuals and laymen of the same country, among the educated and uneducated, among the unskilled laborers and the professional scholars, among the "aristocracy" and the "proletariat." Likewise with the Christianity of the Roman Catholic clergy, of new Catholic converts among the Chinese, Negroes, Hindus, Japanese, Malayans, and many "primitive" peoples — the Catholic Christianity of all these different cultural groups has not much more in common, in its system of meanings, than the mere name Christianity. With the exception of this and a few other traits, the Christianity of the Chinese or Indian or African converts and that of the Roman Catholic clergy differs hardly less than Christianity and Buddhism or Mohammedanism, or some form of Totemic religion.[80] Under the same name we have in all these systems of ideologies and values something profoundly different, in widely diverse cultures. Passing from one cultural atmosphere to another — vertically or horizontally — each of these complicated cultural systems experiences the modification, transformation, or adaptation necessary to a given new cultural atmosphere. And the greater the contrast of the cultures, the greater is the modification. Passage not only from one culture to another quite different from it, but a passage from a variety of a given culture (for instance, the Anglo-Saxon) to another variety (for instance, French, Germanic, Italian)

[80] See, for instance, the most peculiar forms assumed by Christianity among the Zapotecan Mexicans in Mitla; E. C. Parsons, *Mitla,* quoted, pp. 204–210, *et passim;* or the Indian North American tribe, the Antlers; M. Mead, "The Changing Culture of an Indian Tribe," *Columbia University Contributions to Anthropology* (New York, 1932), Vol. XV; or among the Winnebago Indians; P. Radin, "The Influence of the Whites on Winnebago Culture," *Proceedings of the State Historical Society of Wisconsin* (1913), pp. 137–145; or among many other native groups studied in connection with the spread of such cults as the Prophet Dance, the Ghost Dance, and so on. See L. Spier, "The Prophet Dance," *General Series in Anthropology,* No. 1 (1935); A. H. Gayton, "The Ghost Dance of 1870," *University of California Publications in American Archeology and Ethnology* (1932), Vol. XXVIII, pp. 57–82; R. Maunier, *op. cit.,* p. 7. Practically, it is enough to take any more or less accurate description of the real beliefs and rituals of almost any native tribe supposedly converted to Christianity, in order to see clearly the transformation of Christianity as discussed. It is not the fault of the missionaries, but the objective sociological conditions that make the transformation inevitable.

changes a complex cultural value. The parliamentarism of England has never been the same as the parliamentarisms of the other countries which borrowed it from England. Italian Fascism is different from the German, just as the conception of an Emperor (borrowed by Western culture from the Roman Emperor; by them from the Hellenistic conception of Alexander the Great, who borrowed from the Oriental Persian, who borrowed from the Egyptian) has never been the same in all these cultures.[81] The Renaissance of Italy profoundly differs from that of most other, especially Germanic, countries. The "planned economy" of Soviet Russia remains different from that of the Rooseveltian, Mussolinian, Hitlerian, or other "planned economies." And so in regard to almost any complex cultural value, when it passes from one variety of a generic culture to another. The same can be said of the complex techno-economic systems of culture. Capitalism has never been the same in England, Russia, Japan, and Brazil; the machine-manufacturing system is not the same thing in the United States, Japan, China, Russia, and Poland. Physically the factories, the machines, may be identical; and yet the cultural value, meaning, appreciation, functions, of the system are notably different in these different countries.

The same can be said of almost any complicated cultural complex or system, material or immaterial. None of them can help being altered, modified, or disfigured, when it passes from one cultural milieu to a different one.[82]

[81] See L. Wenger, "Ancient Legal History," *Independence, Convergence, and Borrowing,* quoted, pp. 78–79.

[82] The same is applicable to systems of law. As is known, the Roman law has diffused enormously in different societies with different cultures congenial to the Roman Law in their law systems. "Roman law from the earliest times was not so isolated, nor so hostile to other laws of antiquity, as it seemed to Cicero and even to many modern historians." On the other hand, "we must not think that the same Roman Law existed through all centuries and in all countries. Even in antiquity changes were made in it [in different countries of diffusion]; and it was a different law in the Middle Ages, in modern times, in Italy, in Byzantium, in France and in Germany." L. Wenger, "Ancient Legal History," *Independence, Convergence, and Borrowing,* cited, pp. 63 ff.

"Domestication is a common phenomenon in all cultural borrowing. A folk song or a folk story introduced from a distant province is soon revised by nobody knows whom, and, while the main theme — the motif — is always retained, most of the details (names, scenery, fashion, dress, etc.) are retouched with 'local colour!' This modification happened with Buddhism in China. . . . Almost every phase or element of Buddhism has undergone some degree of modification during these twenty-odd centuries. Look at the faces of the deities in a Buddhist temple in China to-day and trace each to its earliest Indian originals, and you will realize how the process of domestication has worked." Hu Shih, "The Indianization of China: A Case Study in Cultural Borrowing." *Ibid.,*

The same is true of the vertical circulation, in so far as the culture of different strata of the same society is different — and usually it is. Taoism, Hinduism, Christianity, Confucianism of the intellectual stratum of either the Chinese, Hindu, or European society is one thing; in the mentality and culture of the respective lower classes it is another thing. Each of these religio-philosophical-ethical systems in its pure form is one of the sublimest and greatest systems ever created. In the mentality and culture of the lower classes of the respective societies, each of them is vulgarized to an enormous degree. What is Taoism or Hinduism of the masses of the lower classes but a collection of so-called "superstitious" rituals, magic beliefs, primitive ideas about God, soul, transmigration, and so on, which have little of the depth and sublimity of the system of Lao-Tse or Qwang-tsu, or of the Vedas, Upanishads and Brahmanas. The same is true of Christianity or Confucianism or any other religious and moral system. There is little in common between the Epicureanism of Epicurus and that of the mass of his followers, during his lifetime as well as after his death. The first was practically "Stoic" and a noble form of ethical eudemonism; the second assumes the most vulgar form of the flat hedonism of "wine, women and song," and *"Carpe diem."* The Darwinian theory of evolution in the mentality of the "enlightened" masses is but an atrocious idea that "man came from a monkey." The ideology of Marxian socialism in the mentality of the proletarian masses is but a call to "steal what has been stolen" and kill and eliminate the exploiters. "Positivism" (of A. Comte or others) means,[83] for the radical high-school or college student, a primitive mixture of

---

p. 232, *et passim.* See there the details of the modification of Buddhism in its diffusion in China.

See in the same volume the facts of the modification of Hellenism, Christianity, of French law, of Jewish folklore, in their diffusion among various cultures. R. Maunier, "La diffusion de droit français en Algérie"; L. Ginzberg, "Jewish Folklore: East and West"; C. H. Dodd, "Hellenism and Christianity."

The same transformation invariably occurs in the folk tales when a topic or hero taken from one culture assumes very different forms in the different culture of its penetration. See the concrete facts in S. Thompson, *Tales of the North American Indians* (Harvard University Press, 1929). See other facts in W. I. Thomas, *Primitive Behavior,* quoted, pp. 626 ff.

[83] This objective fact is the root of the tragedy of vulgarization and decisive disfiguring of any complex and great and sublime system of cultural values when it infiltrates and roots itself among the large masses. Such a success is invariably bought at the cost of its simplification and distortion. Often, after such a success, there remains little of the system as it was created by the author and a selected group of his disciples.

atheism and progressivism. Even such ideas as the concept of a gentleman mean one thing in the culture of England of the eighteenth century; another for a *nouveau riche,* who by hook or crook has made money on the stock market and considers himself a gentleman; and still another for a "proletarian" who is raised by revolution to a position of prominence. The Gothic style, Bach's music, or Dürer's painting mean, for the culture of the lower classes, if by chance these values enter it, something very different from what they represent to the mentality of the connoisseurs and properly trained and qualified persons and groups. Dante's *Divine Comedy* or Shakespeare's *Macbeth* are, again, something quite different in the mentality and culture of the lower and the upper classes. And so with almost any complex system or value.[84]

Vice versa, *when a cultural value migrates upwards, from the lower to the upper classes, it experiences a similar transformation.* In the compositions of Bach, Beethoven, and almost any great composer there are many folk-tunes and songs taken from the repertoire of the lower classes. For instance, in the series of the Razumovsky's quartets of Beethoven, there are many folk-tunes of the Russian people (not to mention those of the German people in other compositions of Beethoven). And yet, they are "Beethovenized" to such an extent that they become quite changed from the initial folk-tunes. In addition, they are set in a configuration quite unlike the original, and mean something very different from what they meant in Russia. When the Negro Spirituals and various folk-songs infiltrated the culture of the middle and upper classes of the United States, they experienced a similar transformation. Only perhaps the skeleton of the

[84] The inevitable vulgarization of education itself, when it becomes universally diffused in all classes, is a further corroboration of the uniformity discussed. In ancient Hellenic society it became most widely diffused in the third century A.D. See M. I. Rostovtzeff, *The Social and Economic History of the Roman Empire* (Oxford, 1926), p. 375. It was so simplified and vulgarized that, among its other effects, we find a complete lack of either great writers, thinkers, or artists in that and subsequent centuries, instead of a great increase of these and a blossoming of culture, as many think. Similarly, the universal diffusion of education in our society has led, among other results, to the emergence of the "yellow press," "yellow movies," "educated ignorance," or, in the totalitarian states, to the diffusion of the governmental "intellectual chewing gum" with all the tabloid pseudo culture and flat mentality of both. And the more "universal" our colleges and universities, our B.A.'s and Ph.D.'s become, the lower becomes the standard of the universities and Ph.D.'s, the greater the superficiality and "trained incapacity" of the majority of the graduates. This is the reason, perhaps, why the crop of real creativeness of cultural values, among all those millions who have successfully passed the present curriculum of schools and universities, has been so disproportionately small.

Negro originals is left in the "arranged" and "jazzed" imitations, while the meaning of the Spirituals and of the Negro songs (dance songs, labor songs, etc.) is now almost entirely changed. The labor song is now a jazz and is crooned in the Follies and night clubs, and various "whoopee" joints. Not infrequently the Spirituals function in the same places and settings. One can hardly imagine a more profound transformation than that!

Again, take the recurrent fashion of the upper classes to go "pastoral," "idyllic," "peasant." When such a fashion invaded the French court at the end of the seventeenth and the beginning of the eighteenth century, with Arcadian and other shepherds and shepherdesses, *paysan* and *paysanne,* and other supposedly pastoral and agricultural personages, heroes, scenes, *paysages,* they all bore factually no resemblance or relationship to the real peasants, the real values in their life and to their real life. Only very remote sugar-coated shells were left of this reality when it became a part of the culture of the French nobility. In a milder form, one can see the same nowadays in observing various "peasant style" objects sold in the fashionable department stores for well-to do customers: the patterns, the styles, the objects taken from the culture of the peasantry are greatly changed and are made to serve purposes and functions quite different from those which they serve in peasant life.

A similar transformation took place in the Renaissance with the Greek cultural values. The leaders of the Renaissance enthusiastically welcomed them and tried by all means to revive and restore them, thinking honestly they were reviving the genuine Greek cultural values (in painting, sculpture, architecture, literature, philosophy, religion, and so on). We know now they were mistaken; their "Greek" values were very different from what they were in Greece and yielded creations only remotely resembling the genuine Greek patterns, forms, and systems of ideas.[85] If the figure of the savage chief — naked but with a top-hat on his head — appears to us comical, we often do not notice that many aristocrats and society persons adorned with some object-value taken from the lower classes, are not less incongruous figures than the savage chief. As a further example, one can identify most of the "literary" personages from the lower classes, when they are depicted by the *literati* who never belonged to these classes. Almost invariably the figures are purely artificial, "sugar-coated," having little or no resemblance to the originals. The same is to be said

[85] As is well known, even such artists as Michelangelo grossly erred in this matter.

of a sophisticated imitation of the "primitive style" in various arts: painting, sculpture, music, architecture, literature, drama. All these "primitive" styles really have little if any relationship to the primitive originals.[86] And so it is with almost any object-value that passes from the lower to the upper classes, or the reverse way. And the greater the difference in the culture of the upper and the lower classes, the greater the transformation. If the difference is negligible, the change is negligible. This explains why the aristocracy and the lower classes cannot have an entirely common language in many spheres of their relationship; using the same terms, they mean — and cannot help meaning — different things; sometimes almost opposite. Justice for the masters and privileged classes is something very different from that for the "under dogs." Truth, beauty, right and wrong, and many other values mean different things to each of these strata.[87]

The above comments are sufficient to illustrate the meaning of the first proposition and its comparatively "universal" character. It operated in the past and continues to do so in the present; in the relationships of various cultures, peoples, societies, groups, horizontally, as well as in that of various strata, vertically. So much for the first proposition.

C. Now to the second proposition. The preceding one, assuming the identity of the cultural value, makes the degree of its transformation in the process of its migration proportional to the degree of difference of the cultures involved. The second proposition assumes this difference is identical or constant. It takes the same cultures A and B between which different values circulate. Assuming that, the proposition contends that the *degree of the change* of various cultural systems tends to be proportional to the degree of special qualification, training, and skill necessary to apprehend the circulating cultural system or value. The *more difficult it is, the more complex, the more special qualification and training and ability it requires to properly apprehend, understand, use, and operate with it, the greater has to be its change in order that it may pass from one culture to a different one — horizontally or vertically. Just on this account some of the values cannot be passed at all, outside of a narrow group of spe-*

[86] See the facts and analysis in W. Deonna, *L'archéologie,* quoted, Vol. II, pp. 453 ff.

[87] K. Mannheim gives a number of cases where the same concept (for instance, "freedom" *Volksgeist* or *Zeitgeist*) means very different things with different classes and political groups. See his *Ideology and Utopia* (New York, 1936), pp. 243 ff. Such transformation of the meaning of the same concept in different social groups or cultures is but a mere case of the general uniformity discussed.

cialists, to most of the other cultural groups of the same society or of other culture.

The greater part of the very complex and refined mathematical, physical, chemical, biological, philosophical, religious, and social-science theories and systems cannot be passed and probably never will enter adequately the culture mentality of most of the cultural groups outside of the selected specialists. The real Plato, Aristotle, Descartes, Newton's *Principia,* I. Kant's *ding für sich und an sich,* Hegel's dialectic principle, the quantum theory, the relativity theory, Thomism, Darwinism, almost all the epistemological and metaphysical systems, calculus — none of these have yet passed into the culture of the majority of the peoples and probably never will. What passes under these names is a vulgarized and distorted shadow of what these systems of meanings are in their real form. This means that the specific qualifications of many cultural values are such that they cannot even be incorporated in most of the cultural milieus different from that of the narrow circle of the specialists.

The other systems and congeries can pass, but in passing they are doomed to be changed, in order to be able to infiltrate the different cultural milieu. They need to be "adapted" and simplified in order to be digestible by the mentality of the bearers of a different culture; and the "adaptation" has to be the greater, the greater the specific complexities of the value. Arithmetic can be taught to a much larger group of people than algebra; algebra to more persons than calculus; and for the passing of arithmetic or algebra to laymen less "adaptation" is necessary than for the passing of calculus. How to grease a car can be passed more easily than how to grind the valves; this is easier to convey than how to make the car. The enjoyment of crooning can be taught more easily and to larger cultural milieus than the enjoyment of Beethoven or Bach. The teachers and popularizers who rashly attempt to make Plato, Kant, Hegel, Darwin, Einstein, Leibnitz, Marx, or any complex scientific, philosophic, moral, or aesthetic theory "popular" commit inevitably a sin of distortion; they circulate not these theories but their poor shadows.

Such is the essential process which takes place when a cultural value passes to a different cultural milieu and such are two of the important uniformities which are connected with it. In so far as these two propositions are valid, they have many important theoretical and practical consequences.

A few of these may be mentioned.

(1) In a *society steeply and rigidly stratified,* with the strata of the population bearing very different culture-mentalities, only a portion of the total culture of the upper and lower strata is common to both; only a portion can and does circulate up and down; and this portion is the smaller and its transformation the greater, the more profound the difference of the total culture of these strata.

(2) Other conditions being equal, the common portion and circulation of cultural values in such a society is less than in a society less steeply and rigidly stratified. Likewise, in the less stratified society, the circulating values need to undergo a less profound transformation in their passage from stratum to stratum than in the more stratified social system.

(3) If instead of the height and rigidity of stratification we take the *factor of mobility,* then, assuming the steepness and rigidity of stratification constant, and the common fund of culture to be possessed by both the upper and lower strata, the portion of the values circulating between the strata will be the greater and the amount of the transformation in their vertical passage needs to be less, the more mobile the society; that is, the more its members move along its vertical ladder. *Ceteris paribus,* in the less mobile caste society, the common fund of the culture of the upper and lowest castes, and the portion of the circulating cultural values, is less, and the degree of their transformation is greater, than in a more mobile, democratic society.[88]

If we take, for instance, Indian and American societies, in the United States of America we shall expect, and in fact do find, a greater common fund of the culture of the upper and lower classes, a greater portion of the circulating cultural values, and less degree of their transformation in the passage, than in India. In American and other mobile societies (where everyone can potentially become everything) this fact manifests itself in the *conspicuous phenomenon of standardization of cultural values,* from Lucky Strikes, fashions of dress, ice-cream, food, tools, cars, to *The Saturday Evening Post,* the best-sellers read by all strata, crooning, jazz, schools, colleges, epidemics of the same fads and hobbies, the same political and other creeds. An enormous portion of such cultural values is common to all strata; an enormous portion of other values intensively circulate up and down, often to the point of monotonous similarity. When, in a given fall, a new style of dress is introduced, it spreads like a fire over most

[88] See, for definition of mobility, its amount, its forms, etc., my *Social Mobility, passim.*

of the strata (with some lag), the main difference being only that the dress of the upper classes is more expensive than that of the lower classes. The same is true of any best-seller (lower strata getting it later, in a cheap edition); of car or radio, telephone or bathtub; political creed — be it Townsendism, Coughlinism, or something else. When the upper classes take up golf or another sport, the lower classes follow, with some lag. When a cross-word puzzle or jig-saw puzzle or other fad starts, it permeates all classes. When college education becomes a rule for the upper classes, with some lag it is adopted by the lower classes; and so on and so forth.

This does not mean that the total culture of the upper and lower classes is identical; nor does it mean that all cultural values can and do circulate successfully; nor that the circulating values do not experience any transformation in their passage from stratum to stratum. But it means that the standardization in the above sense is much greater in such a mobile society than it is in an immobile one, like the caste society of India, or medieval society, or Greek or Roman societies at the period when their strata were rigidly separated and the mobility between the masters and slaves, patricians and plebeians, was insignificant.[89]

(4) As a mere consequence of the above propositions, we shall expect — and, in fact, find — that as a rule the vertical *circulation of cultural values goes on gradually, from a given stratum to the next one above or below, but rarely directly from the lowest to the highest or vice versa.* As mentioned before, a given stratum "apes" its nearest better stratum but not the remotest. One of the reasons for this is that the nearest strata have a greater common fund in their total cultures and are more similar culturally than the widely separated strata. Therefore many cultural values can more easily pass between such similar strata, meet fewer obstacles to circulation, and need to be changed less in the passage, than in the case of the more heterogeneous cultures of the highest and the lowest strata. This is the reason why, as we have seen, the dress or any other value passes usually from the

[89] The same conclusion was reached when I studied the problem in connection with the mobility of individuals and groups. See my *Social Mobility,* particularly Chapter Twenty-one. Investigators of the history of dress and standard of living many times mention and stress the uniformity discussed. See G. Tarde, *op. cit.,* chaps. vi and vii. "The greater separation of social classes in the country [than in the English cities] was less favorable to the spread of upper-class manners and luxuries, which was so prevalent in London." E. Waterman, *op. cit.,* p. 95. See other works quoted on the history of dress.

aristocracy to the next lower class, from this to the middle classes, and from those to the lower classes, or vice versa. Only in exceptional cases are some of the values transferred at one move from the upper to the lower, without passing through the intermediary strata, or vice versa.[90]

(5) Finally, since any sociocultural system is selective (see above, Chapter Two), and since systems and congeries are profoundly different from one another, there is an enormous difference in the matter discussed as to whether the infiltrated culture in the specific field of infiltration represents a *system or congeries*, and whether the infiltrating cultural value is a system or congeries. The main cases here are as follows:

(*a*) The specific field of the infiltrated culture is congeries and the infiltrating cultural value is also congeries. In that case there is neither affinity nor disaffinity between the infiltrated culture and the infiltrating congeries. In these conditions, the success or nonsuccess of the infiltration and the modification or nonmodification of the infiltrating value is decided by purely fortuitous external factors, unpredictable and lacking any uniformity. If the combination of the external circumstances happens to be favorable, the congeries can migrate and settle from one stratum to another (vertically) and from one culture area to another horizontally. Such is the case, for instance, in the incidental passage of the Russian *samovar* into the Western country; or of a Chinese dress, or other congeries, or of some fad or pattern of culture. In these cases, such congeries may pass, but rarely will they have a widespread and successful rooting in the infiltrated culture. Coming fortuitously, they as fortuitously disappear.

(*b*) The specific field of the infiltrated culture is a system

[90] This is again a replica of what we find in the vertical shift of individuals. The uniformity there is formulated as follows: "Except in periods of great upheavals, like the World War or revolutions, the 'ups' and 'downs' in the vertical circulation of the individuals occur gradually and almost imperceptibly. The considerable vertical displacement of a family or an individual demands, as a rule, several years or, more often, one, two, or three generations." Respectively one rarely is transformed from a pauper to a millionaire; from a slave to a king; from a soldier to a commander-in-chief; from an aristocrat to a slave; but one's promotion or demotion proceeds gradually, step by step.

See, for further details, evidences and statistics, my *Social Mobility*, pp. 449 ff. Tarde rightly says that "the thing that is most imitated is the most superior one of those that are nearest. The influence of the model's example is efficacious inversely to its distance as well as directly to its superiority. Distance is understood here in its sociological meaning." *The Laws of Imitation*, p. 224.

and the infiltrating value is a congeries to it. Being congeries, it is again neither congenial nor antagonistic to the system. Therefore, the success of and the degree of transformation in the infiltrating value depends again mainly upon incidental external circumstances, and is similar to the above case in many respects. A phonograph presented to a primitive tribe in central Africa by a missionary or explorer may or may not have some success there; it may or may not change its functions (providing it is a congeries to the infiltrated culture). Everything depends upon the chain of fortuitous circumstances.

(*c*) The special field of the infiltrated culture is a system, and the infiltrating value is also a system. In that case, if the two systems are congenial and have a mutual affinity, the infiltrating system will have an easy and great success and will root itself in the new culture deeply and organically. If the two systems are antagonistic and mutually contradictory, the infiltrating system will meet an active resistance on the part of the other system, and unless it is backed by force or other supporting circumstances, it has little chance to penetrate the other culture. Only by overpowering the competitive system can it root itself in the new culture, and even then only after undergoing considerable transformation. The gospel of Communism in a culture of rugged individualistic proprietors; atheism in the culture of ardent Roman Catholics; the republican political system in the culture of monarchical aristocracy; a system of asceticism in the culture of super-Sensate epicureans; these and millions of other mutually antagonistic systems have little chance of spreading in the areas dominated by the other antagonistic system. If, due to several fortuitous circumstances, they have a little success, it is invariably followed by a profound transformation of such an infiltrating antagonistic system. Communism in such a case would change into the "communism" of Christ's gospel; republicanism into the system of an oligarchy of the court aristocracy; asceticism into a mild form of moderation and abstinence, dictated by the sensate interests of health and bodily comfort; and so on.

On the other hand, as we shall see in the next section, if the two systems are congenial, the infiltrating system will be supported and helped by the infiltrated system.

The above is enough to let us understand that even in the matter of the spatial displacement and circulation of cultural phenomena, the distinction between congeries and systems is urgently necessary. This will become still clearer if we put the same problem in the form of the next question:

X. Why Do Certain Cultural Systems and Values Multiply, Move, and Spread Successfully (Become "Best-Sellers") while the Others Do Not Spread at All or Spread Little?

We know well that some new songs, plays, novels, manufactured objects, creeds, theories, beliefs, paintings, etc., are successful, become "hits," multiply and spread rapidly, turn out to be "best-sellers," while some other books, plays, songs, and similar values either do not have any success or very little. The phenomenon is recurring in various societies as well as at all times. The question arises: Why such a difference? Are there some fairly general conditions which can explain at least in part this "ever-recurring mystery"?

The conditions involved are probably numerous and of diverse nature. Nevertheless, it seems possible to mention a few which appear to be fairly universal. Such are: A, *the nature of the system or value;* B, *the nature of the culture of penetration and diffusion;* C, *development of means of communication;* D, *presence of a force behind it.*

A. *The Nature of the Value.* Assuming other conditions to be constant, the spread of a value or pattern or system in social space — that is, the number of persons and groups who take it and incorporate it into their culture — depends upon the demand for the object, speaking in the terms of economics. The demand for various values and objects is not the same: some are needed or thought to be needed by almost everybody, while others are needed by few. The objects and values which are needed by everybody are, however, in most cases, of such a nature as to be involved in the satisfaction of purely biological needs (food, clothing, shelter, etc.) rather than purely social. Their substance, so to speak, expresses little the individuality of a given cultural value-object. This individuality — their sociocultural style, so to speak — lies not so much in their substance (for instance, food as meat or fish or bread or vegetable; sex as a physiological act of copulation) as in their sociocultural form: how it is prepared and served, with what manner and ceremonies eaten, by what social groups, under what conditions, when it is taboo, etc.; or in which social forms the sex-need is satisfied: by what form of marriage, or concubinage, or prostitution — what are the patterns of these conditions which govern their "proper and improper" use, and so on. So far as the sociocultural forms of these universal values are concerned — and only these forms are really the *sociocultural* (not biological) values — here the distinction of the values needed by everybody and by few does not become as clear as it appears on the first approach. Why in a given culture do most of the people have a polygamic or polyandric form of marriage, while in another only a monogamic? Why in a given society are some forms of food perfectly good from the biological standpoint taboo, while in another the taboo does not concern this food but concerns some other foods? Why are there long fastings in a given group, while in another they are absent? Why, in a culture A, is veiling the face of women universally practiced (has a universal demand), while in another culture it does not have any and is not practiced at all? Why in the same culture or stratum, for instance, in the upper class of the Western culture, are top-hats, formal evening dress, a certain kind of music or poetry commonly spread (are in demand), while in other cultures or in the lower classes most of these value-patterns are neither spread nor in demand?

When these and similar facts are considered, the law of demand becomes helpless, as a mere tautology: those things are spread which are in demand; in demand are those things which are spread, or which are demanded.[91] Therefore we have to change the line of attack on the problem in order to elucidate at least a few points in it.[92] Since the actual spread of a cultural value or object depends upon many conditions — the type of culture, and others — let us first of all assume

[91] Shall I add that the aspect of the supply in the law of demand and supply does not help? Theoretically, the supply of top-hats or evening dress for the lower classes is as great or small as for the upper classes. In fasting period, for instance in Lent, meat or other kind of tabooed food is as abundant or scarce as in the periods when they are not tabooed. Women's veils can be supplied in the nonMohammedan societies as easily as in the Mohammedan. The sex-proportion in many monogamic societies does not differ from that of many polygamic or polyandric societies. Virgins for the role of priestess-prostitutes can be as easily obtained in many a society without such an institution as in the cultures where it does exist. And so on. The law of demand and supply helps little in understanding why, in a culture A, the demand for value C is enormous, while in a culture B it is nil; the same is true of the "supply" part of this problem.

[92] G. Tarde attempted to find some uniformities in the diffusion of various values depending, so to speak, upon the bio-social nature of these values. For instance, he claims that certain drinks diffuse faster and more successfully than certain forms of food; debauchery faster than drinks; some gestures more than certain peculiarities of gait; accent diffuses less successfully than certain patterns of food or dress. "Every city retains a characteristic accent long after its food and dress have become like those of other cities." "All passions and needs for luxury are more contagious than simple appetites and primitive needs." And so on. All these generalizations, being vague in their formulation, are very doubtful. See G. Tarde, *The Laws of Imitation,* pp. 194 ff. Better, but also uncertain and somewhat vague, are the factors of utility, and prestige stressed by R. Linton and others. See R. Linton (ed.) *Acculturation in Seven American Indian Tribes* (New York, 1940), pp. 474 ff., 484 ff.

that *the culture is the same.* Second, since the nature of various values seemingly exerts its influence also upon the success of the spread of the value, let us take, for a starting point of analysis, *the values of the same kind* — that is, values belonging to the same class, but differing from one another by several secondary details. Third, to eliminate the factor of *economic accessibility,* let us assume the various forms of the same kind of value to have about the same economic cost.

Having agreed upon that, let us ask: *Do various forms of the same class of value, of the same price, in the same total culture,* multiply and spread with different success? There is no doubt that such a difference exists. Out of the novels costing, say $2.50, published every month, a few become best-sellers, are spread, bought, and read by millions, while the others do not have any "success." The same is true of newspapers; of books, say, texts in the same field; of the treatises about the same problem; of the musical compositions and songs of the same class: symphony or opera or crooning or what not; of paintings and sculptures; of a brand of cigarettes, of coffee, toothpaste, shaving cream; of the theatrical play; of a brand of suit or tie or almost any other cultural object-value. In some classes of these values, the contrast in the "success" is enormous; in others the amplitude of the contrast is more limited; but this difference in spread or success is found in almost all classes of value-objects. The question now arises: What are the reasons for such a difference? Can it be accounted for, at least to some extent, through indication of a few of its most important "factors"?

So far as we assumed the same culture, the same class of values, and the same economic cost, the "factors" seem to exist in the secondary differences of the values of the same class. They are probably numerous, and we hardly know most of them. But one or two of them can be mentioned.

First, a fairly general proposition can be formulated as follows: *The more "refined" and complex is the nature of the value, the more special qualification and training is needed for its use and enjoyment, the less is its spread within a limited time in comparison with a value of the same class and cost but much less refined, simpler, and demanding fewer qualifications and much less training for its use and enjoyment.*

At the basis of this proposition lies the unquestionable fact that values of the same kind are not all of the same degree of refinement and complexity, but make a kind of pyramid, beginning with the simplest and ending with the most complex. The simplest stratum of values does not require any particular training or gift or ability to be used and enjoyed, while the values of the highest level do require it — and require it more, the more difficult and refined the values are. In mathematics we have a pyramid: arithmetic, algebra and geometry, elementary calculus and analytic geometry, and still more complex levels of mathematics. So also in any scientific discipline. There are the strata of elementary biology, physics, sociology, philosophy, or any other science; and a series of levels of the more and more advanced biology, physics, sociology, philosophy or other science. While the simplest and most elementary level is accessible to a high-school boy, a layman or college freshman, the more advanced levels can be used and enjoyed only by those who have the knowledge of the preceding levels. Not knowing arithmetic, one cannot study algebra or calculus. Not knowing anything in philosophy, economics, or sociology, one cannot use and enjoy the complex problems of Platonic or Kantian philosophy or the difficult problems of advanced economics and sociology. So also in the field of many another cultural value, be it music or painting, literature or law, technology or theology. Hence, the proposition.

Other conditions being equal, as we pass through the pyramid of the levels of the same value and price from the simplest to the most complex and difficult, the smaller becomes the number of persons who can be taught, and who can use and enjoy them. The highest levels of some values cannot even be taught to, or used and enjoyed by most of the people, and vice versa. In brief, the *potential number of users of a given value of the same kind is in reverse proportion to the refinement, complexity, and difficulty of the level of the given value.* Arithmetic in the same society has been and will be spread much more than calculus or still more refined branches of mathematics. Elementary knowledge of physics, biology, or other scientific, philosophic, or religious systems, has been and will be spread more than advanced, real, non-elementary knowledge. In spite of all the popularizations, Palestrina, Bach, and Beethoven have been and will continue to be much less well known than this or that popular song, be it a Hollywood "hit," crooning, or "Sweet Adeline." A cruder form of any religion has always been more popular than a more refined form of the same religion. An intricate form of dance, which requires special training and special skill, say most of the "refined ballet dances," can hardly ever spread as successfully as the simpler forms which can be danced by everybody. Simpler forms of a technical operation within a given field of technical activity, be it agriculture, or applied technology, spreads more than an intricate form of it which demands special training and special qualifications. From this standpoint most of us can paint a little; fewer can design or make pictures; still fewer can do it well; and still fewer can be great artists.

So with almost any cultural value-objects of the same class and price in most of the "compartments of culture." *The highest levels of the values of each class are the real luxuries inaccessible to the majority of persons, not for the economic reasons of high cost, but for the above reason of their complexity, refinement, and special qualifications necessary for their use and enjoyment. In this sense "luxury" can have a much broader and less economic meaning. It denotes a value for enjoyment of which a special ability, special training, special effort and qualification are necessary.* Economically to attend a symphony concert of the great masters of music costs sometimes even less than to attend a "show." And yet, the attendance at such a concert falls short in comparison with that at a show. At the best, only a few thousands, and those not every day, attend such concerts, even in a great metropolitan center, and the concert halls of even famous orchestras are rarely filled to capacity. Hundreds of thousands attend movies and shows daily. A preference for Bach's music is a cultural luxury accessible to a much more limited number of persons than the value of enjoyment of movies and shows. Only a very limited number of persons can understand, and enjoy reading, say, Plato's *Dialogues* or Dante's *Divine Comedy* or Kant's *Kritik der reinen Vernunft*. These are cultural "luxuries," inaccessible culturally but not economically to the large masses: these volumes often cost less than the sum of money spent by the masses for their magazines, novels, popular best-sellers and so on. Kant's works (within a limited period of time) have never been sold by the hundreds of thousands. Will Durant's *Story of Philosophy* has sold over a million copies. The works of the great historians, like Mommsen, or Gibbon, or F. de Coulanges, have never been best-sellers. H. G. Wells' *Outline of History* has sold over a million copies. The totality of the texts in arithmetic are sold in much larger quantities than the texts in calculus. So also with elementary texts compared with the advanced ones in any science. None of the works of the great composers have been sold in the enormous quantities to which some popular "hits" of Hollywood composers have attained. And so on and so forth in practically any kind of cultural value.[93]

The uniformity discussed is fairly general. However, it is not to be overdrawn beyond its legitimate sphere. In other words, it needs to be corrected by the introduction of special reservations, of which the following are the most important:

(1) *Qualifications.* The first limitation is connected with the *span of time* during which the spread of the cultural value is considered. The point is that some of the cultural values become "best-sellers" quickly and spread successfully in a short time, after which their spread is stopped; while other values spread slowly and much less widely within the same period of time, but their spread continues during a much longer or an indefinitely long period. The result is that the second kind of values often spread, when all the time of their "selling" is considered, in a much larger quantity than the first. Many a "best-seller" in literature, art, texts in various sciences, and musical compositions have "great success" and are sold or spread most successfully, but after a few months or years they are forgotten; their spread is ended and their very existence is finished. On the other hand, the works of Plato, Aristotle, Kant or other great thinkers; or of Mozart, Bach, Beethoven and other great composers; or of Shakespeare, Dante, Goethe, or other great writers, never have been sold in great quantities within a short time; but they have been translated and re-translated, issued and reissued, again and again, during decades, centuries, and even millenniums. The net result is that the total number of copies of these works, or the total number of persons who are their users and hearers, exceeds by far the number of copies or readers of the short-lived "successes." In all compartments of cultural creations there are such types of values.

Generally, various "successful" values have different curves of their life-career and life-duration. To one class belong the butterfly values, with an enormous and sudden success: they appear "instantane-

[93] This proposition means that, perhaps with very rare exceptions, a work which becomes a best-seller is a value of the lowest level of the values of that kind. Otherwise, it could hardly become a best-seller that can be used and enjoyed by "everybody." A few exceptions, especially in the field of art, music, and fiction, possibly exist, when the simplicity and appeal of the work is the simplicity of a genius. But that such exceptions are rare is demonstrated by the short life of the enormous majority of best-sellers. They arrive and spread and after a few months are "gone with the wind," for ever. In this sense, the fact that a work is a best-seller is a testimony of its primitive and elementary character. For this reason, I rarely trouble myself with reading a best-seller: its being such is a sufficient evidence of its commonplace nature.

ously," spread over a multitude of users, shine and glow for a short time and then, like a butterfly, fade as quickly as they flared up.[94] At the opposite pole of the successful values are those which spread slowly, sometimes for a long time appearing stationary; but, as time goes on, their spread continues, sometimes increasingly. As a result, their life-duration and life-career slowly rises and continues for a long time, with secondary and temporary fluctuations in success. Between these extreme types, there are a number of varieties of the "life-duration and life-career" of a value; some slowly spread for some time and then quickly decline; others spread rapidly but slowly decline; still others fluctuate, now coming into vogue, now declining, to become, after some time, successful again, after which a phase of decline again sets in, and so on.[95] The greatest values in the main fields of culture are practically immortal and live an indefinitely long time.

Such, in brief, is the first limitation of the discussed proposition. In fact, it is not an exception to the uniformity but a special detail of it that does not contradict but rather corroborates the rule.

[94] An enormous majority of the literary, scientific, artistic, philosophical, religious and other "successes" of our time seems to belong to this kind of values. They have mostly an instantaneous success and spread, but within a relatively short period of time, they are gone and forgotten. Most of the best-sellers in fiction, most of the successful texts in various scientific, philosophical and other disciplines; most of the "hits" in popular music, movie, theater and so on live hardly more than five or ten years. Then they are forgotten and are replaced by other similar, best-sellers in the field. Few of these live as long as a quarter of a century, and still fewer for half a century. Such is their Nemesis. One wonders whether any of such "successes" of the last three decades will be remembered within a century. This rapid turnover is one of the characteristics of our Sensate culture.

[95] Examples of various careers of cultural values are given, for instance, by the careers of composers whose works were performed from 1875 to 1936 by the eight main orchestras in the United States. The survey shows, first, that there are six composers — Beethoven, Brahms, Mozart, Bach, Tschaikovsky and Wagner — who occupy the main place, that is, are performed most frequently in their main works, while all the other composers occupy more modest places. Second, that the first place still belongs to Beethoven, though he slipped from some 25 per cent of all the performed works to some 10 per cent in 1936. In 1910, Wagner was the second, but at the present time he is down and the second place is taken by Brahms, with 8 per cent of the entire repertoire of these orchestras. Mozart's share shrank from 25 per cent to 6 per cent. Considerably neglected during the earlier decades, Bach's music is now rising in demand for the last decade. Wagner was rising up to 1910 and is slowly losing his share in the repertoire of these orchestras (though not in the Opera). Tschaikovsky was rising up to 1910 and declining after that period. Other composers, previously played much more, have been declining. Most of the modern composers occupy very modest places: all the modern composers of England, Italy, and Scandinavian countries taken together are played less than one Beethoven. Other composers, like Dvořák and D'Indy, had two short rises (due to incidental conditions) but all in all, are almost forgotten. Liszt, Schumann, Schubert, Mendelssohn and many others have also been declining, while Gluck, Handel, Haydn

(2) The second qualification in the character of an exception to the uniformity is, as mentioned, the exceedingly rare case when *the simplicity coincides with the perfection of a genius in a given cultural value.* Such a value appeals to the "low-brow" as well as the "high-brow," to a simple man in the street as well as to the most prominent specialists in the field. Such exceptions are found once in a while and seemingly mainly in the field of art and ethical values. A few masterpieces of poetry and literature, like some portions of the *Bible, Mahabharata, Iliad* and *Odyssey, Eddas,* and other great epics; the poems and musical compositions enjoyed by the upper as well as the lower classes; by the nation of the creator as well as by different cultural groups outside it; likewise, some paintings and sculpture are examples of such exceptions in art.

The sublime ethical norms like those given in the Sermon on the Mount, comprehensible and appealing to the simple-minded as well as to the intellectuals, are the examples of such exceptions in the field of ethics. Similar exceptions are possibly found in the field of religion; if not in their dogmatic theology, then in their normal teaching and ritual; and in a few other fields of culture. However, these exceptions are very rare and in no way annul the prevalent rule of the uniformity discussed.

So much for this factor of success or unsuccess in the spread and diffusion of a cultural value.

B. *The Nature of the Culture of Penetration.* The second fundamental factor of such a success or failure is *the nature of the culture in which a value has to diffuse.* Other conditions being equal, *the more congenial to a given value the culture of its penetration and diffusion is, the greater the diffusion, the more chances it has for becoming a best-seller. Vice versa, the less congenial the culture of penetration is to the value, the less are its chances for a successful spread.* We assume here that the value is the same, but the cultures in which it has to make a career are different. The proposition is almost self-evident.

---

have been keeping somewhat modest but stable positions, with some inklings of a slight rise. Finally, a number of composers like Raff, Lindpaintner, Rubinstein and others have practically disappeared from the repertoire in the later period. See J. H. Mueller and K. Hevner, "A Survey of Trends in Musical Taste," *New York Times,* February 27, 1939. These curves of the life-career of cultural values are similar in many respects to those in the achievements of individuals within their life span, of their popularity and fame. See C. Bühler, *Der Menschliche Lebenslauf als psychologisches Problem* (Leipzig, 1933) *passim* and chap. v.

One can hardly expect a successful spread of the gospel of equality in a caste society, and of the gospel of caste inequality in a genuinely democratic society; of the gospel of Communism among the big bankers of a capitalist régime, and of the bankers' gospel among the Communists; of birth-control ideology among Catholics, and of Catholicism among atheists; of pro-British war propaganda among Germans or German-Americans, and of pro-German war propaganda among British or British-Americans.[96] Most of the Sensate ideologies cannot be successful in an Ideational culture, nor the Ideational values in a Sensate culture. Dante's *Divine Comedy,* if published for the first time now, would probably pass little noticed; on the other hand, Maupassant's or O'Neill's or Anatole France's creations would hardly be given a Nobel prize or become best-sellers in a medieval society.

A salesman of car-heaters or oil-burners would have little success in a society which does not have cars, or all the prerequisites necessary for using oil-burners; on the other hand, a salesman of saddles would go bankrupt in a culture which does not have horses. The same is true of

[96] This explains why, for instance, British war propaganda in the United States has been more successful than the German, in the war of 1914–1918 and in the war of 1939. The reason is not a better organization of British propaganda (if anything, it was more poorly organized than German) but the greater congeniality of the British than of the German culture to the American. See the facts and analysis in W. Millis, *Road to War* (New York, 1935); H. C. Peterson, *Propaganda for War* (New York, 1919); H. E. Barnes, "When Last We Were Neutral," *American Mercury,* November, 1939; D. Squires, *British Propaganda at Home and in the United States from 1914–1917* (Cambridge, 1935); H. D. Laswell, *Propaganda Technique in the World War* (London-New York, 1927).

The above also means that the great influence ascribed during recent years to propaganda as such, is enormously exaggerated. If the culture of penetration is inimical or uncongenial to the propaganda value, it will remain ineffective or little effective even if all the radios or papers dissipate it every twenty-four hours. If the culture of penetration is congenial, then even poorly organized propaganda will exert some effect.

Recent experimental studies well confirm these propositions. Typical are the findings of G. W. Hartmann and W. Watson in their experimental study.

One group of 10 believers in a personal deity and one group of 10 atheists were asked to read and evaluate a series of arguments for and against the existence of a personal deity. Both groups were able to recognize the most telling points of their opponents and they remembered these points better than the arguments which they considered weak. The arguments which supported an individual's point of view, however, were better retained than those which were opposed to it.

An increased acquaintanceship with an opponent's philosophy, these investigators found, had no effect upon the subject's religious outlook.

The atheists remained atheistic and the theists retained their belief in the existence of God. The two groups were no nearer together after their new experience than they were at the start. (*Science Service* in *Boston Evening Transcript,* Nov. 7, 1939.)

the sales of Palm Beach suits among the Arctic Eskimos, or heavy fur coats among the dwellers in the tropics. And so on, in regard to any kind of cultural values.

Though the proposition is almost self-evident, it needs a further analysis for elucidation of the terms congeniality and uncongeniality, used in the statement: *Which cultural values are congenial or uncongenial to one another?* The answer is given by the above analysis of the sociocultural system and congeries. Here again its importance comes to the surface. The cultural values that are consistent meaningfully (and expressively) or supplementary to one another (the case of co-ordinated systems), or that are connected by causal ties, or by both, are congenial to one another. The values that are either contradictory meaningfully or unrelated causally are either uncongenial or, at the best, indifferent to one another. In the case of contradiction, they become mutually antagonistic; in the case of a lack of such a contradiction (and also consistency) or of a causal connection, they become indifferent congeries to one another. Such is the answer to the question.

In terms of A. Ferguson, "They borrow often that which they are disposed to invent." This means that when a given system needs a new cultural value its borrowing serves often as a substitute for invention.[97] In the case of congeniality, the penetrating value easily spreads and roots itself in its new home either as its consistent supplement, or enters, in G. Tarde's terminology, into a lucky marriage with the values of the culture of penetration and gives a new invention or new synthesis or new substitution for the old value.[98]

In the case of a contradiction or non-congeniality, there becomes inevitable a struggle for existence between the penetrating value and the respective competitor value of the culture of penetration. In this struggle, the inroad of the penetrating value may be stopped entirely at the very beginning, if the competitive values of the penetrated culture happen to be stronger than the penetrating value. If they happen

[97] *Cf.* R. Maunier, "Invention et diffusion," quoted, p. 7.

[98] Practically all investigators of so-called "acculturation" of the primitive groups by European or other cultures stress this uniformity. Whether the new value is religious, ethical, organizational, economic, or what not, such a value diffuses successfully among the native cultures just for the reason of its similarity or congeniality with the respective values of the native culture. Often it is merely a new dress for the old value of a given culture. See for this the summary of many works given in M. J. Herskovits, *Acculturation,* quoted, pp. 36–37, 38, 54, 65, 80–85.

On the other hand the investigators show that uncongenial values of the Western culture spread poorly, unless they are coercively imposed. *Ibid.,* p. 39. See a good summary of the relevant facts in W. I. Thomas, *Primitive Behavior,* quoted, pp. 726 ff.

to be weaker, the spread of the new value can take place only after its victory over and elimination of its competitor. Even in this case, such a struggle inhibits and slows up enormously the success of the spread of the penetrating value. Only after crushing its competitor can it diffuse unhindered.[99]

For the time being these comments are sufficient to make the proposition clear and its uniformity of a fairly general nature. It explains the success or failure in the spread of a great many cultural values, whether in their vertical or horizontal movement.

C. *Amount of Lines of Communication.* The third important factor is how many, of what kind, how long and swift and accessible are the lines of communication the spreading value has at its disposal. Other conditions being equal, the same value has the greater chance to become "a best-seller" the greater — quantitatively and qualitatively — the number of lines of communication it has. For this reason only, the values originating in the big metropolitan centers diffuse more widely and faster than the values which originate in the small towns or villages, and diffuse mainly along the lines of communication.[100] The same is true of the values of the upper and richer classes in comparison with those of the lower and poorer classes; of the values of less civilized compared with more civilized countries. This factor lies at the basis of the contemporary system of *advertising and propaganda.* Their function and aim consist in bringing the value — no matter of what

[99] See many interesting details in G. Tarde's *Laws of Imitation,* quoted, chap. v. In this work and also in his *La logique sociale* (Paris, 1895), *L'opposition universelle* (Paris, 1897), and *Social Laws* (Paris, 1898; English Translation, 1899), Tarde, with great insight and brilliancy, outlined many aspects of the problem discussed. See further an excellent analysis of the problem in Hu Shih, "The Indianization of China; A Case Study in Cultural Borrowing," *Independence, Convergence and Borrowing* (Harvard University Press, 1937), pp. 219–227; W. I. Thomas, *op. cit.,* pp. 726 ff.

[100] Concrete examples of this are given in H. Earl Pemberton's "Culture-Diffusion Gradients," *American Journal of Sociology,* September, 1936. His study of the diffusion of radio-ownership in the United States shows that the percentage of families with radios in the counties of a metropolitan region tends to follow regular downward gradients from the urban center to the limits of the region. "The urban centers within any given major area are the points at which radio ownership is highest; the hinterlands of each region of metropolitan influence tend to be the areas in which the radio ownership is lowest; in the counties that lie between the center and the limit of the metropolitan region the percentages of the radio ownership tend to be in direct downward gradation from the urban centers. . . . Such diffusion gradients occur because the residents of each unit of a region of metropolitan influence have culture contacts with the urban center of diffusion in inverse ratio to the time-and-convenience distance from the city." *Ibid.,* p. 226. See also quoted articles of R. V. Bowers concerning the direction and spread of such value as "the hobby amateur radio."

kind — to the attention of the possible maximum of its users; in other words, in establishment of a line of communication between the value and a multitude of its consumers. We should not exaggerate their effects; as mentioned before, the success of any value depends upon many other conditions. But the factor discussed has its own effectiveness, especially if the nature of the value and the culture penetrated are not inimical to one another. Of two similar values in the same culture, the value broadcast by papers and radio, by mail and posters, and by other means of communication, has uniformly greater success than the value deprived of these means of communication. Not infrequently, a poorer value proves itself more successful than a similar but better value. This goes equally for commercial commodities, machines, novels, poetry, scientific ideas, philosophical systems, religious creeds, art-creations, and other cultural phenomena.

D. *Support by Force and Other Means.* The important role of force in the successful spread of a value has already been discussed. If to force we add such means as money (for advertising and obtaining the maximum lines of communication) for prizes and rewards, etc., use of prestige and authority of prominent men, organization of a legion of propagators of the new value, and hundreds of other technical means aimed at the support of the value and of its diffusion; then all that has been said about the role of force can be said, with a respective modification, about all these various means of backing and helping the dissipation of the value. They all have some effectiveness.

XI. Curves of the Spread of the Value

A widely accepted belief in the existence of a so-called "normal curve" of growth, of distribution, and of many other "normal curves" has led to a claim that in the matter of diffusion of the sociocultural values there also exists a "normal curve," valid and applicable for an indefinitely great number of diffusions of various cultural values. The example of such a claim is given by H. Earl Pemberton, in his study, "The Curve of Culture Diffusion Rate."[101] On the basis of his study of the rate of diffusion of the use of postage stamps by independent countries of Europe and America, of the rate of state adoption of constitutional or statutory limits upon the taxation rates of municipalities, and of the rate of adoption of compulsory school laws by the forty-eight states of the United States, he concludes that:

[101] *American Sociological Review,* August, 1936.

Within any given culture area the diffusion of a culture trait tends to occur at a rate which may be described by the cumulative curve of a normal frequency of distribution.[102]

It is to be noted that the belief in any kind of "normal curves" for different phenomena in different conditions is generally little founded, and represents, to a great extent, a statistical mythology. Still less can any kind of normal curve of diffusion rate for different cultural values, spreading in different conditions, be expected. The preceding analysis shows that in order for such a phenomenon to take place, among other conditions, the value must be the same, the culture penetrated, the lines of communication, and the backing by force and other means must be identical or essentially similar. Otherwise, no curve applicable to different cultural values diffusing in different conditions can exist, and none does exist. Instead, there exist a wide variety of different curves, beginning with zero-curve for the values that do not diffuse at all; passing through curves rapidly rising and rapidly falling; slowly rising and rapidly falling; slowly rising and remaining stationary for a long time; rapidly rising and slowly falling; slowing rising at the beginning, faster later on, and then fluctuating in most different fashions, for indefinitely long periods, and so on. The curves of spread of our "best-sellers," of Plato's works, of the Bible, and of all the "poorest sellers" are as different as the different curves may be. No "normal" or even "typical" curve for the spread of different cultural values or of even the same value in different cultural conditions is possible. Only by simplifying the situation — the units of spread, the time-units, and so on — can one get for some cases some S-curve or other; but even then the S-curve will be a different shape of S, so different that there are in fact several different S-curves only remotely resembling the normal S. Such a conclusion follows from the above analysis of the factors of diffusion. It is confirmed by our daily observation of the different rate, velocity, and success of diffusion of the best-sellers and the worst-sellers; of long-living and short-living processes of diffusion. It is also confirmed by a systematic study of the curves of diffusion of various cultural and biological phenomena.

If we take, first, the curves of growth and decline of such comparatively identical or similar bio-social phenomena as epidemics, even these curves show a wide variation from one another. The only similarity is that they somehow grow, and somehow decline; but the

[102] *Ibid.*, p. 547. See also F. S. Chapin, *Culture Change* (New York, 1928), where Chapin suggests that culture growth of the diffusion type tends to follow an S curve.

rate of growth, the rate of decline, the rate of intermediary fluctuations, all differ from epidemic to epidemic, from country to country. No "normal" curve exists there. And most frequency curves, namely monomodal frequency distribution curves, are fit only for some epidemics, and even there they vary from one another.[103] If now we compare these curves with that, say, of the diffusion of the Grange movement, measured either by the number of granges or by the membership, the difference appears still greater, and there is hardly any similarity except that they are some kind of curves.[104] Even the Grange curves for various regions notably differ from one another. If these curves are further compared, for instance, with those of the spread of the great empires (measured roughly by the territorial area over which they extended in each decade) such as the Maurya Empire in India, the diffusion of the Spanish conquest on the Western Hemisphere, the conquest of Genghis Khan, of Alexander the Great, of Tamerlane; these very rough curves differ from the preceding ones and from one another. Add to this the curves of the spread of the Reformation or Communism,[105] or the curve of diffusion of the institutions of higher learning.[106] When all these curves are compared they have only one common similarity, namely, they all are some kind of curve. Other than that, there is hardly any similarity, and there

[103] I am not giving here the data collected and analyzed for that purpose by C. Arnold Anderson during his graduate study at Harvard. The data can be found in C. Creighton, *A History of Epidemics in Britain*, 2 vols. (London, 1891–94). Compare, for instance, the curves of diffusion of death from the plagues of 1563, 1636; London plague of 1625; smallpox death in Norwich, 1819; London smallpox epidemics of the seventeenth, eighteenth and nineteenth centuries. All these curves of diffusion or growth and decline of these epidemics notably differ from one another. The same is still truer if these curves are compared with, say, the diffusion of influenza in various cities of the United States in 1918 (see W. H. Davis, "The Influenza Epidemic as Shown in the Weekly Health Index," *American Journal of Public Health* No. 9, 1919, pp. 50–61), or with the curves of diffusion of plague and cholera in various districts of India (See M. Greenwood, Jr., "On Some Factors Which Influence the Prevalence of Plague," *Journal of Hygiene*, Plague Supplement, 1911, II, Vol. I, chap. 45); also Greenwood's "Factors That Determine the Rise, Spread, and Degree of Severity of Epidemic Diseases," *XVIIth International Congress of Medicine (1913)*, Sec. 18, pp. 49–80.

[104] Again, for the sake of economy of space, I am not giving the actual data collected and the curves drawn and analyzed, but they are at my disposal, collected from the main works in this problem. See E. W. Martin, *History of Grange Movement* (Philadelphia, 1913); S. J. Buck, *The Grange Movement* (Harvard University Press, 1913); S. J. Buck, *The Agrarian Crusade* (New Haven, 1920), and many other works devoted to the local agrarian movements.

[105] Again I do not give the data at my disposal for the sake of economy of space.

[106] See the data in W. Lunden, *The Dynamics of Higher Education* (Pittsburgh, 1939), part iii.

certainly is no "normal curve" of their growth, fluctuation, and decline, or their diffusion.

The convincing logical considerations as well as the factual tests do not give any basis for a belief in the existence of any "normal" or even typical curve of diffusion or diffusion rate for all cultural values in all circumstances. Such a "normal" curve is but a myth.

XII. Which Cultural Values Penetrate and Diffuse First: Material or Nonmaterial?

If we have two different cultures that come in touch with one another, which of the traits or values or systems of these cultures begin the penetration of the other culture first and which lag in this process? Is there any uniformity, and if there is, what is it? The main theories give quite opposite answers to the problem. One, represented by G. Tarde, assures us that all in all, the inner imitation in mind precedes an overt imitation in practice. Translated into the language of diffusion, this seemingly means: in order that any "material" value can diffuse, it has to be preceded by the diffusion of the "nonmaterial" desire to possess the material value. In accordance with this, he contends that the imitation-diffusion proceeds from within to without, from the inner meaning-value (or the thing signified) to its external shell or sign.

> Imitation . . . proceeds from the inner to the outer man. It seems at first sight as if a people or a class began to imitate another by copying its luxury and its fine arts before it became possessed of its tastes and literature, of its aims and ideas, in a word, of its spirit. Precisely the contrary, however, occurs. In the sixteenth century Spanish fashions of dress began to diffuse in France, because before that Spanish literature had already won its preeminence in France in the preceding century. In the seventeenth century French fashions began to diffuse over Europe, because before that French literature diffused there successfully. The desire to imitate a certain value must precede and usually does precede the overt diffusion of it.[107]

For this reason the ideas penetrate first, then the material vehicles and actions embody these ideas. The diffusion of religious dogmas precedes that of the ritual; the diffusion of ends that of their means; the diffusion of scientific and philosophical ideas that of their aesthetic and juridical realization; the spread of morals precedes that of manners; and so on.[108] The other theory claims an opposite uniformity.

[107] See G. Tarde, *The Laws of Imitation*, pp. 199 ff.

[108] *Ibid.*, pp. 200–208 ff.

According to it, the material ("civilizational," "societal") values uniformly penetrate first; the nonmaterial ("cultural," "ideological") lag. First penetrate radios, machine-guns, combs, lipsticks; or food, shelter, transportation, arms,[109] and so on; only then the "nonmaterial" values come, like religious beliefs or political ideas or scientific theories or moral norms and so on. First come the soldier and merchant and then the missionary and ideologist. As indicated above, the dichotomic theories of A. Coste, L. Weber, A. Weber, W. Ogburn, R. McIver, K. Marx, A. J. Toynbee, partly W. G. Sumner, A. G. Keller[110] and others,[111] set forth this claim (see above, Chapter Four).

Which of these opposite theories is valid? Neither one, in so far as it claims its uniformity to be general. First of all, as we have seen, the dichotomic division of cultural phenomena is untenable. Untenable also is this deduction from the false premise. Second, factually we can observe no general uniformity of either kind. These pseudo uniformities can be replaced by the following limited uniformities of a very different character.

A. *The kind of values that penetrate first depends, primarily, upon the kind of human agents that first come in contact with the other culture.* If they are merchants, as sometimes they are, then various commercial commodities penetrate first; if they are missionaries, as sometimes they are, then the "ideological values" penetrate first. If they are conquerors and soldiers, then partly material, partly nonmaterial values penetrate simultaneously. If they are students of philosophy or social science (say, Chinese in Western universities), then they bring back and spread the theories and ideologies they studied. If the students are theologians, or engineers, or business students, they dissipate their respective systems of values. And there is no uni-

109 C. Wissler, "Aboriginal Maize Culture," *American Journal of Sociology,* March, 1916, p. 661.

110 See A. G. Keller, *Societal Evolution* (New York, 1931), pp. 208, 218 ff. A. J. Toynbee claims that the first to penetrate are economic; second, political; third, cultural traits. A. J. Toynbee, *A Study of History* (Oxford University Press, 1934), Vol. III, p. 152, Vol. IV, p. 57.

111 See also J. G. Leyburn, *Frontier Folkways* (Yale University Press, 1935). Leyburn also claims that in the frontier society, "The pioneer's first task being to exist, it is in the mores of economic maintenance that changes in the mores are first evidenced and most strongly marked," p. 229, *et passim.* As though the economic maintenance and order can be organized without an establishment of law-order and ethico-religious norms that support it. Similar statements are made by several anthropologists who claim that technical and economic changes come first, and then others. See a variety of such a theory in R. Linton (ed.), *Acculturation in Seven American Indian Tribes* (New York, 1940), pp. 485 ff.

formity as to whether the business or engineering students always are sent first, and students of art, or philosophy, or political science, second.

However, in all these cases, we can talk only about the prevalence of the things that penetrate first. Factually, our merchant leaves in the other culture not only his merchandise but also something of his manners, mores, ideas, beliefs, and so on. Our missionary brings not only his creed, but simultaneously some medicine, often hospitals, knives, rifles, calico, and other material gifts. As to the army and conquerors, they bring and diffuse within the conquered population often the whole of their own culture, with all its material and immaterial values. Whether they were the Aryans in India; the Greeks of Alexander the Great in the Oriental countries; the Romans in the areas conquered; the Arabian conquerors in the subjugated societies; the Spaniards and the Pilgrims in America; the Europeans in their conquered colonies; they all brought and diffused simultaneously the material as well as nonmaterial values; weapons and religion; alcohol and language; merchandise and law-norms; food, knives, and the fashion of using rouge and lipsticks; the rules of elementary hygiene; the prohibition to use the knives or rifles for head-hunting; and so on. Likewise, the Chinese students bring back not only their specialty, but also the Western language, clothes, fashion of shaving or hair-cutting, and hundreds of other material and immaterial values. The situation is not very different in the cases when two societies with different cultures meet peacefully or semi-peacefully. In such cases again we observe that the values of material and nonmaterial character diffuse either simultaneously or nonsimultaneously; in some cases we have a prevalent diffusion of one kind of values, in other cases that of a different kind, without any general uniformity of either. The case of contact and diffusion of values between the Chinese and Western cultures is an example and evidence of that. For instance, "the incidence and sequence of social change in China does not appear to be from material technique to social ideologies. . . . The elements borrowed from Western culture have been (first) in the realm of social ideologies rather than of material technique."[112] In other cases, as

[112] R. T. LaPiere and Cheng Wang, "The Incidence and Sequence of Social Change," *American Journal of Sociology,* November, 1931, p. 401. See the facts in the article. See also Ching-Yueh Yen, "Crime in Relation to Social Change in China." *Ibid.,* November, 1934. Often "fables precede commodities in the intercourse of peoples" states Masaharu Anesaki. See his "East and West," in *Independence, Convergence, and Borrowing* (Harvard University Press, 1937), pp. 249 ff.

the studies of G. H. Danton and H. D. Lamson show,[113] in China there is a simultaneous spread — and in the towns as well as in villages — lipsticks, knives and other material things as well as a series of nonmaterial values of Western culture. On the other hand, a study of the newly arrived or recent immigrants to America from other countries, or any immigrant to any country with a different culture, shows that they take in simultaneously from the culture of immigration a series of material values (in the economic activities of earning their living), as well as a series of nonmaterial values, beginning with language, a few words of which they learn and have to learn as early as any other cultural trait they adopt.[114] To sum up, if in some cases there is an earlier penetration and prevalent diffusion of a certain kind of cultural values, it is conditioned, first, by the kind of the human agencies that first come in contact with a different culture. As there is no uniformity that always merchants, or always missionaries, or always explorers and soldiers penetrate the different culture first, there is no basis for a contention that always material rather than immaterial values penetrate first, or vice versa.[115]

[113] See the facts in G. H. Danton, *The Culture Contacts of the United States and China,* quoted; and the Ph.D. thesis of H. D. Lamson, mentioned. See also Lamson's "The Eurasian in Shanghai," quoted.

[114] The numerous facts of this kind are found in practically any serious study of immigration. See, for instance, the analysis of the Polish immigrants' disorganization in W. I. Thomas and F. Znaniecki, *The Polish Peasant in Europe and America* (New York, 1927), Vol. II, pp. 1646 ff. See there also the "Life-Record of an Immigrant," which in several points shows which of the cultural values of German and American culture the author adopted. See also W. C. Smith, *Americans in the Making* (New York, 1939), chaps. iv–xviii; F. J. Brown and J. S. Roucek, *Our Racial and National Minorities* (New York, 1937); C. M. Panunzio, *The Soul of an Immigrant* (New York, 1921). See the literature in Smith's work and also in R. Park and E. Burgess, *Introduction to the Science of Sociology* (Chicago, 1924), pp. 769 ff. See also E. A. Ross, *The Old World in the New* (New York, 1914).

[115] Many an anthropological work corrobates this conclusion. They show that there is no uniformity in this respect. E. C. Parsons shows that in the Zapotecan town Mitla, there were taken from the Spanish culture not only tiled roofs, and other technical features, but also wedding rites and Catholic religious elements, and "that changes in social organization and in material culture are made more readily than changes in personal behavior." E. C. Parsons, *Mitla, Town of the Souls* (Chicago, 1936), p. 536, *et passim.* R. Redfield tells us that in a Mexican village "the material culture of Tepoztlan, in contrast to the nonmaterial culture, preserves unmodified a large number of pre-Columbian traits," which means that the European nonmaterial culture penetrated more successfully than the material culture. R. Redfield, *Tepoztlan, a Mexican Village* (Chicago, 1930), p. 31.

I. Schapera clearly points out that the kind of European cultural values that penetrated the culture of a South African tribe, Kxatla, depended upon the type of Euro-

B. The second uniformity of limited character in this field can be formulated as follows: *Ceteris paribus, when two cultures A and B come in contact, those values of A which are more congenial to the culture B tend to penetrate earlier than the values which are uncongenial to the culture B (and vice versa).* More specifically, considering that any total culture is a congeries of systems and of single congeries, the systems and congeries of culture A which are congenial (meaningfully and causally) to the respective systems and congeries of B first pass into culture B; and each of these congeries or systems penetrates earlier exactly the most congenial congeries or system of the other culture. If the religious beliefs of the culture A are more congenial to those of culture B, than, for instance, the political or economic systems of A to those of B, then the religious beliefs of A would penetrate B earlier and more successfully (as we have seen) than the economic or political system. And these religious beliefs of A would penetrate first, as a rule, the religious but not economic or political systems of B. If the military organization of A is more congenial to B than the religious

---

peans and their aims. The missionaries "seek essentially to convert the heathen native to Christianity. In pursuit of this policy (they) seek to introduce a new system of morals and general behavior conforming to Christian ideals, and . . . further undertake the secondary task of promoting the general social and material advancement of the people. The Administration is concerned primarily with the maintenance of law and order (and taxes). The trader . . . is there to exploit the natives for his own economic benefit and attempts to develop a good market." Respectively all three kinds of the values of European culture were diffused among the tribe. See I. Schapera, "The Contributions of Western Civilization to Modern Kxatla Culture," *Transactions of the Royal Society of S. Africa,* Vol. XXIV, part iii, pp. 221–252. A. I. Hallowell and F. Eggan show that the change in social organization and religion in the native culture, under the contact of the European, comes as early and can be as deep as the change in economic and technological aspects of such a culture. See A. I. Hallowell, "Recent Changes in the Kinship Terminology of the St. Francis Abenaki," *Atti de XXII Congr. Intern. degli Americanisti* (Rome, 1928), pp. 97–145; F. Eggan, "Historical Changes in the Choctaw Kinship System," *American Anthropologist* (Vol. XXXIX, 1937), pp. 34–52. See also R. Linton, editor, *Acculturation in Seven American Indian Tribes* (New York, 1940). Here, contrary to the generalization of the editor, in a number of cases we see also a nonuniform penetration of now the material, now the nonmaterial traits. A series of studies of acculturation among Louisiana French, Canadian French, among the population and castes of India and other peoples display a similar picture: in the fusion of the cultural traits of the interacting groups are exchanged material and nonmaterial traits, without any uniformity of one of these classes of traits penetrating first or earlier than the second. See T. Lynn Smith and V. J. Parenton, "Acculturation among the Louisiana French"; H. Miner, "Changes in Rural French-Canadian Culture," *American Journal of Sociology,* November, 1938, pp. 355–378. The same is true in regard to the vertical movement of the values. A valet imitates his master not only in the economic and material traits but as much in manners, speech, beliefs, tastes and so on. So do lower classes in regard to the upper, and vice versa.

system of A, then the military organization of A would tend to be adopted by B earlier than the beliefs of A.[116]

The uniformity is a mere application of the proposition discussed before, when we considered the problem of the cultural best-sellers. Therefore, there is no need to dwell upon it at any length. The facts of history well support it. The cases of the penetration and enormous diffusion of the great religious systems, such as Buddhism, Jainism, Christianity, even Mohammedanism, are mainly the cases in which each of these religious systems invaded and penetrated many different cultures first and more successfully, sometimes leaving intact economic and many other systems of the penetrated cultures.[117] The cases of the enormous spread of certain political creeds or systems, like Parliamentarism, Democracy, Communism, Fascism and so on, are again cases where these systems seem to be more congenial to the cultures in which they spread than to several other systems of these cultures left intact by the penetration of these ideologies. The successful penetration and diffusion of the Western technique and forms of economic and military organization for the last century, and especially the last few decades, are cases where the economic or military or technical systems of the Western and other cultures that adopted these Western systems happened to be more congenial. They were adopted while other systems and congeries of Western culture were not.[118] In the seventeenth and eighteenth centuries, from the total Chinese culture which penetrated the Western culture (together with a few other values) came the Chinese pattern of gardening and some other values that later on were called Romantic.[119]

[116] For instance, the Turks (Ottomans) borrowed the firearms technique from Western culture; the Romans borrowed the Oriental "cataphract" military technique; Japan the Western military technique; and so on.

[117] See an excellent analysis of the penetration and diffusion of Buddhism in China in Hu Shih's "The Indianization of China," quoted. See the histories of diffusion of the great world religions. Script of the Syriac culture and art style of the Hellenic culture penetrated the Hindu culture as early as any of the material values of these cultures. For other facts see Albright's and Latourette's works quoted.

[118] "There are in the East some phases of its spiritual heritage which would not admit a wholesale acceptance of (the Western) Scientific culture in its present form," testifies M. Anesaki. "East and West," quoted, pp. 249 ff. See in the same volume the quoted studies of L. Wenger, R. Maunier, L. Ginsberg, C. H. Dodd, Hu Shih, for corroboration of the proposition in the diffusion of the Roman Law, of French Law, of Jewish folklore, of Hellenism and Christianity, and of Buddhism.

[119] See A. Lovejoy, "The First Gothic Revival and the Return to Nature," *Modern Language Notes,* November, 1932; and Lovejoy, "The Chinese Origin of Romanticism," *The Journal of English and Germanic Philology,* 1933, pp. 1–20.

In the light of this proposition, there is neither logical nor factual ground for either one of the two uniformities claimed by Tarde and the dichotomists. If anything, Tarde's statement that "imitation proceeds from the inner to the outer man," is a more general rule in the process of imitation properly than the opposite rule of the dichotomists. But a penetration and diffusion of cultural value is not limited to imitation: some of the values are imposed, some others penetrate before the population has even an idea of these values. Such values penetrate often not because the population want them, but they begin to want them because they have come in contact with them or because they are imposed. In all such cases, the nature of the values is very different. Therefore, one cannot claim that in penetration of the values the inner desire to have them precedes the outer acceptance of them. Our two propositions seem to meet the test much better and are more adequate than the criticized ones.

XIII. Conclusion

The above sums up the main limited and approximate, but real, uniformities in the field of spatial displacement, mobility, circulation, and diffusion of cultural phenomena. It shows that some general rules exist there. Under special conditions most of them admit deflections and deviations from these uniformities, as under special conditions any uniformity — even physicochemical — shows such deviations. But properly interpreted, these deviations are special cases of the rule and not its exceptions.

The above also shows that even in this simplest form of the change of sociocultural phenomena in social space, we cannot either grasp or understand the essential uniformities without a systematic distinction between the sociocultural systems and congeries, and without an adequate conception of the total culture of any population as a conglomeration of systems, supersystems, co-ordinated systems, and congeries of systems and of single elements. As we pass to a study of more complex forms of cultural change in time, the importance of this distinction will grow.

GENERAL INDEX